METTERNICH AND THE DUCHESS

BOOKS BY DOROTHY GIES MC GUIGAN

The Habsburgs

Metternich and the Duchess

METTERNICH
and the
DUCHESS

———◆———

DOROTHY GIES McGUIGAN

Doubleday & Company, Inc., Garden City, New York
1975

Library of Congress Cataloging in Publication Data
McGuigan, Dorothy Gies.
Metternich and the duchess.
Bibliography: p. 557
1. Metternich-Winneburg, Clemens Lothar Wenzel,
Fürst von, 1773–1859.   2. Sagan, Katharina Wilhel-
mine Friederike Benigne, Herzogin von, 1781–1839.
I. Title.
DB80.8.M57M22   940.2'7'0924 [B]
ISBN 0-385-02827-X
Library of Congress Catalog Card Number 79–180089

For B.J.M.
1916—1969

Non omnis moriar

CONTENTS

ILLUSTRATIONS

1. Clemens Lothar Wenzel von Metternich.
2. Princess Eleonore Metternich.
3. Marie Metternich.
4. Clementine Metternich.
5. Three eldest Metternich children, Marie, Clementine and Victor.
6. Austrian State Chancellery, Vienna.
7. Napoleon, 1812.
8. Caroline Bonaparte Murat, Queen of Naples.
9. Pauline Bonaparte, Princess Borghese.
10. Wilhelmine, Duchess of Sagan.
11. The four princesses of Courland as "The Four Graces."
12. Duchess Dorothea of Courland, mother of the four princesses.
13. Adelaide Gustava Aspasia ("Vava") Armfelt, Wilhelmine's natural daughter, with a foster sister.
14. Castle of Sagan in Silesia.
15. Palais Palm, Schenkenstrasse, Vienna.
16. Princess Katharine Bagration.
17. Friedrich von Gentz.
18. Ratiborzitz, country house of the Duchess of Sagan in Bohemia.
19. Tsar Alexander I.
20. Grand Duchess Catherine Pavlovna, the Tsar's sister.
21. Karl August Hardenberg, Chancellor of Prussia.
22. Emperor Franz I of Austria.
23. Prince Alfred Windischgraetz.
24. Prince Karl Schwarzenberg, commander of the Allied forces.
25. The battle of Dresden, August 26–27, 1813.
26. The battle of Leipzig, October 18, 1813.
27. Emperor Franz and his Allies enter Leipzig after the battle.
28. Robert Stewart, Viscount Castlereagh.
29. Charles Maurice, Prince de Talleyrand.
30. Dorothée, Countess of Périgord, née Princess of Courland, at seventeen.
31. Entry of Allied troops into Paris, March 31, 1814.
32. Royalist crowd pulls down statue of Napoleon, 1814.

MAPS

FOREWORD

Few men had a keener sense of history and a more acute awareness of posterity peering over their shoulders than did Clemens Metternich, the Austrian statesman who directed the fortunes of an empire—and, in a sense, of Europe—for some thirty-nine years.

The period between 1810 and 1815 he called "the most important in my life as it was also in the history of the world."

The story told in this book is of the campaign for peace he waged during those years. It is the story also of his intimate friendship through that critical period with Wilhelmine, Duchess of Sagan.

While Metternich gave his name to an age, Wilhelmine of Sagan remained a mysterious, nearly anonymous figure, meriting not even a marginal note in the history of the period.

As her sole biographer, Clemens Brühl, pointed out in 1941, "Historical research on the political woman in the background has barely begun." To which Count Egon Corti, in his preface to *Metternich und die Frauen*, added perceptively a few years later, in 1947: "It is infinitely important to research the role of women in history because it is so much greater than we commonly accept. It is quite right that their influence be felt, simply because they comprise half of humankind."

Neither Brühl nor Corti was able to use the Metternich-Sagan correspondence, which has come to light only in the last decade.

The account presented here of the final drama of Napoleonic times is based to a large extent on the correspondence—for the most part unpublished—of Metternich and his wife, Eleonore, and his cherished daughter Marie, whom he called "my other self." The story of his friendship with the Duchess of Sagan is based on their recently discovered correspondence and on that of the duchess with Prince Alfred Windischgraetz.

A certain mystery surrounded the disappearance of the Metternich-Sagan letters in the last century. In a memoir of her youth published in 1877, Wilhelmine's foster daughter, Emilie Gerschau von Binzer, recalled how her foster mother had once read aloud to her from a packet of letters that had passed between her and Metternich in the early months of 1813, when the two had debated the burning question of peace or war—he resisting the idea of war, she pressing him to join the Allied cause and renewed war against Napoleon. "The prince [Metternich] must have wavered for a long time," Binzer recalled, "for there was quite a collection of those letters in existence. When I asked her about them later on, she told me that at the prince's request she had burned the entire packet."

For years it was assumed that the duchess had destroyed her entire correspondence with Metternich. It is clear now that she burned at his request only those letters of early 1813, so at variance with the late-in-life picture of himself he presented in his *Memoirs* as the farsighted nemesis of Napoleon.

The remainder of their correspondence he himself took care to preserve in a black letter-box bound like a book, with gilded edging, inscribed on the spine in his own handwriting, "Letters of the Duchess of Sagan."

After his death in 1859, his son Richard, aided by archivist Alfons von Klinkowström, sorted and arranged the vast collection of Metternich papers, the correspondence with emperors and kings, with ministers and diplomats, with writers and artists and sculptors and singers, with family and friends. Packed in carefully numbered chests, the archive was stored in the chapel of the old Cistercian abbey at Plass in Bohemia, which Metternich had bought in 1826. Into one of the chests went the black letter-box.

In Plass the archive remained undisturbed until World War II, when the shadow of approaching catastrophe lay over Central Europe, and Prince Paul Metternich, great-grandson of the Chancellor, and his young Russian-born, French-educated wife, Princess Tatiana, felt increasing apprehension for the safety of their priceless historical legacy. If Plass suffered a bombing, as the Metternich castle of Johannisberg on the Rhine was bombed in 1942, or if Bohemia were invaded—as it had been so many times in centuries past—the archive might be completely destroyed.

With the aid of Heinrich von Srbik, renowned Metternich biographer, who had worked in the Plass archive in the time of Prince Paul's father, Princess Tatiana arranged to transfer the dozens of document-filled chests to the Haus- Hof- und Staatsarchiv in Vienna, where they would come under the protection and care of the Austrian Government.

Unluckily an archive employee revealed the planned transfer and Nazi officials in Prague forbade the move. Hastily an alternative solution had to be devised. A cellar under the brewery of the old Plass abbey was thoroughly cleaned, aired, sealed against dampness. Carefully and secretly the chests of documents were carried into the cellar and the door cemented shut.

When the Russian Army invaded Bohemia and occupied Plass in May of 1945, everything in the abbey was smashed and thrown out of the windows.

Forgotten by everyone, sealed away in the cellar under the brewery, the Metternich archive survived intact. Only when the war was well over and a young man of the neighborhood recalled hearing of a treasure buried in the brewery cellar, were pickaxes brought, the cellar broken open. Czech authorities took charge of the historical treasure and the thousands of letters and documents were moved to the Central State Archive in Prague, where they are now in the public domain.

In autumn of 1949, a Czech literary scholar, Dr. Maria Ullrichová, looking for letters of Alexandre Dumas, stopped a few days in Plass and chanced upon the black letter-box bound like a book in one of the chests that still remained in the abbey chapel. Out tumbled some six hundred letters and notes, ivory with age, most in French, some few in German. In 1966 Dr. Ullrichová published in Austria a large portion of the letters.

In Prague in 1968 and 1969 I was able to examine both the Metternich family correspondence and the Sagan letters—many still unpublished—and to piece together the story of that fateful relationship. The papers of the Windischgraetz family, meanwhile, had found their way from Castle Tachau to the Czech State Archive in Pilsen, and they yielded the final link in the story.

There can be little doubt that Metternich's relationship with Wilhelmine of Sagan was the most intense and absorbing of his life. "It is certain that I no longer live except in you—that my life is yours as much as the life of any man has ever belonged to another," he wrote in the grim month of February 1814, when the two had quarreled bitterly across the hundreds of miles that separated them in wartime. Certainly when they were together, he confided his political thoughts and plans to her as he did to no other person. Intently she followed his peace efforts through the last months of the Napoleonic wars, mourned with him at the failure of the Châtillon negotiations, that "advantages bought at so high a price are again abandoned to the chances of war."

Locked in conflict with the Tsar of Russia in a power struggle over the future of continental Europe, Metternich could still beseech the Tsar's help to recover for Wilhelmine possession of her illegitimate daughter Gustava, growing up in Finland. The stormy love affair of those two sensitive and gifted people reached a catastrophic climax at the very moment of worst crisis during the Congress of Vienna, when the world's first great international summit conference threatened to erupt into a new European war.

Less lucky for the historian and biographer than the preservation of the Metternich papers at Plass was the fate of the archive of Castle Sagan in Silesia, which contained not only papers of Wilhelmine but the correspondence of her mother, the Duchess of Courland, with Goethe and Wieland and other leading men of her day, and of Wilhelmine's younger sister, Dorothée,

Duchess of Dino, with Talleyrand. Sagan too was invaded by Allied armies in the closing days of World War II. According to one source, a pair of officers, one in French uniform, the other in American uniform, carried off the entire Sagan archive—of which nothing has been heard since. Other reports relate that books and papers from the Sagan library were dumped into the muddy road so that Russian tanks could pass through.

"It's an evil thing, war," Metternich wrote to Wilhelmine in February of 1814, during the final stages of the campaign in France. "It soils everything, even the imagination. That is why I work for peace despite the protests of stupid people and fools. I want a quick and good [peace]."

Dorothy Gies McGuigan

AUGUST 1974

ACKNOWLEDGMENTS

I want to express my deep appreciation to Dr. Arthur Breycha-Vauthier, director of the Diplomatic Academy in Vienna and a lifelong Metternich scholar, who read the book in manuscript form and offered many useful suggestions.

Prince Paul and Princess Tatiana Metternich not only made available precious family pictures and heirlooms but shared their unique knowledge of family history and the hospitality of Schloss Johannisberg.

My friend of many years, Betty Knorr, chauffeured me on two memorable trips through Czechoslovakia in quest of the past, photographed many of the portraits that appear in this book, shared my interest in the persons and the period and offered many useful insights. To Dr. Maria Ullrichová, scholar and friend, I am deeply indebted for her publication of the Metternich-Sagan letters, which were of such inestimable value in the writing of this book. M. Georges Englebert, of the Belgian Embassy in Vienna, was generous in sharing his exceptional knowledge of bibliographical sources and of the iconography of the Napoleonic period.

Prince Ludwig Aladar Windischgraetz and the late Prince Joseph Windischgraetz, Baron Kenneth Wrede of Helsinki, Hans-Burkhard von Diebitsch of Bielefeld, Countess Ellen Medem of Passau—all descendants of some of the personages who figure in this book—kindly supplied not only family portraits but valuable information and family tradition. My friend Jirina Kadainková of Prague gave useful technical assistance, and I am indebted to Dr. C. v. Braunmühl (Clemens Brühl) of Tübingen, author of the only biography of the Duchess of Sagan.

Dr. Josef Görner and Dr. Jaroslav Honc of the Central State Archive in Prague, Dr. Vladimír Byrtucky, Dr. Antonín Macák and Maria Šimandlová of the State Archive in Pilsen gave me the kindest and most supportive co-operation. The staffs of the University of Michigan Library and of the Haus-Hof- und Staatsarchiv in Vienna have been unremittingly helpful over several years of research, as have the staffs of the British Museum and the Public Record Office in London and that of the Archive of the Ministry of Foreign Affairs in Paris.

Grateful acknowledgment is made to the following for permission to reproduce pictures used in this book: numbers 1, 2, and 5, Prince and Princess Paul Metternich; numbers 3, 4, 17, 19, 26, 36, 37, 40, 41, 42, 44, 48, 49, 50, 51, 58, 59, Österreichische Nationalbibliothek; numbers 6, 15, 52, 61, 62, Historisches Museum der Stadt Wien; number 7, Museum, Chateauroux; number 8, Musées de France; number 9, Mansell Collection, London; number 10, Museum, Castle Náchod, Bohemia; number 11, Prince Biron von Courland; number 12, Count Karl von Hardenberg; number 13, Vava von Essen and the Finland National Museum; number 21, H.M. Queen Elizabeth II; numbers 22, 33, 34, Kunsthistorisches Museum, Vienna; numbers 38, 45, Betty Knorr; numbers 23 and 39, Prince Ludwig Aladar Windischgraetz; number 24, Schloss Orlik, Bohemia; number 28, National Portrait Gallery, London; number 29, Brown University Special Collections; number 30, Petrémand, Réalités; numbers 35, 54 and 56, Trustees of the British Museum; number 46, the Marquess of Londonderry; number 60, Frantisek Preucil, Prague; number 63, private collection. Numbers 14, 18, 25, 27, 32, 53, 55 and 57 are from the author's collection, and numbers 16, 20, 43 and 47 from Hugo Leisching, *Der Wiener Kongress.*

D. G. MCG.

METTERNICH AND THE DUCHESS

I

GUNS OR GREEN TABLE?

Could they not give us this peace that is so necessary for all?
—METTERNICH TO HARDENBERG, OCTOBER 5, 1812

Peace would answer for everything. Has Providence itself dictated Your Excellency's dispatch?
—FLORET TO METTERNICH, NOVEMBER 22, 1812[1]

The carnival season of 1813 was the bleakest anyone in Vienna could remember. Nobody danced. Since the state bankruptcy of 1811, when paper money was devalued by four fifths, everyone in Austria felt the pinch. The price of bread and candles and firewood continued to rise astronomically. Ladies wore old gowns; even some of the very rich had been forced to pawn their jewels.

Around dinner tables that January and February old campaigns were fought out, with silver and saltcellars marshaled for battle lines. And in the two leading political salons, all among the clink of teacups, people argued the probability of war or of peace.

The two salons were in opposite wings of the Palais Palm, a mansion close under the city walls on Schenkenstrasse, only a few minutes' walk from the state Chancellery. In the left wing lived the Russian Princess Katharine Bagration. In the right wing Wilhelmine, Duchess of Sagan, had her town house. "The rivals," they were called in Vienna society, and "the two sybils." Both were young, beautiful, independent and rich. Both were passionately addicted to politics.

In the salons of both ladies that spring the war hawks far outnumbered the doves. Count Clemens Metternich, Austria's suave and astute Foreign

Minister, who was following a firm if difficult peace policy, was often obliged to use his very considerable charm to fend off a barrage of verbal attack and argument.

Katharine Bagration was the widow of that celebrated general who had led the Tsar's army the previous autumn at the battle of Borodino and died of his wounds. In Princess Bagration's house were to be heard the fiercest denunciations of Austria's dilatory policy. From her drawing room, where Vienna's Russian colony gathered, had circulated the very first news of Napoleon's debacle in Russia, together with colorful rumors of the French Emperor's demise in Moscow. Some said Napoleon had lost his mind and been clapped into irons by his marshals; others claimed he had been blown up when the Russians mined the Kremlin.

In the drawing room of Wilhelmine, Duchess of Sagan, some of the more notable Austrian opinion-makers gathered each evening for tea and cards and lively conversation—statesmen and generals, diplomats and journalists—and clever women who had things to say but no other platform from which to say them. Eldest of the four famously beautiful daughters of the last Duke of Courland, Wilhelmine, twice married, twice divorced, possessed enough fortune and social prestige to shape an independent life for herself in a day when few women could exercise such an option. She had besides the spirit and intelligence to make her political thinking valued by some of the most powerful men in Austria. In the duchess's drawing room, too, the talk was most frequently of war.

The hour was certainly one of the greatest delicacy in the affairs of Europe. "Infinitely critical," the political journalist Friedrich Gentz called it.[2]

Although, Metternich recalled later, most people in Austria were weary of war and longed only for peace, a powerful group in the country—"not numerous but important from the position of the individuals composing it"— clamored for Austria to cut loose her tenuous and reluctant alliance with France and to join in a crusading war against Napoleon on the side of Russia and England.[3]

Less than a year before, Napoleon's eagles had seemed to be securely planted from the Atlantic to Poland, from Italy to the Baltic. All of Central Europe had been absorbed into the Napoleonic system in one way or another—by conquest or bribe. Prussia and Austria, defeated on the battlefield, had been shorn of territory and saddled heavily with war indemnities.

Less than a year before, in May of 1812, Napoleon had summoned his German satellites to a meeting in Dresden, one of the one-man political theatricals he enjoyed staging before an audience of kings. From Dresden he had departed eastward for a final military gamble—his *va banque*, Metternich termed it—leading his huge army of a half-million men across the Niemen into Russia, to wrest a conqueror's peace from the Tsar. He planned—so they said in France—to winter over comfortably somewhere in the South, in

Persia perhaps, and in spring to lead his Grande Armée to the East, farther than any army had ever been led before, "to capture India and wreck the countinghouses of England."[4]

Instead, Europe learned in December that a half-million men lay buried under the snows of the vast Russian plains. Of the great army who had swarmed after Napoleon, like a band of mindless lemmings in the sun of mid-summer, hardly 30,000 staggered into Vilna in early December, skeletons of men, half crazed with hunger and cold, dying of typhus along the roadsides and in the hospitals and attics of Vilna.

Even before official news of the catastrophe had been brought to Vienna from Warsaw by a young French attaché, Metternich had seized on the first inkling he got from his own people in Vilna to begin to reweave the subtle strands of European diplomacy into a new pattern. The dynamics of power had shifted at last. It was the moment—so he wrote to his trusted counselor-of-embassy, Floret, in Vilna—to turn his *rêve politique* into reality. That political dream was peace—not a peace that would be only another interlude in the devastating chain of wars Europe had suffered for a quarter of a century—but a final end to the long term of violence.[5] Floret was directed to approach Napoleon's Foreign Minister, Bassano, with a peace feeler. And as soon as Metternich learned that Napoleon had deserted the wreckage of his army in Vilna and was hastening back to Paris as swiftly as sleigh and car-riage could take him, Metternich dispatched an envoy to the French capital to persuade Napoleon himself to make peace.[6]

As the bells of Paris rang in the new year of 1813, Austria's envoy, Count Bubna, patiently listened to Napoleon's four-hour harangue explaining away the disaster in Russia. The short, stout little commander, who bore no worse scars of the catastrophe than a skin reddened by exposure—he had re-turned from Russia, his wife wrote, "fatter than before"—did not sound pacific. He talked of revenge, called the Russians "barbarians of the North," boasted that by spring he would have another 400,000 men under arms. "I'll fight my way back to Russia if I can; if not I'll withdraw behind the Elbe and let the enemy come to me! Fate will decide the rest."

Then he added quickly, "But I am equally ready to make peace if the Emperor of Austria wants it and if he means to do so without stripping France of her conquests. I confess it is a sacrifice to my pride even to speak of peace at this moment."[7]

In the end he assented: yes, Austria might mediate for peace. If the consent of the French Emperor was grudging, Bubna could at least report to Vienna that the people of France wanted peace, that a rumor of Austrian mediation had "created an unbelievable sensation," that nearly all the lead-ing men in France favored accepting the Austrian peace plan.

By the first week of February, Metternich could dispatch his two carefully prepared envoys, one to the Tsar "somewhere in Poland," the other to Eng-land, to persuade Napoleon's opponents to the peace table. He had already neutralized Austria by withdrawing her auxiliary forces from Poland, where y had formed the right flank of the Grande Armée as it advanced into Russia, but had been so skillfully deployed by their commander, Prince Schwarzenberg, that they had avoided battle and suffered no casualties worse than *la grippe* and here and there frostbitten toes.

Presently Metternich would initiate the third step in his peace plan. He hoped to entice Napoleon's satellites—Saxony, Denmark, Bavaria, Württemberg, perhaps even Napoleon's own brother-in-law Joachim Murat, King of Naples—to support his plan for a mediated peace and to form a block to strengthen the peace proposals.

In Vienna that spring of 1813 nothing was quite what it appeared to be. The whole city seethed with rumor, speculation, conspiracy, intrigue. If there was no spirit of carnival, no balls or festivals or masked *redoutes*, there were certainly secret assignations, pseudonyms and disguises.

The Secret Police with their network of informers were everywhere, watchful, suspicious, ready to break up any impermissible gathering. In the Secret Cipher Office letters were opened with a bone knife and resealed so cunningly over a smokeless candle with a carefully replicated seal that one could hardly guess a copyist had been at work. Even the correspondence of the young Empress Maria Ludovica—herself an ardent hawk—was scanned and sent to her All Highest spouse for his inspection.[8]

If Metternich had little support in the upper ranks of Austrian officialdom for his peace drive, he had at least the full backing of Emperor Franz.

With his appearance of imperturbable serenity—"cold, calm, *calculateur par excellence*," Gentz described him—Metternich received the visitors who came and went that spring, most bent on persuading him into war, others, like Gentz, hoping at least to unravel the whole skein of his plans.[9]

Even in the gloomy days of January and February, visitors found the Foreign Minister's study a cheerful room, the tall windows facing south over Ballhaus Square and the imperial palace. A bright fire burned on the open grate; clusters of candles glinted on polished furniture, on books and bibelots that lay everywhere, and on the handsome patrician head of the minister with its clusters of powdered curls.

It was Gentz's habit to call at the Chancellery each morning at ten, when Metternich descended from breakfast with his family, to worm what news of note he could out of the bland and evasive minister.

Skilled journalist, shrewd political commentator, Friedrich Gentz made a precarious kind of living selling information and services where he could. He had left Berlin in a hurry ten years before, leaving behind him a swarm of enraged creditors and a miserable young wife of whom we know little and that sad, for she died conveniently soon after, saving Gentz the trouble and expense of a divorce.

An amusing conversationalist, an incurable gossip, Gentz had turned himself into that useful role, the entertaining extra man at the dinner tables of the titled rich. He maintained a footing in both political salons in the Palais

Palm, taking care to divide his time between the princess and the duchess, both important sources of information. Gentz was a first-class prose writer; his French was clear as a bell, his German nearly untranslatable, crackling and exploding with gutsy adjectives and colorful nouns. Greedy as a child, Gentz had a passion for luxury, for the most expensive chocolates and liqueurs, the most exquisite gloves and shoes and books. His tastes were eclectic; in Vienna it was said that "he loved men often, women sometimes, money always."

"Nobody," Gentz boasted in a letter that spring to the Tsar's chief aide, Nesselrode, "knows Metternich more intimately, has studied him more successfully, penetrated more than I all the springs of his politics."[10] It was not precisely true. For although Metternich had recently endeavored to pin down Gentz's dubious loyalty by turning over to him a lucrative correspondent's post, Gentz's tongue and pen, he well knew, were not completely to be trusted. No secret was safe with Gentz; he was therefore highly useful for publicizing what needed to be publicized.

Among other regular callers at the Chancellery were Baron Wilhelm von Humboldt, envoy of Prussia and ardently pro-war, who tried his best that spring, and in vain, to shift Metternich into some definite military commitment. No more could Count Ernst von Hardenberg, former envoy of Hanover, who relayed reports on the Austrian situation to the Prince Regent of England and called Metternich's peace plan "only temporising."

Other visitors appeared that spring on highly secret missions, slipping in and out of the Chancellery by a private rear stairs. The missions were nearly all designed to pry Metternich and Austria out of their peace stance and into a military alliance against Napoleon.

Prussian General Knesebeck, in civil dress and the strictest incognito, sent by Prussia's Chancellor, Baron Karl August Hardenberg—cousin of Count Ernst—arrived in January to urge Austria to join Prussia in a new war against France.

Prussia, occupied and humiliated by Napoleon after the War of 1806, had been stripped of lands, of men, of food, fodder and horses. Now everywhere in the wake of Napoleon's defeat, people in Prussia clamored to be free of French domination and for revenge against Napoleon. "Strike him dead! The world will call it just!" cried a fiery Prussian poet. Chancellor Hardenberg himself had written the previous autumn how happy he would be "to throw the tinder into the powder keg, to set aflame the world-fire that must destroy the Enemy of Mankind." He found it hard, he confessed, that Austria's hesitation made it impossible.[11]

Knesebeck left empty-handed.

Agents of the Tsar appeared incognito in Vienna as well; Metternich avoided seeing them. Only the Russian envoy, Count Stackelberg, who had been in technical exile in Graz during the Franco-Russian War, was invited to return to Vienna and to come to the Chancellery for an audience.

Stackelberg breezed into Metternich's study, announcing that Russia was quite willing "to come to Austria's rescue if Austria would join Russia in war against Napoleon."

"Wait a minute, my dear Stackelberg," Metternich replied, smiling and gesturing him into an easy chair. "You are like a man who sees daylight for the first time after being shut up in a dark room for six months. The daylight blinds you. Be sure we see better. The Emperor only wants peace. He proposes you go along with it. The French are favorable to it. I invited you to this audience solely to sound out your court in regard to peace."

By the end of the audience the pro-war Stackelberg had been persuaded to write his sovereign "almost under the eyes of Metternich, urging very strong arguments to show the necessity of peace."[12]

England too had her agents in Vienna, reporting back to London on the disposition of the Austrian Government and ready to offer generous subsidies if Austria would go to war against Napoleon.

Besides Count Hardenberg, a second English agent, John Harcourt King, a hotheaded young Anglo-Irishman with a taste for conspiracy, was reporting regularly to the London Cabinet on Metternich and Austrian affairs. With King, Metternich was circumspect; King had been involved in 1811 in a dangerous and explosive plot to foment an uprising in the Tyrol and Vorarlberg—lands lost to France's ally Bavaria—and he might well revive that plot in this new hour of crisis.

But it was a third English emissary, twenty-five-year-old Lord Walpole, who, Metternich feared, might compromise his peace plans. Walpole had been dispatched to Vienna by Lord Cathcart, British ambassador at the Russian court in St. Petersburg, to scent out Austrian plans and to press her into war. Though Walpole arrived in Vienna disguised as an American merchant, Metternich knew that if Napoleon got wind of his mission, he would at once jump to the conclusion that Austria was not intending to mediate peace but rather to join his opponents. Reluctantly he granted Walpole the necessary passport, reluctantly received him at two secret interviews. He knew the young Englishman already to be clumsy and rash; Metternich, therefore, kept *le nez fin*—his nose in the air—as he told Hardenberg, disclosed little or nothing of his plans. Walpole wrote a blistering report to London of Metternich's "weakness of Character," called him ignorant and uninformed, believed the Austrian Emperor "hated" his Foreign Minister, would not keep him long in office. Metternich, Walpole averred, "was even willing to forego hope of regaining lost territory for the sake of a European peace."[13]

While Metternich's peace envoys made their precarious way north through blizzards and ice storms that February—Ludwig Lebzeltern to the Tsar's headquarters, Johann Philipp Wessenberg by way of Denmark and Sweden to England—the balance in Europe tilted ominously toward war.

In Vilna at Christmas, 1812, Tsar Alexander I had celebrated victory over Napoleon and his thirty-fourth birthday, pondering what step to take next:

whether to return to Russia as Marshal Kutusov and his older generals urged and rebuild his devastated country or to march his armies farther and liberate all Europe from Napoleon. His younger advisers, non-Russians for the most part—Anstett, Stein, Pozzo di Borgo, Nesselrode, all with their own irons in the fire—urged him to fight on.

Even while Bubna talked with Napoleon on New Year's Eve in Paris, a thousand miles away, at Tauroggen in Lithuania, General Yorck, commander of Prussia's auxiliary army, had defected from Napoleon's side and turned his troops over to the Tsar. It was precisely the signal the hesitant Tsar needed. A few days later, on the Russian New Year, January 12, Tsar Alexander led his armies across the Niemen. He had accepted Stein's invitation to be "the liberator of Europe."

While the Tsar at the head of his army crossed Poland, inviting Prussia and Austria to join him, Napoleon in Paris worked frantically to put together a new army. He had browbeaten his Council of State, most of whom favored peace; he had got the Senate to agree to a new conscription, arguing that only with a strong army could France buy the peace she needed. "One final effort must be made to drive back the hostile armies that now threaten!" he told them. In a cunning maneuver of fiscal sleight of hand, he had taken over the publicly owned parish lands of France to finance his new army—and a new war if it came.

As fragile and as tenuous as a spider's web woven on a day of high wind, the strands of Metternich's peace design fluttered and hovered over Europe that troubled spring of 1813.

In Vienna the War Party clamored loudly for Metternich's head—or at least his portfolio. There were constant rumors that he would be forced out of office, and that Count Philipp Stadion, his predecessor in the Foreign Office and a leader of the hawks, would take over.

"Not a day passes," the French ambassador, Count Otto, reported, "when [the war faction] does not invent a new way to discredit him, and they are saying loudly that he will soon be replaced by Monsieur de Stadion. . . . Monsieur de Metternich has so little support at court and in society that he has to spend his time with his most determined enemies to get them to pardon him for the direction he has taken."[14]

Humboldt, however, shook his head. Metternich, he said, was shrewder than all the others; he would keep his office.

Never perhaps in his long lifetime—he would live to be eighty-six—would Metternich be under sharper—indeed, nearly lethal—attack than he was in that spring of 1813. Men there were who were willing to murder to force the issue of war.

II

EDUCATION OF A DIPLOMAT

The diplomat must be above all else a man of peace.
—FRANÇOIS DE CALLIÈRES, 1716

Though all his life he would disavow diplomacy—a career, he was fond of telling people, that he had not chosen but that had been chosen for him—Metternich was nevertheless a consummate diplomat, born and bred in the vocation, master of the art of the possible, skilled virtuoso in all the instruments of the negotiating table—compromise, persuasion, improvisation—to say nothing of sharper and more devious tools of political bargaining—ruse, bluff, on occasion deception.

"Between politics and diplomacy," he wrote once, "there exists the same difference as between science and art."[1] He liked to think of himself as a scientist; he was in fact an artist.

He understood the importance of words—in French, of course, the language of diplomacy—not only for the sake of clarity but sometimes for diversion and ambiguity, for their hidden meanings and glimmers of meanings. He understood the unspoken language of the game where the flicker of an eyelid, a change of inflection, the use of a single shaded word in a *note verbale* could hold as much meaning as a recalled ambassador.

He wore his career with well-bred nonchalance, like his artfully cut *fracs*, as if their beautiful fit were the merest accident and not the result of a long series of studied adjustments between him and his tailor. The air of casualness and easy indolence with which he performed routine diplomatic chores was the style of the eighteenth-century diplomat-aristocrat; it lent credence to the accusation of frivolity so frequently leveled at him. "A pretty windbag," Napoleon once called him.

In fact, like most gifted and ambitious men—though Metternich was vain enough to deny the ambition—he was capable of periods of intense, concentrated work, when he could go nearly without sleep for days and nights, carrying a staggering work load and more than staggering responsibility.

Perhaps most of all he was a consummate playactor, and he thoroughly enjoyed playing the part he had created for himself. With care he polished the image he presented each day to the world—an image of cool, easy composure and of a certain imperturbable irony with which he surveyed his natural habitat, the drawing room. He was master of all the arts of the salon, the ricochet of small talk, the mine of amusing anecdote, the gift for mimicry and caricature, a touch now and then of malice.

Even his enemies were inclined to agree that he was a man of indisputable charm, that quality that travels least well down the long avenue of history.

He was not Austrian by birth; he would never feel quite at home in the capital. "I don't like Vienna and I've never liked it," he told his friend the Duchess of Sagan.[2] Four years younger than Napoleon, he had been born in 1773 in the Rhineland, where his father's estates, near the confluence of the Rhine and Moselle rivers, lay not far from France. Like so many citizens of border territory, Metternich's nationality remained all his life a little blurred.

He was French in education and in tastes; he spoke French in his profession and at home with his family as well; he made love in French; but he remained all his life loyal to that eighteenth-century universality of culture by which men could call themselves Europeans first of all, and only second, Austrians or Russians or Frenchmen.

In the late afternoon sunshine of the old regime, when a still feudal class of wealth and privilege ruled unchallenged in Europe, it had been Metternich's good fortune to be born into the top layer of that hierarchical society.

From his mother, Maria Beatrix Kageneck, of an old noble family of the Breisgau, beautiful, intelligent, ambitious and young—she was only seventeen when this adored older son was born—he got his blond good looks, the slender eagle nose that gave a certain look of arrogance to his face, his gift for amusing conversation, and his ease and grace in the drawing room. His mother's undisputed favorite and no doubt more than a little spoiled, he had been reared on honey as well as milk, endowed for life with the sunny optimism that enabled him, as Gentz said, "always and in all circumstances to view the world in rose-colored light."

His father, Count Franz Georg von Metternich, held a series of diplomatic posts under the Elector of Trier and then as resident minister of the Austrian Netherlands for the Habsburg emperors. Young Clemens had been quite literally born into the international freemasonry of diplomacy —which his father practiced, it might be added, with a certain Venetian style and more than a little insouciance. "This matter like most others," he would say with a shrug, "will be settled in one way or another."

The Metternichs were a warm and affectionate family circle, more closely knit than most aristocratic families of that day. The other two children decidedly took second place to Clemens in their parents' affections—the elder sister, Pauline, plain, heavy-featured, inclined to plumpness, but "very nice," people said, "well brought up"; and Joseph, the younger brother, called Pepi, a perfectly nice boy of mediocre ability, who would live all his life in the shadow of the talented elder brother. To Clemens his mother wrote once: "You are the favorite child of your mother—I could almost say of God."[3]

On the Habsburg throne in Vienna in the 1780's sat that irascible, impatient, disgruntled, incontinently dedicated reformer Joseph II, most generous of the enlightened despots, who, a whole decade before the French Revolution, was taking giant steps toward a more egalitarian society. Serfs were freed, the nobility taxed, Church and state separated, restrictions on the press lifted, civil rights granted Jews and Protestants, and a decent basic education decreed for all children. The privileged classes, especially in Hungary, resisted violently; by the time the Bastille fell in Paris, Austria was into a counter-revolution. Nevertheless the heady air of Josephinism never completely evaporated in Austria. Unquestionably Joseph II staved off an Austrian revolution for years.

The political and cultural climate of Metternich's youth was that of Joseph II and of the *Aufklärung*. His tolerant young parents, eager to prepare their sons for a place in the great world, designed an exceptionally liberal education for them. A learned abbé tutored them in the classics and the humanities. But when Clemens was thirteen, his parents engaged a young Protestant tutor, Johann Friedrich Simon, who was not only a disciple of progressive education on the model of Rousseau and his German parallel, Basedow, but a political radical as well. Clemens was a hypersensitive boy, rather too easily moved to tears, and it was one of Simon's first tasks to toughen him a bit: fencing and swimming were prescribed.

With Simon as guide and tutor, and with the abbé for conservative ballast, fifteen-year-old Clemens and his brother Pepi were enrolled at the University of Strasbourg in French Alsace, probably the most cosmopolitan of European universities in that day and celebrated for its school of international law.

Under the eminent professor Christoph Wilhelm Koch, potential young diplomats like Clemens Metternich absorbed the highest thinking of the Enlightenment on problems of international order.

The previous century and a half had seen the development of the earliest models of peace-keeping institutions. Poets and prophets had imagined a world free from violence; philosophers and statesmen had attempted to design such a world—on paper at least. Emeric Cmcé had suggested a permanent congress in Europe to arbitrate international disputes, while Sully, minister of Henri IV of France, proposed in his "Grand Design for Peace" a General Council of Europe with a joint army to make common decisions work. Some hundred years later, in 1713, the Abbé de St. Pierre detailed a more comprehensive plan for a union of sovereigns to preserve order and tranquillity, with a neutral City of Peace designated, where plenipotentiaries might meet to negotiate their differences and a court of arbitration be set up to decide international disputes.

Out of the humanist values of the seventeenth and eighteenth centuries had developed the basic concept of a Law of Nations, a kind of code of accepted conduct to guide nations in their relationships with one another, and to bring the use of force on the international level under a rule of law. The codifiers of that law, Grotius and Pufendorf and Vattel, urged a spirit of conciliation among nations, and the use of mediation, arbitration and of peace congresses to settle disputes.

While the art and practice of diplomacy—the management of international relations without the use of force—took an increasingly important role in the operation of government in the eighteenth century, war itself appeared to be declining, and wars when they occurred were less intense, less widespread.

In the climate of the Enlightenment peace no longer seemed an ideal state, but a possibly normal condition of human society. It was in this climate that Clemens Metternich grew to young adulthood.

The French Revolution erupted during his second year at Strasbourg. Metternich's first reaction to revolution, as described years later in his *Memoirs*, was certainly written with the hindsight of age and hardening conservatism. His tutor Simon was an enthusiastic supporter of the Revolution, and the revered Professor Koch became a member of the National Assembly. Probably Clemens viewed his first mob scene less with shock than with plain adolescent curiosity.

When he left Strasbourg in the summer of 1790 it was to accompany his father to the majestic spectacle of an imperial coronation in Frankfurt, a ceremony in which he too played a part. Joseph II had died; his brother, Leopold II was crowned Holy Roman Emperor with medieval pageantry. Only two years later, after Leopold's sudden death, Metternich took part in another imperial coronation, that of Leopold's son, Franz II, a slight, unimpressive, long-faced young man, only four years older than Clemens.

The guests who ate and drank at the banquets and danced at the balls could not have dreamed they were dancing on the grave of a feudal world. It was the last imperial coronation, and Franz the last Holy Roman Emperor.

While the French Revolution gained impetus and the monarchs east of the Rhine considered intervention, Clemens enrolled at the University of Mainz under the tutelage of the historian, Nicholas Vogt.

In the drawing rooms of Mainz, and in Brussels, where he spent holidays with his parents, he polished the useful arts of conversation and lovemaking among a decimated cast of French émigrés who continued to perform the graceful rituals of a drama that no longer had a stage.

In 1794 the revolutionary armies of France swarmed over the Rhineland, occupying the Metternich estates and cutting off that comfortable income that had enabled Count Franz Georg to maintain his family in easy luxury. At the same time Franz Georg lost his post as resident minister of the Austrian Netherlands in Brussels.

It was a bleak moment for the family, to find themselves reduced to not very genteel poverty.

Despite their troubled circumstances, the master plan for the elder son's education was carried to completion. In the spring of 1794 he accompanied a Belgian official to England for several months, to perfect his English and to observe parliamentary government in action.[4]

When he returned to the Continent in late autumn, his family had settled in Vienna. In the Austrian capital, where three hundred families of ancient feudal lineage made up the most exclusive court society in all Europe, the Metternichs, newly poor and with a full share of enemies in high places, did not cut a great figure.

It was Clemens' ambitious, strong-willed mother who took the simplest, most direct way of mending the family fortunes. She led her good-looking elder son, with his beautiful manners and ease of conversation—perhaps just a trifle glib in one so young—into the Kaunitz drawing room to meet Vienna's most eligible heiress. Countess Eleonore Kaunitz was not only heiress to a fortune but to one of the most distinguished names in European diplomacy; her grandfather, Prince Wenzel Kaunitz, had been Chancellor to Empress Maria Theresia and architect of that Austro-French alliance that had shattered the old power relationships of eighteenth-century Europe.

It had not been the easiest marriage to bring off. The young countess was courted by a number of top-drawer aristocrats, and neither her father nor her aunt, Princess Eleonore Liechtenstein, arbiter of Vienna society, was impressed by the young Rhinelander.

But the heiress herself had settled matters by falling irrevocably in love, and by moving heaven and earth and both her father and her aunt to have him. They were married at the Kaunitz castle at Austerlitz in Bohemia in the autumn of 1795, and if Clemens was not in love with his bride, he understood perfectly his role in the eighteenth-century marriage of *partis:*

> I was married only a few months after coming to Vienna [he wrote later]. My parents arranged the marriage; they left the decision up to the parties concerned. I was sorry to marry; my father wished it and I did as he wanted.[5]

The first years of his marriage he spent as an aristocratic dilettante, enjoying the society to which his wife's family connections brought instant entrée, reading for pleasure, attending lectures in geology, chemistry, physics, medicine. "I lived in the hospitals," he wrote of those years, "passing through all the *dégoûts*." All his life he would take a great interest in medicine.

Children were born to the couple, a daughter, Marie, who became Clemens' most cherished child, two little boys who died, one after the other—a not uncommon occurrence in families of that day—then a son, Victor, and two more daughters, Clementine and Leontine.

In 1801, when he was twenty-eight, the Austrian Emperor offered him his choice of three diplomatic posts. He chose Dresden, the rococo capital of the little country of Saxony, as safe a shelter as could be found in the whirlpool of European politics—and an excellent listening and learning post.

Already Napoleon had made himself First Consul of France. He had defeated Austria in battle and the Peace of Lunéville had been signed.

Napoleon's background and education could hardly have been more different from Metternich's. From Corsica he had been taken as a boy of nine to the military school at Brienne in France, where he was a scholarship pupil. An outsider, lonely, moody, *farouche*, speaking French with the accent of his island, he had turned the full power of his keen intellect on mastering the techniques of waging war. At fifteen he had gone on to the École Militaire in Paris, where he was commissioned a second lieutenant at sixteen.

During those formative years of his life, while he applied himself to his studies—studies primarily useful for a military career—Napoleon lived, so far as is known, without affection, without the gentling influence of family life. There were no women in the world of the military; he saw his mother and sister only once during those seven years. With the world of play, of leisure, of the uses of civility, he made no acquaintance. His ego, his whole sense of self, of masculine identity, was closely bound up with physical combat, with concepts of conquest and power and the inadmissibility of defeat.

In the year of Metternich's marriage, 1795, Immanuel Kant published his *Perpetual Peace*—the last great work of the Enlightenment on the solution of conflict by non-violent means. In it Kant envisioned a world republic with universal citizenship that would by law put an end to war.

In October of 1795 Napoleon walked into the Convention in Paris—or so he told the story later—on a day when it was threatened by dissension, perhaps dissolution. One of the leaders, Cambacérès, asked his advice. "I replied by asking for guns." That famous "whiff of grapeshot" was the first major step in Napoleon's climb to the pinnacle of European power. At the end of 1804 he had himself crowned hereditary Emperor.

Metternich, meantime, through the use of skills that were precisely the reverse of Napoleon's, was rising swiftly on the diplomatic ladder. At the end of 1803 he had moved up to the more important post of Berlin, where he was charged with the task of making an alliance with Prussia against

Napoleon. But King Friedrich Wilhelm III delayed, and in 1805, without the aid of Prussia, Austria and Russia went down in defeat before the French at Austerlitz, that battle Napoleon called his "masterpiece."

The following year Napoleon, having heard Metternich described as "bland" and of "imperturbable politeness," asked for his appointment as Austrian ambassador to Paris. There he began to learn to know Napoleon— as well as any man could know him. Disdainfully the polished Austrian recalled that first meeting, where the French Emperor "showed himself the parvenu" by keeping his hat on, against the rules of protocol. Yet Metternich found himself fascinated by Napoleon. "Conversation with him always had a charm for me, difficult to define."[6]

Napoleon had proposed to his sister, Caroline Murat, that she cultivate the Austrian envoy so that she could provide her brother with useful information. Talleyrand described Napoleon's younger sister as having "Cromwell's head on the shoulders of a pretty woman." Whether Caroline learned more from Metternich or he from her remains a question, but their friendship survived even the debacle of Napoleon.

In 1808, when Talleyrand, Napoleon's Foreign Minister, disillusioned with the war in Spain, where Napoleon's army was meeting bitter and unyielding opposition, began to work secretly for the Emperor's overthrow, he sold information to Austria, and subtly, with the utmost caution, sought to entice Austria into another war against France. Metternich relayed Talleyrand's information in cipher to the Austrian Foreign Minister, Philipp Stadion.

Aflame with patriotic zeal to defeat Napoleon and win back territory lost to France in 1801 and 1805, Austria declared war on France, and in May of 1809, under the Emperor Franz's brother, Archduke Karl, delivered a serious defeat—the first of his career—to Napoleon at Aspern.

Metternich, sent back to Austria in exchange for a French diplomat, arrived in time to stand at the side of Emperor Franz on July 5, 1809, on a hill a few miles below Vienna, with a telescope turned on the battlefield of Wagram.

"Very well," said the Emperor at the end of that day, so disastrous for Austria, "we shall have much to retrieve." In a gesture of despair he handed the portfolio of Foreign Minister to Metternich.

To take over the helm of a defeated country at a black low of morale and of material resources demanded courage and stamina far beyond the ordinary. Resourceful, flexible, armed with patience, Metternich would do whatever was necessary to survive in Napoleonic Europe. "We must buy time," he murmured to Prince Karl Schwarzenberg, who was replacing him at the embassy in Paris. To Emperor Franz he wrote:

> We must confine our system solely to tacking, to effacing ourselves, to coming to terms with the victor. Only thus may we perhaps preserve our existence until the day of general deliverance.[7]

Three months later, with the help of his wife, whom he had left behind in Paris, Metternich executed that most audacious coup of sauve-qui-peut politics; he married the Emperor's daughter, Archduchess Marie Louise, to her country's conqueror, Napoleon. "For Austria's sake and for Europe," the girl was told; she left for Paris in floods of tears. The old Viennese aristocracy, suspicious already of an outsider who had risen so quickly to the top post in the imperial government, were outraged at the marriage. A Habsburg princess wed to the Corsican tyrant! "A heifer sacrificed to the Minotaur," quipped the old Belgian wit the Prince de Ligne.

Metternich had hoped to buy important concessions with the marriage —at the very least, the return to Austria of her Illyrian possessions on the Adriatic. Napoleon presented him with a splendid silver dinner service crafted by the best goldsmith in Paris. Austria's rewards were chiefly negative. Metternich had prevented Napoleon's marriage to the sister of the Tsar and a renewed Franco-Russian alliance—not unimportant in the long range of his politics. Napoleon refrained from dismembering or invading Austria— at least for the moment.

Carefully Metternich continued to steer his course among the shoals and shallows and the hidden mines of Napoleonic Europe. With Austria in the middle ground between the two colossi of France and of Russia, his politics would always demand playing off one against the other. Above all, he had vowed, Austria would not again become a battlefield.

From 1809 he began to design a European peace—not a Napoleonic peace, which was only an armed truce, but a permanent peace that might be safeguarded by a co-operating society of nations.

In the Austrian Chancellery, the handsome baroque building on Ballhaus Square, Clemens Metternich both worked and lived.

His private apartments adjoined the offices of the ministry on the second floor. Each morning his valet Giroux drew back the curtains of the canopied bed and made his master ready for the day, performed all the little rituals that enabled Metternich to appear in public fastidiously soigné, every powdered curl in place, the snowy white stock at the neck tied in the most fashionable of knots.

Besides the ordinary chores of grooming, Giroux also provided—unwittingly, to be sure—the comedy relief in Metternich's day. He was a valet out of Molière, and all Metternich's friends waited for the latest Giroux anecdote.

Countess Eleonore Metternich, Laure to her husband and friends, lived with the children in the family apartments on the third floor. His life and hers moved along parallel paths. Most days Metternich breakfasted with Laure and the older children. When it suited his plans they dined together. Occasionally they slept together. It was a perfect arrangement—at least from Clemens' point of view.

From his father he had learned the importance of courting the older ladies of society, "who by their gossip have much more influence than you can imagine on the opinions formed of young people."[8]

From his mother he had learned the pleasure to be found in the company of spirited and intelligent women. He valued women for brains as well as beauty, even thought it quite possible—as he told a fascinated circle at a soiree one night—that a woman could carry out the duties of Minister of Foreign Affairs.[9]

Aristocratic society on the Continent had always followed the traditions of courtly love: marriage was a practical institution for the preservation of property and lineage, but poetry and romance were sought outside the bounds of marriage. "We marry to have children and not to satisfy the desires of the heart," Clemens wrote.[10] Clemens Metternich simply found it impossible to live without *une amie*, an intimate woman friend. He loved with grace and with great loyalty. He never broke ties; more often than not he transmuted his love affairs into friendships that lasted for life. He was a man who not only loved but liked women—a quality more rare than might be presumed.

During Clemens' first embassy in Dresden, Laure had shed most of the tears she was likely to shed in the course of their marriage. The whole world had known then that her young husband spent most of his nighttime hours —and a good many of his daytime—in the company of Princess Katharine Bagration. Princess Bagration bore him a child whom she named quite coolly after the father: Clementine. So he had two daughters named Clementine, a few years apart in age. In the narrow world of Central European society the two little Clementines occasionally met without ever guessing their close relationship.[11]

There was gossip then and later that Laure had retaliated in kind, and that the two middle Metternich children, Victor and Clementine, who were as dark as the others were fair, were not Clemens'. However that may be, Laure had learned after a time to keep her mournful brown eyes closed, sometimes for rather long periods of time. She remained his incomparable partner. He relied on her for the thousand tiny ways in which his personal life was arranged to suit his tastes, his comfort and his convenience. Her shrewdness, her discretion, her understanding of the diplomatic world and the fine gradations of protocol and precedence contributed not a little to Metternich's success.

During the Paris embassy she had handled adroitly the odd manners of the Bonapartes.

One January morning Pauline Bonaparte had invited Laure to bring her children calling. They had found Napoleon's beautiful sister reclining on a sofa in her boudoir as nude as Canova had sculpted her, while a black male friseur arranged her hair and a white maid drew on her undergarments and stockings. "We were present at her toilet from head to foot," Laure wrote her husband. "She had herself dressed even to her undershirt and hose in front of us and during the whole time she sang only your praise."[12]

Laure had not allowed herself to be ruffled by Napoleon's ill-mannered jokes. One night, receiving diplomats' wives at a *cercle* in the Tuileries, he stopped in front of her to remark, "Countess Laure, we are getting old and thin and ugly!" She had smiled and curtsied, as if he had paid her the nicest of compliments, which delighted him even more. "You certainly have more *esprit* than all these ninnies around you!" Later that evening he had remarked to a group within her hearing, "Madame Metternich is a charming woman whom I especially like because she never talks politics."[13] Laure did, of course, talk politics—only not before Napoleon.

Her husband had reason to thank Laure for her cool handling of a certain blood-chilling scene in the Paris house of General Andoche Junot just at the time when the Napoleon-Habsburg marriage was in negotiation. The paranoic Junot had discovered certain compromising love letters in his wife's possession, purportedly written by Clemens Metternich, and had summoned Laure Metternich to witness his revenge. In her presence he threatened to kill his wife with sewing shears, to kill the Metternich children as well and to challenge Clemens to a duel. "You will be hanged for it," said Laure Metternich shortly, "and I shall meanwhile put my children under the protection of the Emperor." The letters, she declared, were not in Clemens' handwriting; General Junot must be mad—his own extramarital escapades hardly left him grounds for accusing his wife. With that she left the Junot house, promising to send help to the wretched wife. A day or two later Napoleon packed both Junots off to Spain.[14]

The Junot scene was presently the talk of Paris, and Clemens Metternich in Vienna got reports from several sources on Laure's levelheaded valor.

Laure was an excellent mother; the four Metternich children were admirably brought up.

The eldest, Marie, her father's favorite, had just passed her sixteenth birthday. She wore her hair up in an arrangement of braids with curls hanging from each temple, and she looked out on the world with the gayest of bright spirits. Between Marie and her father existed one of those little hidden alliances that tie silken knots under the surface of family life. "She is me," he wrote of her, "and such is the fact in all essential ways. The movement of her mind is entirely like mine. She has most of my ideas and especially the same way of expressing them."[15] Sometimes when he worked late, Marie would tiptoe to the door, knock softly and sit waiting until he had time to talk to her. "*Nous deux*,"—we two—she would write again and again in letters to her father.

Victor, the Metternich son and heir, a bright, likable ten-year-old, worked hard at his studies to win his parents' praise—what else could fond parents ask? Once when he was ill his father wrote of him, "I have only this one son, and if I had sixty-five like the Shah of Persia, I would not love him the less."[16] Nine-year-old Clementine was described by their friend Prince Schwarzenberg as "an angel"; the baby Leontine was a delightful toddler of two.

Unlike most aristocratic fathers of his day, Metternich was a warmly affectionate father who spent a good bit of time with his children. He could romp with them, joke with them, pound out "Trempe ton pain, Marie" on the piano in such a comical way that the children shouted with laughter. He had a special gift with children; years later he remarked, "If I had not been a minister of state, I would have been a nursery governess."[17]

His marriage had, on the whole, worked out very well. A *mariage de convenance* on his side at least, the attachment had deepened and stabilized over nearly twenty years. The children, both living and dead, bonded them. They shared the common language that long marriage creates and a kind of dry ironic humor in looking at the world. Between them Napoleon was always *"le petit homme."*

> I am very far from regretting it today [Metternich wrote of his marriage]. My wife is excellent, full of intelligence, possessing all the qualities that make for inner happiness . . . [She] has never been pretty; she is lovable only to those who know her well. There is nothing in the world I would not do for her.[18]

So he came and went as he pleased, enjoying his life both public and private. He and Laure had worked out a modus vivendi, and if it was Metternich's modus more than Laure's, well, so Providence had ordained the world!

Women's options were few; their status derived from their husbands'. Laure could enjoy her position in the top circle of Vienna's social hierarchy.

"A few friends I am sure of," Clemens wrote, "really devoted, counting on me as on themselves, *une amie*—there is my fortune. A gentle tranquil home, an excellent wife, mother of good children whom she is raising well—there is my whole life."[19]

For some time there had been no *amie*, no intimate woman friend and political confidante. In the spring of 1813, target of unceasing criticism as he pursued his unpopular political course, Metternich felt more acutely than ever that lacuna in his life.

More and more often in the late evening, when he had written the last letter, signed the last dispatch of the day, he would walk briskly from the Chancellery across Minoritenplatz to Schenkenstrasse and climb the right-hand flight of stairs that led to the house of the Duchess of Sagan.

III

THE DUCHESS OF SAGAN

Wilhelmine of Sagan had spent most of the year 1812 on her estates in Bohemia, trying to bring some order to her tangled financial affairs. Her duchy of Sagan in Silesia had been occupied by the French Army after 1809, and she found herself so short of cash that she had enlisted Metternich's help to try to sell her diamonds—a chore at which he had abysmally failed.[1]

The two had known one another casually for years. They had met in the days of his Dresden embassy, and their paths had crossed from time to time in the spas and in the drawing rooms of Prague and Vienna.

They had carried on a gossamer-light flirtation, that conversation of the salon both understood so well, a pleasant game of words and eyes, of light bantering notes, of graceful badinage, that might lead equally well to bed or to a ball. He admired her beauty and intelligence; her political insights were nearly as keen as his own. But she had been twice divorced, and her succession of love affairs—even in the comparative freedom of Vienna society—gave him pause.

"I thought you had much *esprit* and little heart," he wrote her later, "that you were calculating but with little depth. You were beautiful—but I did not think you were good."[2]

They had not really become friends until the spring of 1810, when the newly appointed Foreign Minister had shocked Austrian society with news of the Habsburg-Bonaparte marriage. In her drawing room he had appeared, his newly acquired Golden Fleece gleaming about his neck, to fend off the vitriolic attacks of her sister Pauline and their friends who condemned the marriage as "a vileness, villainy of villainies."

That spring of 1810 he and Wilhelmine had embraced, as lightly as one might touch a champagne glass. If she had come close to falling in love with him then, he had kept sex and love well separated, had gone off to Paris with the wedding cortege and had resumed his old friendship with Caroline Murat.

When he returned to Vienna in the autumn of 1810, Wilhelmine was deeply in love with a young officer and hero of the War of 1809, Prince Alfred Windischgraetz. "Where were we in 1810?" Metternich would write her sadly later on. "Where then did I keep my heart? Where my head? Ah, my dear, what years of lost happiness, what years lost to me."[3]

Generally considered the loveliest and most gifted of the four princesses of Courland, Wilhelmine's childhood had been passed in her father's little sea-swept Baltic duchy, with its eight-months-long winters of bleak fog and storm blowing in across wide stretches of gray sands. Her father was Russian, her mother of an old noble Courland family, the Medems; the duchy itself was an uneasy fief of the King of Poland. Her cosmopolitan background was reflected in her given names: she was christened Catherine Frederica Wilhelmina Benigna, for the great Empress Catherine of Russia, for Crown Prince Friedrich Wilhelm of Prussia and for her paternal grandmother, the Duchess Benigna.

Like many exceptional women of her day, Wilhelmine was the eldest daughter of a father without sons, who lavished on the pretty, precociously bright little girl all the affection and pride of his somewhat dour and tyrannical disposition. He took her about with him everywhere, on her second birthday gave a grand ball in her honor, leading the tiny child out in a sweetly cut ball gown, to open the dance with a polonaise.

The critical years of Wilhelmine's adolescence were the volcanic years of the French Revolution; repercussions of that hurricane reached even the distant shores of the Baltic. When Poland's King Stanislas announced a liberal constitution and a parliamentary government for his people, it was an excuse for Catherine the Great, abetted by Friedrich Wilhelm II of Prussia, to perform a third and last surgical operation on Poland, Catherine taking Courland for part of her plunder. In exchange for withdrawing peacefully as ruler, Duke Peter was rewarded with two million rubles and a princely income.

Whatever had been his shortcomings as ruler, Duke Peter was not only a man of exceptional taste—he had accumulated a superb collection of fine paintings, sculpture and engravings—but of shrewd business sense as well. He had had the foresight to feather his nest and long before his exile from Courland in 1793, when Wilhelmine was twelve, he had already acquired the duchy of Sagan in Prussian Silesia, as well as estates in Bohemia and palaces in Berlin and Prague.

He was in fact one of the richest men in Central Europe. When the King of Prussia died in 1797, the royal family, embarrassingly short of cash, had borrowed from the Duke of Courland to pay for the king's funeral.

In the castle of Sagan the family lived a life of feudal luxury. The duke had his own troupe of Italian musicians and comedians to perform in the castle theater—some of the early performances of Mozart operas were given for the duke. There were house parties and hunting parties where fifty or a hundred guests would arrive to hunt, to dance, to banquet for the better part of a winter.

Of warm family life, however, Wilhelmine and her three younger sisters had singularly little. Aristocratic marriages were property bonds; their parents' marriage was anything but happy. Her mother, the pretty and still youthful Duchess Dorothea, escaped as women of her class had frequently escaped, into the arms of a younger lover, a Polish Count Batowski, almost certainly the father of Wilhelmine's youngest sister, Dorothée. The duchess bought herself a summer castle in Saxony, contrived to spend six months of every year there in the company of her lover and their child. The latter the Duke of Courland conveniently continued to acknowledge.

Although Wilhelmine's parents were cultivated people, the education bestowed on the three elder princesses was meager at best. Had Wilhelmine been born a boy, she would have had, like Clemens Metternich, carefully chosen tutors to direct her curious, bright mind, to accompany her to one of the great German universities, to guide her on her grand tour of Europe. Eventually, as the eldest child, she would have sat in her father's place in the Bohemian estates, and from there in all likelihood, with her birth and her natural gifts, have risen as Metternich had, in the diplomatic and political world of Central Europe.

But only one career was open to women: marriage to a man of equal or, preferably, of superior rank.

When Wilhelmine was twelve an excellent governess, Antonie Forster, sister of that Georg Forster who had accompanied Captain James Cook around the world, came to teach the princesses. Fräulein Forster had a broad grasp of scholarship and a liberal mind in close touch with the Enlightenment. She had lived many years in England; she taught the princesses fluent English—already they spoke French, German, Russian; she opened for Wilhelmine an enticing glimpse of the limitless world of learning. But she remained with them only two years, when it was assumed apparently that the girls' education was complete. All her life Wilhelmine would regret that far from adequate education; years later she would bring Fräulein Forster back to live as an honored guest under her roof and teach her foster daughters more than she herself had learned.

When Wilhelmine's father, Duke Peter, died in January of 1800, he left behind an immense fortune, a lovely, still youthful widow, suddenly emanci-

pated from an unhappy marriage, and four daughters, precociously beautiful—three of them now perilously rich.

It happened that sixteen-year-old Jeanne had been disinherited on her
father's deathbed for one of those unlucky sexual misadventures around which
nineteenth-century fiction would spin a hundred plots. During the summer of
1799 the Duchess of Courland had taken Wilhelmine to the elegant spa of
Karlsbad where Central European aristocracy customarily displayed mar-
riageable daughters. Her sisters Pauline and Jeanne had stayed behind
with their father in his Bohemian castle at Náchod, where he liked to spend
summers. Jeanne had fallen in love with a young Italian actor-violinist
named Arnoldi, who played in her father's private orchestra and gave the
sisters music lessons. The little summer romance had ended as such affairs
often did. Jeanne became pregnant. In fearful desperation the young pair
fled from Náchod to Germany, hoping to marry and take ship to America,
with Jeanne's little box of personal jewels to buy them passage.

Jeanne's father, the duke, outraged at the thought of such a mésalliance,
sent servants and soldiers in pursuit of the pair. In Erfurt a Prussian
officer found Jeanne and brought her back home. Her father would not see
her or forgive her. Just before his death, two months later, he settled her
share of his vast fortune on her three sisters. A few months later Jeanne bore
a little son, Fritz, who was put to nurse with a goldsmith's wife near her
mother's castle in Saxony, and later placed with the Partheys, a cultivated
family in Berlin, who educated Fritz with their own sons. As for Jeanne's
lover, Arnoldi, he wrote letter after letter to Jeanne, beseeching her to flee
with him. Eventually, probably through a letter forged in Jeanne's handwriting, he was lured back to Bohemia, seized, imprisoned and executed by
order of the girls' guardian, Count Wratislaw, Chief of Bohemian Police.
Punishment for seduction was in inverse relationship to one's rank in society.[4]

That spring of 1800, in the months after the duke's death, all the most
eligible princes of Central Europe flocked to pay court to the two eldest
sisters. Wilhelmine remained coolly aloof to all suitors, but Pauline, to whom
marriage meant a kind of emancipation, married the Prince of Hohen-
zollern-Hechingen in April of 1800. She was not in the least in love with
him and after bearing him a son would live separately from her husband
most of her life.

A month later, in May of 1800, Prince Louis Ferdinand, cousin of the
King of Prussia and a man of unusual gifts, handsome, intelligent, musically
gifted—he would be one of the great heroes of Prussian history—appeared
to pay court to Princess Wilhelmine. He was also, to be sure, a bit wild and
over his head in gambling debts. His father had warned him sternly that
he must marry an heiress and soon. Still Louis Ferdinand seemed to be an
ideal match for Wilhelmine, and their first meetings, under the duchess's
careful eye, went off well. The prince seemed to be completely enchanted
with the girl. But before the wooing was well under way, he got orders from

the royal palace in Berlin to drop the courtship at once. The reasons for the order have never been clear. Some sources believe Queen Louise of Prussia persuaded the King to retract his permission for the match because the Courland family was not of equal birth with the Hohenzollerns. Others believe that certain rumors concerning Wilhelmine had reached the ears of the Prussian court.

Certainly the abrupt end of the courtship by royal order was humiliating to the prince, equally so to Wilhelmine.

But the truth was that her affections were already engaged. That spring of 1800 she was deeply in love with Baron Gustav Armfelt, an exiled Swedish statesman and adventurer more than twice her age, with a wife and children of his own in Sweden. Armfelt had been forced to leave Sweden during the regency that followed the assassination of Gustav III. Wilhelmine's mother had met him in Karlsbad, and unwisely had brought him to live in the Courland palace in Prague after her husband's death. Armfelt called it his "isle of Calypso."

Promising to superintend the duchess's financial affairs and to complete her daughters' education, Armfelt turned his practiced charm on the duchess and persuaded her to end her long liaison with Batowski. He taught seven-year-old Dorothée to read, and under the mother's sweetly myopic gaze, while he talked philosophy and art and Rousseau, the accomplished rake of forty-two introduced Wilhelmine to all the erotic refinements acquired in the choicest alcoves of Europe. Choderlos de Laclos could hardly have imagined a more dangerous liaison.

Armfelt had gone along with the Courland ladies to Leipzig when Prince Louis Ferdinand had been introduced to Wilhelmine, and he may have been instrumental in bringing about the rupture of the suit.

In any case, only six weeks after the departure of Prince Louis Ferdinand from the scene, Wilhelmine was hastily married to Prince Louis Rohan-Gué-menée, penniless younger son of the ancient noble French family which had emigrated to Prague during the Revolution. Wilhelmine was already two months pregnant with Armfelt's child, and the dowry arrangements were of a suitable magnificence to insure the complaisance of the bridegroom to the somewhat unusual terms of the marriage.

Late that year of 1800 Wilhelmine left Sagan to journey alone to Hamburg, supposedly to visit a half sister. There in January of 1801, with Armfelt at her bedside, she bore a little daughter, whom they named Adelaide Gustava Aspasia Armfelt—called "Vava" for short. The child was whisked off to cousins of Armfelt to rear, with Wilhelmine named as godmother so that she could settle a sizable portion on the child. The birth had been difficult, the midwife's ministrations clumsy, and she was slow to recover. When she returned to Sagan, ill and thin, it was given out that she had been injured in a carriage accident. Never again would Willhelmine conceive and bear child.[5]

That Vava Armfelt was Wilhelmine's illegitimate child remained a well-kept secret within her immediate family.

In the early days of the nineteenth century, as Napoleon rose to be First Consul, then Emperor of the French, that interesting ménage à trois, young Prince and Princess Rohan with their live-in friend, Armfelt, traveled about from Prague to Paris, to London, to Dresden, leasing a palace here and there, entertaining lavishly, both husband and lover freely spending Wilhelmine's fortune. She wearied of Armfelt first, then of Rohan, whom she divorced in 1804. She remarried almost at once a tall, melancholy Russian, Prince Wassily Troubetskoi, whom she met in Dresden. The second marriage lasted scarcely longer than the War of 1805. Troubetskoi too she divorced, paying heavily again for her independence. It was simpler and much less expensive, she found, to take lovers.

In the eighteenth century, in France and in Central Europe, women had enjoyed increasing social freedom. While the fine slogans of the Enlightenment, equality and the brotherhood of man, said nothing of the equality and sisterhood of women, and while even the most radical of the French revolutionaries declined to extend citizenship to the female sex, still some women —Mary Wollstonecraft in England, Madame de Staël and Olympe de Gouges in France—had spoken out strongly for better education, greater autonomy— even the possibility of civil rights for women.

In the Protestant countries on the Continent open separation and divorce were increasingly common. As Madame de Staël wrote, marriage in Germany was becoming "less an association which has for its result affection than an affection of which the consequence is association." If the Revolution in France had failed to bring women any participation in government, nevertheless it had eased the legal restrictions that prevented their living as individuals with free choice.

The changing attitude of women toward themselves at the turn of the eighteenth century was reflected clearly in the revolutionary design of their clothing. Hoops, panniers, constricting whalebone corsets were gone, along with the powder, wigs and beauty patches of the old regime. Dresses were cut loosely and comfortably, to follow the natural lines of the body. Women suddenly had complete freedom of movement. They could walk, stride, even run, jump in and out of carriages—impossible for a fashionable woman a few years earlier. Under the new gowns, often transparent and slit to the thigh, was worn only a lightweight clinging shift, with bare legs and sandals *à la Grecque*. Hair was cut and worn *au naturel*, in ringlets hanging loose about the face or pulled back into a simple Grecian knot.

But Napoleon's rise to power and the development of a military regime in France spelled an end to the brief period of greater legal and social freedom women had enjoyed. The Code Napoléon declared married women the property of their husbands, curtailed their legal and property rights for well over a century. The Code itself was drawn up by Napoleon's large staff of legal experts, but the laws applying to women had been amended into stricter terms in Napoleon's own handwriting.

Napoleon abhorred the idea of women influencing politics; he blamed the moral laxity in France on the social freedom of women under the old regime. He did not feel comfortable in the society of women. "Love," he remarked to his Council members once, "is an exchange of perspirations." Also it took too much time from really important things—such as making war. "It takes time to make oneself loved and even when I had nothing to do I always vaguely felt that I had no time to waste."

In any case, the biology of the sex was their destiny. Women, he declared, were "machines for making babies."

> What a mad idea to demand equality for women! Nature intended women to be our slaves; only through our stupidity do they try to rule us. They are our property, we are not theirs. They belong to us, just as a tree which bears fruit belongs to the gardener.[6]

Wherever the Code Napoléon was carried by the empire's conquering armies, it brought half of humanity less liberty, less equality under the law.

The Courland princesses had not been untouched by the earliest currents of French and English feminism. Wilhelmine's aunt, Elisa von der Recke, had left an unhappy marriage to make an independent life for herself as a poet and writer and a central figure in the literary circles of Goethe and Wieland and Schiller. She had been one of the first women in Germany to read and absorb the importance of Mary Wollstonecraft's *A Vindication of the Rights of Woman*. And if her frank espousal of feminist views was not quite the style of her nieces, still they were fond of Tante Elisa, and in their mother and her sister the four princesses had before their eyes models of women who in differing ways had shaped independent lives for themselves.[7]

Gradually, out of the unwisdom, the shipwreck and disillusionment of her youth, Wilhelmine matured and created a life of her own quite unlike that of most women around her. Discarding the names of both her former husbands, she assumed the title of her inherited lands and remained to the end of her life the Duchess of Sagan.

Her closest family ties were with her two sisters, Pauline and Jeanne. After the birth of her illegitimate child in 1800 Jeanne had been provided with a tempting dowry and married off to an unpleasant Neapolitan with a somewhat dubious title, the Duke of Acerenza. Both Pauline and Jeanne lived apart from their husbands, sharing a town house in Vienna not far from Wilhelmine's. Their youngest sister, Dorothée, married for political reasons in the spring of 1809 to a nephew of Napoleon's Foreign Minister, Talleyrand, now lived in Paris.

A little troupe of children of complicated provenance followed in the three elder sisters' wake and shared their affections. Three young girls who called Wilhelmine *Maman* were being carefully educated in the private school of Madame Brévillier in Vienna. Thirteen-year-old Emilie was actually Wilhelhelmine's niece, child of an illegitimate son of her father. Eight-year-old Marie Wilson had been born of a brief liaison between Pauline and Wilhelmine's first husband, Louis Rohan. The third child, Clara Bressler, was not blood-related, but was the child of an impoverished girlhood friend of Wilhelmine's.

As for Wilhelmine's only natural child, Gustava was growing up in faraway Sweden with the Armfelts. After the annexation of Finland by Russia in 1812, the child's father, Baron Gustav Armfelt, had become governor and was working in close association with the Tsar. It was the bitterest regret of Wilhelmine's life that she had surrendered her child to the father thirteen years before, in the confusion and pain and uncertainty of her youth. In 1813 she began to ponder how she could regain possession of her daughter.

In the spring of 1813 Wilhelmine had just passed her thirty-second birthday. Neither men nor women disputed that she was one of the loveliest women of her day; over and over, the word used to describe her was not *jolie* but *belle*.

Her looks were not easy to capture on canvas. Although in her portraits she appears to be brunette, she was actually a dark-eyed blonde "with great brown eyes and the finest forehead," Emilie describes her. Wilhelmine did not completely approve of her nose, slender and curved like her father's, but it gave a stamp of distinction to a face that might otherwise have been too soft in outline. She was not tall—she used to joke that her height was exactly that of Napoleon—but she carried her beautifully proportioned figure well, so that she had the appearance of regal height.

The Italian Grassi painted all four sisters in fashionable Grecian poses, Wilhelmine's face extraordinarily expressive, her dark eyes sparkling, lips just parted in a mischievous smile, as if she were trying to keep an enormously funny secret to herself. "For some years Grassi has been painting your expression on all the faces that pose for him," Metternich told her once.[8] Perhaps only the subtler pencil of the English portrait artist Sir Thomas Lawrence captured something of the seductive and elusive charm that left so indelible an impression on her own generation and the one after.

A woman of great warmth and humor, Wilhelmine was surprisingly without vanity. Her foster daughter recalled how she often received visitors in the morning in déshabille, in her old wadded dressing gown, her hair in a black sleeping cap, with two slices of lemon bound to her temples. Extravagantly generous of herself and her worldly goods, she was always ready to empty her purse, lend her jewels, add another penniless exile to her household.

Because she was beautiful and because she rebelled against the double standard of sexual morality, by which, as her contemporary Rahel Varnhagen pointed out, men and women formed "two different nations, one moral, the other not," it would be in terms of her sexual life that contemporary memoirists and later biographers would define Wilhelmine.

Barred by her sex from participation in government, she found in politics nevertheless the consuming interest of her life.

She had a thorough understanding of the complex history and political machinery of Central and Eastern Europe. Multilingual, with a network of relatives and acquaintances in England, France, Prussia and Russia, she kept in close touch with the latest news, nuances, gossip, rumor.

Wilhelmine held no position of power, nor did she leave any political writings, as Gentz did, by which a later generation could assess her skill of analysis and her political discernment. All we know of her gifts was the influence she exercised on the minds of the men around her. Gentz remarked somewhat grudgingly, "Even women at that time took such an active part in [political] affairs that I must acknowledge I learned much in my confidential conversations with the shrewd and intriguing Princess Bagration, the enthusiastic but excellent Countess Wrbna, and the restless but very clearsighted Duchess of Sagan."[9]

And Metternich told Wilhelmine:

> If you had been a man you would have been my friend. We would have carried on great and successful business affairs together. You would have been an ambassador and I a minister—or vice versa.[10]

Hastily he added that he preferred her as she was.

The tragedy of her life was its lack of purpose, the waste of a keen mind and exceptional natural gifts. She was easily discouraged, she had no faith in herself or her future, often fell prey to periods of deep depression. The sixty-hour migraines from which she suffered all her life stemmed no doubt from the unresolved tensions of her life, its frustrations and emotional insecurity. Never could she believe in the possibility of her own happiness and fulfillment. "The faculty of tormenting myself, that of being unhappy, is much stronger in me than that of being happy," she wrote.[11]

In the circles of society where power was held, women as well as men were divided on the question of war or peace. Empress Maria Ludovica, whose family had lost their duchy of Modena to Napoleon, was strongly pro-war. Caroline von Humboldt, wife of the Prussian envoy and an ardent Prussian patriot, cried, "Oh, that I could buy the beginning of this victory with my heart's blood! Nature has made women wonderfully—so limited strength and so unlimited desires!"[12]

Wilhelmine's sister, Pauline Hohenzollern, had been so outspokenly critical of Austria's peace policy that her name had appeared in police records more than once the previous autumn and Metternich had had to write Wilhelmine to shut her sister up.

Wilhelmine herself was torn by uncertainty: war appeared to be inevitable —and yet if Clemens Metternich were right, then it was still possible that war might be avoided. To Alfred Windischgraetz she had written once:

> I am not a heroine, and as a woman I can only deplore the miseries of war, and I am sure if there were only women ruling there would never be war and the world would not be the less happy for it.[13]

IV

DANGERS OF THE TRADE

Toward the end of that February of 1813 Clemens Metternich narrowly escaped assassination.

He was to have been set upon late one night, either strangled or stabbed, as he emerged "from a certain house he frequented." So much is clear from the police report which Otto, the French ambassador, quoted in his dispatch to Paris.[1]

The "certain house" was beyond doubt the Palais Palm, and it may well have been on Wilhelmine's threshold that the murder was to have taken place.

Of the would-be assassins the report detailed nothing except that they were army officers, that they belonged to a secret society pledged to bring Austria into war on the side of Russia.

The Austrian Secret Police, ubiquitous if by no means so efficient as Napoleon's, got wind of the plot in time. The officers were apprehended, the secret committee rounded up and everything quickly hushed up "so as not to excite people any further."

But there was more than one plot afoot that troubled and suspenseful spring, and more than one conspiracy to rid Austria of her Foreign Minister.

Among the visitors to the Chancellery in the first week of February was the young Anglo-Irish agent John Harcourt King. He came to ask Metternich for a passport for his courier, a man named Danelon, who was to carry dispatches to St. Petersburg.

Sixth and youngest son of the Earl of Kingston, who had large estates in County Cork, King had come to the Continent in 1802—the same year Metternich had begun his Dresden embassy—hoping to forge a diplomatic career for himself. Attractive and personable, "certainly very amusing," a compatriot described him, "but terribly harum-scarum, even for an Irishman," King had a strain of intemperate eccentricity.[2] He was brash, incautious, hotheaded— qualities singularly unsuited to diplomacy. In the eleven years since, while Metternich had risen to the top post in the Austrian Government, King had not succeeded even in winning diplomatic accreditation from his government.

For a number of years after her second divorce, the lively and fascinating King had been Wilhelmine's lover, and it had been in her house that Metternich first made his acquaintance. The two men disliked each other at once. Exact opposites in temperament and in political philosophy, they viewed one another with distrust and suspicion, not unmingled with personal jealousy.

King had not, however, hesitated to make use of his personal acquaintance with the Austrian minister to persuade the English Foreign Office to send him back to the Continent as a secret agent in 1811. He was to keep Castlereagh informed on Austrian plans and to perform such other chores for his country as might come his way.

Metternich had granted King a renewed passport, he told Emperor Franz, in order to keep a watchful eye on him. King's love affair with Wilhelmine had long since ended—at least on her side, though by no means on King's. The watchful eye would be needed, for one of the little chores King hoped to perform for his country was to aid in stirring up a revolt against Franco-Bavarian rule among the Alpine lands that had once belonged to Austria.

Ever since the War of 1805, when Austria had been forced to cede the Tyrol and the Vorarlberg to Napoleon's ally Bavaria, a strong party of Tyrolean patriots had fought against Bavarian-French rule. During the War of 1809 under the courageous Andreas Hofer, they had freed the province for a time, only to lose their liberty again by the Peace of Schönbrunn at the end of that year. Andreas Hofer, looking on that dictated peace as a betrayal, continued to fight on. He was taken prisoner by the French and shot at Mantua by order of Napoleon in February of 1810. The short tragic struggle of the loyal Tyrolese had aroused wide sympathy in Austria and deeper resentment of Napoleon.

After 1809 a series of plots to free the Tyrol simmered under the surface of the Austrian political scene, secretly encouraged by English agents on the Continent with promises of support and money. Anti-Bonapartists believed that a revolt sparked in the Tyrol would spread quickly to French-dominated Switzerland, to northern Italy and down to the Illyrian coast. In 1811 such an uprising had been planned but had foundered for lack of money and of leadership.

A group of ardent anti-Bonapartists formed a political club that met on Mondays at King's house to dine and talk. Among them were General Wall-

moden, highly respected in the Austrian Army and a close friend of the Courland princesses, Irish-born General Nugent, who also served in the Austrian
Army, the Sicilian ambassador, Count Ruffo, and not least of all Gentz, who
certainly reported back to Metternich on anything worth reporting.

King, meantime, totally committed to the overthrow of Napoleon by
violent means, viewed with a jaundiced eye Metternich's peace plan—what
King termed "cold, selfish politics." At Metternich's specific urging he wrote
inquiring the views of His Majesty's ministers "on the practicability of negotiations and on what bases they would be inclined to negotiate." Metternich's sole object was "a general peace and provided he attains that end," King
averred, "he is not anxious what the conditions of it may be," adding, not
without a grain of personal animus, "His only ambition is to be pointed out
as the pacificator of Europe, for no other reason than to satisfy his vanity."[3]

With news of the disaster that had befallen Napoleon's army in Russia,
the hope of the Tyrolean patriots revived, and the plot to spark a revolt in
the Alpine lands was resurrected again. By the end of January the conspiracy
had ripened and had acquired a leader and the promise of money.

Among the conspirators were such well-known Austrian officials as Joseph,
Baron Hormayr, director of the imperial archives, and Anton Roschmann,
former *Kreishauptmann* of the Tyrol. It was General Wallmoden apparently who had persuaded Archduke Johann, the younger brother of Emperor
Franz, to lend his name as leader to the risky undertaking. A kindly, idealistic man, with a penchant for Rousseau's simple life and a keen sympathy
for the Tyrolean peasants, the archduke agreed to leave Vienna as soon as
the weather permitted to take charge of Tyrolean volunteers. The signal for
the uprising was set for Easter Monday, April 13.

King for his part promised to furnish the plotters with up to thirty
thousand pounds for guns and powder. The money was to come from a fund
which Lord Cathcart, English ambassador at the court of the Tsar, was holding for just such useful purposes.

Certainly the Austrian police were on the track of the plot from early
January, for young Walpole during his visit to Vienna had indiscreetly made
connection with one of the leading conspirators, John de Salis, and had
carried back to St. Petersburg a full report of the plot. King had met twice
with Archduke Johann in January, as well as with the other conspirators.
Probably all King's letters had been opened, read and resealed. Metternich
had allowed the dispatches to pass.

But the political situation was growing more delicate each day. If feelings
of hatred against Napoleon and the French continued to crystallize, such a
revolt indeed might, as King and his friends believed, set Central Europe
in flames, totally destroying any hope for peace.

In response to King's request for a passport for his courier Danelon in
early February, Metternich did not expressly refuse to grant one, but he de-

layed issuing a pass until his peace envoys were well along on their respective journeys to the Tsar and to England. He explained quite frankly to King that he feared King might express himself in his dispatches in such a manner as to counteract his project of negotiation.[4]

King fretted and fumed. Not until February 23 was the precious pass furnished so that Danelon could take his departure for the North. Orders apparently were sent on ahead that Danelon was to be watched on his journey through Austrian territory to make sure he passed no papers to anyone. At Brünn and again at Olmütz he was delayed by the authorities.

On the night of February 25 he left the Moravian town of Weisskirchen. A half hour outside town, on a lonely dark road, as he was dozing in the back of his carriage, it was suddenly set upon by highwaymen, the vehicle overturned, he himself pulled out, bound, gagged, blindfolded and led into a nearby wood, where he was searched down to his boots. He was not injured and before long an officer in a passing carriage rescued him. The courier's carriage had been ransacked and even the pillows taken—pillows stuffed full of secret dispatches for St. Petersburg and London.[5]

In Weisskirchen he notified the authorities and waited several days, hoping the bandits might be apprehended and his dispatches returned. No trace of either was ever found, though he picked up rumors that the holdup had been planned.

King did not learn of the robbery until a full week later, in the first week of March. Furiously he hurried to the Chancellery, certain, as he exploded in a letter to Castlereagh, "that this infamous and atrocious deed" had been perpetrated by Metternich's orders. The Austrian minister received him in the friendliest way, "feigned to be totally ignorant of the transaction," and expressed guileless concern lest King's dispatches "fall into improper hands."[6]

A day or so later, on March 7, the last Sunday of the carnival season, Count Otto had an appointment with the Austrian minister. But Metternich sent a message asking to postpone their meeting because of "urgent business." All that day Metternich worked with the Minister of Police, and in the evening police fanned out over the city rounding up the suspects in the Alpine conspiracy. "A great number of personages, even very highly placed, were arrested," Otto reported to Paris.[7] Hormayr was arrested in evening clothes, about to leave the house to celebrate his daughter's birthday.

Justice was swift. There was no trial, and all news of the conspiracy was kept out of the official press. The plotters were whisked away, some, like Hormayr, to prison in Hungary, others into exile.

Archduke Johann was given a stern dressing down by the Emperor and placed under house arrest. For many years afterward the Emperor refused to trust his younger brother with any post in the government.

Wallmoden had already, a few days before the denouement of the plot, had a stormy interview with Emperor Franz when English newspapers had disclosed that the Austrian general had accepted a commission in the English Army before he had resigned from the Austrian. The sovereign informed him he could be sent to a fortress for life; two days later Metternich told Wallmoden he might leave Austria, "enjoining him to leave immediately."[8]

The sequence of events in the tense days immediately preceding March 7 is not entirely clear. Certain it is that Anton Roschmann, perhaps as early as February 19, had confessed the whole conspiracy to Metternich. For turning state's evidence Roschmann went free. While there is no proof of Metternich's complicity in the Danelon robbery, circumstantial evidence points strongly to him. And certainly he had motive. King's dispatches provided him with evidence needed to move in and crush the conspiracy.

King was invited to leave Austria, or rather desired, quite civilly, according to Cathcart, "to chuse another Residence." Even then, on the brink of exile, King did not have the sense to bridle his tongue. He accused Metternich and Count Hardenberg of complicity in "the late atrocious crime"— the Danelon affair—not even bothering to veil his accusations in cipher in his dispatches to Castlereagh. Gentz, writing to Wessenberg in England, called the Alpine conspiracy "fatal beyond measure." Metternich had seen in King only "a conspirator and a personal enemy," while King saw in Metternich "nothing but a minister-bandit."[9] The plot, Gentz observed, was "clumsily conceived and very foolishly imagined and carried out."[10]

Metternich had handled the Alpine conspiracy with toughness, but also with considerable restraint. Had the plot taken place it would have smashed like a hammer blow the delicate and fragile vessel of peace. It could have cost, quite futilely, hundreds or thousands of lives, as Metternich himself pointed out, delivered over to French or Bavarian military authorities to be shot. Metternich intended to win back the Tyrol for Austria—but he intended to do it through a negotiated European peace.

On the very eve of his departure King wrote Castlereagh that Metternich "has not yet abandon'd his hope of a general peace," that he thought Bonaparte, realizing the difficulty of his position, would be ready to listen to terms, and that the basis of those terms would be a France retiring within her "natural boundaries" of Rhine, Alps and Pyrenees.[11]

It had been during the days just preceding the exposure of the Alpine plot that Metternich showed Otto the police report detailing plans for his assassination. "He made me read other reports revealing plots woven in the same vein under Russian auspices," Otto said.[12]

Roschmann, moreover, in his confession warned Metternich that his life was in danger. "They think," he told the Foreign Minister, "that the politics of the Austrian Cabinet would change if you disappeared from the scene."[13]

Metternich's cool physical courage in those days amazed and impressed Gentz. The minister continued to go about the city unarmed, without bodyguard, continued to walk nearly every night to the Palais Palm, quite as if nothing had happened. He had to prove, Gentz wrote Nesselrode immediately after, that "he was not a man to be trifled with in these things and he would find his path himself without having others trace it out for him."[14]

CENTRAL EUROPE: 1813

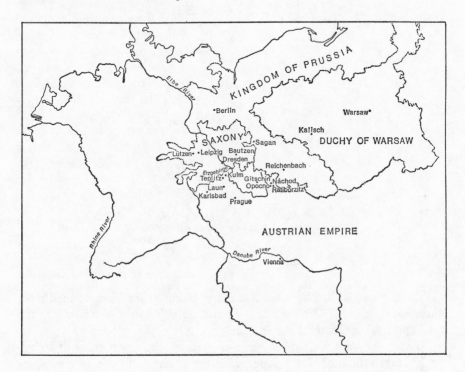

V

GLOOMY SPRING

*It is Austria! Austria! which holds the balance, and it is
to Austria that we should direct all our thoughts.*
—SIR ROBERT WILSON

1

The Alpine plot had been frustrated, but prospects for peace seemed more uncertain than ever. "We are rushing headlong either into peace or into the total upheaval of Central Europe," Metternich told Otto gloomily.[1]

Despite his sangfroid and seeming composure, the tense weeks of February had taken their toll. Immediately after the arrests in the Alpine conspiracy Metternich took to his bed. Ill he remained through the critical weeks of March and April while the hope of peace quivered uncertainly in the balance against the threat of renewed war.

Whatever was the nature of his illness—perhaps the "rheumatic catarrh" to which he was susceptible—his friends were sufficiently concerned to beg him to spare his health, and the Emperor took the unusual step of crossing the square from the palace to the Chancellery to confer with his minister in his chamber.

It was in every way a gloomy spring, and Metternich's usual cheerful optimism was surely sorely tried. The snows that had buried the Grande Armée in November and December lingered long on the slopes of the Giant Mountains and the Tatras, and in the river valleys of the Elbe and the Oder and the Danube. After the snows melted, a steady cold rain fell day after day.

Metternich himself was still ill in April when all four Metternich children came down with whooping cough—a disease all too often fatal to children in that day. Upstairs in the third-floor apartment Laure Metternich watched anxiously at their bedsides, and every day Dr. Staudenheimer climbed the stairs to visit Clemens and then a flight higher to dose the children with great spoonfuls of a bitter brown medicine.

"Nothing breaks me down like a sick child," Metternich would remark. "Never anxious about myself I am always so for the children."[2] Nine-year-old Clementine, usually the sturdiest of the Metternich children, was the most dangerously ill.

If only spring would come! As soon as the weather permitted, Laure intended to move the family out of the damp, chilly apartments in the Chancellery to their summer villa on the Rennweg. A year or so before the Metternichs had bought the pretty country house in Italian style, surrounded by lawns and fine gardens, just twenty minutes' carriage ride outside town. The younger children would have room to romp and play in fresh air and sunshine. Metternich himself "hungered and thirsted" for the garden. "I am a child of light and need brilliant light to be able to live," he wrote.[3] He would go riding with the children each day; it would be good for his nerves; horseback riding was Dr. Staudenheimer's prescription for nearly every complaint.

Meantime, he lay in bed, listened to the sound of rain falling outside his windows, read the dispatches his assistant Hudelist brought him, saw the most important visitors.

One of these was Louis Narbonne, the new French ambassador whom Napoleon had sent to replace Otto. Otto had been writing a bit too persuasively of Metternich's peace designs, and Napoleon was certain Otto was in Metternich's pocket. He warned Narbonne "not to fall victim to Metternich's siren charms."

Narbonne was an authentic survivor of the old French monarchy; indeed, French society gossiped that Narbonne with his exquisite manners and his huge Bourbon nose—rosy from a lifetime of good living—was in fact a natural son of Louis XV, whom he strikingly resembled. Like Talleyrand Narbonne had transferred his allegiance to Napoleon. Napoleon had been enchanted when Narbonne introduced him to the forms of old society, delivering dispatches to the French Emperor on the flat of his sword accompanied by a sweeping bow.

In Metternich's view it was not a happy exchange of ambassadors, but from his sickbed he sent off a friendly note of greeting:

> I am not looking a bit like myself alas! at the moment of your arrival. I am really ill—I who am never sick. . . . But come around and see me tomorrow in your off-duty clothes, without your pearls or keys or diamond buckles.[4]

He managed to extract at once the crucial piece of information he wanted. For all the splash of his arrival, with a string of fine carriage horses, a fleet of servants liveried in red on red, four dozen place settings of wrought silver and the finest Sèvres, Narbonne had only ordinary credentials and no powers to negotiate even a preliminary peace.

For his part Narbonne found that Otto had not exaggerated the virulent anti-French sentiment in Vienna. Everywhere he went he met the outspoken wish that Austria would soon free herself of the heavy boot of France.

No more than Napoleon was Narbonne convinced that Metternich's peace talk was genuine. Unlike Otto he was prepared to report exactly what Napoleon wanted to hear. Later, on St. Helena, Napoleon wrote of that spring, "Until Monsieur de Narbonne's embassy we had been dupes of Austria; in less than 15 days [he] had penetrated everything, and Monsieur de Metternich found himself very embarrassed in this nomination."[5]

Just before Narbonne's arrival Metternich had got the first report from the peace envoy he had sent to the Tsar. At first the Tsar had refused to assent to Austria's intervention until he knew precisely what kind of peace Metternich had in mind, and what Austria planned to do in case the peace effort foundered. In the end he agreed to the peace attempt, provided his Allies agreed as well. The assent of the Russian sovereign had certainly been reluctantly given—and only to win Austria to the Allied cause. Still that assent, reluctant or not, was essential to the unfolding of Metternich's peace plan.

Meantime, a new complication had arisen, of which Metternich was well aware even before he had the news from Lebzeltern. In Breslau in late February the Tsar and the King of Prussia had met and agreed on terms of an alliance, which was signed a few days later at Kalisch. The treaty guaranteed that Prussia would be restored to the territorial size she had had before the War of 1806. Which lands she would be given were not spelled out, but the treaty was so worded as to give the Tsar a free hand in annexing Poland, with Prussia getting territorial compensation in Germany—probably Saxony. Both countries agreed not to sign a separate peace. The Kalisch treaty would bring a mare's nest of problems in its wake.

Metternich's next step was to send Schwarzenberg to Napoleon, to persuade him to postpone his planned second campaign against Russia, and to send instead envoys to a peace congress.

Throughout that month of March, in and out of his sickbed, Metternich worked with enormous care drawing up Schwarzenberg's instructions. Never had he weighed with greater thought every persuasive word and argument that could be put into the balance. Gentz described that polished and lucid diplomatic document as "a masterpiece of principles and reasoning with which Napoleon himself was struck."[6]

Struck perhaps, but not persuaded.

2

On April 8 at St. Cloud, at the end of Napoleon's levee, the French Emperor led Schwarzenberg into an inner room, where the two talked for several hours.

If Schwarzenberg had feared a storm of anger and reproaches for having withdrawn his auxiliary corps from combat, Napoleon only smiled and said with a note of irony, "*You* certainly conducted a fine campaign!" He kept calling Schwarzenberg "*mon cher ami*"; his tone remained gentle and friendly throughout.[7]

At first he talked of the Russian campaign, as he had earlier to Bubna—not in terms of the human tragedy but rather of the damage to his military prestige. It was the weather, he repeated over and over, that had destroyed the Grande Armée. But he had already put together a new army; in a few weeks he would have a cavalry corps as fine as the one he had lost. "I have just ordered up a new levy of 180,000 men," he said. "All my ministers turned pale, but I know the spirit of my people better than they do. Just talk to the French of *la gloire* and they are seduced at once!"

"But the Emperor of Austria," Schwarzenberg put in, "believes that war can still be avoided and peace made. He is ready to dedicate everything to it."

Napoleon cut him short. "For four months they've been chattering to me about peace. I didn't hesitate to accept your offer of intervention with pleasure. What has it got me until now? I'm ready to make peace! What do they want me to do? I can't take the initiative—that would be surrender. It's up to others to offer proposals to *me!*"

But the distances between capitals in Europe were so great, Schwarzenberg pointed out, it took weeks and months for messages to go and come. "It makes peace efforts slow and difficult. Moreover," he added, "Your Majesty's utterances have not sounded very peaceful of late."

Napoleon smiled and shrugged. "*Mon cher ami*, you've got to talk like that to the Senate and the public to get them to co-operate. As for the English, they'll never make peace until they can reduce the French Navy to thirty vessels!"

Metternich had instructed Schwarzenberg to try to find out what sacrifices Napoleon would be willing to make for peace. If England refused to take part in a general European peace at the present time, would Napoleon still be ready to negotiate for a continental peace, and on what terms?

To be sure, Napoleon replied in his most conciliatory tone, he was always ready to listen to talk of a real peace. So Metternich was proposing a peace congress in Prague? "Very well, let them assemble a congress in Prague or anywhere else—only not at Russian headquarters. But you [Austrians] will have to raise an army, camp in Bohemia, and threaten Russia with it."

Neither in that first audience nor in a second one a week later could Schwarzenberg extract from Napoleon any statement of the bases on which he might make peace. Schwarzenberg came away empty-handed. It was clear, he reported to Metternich, that Napoleon "burns with desire to avenge his immense losses. In the end everything depends on one man alone: that man is Napoleon."

Nor did Schwarzenberg have better luck with Bassano, Napoleon's

Foreign Minister and the only man in his confidence. Bassano headed the war party within France, and Schwarzenberg's pleas that Bassano dissuade his master from going to war out of injured male pride, "risking a new campaign to reaffirm it," fell on deaf ears.[8]

Schwarzenberg's disappointing reports reached Vienna in mid-April. Even while Metternich scanned the dispatches, Napoleon was kissing his wife and son good-by in St. Cloud and riding away to join his troops in Mainz. By April 25 he was in Erfurt, on April 29 in Naumburg, on May 1 on the plains of Lützen, just south of Leipzig in Saxony. "My pen," wrote his secretary Fain, "cannot follow the speed of the launching of this campaign; it can only follow his steps."[9]

Austria's only hope, Schwarzenberg advised in his report, was to build up her army to make her voice for peace effectively heard, and "to serve as a weight to whatever negotiations take place." Napoleon needed another two to three months, Schwarzenberg judged, to build his reserve for a full-scale campaign. He might accept a temporary armistice with Russia to help him through that time.

Immediately after Schwarzenberg's dispatches from Paris came the first news from Wessenberg in London. England flatly rejected Metternich's peace proposal. Very cold had been Wessenberg's reception in London at the end of his harrowing eight-week journey. Castlereagh informed him at once that he could not be received officially but only in private audience; a peace mission at that moment was in fact "an embarrassment to the English Government."[10]

Napoleon's bellicose address to the Legislative Corps in Paris, his declaration not to yield up territory incorporated into the French Empire or to remove a Bonaparte from the throne of Spain had hardened English resolve, and ended any hope that England would agree to take part in negotiations.

Instead of working for peace, Castlereagh urged Austria to join the other powers in concerting for war "for their common Interests and Honour." He spoke of "the Liberties of Europe," but it did not escape Wessenberg that freedom of the seas—a crucial issue of conflict between England and France as between England and the United States—was not included among the liberties under discussion. England, wrote the embittered Wessenberg, would continue to back a system of war "as long as she is attached exclusively to a monopoly of sea commerce."

If Schwarzenberg's report had been discouraging, Wessenberg's dispatch dealt Metternich's hopes a yet more severe blow. According to Gentz and Hardenberg, he was "singularly affected," and "deeply grieved" by the reception the London Cabinet accorded to his peace envoy.[11] England was Russia's ally; the attitude of the English Cabinet toward the mediation effort would certainly influence the Tsar.

In that depressing month of April Metternich could count only one small victory. He had been attempting to pry loose some of the German states from Napoleon's Rhine Confederation, persuading them to join instead a concert of powers to support his peace move. He had made overtures to Saxony, Bavaria, Württemberg, and to Caroline and Joachim Murat, rulers of the Kingdom of Naples. Bavaria and Württemberg, frightened of reprisals if they offended Napoleon, declined.

But when the Prussians under General Blücher marched into Saxony, the old King fled his capital, and Metternich was able to persuade the Saxon Prime Minister "to make common cause with the Austrian Empire to make our armed mediation work." The treaty was, of course, a deep secret. When Narbonne learned that the King of Saxony was in Prague, Metternich explained with an air of innocence, "Oh yes, he fell on us like a stroke of lightning."

"Maybe like lightning," Narbonne retorted, "but I suspect you're as clever as Franklin in making use of it."

3

Metternich went to work at once to reconstruct his design for peace. Never had his toughness, patience and flexibility been more apparent than in those late spring days of 1813 as he worked against time with no other weapons than those of his diplomatic trade to prevent Europe from again exploding into war.

The maneuvering space had grown narrower. So England refused to talk peace! Very well: he would design a continental peace without England. If he succeeded, then certainly England—left to face Napoleon alone—would be ready to take part in a general peace.

First, he needed a clear statement of the combatants' war aims: what were the minimum demands of Russia and Prussia, and what were the maximum concessions Napoleon would make? Well Metternich knew it would be no easy task; both sides hoped to win more on the battlefield than could be won by compromise at a peace table. Whatever peace was made, it must be one that restored a true equilibrium of power. "Not a precarious state of affairs," he wrote in the instructions for his envoys—such as had been the dictated peace settlements of Napoleon—"but a general arrangement which will put back the geographical and political relations of the powers on just and lasting bases."[12]

Never did Metternich make more subtle and delicate use of diplomatic techniques than in those weeks of May and June. With both of the warring parties he strove to touch the right note, "to think of what is in their minds," as the classical teacher of diplomacy Callières had instructed, to weigh out the precise bribe, unveil the precise threat, that would win them to his plan.

To the Tsar Metternich planned to send the one man in Austria who could best overcome the Tsar's distrust of what he called "Austria's delaying tactics," his suspicion that Austria was secretly committed to Napoleon's cause. That man was Count Philipp Stadion, Metternich's predecessor in the foreign ministry and chief spokesman for the War Party.

Stadion was to persuade the Tsar to accept an armistice, with a peace congress following it; he was to ascertain in writing the minimum bases on which the Tsar and his ally the King of Prussia would agree to negotiate. The carrot on the stick was the Austrian Army. If the Tsar co-operated and accepted Austria's armed mediation, and if the negotiations were unsuccessful, then Austria would "appear on the scene as the principal intervening power," backing the peace proposals with force. It was almost—but not quite—a promise to join the Russian-Prussian coalition if the peace plan failed.

To Napoleon Metternich was sending Count Bubna again, a suave diplomat and an experienced general, whom Napoleon liked and respected. Bubna was to persuade Napoleon to accept an armistice and a peace congress and to try to find out what he would give up for a peace. The colonies England had taken from France, which Metternich had hoped to use as a bargaining tool, would not be forthcoming at once.

The mission to Napoleon would be extremely difficult, but Metternich had one weapon of enormous weight on his side which he would not hesitate to use again and again in the next months in his efforts to force through a peace. That weapon was public opinion; Metternich was certain that the French—even Napoleon's marshals and his officers—overwhelmingly desired peace and were willing to make sacrifices for it.

A wave of nerves and apprehension swept over Vienna in early May. Everyone knew that some hundreds of miles to the northwest two great armies prepared to do battle. People kept their windows open to listen for the sound of cannon, and there were generals who claimed they had heard the sound of gunfire on the day of the battle of Lützen.

Anxiously Metternich waited for news. The outcome of that battle was certain to affect the mission of his two envoys, and he must keep all possibilities in mind.

In April Narbonne had boasted to Metternich of the size of the new French army Napoleon could put into the field—840,000 he declared. With the army in Spain, and the National Guard, he had an effective force of over a million men.

And what of cavalry, Metternich had asked? Napoleon had only a small force of cavalry, "and without this powerful arm how can he hope for great successes against the enemy?"

"The Emperor has taught us many things," Narbonne retorted loyally, "and he will no doubt teach us what one must do with a smaller cavalry force."[13]

Metternich had guessed that Napoleon would win the next battle; he had guessed too that it would be an incomplete victory.

The first reports reaching Vienna of the battle of Lützen, fought on May 2 some twelve miles south of Leipzig, claimed a victory for Russian-Prussian forces and occasioned short-lived rejoicing in Vienna. Almost at once the news followed that it was Napoleon who had won—his forces had outnumbered the Russian-Prussian army by two to one. It had not, however, been a decisive battle; as Metternich predicted, lack of cavalry had prevented Napoleon from pursuing his enemies and delivering a final blow. The Allies had retired in good order.

Nothing had been gained at Lützen. Casualties on both sides were heavy.

As soon as he had news of Lützen, Metternich dispatched Stadion to find the Tsar and the King of Prussia somewhere east of the river Spree, whither their forces had withdrawn. He kept Bubna in Vienna a day or two longer, changing his instructions a bit to fit the new military picture, then dispatched him to Napoleon in Dresden.

The minimum bases Metternich proposed on the part of Austria were moderate ones. Austria should be restored to the territorial extent she possessed before the War of 1805, Prussia to the size she had before her defeat by Napoleon in 1806. The duchy of Warsaw—that is, French-controlled Poland—was to be dissolved. France must retire within her natural boundaries of the river Rhine, the Alps and the Pyrenees.

Stadion was warmly received at the headquarters of the Allies, but differences of opinion on the peace bases arose at once. In the little town of Wurschen, where the Tsar was staying, his ministers drew up *their* list of demands—a far more extensive recharting of Europe, which Metternich, when he got Stadion's report, found impossible, in fact "overwhelming." Metternich wanted to present Napoleon with such demands as he might conceivably accept, in order to win him to the negotiating table. The Allies, bent on war, wanted to present him with demands he was certain to refuse.

Moreover, neither the Tsar nor his chief minister, Nesselrode, nor the Prussian Chancellor Hardenberg wished to accept Metternich's plans for negotiation unless a definite time limit—and a brief one—were fixed for Napoleon's reply, and a definite promise made by Austria to commit her Army to the Allied cause if Napoleon refused.

While Stadion discussed bases at the Russian-Prussian headquarters, fifty miles away in the palace in Dresden Bubna had a stormy audience with Napoleon.

For more than five hours, far into the night of May 16, Napoleon harangued Bubna "with a burning vehemence that is difficult to describe," the placid Bubna reported.[14] Napoleon's diplomatic style closely paralleled his military technique. It was based on a barrage of verbal artillery, on heavy weapons and rapid maneuvering. It was designed to overwhelm, to intimidate, not to conciliate. It could, however, be called neither a battle nor a duel, since Napoleon usually controlled the cannon.

For the first moment or two that night he appeared to be friendly, inquiring after his father-in-law's health and that of the imperial family. Then
suddenly turning on Bubna he shouted, "What are you doing there in
Austria? You're arming! Against whom? It can only be against me!"

Entering the palace in Dresden after the battle of Lützen, he had
found on the King's desk a copy of the treaty Austria had just drawn up
with Saxony. He was outraged; what did Austria mean trying to lure
Saxony out of her alliance with France? He had taxed the old King with
treachery; the King pleaded that he had yielded to Austria under pressure
and only with the thought of saving his subjects from suffering.

Metternich had made overtures to Bavaria and Württemberg too, Napoleon had heard. "I don't want your armed mediation," he cried. "You're
embroiling affairs even more. Let me handle my own business with the Tsar.
We'll come to an agreement. I accepted your intervention for peace when
you were my allies. When you withdrew your auxiliary corps you ceased
being my ally!"

The principles of neutral intervention and mediation meant nothing to
Napoleon.

"I'll yield nothing—not a village of everything that is constitutionally
joined to France! A man who has come to the throne from a simple private
person, who has passed twenty years under grapeshot—he is not afraid of
cannonballs! He fears no threats! I don't hesitate to sacrifice my life. I
don't value it any more than those of 100,000 men! I'd sacrifice a million
men if it's necessary!"

Back and forth Napoleon paced, now and again stopping to pound the
table for emphasis. He was clearly into one of his tantrums. Bubna stood
silently waiting, gifted by good fortune, as Lebzeltern once remarked, "with
imperturbable phlegm." He needed it that night. Whenever Napoleon
paused, Bubna tried to put in a word and to hand him the letter he was
carrying from Emperor Franz.

Napoleon brushed the letter aside. So Austria was trying to threaten
him—Napoleon! Well, he could do his own threatening. "I bought Illyria
with the loss of a million men. You won't have it back without sacrificing
as many! One doesn't win provinces with rosewater! Those are ways one
uses to seduce women! You can't make war against me with your forty-five
million new bank notes. You'll need 400,000 men under arms to fight me
with any success. . . . If you want provinces blood must flow!"

As for his marriage, he repented it, he declared. A moment later, however, he retrenched. "What I hold dearest is the fate of the King of Rome.
Certainly nobody reproaches me with having too tender a heart, but if I
love anything in this world it's my wife." He paused a moment and added
—words that Metternich certainly carried with him during the months that
followed—"If I go under you will plunge France into anarchy. You'll kill
my wife and child, issue of your blood."

Austria had three choices. If she joined Russia, very well, it was a system, though Austria would end up doing most of the fighting. Or she might ally herself with France; he would pay well. The third choice, neutrality—that would be the worst bargain. "We'll make our arrangements at your expense," he warned—precisely what Metternich most feared.

In the last half hour, toward two in the morning, Napoleon calmed down. Bubna had a chance to speak. He described the sincerity of Metternich's peace aims, named the bases on which negotiations might begin, spoke of the peace congress Metternich proposed to meet in Prague.

"Do you have power to negotiate?" Napoleon asked Bubna. Bubna admitted he did not.

"In that case," said Napoleon, "you can go back to Vienna and tell them officially that I am ready to make sacrifices for the house of Austria. I want my father-in-law to play a fine role, and even in case of war to remain on good terms with him."

He added that a battle was about to take place, and Bubna could not remain in Dresden.

Next morning before seven, Caulaincourt, of all Napoleon's close associates the firmest supporter of peace, appeared at Bubna's door. As soon as Bubna had left Napoleon, the Emperor had summoned Caulaincourt, talked with him at length about the Metternich proposal, and had read his father-in-law's warm and pacific letter. He sent Caulaincourt to gather further details—who, for example, was to get Poland if he surrendered the duchy of Warsaw?

Carefully Bubna explained to Caulaincourt what he knew of the proposed program. "He listened to me calmly," Bubna reported, "and I can say with sympathy, and promised to bring the Emperor around."

In the afternoon Bubna was summoned to the palace again for a last brief interview with Napoleon.

"Write that I am inclined to peace," Napoleon told him. "The sovereigns should send plenipotentiaries and explain what they wish. I have spoken the first word, now it is up to them to speak."

And yes, he would also agree to an armistice. "If while we are discussing arrangements, another battle is fought, it can be either lucky or unlucky for me. I'll still accept an armistice."

He said nothing of accepting Austria's armed mediation.

At the end of their conversation Bubna took his courage in his hands and spoke of Europe's deep longing for peace. Would the Emperor not put away the actions of a military ruler and become a true ruler of France? Napoleon laughed out loud and replied, "I have to show myself at the head of my armies."

As Bubna departed, Napoleon called out after him, "Forget my fireworks. I don't speak so frankly with everyone!"

Bubna, summarizing the tenor of his conversations with Napoleon, wrote in one of the understatements of that century, "It lies in the character of the man not to give in easily."[15]

Hurriedly that afternoon Bubna wrote to Stadion telling him that Napoleon would agree to an armistice. Had he been able to travel directly to Görlitz to the Tsar's headquarters, Bubna might have been able to deliver that important letter within hours, and perhaps have averted the impending battle. But two great armies lay between Dresden and Görlitz—and Napoleon had his own plans for arranging the armistice. He meant to cut Austria out of the mediating role and keep the power in his own hands.

Bubna drove southwest to Teplitz in Bohemia, where he gave the precious letter to an Austrian diplomat, Philipp von Neumann, to carry northeast to Görlitz while he himself hurried back to Vienna.

Scarcely had Bubna left Dresden when Napoleon dispatched Caulaincourt to the advance posts of the Russian-Prussian armies to talk with the Tsar about an armistice.

It was the eve of the battle of Bautzen.

It was also the moment of crisis Metternich had most feared. If Napoleon and the Tsar came to terms together, Austria would lose her role in the peace—and might lose far more besides. If there were another Tilsit—and the two colossi divided Europe between them?

4

"Never," wrote Count Ernst Hardenberg during those tense days of May 1813, "has Count Metternich so completely lost his composure as in the days between the departure of Count Stadion and of Monsieur Bubna for the headquarters of Tsar Alexander and of Napoleon, and that of the arrival of their first reports."[16]

Never were couriers awaited more impatiently in the Chancellery.

Metternich's position during those critical days was a singularly lonely one and his responsibility immense. More precariously than ever war or peace hung in the balance. One false move—a lost battle, either diplomatic or military—could cost Europe the hope of freedom from the domination of any one power, either France or Russia, could cost Austria all hope of restoration to a leading position in the councils of Europe.

Never had Metternich been in greater need of a close friend and confidante, someone reasonable and sympathetic, whose personal loyalty he could trust. Increasingly that spring Metternich turned to Wilhelmine. With her he discussed more frankly than with anyone else the terrible anxieties, the chances for war, the hopes for peace, the whole spectrum of political ambiguities he must somehow unravel—making his fateful moves among forces over which he exercised no control.

Later he recalled that period to her when he had been "unappreciated by millions, object of suspicion to all the powers—misjudged by the universe except by two or three persons—my dear, you were one of these."[17] In the nearly unbearable tensions of those days Metternich found reassurance and support in her "astonishingly shrewd judgment and inperturbable serenity."[18]

Though she herself was convinced that war was inevitable—how else deal with a man of totally military mentality like Napoleon?—and that Austria's only course was to join the Allies, she had moments of doubt. Was it possible that Napoleon might be persuaded to listen to reason, that a balance of power could be restored without war, that other methods might succeed—diplomatic weapons too seldom used by men in power to avoid conflict?

Yet if she too felt torn on the very question that tormented Metternich, she did not have the confidence in her own powers of judgment to support him firmly in a path toward peace: that much is clear from her letters to Alfred Windischgraetz at that period.

But she gave Metternich a sympathetic ear and a listening intelligence. Not only did they see one another often, but, as friends did in that era, they exchanged frequent letters and notes. When he had been bedridden during March and April they had certainly written one another. When he was not able to talk with her alone, or if one of their conversations was left unfinished, he would write to clarify a point or a position, late at night often, by candlelight at his desk in the Chancellery.

Significantly, all the letters and notes the two exchanged during the critical spring of 1813 were destroyed later on, at Metternich's specific request.

Many years later, Wilhelmine's foster daughter, Emilie von Binzer, setting down recollections of her youth, wrote of those letters that had passed between Metternich and Wilhelmine during the spring of 1813:

> Before Austria declared herself against Napoleon, the Duchess had a long correspondence with Prince Metternich, in which she used all the levers of a beautiful woman of high intelligence and of a patriotic German, to further the union with the Allies; the Prince gave her these letters to keep, I do not know for what reason, and she read them aloud to me. They glowed with enthusiasm, they contained statements of the political circumstances of that time which did honor to that statesman. The Prince must have wavered for a long time, for there was quite a collection of those letters in existence. When I asked her about them later on, she told me that at the Prince's request she had burned the entire packet. How few people would have destroyed those documents [that revealed] the great and noble influence of her person on such an important time![19]

It was, apparently, the only portion of their correspondence of several years that was destroyed; all the other letters and notes—Wilhelmine's going back as far as 1810—Metternich kept carefully in a black letter-box bound like a book on a shelf in his private study, that study that was always kept locked in his absence.

Curiously too, the entire section of Gentz's diary covering the same period, from January through June of 1813—when he too was talking with

Metternich nearly every day—was ripped out later on, probably by Gentz himself. Certainly the hand of Metternich was visible in both events, the post hoc censor of history, clipping and editing his political past as adroitly as he rewrote it for his *Memoirs*.

If Metternich shared all his secrets with Wilhelmine that spring, she too shared hers with him. All spring her liaison with Alfred appeared to be approaching an end; she confided the story of their quarrels, of the jealousies and disagreements, the coolnesses and ruptures and reconciliations to her friend Clemens, who was certain that all would soon be over between her and Alfred. He found their relationship hard to understand. "Alfred is a child and less than a child compared with you. You, mistress of a child whose life you have not even succeeded in absorbing—and you, the woman you are—happy? No, my Wilhelmine," he wrote her once, "you will pursue happiness a long time without meeting it along that road. A liaison like that does not fill one quarter of your soul—"[20]

That spring Clemens and Wilhelmine began an intimate relationship— perhaps during some period of her estrangement from Alfred. And if Clemens was scarcely aware that the friendship was for him at least deepening into something far more serious, his close circle of acquaintances took note and talked among themselves of the minister's ensnarement in the wiles of a lovely Circe. Certainly in the weeks of April and May Wilhelmine turned on him the full charm of a radiant and seductive personality.

5

While Metternich waited anxiously to hear from Stadion and Bubna, a second fierce battle was fought on May 21 and 22 near the village of Bautzen in Saxony. Again as at Lützen the battle was costly in casualties but indecisive. Though Napoleon succeeded in driving the Allies from the field, he had not inflicted a real defeat. The Russian-Prussian army withdrew in good order, retiring deep into Prussian Silesia and as close as possible to the borders of Austria—a move, Metternich wrote later, designed to corner Austria and force her into the war.

On the eve of Bautzen Caulaincourt had waited in vain at the Allied outposts for a reply to Napoleon's armistice proposal to the Tsar. Not until after the battle was fought did a reply from the Tsar's chief minister, Nesselrode, reach Napoleon.

It was a reply that astonished and infuriated him. Russia and Prussia, Nesselrode wrote, had accepted the mediation of Austria. They would therefore only treat for peace through the offices of their mediator. Napoleon must address his request to Austria.

It was a major diplomatic triumph for Metternich. Napoleon, who had treated Austrian mediation with some contempt, who had intended to arrange an armistice directly with the Tsar, had failed. For the first time, he was forced to consider Metternich's total peace plan with seriousness.

Stadion, meantime, at the Tsar's headquarters, had Bubna's letter about an armistice and had addressed a proposal at once to Berthier, Napoleon's chief of staff.

Bubna himself, back in Vienna, was reporting on his conversations with Napoleon. If England could only be persuaded to participate in negotiations, to make certain maritime concessions, then Napoleon might agree to withdraw from Germany, Bubna thought. "If I get a maritime peace," Napoleon had told Bubna during their second audience, "I can bring greater sacrifices for it, for I can say to my people, 'I made these sacrifices for your commerce, for your well-being.' "[21]

Napoleon would welcome a congress, Bubna reported, and one that included not only plenipotentiaries from England, but also from the United States—to end the Anglo-American conflict—even from the Spanish insurgents, so that all facets of the widespread war might be dealt with at one peace table.

But if England refused to participate, then Bubna believed Napoleon would refuse to surrender his hold on Germany. "He holds to his lucky star. . . . His sole desire is to work on history. What his country suffers, even what happens to his dynasty if things do not turn out well, is of secondary importance to him." What Napoleon wanted above anything else, Bubna concluded in his report, was to furnish material for his future biographer to write, "Napoleon accomplished more than any mortal man."

The one auspicious result of Bubna's mission was that Napoleon had, for whatever reasons, agreed to a congress. In the official French *Moniteur* on May 25 Napoleon announced that there would be a peace congress in Prague, quite as if it had been his own idea—excellent propaganda for home consumption to counteract the shock of the high casualties of Bautzen and Lützen.

Bubna was sent back to Dresden to win Napoleon's specific acceptance of Austria in the role of mediator, and to try to elicit very precise details of his war aims or peace bases.

Traveling through Saxony during the last days of May Bubna saw everywhere the terrible debris of the last battle. Roads were jammed with peasant carts laden with sick and wounded. The town of Bischofswerda had burned to the ground—nobody could say how or why. The hospitals and private houses of Dresden were filled with wounded; thousands of men ill with typhus, rampant in the wake of the armies, were shipped on barges down the Elbe to be cared for in villages along the river.

Hunger was widespread. The armies had scraped the cupboards of Saxony bare, and Napoleon had had to send all the way to Nürnberg for bread to be brought back to Dresden by post chaise. The Russians had killed and roasted even the precious Merino sheep the Saxon King kept to grow wool for the royal family.

Because Metternich's earlier peace proposal had not been accepted, some forty thousand men had been killed in battle, thousands more wounded, villages destroyed, the lives of countless men and women made nearly unbearable.

In the French army morale among the raw young troops, and even among seasoned veterans and officers was low. "What a war!" they exclaimed. "We shall all of us be dead before the end."

In vain Napoleon railed at his marshals. "I can see, messieurs, that you don't want to make war any longer! Berthier wants to enjoy himself hunting at Gros Bois. Rapp wants to live in his fine mansion in Paris. I have to agree, sirs, that I am not very well acquainted with the pleasures of the capital!"[22]

The lucky star of which he used to boast no longer seemed to be in the ascendant. In a farmyard in Silesia where Napoleon spent a night, all his baggage wagons, with his uniforms, his jewels and the army's pay, caught fire and burned. Napoleon had to have a pair of pants hastily sewed up for him in Breslau—one of those little accidents of war that can be so vexing even to a supreme commander.

News of the battle of Bautzen reached Vienna at four o'clock in the afternoon on Saturday, May 29. Metternich ordered his carriage at once and drove to the imperial summer palace of Laxenburg, where the Emperor was staying.

Austria had to act quickly; there was no time to lose.

It took five days for a courier to journey north from Vienna to French or Russian army headquarters, another five days to return. Would there be— could there be—an armistice? Or would there be still another battle—and another and another?

On the single slender thread of Metternich's negotiations hung all hope for peace. He himself would go north to the war zone—and he would take the Emperor with him.

VI

HOUSE PARTY IN BOHEMIA:
THE ARMISTICE OF JUNE

It is a terrible thing to have all of Europe on one's shoulders . . . when one thinks besides that the entire universe is turning its gaze on one, that the safety of eighty million men hangs on us here at Gitschin—well, it gives one something to think about!
—METTERNICH TO MARIE, JUNE 8, 1813

1

In the gray dawn of June 1, 1813, while the city of Vienna slept, Metternich, Emperor Franz and his aide, General Duka, in carriages harnessed to the swiftest horses in the imperial stables, galloped across the Danube bridge and sped north toward a certain Castle Gitschin in Bohemia.

Metternich had left in such a hurry, ordering his baggage to follow in another carriage with his valet Giroux, that he forgot to take along the black china-wood box holding his money and travel necessities and he had to scribble off a note to Laure from their first dinner stop at Budweis.

As carefully as a general choosing terrain for a battle, Metternich had examined the map, put his finger on a spot nearly midway between Napoleon's headquarters at Dresden and that of the Tsar and the King of Prussia at Reichenbach in Silesia. Gitschin—Ratiborzitz—Opocno—all those Bohemian towns with the crazy names, Gentz wrote that month, suddenly became the focus of Europe's politics.

In that arena in the heart of Europe more than half a million men waited only a signal from the sovereigns to begin war anew. Would there be an armistice? Who could tell? Everything was touch and go. Certainly there was not a moment to lose if peace were to be plucked out of that forest of serried guns and sabers. "The tinder," Baron Fain wrote, "still burned under their cannon."

The second night the imperial party did not stop to sleep but drove on through hours of black downpour over roads axle-deep in mud, the carriage jolting this way and that, now and again mired so that coachman and lackeys had to dismount and tug and heave to pull it loose—hardly a comfortable journey for an emperor. But luck, it turned out, was with them. At the little inn in Kolin not far from Prague, when they stopped to rest and warm themselves, a carriage bearing the imperial arms of Russia drew up behind them, and out jumped the Tsar's own minister, Count Nesselrode.

In a last effort to induce Austria to join the war at once, the Tsar had sent his minister to Vienna to speak directly with Emperor Franz. Halfway there, at the town of Brünn, Nesselrode learned the Austrian Emperor had already passed through on his way north; he had turned his carriage and gone full speed in pursuit, overtaking them at three in the morning.

The Tsar wanted an answer to two crucial questions. Would Austria go to war if France did not immediately accept the proposed bases for negotiation? If so, when would Austria declare?[1]

Meantime, the armistice dangled in the air. The fifty-six-hour cease-fire was expiring, and the commissioners meeting to discuss an armistice could not agree on terms. Russia, quite frankly, said Nesselrode, did not care whether an armistice were signed or not; the Tsar was determined to carry on the war. If Austria wanted an armistice signed—very well, what was she prepared to bargain for it? Her promise in writing to war when that armistice came to an end? Metternich would not answer yes or no.

"Come with us to Gitschin," was his reply, and Nesselrode followed them to Wallenstein's gloomy old castle in the tiny town near the northern border of Bohemia.

In Gitschin that Thursday afternoon, with an hour or two of sleep behind him, Metternich sent off a courier to Stadion at the Tsar's headquarters in Reichenbach, ordering him to press hard for the armistice. "More than anything else the armistice would serve us," Metternich wrote. Once it was signed, Stadion was to hold everything in abeyance until Nesselrode's return; then he was to draw everyone and everything into the mediation effort. He promised that Nesselrode would return in the happiest frame of mind, convinced "that we shall in no case abandon the affair." Meantime, "I shall consider the truce the greatest of all goods at the moment."[2]

The following day, June 4, the armistice between France, and Russia and Prussia was signed at Pläswitz and ratified a day later. A pair of young officers, one French, one Russian, rode up and down the lines of both armies, sounding a bugle call to announce that arms were to be laid down for six weeks, until July 20.

Cheerfully Metternich could inform his wife:

> The first step is taken, *ma bonne amie*. The armistice is concluded and on very good bases. If we had arrived a single day later, the armistice would not have been made, because Tsar Alexander, who is behaving like an angel toward us, called on us directly for a decision.[3]

For the next three days, in the draughty chill of Gitschin—"unheated," Metternich wrote Laure, "since Wallenstein's day"—the two ministers, Austrian and Russian, tried to out-maneuver one another in the intricate game of war versus peace.

They had met before in Paris and again in Vienna in 1811, these two gifted diplomats whose careers paralleled one another so closely. A few years younger than Metternich, Karl Nesselrode too came from a family of German counts of the Holy Roman Empire, and had been, like Metternich, virtually born into the world of professional European diplomacy. Though his father was in the service of the late Tsar, Nesselrode had never seen Russia until he was a grown man, would never speak really fluent Russian. He had tried a stint in the Russian Navy, but he had disliked it intensely—perhaps because of his stature, for he was a tiny man, standing scarcely five feet tall.

Adroit, genial, sharp, articulate, he had risen rapidly to be the Tsar's most trusted minister and right-hand man. With his own brand of wry humor Nesselrode ascribed his success to his ability to jump on and off a horse during the late campaign.

At Gitschin he and Metternich found they could work together; it was fortunate, for during the next three years they would find themselves often at close quarters and on opposite sides of the bargaining table.

But at Gitschin—and during the months that followed—Metternich proved to be the smoother and tougher bargainer.

Nesselrode had arrived prepared to use every weapon to bring Austria into the war. Russia, he pointed out, could make no peace without her ally England, and England refused to treat for peace now. True, replied Metternich, a general Europe-wide peace would only be possible when England agreed to take part. But they could make a "preliminary," a continental peace—and surely such a peace would be the quickest way of drawing England into a final general peace.

In the end, when Nesselrode rode away from Gitschin on Sunday, June 6, he had not got the clear-cut answers the Tsar had sought:

> Count Metternich had conceived the plan of proposing to Napoleon moderate conditions for a general peace in the European interest. . . .
> To my regret I could not obtain a more positive result and carried away from Gitschin only the mission of explaining to the two sovereigns Metternich's ideas. It was to be foreseen that they were not to their taste.[4]

Nesselrode's message from Metternich was an urgent plea to the Allies to join Austria in a "preliminary" peace congress with Napoleon, using Austria's four moderate bases as a foundation. And Nesselrode was to extend a warm invitation to the Tsar to meet personally with Metternich—perhaps at Castle Opocno near the eastern border of Bohemia, within a few miles of Silesia. The Tsar's two sisters, the Grand Duchesses Catherine and Marie, had been staying in Prague; a meeting with their brother could furnish the ostensible reason for his visit on Austrian territory.

2

Metternich's departure from Vienna had been, of course, less secret than he had hoped. Two old servants of French émigrés living in Vienna had got wind of it from a groom in the imperial stables and hurried off to inform Narbonne, the French ambassador, that carriages of His Majesty were being readied for a journey of some length.

Narbonne had gone straight to Metternich to demand the reason, and the Austrian minister had replied frankly that he and the Emperor were journeying north in the hope of negotiating a peace. "May heaven, my dear Count, support our good intentions, and I shall ask no better than to go to rest for the remainder of my life!"[5]

Narbonne did not believe a word of it. He had already been informing Napoleon in every dispatch that Austria was building up an army to go to war against him. The day after Metternich's departure Narbonne was driving full speed toward Dresden. Napoleon must be warned.

In those days of early June Saxony and Silesia were full of rumors of Napoleon's death, the wish-dream of a people sick for peace. There were Saxon farmers ready to swear that the stocky figure in the general's uniform they had seen passing along the roads on his way from Bunzlau to Dresden was not the French Emperor at all but a mechanical marvel with a face of wax, that Napoleon was really dead, and a coffin had been smuggled into the palace in Dresden. The rumors had spread as far as Vienna, where they gained such credence that Laure wrote her husband she had almost come to believe in the death of "the little man" herself.

Far from dead, in his study in the Marcolini Palace outside Dresden, with Narbonne's news that Metternich and the Austrian Emperor were in Gitschin, Napoleon bent over his map of Bohemia, studying the mountain passes that led from Saxony south into Austrian territory—and the shortest route an army could take to Vienna.

His marshals and generals had pressed hard for the armistice and for his agreement to peace talks. Perhaps for the first time in his life Napoleon had surrendered something of his own accord. He had evacuated Breslau and a wide belt of occupied territory, agreeing to make it a neutral zone for the duration of the armistice. He had only agreed to the armistice, he wrote his Minister of War, because he needed more cavalry, and "because of the hostile attitude of Austria." By September, he wrote, he would "be in a position to crush my enemies."

Yet there were signs too that he might take peace talks seriously. "If the Allies do not want peace in good faith, then this armistice can be fatal for us."[6]

Meantime, he prepared for war. He inspected bridges and fortifications, kept an eye on the training of the raw young recruits arriving from France. And he avoided talking to Bubna.

Bubna's requests for an audience got no response. Dispatch after dispatch from Metternich in Gitschin urged Bubna with increasing impatience to arrange an invitation for Metternich to come to Dresden for a personal talk with Napoleon.

Not until the early evening of June 14 was Bubna summoned at last to Bassano's house, where he was told to cool his heels while that minister finished supper. Bubna waited two hours. Admitted at last to Bassano's study, the French minister apologized for his tardiness and informed Bubna that Napoleon would see him that same evening at the Marcolini Palace outside the city.

Hurriedly Bubna jumped into his carriage, for it was growing late, and ordered his driver to take him with all speed out to the suburbs. It was half past ten when he was ushered into a waiting room outside the Emperor's apartments. Once again he sat down, hat in hand. When an aide appeared at last, it was to inform Bubna regretfully that he had come too late, the Emperor Napoleon was going to bed.[7]

3

In Allied headquarters in Reichenbach a stormy conference followed Nesselrode's return without Austria's commitment to war. The armistice was roundly censured for the most part, according to Humboldt, and nobody wanted to hear about peace negotiations. The young hawks around the Tsar pressed him to continue the war; Anstett and Knesebeck hinted, not too subtly, that Austria might be leading them on to ruin with her delaying tactics. Even Stadion found the idea of further negotiations abhorrent. "Leave me out, I beg you, of any peace congress," he wrote, adding that if asked he would refuse to serve.[8]

Several factors contributed to the reluctance of most of the Russian and Prussian leaders to postpone the war. The English were dangling tempting promises of large subsidies if they continued to fight, and both Lord Cathcart and Sir Charles Stewart—British envoys to Russia and Prussia—looked with great disfavor on Austria's efforts toward negotiation. It was not in England's interest to negotiate a peace—not yet.

There were other reasons why the Allied leaders were anxious to get on with the war. Army coalitions seldom work smoothly; there were grating disagreements among Russian and Prussian officers. The Cossacks had swept across Prussian Silesia like a horde of locusts, foraging in the fields of young grain, with a host of camp followers plundering in their wake. Much better to carry the war into someone else's lands.

If Nesselrode had failed to win Metternich, the Allied leaders decided at the conference on June 10, then the Prussian Chancellor, Baron Karl August Hardenberg, must go to Gitschin and try to wring out a better bargain.

First, he must insist that the Russian-Prussian bases of Wurschen—entailing far greater sacrifices for Napoleon and therefore unlikely to be accepted—be used as the bases adopted for negotiation. Secondly, he was to insist that Metternich put into writing Austria's promise: if Napoleon refused the bases, Austria would go to war.

So it was the turn of Chancellor Hardenberg to spend two days talking with Metternich in Gitschin. He took along his cousin Count Ernst, the "Vienna Hardenberg," as they all called him, both to keep him company and to lend an extra pair of ears. Those extra ears were needed, for the elderly Chancellor was extremely deaf. On Friday and Saturday, June 11 and 12, first Metternich, then Count Ernst shouted in the old baron's ear.

Metternich had known Baron Hardenberg since his Berlin embassy days and the two men understood and respected one another. A charming, gentle, cultivated man, Hardenberg too had come into his career of diplomacy and public service as an aristocratic birthright. A generation older than the Austrian minister—he was now in his sixties—Hardenberg came from a distinguished Hanoverian family. Like Metternich he had studied international law at Strasbourg, served the governments of several small German duchies, and had finally risen to the top government post in Prussia, where he had contributed importantly to that country's administrative reform.

Though he and Metternich disagreed now on procedures for achieving a new order in Europe, the design both men envisioned was not too different. Both agreed that a balanced and therefore peaceful Europe could only be achieved with a strongly united Austro-Prussian block as a central axis.

At the moment, however, Hardenberg objected strenuously to Metternich's four moderate bases as a foundation for peace talks, declaring England would never accept them, that Prussia would lose the golden subsidies England was promising as a price for continuing the war. Patiently Metternich explained again that since England refused to participate in negotiations, she could hardly expect her interests in Holland and Spain to form part of the foundation of the negotiations. When England agreed to negotiate, they could discuss the terms of a general peace.

Firmly Metternich held to his four moderate bases, terms he thought Napoleon might be persuaded to accept.

On the second Prussian demand Metternich had to yield. If Napoleon refused to accept the proposed bases by July 20 and to take part in a peace congress, then Austria would join the Allies. The two days with Hardenberg had been days of tough, hard bargaining, and Hardenberg returned to Reichenbach with more than Nesselrode had.

How unwillingly Metternich had agreed to the promised treaty was evident from the letter he wrote next day to Stadion. Such a treaty was "either superfluous or incompatible with our role of mediator," he pointed out. "What would the Allies say if they learned that we drew up such an agreement with the French Cabinet?"[9] There had been no other way to win agreement to negotiations, but the treaty must remain the deepest secret.

Stadion had already agreed that the Allies might send a military representative to Gitschin to discuss with Schwarzenberg the state of the army and joint campaign plans—if it should come to war. The Allies made the most of that opportunity to compromise Austria by sending Russian General Toll in full military regalia, accompanied by a bevy of uniformed aides, so that the world would know military talks were taking place.[10]

4

"I'll be back in three weeks," Metternich had promised Laure when he embraced his family on the eve of his departure from Vienna.

From Gitschin he wrote them nearly every day, tender affectionate letters in French, *mes bons amis,* often written late at night by candlelight after a long day of diplomatic dealing.

He wrote Laure for things he needed—their cook Chandellier and a scullery boy, to be sent at once in the court calèche. Daily life in Gitschin was not precisely cheerful. The cold rain pelted down. "It takes an hour to go a quarter of a league the mud is so black and deep," he wrote. For amusement one could walk in the sodden, rain-swept gardens, listen to the sound of an organ being tuned in a nearby church, and the cracked bell ringing for services. On rare days when the rain stopped and the Emperor went hunting, Metternich did not join him; he was no sportsman and shooting did not appeal to him in the least.

Often he had a droll little story to tell of Giroux—how arriving at Budweis Giroux had been mistaken for the Emperor of Austria and the local militia had turned out to receive him. Hearing "an infernal noise" Metternich had gone to the window of the inn in time to see Giroux, hatless, leaning out of the carriage window, gesticulating wildly and shouting in French that he was *not* the Emperor, while the militia, understanding only Czech and a bit of German, thought the Emperor certainly eccentric, but went on presenting arms, beating their drums, saluting the flag:

> They take his gestures for affable approval and the drums roll more loudly than before. He is alone in his carriage; the two chasseurs are on the box. He is superb!

Of political affairs Metternich wrote Laure, that he would presently be talking to the Tsar and the King of Prussia, perhaps also to Napoleon. There would be a congress meeting soon in Gitschin, he thought. "Bubna should send us news at any moment from Dresden." Meantime, his foot was in the stirrup, so to speak, to leave on a moment's notice "for the right or the left" —toward the French or the Russians.[11]

From Vienna Laure and the children wrote him every day as he had directed—he chided them at once if a letter did not come in the diplomatic pouch—regaling him with tidbits of Vienna gossip and the small happenings of their domestic circle.

Laure's tiny cramped script, crossing the page like the print of an exotic bird's foot, told of their new cook, "an excellent little cook—we've never dined better," of the mysterious death of two of Metternich's pet spaniels, of the children's improving health. Dr. Staudenheimer was prescribing Eger water for Clementine; soon she would be permitted to get out of bed and go for a short walk with her governess. The color was returning to Marie's pale cheeks—or perhaps it was the pretty dress, *couleur de rose*, made from material in the surprise box of gifts for the children which kind Monsieur Lebzeltern had sent from Reichenbach. "Adieu, my very dear one, may Heaven keep you from all evil and bless all your enterprises."

The children took turns writing too, Victor and Clementine in large round copybook hands on carefully ruled sheets:

> I am happy to be able to write you, dear Papa [Victor wrote]. I should prefer, however, to see you and to embrace you. Come back soon, dear Papa, and we shall go riding together.

But it was his darling Marie who turned out to be the most charming of correspondents, recounting all the happenings of family life with a touch of dear Papa's own dry humor. She could describe the solemn figure of Monsieur Hudelist climbing the stairs to their third-floor apartment "like a ghost—one would think from his face he brought us the most awful news," and their governess, timid, twittery Madame Revel, so terrified of thunderstorms she always wanted to run and hide in the cellar—and there were frequent thunderstorms that June.

"My whooping cough is disappearing at a great rate," Marie reassured her father. She missed him terribly; she awaited her turn to write "with impatience, for it is a very agreeable occupation to talk with my dear Papa":

> This has really been a year of trials. I've never before needed so much patience. First a winter without balls, then two months of whooping cough, and now your absence that may perhaps last a long time.

She hugged him "thousands and thousands of times."

> It seems like a thousand years since I saw you, dear Papa, and it will probably be as long before I see you again. . . . You would not believe how sad and silent this house is since you are no longer here.

She added that their dog Gips "will die of grief and loneliness if you stay away long. His hair is already turning white."[12]

The sudden departure of Metternich and the Emperor had thrown the city of Vienna into consternation in those first days of June. Our Emperor gone! And with Metternich! More like an abduction! Timid souls shivered, expecting to see Napoleon with his army at the gates of the city within hours.

The hawks of the War Party, on the other hand, were equally dismayed, declaring that journey north could only mean another shameful appeasement of Napoleon.

> Everyone here is in the greatest state of tension [Laure wrote]. May we soon have news and may it be good news above all.[13]

News of the armistice brought more excitement—relief to some, consternation to others. "Fools will shout against the armistice," Metternich warned Laure. "Such as it is, it will save the world."[14]

One rumor after another swept the city, which had to glean its news chiefly from the carefully filtered government pronouncements in the official *Austrian Observer*.

Marie wrote her father:

> You've no idea of the stories they tell here. Among others that you've quarreled with the Emperor and that the Emperor would be back here by yesterday. Quite a crowd gathered in Bellaria to meet him.[15]

Metternich was far too thin-skinned to shrug off the critics and rumor-mongers lightly—the Vienna *crieurs*, he termed them—those who criticized his policies while he was working his heart out to save Austria and all of Europe from the devastation of another war.

Meantime, in the days that followed the Emperor's departure and the armistice, dozens of carriages poured out of Vienna, like a flock of gulls in the wake of a ship, taking the road north to Bohemia—diplomats, generals, secretaries, servants, curiosity-seekers, young men and old who thought war was coming and who hurried to enlist again in the Army.

Presently Laure could inform her husband:

> Vienna is becoming a real desert. Every day there are more leaving and almost all for Bohemia. Of this number are the Duchess of Sagan and her sister Pauline, the former going to her estates, the latter to see her mother in Karlsbad. . . . Prince Windischgraetz is also leaving as a volunteer for the army.[16]

With Laure's news in hand Metternich dashed off a gay little note of greeting to Wilhelmine in Ratiborzitz. So she had followed his advice and come to Bohemia! Could they not meet somewhere soon? His regular courier to Reichenbach passed close by Ratiborzitz and he would keep her posted on all the news. She was not to split her brain apart trying to puzzle out why he was in Gitschin.

At last, on June 15, came the first real break in his peace plans. Stadion wrote that the Tsar had decided to accept Metternich's invitation, would meet him at Castle Opocno on the border of Bohemia in two days' time.

> My journey will influence to a great extent the fate of poor humanity [he wrote Laure]. So pray God to comfort me and that he will make everything turn out well.[17]

Castle Opocno lay less than two hours' journey from the country house of the Duchess of Sagan. He would spend the night before the meeting with the Tsar under her roof.

5

Wilhelmine had found Metternich's note awaiting her when she alighted from her traveling carriage at her country house in a driving rain on the late Thursday afternoon of June 10. Exhausted from the four-day journey, chilled to the bone, she had gone straight to bed with one of her severe migraines.

It had not been only Metternich's word in her ear that had changed her summer's direction and brought her to Bohemia instead of Baden. Alfred Windischgraetz—like dozens of other young men—was hastening to rejoin his regiment in the belief that Austria would soon be at war. On her journey from Vienna she had stopped to spend a few blissful hours with him in the inn at Czaslau before they had parted—he for his regiment at Pardubitz, she for her country house at Ratiborzitz, near the border of Bohemia.

On Friday sitting before the tall windows of her sitting room that looked out over the meadows to the serene river Aupa, gray now and misted over with rain, she wrote Metternich:

> I flatter myself that I've guessed only too well what brings you to this part
> of the world to break my head trying to find other reasons.

She would send horses to the nearest relay station to meet him if he would let her know when he was coming. She promised not to talk politics if he came. "I want the few moments with you here to be moments of rest for you—." Still she could not forbear pressing him just a little to make up his mind in favor of the Allies:

> Be sure that I have often thought of you and always with the warmest
> friendship—without forgetting that nothing in the world would make
> you more attractive in my eyes than to be the greatest enemy of that
> man who is everybody's enemy. Adieu, dear Clemens, I am waiting for
> you soon, soon—here if it is possible, if it is absolutely impossible, wher-
> ever you can arrange a rendezvous.[18]

She was just sealing her letter when the sound of carriage wheels on wet gravel announced the arrival of the first of the numerous houseguests who would sample the hospitality of Ratiborzitz during that critical month of June 1813.

It was Gentz with his valet Leopold, drenched through and through, shaking themselves like a pair of wet dogs on the stone-floored reception hall.

Like Wilhelmine and Count Ernst Hardenberg, Gentz had taken Metternich's hint and come to Bohemia, "to be," he wrote Nesselrode, "as near Gitschin as possible without actually being there."[19]

Gentz at once fell in love with Ratiborzitz, which, he wrote his friend Pilat in Vienna, "joins the serenity of paradise with all its beauties. It is hard to describe all I am enjoying of fine hospitality, of the comforts of life, of heavenly peace, of magnificent cuisine (that special art that interests me so deeply)."

He felt truly ashamed, he added complacently, to be "so indecently comfortable," while Metternich led "such a sadly tormented and joyless life" in Gitschin. He heard the count spent his evenings "most often with his pipe and tobacco, lonely and alone."[20]

The day after Gentz's arrival, on Saturday, the two Hardenbergs stopped in Ratiborzitz on their way back to Reichenbach from the talks at Gitschin, bringing news of the visit with Metternich and another letter for the duchess.

That evening in the library, while Wilhelmine poured tea, the men talked of serious and of frivolous things until, she wrote Metternich that night, her head was spinning. "They are talking only Egypt, Greece, the plateau of Hindustani, transmigration, people, science, poetry, Slavic, Finnish, Sanskrit . . . You see politics do not absorb these gentlemen completely."[21] The two Hardenbergs stayed for the weekend and left early Monday morning.

Before the end of June most of the leading men in Central Europe would warm their hands at the white-and-gilt porcelain stoves, sleep on goose-feather beds, breakfast on thick cream, fresh-churned butter and new-baked bread, dine in the gentle candlelight of the pretty pink-and-gray dining room whose windows looked out on the treetops of the dripping garden.

Wilhelmine had inherited Castle Náchod and the surrounding estates, but she had chosen for a summer residence, instead of the castle with its ghosts, its empty high-ceilinged rooms and gloomy drafty corridors, a charming little manor house that crowned a hill above the placid Aupa River. A simple, square, pale yellow country house, Ratiborzitz caught the sun like a bird-cage set in light. She had restored it and furnished it with exquisite taste. Behind the house terraced gardens sloped steeply down to broad meadowlands through which coursed the river Aupa between banks bordered by immense old oaks. The fine woods and meadows on the estate had been left in their natural state, a great wild park in the English style, only judiciously pruned here and there, to open up a rustic woodland walk or bridle path.

There was about the whole place a sense of refuge, of idyllic remoteness from the bustle of the world, and she had come to love it above anywhere else. She loved to awaken to the sounds of farm life—of cocks crowing in the barnyard, horses neighing, dogs barking. In the country she lived simply, with few servants, worked about the house and garden herself in a smock-like peasant dress, roamed the countryside on foot or on horseback, spoke Czech with the accent of the neighborhood, knew all the village and farm people by name, took part in the festivals of midsummer and harvest.

For Wilhelmine Ratiborzitz was inextricably bound up with the deepest love of her life.

In the spring of 1810 Wilhelmine had been at the dreary low point between liaisons, in the wretchedly empty limbo of not loving. Meantime, Alfred Windischgraetz had lain perilously ill with a lung inflammation. Her kind-hearted sisters had brought him to their house in Vienna to nurse him back to recovery. She had urged him to come to convalesce in the good country air of Ratiborzitz. What began for both of them as a light-hearted flirtation deepened into an absorbing love of such intensity it would be all but impossible for either of them to pluck out the roots.

In the sunshine of May and June 1810, they had passed idyllic days together at Ratiborzitz, awakening together to walk in the meadows and pick wild strawberries for breakfast, riding along the bridle paths in the beech forest and under the giant oaks by the river, going to bed together at sundown, laughing like children, draining the sweetness out of those first rapturous weeks together.

"I think it would not be possible to love you more than I do today," she had written after his departure that June. She recalled to him the walks they had taken together in woods and fields. "Now following those same paths brings back the precious hours we walked there together. There you stopped to look at me—here I took your arm—there we chatted—I lived only happiness when you were with me—May heaven bless you and bring you back soon to us—no, not to us, to me—I will share you with no one."[22]

A few weeks later she wrote him:

> I love you too much ever to know peace of mind. It seems to me I understand perfectly the life of a miser. . . . I want to watch always over my treasure, and I know no one to whom I would trust that care.[23]

Later on there were less idyllic moments. Again and again stormy quarrels tore apart the fabric of their relationship.

For Alfred, Catholic and head of one of the old Austrian families of feudal nobility, marriage to a twice-divorced woman six years older than himself was out of the question. His mother and his sisters pressed him to break off the affair that seemed to absorb his mind and heart so perilously. On her side, Wilhelmine, with her habit of independence, her sense of personal identity stronger than in most women of her day, was not the docile, self-effacing partner that Alfred possessively demanded. She enjoyed the company of lively intelligent men. Her beauty drew them like a magnet, and she flirted as naturally as birds fly in summer. Alfred, touchy, proud, could not bear another man's eyes on her. Driven to violent jealousy, he punished her by attention to other women, or by retreating into icy, sullen silence. Both suffered profoundly, yet the sexual attraction between them was so powerful that neither could bear to give the other up.

During the summer of 1812 they had quarreled bitterly and finally parted.

> For a long time you have been breaking my heart [she had written him].
> Yesterday you treated me with a humor and a coldness that drove me
> to despair. Why? I do not know. I find nothing in my heart or my con-

duct to justify it. My anxiety, my tears—nothing touches you—my presence bores you—

She begged him to sever their tormenting relationship, once and for all. Instead, Alfred had come to Ratiborzitz in the late autumn for a reconciliation as piercingly sweet as any in their troubled liaison.

You have been so good, so perfect toward me that I cannot doubt [you] without being a monster of ingratitude. . . . For the last two and a half years I've sometimes believed that I pleased you, sometimes that you wished me well. Only for the last few days have I felt that you truly love me. . . . *N'est ce pas être trop heureuse?*²⁴

On the yellow stucco walls of the stables at Ratiborzitz she had painted the figures of a great sundial to remind her of the Indian summer sunshine of that lovely autumn.

In Vienna, during the spring months of 1813, she had again premonitions that their love affair was waning. Yet with war hanging over their heads, the thought of parting from him was unbearable. However crowded the manor house became that June, Alfred's bedroom and study adjoining her own boudoir and sitting room were lent to no other guests but kept for him alone.

On the morning of June 15 Alfred still lay sleeping in that adjoining room—he and his friend Major Trogoff had arrived late the evening before on leave from their regiment—when Wilhelmine's maid awakened her to say that Baron Marschall, Austrian attaché at the Tsar's headquarters, had arrived and would speak to no one but the mistress of the house. Hastily throwing on a morning gown, Wilhelmine went to meet him. His Imperial Majesty the Tsar, Marschall informed her, would be pleased to dine with her the following day, toward two in the afternoon, on his way from Reichenbach to Opocno, where he was to meet the Austrian Foreign Minister.

The Tsar's message threw the whole manor house into a flurry of excitement and consternation. The world might be teetering on the brink of war —Austria might be forced to choose sides within twenty-four hours—nevertheless, the fact remained that the Tsar of All the Russias—from whom, incidentally, came her mother's entire income and a good portion of her own —was about to descend on Ratiborzitz, and its mistress was completely unprepared to entertain a sovereign. She had no chef—in summer as always some of the farm women took over her kitchen; the one butler she had brought from Vienna was ill in bed; she had not a single trained servant save her lady's maid Hannchen.

She sent a messenger with a panicky little note to Metternich six hours away in Gitschin. He simply must rescue her and send a pastry cook; was she not entertaining the Tsar for his sake and for Austria? But Metternich had no pastry cook and the Emperor's could not be spared. He sent her in-

stead an aide, Count Bombelles, one of those versatile men who can put
their hand to any emergency, together with a valet de chambre, and a case
of bonbons, cakes, macaroons and tiny sweet soufflés. The pastries would
undoubtedly arrive shaken to bits in the post chaise over the rough roads;
she would have to explain them to the Tsar, Metternich wrote lightly, as a
newly invented macédoine of pastry particles. And would she permit him,
Metternich, to spend the following night under her roof at Ratiborzitz, on
his way to meet the Tsar at Opocno?

Later on, in an entertaining letter to Laure, Metternich described the
episode of the Tsar's dinner party, declaring that Wilhelmine and Gentz together "had nearly died of fright," that Bombelles had saved the day, "even
making the ices, which they say were excellent."[25]

Wilhelmine however, had risen to the emergency; she could work like a
whirlwind when the occasion demanded, as her foster daughter Emilie testi-
fied, making rooms ready for guests, taking a hand in the kitchen. This time
she packed Alfred and Trogoff back to their regiment, keeping only Alfred's
valet François to help serve. All the resources of her house and a good many
borrowed were thrown into the emergency. She sent wagons to collect food
from the hundred farms of Náchod, created a dozen servants out of her
farm people. By that Tuesday night Gentz could write his friend Pilat, gleefully announcing the impending visit:

> Tell Princess Bagration (but spare her life) what a great day awaits her
> mortal enemy tomorrow when the Tsar dines here.[26]

As it turned out, the Tsar's visit went off beautifully.

The rain had ceased, the day was bright and miraculously clear. The Tsar
was to have crossed the border before noon and be at Ratiborzitz by two. A
gala reception at Náchod delayed him, and it was after four when his carriage drew up before the steps of the manor house where Wilhelmine waited
to receive him. All charm and gracious good manners, he raised her from
her curtsy to kiss her affectionately on both cheeks and ask at once after her
mother, his old and dear friend, the Duchess of Courland.

"No one could be more friendly, more affable, more obliging and more
gracious than he," she wrote Alfred that night.[27]

Though, like Metternich, Wilhelmine counted herself Austrian by adop-
tion, she had not forgotten her ancestral ties to Russia, that her grandfather
had won his high place in the world of Eastern Europe from the Tsarina
Anna, that her own father counted himself Russian to the end of his days
while she herself had been christened for the Tsar's grandmother, the great
Catherine. Her mother had spent some weeks in St. Petersburg and had sub-
sequently entertained the Tsar at her castle in Saxony, where Wilhelmine's
three sisters had made his acquaintance, but Wilhelmine now met him for
the first time.

It was certainly not by chance that the Tsar had come to dine with her
at Ratiborzitz. "Stadion chose me to provide an agreeable impression of Bo-

hemia to His Majesty," Wilhelmine wrote Metternich.[28] But it was more than an impression of Bohemia that Stadion and Lebzeltern expected when they engineered that dinner party. The Tsar was intent on drawing Austria into war; if the Duchess of Sagan had great influence over Metternich, as it was rumored, then she must be pressed to use her persuasive powers on the resistant Foreign Minister.

Most observers at that time accounted the Tsar a handsome man, blond and blue-eyed like his grandmother. And though at thirty-four he was growing a trifle stout, so that he had to be corseted into his skin-tight uniforms, and his short neck and heavily padded uniform shoulders gave him a curiously top-heavy look, still he moved lightly and gracefully on his feet, had great personal charm and irresistibly winning manners.

Wilhelmine showed him about the gardens and the house; he admired the taste and imagination that had gone into the work of restoration, and the beauty of the natural landscape.

Dinner had been laid for the Tsar in solitary splendor, as protocol demanded, in the long dining room lighted by shafts of late afternoon sun. Not even the hostess could sit down with an emperor uninvited.

But graciously the Tsar insisted that the whole company dine with him, Wilhelmine, of course, at his right hand. Besides the single aide, Count Tolstoy, who accompanied the Tsar, at table that day were Stadion, Lebzeltern, Gentz, Bombelles, Marschall, and a half brother of Wilhelmine, Schwedhof, who was an officer in the Prussian Army. Everyone joined in the lively conversation, "as free," Gentz told Pilat, "as at Count Metternich's when we sit around like a little committee."[29]

The conversation touched on everything, especially everything military— on Napoleon and his Russian campaign, on the weakness of his pursuit of the Allies after Bautzen, on the state of the armies and the prospects for continuing the war.

The Tsar, who was noticeably deaf in one ear, leaned toward Wilhelmine to catch her words, fixing his eyes on her face with flattering attentiveness. He inquired after her mother's health again and if she would be returning soon to Paris. It was a somewhat delicate subject, for her mother, when she went to Paris in 1809 after marrying her youngest daughter to the nephew of Napoleon's Foreign Minister, Talleyrand, had become an ardent Bonapartist. Later, along with Talleyrand, her sentiments had undergone a decided change and now she was as much anti-Bonaparte as she had been pro- before. It was a reversal the Tsar himself should have understood, but he did not like to be reminded of his camaraderie with Bonaparte at Tilsit.

Since Napoleon's Russian campaign, not a ruble of her mother's income had been paid her, and now Wilhelmine tried tactfully to set matters to rights. "I think I rendered my mother a good service," she wrote Alfred that night.[30]

But there was another matter involving the Courland family that the Tsar for his part wished to set to rights. At the Congress of Erfurt in 1808, when Napoleon had basked in the unctuous subservience of the German satellite sovereigns, Talleyrand had supplied certain invaluable information on Napoleon's plans to the Russian Tsar. As a favor in return Talleyrand asked the Tsar to intervene and secure the hand of the youngest—and immensely rich—Courland princess, Dorothée, for his nephew and heir, Edmond de Talleyrand-Périgord. The Tsar obligingly stopped on his way back to Russia at the *Schloss* of the Duchess of Courland in Saxony and in the smoothest and politest of blackmail—for he controlled the duchess's entire income—made known his wishes for the marriage of her daughter. Fifteen-year-old Dorothée was tricked into foregoing a betrothal she had long dreamed of with the Polish Prince Adam Czartoryski for what turned out to be a wretched marriage, and forced to leave her own country to live in the country of the enemy—France.

Dorothée's three older sisters had been shocked at what they considered their mother's betrayal—a betrayal both political and personal, for she had promised never to force her daughters into a marriage against their inclinations. All three sisters boycotted the wedding, a sad little proxy affair in Frankfurt, on the way to Paris, in April of 1809, with the Duchess of Courland's old friend—and Napoleon's—the Prince Primate Dalberg presiding. For some three years the Duchess of Courland and her three older daughters remained estranged. Not until the previous summer of 1812, when she had come to Karlsbad, had they been reconciled.

The Tsar was well aware that Wilhelmine and her sisters had been furious at Dorothée's marriage, and might still harbor a certain prejudice against him for his unsavory role of marriage broker.

Now, at the dinner party on June 16, the Tsar turned to Wilhelmine and declared that "people had wanted him to mix in the marriage of my sister but that he hoped we were persuaded he would never be part of such an affair."[31]

It was an outright lie, and Wilhelmine knew it, but this was not the moment in history to hold a grudge against the Tsar. Wilhelmine only smiled and nodded and turned the conversation to more general topics.

On the subject of the war the Tsar made his views perfectly clear to her:

> The Tsar talked a great deal of his firm desire to continue the war provided that Austria will help; his hope was in her.[32]

In the library after dinner Wilhelmine poured tea, and the Tsar sat at her elbow chatting in the most engaging manner. Just after seven he left with his party for Opocno, pronouncing himself enchanted with everything at Ratiborzitz, with the house, the gardens, the exquisite dinner—most of all, with his lovely hostess. He promised her he would return to dine again with her within a week, on his journey back to Reichenbach.

An hour after the Tsar's departure Metternich's carriage drew up before the steps of the manor. He had timed his arrival carefully; it might have been diplomatically awkward to encounter the Tsar prematurely. He had thanked Wilhelmine for inviting him to dine with them, but he had declined;

he did not wish to dine, he wrote, "where I am not certain of finding friendly powers."[33]

He had hoped to find Wilhelmine waiting to greet him; he had hoped to hear her recount in her warm voice the tale of the day's events. But Wilhelmine, exhausted by the preparations and by the excitement of the day, had retired, leaving only a cool little note thanking him for the loan of his servants and for the good things they brought. Instead of Wilhelmine, it was Gentz who poured out an account of the day, dwelling effusively on the Tsar's intelligence and charms. Never before had Gentz sat down to dine with an emperor, and his life would never be quite the same.

In her boudoir that evening Wilhelmine sat writing a long letter to Alfred, who had been not a little cross at being dispatched back to his regiment instead of spending blissful days at Ratiborzitz. Moreover, the Tsar's reputation for conquest included women perhaps even more than armies, and Alfred was certain to be working up a case of jealousy.

> The Tsar [she wrote Alfred that night] was very nice, but he would have had to have many more perfections to console me a little for what he forced me to sacrifice for him. . . . They steal the best part of my existence in depriving me of your presence, dear dear Alfred.

Of their conversations over dinner she told Alfred what he most wanted to hear:

> They appear decided on war. You can imagine what I suffer having to hide in my heart what my true feelings are. . . .
>
> Adieu, think of the sad night that awaits me and that will be followed by so many others until I can press you to this heart that loves only you. I kiss you thousands and thousands of times. Adieu, dear Alfred, my everything. . . .[34]

That night of June 16 with the Austrian Foreign Minister under her roof, was a sleepless one for everyone in the house. Couriers from Vienna, couriers from Dresden—sent on to Ratiborzitz from Gitschin—came galloping up the road from the village in the middle of the night, pounding at the door and clattering up the stone stairs, with dispatches for Metternich that could not wait till morning.

Bubna's courier from Dresden brought no definite word of a meeting with Napoleon or Bassano; he was sent immediately back to Dresden with the news of Metternich's approaching meeting with the Tsar. It would do no harm to pique Napoleon's curiosity a bit.

In the morning over an early breakfast Metternich saw Wilhelmine, but she did not try to influence him in his talks with the Tsar, as Alfred had evidently urged her:

> . . . with the liberty that I have of talking sometimes to certain persons I perhaps ought to have tried to raise his soul toward a great end, but I admit I exhausted all my strength in the conversations in Vienna I told

you about. I did everything then that I could and this time I remained completely passive. Besides what could my feeble remonstrances do— they are nothing for the public good and I have paid dear for them.[35]

With Lebzeltern and Bombelles for company Metternich drove on to Opocno and the meeting with the Tsar.

6

It was not the first time the Russian sovereign and the Austrian minister— whose relationship would have momentous consequences for Europe in the next months and years—had met. Seven years before, in 1805, when he was a rising young diplomat at his second post, in Berlin, Metternich had so won the Tsar's esteem that Alexander had requested Metternich be sent as ambassador to St. Petersburg. Napoleon too had asked for Metternich—and it was to Paris he had gone.

But the political ambience had changed since then. Russia had refused aid to Austria in the War of 1809. Austria had fought alone against Napoleon and gone down in defeat. The Tsar had not hesitated to accept a share of the spoils of that defeat by acquiring Austrian Galicia. Metternich's policy of rapprochement with France had followed, the Austrian marriage, and the alliance with France in the spring of 1812 as Napoleon prepared for his Russian campaign. A deep personal enmity between the Tsar's chief minister, Romanzow, and Metternich had not improved Austrian-Russian relations.

Since the disaster to the Grande Armée and the triumphant advance of the Russian army halfway across Europe, Metternich, while protesting Austria's friendship for Russia, had steadfastly refused to join Austria's arms to Russia's.

When the two men met again in the hastily furnished salons of Castle Opocno, there was little trust between them. Metternich, striving for immediate European peace, feared another Tilsit, with the Tsar and Napoleon embracing, perhaps making a pact to dismember Austria. The Tsar on his side feared that Metternich was simply holding out until Russia exhausted herself in a conflict with Napoleon, when Austria would step in and pick up the pieces.

Speaking of the Tsar three years earlier, Napoleon had told Metternich, "It would be difficult to have more intelligence than Tsar Alexander, but there is a piece missing. I have never managed to discover what it is."

"Quick and versatile mind," Metternich described the Tsar, "easily led to change his ideas."[36]

More than in most men the opposites in Alexander's nature warred with one another. A strong vein of sensuality battled a strain of deep religious mysticism. Intelligent, educated in the ideas of the Enlightenment by the liberal Swiss tutor Frédéric de La Harpe, whom his grandmother, Catherine the Great, had chosen for him, he envisioned himself a philosopher-king righting wrongs, putting his philanthropic ideas to work among his people. But the strain of romantic liberalism feuded with the realities of still medieval Russia, and philosopher-kings were long out of date in Napoleonic Europe.

Never would he contrive to bring consonance either to his political ideas or to his complex emotional makeup. He would be forever haunted by the guilt of parricide for that night in March 1801, when he had dozed in the Winter Palace in St. Petersburg while a band of plotters broke into the apartment of his father, the mad Tsar Paul, and strangled him.

Alexander suffered from a deep-seated insecurity, doubted his own manhood, had an almost pathological fear of being thought cowardly. With everlasting shame he would remember the night of Austerlitz, when he had sat weeping under a leafless apple tree while his armies fled in disarray before the French.

He had acquired a passion for things military; he could explode in a tantrum, shouting, "I am a soldier! I trust only soldiers!" His beloved sister Catherine had driven him quite frantic during the French invasion the previous year. At first she had urged him to leave the Army to his generals; then, after the burning of Moscow, she had all but accused him of cowardice and loss of honor for abandoning his armies and waiting out the war in St. Petersburg. There had been a dangerous moment in the year 1812 when the Tsar's popularity and his people's faith in him had sunk so low that there were demands that he be replaced on the throne by the energetic, single-minded young Catherine.[37]

Yet Catherine remained his adored sister, closer to him than anyone else in the world—far closer than the prim and virtuous Tsarina Elizabeth, to whom he had been married as an adolescent, who bored and annoyed him unspeakably, and whom he kept at as great a distance as possible.

Catherine was endlessly amusing—and disturbing. Things were always livelier when dear Katya was around. They could play at being children again, sit up most of the night chattering and laughing uncontrollably. "I love you none the less madly though you are a little mad yourself sometimes," he told her.[38]

Catherine could wheedle and needle almost anything out of her brother. When her husband, Grand Duke George of Oldenburg, died of typhus the previous December, Catherine let no grass grow under her feet. War or no war she set out at once on a campaign for another husband, preferably one who would wear a crown. She played her widowhood to the hilt, had opportune fainting spells that necessitated her immediate departure for the spas of Bohemia, where the society of Central Europe still met. She rather thought that Archduke Karl, brother of Emperor Franz of Austria and a distinguished general in his own right, might do.

The Tsar's two sisters, Catherine and Marie, had arrived at Opocno from Prague the day before Metternich, so that a kind of Romanoff family reunion formed the background for the Opocno talks.

Metternich did not expect his meeting with the Tsar on June 17 to be an easy one. To his relief and pleasure he found Alexander in great good spirits, receiving him with friendly warmth, ready to talk with engaging frankness.

In his *Memoirs*, written years later, Metternich declared of the Opocno conversations that he had assured the Tsar it would not matter whether Napoleon accepted the proposals offered or not, so long as time was gained to improve their armies "and from which we may ourselves take the offensive." In other words, Austria was already determined on war.[39]

But contemporary documents clearly refute Metternich's recollections. Indeed, if such had been the case, the fierce and bitter arguments between Metternich and the Allied sovereigns and ministers in the ensuing days would never have taken place.

On Thursday, June 17, he and the Tsar talked together for over two hours without reaching any agreement. The next day Nesselrode and Stadion joined in the talks, with the Russians urging again that the six bases of Wurschen be presented to Napoleon as an ultimatum. Metternich refused. He proposed that no peace bases at all be named beforehand, in order to draw Napoleon to the peace table, and that only the four moderate Austrian bases be used if any at all were to be named.

In the end the Tsar agreed to take part in a congress. But Metternich had to give his word that if the peace negotiations failed, Austria would join in war against Napoleon.

7

Metternich had won Russia to try for peace. Now he must win Prussia. He sent a courier off to Reichenbach inviting Hardenberg to meet with him, Nesselrode and Stadion on the following day, Saturday, June 19, at Ratiborzitz.

In his *Memoirs*, again glossing over his peace effort of 1813, Metternich wrote that from Opocno, "I went straight back to Gitschin," omitting any mention of the crucial two-day meeting at Ratiborzitz in which he fought for Prussia's consent to a peace congress.[40]

Wilhelmine, who was so close to all the events of that June, wrote of that conference:

> The meeting of Metternich, Hardenberg and Nesselrode to take place here will probably decide the fate of Europe. It is in my humble house that they will make their plans for a peace—which will take place only if the chief monster finds it in his momentary interest—for on him depend war and peace, and these earnest personages know nothing about it.[41]

Metternich had planned to drive back to Ratiborzitz from Opocno to sleep under her roof that Friday night and have more than the brief glimpse of her he had caught the previous day. But a battering thunderstorm intervened, followed by a long deluge of rain. He dispatched a note that she might expect him instead early Saturday "at the very moment you open those lovely eyes of yours which the Tsar is pleased to describe to anyone who will listen."

He adds teasingly that she must not think it is for her he is coming to Ratiborzitz, but rather to meet with Hardenberg "in a spot which is becoming entirely diplomatic." He will spend Saturday and Sunday with her. On the back of the note he adds a postscript:

> I may bring Nesselrode. The Tsar is in love with you. Say hello to Gentz.[42]

By Saturday the storm had passed, leaving a day cool and brilliant as a polished diamond.

True to his word Metternich's carriage drove up to the door of the manor house very early. Bombelles was with him, but not Nesselrode.

Over breakfast with Wilhelmine and Gentz he detailed his visit at Opocno. The talks with the Tsar had gone well, Metternich reported, and he declared himself, according to Wilhelmine, "enchanted with Tsar Alexander —he who is scarcely ever excited about anything."[43]

An hour later Hardenberg drove in from Reichenbach, accompanied by Humboldt, who had not been invited, and the councillor Barbier.

Prussia was going to prove the harder nut to crack. And the Tsar's assent to a congress was contingent on Prussia's agreement.

From the moment of his arrival in Reichenbach a week earlier Humboldt had worked to push through the subsidy treaties with England and to press for continuing the war. Four days earlier, on June 15, the Anglo-Prussian treaty had been signed, "a decisive step," Humboldt wrote his wife, "to show that after the armistice we are not steering toward peace."[44]

But all that week Humboldt fretted about the possibility of Prussia and Russia giving in to Austria. The Tsar, he guessed, would yield to Metternich on the bases. The King of Prussia might too, since he declared it would be impossible to go on fighting without Austria.

> Things look bad [Humboldt wrote on Thursday night]. Austria is work-ing with all her strength for peace, and proposes bases which give the peace neither safety nor benefit nor even honor. . . . Austria will give no ultimatum to Napoleon [but] will hold a kind of congress and is already talking about it in notes.[45]

It was a contentious Saturday at Ratiborzitz, a day of "tête-à-têtes, of half and whole conferences."

Clearly the Prussians were determined on war and averse to holding out any offer to Napoleon that he might conceivably accept. Prussia again insisted that the six conditions of Wurschen be presented to Napoleon as an ultimatum. Metternich refused, declaring that any demands should be presented when the negotiators met together in a congress. The point was to get the conflicting parties to sit down and talk.

Had the negotiations of mid-June been merely a diplomatic *Schein-Krieg*, as many historians have written, to cover Austria's real intention of going to war against Napoleon, there would have been no arguments, no disagreement between Austria and Prussia. But Metternich was as determined as ever to try for peace.

In the library Metternich shouted at Hardenberg, "deaf as a pot," Wilhelmine reported, "but otherwise polite and friendly." Humboldt stayed close beside him, providing the extra ears and the encouragement to resist Metternich's proposals.

Around the dinner table that afternoon the debate continued. Hardenberg and Humboldt brought all the pressure they could to bear on Metternich to give up his effort to negotiate. Napoleon could not possibly want peace, they argued. Why dally and give him more time to build up his armies? Why not join the Allies at once, make war the moment the armistice expired?

As to the bases Metternich proposed, Hardenberg declared flatly that he would resign his post if the Prussian King were to sign "a bad peace"— that is, a peace which failed to give Prussia all her claims.

Everyone at the dinner table supported the Prussian stand, Humboldt wrote his wife later.

> Gentz is an unbelievable help, and the duchess supports us too. Poor Lebzeltern has fallen out of grace, for he thinks as we do, and Stadion is always looking for an honorable way out.[46]

It is unlikely that Wilhelmine really supported the Prussian position. Torn by the question of peace or war she wrote to Alfred that night:

> Hardenberg . . . talks only of fighting well. Mon Dieu! what a grief all these people are to me. They wouldn't talk so freely if they could imagine with what disquiet I hear the question of peace or of war discussed, and how I suffer to have to pronounce sentiments so opposed to those I carry in the depths of my heart.[47]

To calm ruffled tempers Wilhelmine proposed a long walk in the last sunshine of the June afternoon. She led them through the lovely gardens, sparkling still with the night's raindrops and smelling of late roses, across the broad meadow where now and again a stork rose to skim away over the treetops toward the Giant Mountains in the misty distance.

The whole place Metternich found perfectly enchanting:

> . . . a masterpiece [he wrote Laure]. Imagine a small house, very beautifully designed, furnished like a jewel, on a hill which forms one side of a charming valley, the whole valley a meadow crossed by the pretty river Aupa.[48]

Whatever calm the walk produced, it was not for long. In the evening there were more discussions, and "much ill humor and irritation," Humboldt declared, which might have led to most unpleasant scenes had he not "led the group back through more general conversation."[49]

In Metternich's memory of the evening, it was Wilhelmine who with tact and gentleness kept the conversation from erupting into an explosion of anger and hard feelings.

Never in all the difficult weeks of spring had Metternich felt so deeply discouraged, so frustrated as he felt that Saturday evening of June 18 in Ratiborzitz. Discussions with Prussia were at an impasse. Never had he come so close to abandoning his effort to bring everyone around to negotiations for peace. While Humboldt and Hardenberg emptied their teacups, and Gentz and Stadion leafed through the folios of fine engravings her father had collected, Wilhelmine in her favorite chair worked at the needlework she always had at hand. Sitting beside her in one of his most gloomy hours, depressed by the intransigeance of the Prussians, Metternich confessed that he considered resigning his post.[50]

Later that evening in her boudoir, writing to Alfred of the day's events, Wilhelmine labeled the bitter debate over peace bases a lesson in pure futility:

> Everything depends solely on the great personage who sometimes promises to give in to demands made upon him, sometimes refuses and makes fun of all of them in the bottom of his heart. It's on him our fate depends; if he sees war as inevitable, he'll send this whole mob packing. If his resources are not sufficient, he'll give in for a moment, so that he can teach them all a lesson, separately, one by one.

She knew Alfred would be gnawing his heart out with jealousy, not only for these men around her, but for her absorption in political affairs. She tried to reassure him:

> What matters to me the fate and existence of empires, what matters to me who and how they are governed, and if the world trembles a little more or a little less—Once this interest was more important to me than anything—today I see only you, dear Alfred.[51]

After the others had gone off to bed, Gentz and Metternich—both by nature nighttime people—stayed up talking "for seven hours," Gentz wrote Pilat jubilantly, until dawn broke in the skies.

At a final conference on Sunday morning Metternich and Hardenberg reached an agreement. Prussia would send delegates to a "kind of a congress" in Gitschin. No ultimatum would be presented to Napoleon, nor would peace bases be named beforehand.

But the Allies had exacted their price: Austria would be bound to go to war if the negotiations failed.

When Metternich left at noon for Gitschin, Bombelles and Lebzeltern beside him in the carriage, he felt he had carried off the victory. "I shall bless this fate which has become mine if I succeed in pacifying Europe," he wrote Laure.[52]

He intended to invite England once again to take part in the negotiations. Stadion was to propose that Russia and Prussia ask their ambassadors in London to join Austria in urging English participation in a peace effort.

An hour or so after Metternich's departure that Sunday Nesselrode drove over from Opocno, bringing an invitation to Wilhelmine, Gentz and Humboldt to dine with the Tsar and the King of Prussia the following day.

But on Monday morning Gentz and Humboldt went on without her, while Wilhelmine stayed behind in Ratiborzitz on the pretext of a migraine. She had made the mistake of describing the Tsar in rather too flattering terms to Alfred, and had added:

> Gentz with his usual penetration claims that I have a grand passion [for the Tsar]. One must pardon him for being so stupid.[53]

She got in return a sarcastic little note from Alfred, congratulating her on her success with the Russian Emperor. It was childish of Alfred, but he was jealous and he would have been furious had she gone to Opocno. With the house at last quiet and empty of guests, she wrote him that day:

> Everybody speaks of the attraction the Tsar feels for me, which wounds me. . . . I can't help receiving him here, but I do not want to appear to be seeking a meeting with him . . .

She had already assured Alfred that "only one success would please my heart and soul alike—to make sure of your love. . . . Be sure, dear, that I think the best of my qualities that of belonging to you—of being accepted as yours. . . ."

She was weary now of entertaining. If this constant brouhaha were to continue, with guests coming and going at all hours, couriers awakening her in the middle of the night, the exhausting round of entertaining—to say nothing of the heavy expense involved—she would soon be quite ill. She was already sick with the privation of not having him with her:

"With friends one counts the days," she wrote, "but with you I count also the nights. I want to miss none of them."[54]

In Opocno Gentz and Humboldt found everyone in full court dress, for the King of Prussia had arrived and there was to be a gala banquet that day. Gentz, embarrassed to find that he alone wore ordinary street dress—having forgotten, he wrote Pilat, to bring "my wedding clothes"—refused at first to join the glittering company at table. But he yielded in the end to the Tsar's entreaty, wine flowed, his tongue was loosened, and Gentz enjoyed himself thoroughly as always when he had a chance to talk.

After dinner he talked with the Russian sovereign for three whole hours, he boasted to Pilat. The Tsar admitted he had long been prejudiced against

Metternich's political principles and character, that Romanzow's enmity for the Austrian minister had contributed to his own distrust—but that since his own conversations with Metternich, he felt much reassured. The Tsar "would give a kingdom," Gentz added, "if he could stir up Austria to seize arms without any attempt at peace."[55]

Humboldt, Nesselrode, Stadion and Gentz closeted themselves to draft the treaty that was to bind Austria to the Allies if the negotiations should fail. The treaty was finished on Tuesday, and early Wednesday morning Nesselrode left to carry it to Gitschin for Metternich's approval. He intended to make a last-ditch effort directly with Emperor Franz to persuade him to adopt the harsher Wurschen bases as an ultimatum to Napoleon.

Gentz left at the same time as Nesselrode, to return to Ratiborzitz and to be on hand when Wilhelmine again entertained the Tsar at dinner.

This time the Tsar visited Ratiborzitz with a whole bevy of aides and generals in attendance and with a regiment of Cossack guards, his elite troops, all over six feet tall and in the most splendid of uniforms.

With him too was his brother, Grand Duke Constantine, who had neither Alexander's good looks nor his personal charm. A neutral witness would describe Constantine as having "a dreadful face resembling a hyena in fury."

That Wednesday, June 23, was another cold wet day when all the stoves in the manor had to be lighted to drive out the dampness and chill. The guests had barely sat down to dinner when one of Wilhelmine's estate stewards rushed in. "Your Highness!" he cried. "The Cossacks are chopping down the oaks along the riverbank! They're burning them for firewood!"

Before Wilhelmine could reply, Constantine leapt to his feet, pulled out his sword and yelled to his adjutant, "Hang every one of the devils that's laid a finger on one of the duchess's trees! Hang them from the oaks!"

At Constantine's words Wilhelmine burst into tears, crying, "I'd rather they cut down every one of my trees than that a single man be hanged!"

The Tsar intervened, gave orders to an aide. Cossacks and trees were spared. Wilhelmine dried her tears and the dinner resumed—not quite with the same gaiety as before.[56]

The next day the incident of the Cossacks and the oaks was forgotten. A note arrived from Metternich that threw the whole house party into excitement. He was on his way to Dresden to talk to Napoleon.

> I shall stay twenty-four hours and be back at Gitschin on Saturday, 27.
> I need not tell you how *happy* this journey makes me. I come like the
> proverbial man of God bearing the weight of the world! How I wish I
> were not weighted with that burden![57]

8

In the middle of June, despite the torrents of rain, Laure moved her household bag and baggage out to their garden villa in the country on the Rennweg. She hoped—and Dr. Staudenheimer too—that fresh air and sun-

shine—if there were any sunshine in this gloomy and endlessly wet summer—would restore the roses in the children's pale cheeks. The Chancellery
apartments were hopelessly damp and chilly, and the children, especially
little Clementine, continued to cough.

Despite the wretched weather the children's health did indeed improve.
They could not play outdoors but they could dine in the conservatory and
look out through the glass panes from between the palms at the brilliance
of the roses blooming pink and white and red in the wet gardens. Dr.
Staudenheimer paid a visit to the villa, inspected the rooms and pronounced
them satisfactory. The children might stop taking the dreadful brown
medicine; Marie and Victor were to start riding horseback just as soon as the
weather improved, to complete their cure.

They had bought the pleasant villa just outside the city so that every
spring and autumn they could enjoy the pleasures of the country. Their summers they intended to reserve for the gay little spa of Baden. The villa was
not too far for the children to go into town for their lessons, and for dear
Papa to go and come each day to the Ballhaus. They could breakfast together in the garden, to the sound of birds and the bells of the Salesian
convent opposite calling the nuns to prayer.

Metternich had given much thought to remodeling the place, had himself designed the gardens. Even in the rain of this miserable June people
drove out to visit the gardens, where roses bloomed in outrageous profusion.
Laure wrote her husband that Ferdinand Palffy was "quite jealous of our
flowers and of the landscape design," that everyone was calling the Metternich gardens "the most divine in Vienna"—and all credit to her husband.
Even Laure's old uncle, Franz Wenzel Kaunitz, drove out and had to be
shown the gardens in a drizzling icy rain. As for Count Razumowsky, the
Russian envoy, his visit was prompted perhaps less by an eagerness to admire the landscape design than to pry the latest news of the political scene
in Bohemia out of Countess Laure. As Marie wrote her father,

> Maman has the reputation of being the most discreet woman in the
> world, for no one wants to believe her when she says she doesn't know
> anything.[58]

Despite her anxieties that June, and the absence of her husband, Countess
Laure kept the household running smoothly, had friends in for dinner,
took the children to their lessons and saw that they enjoyed pleasures suitable to their years. All the children went to a puppet theater, where they
could rock with laughter at the antics of the Viennese Punch, Hans Wurst.
Marie was old enough to accompany Maman to a performance of a play,
Manon, over which she wept buckets.

Most exciting of all turned out to be a production of *Don Juan*. Count
Palffy, an old friend of theirs and director of the imperial theater, had dined
with them in the Rennweg villa, and lamented that the police were taking

away most of the devils in his *Don Juan* for fear they would set fire to the theater.

But when Marie and Clementine went with their governess to the theater one night, sure enough, just at the climax, the devils running around the stage with lighted torches set fire to the curtain and general panic ensued. Madame Revel was terrified and cried out in a trembly voice, "Come, hurry, my good children, put on your shawls! There's not a moment to lose!" The fire was doused and no harm done, but Marie had enjoyed every moment of the excitement:

> All the extras rushed out from backstage with indescribable shouts and fracas; Don Juan's supper table was torn apart and broken into a thousand pieces.

Except for the fire, Marie concluded in her account to Papa, the play had been pretty much a bore, with Don Juan stiff as a stick and speaking in Viennese dialect.[59]

On June 18, the day Metternich dined with the Tsar in Opocno, there had been a family birthday party in the villa for two-year-old Leontine. "Today we celebrate a little birthday," Laure wrote, "which you are permitted not to think about with all the affairs in which you are immersed." Laure thought he had probably already left for Dresden and she added, a bit wistfully, "You were here only on the day of her birth; the other two birthdays you have been away, both times in Dresden."[60]

Metternich was not likely to forget the day of Leontine's birth, in June 1811, for Laure had very nearly lost her life in the agony of a long and difficult labor.

Leontine was a merry, bright child, and Marie wrote her father of her little sister:

> You'll see how sweet Leontine is and what progress she has made. She speaks very prettily and astonishes everyone by her intelligence and her gay and even humor.[61]

In those last days of June no letters at all came from Metternich.

Nearly every day Laure dressed and took a carriage into town, leaving Victor for his lessons with his tutor, then going on to the Chancellery to learn if Hudelist had any news that day from Gitschin. One day Hudelist could inform her with certainty that Metternich was indeed in Dresden, perhaps at that very moment confronting *le petit homme*, "who they say is neither gentle nor understanding right now."

A long week of anxiety, of rumors, of black pessimism stretched out into ten days. Still no news came.

> Louis Starhemberg [Laure wrote her husband] is spreading a rumor in the city that you've resigned and that Stadion has taken over your port-

folio. He is not one of your friends, nor is the Prince de Ligne, who is also free with his opinions.

The weather, wet and chilly before, grew worse; it rained steadily until the streets of the city coursed like rivers and the Danube threatened to over-flow its banks.

Everyone here is in a most painful state of tension, as you can imagine. There are some here who go in the enchantment of hope, others who already see the French in Vienna. Everyone is agitated in one way or another and no one is happy.[62]

Her cousin, Wenzel Liechtenstein, who rather enjoyed being a purveyor of bad news, drove out to the villa to tell Laure of a terrible epidemic of sickness in Dresden.

Though Hudelist had told her that Monsieur de Metternich would be back from Dresden by Saturday, only a long silence followed.

I am not at all pleased when I have no news of you [Laure wrote in her daily letter], and if Monsieur de Gentz did not write regularly to Pilat, we could believe you dead and buried. . . . I am going to take my letter in to town and talk to Hudelist, who may know something although he is scarcely communicative.

Laure added a bit tartly, "It is the first time I have reason to thank Gentz's chatter and that I find him good for something." They were, she wrote, "awaiting news from day to day, almost from minute to minute."[63]

Even Marie, who "never thought political affairs could interest me" now thought of nothing but politics and dear Papa. She embraced him "thousands and thousands of times," adding, "The roses in the garden are lasting longer than usual, as if they wished to await your return before losing their petals."[64]

VII

ENCOUNTER IN DRESDEN: METTERNICH vs. NAPOLEON

*I shall leave for Dresden tomorrow evening. I shall stay
24 hours. Those 24 hours will be the hardest of my life;
they will decide the fate of the world.*
— METTERNICH TO LAURE[1]

1

Metternich had made sure that news of his meeting with the Tsar and
the Prussian King at Opocno would reach the ears of Napoleon through
Count Bubna. The French Emperor would be suspicious, irritated, vexed—
but most of all, burning with curiosity.

Returning from Ratiborzitz Metternich found a "most pressing" invitation from Bassano to come to Dresden. He was awaited, Bubna wrote, "with
some anxiety," and should come "as soon as his affairs permit." He had to
wait in Gitschin, however, for Nesselrode to arrive, bringing the draft of the
fateful Reichenbach Treaty. Metternich made a few changes on Wednesday
evening. On Thursday morning early he climbed into his carriage, rode all
day and all night, was in Dresden on Friday afternoon, June 25.

Ominously the city presented the appearance of a huge armed camp. On
the outskirts hundreds of men were at work, digging trenches, putting palisades in place, rebuilding the walls. On the plains troops of young conscripts
were drilling. Inside the city the streets were filled with French uniforms;
French peddlers cried their wares, even French bootblacks shouted, "*Cirez
les bottes!*" Once his carriage had to halt to wait for a troop of recruits to
pass—not yet in uniform, fresh-faced, incredibly young, looking as if they
had just been scooped up from the farms of Normandy and Champagne.

From Count Bubna he learned that Napoleon was out of town, inspecting military installations along the Elbe. He had his replies to Bassano's memoranda delivered at once; his notes urged again the negotiation of a preliminary peace whereby men would disarm and make ready for the final peace that must include England. He proposed Gitschin as a meeting place for such a peace conference.

He did not have to wait long. The next morning, Saturday, June 26, a messenger summoned him to an audience with Napoleon at the Marcolini Palace, just outside the city.[2]

In the anteroom Napoleon's generals and aides stood about with long faces. Berthier, conducting Metternich into Napoleon's suite, whispered urgently, "Remember, France will have nothing but peace!"

In the inner reception room Napoleon stood waiting alone, his sword at his side, his hat under his arm. He had changed noticeably since the wedding festivities in Paris in 1810, changed even since the days in Dresden in May of 1812, when he had arranged the glittering gathering of his allies to see him off for Russia. The stocky figure in the green uniform had grown stouter, the face more jowly and deeply creased, the hair thinner, combed over a balding skull. He did not appear, as Schwarzenberg had described him in April, "gentle and preoccupied."

Anyone who was not for Napoleon was against him, and he was filled with suspicion of Metternich's motives. What did he mean by consorting with the enemy? French army police had intercepted dispatches of Stackelberg to St. Petersburg bragging that Austria was drawing closer to the Coalition. Napoleon pictured Metternich at Gitschin surrounded by English agents pressing huge subsidies on him if he would join their cause.

Napoleon began by inquiring after the health of his father-in-law. Then, his face fixed in a scowl, he stopped directly in front of Metternich and cried: "So here you are then, Metternich! If you wanted to end our alliance, why didn't you tell me sooner? Meantime, I've won two battles. My enemies are licking their wounds. Suddenly you come gliding into the middle of things, spouting all this talk about armistice and mediation. Without your interference everything would be settled between me and the Allies.

"So you too want war! Well, you shall have it! I've annihilated the Prussians at Lützen; I've beaten the Russians at Bautzen. Now you want your turn. Very well; the rendezvous will be Vienna!"

Metternich put in gravely, "Peace and war lie in Your Majesty's hands. The world needs peace. Today you can still conclude peace. Tomorrow may be too late."

Napoleon interrupted him. "What do they want me to do? Degrade myself? Never! I'll know how to die, but I shall never yield up one handsbreadth of soil. Your sovereigns born to the throne may be beaten twenty times and still return to their palaces. I'm the child of fortune—my reign won't outlast the day I lose my strength and people stop fearing me."[3]

Metternich tried to assure Napoleon "in the most positive manner of the sincere desire of the Austrian Cabinet to lead the warring parties to at least a continental peace." Metternich pointed out that what Austria wanted was "an enduring peace, one honorable and satisfying to all."

"But England," Napoleon cried, "wants no peace!"

True, Metternich replied, a general peace including England did not appear probable at this moment. But continental Europe might be restored to peace and equilibrium, and that peace could be permanently guaranteed by placing it in the hands of a society of independent states.

Thus early, in June of 1813, was Metternich envisioning a "concert of nations" uniting to insure a permanent European peace—and it is Baron Fain, Napoleon's secretary, who reports it.[4]

"Speak more clearly," Napoleon interrupted. "Come to the point! I've offered you Illyria to remain neutral. What does my father-in-law want?"

Metternich named the bases on which Austria, Russia and Prussia had agreed as the minimum terms for negotiation: a France restored to her natural boundaries of the Pyrenees and the Rhine; the dissolution of the duchy of Warsaw; the restoration of Prussia; the return of Illyria to Austria.

"The Emperor has offered the powers his mediation, not his neutrality," Metternich went on. "Russia and Prussia have accepted that mediation. It is for you to reply to it today." If Napoleon accepted, they would fix at once a time and a place to negotiate. If Napoleon refused, Metternich pointed out that Austria would soon have 250,000 men in Bohemia— and they could only be kept there, he threatened not too gently, for a few weeks because of shortage of subsistence.

Napoleon interrupted. Bah! he knew precisely how many soldiers Austria had—and not only how many she actually had, but how many she was capable of raising. Narbonne had sent spies into the field who had counted even the drummer boys. "But," added Napoleon, "I prefer to rely on my own mathematics, which always prove to be exact. No country can have a bigger army than it is capable of raising."

He led Metternich into his inner study, expanding on the economics of the military, and showed him lists of the Austrian Army, regiment by regiment. For more than an hour they argued over the details of those figures.

When they returned at last to the reception room, Metternich remarked, "In ordinary times armies are made up of only a small part of the population. Today you have called a whole people to arms. I have seen your soldiers—they are nothing but children. If this children's army you raised yesterday should go down in defeat, what then?"

At Metternich's words Napoleon flew into a fury. He turned on his visitor, his face contorted with rage, and yelled: "You are no soldier and you don't understand soldiers! I was brought up in the field. For a man like me the lives of a million soldiers are just so much shit!"[5] He slammed his hat with all his force against a corner of the room.

Metternich was leaning against a console that stood between two windows. Gesturing toward the world outside, he said softly, "Why have you chosen to say this to me within these four walls? Open the doors and let your words be heard from one end of France to the other."

Napoleon continued to pace up and down the room excitedly. Once he gave his hat a kick. "The French can't complain of me. To spare them I sacrificed the Germans and Poles. I lost 300,000 men in the Russian campaign, but there weren't more than 30,000 Frenchmen among them."

"You forget, Sire," said Metternich, "that you are speaking to a German."

Presently Napoleon grew a bit calmer. He continued to walk up and down the room; at the second turn he stooped and picked up his hat. "I can defy man," he said, "but not the elements. It was the cold that ruined me. In a single night I lost 30,000 horse. I lost everything except my honor and the feeling of what I owe my brave people. I made up for last year's losses. Only look at my army and the battles I've just won. I'll hold a review for you!"

Remembering Berthier's urgent whisper in the anteroom, Metternich put in, "It is that very army that wants peace now!"

"Not my army," cried Napoleon quickly. "It's my generals who want peace. I have no more generals. They were all demoralized by the cold of Moscow. I've seen the oldest of them cry like children. A fortnight ago I might have concluded peace. Today I can do so no longer. I've won two battles; I shall not make peace."[6]

Napoleon proceeded to give Metternich a full account of the Russian disaster—an account, Metternich recalled later, that occupied several hours of that day. There were many digressions in the marathon conversation; often they jumped from one subject to another. "Those who have known Napoleon and transacted business with him," Metternich wrote, "will not be surprised at that."

It was Metternich's boast to the end of his life that he had studied Napoleon and understood him. He intimated that his comprehension of Napoleon's character enabled him to lead him to his doom.

It was not, of course, true. The two men were constitutionally incapable of understanding one another, though each harbored a grudging respect for the other.

Napoleon had gone from the climate of Corsica, where Latin *machismo* ruled, where feuds were settled by physical violence, where traditions of an eye-for-an-eye still held sway, directly into the world of the military that taught power bought by arms, political solutions imposed by superior force.

Metternich, on the other hand, ingrained with a profound hatred of violence and of disorder, had been bred up from childhood to respect diplomacy and the discourse of reason. His whole education had directed him into the rational methods of conflict resolution. He believed that reason and the laws of mechanics could govern international relations, as surely as in the eighteenth-century view they governed the world of nature. Nor had Metternich at this period hardened into the inflexibility that is always the politician's most dangerous enemy; his brain was still extraordinarily supple, gifted at discerning possible avenues of conciliation, of compromise.

The confrontation that day in Dresden was the encounter between the primitive law of the club and the rational man's uses of civility in arranging the affairs of nations.

Proudly Metternich wrote later that he had felt himself at that crisis "the representative of all European society."[7]

Napoleon's view of their dialogue that day was quite different. Already determined on war, he had no intention of being dissuaded, only of pretending to be. To Caulaincourt that night he would try to justify himself on the grounds that he needed revenge. He called Metternich's demand for a mediated peace "blackmail without fighting." And he added indignantly to Caulaincourt: "A conqueror everywhere, I don't have to receive the law of the conquered—still less those who haven't fought!"[8]

To Napoleon boundaries were something one bought at the world's counters with the blood of armies. Why should France disgorge territories she had conquered?

To Metternich he cried out, "You want me to give up more than I'd have to with four lost battles? And it is my father-in-law who entertains such a project! He deceives himself if he thinks a mutilated throne can be a refuge for his daughter and his grandson.

"You think I'm going to evacuate all Europe when I'm occupying half of it—lead my legions back across the Rhine, the Alps, the Pyrenees? Sign a treaty which is nothing but a huge surrender? Deliver myself up like a fool to my enemies when my flags are flying on the shores of the Vistula and the Oder and my victorious army is at the gates of Berlin and Breslau?"[9]

Napoleon led Metternich into his map room. Metternich must have seen there, ominously spread out on a table, Müller's great map of Bohemia, over which Napoleon had been poring in those days, marking with pins every road and mountain pass leading from Saxony into Austrian territory.

Outside the closed doors of Napoleon's suite the aides and generals who stood about anxiously through that long day, afraid to leave, caught now and again fragments of the conversation, often heard their master's voice shouting in excitement or anger. Metternich's voice, low-pitched, controlled, most of the time could not be heard.

Now Napoleon's secretary Fain heard his master shout: "I'll not give up an inch of ground. I'll give up part of the duchy of Warsaw to Russia. I won't give anything to Austria because you haven't beaten me. I'll give nothing to Prussia because she has betrayed me. Illyria cost me 300,000 men; if you want it you'll have to fight for it!"

It was outrageous to Napoleon that Austria could ask to have conquered territory restored to her at the negotiating table without going to battle. "Without drawing a sword!" cried Napoleon. "These claims of yours are an outrage! Ah, Metternich, how much has England paid you to make war on me?"[10]

Metternich must surely have blanched at the insult. He had given his word that he was free of commitments at that moment. The Reichenbach Treaty with Russia and Prussia was not yet signed, and as for England, Metternich's only direct contact had been the peace mission of Wessenberg. With great effort he retained his composure and said nothing. His self-possession astonished and impressed Napoleon, who would remark later that night to Caulaincourt, "Since this couldn't be Metternich's first affair with money, the reproach must have shocked him a bit." And he added, "Metternich is well trained. He learned his lessons well in Paris. He has really become a statesman, have you noticed?"[11]

All day long the marathon conversation had lasted. Toward the end of the day the two men were pacing up and down the length of the room together. Napoleon's hat had again fallen to the floor, and they had passed it several times. Metternich refused to stoop to pick it up; in the end Napoleon reached down and retrieved it.

At some point during the long day they touched on Metternich's personal affairs. Napoleon, who believed every man had his price, may have offered Metternich a princedom if he would maintain Austria's neutrality.

> I do not know what I would give [Metternich wrote his wife afterward] to have had a witness to that audience. Four times the Emperor threw his hat into a corner of the room, swearing like the very devil. Every time I saw him go into one of his rages, I carefully laid my own hat gently on a chair, to show him that I at least knew how to retain possession of my temper.
>
> Each time, after one of those rages, he became quite calm again. He ended by declaring at the ninth hour that I was one of the men he liked best in the whole world, and that if we made war on each other tomorrow, he would not like me the less.
>
> It would be hard to believe scenes like that could happen. The good God who gave me my unshakable calm permitted me to overcome everything, and He will protect me up to the end of my enormous task.[12]

The long afternoon had come to an end; twilight had fallen on the city outside. Slowly the room had darkened, but Napoleon's servants had not dared enter the room to light the candles.

Toward the end of the day Napoleon had grown calmer. He spoke of his marriage: "So I have committed a stupid folly in marrying an Austrian archduchess!"

"Since Your Majesty desires to know my opinion," Metternich replied, "I will candidly say that the conqueror Napoleon has made a mistake."

"But the Emperor Franz will not dethrone his daughter?"

"The Emperor knows only his duty, and he will fulfill it. The Emperor Franz is first of all a monarch, and the interests of his people will always take first place in his calculations."

Napoleon cut him short. "What you say doesn't surprise me. I know I've made an inexcusable mistake. It may cost me my throne"—he paused an instant to deliver his final thrust—"but I will bury the world beneath its ruins!"

By then it was nearly half past eight at night; they had been talking since half past eleven in the morning. The two could hardly see one another's faces. Napoleon led Metternich by the arm to the folding doors and said, "We shall see each other again!"

Metternich, physically and emotionally drained by the nine-hour ordeal, bowed. "At your pleasure, Sire, but I have no hope of succeeding in my mission."

"Well now," Napoleon touched his shoulder lightly, "do you know what is going to happen? You will not make war on me?"

"You are lost, Sire," Metternich said quickly—or says he said. "I had the presentiment of it when I came. Now I am certain of it."

In the anterooms Metternich found the same generals and aides and secretaries standing about as in the morning. They crowded around, trying to read something in his face. Berthier, handing him into his carriage, asked if he felt satisfied with his reception by the Emperor. "Yes," he replied grimly. "He has explained everything. It's all over with that man."[13]

Returning to Bubna's apartments that night, Metternich felt utterly exhausted, deeply discouraged. So he had lost his gamble for peace! Napoleon had agreed to nothing, had evaded his overtures with accusations, with bombast and threats. He had made it clear he intended to go to war.

In a mood of black depression that night, Metternich sent off an express courier to Schwarzenberg at his army headquarters near Prague, asking how much time he needed to bring the Austrian army up to maximum strength. Two days later, on June 28, the reply reached Dresden: Schwarzenberg needed twenty days to train an additional 75,000 men.

While Metternich sat up late talking with Bubna that Saturday evening, June 26, Napoleon in the Marcolini Palace was giving Caulaincourt his own account of the meeting. He remarked bitterly that Metternich had "this word peace in his mouth all the time, as if it depended on me or on him to make it. That word is just a pretext for his demands; later it will color over his treason."

Caulaincourt, who wanted above all to see France restored to a state of peace, listened to Napoleon, appalled. When he ventured to propose that his master accept the opportunity for a negotiated peace that Metternich was holding out, Napoleon brushed him aside.

"Bah! You don't know Europe; you don't know the effect produced by my last victories on the conscripts. Everyone is trembling! We must profit by this moment to deliver the last blow and enjoy without humiliation a long rest. You talk like a schoolboy of Metternich and the Austrians. If I can have just two months more to build up my cavalry I'll dominate everything. If I had had 4,000 more horse at Bautzen the Russians would be back across the Vistula, and Metternich, who plays the bully today, would be on his knees!"[14]

Next morning at eight Metternich found Bassano waiting in his drawing room. But Bassano had nothing to add to his master's utterances of the day before. Metternich informed him that he would send at once an official proposal of Austrian mediation, and that he would await an immediate reply.

News of the stormy conference between the French Emperor and the Austrian Foreign Minister had already carried from one end of the city to the other. "You have no idea of the effect my presence here has produced on the public of Dresden," Metternich wrote his wife. "There are crowds continually gathered under my windows—people who want to see what I am doing." He added, "Perfect strangers come up to me on the street to ask if I think there is a possibility of peace."[15]

Only too well the Saxons knew that if it came to war, their capital and their country were the likely battlefields.

Napoleon had ordered the cellars of his treasury in the Pavillon Marsan in Paris opened, and his reserves of gold brought out—gold that came from the tribute imposed on defeated Austria and Prussia after Austerlitz, Jena, Wagram. Smiling perhaps at the irony of using war indemnities paid by his defeated enemies to buy a new war against them, Napoleon ordered all his troops to be given their back pay. A veritable rain of gold showered on Dresden.

Innkeepers, restaurateurs, bootmakers and tailors did a rush business. Every map of Saxony and Bohemia was sold out of the bookstores to French officers studying the terrain where they expected to do battle.

Everywhere were grim reminders of the recent campaign. Hundreds of wounded from Bautzen and Lützen had been loaded on boats at Dresden and dumped in villages up and down the Elbe.

> You have no idea of the misery and horror that reign here [Metternich wrote to Laure from Dresden]. The last battles cost the French over 80,000 dead and wounded. Every house that can possibly be put to use has been turned into a hospital. There are probably still at least 25,000 wounded and sick here in Dresden and the suburbs.[16]

2

In the days that followed the interview with Napoleon, while he waited for a reply that did not come, Metternich wandered about the streets of the lovely city, filled for him with memories of a decade before, when it had been a delightful first post for a rising young ambassador. Long after political storms had shaken all Europe awry, the world of the rococo had lingered on in Dresden:

The French Revolution after overthrowing the old monarchy had reached
the stage of Bonaparte's consulate [Metternich wrote of those early
Dresden days], but at the Saxon court hoops had not yet been discarded![17]

But now it was an armed and arming city. At night the surrounding hills
glowed with the bivouac fires of huge encampments. The whole town bustled
with military preparations. All the streets between the great city gates had
been transformed into batteries of cannon, he wrote his wife. One day
Metternich crossed the bridge to the New Town and walked for a few
moments in the lovely Japanese Gardens, where grew

> the most beautiful roses in the world. . . . I went in for a moment and
> I could have wept for those continuous upheavals they call the history of
> empires.[18]

Sunday, Monday and Tuesday passed. There was no reply to Metternich's
mediation offer. In the Dresden shops he bought gifts for his family, silk
for gowns for Laure and his daughters. One night he went to a performance
by the troupe from the Théâtre Français, and he might as well have been, he
wrote his wife, back in St. Cloud.

Metternich, usually so ready to see life, as Gentz remarked of him, in
rose-colored light, grew increasingly pessimistic during the days in Dresden.

Napoleon was obviously unmoved by either pleas or arguments for
peace.

On Tuesday night a messenger brought the draft of a proposal from Bas-
sano that had nothing in common with the mediation plan proposed by
Metternich. The Austrian minister sent word to Bassano that he would leave
Dresden very early the following morning.

Accordingly, on that Wednesday morning, June 30, his carriage was
harnessed, his baggage loaded. Metternich himself, in traveling clothes, was
about to mount his carriage when a messenger galloped up to the door with
an urgent note from Bassano. Napoleon wished to speak to him at once; he
was awaiting him in the Marcolini gardens.

A few minutes later Napoleon greeted him almost affably: "So, you are
pretending to be offended? What for?"

Metternich replied shortly that his duty required him to lose no more
time in Dresden.

Napoleon pulled from his pocket a copy of the draft Bassano had sent
Metternich the night before. He read it quickly and threw it down, saying,
"Perhaps we shall understand one another better, you and I. Come into my
study and let us come to an agreement."

He asked Metternich if Bassano might join them and serve as secretary.
In Napoleon's private study the three men sat down before a small table
where writing materials were laid out.

"Write out your articles as *you* wish them to be," Napoleon directed.

Metternich set down clearly and briefly a draft of his mediation plan:

1. The Emperor of the French accepts the armed mediation of the Emperor of Austria.
2. The plenipotentiaries of the belligerent powers will meet the mediating court at a conference to be held in Prague on the tenth of July.
3. The tenth of August shall be fixed as the last day of the negotiations.
4. All military operations are to be suspended until that day.

The three men signed at once. Napoleon raised a single difficulty. The armistice signed with the Russians and Prussians was due to expire on July 20. Could Metternich guarantee an extension of that truce until August 10? Metternich replied that he had no official power to do so, but he would on his own word guarantee that extension. An additional clause was added at Metternich's request that grain to feed the Russian army—now foraging freely in Silesia—could be exported for them from Bohemia and Moravia.[19]

An hour later Metternich was in his carriage, jubilantly bound for Gitschin, the French assent to his mediation signed and sealed in his pocket.

This at least was his recollection, written down many years later, of the closing episode of that famous Dresden encounter.

Writing to his daughter Marie immediately after his return to Gitschin, Metternich tells a rather different story:

> Tell your Mama that I returned very pleased from Dresden. That the last day there I had another battle of over six hours with the Emperor [Napoleon], but that I emerged from it so victorious that he ended up embracing me.[20]

A day or so later he wrote his wife that Napoleon's parting words to him had been, "It may be you'll be unhappy, but you don't deserve to be, for your conscience must tell you you've done everything a good man and a clever minister can do!"[21]

Those words sound far more Metternichian than Napoleonic; we may conclude that Metternich exercised a husband's right to edit his accomplishments for his wife's benefit.

Whatever was the text of their discussion that last day, it certainly turned on what sacrifices Napoleon was willing to make at the proposed peace congress. Gentz reported to Wessenberg a few days later "that Napoleon would bring the greatest sacrifices to a general peace"—one that included England. He would sacrifice something—but far less—for a continental peace. He would only engage in a continental peace to avoid war with Austria.[22]

What had brought about Napoleon's sudden reversal, his last-minute decision at the hour of Metternich's departure on June 30 to agree to the peace congress?

Quite probably the answer lies in a little-noticed sentence in Baron Fain's account of those critical Dresden days. Napoleon's secretary tells us that on June 30 an express courier brought news to Napoleon of the terrible defeat inflicted on his armies in Spain under the walls of Vitoria.[23]

Very likely that news—disastrous for his military plans—reached his bedside early in the morning. Certain it is that Napoleon confided that news to no one, not even to his Foreign Minister, for three days. He knew that every hour now was precious to him, before the Allies had the news and made their own uses of it. Knowledge of that catastrophe could be enough to push Austria into the arms of the Coalition, to begin war at once before his raw recruits were trained and his cavalry assembled. The defeat at Vitoria would have a powerful effect on French public opinion, already clamoring for peace. He could not afford to turn down the Austrian peace attempt—and any delay would help him complete his military preparations.

Metternich did not learn of the French defeat at Vitoria for some days, when Bubna, according to Gentz, wormed it out of someone at Napoleon's headquarters. Rather than using it to arouse popular feeling against the French, Metternich hushed up the news of Vitoria for a time; the Prague Congress had begun and he hoped—rather vainly—to preserve a neutral atmosphere in the city.[24]

There was a small postscript to the Dresden interlude, one of the little complexities that face even the most skillful of diplomatic jugglers. After the Dresden visit Napoleon sent Metternich a jeweled snuffbox, the customary perquisite for the successful completion of a piece of diplomatic business—the boxes always carefully scaled to the importance of the business and the rank of the recipient. This particular snuffbox was of dazzling extravagance, studded with sixteen enormous diamonds.

> The box is so beautiful for such a small affair [Metternich wrote Laure] that you can see from its choice that Napoleon is afraid of us.[25]

He sent the box off at once to Laure in Vienna; she was to get Hoppé—a Chancellery official who also took care of certain of Metternich's private affairs—to appraise it, so that a token of the precise same value could be dispatched to Bassano in the name of the Austrian Emperor. She was to show the box to no one else, for the public, "always so good-natured," he commented ironically, might jump to the wrong conclusions, and suspect that Metternich had been bribed. He made her a gift of it—she could have the diamonds pried off to enlarge her necklace from three to four strands. It was appropriate no doubt that Laure—who had been so helpful in arranging the Napoleonic marriage—should glitter on great occasions with Napoleon's last gift.

3

Just before leaving for Dresden Metternich had dashed off that brief note to Wilhelmine, promising that he would be back in twenty-four hours:

Remember me to your daily guests, and tell them that I'd be very happy
if one or another would like to take my place on the banks of the Elbe
and yield me his on the shores of the Aupa.[26]

Through the long week that followed, the guests in the manor house
argued and talked and waited for his return. Surely he would fail in his
mission, war would be declared promptly on July 20, the last day of the
armistice, and everything would be clear as crystal again. Gentz boasted to
Pilat:

If you were in my place and knew everything I knew, you would hold
the war for certain and inevitable.[27]

During that last week of June, with the weather bone-chilling cold and
rain falling intermittently, the house party took on an increasingly gloomy
air. Ratiborzitz was crowded to bursting with guests; "not a soul more could
be sheltered," vowed Gentz.

Baron Hardenberg was there, and his brother Karl Philipp, a Hanover
judge. Windischgraetz and Trogoff had come on a week's leave from their
regiment.

Humboldt's sixteen-year-old son Theodore, wounded fighting with the
Prussian army at Bautzen, had found his way to headquarters looking for his
father and been sent on by Lebzeltern to Ratiborzitz. Humboldt—who
firmly believed every able-bodied man should fight for his country (he
was quite cross with his famous explorer brother Alexander just then, sitting
out the war in Paris)—was tenderly proud of his eldest son. But he could
find little to say to him. The immense canyon of years loomed between
them. He could only fret in his letters to his wife that Theodore still sat a
horse poorly; how could he hope to rise in the Army if he could not ride
properly?

That week too an unexpected guest arrived from Vienna, a close friend
of Princess Bagration, a French émigré named Fontbrune. In letters to
Vienna Gentz had made a bit of malicious fun of the princess, who he
knew was fretting her heart out in Vienna over the successes of her rival,
the Duchess of Sagan—entertaining even the Russian Tsar! The princess was
almost decided herself to leave for Bohemia—if only she knew war were not
going to break out at once. So she had sent Fontbrune to reconnoiter and
report back precisely what was going on in her rival's drawing room.

On the very Saturday that Metternich was debating with Napoleon,
Hardenberg and Humboldt had left briefly for Reichenbach headquarters, to
return again to Ratiborzitz a day or so later. On Sunday, June 27, the treaty
was signed in Reichenbach, by the terms of which Austria was bound to the
Coalition if Napoleon failed to agree to a negotiated peace by July 20. In
exchange for Russia's and Prussia's agreement to a peace congress, Metternich
had been forced to agree to the treaty; Stadion signed in his absence. The
Tsar and the Prussian King were jubilant: there would be no backing out

for Austria now; she was definitely committed—and surely Napoleon would not agree to negotiate!

Outside the manor house the rain fell steadily; no one ventured to go walking. The stoves were kept lighted. Humboldt, with his wide-ranging scholar's mind, usually carried his learning about with him like a treasure he could draw upon to pay for life's harder moments.

> There must be a special world of the Inner Man [he wrote his wife, Caroline] over which the breakers of life only pass, which continues to exist, hidden and still.[28]

But in those days in Ratiborzitz Humboldt could not sit still or concentrate on a book. He could only pace back and forth in his room and stare out of the long windows onto the meadows and distant mountains.

> There are plenty of fine books and very learned people in the house, but I am not in the mood to read. I am mostly idle, look out on the long valley and the hills beyond and think of the future. I still talk a great deal with Gentz, though talking with him . . . can no longer help. My point of view must remain what it is. He has another that is of no use to me.[29]

In midafternoon the little company met at the long dining table. Sometimes the tension between Gentz and Humboldt broke into bitter argument —usually over the Tugendbund, the League of Virtue, a Prussian patriotic society that Gentz denounced as revolutionary—"bloody battles" of the dinner table, Gentz called them.

In the evening everyone met in the library, to drink tea, to talk and argue and play cards. Humboldt sat with an open book before him, staring at the same page. Some of the gentlemen took snuff, others puffed on their small pipes; Alfred alone smoked a long elegant cigar, a habit he had introduced into Austria from Brussels.

Three, four, five days passed—no sign, no word from Metternich.

Gentz described the week to Pilat in Vienna:

> All day Tuesday awaited with a good bit of impatience news from Gitschin. Wednesday morning we confidently expected to hear. The whole day stretched out without our getting any message. Thursday—yesterday—dawned. Mounting anxiety. All dead from it.[30]

Across the border in Silesia, a few miles from Ratiborzitz, the Tsar and the Prussian King grew increasingly anxious over Metternich's silence. Alexander arranged two troop reviews to relieve the mounting tension at headquarters; he and the King no longer felt jubilant.

In God's name, what was going on there in Dresden, a couple hundred miles away, between those two men, Napoleon and Metternich, neither of whom could be trusted? There they were, by a singular stroke of unlucky chance, holding the fate of the world in their unreliable hands!

Letters flew from Reichenbach to Ratiborzitz; Humboldt and Hardenberg admitted glumly that in headquarters "they knew no more than we. We were in despair."[31]

What on earth could be happening? Had Napoleon bought Metternich off? All sorts of rumors flew about in Reichenbach.

In Ratiborzitz the little group of houseguests held a council of war. The suspense had become unbearable. On Thursday, July 1, Hardenberg dispatched his cousin to Reichenbach to see if by any chance a courier from Gitschin had bypassed Ratiborzitz and brought news straight to the sovereigns.

Gentz at the same time sent off his valet Leopold in the opposite direction to Gitschin. Leopold was instructed to ride at top speed, find out exactly what had happened. He was not to remain in Gitschin longer than to change horses and gallop back with the news to Ratiborzitz. With the duchess's relays sent ahead, Gentz figured that Leopold could make it to Gitschin and back by midnight Thursday—or daybreak Friday at the latest.

Thursday evening there was a desultory card game. Hour after hour the gentlemen sat up and waited. Midnight struck. One by one they drifted off to bed, Gentz going the very last, to sleep fitfully and listen for hoofbeats.

Friday morning came and went without Leopold. Gentz was beside himself. He had ordered his valet not to delay a minute; it was intolerable that he could not obey orders!

That evening he wrote his friend Pilat in an uncertain temper:

> If anyone had told me that on Friday, July 2, I would still be without any news from Count Metternich, I would have called him a dreamer. . . . Still I have just had—I am writing this at 7 in the evening—such an absolutely heavenly dinner, and during the course of it fought so bitterly over the League of Virtue that for today I dare not complain any more.[32]

He had not yet sealed his letter when he heard the sound of hoofbeats pounding up the road from the village into the stable yard of the house. It was indeed Leopold. Yes, His Excellency had returned from Dresden; he had made Leopold eat and sleep a few hours, told him nothing of his trip, not a word, but sent him off with a tiny sealed note for the duchess.

In the library Wilhelmine opened the note and read it aloud. Absentmindedly Metternich had written across the top, "Dresden, 2 July" instead of "Gitschin," where he most certainly was.

> It is said, my dear Wilhelmine, that Ratiborzitz will be marked by the finest pen history holds in her hand; this place is becoming quite the diplomatic center of Europe at a moment when poor Europe is the center of the world's griefs.[33]

He would come to Ratiborzitz the next day, he told her, on Saturday, to meet with Count Stadion and Monsieur Nesselrode. He would give them all an account of his journey to Dresden; he would remain with the duchess overnight; he would need a room and would bring one servant only. Besides that servant he would bring "a windfall of good news for the curious denizens of Ratiborzitz."

Everyone pored over the note; not a clue to what that windfall would be! Certainly Metternich had told Leopold nothing; he had no intention of surrendering the lead in his own drama to a mere bit player. "So you can imagine," Gentz added in his letter to Pilat, "what excitement has reigned here in this little castle."

Late Saturday afternoon Gentz borrowed a carriage and drove out on the highway in the direction of Gitschin. He could wait no longer—he had to be the first, or as nearly as possible first, to hear whatever the news would be. Toward five he met Metternich's traveling berline, in it Lebzeltern, who good-naturedly changed places with Gentz.

> On the way back the recounting of his most distinguished adventures in Dresden! He had a very hard time there, but through his great presence of mind, his decisiveness, his cleverness, he brought all the storms in the end to tranquillity.[34]

During his lifetime Metternich would relate the story of his Dresden encounter many times, but certainly never did he tell it with more dramatic effect than that night of July 3, in Wilhelmine's drawing room in Ratiborzitz. With his flair for acting, his gift of mimicry, the tale of his verbal duel with the French Emperor certainly lost nothing in the telling— Napoleon scowling, stalking back and forth, giving his hat a kick, assuming the poses and flailing the air in the gestures he had learned from the great actor Talma. Metternich no doubt embroidered a bit more colorfully his own cool and valiant replies. And never would he have more intent listeners— Hardenberg, Nesselrode, Stadion, Humboldt, who could barely wait to hear the denouement that concerned them so critically; the younger men, hot-headed patriots all, aching for war to begin again—Alfred, young Theodore Humboldt, the Prussian aides who had ridden over from Reichenbach. And Wilhelmine, who feared war was inevitable but wished it were not, put down her needlework to listen, utterly absorbed in Metternich's tale.

When he reached the climax of his story—Napoleon's sudden about-face and his last-minute agreement to a peace congress—pandemonium broke out in the room. Nobody had expected that ending—Metternich triumphantly holding up the signed agreement of June 30. The Russians and Prussians were dismayed and angry and made no bones about it. They had been certain the Dresden journey would be a failure, that Austria, committed now by the Reichenbach Treaty, would join the Coalition at once.

Furious, they pointed out that the Reichenbach Treaty, the ink of which was barely dry, stipulated July 20 as the deadline for the armistice. But the treaty was not ratified, Metternich replied—nor would it be by Austria—unless the armistice were extended until August 10.

Shutting themselves up in the library, Hardenberg, Nesselrode and
Stadion assailed Metternich. How had he dared agree to an extension of the
armistice without consulting them—and an extra twenty days—when the
Prussian and Russian generals could scarcely be prevailed upon to wait until
July 20!

They had wanted from Napoleon either everything—or nothing. Disappointed and angry, they railed at Metternich; long afterward he would
speak of his "hard hours at Ratiborzitz."[35]

The next day, Sunday, the diplomatic battle raged on behind closed
doors.

> This conference [Nesselrode recalled afterwards] was one of the most
> stormy at which I've ever been present, but the importance of drawing
> Austria to our side was so great that we had to agree to all the conditions
> she stipulated.[36]

Nesselrode well knew that the Tsar, so honey-sweet and conciliatory toward Metternich at Opocno in his effort to win Austria to the Coalition,
would be furious at the new delay. Someone had to be sent to get the Tsar's
agreement to the armistice extension. Stadion refused to go, saying he would
rather resign his post. It fell to Lebzeltern, who left grumbling and protesting that he was reserved only for such nasty errands as this one.

There was in fact a most unpleasant scene. In Reichenbach the Tsar flew
into one of his tantrums, talked of Metternich's treachery, called him "nothing but a valet of Napoleon," and declared he would never agree to such a
measure. Only when his anger subsided a bit and Lebzeltern explained that
Austria needed that armistice extension chiefly to complete her military
preparations, would the Tsar reluctantly assent.[37]

So it was that Metternich won a less than halfhearted agreement from
France, from Russia and Prussia for twenty precious extra days in which to
talk peace. He needed England's participation too, and he thought of sending Gentz to England as a courier to bring fresh persuasion to bear on the
London Cabinet. But there was scarcely time in the short space of the
armistice. On the whole, he decided, it was hopeless to try to engage England.

Just after daybreak on Monday, July 5, he climbed again into his carriage
for the return ride to Gitschin, some ten hours away. Gentz rode with him
as far as the first relay station of Jarowicz. Only when Gentz had left, and
he sat alone in the carriage with the silent Giroux, did the long-drawn-out
tension, the nerve-racking anxiety of the last days and weeks overwhelm
him.

> I lead a life, *ma bonne amie* [he wrote Laure], which gives me a longing
> for rest I cannot describe to you. Always between France and the Allies,
> required to speak French one day, Russian the next, in between to attend
> to all my Austrian business, alone in the world for I have not even a

friend I can trust to write a letter, I give you my word if this pace continued very long I could not endure it. My health has borne up without any sleep. In 15 days I have not spent four consecutive hours in bed.[38]

Other thoughts besides the armistice occupied Metternich too. Jolting over the wretched roads, axle-deep in mud, half dozing from exhaustion, his thoughts were certainly never far from the lovely woman under whose roof he had slept for exactly three nights.

In the brief hours at Ratiborzitz, keyed up in the high tension of the Napoleonic drama, he had realized with absolute clarity that he was irretrievably in love with Wilhelmine.

She could fill so perfectly that special relationship he needed, of a close woman friend, *une amie*, a romantic confidante, a silver satellite to reflect the dazzle of his own sun. Nor was it only Wilhelmine's singular seductive beauty that made her desirable. There was about her a wonderful tranquillity, he thought, an unshakable calm. She listened admirably, presented her own views with clarity. Often her keen intelligence pierced to the heart of a discussion while everyone else was talking around it. And when the conversation in her drawing room grew dangerously ferocious—as it had at times in the last days—she could intervene with warm humor, a quick remark, an engaging laugh, and turn it into safer paths.

In the terribly difficult days just past, when he had felt himself almost unbearably alone, Wilhelmine had understood what he was attempting to do—and why it mattered. She did not believe his peace effort would succeed, but she believed he should make it. She alone had given him words of understanding and gentle encouragement.

Did she already love him in return? Or would she come to love him? He simply did not know. Metternich, usually so confident in matters of love—and why not? women had been on the whole most accommodating—felt the ground slipping away like quicksand. He was bewildered by the intensity of his own feelings.

In nothing was Metternich's vanity more vulnerable than in affairs of the heart. Never having been a soldier, his masculine ego had a special need for the victories of the sexual battlefield. They had been for the most part easy victories. Veteran of dozens of skirmishes in drawing room and alcove, master of the delicately erotic passage, the graceful compliment, the charming letter and pretty gift, he understood not only how to win and with grace, but far more difficult, how to withdraw from the field without a scar. He could boast with some truth that his mistresses remained his friends.

Yet he had already an uneasy presentiment that this love of his would be unlike the others. Here he was, a man of forty, worldling of worldlings, a man of cool reason, with that sangfroid Gentz so rapturously admired, flung into a vortex of wild emotion he had not known existed.

He wanted her for his mistress, not for a few nights or weeks or months, but for the next years—how many, who could say? He wanted her more than he had ever wanted any woman in his life. But with the prescience of a sensitive man in love he knew already that his love might be without hope.

Sometime during those last crowded hours at Ratiborzitz, in a manor house filled to the brim with guests, he had found some moments alone with her to tell her that he loved her. She had answered with an affectionate smile that he was her dear and trusted friend.

Surely, he thought now, that liaison with Alfred had long been approaching an end. He had read all the signs, knew the bitter quarrels that had rent the fabric of the relationship with increasing frequency.

And yet? And yet? He simply did not know.

Writing to her from Gitschin a day or two later, he thanked her for the hospitality of Ratiborzitz. Her charming manor would become what it had been before—the prettiest spot in the world. No more emperors, no more ministers of foreign affairs, no more questions of war and peace "lacerating your salon." For him Ratiborzitz would always be a place filled with "memories of happiness, of gratitude, of so many regrets, so many wishes!" And he wrote:

> My dear W. Don't forget me; hold me a little always in your memory, and tell yourself that I love you from the bottom of my heart and much more alas! than I ought to for the good of this poor heart and for the situation in which we find ourselves! I hold a grudge against fate for having reserved such a painful school for me. . . . It is a strange thing to have you *as a torment* over and above all the other torments of my life![39]

VIII

---◆---

COLD PEACE IN SUMMER:
THE NON-CONGRESS OF PRAGUE

1

In the early days of July the tardy summer dropped like a smoldering bomb over Central Europe, as if all the sun and warmth of the absent spring had been bottled up to explode belatedly in a burst of brilliant hot sunshine.

Into the ancient city of Prague with its baroque palaces and sgraffiti-painted houses flocked an international society of diplomats, army officers, hangers-on of officialdom, and a throng of the merely curious—everyone who wanted to be near whatever might happen, or have at least a last gay fling before Armageddon. In the narrow streets on both sides of the river Moldau carriages with armorial bearings clattered, and uniformed couriers with urgent messages jostled liveried lackeys bearing invitations to dine.

Prague was scarcely the ideal neutral setting for a peace congress. The temper of the city was passionately anti-French, anti-Napoleon. After Eylau, after Tilsit, after Wagram, disaffected Prussians and Russians and Austrians had fled to Prague to join any kind of secret effort to dislodge the French from Central Europe. Baron vom Stein, ardent patriot and spearhead of German unification, lived in Prague for a time. He called it "a land of rectitude"; Napoleon called it "a home of madmen."

In the streets of Prague in the summer of 1813 comedians on movable stages acted out anti-French pantomimes and playlets to the hoots and acclaim of the street crowds. In the theaters of Prague actors ad-libbed anti-French political jibes to the wildest applause.

News of the defeat of the French army at Vitoria in Spain reached

Prague soon after the congress began to assemble and turned the city into a riotous celebration. Rockets went off, bonfires were lighted, everyone went a little crazy with joy. At Russian army headquarters in Silesia, the Tsar ordered a Te Deum sung, the first time such a hymn of thanks was ordered for a battle in which no Russians took part.

And now in the middle of July Metternich began to bend all his efforts to a final bid for European peace. Within the narrow span of the extended armistice he hoped to bring the belligerent powers to the negotiating table. Yet who believed in that chance for peace? "Peace," Humboldt wrote his wife, "is very improbable."[1]

"Only Metternich and Emperor Franz," Gentz observed, "are going to work in good faith. Nobody really wants peace except he."[2]

Metternich himself was realistic enough to know the odds:

> If God seconds me [he wrote Laure on July 8] I shall be in a fair way to finish with all this in short order; if not, then come weal, come woe, the die is cast; and I shall pull my hat down over my eyes so I need not look around but only in front of me.

He begged his wife to keep up her courage and "not to believe in war. There is just as much to bet against it as for it, and maybe more against it."[3]

Moving from Gitschin that first week of July, Metternich stayed for a few days with the Austrian Emperor in his palace in Brandeis outside Prague. Then he moved into the Schönborn Palace in the Malá Straná, the Little Side of the Moldau River, that charming precinct of narrow streets and fine baroque squares that clusters around the foot of Prague's great hilltop castle, the Hradschin.

He had written his wife to dispatch a coachman, groom and lackey, an everyday carriage with four good horses, and silver and table linen, for he must be prepared to entertain the delegates in style.

But what delegates? was now the question.

In Dresden Napoleon had indicated his choice of Caulaincourt as first plenipotentiary for France and Louis Narbonne as second. Armand Caulaincourt, Duke of Vicenza, known to be a firm advocate of peace, had served as secretary at the French embassy in Petersburg, and was on friendly terms with the Tsar. No choice could have pleased Metternich more.

To his deep disappointment, however, Russia and Prussia, instead of treating the congress as a summit conference of great international importance and sending Hardenberg and Nesselrode, who had carried out the Reichenbach and Ratiborzitz negotiations, designated for the Prague discussions only lower-echelon diplomats—Jean Anstett for Russia and Wilhelm von Humboldt for Prussia.

The two appointments were a clear indication that the Tsar and the King of Prussia put little value on the Prague negotiations. Anstett had had no experience in major negotiations; he was known to be ardently pro-war; his appointment, moreover, was an indelicate insult to France—or at least Napoleon took it to be—for he was not Russian at all, but Alsatian-born, a defector whom Napoleon termed a "traitor to France." Humboldt himself did not like being paired with him; Anstett's reputation, he wrote his wife, was not a good one either in Vienna or in Prussian-Russian headquarters. Humboldt thought the disparity among the negotiators was so great that Metternich himself could not appear but would have to send his assistant Baron Binder.

Bristling with anger when he heard of the appointments, Napoleon refused to send Caulaincourt. Narbonne was dispatched to Prague with neither instructions nor negotiating powers.

Anstett's name was "not sufficiently distinguished to figure beside his own," Narbonne declared openly when he got to Prague, adding airily that "he knew nothing of a congress—he was only a traveler sojourning in an inn."

The Tsar and the Prussian King did not appear in Prague at all during the time of the congress. They had gone off to Trachenberg to a rendezvous with Crown Prince Bernadotte of Sweden, with whom they discussed plans for the next campaign. Their agreement to negotiate had been wrung out of them reluctantly—and only to induce Austria to join them in war. From Trachenberg the two monarchs went their separate ways to Silesian spas to splash out the hot days of summer and await the end of the armistice.

Whether by accident or design the Tsar had neglected to leave with his generals meeting at Neumarkt instructions for signing the official extension of the armistice until August 10. Further wrangling and delay over the terms ensued, Napoleon declaring he could not send a plenipotentiary until the renewal had been guaranteed. Metternich protested that he had given his word of honor and a written notification, so that the French plenipotentiary might have been dispatched to Prague at once, "which would have satisfied those duties of politeness that are as much an obligation of one state with respect to another as they are upon individual members of society."[4] But politeness in personal or international affairs had not been part of Napoleon's training.

Already on July 14 the prospects for peace were so disheartening that Metternich wrote his wife:

> My burden is enormous, and every day a little heavier; my life certainly
> is not strewn with roses! When I leave here I shall collapse on a sickbed,
> and I shall have aged by 20 years![5]

One of the futile but fascinating exercises of history is to conjure up what might have been, had a single element in the equation of events turned out differently. Metternich might have succeeded in the peace effort of 1813 had he received a single crucial message making its painfully slow way by ship and horse from London—a message that was in the end carefully concealed from him.

On July 14, 1813, when Metternich wrote Laure in deep discouragement, he might have been jubilant had he known of the dispatch that Lord Castlereagh, England's Foreign Secretary, was at that moment handing to his courier Remus.

England had flatly rejected Metternich's first peace feeler, carried by Wessenberg in spring. But during the weeks of June, as England anxiously watched herself increasingly isolated from the ongoing negotiations, Castlereagh began to have second thoughts. The victory in Spain had improved England's bargaining position with Napoleon. At Metternich's request, both Russian and Prussian ambassadors in London—though hardly with enthusiasm—had urged the British Cabinet to join peace talks.

Now in mid-July the English Cabinet did in fact agree to participate in negotiations.

On that July 14 Castlereagh sent off a carefully worded dispatch to Lord Cathcart in the Tsar's headquarters in Reichenbach, informing him that England would accept Austrian mediation. There were two provisos. England's maritime rights were not to be discussed at the congress, and Cathcart must get the assent of Russia, England's ally. Cautiously Castlereagh refused to inform Wessenberg, Metternich's own on-the-spot envoy in London, of the fatefully important decision.[6]

The agreement of England to take part in preliminary peace talks in the summer of 1813 was a factor of immense international importance. Napoleon had reiterated again and again that the participation of England was essential to any general peace. The co-operation of England would give Metternich the powerful tool he needed to force Napoleon to the bargaining table.

Unluckily the seaport of Hamburg had been recaptured in late May by the French, so that dispatches from London had to thread a slow, precarious route to reach Silesia. Precious weeks would pass before this crucial dispatch would reach Cathcart in Reichenbach.

Meantime, Metternich proceeded with his design for negotiation. It was his plan to receive from the delegates of the two belligerent powers a clear statement in writing of their minimum demands. On the basis of their demands, he hoped to propose so reasonable a compromise as to make the act of going to war a clear absurdity in the eyes of the European public— most particularly, that of France.

First of all, he needed the absolute backing of his own Emperor. Precisely what Metternich thought of his sovereign nobody will ever know. Certainly from time to time he had thoughts rather different from the unctuously flattering description he has left us in his *Memoirs*. At least once that summer, in a moment of despair, he would write Laure a sentence or two of revealing frankness.

But Metternich was not an elected official, he was an appointed employee. His constituency was one man—and his entire power was built on the continuing support of that curious, phlegmatic, cautious mediocrity on the Austrian throne, who combined an instinctive self-protective shrewdness with the marvelous Habsburg staying power.

Quite obviously Metternich did not entirely trust his hesitant sovereign. He wanted now his pledge of support—and he wanted it in writing:

> I must allow no shadow to pass over my soul [he wrote], otherwise all my steps in Prague would, without the most precise definition of the will of Your Majesty, bear the impress of ambiguity.

He asked carte blanche to mediate with a free hand, backing whatever compromise plan he offered with the threat of force: the expanded Austrian Army would be that threat.[7]

So delicately were the forces of the warring powers balanced—France versus Russia and Prussia—that the additional weight of the Austrian Army —now approaching 250,000—would assure almost certain victory to either side.

In that carefully written and cunningly flattering memorandum to the Emperor, Metternich outlined with clarity the paths that still lay open to Austria, and the bases on which European peace might still be made. It would be a preliminary peace to be sure, since England had thus far refused to be party to it.

He reviewed the disaster that had brought Austria to her knees in 1809, and the manner in which she had arisen again in the brief space of four years to "the first position in Europe"—the position she now occupied as mediator and balance wheel. Implicit was a reminder that it was his own— Metternich's—wisdom that had restored Austria.

As mediator Metternich needed to have in hand some tool for compromise, and he pressed his Emperor now for an important decision. He could count on no self-sacrificing offers from France, or from Russia or Prussia; any surrender at the bargaining table on one of the proposed peace bases would have to come from Austria. Metternich proposed therefore that Austria if necessary be ready to give up Illyria, her old possessions along the Adriatic seacoast, so precious to a landlocked country. He hedged, however, by adding that if Illyria were to be sacrificed now for the sake of a preliminary peace, it would be returned to Austria when the final peace was made—that general all-European peace that would have to include England as well.

And finally, Metternich reminded the Emperor, if Napoleon turned down the peace proposals offered him in Prague, the Austrian Emperor must be *unalterably determined* to "remain true to your word and seek for preservation by the closest union with the Allies." He must leave everything in Metternich's hands:

> Your Majesty can only save yourself and the Monarchy if Your Highness acts with the greatest decision, and if I can rely with the most perfect

confidence on the greatest perseverance being shown in the course prescribed for me, when once decided on. Without this decision my steps
from day to day will be hesitating and incoherent, and even dangerous to
the last degree.[8]

Emperor Franz's reply was brief and to the point. Metternich was to
hold fast "to what I have already declared as the minimum." If all other
means were exhausted, Illyria might be sacrificed.

2

During that month of July 1813, life took its leisurely course in Prague.
Everyone waited for Napoleon's delegate to arrive. Jokes flew around—Anstett was particularly witty on the subject—about the ridiculous congress that,
as Gentz put it, *"in der Geburt ersticke"*—refused to be born.

Scholarly Humboldt made good use of his spare time; he sent home for
his Czech grammar and engaged a teacher to give him lessons. Narbonne
spent his days in Prague doing what he liked best—dining, drinking, engaging in light-hearted conversation.

The Duc de Broglie, secretary of the French delegation, passed his days
sightseeing, roaming about the network of little cobbled streets around the
castle, where the Danish astronomer Tycho Brahe once worked. De Broglie
was also engaged in spying. With considerable success he gathered very precise data on the size of the expanding Austrian Army. Later on, when he delivered his information to the French Emperor in Dresden, Napoleon laughed
at him, Broglie says, declaring "our figures were a myth and we were idiots."
It is quite possible, as De Broglie suggests, that Metternich himself made
those figures easily accessible to the French, in the hope that the impressive
size of that army would give Napoleon pause.[9]

As for Gentz, his days in Prague were the most memorable of his life. He
had wangled the choicest apartments in all Prague, in the beautiful Waldstein Palace, rooms that gave onto exquisite formal gardens with fountains,
sculpture and graveled walks.

He engaged an excellent cook, Bastien, from whom death alone would
part him, and a dependable private secretary. Before long he would add to
his household an interesting young Saxon named Karl Leiden, a defector
from the French Army, who, as Gentz discreetly explains, "climbed high in
my favor." Just how high Gentz, with his ambiguous sexual proclivities, allowed him to climb is not certain, but the quarrels he relates in his *Diary*
have the sound of lovers' quarrels.

> My domestic life [he wrote of this period] was entirely after my wishes
> —comfort and elegance—a distinguished unmarried gentleman.[10]

In those days of waiting, Metternich worked mornings in his cabinet,
wrote dispatches, received visitors, conducted all the complicated Austrian

business he must now handle by long distance and daily couriers to Vienna. He began the practice of dining late, at five, often inviting guests. Sometimes in the cool of the day he walked about the terraced gardens that rose enchantingly behind the Schönborn Palace up to a little *temple gloriette*. He had borrowed one of the Emperor's fine saddle horses, and some days he rode out of town to visit Schwarzenberg at the Austrian army headquarters. There he dined at the general's long refectory table, about which were ranged "like so many onions on a string" the well-born young counts who were Schwarzenberg's aides, "40 or 50 moustached faces in all colors and shapes," he wrote to Marie, "who wouldn't dream of coughing or spitting or speaking without official sanction."[11]

It did not occur to Metternich to send for Laure and the children to come to Prague to be with him, though other wives were there. Paul Esterházy and his pretty young wife, Thérèse, who was nursing their firstborn child, moved into rooms in the Schönborn Palace, and Metternich could enjoy a glimpse of felicitous domesticity.

Schwarzenberg's wife, Nani, was in Prague too—little, dark, lively—and more than a little eccentric, the Metternichs thought. Schwarzenberg doted on her, and as often as not that month of July Nani would be presiding at the officers' table at Lieben, looking, Metternich thought, "like a flea in a cluster of June bugs." The Schwarzenberg marital relationship was "a great enigma" to Metternich.

Evidently Schwarzenberg's connubial activities exhausted him, for since Nani arrived, "Schwarzenberg does nothing but sleep; he goes to sleep on her shoulder at the theater." If Nani died at the same time as her husband, Metternich thought, "he would risk not waking up for the next life at all."[12]

He could make jokes about the Schwarzenbergs' marital devotion—certainly rare enough in aristocratic marriages of the day—but his own affair of heart left him in the black depths of depression.

On the way to Prague he had written Wilhelmine a first clear declaration of love. He had asked her to reply to him at Prague, but the letter he found waiting for him was not a reply to his ardent letter—had indeed nothing to do with him at all. She had got an impudent flirtatious letter from a Dutch officer in a French regiment occupying her sister's estates in Silesia; the officer expressed his admiration for the three beautiful Courland princesses, whose portraits he saw all about the castle; Wilhelmine's portrait, he added, he was having copied. Indignantly Wilhelmine forwarded the letter to Metternich—what should she do about it?

Metternich wrote her two letters at once. One, in diplomatic style and ostensible, was a charming witty reply she could read aloud for her guests' amusement. The Dutch officer was *bête*—stupid; one must never be angry with *bêtes*—beasts. As for her portrait, since the original could not possibly have captured her loveliness, how could the copy of a copy? However, he added, if she would like the officer killed, he would see to her pleasure at once. "Adieu, beautiful princess! You must be beautiful if even the beasts offer you homage."[13]

The second letter was written for her eyes alone. It was the beginning of a long series of letters Metternich would write Wilhelmine in the months that followed, letters that are totally unlike any others he wrote in his lifetime—indiscreet, unself-conscious, an outpouring of his deepest feelings of passion, pain, longing.

> Have you not found a single moment to write me a small word of kindness . . . ? How easily one finds a minute to say what one feels; one never has time to say what one does not feel. No, my dear Wilhelmine, you do not love me, and how unhappy I am for loving you too much!
>
> Fate has willed it; that is all I can say to comfort myself; I should never have fallen into this terrible trap. I told myself so—I tried reason; they reason in vain who struggle against the heart. One minute with you and I think my reason is restored, a few days without you and I feel nothing but my sorrows!
>
> I watched you for years; I found you beautiful; my heart remained silent; why has that sweet peace deserted me? why out of *nothing* have you become for me *everything*? Dear Wilhelmine, why out of *nothing* have I become for you only *peu de chose*—a little something?
>
> Good night, my dear. I am in a black mood today and I do not want to pass that feeling on to you. You are made for happiness; yours will always be mine; I foresee that my suffering can only increase. I am resigned to it. . . . I love you as I do my life; be willing to bear with it: it is the easiest of all permissions to grant and the hardest to receive, the most impossible to refuse, the most humble to ask.[14]

Two days later, when Gentz came to Prague from Ratiborzitz, he brought him Wilhelmine's reply.

She had been astonished and touched by Metternich's frank profession of love. They were such old friends, she and Clemens; they had carried on their playful, bantering flirtation for so long, the conversational coin both spent so easily, she could scarcely believe in the sudden change, the deep intensity of his new feeling for her. In the crowded June days at Ratiborzitz she had, to be sure, sensed his eyes fixed on her again and again in a new absorbed way, detected the different, pressing inflection in his voice. But she —what did she feel for Metternich?

> If you know a word, dear Clemens, that says more than emotion, sensibility, gratitude, friendship and tenderness, I beg you to use it to give you an idea of the way I felt when I got your letter of the 6.

That he could find time for her at such a moment, overwhelmed by the immensity of the problems he faced, pleased and flattered her, of course. But he had written, "It is a strange thing to have you *as a torment* over and above all the other torments of my life." Now she begged him:

Don't regard me as one more torment—if our position is not what you desire, still it has its good side—let us hold to that—and allow me the satisfaction of believing that I may sometimes lighten your position, make you forget for a moment the burden you bear, that burden that is very nearly the whole world—[15]

She herself would be coming soon to Prague, she promised; she could not say which day, but "it is definite."

It was not the letter he had hoped to have from her. That gentle affectionate letter of hers was, he told her later, "a blow of a fist on my heart."[16]

In those difficult July days in Prague Metternich had one single relaxation.

Sometimes in the evenings around ten, when the last official visitor had gone, Gentz and Humboldt would appear on Metternich's doorstep, and the three men would wander around the moonlit streets of the old city, "talking sense or nonsense," Gentz recalled, "or playing jokes on one another."

Nobody could be a gayer, more amusing companion than Metternich, and he needed desperately just then, some moments of respite from the terrible burden he carried. Across the ancient Maltese Square, its fountain silvered in the moonlight, under the shadow of St. Nicholas Church, lingering on the Charles Bridge to watch the Moldau flow by the sleeping city, they would walk, talking of history, of man's fate in peace and in war:

We argue the great questions of the moment [Gentz wrote] as if the count, on whom the fate of the world certainly hangs to the highest degree—were a philosopher, like us, and we talk of war and peace as if we were three simple *Landjunker*—country gentlemen. Most often Metternich and I are in the lists against Humboldt.[17]

Humboldt too described those midnight walks to his wife, and the remarkable conversations. "Even when one disagrees with Metternich, he always listens, enters in and is never unfair."[18]

On those "unforgettable walks" of theirs, Gentz became Metternich's confidant—that position he had so longed for and never before attained—if not wholly in the political affairs of the moment, at least in that matter closest to Metternich's heart, his love for Wilhelmine.

Earlier Gentz had warned Metternich against her as "a terribly dangerous person." Now he praised Wilhelmine to the skies; she was "good, clever, intelligent, had great depth of character."[19]

He could also be incredibly clumsy in his new role of Eros' helper. One Sunday, as they were about to go to dinner, Metternich broke open a packet that had just arrived from Berlin and exclaimed, "Here is King back on the scene again!" John Harcourt King, whom he had banished from Austria in March, was back on the Continent again, asking for a passport to Austria.

"Ah," says the blundering Gentz, plunging in the sword, "I see what is going on. King can't possibly have any commission; he hasn't come to the

Continent for nothing—he is going to Ratiborzitz and I must warn the duchess!"

Instantly Metternich was a prey to the torments of jealousy. "My dear, I could not have been more floored by the blow of a club! I could die at the very thought." If King ever went to see her, she must promise to tell him at once. He could not bear the thought; he was certain she was afraid of King and also that she had once loved him a great deal. "That miserable Gentz —why did he say that?—I would never have guessed, never invented for myself this new mode of torment."

And he begs her—will she not come soon to Prague? If she does not come soon, events might take him away from Prague. There could be troop movements too very close to Ratiborzitz. "Our questions turn furiously toward war. The days are passing; soon there will be no more to pass; the bomb will explode!"[20]

But her sister Pauline had come to visit, then her cousin Biron; Wilhelmine postponed her trip to Prague from one day to the next. She sent Metternich her "tender friendship."

3

One by one the days of the hard-bought armistice slipped by, and still Napoleon did not send a negotiator to the peace congress.

> We are still waiting for what will transpire [Metternich wrote Marie] . . . and I defy anyone in the world except for God, who is not letting us into his secret, to know how the whole thing will end. . . . If it comes to war, tell *Maman* to remain calm. It would be difficult to decide which side will have the better game and the time that we have won serves us in a very good way.[21]

And to Laure he wrote, "Wait and pray God for peace. It is the first of my wishes, and if anyone in Europe can bring it, I can."[22]

On July 19 official notice of Caulaincourt's appointment reached Prague. Metternich was cheered: the choice gave "new birth to the hope of peace." There were twenty-two days left of the armistice, and much could happen in those days.

Caulaincourt's secretary reached Prague—but not Caulaincourt. The Prussians and Russians made no bones about their delight at the way things were going—or not going. Was it not all turning out exactly as they had predicted? Of course Napoleon would not negotiate!

Gleefully Humboldt wrote his wife, "Anstett and I do not even notice [Caulaincourt's absence], for we did not come here to negotiate. Only it isn't very nice for Austria."[23]

"Never was a Congress more of a joke," Nesselrode wrote later. "At bottom nobody really wanted peace."[24]

Nobody, that is, except Metternich. He was disheartened and—as a professional diplomat—humiliated. "We are still waiting from moment to moment the arrival of Caulaincourt," he wrote Laure. "The thing is becoming ridiculous, and we would look like pretty fools if we had not taken the attitude that has been ours, without illusions, without exaggeration."[25]

Bitterly he described to Laure how Narbonne was "running around town like a poisoned rat with enormous visiting cards that he leaves everywhere, on which are inscribed 'Count de Narbonne, plenipotentiary for the Congress.' As he has no instructions for negotiating, it is as if he were not here."[26]

From Reichenbach Tsar Alexander wrote his sister Catherine, who was taking the waters at Eger in western Bohemia, that "every day people grow more warlike, and I have the best hope that things will go as they should."

Coolly he proposed to her in a letter written July 20 that she should apply herself to the bribing of Metternich, "and what is needed to have him wholly ours. I give you back the 1,700 ducats and authorize you to pursue those tactics wherever needful."[27]

It would have made an amusing backstage scene—blunt, tactless, mischief-making Catherine attempting to bribe the most polished diplomat in Europe with a few thousand ducats—where Napoleon had failed with the offer of a princedom. But Catherine did not go to Prague until after the armistice had expired, so the scene never took place.

While everyone waited for Napoleon's delegate, another interesting visitor from France made his appearance in Prague on July 20. This was Fouché, Napoleon's former Minister of Police, who had fallen out of favor and was on his way to a kind of exile as governor of Illyria, a good safe distance from Paris and association with Talleyrand.

Fouché was to replace General Junot, "who," Metternich wrote Laure— he knew she would be titillated by this morsel of news—"has just gone to the trouble of proving that he is mad. I suppose," Metternich went on, "that you've not doubted for a long time that he has been mad, more or less incognito. Now he has just gone out for a walk quite naked and had the cannons fired to salute him. He was certainly already crazy in January of 1810" —a reference to that extraordinary scene in which Laure played a valiant part—"without going walking naked."[28]

Fouché in his audience with Metternich that month in Prague told him of the rising sentiment for peace in France. In Dresden Fouché had had the courage to tell Napoleon that if he did not conclude peace at once, he would endanger both his own survival as Emperor and that of his dynasty. Napoleon had replied that the moderate terms offered him by the Allies were only a trick to get him to negotiate, when more demands would be made on him. "One or two battles will settle everything," Napoleon promised Fouché. They were scarcely sentiments to encourage Metternich's peacemaking hopes.

In Dresden each morning Napoleon reviewed the troops newly arrived from France. They paraded before him, saluted him thrice and cried, "*Vive l'Empereur!"* After breakfast he devoured his masses of paper—dispatches from Paris, police reports of arrests of disaffected persons, bulletins from various parts of the French Empire, reports from officers on the outposts along the Elbe and the Oder and along the borders of Bohemia.

Certainly the Prague Congress had encouraged hopes for peace among the French people. Underground opposition to Napoleon's war plans was growing more vocal, as Fouché had reported.

Later, on St. Helena, Napoleon spoke of the tribulations and harrassment he had to endure during the period of the Prague Congress, "with the Coalition threatening my existence and even my ministers urging me to make peace."

To his staff that summer in Dresden urging him to the peace table, Napoleon repeated that he would be ready to yield much for a "general peace" that included England. But he insisted that Metternich's offer was not genuine, that Austria had already ranged herself on the side of the enemy. "Don't let Metternich's fine words mislead you!" he told them. [29]

During those days of crisis in Prague, as hopes for even a continental peace dwindled, Metternich expressed himself sternly to Narbonne on the conduct of Napoleon in delaying the sending of his plenipotentiary. Austria, he promised Narbonne, was at that moment free of engagements to any country, but once the armistice terms had expired, let Napoleon be under no illusion:

> At midnight on the 10th of August we shall have entered into engagements with all the world except France, and on the morning of the 17th you will have a force of 300,000 Austrian soldiers added to your enemies.

If Napoleon counted on the fact that his father-in-law would not take arms against him, Metternich warned him that Emperor Franz would be grieved, but "his duty to his people, to himself, and to Europe demands that he put an end to the existing state of affairs."[30]

Convinced at last that Austria was in earnest, Narbonne wrote to Bassano that France must "either negotiate seriously or be at war with all Europe," that the Russian and Prussian plenipotentiaries were threatening to withdraw from the congress since the French delegate had not appeared, and that if they left, all would be at an end.

Not until the last week of July did Napoleon dispatch Caulaincourt to Prague—but, like Narbonne, without credentials to negotiate and with instructions to raise procedural points that would block Metternich's mediation.

Like thousands of others in France, Caulaincourt had long ago wearied of Napoleon's military adventures, wanted only peace. For a moment Metternich thought he might succeed. "It would be hard to tell you how pleased I am with Caulaincourt," he wrote Laure. "Nobody could have more *esprit* and good *esprit* than this man."[31] Given some leeway, the two might have come to an understanding.

Caulaincourt dined with Metternich on the day he arrived in Prague, Wednesday, July 28, and Metternich proposed they set to work at once. Only thirteen days were left of the precious armistice period. To save endless delays over protocol and procedure and to keep tempers at an operating cool, Metternich suggested both sides adopt the system of mediation that had been used at the Congress of Teschen in 1779. Each side would submit their basic demands to him as mediator; he would work out compromise solutions.

The Prussian and Russian delegates accepted the proposal at once. The French delegates, however, replied that their instructions did not permit the Teschen system, but required that they meet the other delegates face to face. They would have to write back to Dresden for permission.

This is Europe's last chance for peace, Metternich reminded Caulaincourt at the end of their first frustrating conference. He repeated the warning he had given Narbonne. Austria is free of commitments today, but if France refuses to negotiate in good faith, as Napoleon agreed to do in Dresden, then Austria will join the Coalition against her.

Caulaincourt sent off an urgent dispatch to Napoleon:

> Everything I see confirms for me what Count Narbonne says, that Austria has already chosen her side. The moment is grave. Your Majesty will find himself in war with the world if peace is not made in ten days. I beseech you, Sire, let all the chances of war be weighed in the balance with peace.[32]

As the days of July passed, mounting pressures began to erode Metternich's will to peace. Gradually he too had become convinced of Napoleon's intransigeance. His friends and enemies alike, even the officials of his own Chancellery—Hudelist at the head—saw war as inevitable. Only Emperor Franz had really supported the peace effort; the war-minded Empress that summer wrote her husband letter after letter urging him to war. "Only don't give in any more—either conquer or die! If half the monarchy is lost, the other half must hold out until the enemy is defeated!"[33]

"The congress is finished," Gentz wrote Nesselrode. "Even if Napoleon suddenly became as tractable and as moderate as he has been harsh and insolent, he could not bring affairs back to the point they were at two months ago." Napoleon's conduct proved clearly, Gentz thought, that "this monster's head is absolutely deranged."[34]

At the end of a futile conference with Caulaincourt on Friday, July 30, Metternich handed to Gentz the sketch for a war manifesto he was to put in readiness.

In an hour of depression and discouragement he wrote to Laure:

> If I were Emperor I would have stopped negotiating a long time ago; as I am only his minister I shall negotiate until all human opportunities are

exhausted for arriving at peace—and it may be the very last moment that gives it to us perhaps.

His cool composure came very near to shattering at that point:

> I shall regard the 10th of August as one of the happiest days if one way or another I am delivered of the frightful burden that weighs on me at this moment. Peace or war; the interval that separates them is a fearful thing![35]

4

The War Manifesto had been sketched in Metternich's mind while he walked in the country one day with Wilhelmine. For she had come to Prague at last, on the same day as Caulaincourt, to share the excitement of the final days of the congress, and to be with Alfred.

The Courland palace in Karmelitergasse had been sold two years earlier in the wake of the Austrian state bankruptcy. Wilhelmine borrowed a suite of rooms adjoining Gentz's in the beautiful Waldstein Palace.

Each evening a group gathered in her drawing room as in Vienna and Ratiborzitz, to drink tea, to exchange the day's political news. Gentz was always there, Humboldt, Fontbrune, Louis Rohan, Alfred and his friend Trogoff, and some of Wilhelmine's old Prague acquaintances. Late in the evening Metternich would walk up the castle hill to the Waldstein to find Wilhelmine moving like a queen bee in a cloud of ever present admirers.

Sometimes she dined with him at the Schönborn Palace, and her grace and tact lightened the conversation on the days the French group were his guests.

Once she sent Metternich a hasty note that her aunt, Elisa von der Recke, had arrived unexpectedly from Karlsbad, along with her friend and traveling companion, the odd little poet Tiedge. "Bring them to dinner," Metternich replied. The talk that day divided between war and poetry. They had found Goethe "very morose" in Teplitz, while in Karlsbad Elisa had succeeded in nursing back to health her sister's godson, the gifted young poet Theodor Körner, badly injured in a skirmish with the French three days after the armistice was signed.

Sometimes when he could spare an hour or two during the day Metternich would invite Wilhelmine to walk with him in the palace gardens or ride out into the countryside. On the days when he could not see her, he sent a servant around to the Waldstein Palace with a little note to greet her when she awoke:

> I am writing because I shall not see you this morning, and I must tell you that I love you more than my life—that my happiness is nothing unless you are very much a part of it.[36]

In those days of mounting suspense and anxiety at the end of July and in early August, as Metternich saw with despair that his peace plans were foundering, he was suffering a kind of personal anguish he had never before experienced.

Never before had he loved a woman who did not at once return his affection. Never before had a woman been so elusive, so difficult to win. He could not understand her, nor could he understand the terrible trap into which he had fallen. A middle-aged man of great worldly experience, who prided himself on his understanding of women, on his perfect self-mastery, who had kept his life and his feelings on a careful rein, he found himself prey now to all the passion, the jealousy, the self-torment of a green adolescent in the throes of first love.

He had been so certain that the love affair with Alfred was finished. Was he, Metternich, not equally attractive, far more intelligent than Alfred, infinitely more important in the eyes of the world, a man whose hand lay now on the very pilot wheel of Europe?

Would she ever love him? He simply did not know. His whole life seemed wrenched asunder. He could not get his bearings. He slept badly. The ordinary pleasures of life no longer pleased him. Later on he recalled those unhappy days in Prague:

> Those were the days of the declaration of war. My public life began to develop; the alliance threatened to collapse either because of me or on top of me. And my soul—the only good side of me—was splitting apart even more than the political structure.[37]

His passion for Wilhelmine was no secret that summer in Prague. Everyone gossiped, and certainly some of his friends—Gentz and Paul Esterházy among them—tried to talk him out of it. She was a *femme fatale*, Paul warned him; she had loved many men already, would love many more.

Wilhelmine was charming, friendly, affectionate to Metternich. But it was for Alfred she had come to Prague, and it was Alfred's impending departure to war that worried her, not Metternich's.

In that scalene triangle—Wilhelmine, Alfred, Metternich—nobody's love matched anyone else's. And there was, of course, Laure as well.

5

In Vienna in early July Countess Laure had packed the whole family up again and moved them—children, nurses, governesses, cooks, even the dog Gips—out to Baden, the charming little spa a few miles from Vienna. She hated to leave the garden villa on the Rennweg just as fine summer weather was beginning, "but the apartment in Baden is so expensive one must at least enjoy it."

Besides, the warm sulphur waters of Baden would be good for all of them, Dr. Staudenheimer declared.

The children adored Baden; they ran about on their first day joyfully recognizing every familiar walk and hill and hiding place:

> Everything is just the same, each piece of furniture in the same place as last year. The only difference is that you are not here.

Marie called it her "earthly paradise." Wouldn't dear Papa soon be finished with "these adorable negotiations" so that he could come and join them?[38]

Life for the summer visitors was a round of gay and leisurely amusements. All their intimate circle of friends in Vienna moved in the summer to Baden. There were luncheon parties in someone's garden, and picnic excursions in the country. Ruins were extremely fashionable just then, and the little Metternichs were enchanted when they went to visit the ruins of Rauhenstein and a terrible thunderstorm came up at just the right moment, adding to "the holy terror and veneration that ruins and rocks inspire."

There were always amusing things going on, as when dear Lory Fuchs danced a ballet with Monsieur Borel and Count Schönfeld on the name day of Jeanne Acerenza, Wilhelmine's sister. Monsieur Borel, who was Jeanne's long-time lover, had grown comfortably stout in his ten years in Vienna, and the thought of him engaged in a pas de deux was enough to send Marie into peals of laughter. If one had nothing else to do one could go and watch the female bathers in their voluminous gowns splashing about in the Women's Bath:

> There are 60 of them [Laure reported]. I've never seen such a hideous sight—funny too—fat Nano and skinny Princess Trauttmansdorff.

She thought the whole thing a sight worthy of Hogarth.

On the promenade young dandies like Prince Reuss and Count Schönfeld watched "the beauties and uglies of Baden," and thought it frightfully amusing one day to inquire of every passerby whether he was a lackey for hire.

When the Empress came to Baden to visit Archduke Anton, there was a fete in her honor at the Casino, and Countess Laure permitted Marie to dance. In fact everyone danced—old and young, fat and thin—joining in the newfangled waltzes that had become all the rage of late. Marie declared, "I laughed as I have never laughed before at the ridiculous figures one saw waltzing."

That Sunday the priest at Mass denounced Baden as another Sodom, Laure reported.[39]

Ten-year-old Victor's name day was celebrated with a succession of delights for the Metternich children. "Never," wrote Marie, "was an emperor feted with more splendor than Victor." First, Lory Fuchs gave a luncheon in her garden, with Victor ensconced at the head table like a young prince.

"As we sat at the festive table there was a fanfare of trumpets, then a celestial harmony charmed us all through the meal." Everyone went for a long walk, then repaired to the Metternichs' for a second feast, with Victor's health drunk in champagne. Another excursion followed, this time into the lovely Helena Valley, then back to town to Count Batthyáni's, who gave a party for all the children of Baden in Victor's honor, "which surpassed in splendor and magnificence even Madame Fuchs's." Next came a pantomime by a group of Baden comedians, then home for supper—"our 4th meal of the day," recounts Marie contentedly, and to bed "very tired."[40]

Papa sent an envelope of ducats to Victor from Prague, with which he was to buy his heart's desire.

But even Baden was not really carefree that summer. The air was full of the rumor and rumblings of war. In the baths limped wounded officers, Russian and Prussian mostly, casualties of Bautzen and Lützen and even of the Russian campaign, many with wooden legs or on crutches, hoping to regain their strength through the magic of Baden's waters.

The women in Metternich's family all hoped for peace. "What glory for you and for our whole family," his mother wrote, "if you succeed in making peace for the world. How happy we shall be when you come back to us, not with laurels but with an olive branch in the hand. That is what all of humanity needs."

And Marie: "Everyone here believes in war except I, who have great confidence in you, cher Papa. . . . Only we two see all in *couleur de rose, n'est-ce pas?*"[41]

In the countryside conscripts were being rounded up, not always willing and eager to be part of anyone's War of Liberation. Laure saw a cartful of those future soldiers one day, including the fifth and last son of a peasant, a boy of sixteen who sat in the cart crying bitterly:

> They took him by force [she wrote her husband]. As he was being led across the square he saw his mother and asked to be allowed to speak to her. The soldiers would not consent. The mother began to scream and throw herself on the horses. Passersby stopped and began to interfere in her favor. The commissar of police had to be called to address the crowd very firmly.[42]

Metternich's letters with their meager news from Prague were seized upon and devoured "with such haste that one hardly has time to unseal them, and they are read and reread thousands and thousands of times. What a long, what a terrible absence!"

Metternich begged his wife to remain calm, and continued to reassure her that peace was as likely as war. But he summoned Hudelist to Prague from the Chancellery in Vienna and gave him instructions in case of war and invasion. He directed Laure to make plans to move the family to an estate of theirs in eastern Moravia, which would certainly be as safe as any-where in Europe, he thought.

In the last difficult days of the armistice term, the family in Baden got no word at all from Prague to allay their growing anxiety. People kept com-ing to their house to beg for a morsel of news. Laure could easily remain close-lipped now, for she had no news herself to give. Not a note, not a letter came from her husband.

In Vienna people were packing their trunks and preparing to flee, as if the French would descend on the city in a flash.

> There is confusion, agitation, perplexity, no greater nor less than if the
> last judgment were about to happen [Laure wrote]. All the men are
> leaving to join the Army.

Martial tunes were played in the Baden Casino, but nobody danced these days, "and the dancers only talked politics."[43] Young Victor Metter-nich declared with tears in his eyes that if only he were a bit older, he would go and fight the French himself.

Laure was quite beside herself. What should she do, she wondered. Should she pack them all back to Vienna and make ready to flee? When at last a packet arrived from Prague, Laure tore it apart in her haste and anxiety. Gloves and ribbons! Her husband had ordered them from Paris for her and Marie. She could have wept. How could he think they wanted ribbons when the world was about to collapse around them!

Meantime, a delicious morsel of gossip was going the rounds of Baden. Wilhelmine's flighty, impulsive, indiscreet sister, Pauline Hohenzollern, had just arrived in Baden from her visit in Ratiborzitz and Prague. Gleefully she reported that Metternich was head over heels in love with Wilhelmine, who —as everyone knew—was going to marry Alfred Windischgraetz. Metternich, the calm imperturbable statesman, the minister who had talked face to face with a ranting Napoleon without once losing his self-control, the man on whom the life of every person in Austria, perhaps in Europe, now depended —had quite lost his head, taken leave of his senses. Wasn't it delicious? Too amusing for words? Baden was small; news carried fast; a kind friend brought the tidbit to Laure Metternich.

For three years now, since the Junot episode, in which she herself had emerged as the quiet victor, Laure had had no moment of real disquiet over her husband's affairs of heart. Their domestic life had settled down into a pattern of cheerful, affectionate routine. Must she now go through it all again—stand by while he fastened his attention and heart on a beautiful woman—most painful of all, a woman of their own intimate circle of friends?

Laure wrote her husband at once:

> I will not hide from you that Pauline has related something that astounds
> me. They say the Duchess of Sagan has moved to Prague to stay until the
> end of the congress—and for whose sake? Guess if you care to.[44]

The days of early August passed. There was still no word from Prague. Why did he not write, at least a word, a note? One of Metternich's employees, the careful, noncommittal Pilat, who purveyed the filtered news the public got through the government-controlled *Austrian Observer*, returned from Prague, whither he had been summoned by his chief. He came out to Baden at once to see Countess Metternich, bringing her husband's fond regards. In answer to persistent questions, the unimaginative Pilat explained lamely that the count "had had a sore finger and had therefore been unable to write."

Mournfully Laure wrote her husband: "Never have you left me so long without news, my dear."[45]

6

The Congress of Prague was again at a standstill, for Caulaincourt could do nothing until Napoleon replied to his plea for power to negotiate, and Napoleon had gone to Mainz to meet Marie Louise and to give her final instructions.

Napoleon found Caulaincourt's urgent message waiting for him when he returned to Dresden on August 5. Perhaps his wife's pleas not to go to war against her father had softened him a bit. Now Caulaincourt's letter declaring that Austria meant business moved him to action. Napoleon had certainly determined to carry on the war. "The Emperor makes his decision," his secretary recalled, "he thinks only of negotiating through fighting."[46] But he had not really believed that his father-in-law would go to war against him. In his own clannish Corsican family, the ties of blood meant more than the welfare of the French nation. The Habsburgs, on the other hand, trained for generations in the monarchical system, identified family ties with political *sagesse*, readily sacrificed daughters, nieces, brothers, cousins, whenever the exigencies of state demanded it. Napoleon had not counted on Austria joining his enemies.

Now belatedly he began to take Metternich's threat seriously. Cynically he had believed he could buy Austrian neutrality, assuming, as he always did in his dealings with men and nations, that everyone had his price.

He was furious that Metternich had managed affairs so adroitly as to win a dominating position for Austria in the decision-making process.

"I would feel," he told his staff, "a real repugnance in seeing Austria as her price for the crime she committed in violating our alliance, reap the fruit and honors of the pacification of Europe."[47]

If he could buy Austrian neutrality, he was certain he could easily defeat the Russians and Prussians, this time a real defeat. After that he would deal with Austria separately—and he would make her pay for her presumption in assuming the role of Europe's mediator.

The message Napoleon sent off to Prague ordered Caulaincourt to find out at once what was Austria's asking price. On Friday, August 6, Caulaincourt got the message, so secret that he did not even divulge it to Narbonne at first. Napoleon had added a second instruction. The French delegates were to accuse the Russian and Prussian delegates of "not opening the negotiations with the aim of peace but with a view to compromising Austria with France.[48] The language of the note was hardly diplomatic, and the accusation was designed to inject further disharmony into the peace conference. Humboldt and Anstett declared at once that they were shocked and insulted, and Metternich had to agree they were justified.

Only four days remained of the armistice to make peace for the continent of Europe. The moment was one of final crisis. Caulaincourt asked and got a private audience with Metternich at once.

On Friday night, August 6, when the group of friends met to drink tea in Wilhelmine's salon in the Waldstein Palace, Humboldt noted that Metternich was not at all his usual buoyant self; he appeared downcast, troubled, dispirited. He had told no one of France's secret offer, but late that evening, he knocked on Gentz's door, told him of the offer and how he planned to reply.[49]

On Saturday evening he invited Humboldt and Anstett to the Schönborn Palace, showed them his memorandum, now bearing Emperor Franz's countersignature.

To Napoleon's query about Austria's asking price, Metternich replied that Austria would make peace only on the bases already agreed upon with Prussia and Russia. In a last-ditch attempt to appease Napoleon, Metternich might have withdrawn the demand for Illyria, and given up the freedom of the Hanseatic cities, but he included both these points. And he added a final important one: the independence of the small and large states of Europe must be guaranteed by a concert of powers, which would maintain them unchanged "except by common agreement."[50]

The memorandum added that there could be no extension of the armistice, that only through August 10 was Austria free to negotiate and to impose terms on Russia and Prussia. After that Austria would be bound to her allies.

Anstett and Humboldt, fearful that Napoleon might accept these reasonable terms, urged Metternich to rewrite the memorandum in stiffer terms. This Metternich refused to do.

On Sunday he handed the reply to Caulaincourt. The French courier locked the sealed memorandum in his saddlebag and rode off over the Bohemian mountains to bring the reply to Napoleon.

Only hours now remained to make use of the armistice.

Napoleon got the dispatch at three in the afternoon of Monday, August 9. There was still time to reply—but not a moment to delay if he were to accept the terms and make peace.

Napoleon's name day fell on August 15, but this year he had moved his saint's day up to August 10, as if that final day of the armistice were to be a day of celebration—or as if he expected to be otherwise occupied on August 15. Laure Metternich and many others had hoped Napoleon would mark his name day by some dramatic gesture of conciliation, turning it into a peace festival. But the festivities in Dresden that day were almost purely military. There were parades and troop reviews, and Te Deums in the churches, though nobody was clear as to precisely why God was being praised at that moment. Banquets lasted into the night; the French acting troupe put on a special performance in the Orangerie.

In Prague on August 9 Metternich adroitly arranged to send Alfred out of town on an errand to the Emperor in Brandeis, so that for once he might enjoy Wilhelmine's company alone. But he found her deeply depressed, not to be cheered.[51]

The armistice was to come to an end at midnight on Tuesday, August 10.

That morning Metternich wrote Wilhelmine a letter of farewell—for no one knew what the next days would bring. She would be among his guests that evening at the Schönborn Palace, but he would not be able to see her alone, and the following day, August 11, she would leave Prague very early to return to Ratiborzitz, where she was to entertain the Tsar again at his express wish.

> My dear [Metternich wrote her], let me take leave of you in writing—I have not the strength to see you tomorrow; you know the reason and I respect those moments that cannot belong to me! Love of my heart— you possess it entirely—nothing is so true and so pure as the fire with which I burn for you—love me when you have time for it; don't think of me tomorrow; of all the sacrifices I can make for you it is the most painful, this oblivion I ask of you. Take care of yourself on your journey. Think of a return that will make me forget all these very painful moments. If you find my name in your heart tell yourself you have been loved—but never as by your poor friend—[52]

He did not sign it; only rarely did he sign his letters to her.

To Laure that morning of August 10 he wrote:

> The great moment has come, *ma bonne amie*. The official negotiation comes to an end today with nothing at all accomplished. There remain 6 days of confidential negotiation. Will it lead to something or not? The congress will be dissolved today, and tomorrow an auxiliary army of 150,000 Russians and Prussians will enter Bohemia to form with ours a mass of 340,000 men, all under the command of Prince Schwarzenberg. Say nothing about it.[53]

No reply had come from Napoleon, yet even then Metternich did not quite give up hope. Like the French he interpreted the terms of the armistice agreement as allowing six days' grace after its termination before shots could be fired. He clung to the slender thread of hope that a miraculous arrangement might possibly be made in those days of grace.

Humboldt and Anstett had been fretting anxiously through the last remaining hours, fearful that Napoleon *might* in fact reply and so delay the beginning of hostilities. Humboldt trusted neither Napoleon nor Metternich, feared some collusion of the two would produce a postponement of war even at this zero hour.

On that Tuesday evening, August 10, friends and future allies gathered in Metternich's salon. Wilhelmine was there, of course, the young Esterházys, Paul and Marie Thérèse, Paul's sister, Leopoldine Liechtenstein; Gentz, Windischgraetz, Trogoff and Fontbrune.

Humboldt paced nervously up and down the room; Anstett, sure of his victory, sat, watch in hand, counting the minutes.

Present too that night was Prince Karl Schwarzenberg, who was to be supreme commander of the Allied forces. If it came to war, Metternich had long ago decided, neither a Russian nor a Prussian would have the high command, but his old friend and fellow diplomat.

A few minutes before midnight conversation came to a lull. It was not impossible that even now at this final hour an express courier from Dresden might bring a reply from Napoleon.

Across the Moldau, above the sleeping city of Prague, the door of the Gothic clock in the Town Hall sprang open. Out stepped the little wooden Christus and the twelve apostles to bow and retreat as the strokes of midnight sounded. In Metternich's salon a silvery-chimed clock repeated the hours. Humboldt and Anstett leapt to their feet, jubilantly declared their powers as delegates had expired. The congress was at an end, without—as Gentz said—ever having been born.

Whatever joy shone on the faces of others in that room, there was none on Metternich's. He accepted the pen Wilhelmine held out to him and gravely signed the declaration of war. Deeply moved, he rose and held out his hand to Schwarzenberg "to wish him success in the terrible enterprise that lay ahead."

"Then," he wrote afterward, "I had the beacons lighted from Prague to the Silesian frontier, as a sign of the breach of negotiations." From the castle hill of the Hradschin, all across Bohemia, the bonfires leapt up into the black skies, bringing word to waiting Russian and Prussian troops that they might march across the border into Bohemia to form part of the Allied army.[54]

Relief Metternich must surely have felt after the terrible tensions of the last weeks and months. But there is no doubt whatsoever that it was with the deepest sense of frustration and of bitter disappointment that he had seen his peace efforts crumble to nothing.

He wrote to Caulaincourt the next day:

> It is with deep regret that the undersigned sees an end to his functions of mediator, without obtaining out of that sterile attempt to arrive at a satisfying peace between the belligerent powers any other consolation than that of not neglecting on his side any means to complete so valuable a task.[55]

At their farewell meeting he told Caulaincourt: "We two alone wanted to make peace."

Caulaincourt sent De Broglie next day to pick up the passports for the French delegation. So unpopular were the French in Prague in those days that De Broglie did not dare appear until nightfall "to avoid any unpleasant adventure, for we could not pass through the streets without being insulted."

At the Schönborn Palace De Broglie found the waiting rooms crowded with Allied officers who turned hostile glances on the Frenchman. Metternich appeared from an inner room, took him courteously by the arm and led him into his private study, where they chatted for an hour. De Broglie describes Metternich as he saw him on that night of August 11 as "a soul filled with patriotic and personal anguish. . . . His eyes were moist, his hands worked nervously, and his forehead was covered with perspiration."

Metternich told De Broglie that this war would be unlike the previous wars against Napoleon. Even if there should be another Austerlitz or Wagram, the Austrians would refuse to surrender and would fight on as partisans. Metternich reviewed his own efforts to make peace. "He called to mind the attacks to which he had been subjected, the reproaches he had endured."[56] Scarcely a person in the higher ranks of society—except for Emperor Franz—had encouraged or supported Metternich in his attempt to negotiate peace. Even his friends, his fellow diplomats, his own Chancellery employees, all had urged him to abandon his peace effort and agree to the war.

On the morning of August 12, two days after the end of the armistice, the credentials of the French negotiators finally arrived from Napoleon, together with a counterproposal that was totally unacceptable. Caulaincourt and Narbonne brought the documents to Metternich:

> I told them it would no longer be possible to make use of these letters. The die was cast, and the fate of Europe was once again left to the decision of arms.[57]

Caulaincourt asked if he might remain a few days longer on the slender chance that further negotiation could be arranged. Everything was too late; his last talk with Emperor Franz on August 16 was fruitless. The armies were already on the march. Caulaincourt returned to Dresden, and from thence to France.

"So the last attempt has foundered," Metternich wrote Hudelist, "and Caulaincourt leaves us tonight. He is inconsolable over the way things have gone, and from the beginning to the end he has behaved like a truly honorable man."[58] Months later, in April of 1814, just before he attempted suicide at Fontainebleau, Napoleon would tell Caulaincourt, "I was wrong not to sign the peace at Prague. I could not really believe Austria was so determined."[59]

Yet it was not Napoleon's intransigeance alone that brought about the failure of the Prague Congress and of Metternich's great effort to bring peace to Europe. Repeatedly Napoleon had told those around him that he would take part in negotiations if England could be induced to join. Any European peace, he said more than once that summer, "is only an armistice while England is renewing the coalitions." He would be willing to surrender a great deal for the sake of a general peace, one in which England took part.[60]

England's assent to take part in the peace negotiations had in fact reached Allied headquarters in Reichenbach during the first week in August, several days before the armistice expired. Cathcart had taken the crucial dispatch directly to the Tsar, as Castlereagh had instructed; it was up to the Tsar to decide whether to inform Metternich of England's agreement. The Tsar and Cathcart together made the fateful decision to keep England's consent a secret from Metternich, and to allow the armistice to expire, because, Cathcart wrote blandly to Castlereagh on August 12, "war was inevitable." Actually, as Sir Robert Wilson wrote later, it was because of their fear that Metternich would insist on continuing negotiations.[61]

Little wonder that Anstett and Humboldt had waited so nervously through the last hours of the armistice on August 10.

IX

DEFEATS AND VICTORIES

If the world were like us, my dear Marie, there would be
no wars. They are really a hateful invention, but unhappily
they lie in the nature of man.
           —METTERNICH TO MARIE (SEPTEMBER 4, 1813)

1

So it was war.

Prague was delirious with joy over the declaration. The Russian and Prussian corps crossed the border at once from Silesia into Bohemia to join Schwarzenberg's Austrians. The streets of Prague were filled with Russian uniforms. The whole city looked, said Metternich, "like a Russian camp. . . . One meets here only Cossacks and bearded faces."[1]

All three sovereigns together with their chief ministers and their staffs were to follow the armies into the field. One of the odd sights of that last campaign of the Napoleonic Wars would be the two-mile-long string of assorted vehicles—elegant carriages, lumbering berlines, baggage wagons—with their precious cargo of top-level civilians, secretaries, valets, cooks, camp beds, folding desks and traveling kitchens—trailing along behind the armies.

Metternich hated the thought of the coming campaign journey, but there was no choice.

He had hoped the whole nightmare of impending war would end by August 10, and he could return to Vienna in triumph, waving his preliminary peace treaty, to begin preparations at once for the general peace he had planned many months before. He had left Vienna the first of June, hoping to be away only three weeks. Who knew now how long it would be?

He would have to give up the order and elegance of his daily life at home, that comfortable and comforting life he had shaped so carefully to his personal needs for privacy, for family life, for society:

> The greatest sacrifice I can bring to the Cause [he wrote his wife on August 13] is the kind of life I am going to lead. I detest camp and camp life. I was put here for gentle, peaceful kinds of pleasures and enjoyments, and I hate everything that takes me away from them.[2]

His campaign carriage and *fourgons* for baggage were ready, and the seventy horses needed to transport himself and his mobile chancellery. "I could weep looking at all of it." Laure must be very careful and very economical from now on, he wrote, for he would have two households to support, his own and his family's in Vienna, and they would most certainly be short of money. Emperor Franz was not an especially generous employer, and Metternich had to pay his own traveling expenses in wartime, furnish his own kitchen and table. The Army lent him horses, however, so that his own could be sent back to his stables in Vienna.

Reluctantly too Metternich prepared to part with those of his servants who were enemy nationals. That meant sending back to Vienna his French cook, Chandellier, his footman Joseph—whom Laure was to train to serve Victor—and, most awkward of all, his invaluable valet Giroux. Not only did Giroux understand perfectly how to keep his master impeccably dressed and groomed, every powdered curl in place, but Giroux was a source of endless amusement to Metternich. Who would make him laugh now? At first Metternich wrote Laure that he would send for Giroux, sub rosa, just as soon as the anti-French temper at headquarters subsided a bit, but in the end Metternich refused to part with Giroux at all, and the French valet stayed with his master to the end of the campaign.

The days following the end of the armistice were days of deep depression for Metternich. Again and again he reviewed with himself and with others —with De Broglie, with Laure, with Wilhelmine, with Gentz—his long and futile effort to make peace.

He felt better, he wrote Laure that week, because he had put down his "immense burden," and ended "the most painful task his political life had ever handed him."

He was not afraid of what lay ahead, he declared. "I am going to become for some time the Minister of Europe. Think of me often, *mes bons amis,* and pray the good God to give me strength and courage. I am as calm as if I had a game of checkers to play."

The handwriting in that letter of August 13 belies his boast of calm. In place of his usual clear, flowing script, it is nervous, jerky, in places nearly illegible. He often made a mistake in date when under severe nervous strain, and on this letter he wrote "May 13" instead of "August 13."

Having reassured Laure that she and the children might remain for the time being in Vienna—there appeared to be no danger of immediate attack in that direction—Metternich replied now to that indirect—and, he well knew, anxious—question she had asked about the Duchess of Sagan. Was the gossip she had heard true?

> I laughed at what you told me in your last [he wrote Laure] of the journey of W. of Sagan. I am certainly glad the public is busy with my love affairs while my head is splitting apart over the negotiations. I would be very flattered if she came here for my sake; what ought to prove a bit the contrary is that she was with Prince Windischgraetz for twenty-four hours and left here the same day he did. Windischgraetz is not to be recognized. He has changed regiments and we saw him the last day without moustaches.

He wrote Laure now with special tenderness:

> Adieu, my good Laure. You know that I love you with all my heart, and I shall never console myself at not being with you. Kiss the children and pray that all goes well. I expect to hear nothing more but cannon, to see nothing except the dead and the dying.[3]

Wilhelmine had left Prague the day after the declaration of war, in order to entertain the Tsar one last time at Ratiborzitz at his special request. She had promised Metternich she would come back to Prague the very moment the Tsar had left. Paul Esterházy, whom Metternich sent with two footmen to help her receive the Russian imperial party, carried a tiny note for her:

> I wish I were he. I wish I were my letter. I wish I were almost anything outside myself, and still I shall not trade this *myself* with anyone. . . . I count on the pleasure of seeing you the 16. If I were disappointed in that hope I should be very unhappy. I do not know what makes me think I shall be—probably only the unfortunate habit of no longer believing in my happiness—I who on the other hand am the happiest person on earth!
> Adieu, dear W. Don't please the Tsar *too* much and still enough to follow him to Prague.[4]

During that hectic week after the armistice ended, as the sovereigns and their ministers and generals met to thresh out problems of leadership and campaign plans, Metternich had a thousand things to do, people to see, arrangements to make.

The molding of public opinion in Europe would be a matter of deep concern to him during the coming months. The War Manifesto he had framed and turned over to Gentz to finish, explaining the course of events and of negotiations that had finally led Austria to war, was considered in Europe one of Gentz's most brilliant pieces of political writing. "The facts and general drift are mine," Metternich wrote Laure, "the style is Gentz's and this last is in my opinion a masterpiece of simplicity and force."[5]

Metternich had learned much from Napoleon about the art of propaganda. His next step was to draft an Order of the Day for the Allied
armies, to be published over Schwarzenberg's signature. That Order of
the Day, reflecting Metternich's political thinking, the philosophy that
would dominate his actions during the entire campaign, set forth the limited
war aims of the Allies: "Not against France but against French preponderance
outside the borders of France this great alliance has arisen." He stayed up
most of one night drafting the order—"one of my nocturnal operations,"
he called it. "I sent it to Schwarzenberg so he could add a few military
phrases—you know each of us must speak his own language—and we've
made a good job of it."[6]

He had that Order of the Day read aloud to the troops in the presence
of the Tsar and the Prussian King at Wrany on August 19, and later
circulated in Saxony in the vanguard of the invading armies.

The Tsar, who loved nothing better than to be the center of a military
parade, made a festive entrance into Prague on Sunday afternoon, August
15, with bands blaring and a tumultuous crowd cheering him, "with an
enthusiasm difficult to explain," Metternich wrote dryly to Laure.

Already he resented the Tsar. In that subtle, intricate tug-of-war he
had carried on with the Russian sovereign for the last eight months—the
Tsar endeavoring to draw Austria into war, Metternich striving to bring
Russia into a mediated peace—the Tsar had won. Metternich could not
console himself that the plays he had made as loser were far more brilliant
than those of the Tsar as winner. From the month of August onward
Metternich would manipulate his immediate past to make it appear that he
had, in fact, planned things exactly as they had happened.

Wilhelmine was to arrive in Prague the day after the Tsar, on Monday,
August 16. All that day Metternich waited eagerly for the message from the
Waldstein Palace informing him she had come. Instead, just at nightfall,
when he was about to send a servant to inquire, one of the duchess's people
from Ratiborzitz brought a letter from her. Contritely she explained that
she had been ready to leave, Stadion had even ordered her horses brought
to the door, when she was seized with one of her terrible migraines.

A pity, she added, that Metternich himself had not come to her dinner
for the Tsar instead of sending Paul Esterházy—what an unfortunate idea
that had been! "You will not forget to keep me *au courant* of all that is
happening," she begged. "Adieu, dear Clemens, I count on you as one of
the truest, most faithful, dearest friends I could have."[7] It was a thoroughly
nice letter—and Metternich was crushed with disappointment. Her messenger
awaited his reply.

> I calculated exactly the moment of your arrival [he wrote her]. I looked
> forward to this blessed moment. I waited for it with such a feeling of
> happiness, of gratitude—and then they brought me your letter! I shall
> not reproach you, my dear. What use would it be? You do not love me.
> If you loved me, you would have come.

In the misery of the moment he nearly decided that he must put her out of his mind forever:

> I ought never have flattered myself with what could not be. . . . I promise you I shall do everything possible to cure myself of a pain that is killing me. *Mon amie*, I do not yet imagine what life without you can be. Be happy. I would give my life a hundred times over for you.

He would prove to her, he added, that he could suffer and be silent. That was the one thing Metternich could not do. Having promised not to reproach her, he rained reproaches on her head. Why had she deceived him? Why had she promised to come, only to frustrate his happiness once again? He had "sacrificed the impossible" to prolong his stay in Prague in order to see her. He had turned all his plans upside down; he had lost his head. "I have no head on me at this moment—only a heart and that heart is broken. The most *difficult* moment of my life has just passed. Why did the most *cruel* have to be reserved for me as well?"[8]

But instead of coming to Prague Wilhelmine stayed on in Ratiborzitz through the last weeks of August. Alfred had left to join his new regiment, the O'Reilly Light Horse serving under the Prince of Hesse-Homburg; perhaps there was nothing now in Prague to draw her.

A few days after the Tsar had dined at Ratiborzitz, the King of Prussia rode across the border from Reichenbach at the head of his army, and she stood in the tower of Náchod Castle with Tante Elisa to watch the splendid sight—the fine Prussian cavalry, banners flying, the infantry high-stepping along the highroad to Prague. On an impulse Wilhelmine—though Protestant and lukewarm at that—ordered a Mass said in the little baroque chapel of her castle that had once belonged to the Piccolomini family.

Imbued like Metternich with the romantic sensibilities of the period, Wilhelmine too set down all her emotions on paper. She was in a state of black dejection, she wrote him:

> I know that I am less good to you than I would like to be, dear Clemens, forgive me, it is impossible to be otherwise. An immense weight lies on my heart, I suffer impossibly, there are moments when I think I shall die of it. Don't hold it against me then. Know that my heart suffers in causing yours pain and that I am sincerely attached to you.
>
> I feel my pulse to see if I am not ill. Alas! it is only my soul that is ill, and for ills of this kind there is no remedy. . . . Adieu, dear Clemens, you whom I look on with gratitude and pride as my friend. Adieu.

And at the very end she added, half a jest, half a promise—knowing how he hated that word "friend" in the context of their relationship: "I don't tell you always to be [my friend]—I might offend your heart by a doubt—Adieu."[9] Did she mean that he would be something more?

The hot days of that briefest of brief summers came abruptly to an end. Stormy skies poured down sheets of rain; the weather turned cold; along the

Bohemian roads sloshed the armies, over their boot tops in mire. Everyone went around with chills and fever and sore throats.

Metternich too became ill and took to his bed in Prague.

Extraordinarily strong physically—he would live to be eighty-six—his tensile, wiry strength enabled him to endure long periods of hardship and physical fatigue. Nevertheless, he nearly always fell ill after any intense nervous strain.

He wrote Laure matter-of-factly that his illness was nothing but a head cold; to Wilhelmine he gave a more romantic diagnosis:

> Nature always ends up by paying for the demands of the soul. Mon amie, I am on my sick-bed. My doctor does not know what illness I have; you and I know. I must close now because my head aches, and because some-times I remember that it would serve my country ill if I departed leav-ing an immense task begun and not finished.

Her letter from Náchod had lifted his spirits and hopes. It was the most revealing of herself, and the most affectionate she had written him. "It is your soul that speaks in this letter." He began to believe that she might come to love him:

> Adieu, my W. You belong to me and my heart tells me you will belong to me even more; this heart has never deceived me—it loves only those who have complete ties with it; would I have found you to have you be the sorrow and torment of my life?[10]

For the first time he addressed her with the intimate *tu*. He longed too for her to claim him within her intimate circle of *thou*'s, but for Wilhelmine that linguistic barrier to total intimacy was the very last to be scaled. She could sleep with a man and still he remained *vous*. Sexual relationships could be for Wilhelmine a matter of warm friendship, not necessarily love, but the use of *tu* was a final bonding, an inner surrender of her own deepest self. It was reserved inviolably for those she loved—for her sisters, for her foster daughters, for her maid Hannchen—and for two or three men only in her whole life.

2

Before he was completely well again Metternich climbed into his carriage —the small, light traveling carriage he had bought especially for the campaign—and drove first to Komotau, where the Tsar had his headquarters, then in the wake of the huge Austro-Russian-Prussian army on its way across the mountains into Saxony to battle the French.

The forty days of the armistice had been, it turned out, only a breathing space in which both sides could train more troops, forge more cannon, hatch out their military plans.

Napoleon had been everywhere those last days of summer. He had ridden over every road near Dresden, examined every bridge and every redoubt, visited fortresses, studied on his maps every stream and every pass in the Bohemian mountains.

Yet his officers and those around him detected a change from the Napoleon of the old days. No longer was he the quick, energetic commander who made instant decisions, divided his enemy with knifelike strokes, moved his troops with the lightning-quick maneuvers that had won him victory after victory.

He was middle-aged now, stout, short of breath, suffering all the ailments of advancing age—prostate trouble, a recurring kidney ailment, hemorrhoids. He preferred not to ride but to follow his armies when he could in his comfortable little low-slung green carriage, with a portable desk and a seat that folded out into a bed. He pondered longer about taking the offensive. He played a waiting game.

The balance of numbers was now on the side of the Allies. With the addition of the Austrian Army, the Coalition could count nearly a half million men to put in the field against Napoleon's main army of 300,000. More crucial than mere numbers was the decisive factor in every battle of that day—the cavalry that gave an army mobility, flexible muscle and pursuing power. Napoleon had only 40,000 horse to put in the field against the Allies' 100,000.

But all the advantages were by no means on the Allied side. Napoleon was still the best general in Europe—and he held his high command indisputably in his own hands and head.

The Allies, meantime, wrangled bitterly over their own supreme command.

Metternich had thought the matter quite settled. Part of Austria's asking price for entering the Coalition and for supplying the largest number of troops was that an Austrian would hold the supreme command. He had determined that Schwarzenberg should have it—though many Austrians in government circles favored Archduke Karl, the Emperor's brother. There were important reasons for choosing Schwarzenberg. Schwarzenberg, an experienced diplomat as well as a competent general, would understand clearly that political decisions must take precedence over military—the reverse had too often been true in wars in the past. With Schwarzenberg in command, Metternich could remain close to every military decision, while he kept control of political ends in his own hands.

But the Tsar considered himself the natural choice to lead the armies. He had a whole clutch of generals on his staff to help him, he pointed out, including two of Napoleon's own defected generals—Moreau, who had been living in America until he got the Tsar's invitation to join the Russian general staff, and the Swiss tactician Jomini.

At Komotau, with the Allied armies poised to march into Saxony, there was a fierce battle at headquarters over the command. At last, against the

Tsar's stubborn insistence on himself, Metternich replied curtly that if the Russian sovereign took supreme command, he would withdraw the Austrian forces. The Tsar gave in; Schwarzenberg retained command. Metternich returned from Komotau that night of August 23 "as weak as if I had just got over a severe illness"—which indeed he had.[11]

Whatever Schwarzenberg's title—and he was careful not to flaunt it —the Tsar considered himself the real leader of the Allied forces. He did not know the old army saying, "One bad general is better than two good ones," and he continued to ask advice from half a dozen, no two of whom ever agreed. Over and over Schwarzenberg would write his wife of the impossible position he was in. "It's a chaos of would-be doers around here, my Nani."[12]

Dependable, quiet, humane, Schwarzenberg would be labeled more "ministerial" than military. The Prussian Clausewitz would deride Schwarzenberg's old-fashioned ideas of strategy, his deliberate movements, the miserliness with which he hoarded the lives of his men. Neither a brilliant tactician nor a bold strategist, Schwarzenberg proved in the end to be a good choice for that difficult and thankless post. He brought patience and diplomacy to the confusion and infighting at headquarters, with three sovereigns and a swarm of generals of several nationalities underfoot.

Metternich's quarrel with the Tsar over the high command was the first in a long series of bitter disagreements the two men would have during the course of the campaign, disagreements that would threaten to wreck the Coalition and eventually even the peace.

Nor was the question of supreme command the only question in dispute among the Allies; there was also the question of campaign strategy.

According to the Trachenberg plan devised in July, the Allied forces were divided into three main armies. The smallest, the Army of the North, comprised of Swedish and Russians under Crown Prince Bernadotte, was to remain in the lower Elbe, to attack the French fortresses there and to cover Berlin. The second, the Army of Silesia, chiefly Prussians with one Russian corps, under the Prussian General Blücher, was to move north from the Silesian encampment and try to retake Breslau. The third and by far the largest, the Army of Bohemia, under Schwarzenberg, comprising Austrians with a Russian and a Prussian division now encamped in northwestern Bohemia, was to be the main attacking force.

Drawing a lesson from the Russian campaign, the Allied strategists had agreed it was best to avoid direct confrontation with Napoleon in a large-scale battle; better to harass his forces, cut supplies and communications, wear him out—but retreat if there were danger of direct attack.

Each side now tried warily to assess the best chances.

Napoleon, believing that the main Allied force was in Silesia and would attack from that direction, moved eastward from Dresden to Stolpen, considering also the possibility of swooping down suddenly through one of the mountain routes onto the city of Prague.

When the Allies learned that Napoleon had left Dresden and was many miles to the east, their original plan was changed on the advice of Moreau and Jomini, who thought it the perfect moment to strike at Dresden and capture Napoleon's headquarters.

Dresden lay only thirty miles north from Allied headquarters at Teplitz, as the crow flies, across the curtain of the Giant mountains that border northwestern Bohemia, but men were not crows, and in that stormy week in late August, over hazardous, nearly impassable mountain roads, the crossing took two nights and two days.

"The roads through the Erzgebirge have to be seen to give one an idea of what the will of man is capable of," Metternich wrote his wife.[13] In his light campaign carriage, with Paul Esterházy at his side, Metternich followed the army, traveling behind an artillery unit in which two batteries of large-bore cannon had to be dragged by main force of men and horses through deep mud, up steep slopes and across passes so narrow his own small carriage could barely squeak through. It had been a terrible journey. Heavy rains beat down, soaking them "like spaniels." Again and again they had to dismount to help push some vehicle out of the mire. Wagons and cannon lay abandoned in the mud blocking the road; worse yet, provision wagons, so that many of the troops were without food for days.

Still the prospects on August 25 and 26 looked rosy and promised a quick and easy victory. Wittgenstein and his Russian corps captured the town of Pirna, the gateway to Dresden, and one by one all of Dresden's outlying defenses fell to the Allies. Even the weather cleared for a time. By the afternoon of August 25 most of the army had crossed the mountains and lay encamped in a great semicircle on the heights above Dresden.

Schwarzenberg wanted to order the attack at once; Jomini agreed, but the Tsar and King of Prussia argued against it. Their men were tired, and the last unit, the Klenau Corps, had not yet caught up with them.

Napoleon, meantime, had been summoned from Stolpen by an urgent message from Saint-Cyr, the commander in Dresden, who declared he could not possibly hold the city against the vast Allied army unless Napoleon came to help. Marching double quick Napoleon was back in Dresden on the following morning of August 26. Quite clearly from their encampment the Allies could see the double column of Guard troops crossing the Elbe by the Old Bridge into the city gate, and they could hear in the distance those ominous shouts, "*Vive l'Empereur!*"

At three that afternoon, August 26, with three cannon blasts, Schwarzenberg gave the order to attack. Column after column of Austrian infantry, each column preceded by fifty cannon, marched down the slopes and across the open plain toward the heavily walled city.

"Everything is going marvelously," Metternich crowed in a letter dashed off to Laure from headquarters at four in the afternoon.

A courier was about to leave for Vienna, and he wanted her to have the good news first:

Napoleon, entirely deceived about our movements, has thrown his whole
army toward Silesia, where he thought he would meet the Russian and
Prussian armies. We've executed a very bold maneuver. . . . While I am
sitting here writing the earth is shaking in a terrific cannonade before
Dresden. . . . The Cossacks spent last night in the Great Gardens. The
whole army is on the move. Great events are in store.[14]

Two regiments of Westphalian hussars—Napoleon's unsteady allies of the
Rhine Confederation—had gone over to the Allies that morning.

Certain that victory was a matter of hours, or a day or two at most,
Metternich and Paul jumped back into the little carriage and started back
across the mountains to bring the good news to the Austrian Emperor,
waiting at Teplitz.

Twenty-four hours later, having dined comfortably with the Emperor in
the Clary Palace in Teplitz, Metternich wrote a long, exuberantly optimistic
letter to Wilhelmine. The attack on Dresden, he declared, "had turned
entirely to our advantage":

My hard moments at Ratiborzitz are forgotten; everyone is saying that I
alone have sense and calculated everything well—one must act according
to one's convictions and let everyone else talk—that is the simple very
simple adage of my public life and has always led me well. Fools and
imbeciles wanted to begin when nothing was ready. . . .[15]

He could not have been more wrong about Dresden.

On the night of August 26—the night Metternich was driving back to
Teplitz—heavy drenching rain began to pour down once more. There was
no discernible daybreak. "The worst English December day was never
more bleak or soaking," wrote Wilson on August 27.[16]

All that day torrential rain poured down out of an ice-gray sky. French
sentinels on the walls of Dresden could see Allied soldiers a mile or so
away shaking water from their tents and their clothing.

Everything went badly for the Allies. Their cavalry slipped and skidded
on the muddy slopes; horses and cannon foundered in the deep mud of the
plain. More than half the men were barefoot. Wet powder would not fire;
heavy cannon failed to shoot.

Try as they might, pounding away with their heaviest cannon, the
Allies could not penetrate the heavy walls of the city.

The Allied leaders had neglected to bring ladders and scaling equipment—perhaps they thought the thick walls would crumble under artillery
fire. Orders were given for an assault on the outer walls, and the men tried
to scale them using bayonets for foothold. Robert Wilson and Charles
Stewart led one such daring assault on the walls:

I remember what I owed to Austria, [wrote Wilson], to England and
to myself. I dismounted, climbed over the palisades, with extreme difficulty reached the crest of the parapet, sprang on it, took off my cap and

gave three cheers, Charles at my side. Instantly hundreds mounted and manned the redoubt.

Count Colloredo came up to me afterward, gave me his hand, said various handsome things, so did all the other generals.

With marvelous British understatement he adds, "It was a satisfactory moment."[17]

But it was in vain; hundreds were killed in the futile attempt to scale the walls of Dresden.

There was nothing tidy about such battles; they were fierce, murderous—and more often than not, bogged down in utter confusion. Black smoke made the whole battlefield nearly invisible, and at times it was almost as easy to be shot by one's friends as one's enemies. At one point that day Wilson and Stewart and Moritz Liechtenstein found themselves galloping along in the midst of Napoleon's Guard troops; only the darkness, rain and disorder saved them from recognition.

The deafening noise of artillery fire did not quite drown out the shrill neighing of dying horses, the screams of the wounded lying everywhere untended. Not until the battle was over—and maybe not then—might they be carried off the field and carted to the nearest city. The severely wounded were simply left on the field to die.

On the early afternoon of that day, as the Tsar, the Prussian King, Lord Cathcart and Moreau rode along at the edge of the field, there was the sound of a cannon shot quite close by. "General Moreau is hit!" Wilson cried. The stray cannonball had plowed through Moreau's horse and smashed both his legs. From the ground where he was thrown, he lifted himself a little, looked at his legs and said, *"C'est passé avec moi; mon affaire est faite."* Carried to a tent close by—he was lucky or unlucky enough to have the Tsar's own field doctor at hand to amputate both legs at the hip, without anesthesia except brandy, and with one of the Havana cigars he had brought from New York clenched between his teeth. That night he was borne back across the mountains to Bohemia on the pikes of twenty-six Russian soldiers.

Napoleon that day had ordered a great bonfire lighted so that he could see to direct the battle. One of the marks of his peculiar genius was that he could look at such a dark chaotic welter as the battle of Dresden, and know precisely where to send his fresh cavalry, where to aim his final blows. Watching the enemy, glass in hand, he thought he perceived a gap in the great half-circle of Allied troops—it was the space that had been left for the Klenau Corps, just now struggling to the field, exhausted from the mountain crossing.

Napoleon at once ordered his cavalry in to attack at just that breach. The brightest spot on that desolate day was Joachim Murat, the flamboyant King of Naples, leading a cavalry charge in the rain, a figure straight out of grand opera in a gold-embroidered mantle, yellow boots and amaranth breeches, his horse in sky-blue trappings—on his head a hat topped with ostrich plumes and a heron aigrette. The cavalry attack succeeded.

In the late afternoon it was clear to the Allied leaders that the assault on Dresden had failed. The battle was lost. In the streaming rain they held council at the edge of the field around a wet wood fire—Schwarzenberg, the Tsar, the Prussian King and their generals. Standing on planks so as not to sink deep in mud, they gave the order for retreat.

And now that immense unwieldy mass of men—hundreds of thousands, soaked to the skin, shivering with cold, hungry, sick with fatigue, thousands wounded—struggled back across the mountains to Bohemia.

Behind them they left 20,000 dead and wounded. And herded into Dresden that night were some 13,000 prisoners, mostly Austrian, exhausted and famished, jammed into the Protestant church and in the open air of the Brühl gardens.

Napoleon himself caught cold that day, rode back into the city, water streaming off his clothes, the brim of the famous bicorne hat hanging down to his shoulders. He was too sick to leave his bed in the next days to join the pursuit of the defeated Allied army.

Everyone at once blamed everyone else for the disaster of Dresden.

The Tsar and the King of Prussia blamed Schwarzenberg and wanted him removed at once from his command. The King of Prussia berated him openly.

Schwarzenberg blamed the fact that his orders had not been followed. Throughout the battle, the Tsar had paid little attention to him, had ordered the Russian troops about as he saw fit. Charles Stewart wrote that "only half of Schwarzenberg's plans were adopted" and half the Tsar's, "while Jomini filled up the measure of embarrassments."[18]

Bitterly Schwarzenberg told Wilson "he will either resign or make over the command to the 'military college' that accompanies the army."[19]

If only Schwarzenberg could lose his temper, be really angry, Metternich wrote. But proud, dignified Schwarzenberg could not vent his feelings except to his wife:

> My head [he wrote his dear Nani] feels as if it is exploding. . . . Often
> I think of resigning but the goal is so exalted, so hallowed, and the situ-
> ation of such a kind that I perceive any other would be able to bear
> even less in my place.[20]

So he stayed.

Fortune in any case had another word or two to say.

Napoleon had planned to encircle the retreating Allies, trap them in the Bohemian mountains and finish them. He had sent General Vandamme with an army of 100,000 to await them on the heights of Peterswald. Vandamme, his eye on a marshal's baton, thought he knew a better way. His army was astride the shortest and best road into Bohemia, only a few miles above Teplitz, where the Allies were headquartered. He decided to move swiftly down on Teplitz, cut off the Allied retreat, and open up for Napoleon the road to Prague and Vienna.

He ran into a Russian guard unit of some 8,000 men under Count Ostermann, who managed to hold him until Austrian reinforcements hastened up from Teplitz. Meantime, by lucky chance the Prussian General Kleist, retreating after Dresden, took a different route from the one assigned and caught up with Vandamme from the rear. Clamped in a vise between two strong forces in the narrow mountain defile, the French corps was annihilated; Vandamme was taken prisoner and brought back to Prague, thence to Russia.

Metternich had had a share in the victory of Kulm. Schwarzenberg could not be found, and it was he who had given the order to Austrian troops to move at once into the breach.

Dresden had been a bitter blow to the Allies; Kulm lifted their spirits. There was good news from the other armies—Blücher's Silesian Army defeated the French under Macdonald on the Katzbach River. In the north General Bülow won another victory at Dennewitz.

From Teplitz that evening of August 31 Metternich could send the good news to Wilhelmine: "I want to be the first, my dear Wilhelmine, to announce the beautiful victory we've just carried off."[21]

Gentz was now in charge of public relations in Prague, and he threw himself heart and soul into the job. He loved being the one to receive couriers with dispatches hot from army headquarters, loved being the purveyor of the freshest of fresh news. It made him very popular in Prague; in the weeks that followed people flocked to his rooms in the Waldstein to ask the latest, and his rooms "were seldom empty of visitors."

Metternich was fully attuned to the importance of manipulating public opinion. As always with war news, the facts were carefully measured and seasoned so that the whole grim business could be presented neatly and palatably to the public.

Rumors of the disaster at Dresden had reached Prague, and Gentz was worried sick lest something had happened to Metternich on his journey to and from the battle:

> I saw you, not yet wholly recovered from your last illness, exposed to great physical exertions, to heavy anxieties, to sleepless nights . . . and finally returning with carefully repressed but nonetheless gnawing grief. This was a bad dream; everything will go excellently [now].[22]

Word of the victory at Kulm reached Gentz at eleven on the morning of August 31. He got the presses going in record time. By four in the afternoon extras of the Prague *Gazette* were being hawked in the streets; Gentz had wanted to rename the battle for another village, Nollendorf, because it "rolled about so nicely on the tongue."

In the official *Austrian Observer* the battle of Dresden was reported in a dozen words that implied the French had retreated with losses, while Kulm was described in exuberant detail as a glorious victory—which, of course, it was. Gentz admitted ruefully to Pilat that they had perhaps gone a bit too far in hiding the facts of Dresden, and their credibility gap was showing: "Between you and me, we hushed up the real story of those days a bit too much in the beginning."[23]

The irony of their profession did not escape those two veteran journalists, and they could laugh together over how the French had reported the precise same news in the precise opposite sense. Napoleon's *Moniteur* described Dresden in glowing detail. Kulm was dismissed as a minor mishap of no real importance: "General Vandamme," stated the *Moniteur*, "met with certain difficulties near Teplitz."

3

In Ratiborzitz, that lovely isolated corner of the world, some thirty hours' distance from Prague and twice again as far from Teplitz, Wilhelmine felt herself totally cut off from the only world that mattered to her. The future of Europe might be decided at any moment—and she might as well be a million miles away as in Ratiborzitz.

In those last days of August she wandered about the house disconsolately, listening to the endless rains beat down. It was so cold that in spite of the porcelain stoves her teeth chattered. She could not concentrate to read. She had packed up her precious library ("I have a great tenderness for my books," she wrote Metternich) in case Ratiborzitz should be occupied and ransacked, as Sagan had been.

> Here everything contributes to making me sad—a house all empty to make one afraid—rain pelting down night and day, and always the same faces, whom I love certainly but who are not made to cheer me up.[24]

Fontbrune had stayed on, a lingering houseguest, and Tante Elisa and Tiedge. Madame Trogoff, wife of Alfred's boon companion, remained too; she would now become a kind of permanent resident-companion in Wilhelmine's generous and flexible household. A little stout woman with bright black eyes, Breton by birth, Madame Trogoff kept her snuffbox close at hand, and in moments of gloom and uncertainty flicked through her pack of worn tarot cards. She was easy to have around, and she made herself useful to Wilhelmine in all sorts of ways. She knew when to talk and when to be silent; she carried around in her head a whole apothecary of Breton herb remedies for everything from rheumatism to migraine; she would keep track of Wilhelmine's dressmaker and millinery bills, which were apt to be astronomical and not always paid on time.

The countryside around Ratiborzitz was a sea of rumor. It was said that the local postmaster, a Pole, was really a French spy, and that if one listened one could clearly hear the firing of distant cannons—though Blücher's forces were a good hundred miles to the north.

She thought she would go back to Prague, where she might at least hear the latest war news.

> This state of uncertainty is killing me. . . . Tell me where I can go to be nearer my friends. Tell me what you think, dear Clemens, give me good advice—and especially advice that will make me leave here—this solitude is driving me to despair.[25]

Her warm, affectionate letter was waiting for Metternich when he returned to Teplitz from the Dresden battlefield on August 26, in his mood of joyful optimism. He sat down at once and wrote a long, tender letter in reply, describing his taste of battle, bragging that God had given him a good share of courage—he almost wished he were a soldier instead of a diplomat. (If it was military heroes that she admired, he thought, he too could fill the bill!)

Did she still think he was "so cold, so reserved, so self-centered, so haughty" as many people who did not know him always thought?

> I shall prove to you that I love you more than myself . . . that I consult only your interests. . . . don't reproach yourself—you are innocent of the ills I have caused myself. The day of my death . . . I shall ask pardon for many many torments, and a single tear of regret!

The letter was quite in the mood of a young Werther. But Metternich's intuition did not fail him when he wrote:

> You will never love me perhaps, but I shall end by becoming necessary to you.

If she wanted to be closer to the scene of great events, he thought she should go to Prague. But she must travel light, taking few servants, and with her own horses, "for Prague could be in danger as is all of Bohemia. The war has taken so singular a turn that it is impossible to predict where we shall finish."[26]

In the loneliness and isolation of Ratiborzitz her feelings for Metternich began to change. She had heard nothing from Alfred. Metternich had promised to forward her letters to Alfred by special messenger, and had offered Alfred to send on his letters to Wilhelmine by army courier. But no letters at all from Alfred had reached her.

In those days of deep depression, of sleepless nights, of recurring migraine, Wilhelmine was touched by Metternich's romantic and beautiful letters, by his constancy and devotion—and not least by his dispatch of the latest political and military news. She would have been less than human not to be flattered that so attractive a man, near the very pinnacle of leadership, was deeply in love with her. If she could not herself be a political mover, she wanted to be close to those who did move. And she wanted to fix her affections permanently on a man she could wholly rely on. Her long friendship with Clemens, his poetic and passionate letters, his eminent position and his confidence in her judgment—slowly her imagination began to kindle this friendship into something that—if not passion—was more than affection. She was persuading herself into love. She counted on his love, she wrote him,

> with the certitude of maturity and the confidence and abandon of childhood. I count on you, dear Clemens, in life and in death. . . . So few people keep the promises they make, and you, dear Clemens, whom I call my friend with rapture and pride and the deepest satisfaction—the best feelings of my heart—you not only fulfill my expectations but the dreams of my imagination.

He had told her that she understood him better than anyone in the world did, that they two were cut from the same cloth, walked the same road.

> . . . nobody knows you better than I [she agreed] and far from you my memories help to perfect this acquaintance and to love you as much because you deserve it as because of the inclination that for so many years attracted me to you—

She was delighted one day to come upon a packet of sugared almonds he had sent her a couple of weeks earlier by Karl Leiden, intended perhaps for the Tsar's dinner party. She gobbled them up all by herself, thanking him for remembering how she adored them. He had ordered Gentz to send her copies of the manifesto, the Order of the Day and his press releases, so that she would get at least the good news.

After his last long letter of August 27 from Teplitz she wrote him gratefully:

> My dear good Clemens, I love you with my whole heart; if this love is perhaps not everything that you could wish, in many ways it is more, that I'll answer for.[27]

Yes, she would go to Prague—and if Clemens wished to see her, she would go wherever he wanted.

Early Thursday morning, September 2, Wilhelmine, with Madame Trogoff beside her and her invaluable maid Hannchen, who happened to be eight months pregnant, left Ratiborzitz in the heavy traveling berline. On Metternich's advice she took as well her fast little calèche and eight good carriage horses.

It was an exhausting and at times terrifying journey for women alone, for the roads were filled with troop reserves, with stragglers and deserters, and even, they had been warned, with Cossacks and bandits. "I had some fearful moments," she said afterward, and her courage nearly left her at times. The journey took far longer than usual, and it was late Friday night when they reached Prague, exhausted and nearly ill. The gates of the city were locked, but Gentz had left word with the watchman.

In the Waldstein Palace, supper was waiting for them, and her old friends, including Gentz, who could not wait to relate all the news—good and bad. Among the packet of letters were two with Metternich's seal—a letter of greeting, which had crossed the one she wrote him from Ratiborzitz, proposing, like hers, that they meet halfway between Prague and Teplitz. She was pleased that the idea had come from her at precisely the same moment as he had written. Would she, he asked, be brave enough to take the roads just now and meet him halfway between Prague and Teplitz, at Laun? She must bring Gentz along, "for it is necessary to have a man on the main highways now, however little a man our good Gentz may be. . . ."

His second letter gave precise instructions for her journey. She must send relays of horses ahead on Sunday and leave Monday morning early in her calèche. He had engaged four rooms for them in Laun, sent his own cook and Karl Leiden on ahead to make preparations to receive her. He warned her:

> We shall have to spend the night there, because it is impossible to think of traveling at night on account of Cossacks and marauders, unless you have an escort.[28]

That brief, sweet meeting of Metternich and Wilhelmine in Laun, short hours stolen out of the disorder and danger and confusion of war, was one of the happiest of their friendship.

In those early September days, in the wake of the first battles, the road between Prague and Teplitz was choked with the appalling debris of war. There were captured French cannon and baggage wagons, reserve troops on the move—and an endless stream of prisoners, tattered and dropping with fatigue, endless wagons piled high with wounded and dying, victims of the battles of Dresden and Kulm. More than once Wilhelmine wondered if she should indeed have started out.

But once in Laun all the horrors were forgotten.

Metternich arrived in the highest of high spirits, having invented a pretext of urgent business to absent himself from headquarters for two whole days. Gentz described him "in such a humor, so well, so handsome, so cheerful, so full of strong and serene hope, I never saw him! On his face stood written quite unmistakably the happy outcome of the war."[29]

Months later Metternich looked back on their rendezvous in Laun, writing her:

> I saw you at Laun! Never shall I forget those few hours I spent there—they were the first good moments in our liaison. If I live a long time—which will not happen to me—I shall have myself carried quite old to Laun again, and there I shall shed tears over the most precious of all my memories![30]

The three friends lingered long over dinner.

Metternich could relate now in all its grim detail the terrible lost battle of Dresden. He told them too of the tragedy of General Moreau, who had died here in Laun only days before. The Tsar had ordered his body embalmed and sent to St. Petersburg, where it would be buried with great honor.

But the battle at Kulm and Blücher's victory on the Katzbach had restored all of Metternich's buoyant optimism. It was only a matter of time now—weeks perhaps—and the war would be over.

Gentz, delighted at being part of the lovers' rendezvous, wrote afterward, "The hours I spent with Count Metternich in Laun were unforgettable— among the happiest in my life." And he added, "Between Metternich and the duchess there stood then a very intimate relationship."[31]

They had to bid one another good-by the next day and drive off in opposite directions—Metternich back to the army in Teplitz, Wilhelmine and Gentz to Prague. Clemens had promised her he would come to Prague before the army moved again, if a way could be found. Rapturously he wrote her a day or two later from Teplitz:

> I dreamed, my dear, that I was banished to a country of sorrow and death. Everything around me was a scene of killing; my heart was oppressed, my soul suffering, my life extinguished. A dreadful night covered the earth. . . . Suddenly I am transported into the loveliest, most blessed spot on earth. Everything smiles at me; I breathe only pleasure and happiness; I see a good angel who consoles me for all my past troubles, who exhorts me to bear those of the moment. My dear, it happens that all that is true, and I have returned from Laun.
>
> You have made me drunk with happiness. I love you, I love you a hundred times more than my life. I do not live, I shall not live except for you.[32]

Wilhelmine, less ecstatic, thanked him "a thousand times for the good moments" he had given her in Laun. With him she felt safe and reassured; her anxieties melted away:

> I do not know how I love you, but I love you very much and with my whole heart.[33]

She still addressed him as *vous* in her letters. The word was like that door between their rooms in Laun, unlocked but standing closed. They had made love, to be sure, but Wilhelmine, when she wanted to speak with him, had always knocked on the door between, which both amused and baffled him:

> I shall do everything you want [he wrote her]; I shall even learn to knock on the door as you do, however *ennuyant* it seems to me. My dear, I would knock, I would kill myself, I would do everything providing that you open to me.[34]

Metternich remained for a few days in that heady state of bliss in which he returned from Laun. He felt certain now that she loved him, that she would come to fill that place he had made ready for her in his life.

Wilhelmine, on leaving Laun, returned to all her old anxieties, her uncertainties, her uneasiness about herself and her future. "I have a presentiment of trouble," she wrote him. "To my usual fears is joined now, I don't know why or how, a fear of some event that will separate me entirely from my friends. . . ."[35]

Just after daybreak on the Saturday morning following the trip to Laun, Alfred Windischgraetz appeared at the door of her apartment in the Waldstein Palace in Prague, having ridden all night from Leitmeritz to see her.

Gentz, in rooms adjoining Wilhelmine's, learned at once of Alfred's arrival. The day before Gentz had heard from English diplomats in Prague that the French had crossed the mountains into Bohemia again, and that there was fighting near Kulm. He expressed surprise at seeing Alfred when the whole Austrian army might be in grave danger again. How did he dare absent himself from his regiment? The day and night were spoiled for Alfred—and for Wilhelmine. He could not wait to ride off at dawn on Sunday.

Gentz wrote Metternich at once to report Alfred's visit to Wilhelmine. "[Alfred] is now in the most terrible anxiety because he fears that his regiment will be called to action and he doesn't know which way to take to rejoin it fast enough. . . . I await with great longing Your Excellency's letters and further commands."[36]

Wilhelmine too wrote Metternich of the visit. "Gentz will have informed you, *mon bon ami*, of the surprise I had yesterday." Windischgraetz had ridden off in a white heat, she added. "It would have been too cruel not to be involved in an engagement where it meant leading his regiment for the first time under fire."

She tried to reassure Metternich of her affection, but it was a cool, reasonable letter:

> I think of you often, *mon ami*, and I assure you that you can be very pleased with my behavior. I shall never regret what I am able to do for your happiness—count on it—and I am persuaded as much as anyone can be that you truly love me—I rest so to speak on this conviction—when the storm that swirls in me and around me exhausts me too much I think of the friend Heaven led me to find, of the feelings he wants me to believe are sheltered from time, and serenity is born again in my soul. I don't find myself any longer alone in this world, thinking of the person who wants to love me *always*.[37]

In Laun he had asked her to make some small purchases for him in Prague. She had bought the gold cord and tassels he had asked for his uniform—they were not pretty "but there was no way of finding others." Tomorrow she would send the bonnet and the taffeta which were to go to Laure.

But in Teplitz Metternich was already in the depths of despair where Gentz's letter had plummeted him:

> I have not written you because G[entz] warned me of W.'s arrival and dead men do not write letters. There are so many moments of my

life when I would as soon not exist. . . . How often during these last two days have I felt the sensation of a *broken heart.** My heart in such moments seems physically to break, I feel little except fever, agony, death. For three months I have no longer known who I am, I know only that I love you more than my life, more than I have ever loved, and that my whole existence has been turned upside down.

The courier did not come as usual next morning to pick up Metternich's mail. He unsealed the letter again to add a few lines:

My good W., why must I love you so much? Don't you know a way to lead me back a little to myself? . . . Good day to you who are my life and my death, my joy and my sorrow, my good and my evil— and whom I wish I had never known.[38]

* In English in the original.

X

WAR CAMP IN TEPLITZ

1

On that morning of September 11, when Alfred Windischgraetz had appeared at Wilhelmine's door in Prague prepared for a blissful week-long reunion, Metternich was sitting at his desk in his quarters in Teplitz, weary but too keyed up to sleep, writing to Laure of his adventures of the night before:

> I am writing you at an unheard-of hour [eight o'clock in the morning], *ma bonne amie*, because I spent the whole night on foot following a pretty affair that has been going on since yesterday noon.[1]

There had been bitter fighting in the mountains only three miles from Teplitz. The Allies had succeeded in holding the French back; Metternich had remained with the Austrian forces that day and night.

In the early days of September the Allies had resumed their agreed-upon tactic, copied after Kutuzov's maneuvering during the Russian campaign. The game was to attack wherever Napoleon was not, to cut supply lines and communications, to beat down the French army, to wear it out, rather than face Napoleon's superb generalship in another large-scale battle such as Dresden.

When Blücher had attacked the French under Macdonald in Silesia with great successs, Napoleon had turned eastward to halt his advance, whereupon Blücher withdrew. Napoleon learned then that the Russians under Wittgenstein were advancing again from Bohemia toward Dresden and had captured Pirna. He wheeled toward the west, forced the Russians back, advanced through the Bohemian mountains until he stood nearly on the spot where the battle of Kulm had been fought only days before, on the heights above Teplitz.

In a panic, the Allies prepared to evacuate their headquarters; all the baggage and movables were sent to the rear, and for a few days Emperor Franz moved to safer quarters.

For some days the French remained on the mountain crests, so close that from the windows of his quarters in Teplitz Metternich could clearly discern with his pocket spyglass the movement of men and horses in the French encampment. All day long the sound of intermittent musket and cannon fire could be heard in the valley, and at night "the hills were lighted to their crests and the valleys blazed in a sheet of fire."

French prisoners reported that Napoleon was there looking down on them, that he had a horse shot out from under him in one engagement.

The climax of the invasion came on September 17, when a fierce battle in the mountains lasted far into a night of impenetrable fog:

> What a night! [Metternich wrote]. It's a wonder our brave men did not kill one another. I came back by the light of cannon fire, for never was there a blacker night.[2]

Soon after, the French quietly withdrew back across the mountains to Dresden again. It would have been the height of folly, Napoleon decided, to fight a major battle with the mountains at his back, or to descend on Teplitz by a defile so narrow and steep "a single broken wheel would have stopped a whole army."[3]

The rains of that peculiarly desolate year had begun again in August, continued through the autumn days of September and October. Most of the rivers of Central Europe overflowed their banks. Bridges washed away; a whole French division fell into Allied hands—some drowned trying to swim to safety—when they could not find a single bridge left standing to cross the river Bober.

Over all but impassable roads the armies trudged, losing boots and equipment, sleeping outdoors under pouring skies, ice-cold and drenched to the skin. The toll from illness—especially among the young troops of Prussia and Austria—was appallingly high.

In and around Teplitz the stench of death and of life, of men and of horses, was all but unbearable. Metternich asked Wilhelmine to find him a little pocket flask to hold vinegar to protect him from the fumes.

The army hospital in Teplitz was filled to overflowing. Every army had its medical and sanitation corps—that of the Austrian Army probably among the best—but medical care was primitive and medical resources woefully inadequate to handle the debris of a great battle.[4]

In the Clary gardens of Teplitz, where only weeks before ladies in summer dresses had strolled and chatted and sipped the beneficent waters, now French prisoners and French wounded lay all about:

pitiful to see [Metternich wrote Marie]—all really children, hardly old enough to be bearing arms. Everything here is filled up with wounded; in the ballroom beyond the garden they do nothing all day but amputate arms and legs.[5]

Often he went to the gardens to talk with French prisoners, one day chanced upon a young man who had kept a toy shop in the rue St. Denis in Paris, where Metternich had often gone to buy toys for his children. The youth had been wounded in the arm, the wound had turned gangrenous; Metternich gave him ten florins to have the arm amputated. Surgery existed chiefly for prisoners who could pay.

If Metternich had hated the idea of war, his first-hand view of battle-fields filled him with undiluted horror:

I detest everything that is war or that even resembles war [he wrote Laure]. To see only dead and dying and cripples, to have to look carefully wherever one walks so as not to step on a corpse, to be deprived of all the pleasures of living—if there were not something exciting in danger itself, I do not know how one could endure all this.[6]

Marie was moved to tears by the story of the young French soldier who had once sold toys to her and her little brother and sister. She shared her father's views on war as on all else:

I was sure you think as I do [she wrote him] that war is a horrible invention. It is unfortunate that everyone doesn't think as we do. We must be going quite against nature, we two, since you say that war is part of human nature.[7]

Among the 150,000 casualties the Allies counted by mid-September was the gifted young poet Theodor Körner, killed by a cannonball at twenty-two, just two weeks after war had been declared. In his pocket when he died was a little green silk-covered notebook filled with scribbled verses. In the very last poem, written on the eve of his death, he addressed his sword as his bride—in the very height of the romantic tradition—and bade her come forth for the wedding of the battle day. Set to music, Körner's "Song of the Sword" would be sung and wept over in parlors that winter wherever German was spoken.

Metternich sent the words and music to Wilhelmine; her mother had been young Körner's godmother.

Metternich and Humboldt debated hotly over Körner's death; their views on war differed radically. Metternich believed the aristocracy of genius was too precious and irreplaceable to be squandered in war.

I wish there were a law [he wrote Laure] that any individual marked by a very superior talent would not be exposed to the fate of battle. Körner, who promised so much, rendered no more service than any clown.[8]

Humboldt thought that death "in a brave and just battle" was an enviable and noble death, that it was every man's duty to fight for his fatherland. "Aeschylus [he wrote his wife, Caroline] would have found it remarkable if one had tried to hinder him from fighting at Marathon." While he grieved for Körner's parents, whom he knew well, ". . . still I can't regret that he went to war, though Metternich has argued again very bitterly with me over it."9

2

In that uneasy month of September, as the Allies reorganized their armies after the Dresden disaster and waited in Teplitz for a French attack, Metternich proceeded with his own business of diplomacy—to clarify Allied war aims, to bring the war to an end as quickly as possible, and to plan ahead for the peace.

Only rarely in history has the apparatus of diplomacy and peacemaking been harnessed directly to the warmaking, as it was in this last phase of the Napoleonic Wars. While cannon blasted away only a half hour from Teplitz, the diplomats of Austria, Prussia, Russia, England met nearly every day, dined together, smoked together, discussed, argued, planned. An Allied military victory might force Napoleon to the negotiating table, Metternich thought. Equally helpful in weakening Napoleon's resolution would be a show of Allied unity, and the prying loose of Napoleon's satellites, especially the German princes of the Rhine Confederation. With all the finesse at his command, Metternich engaged in persuading Bavaria—a powerful Ally of the French, with a well-trained army of 60,000 perched on Austria's western frontier—to join the Coalition against Napoleon.

Even with fighting in progress close by, there was a certain order to daily life at headquarters. Most of the day Metternich worked at his desk with his secretary, Baron Binder. Often he had friends to dine with him, and if the food was more meager and less elegant than in the Ballhaus, still—until the end of the month, when he dispatched his extra equipment and servants back to Vienna—the men sat down to a table set with spotless linen and crested silver.

The curious all-male world of the army encampment fascinated both Metternich and Humboldt. Often in the afternoon they tramped together across the fields to visit one or another of the vast camps that stretched for miles around Teplitz. Often the two argued political matters—especially the future of Germany—but they enjoyed one another's company, could watch fascinated the special way the Cossack soldiers shod their horses, the way they cooked their supper without a pot:

They take a whole unskinned ox's head [Humboldt wrote his wife]
and stick it over the fire. The skin serves as pot—the meat and

brains sizzle away inside. Lebzeltern claims it tastes very good. Certainly the ox head with horns on looks wonderful over the fire.[10]

Metternich struck up a friendship with Hetman Platov, leader of the Cossacks, who gave him one of his finest Cossack horses "that looks infamous but can go twenty leagues in a day." In Prague Gentz complained that instead of replying to his political questions, Metternich wrote "a half-page joke over these disgusting Cossacks, their barbaric general, his damned caviar and dried fish."[11]

In the evening a group often gathered at Metternich's for what Humboldt called the Tobacco Collegium, everyone smoking his favorite pipe and engaging in a free-for-all discussion of military and political prospects.

A new recruit to Metternich's circle of regular companions was the new English ambassador to the court of Austria, twenty-nine-year-old Lord Aberdeen, fresh out of England with injunctions from Castlereagh to keep a watchful eye on Metternich's negotiating tendencies. Within the English Cabinet and in England in general there was great suspicion that Austria was still "soft" on Napoleon, that she was not waging war quite as energetically as England desired.

Gentz, meeting Aberdeen in Prague en route to Teplitz, was not impressed. "Very self-conscious, embarrassed and embarrassing, gloomy, stone-cold-dead . . . an unrefined bear," he pronounced.[12]

But young Aberdeen was neither uncultivated nor a bear, only locked into a posture of stiff reserve by his natural shyness, and the circumstances of his life and upbringing. Of a Scottish noble family, orphaned as a child, Aberdeen had been early initiated into the high councils of the English political scene as a ward of Pitt, had had the good fortune to marry happily for love, only to lose his beautiful young wife to consumption. Very serious, very sensitive, very introverted, young Aberdeen would have preferred poking about unearthing temples in Greece or writing essays on the marvels of classical architecture, to being sent as a diplomat to a post in the very war zone, a hotbed of dissension and intrigue, where even—he wrote home appalled—Metternich and the Austrian Emperor had been sleeping on straw! "I never expected to be in such a scrape," he wrote. "Wretched habitation—no food—the air pestiferous with dead bodies of men and horses—"[13]

He was horrified at the sights and sounds and stench of Teplitz, haunted by the sight "of poor wounded wretches of all nations," on one of his very first days had stumbled "over a great heap of arms and legs which had been thrown out of a summer house in which they had been cut off."[14] Almost at once Aberdeen fell ill of dysentery.

"He may be knowledgeable and interesting," Humboldt wrote of him, "but no one can get anything out of him, so stiff and silent he is."[15] Like most English diplomats, Aberdeen spoke little French and no German.

But Metternich who had learned English in England welcomed him warmly, put him at ease, made his life as comfortable as possible, talked to him with confidence and candor. Aberdeen melted at once under Metternich's charm.

In the tricky power balance within the Coalition itself, Metternich stood desperately in need of English support, for the Tsar and Prussian King could be counted upon to reflect the same views. Aberdeen presently was reflecting Metternich's, and writing glowing accounts of the Austrian minister's prudent and skillful handling of the intricate questions of the day, assuring the English Cabinet of Austria's firm adherence to the Good Cause.

It was easy enough for Aberdeen to learn to hate war; very soon Metternich, in his private conversations with Gentz, could call Aberdeen "a conspirator for peace." When Aberdeen returned to Prague for medical treatment, Gentz was amazed at the change. The young Englishman was quite another man, Gentz wrote Metternich, adding unctuously, "Your sheen is reflected in his face."[16]

The unity of the Coalition—badly splintered by the Dresden defeat and threatened further by continuing dissension over the high command—was welded together more firmly by a trio of pacts signed just after Aberdeen's arrival in Teplitz. Austria, Russia and Prussia promised to guarantee one another's territory, not to sign a separate peace with Napoleon, to re-establish a "fair equilibrium" of power in Europe.

Secret clauses spelled out more precise war aims. Austria and Prussia were to be restored to their pre-Napoleonic strength. Hanover was to be returned to the English Crown. The Rhine Confederation would be dissolved, and "a friendly agreement" reached on the future of Poland. Finally, the "entire and absolute independence" of the various states of Germany was assured.

The Teplitz treaties were intended not only as glue for the unsteady Coalition, but to entice Napoleon to the negotiating table by a show of united strength. Russia and Prussia were already bound to England by treaties, and now Aberdeen and Metternich were to work out a joint agreement.

The Teplitz treaties were followed by a great show of togetherness. Everybody presented everybody else with orders and decorations, there was much mutual embracing and kissing of cheeks. The Tsar presented Metternich with the St. Andrew's Cross in diamonds, which brought nine minor ones in its wake. Humboldt got his share and wrote his wife, "I'll soon be frightfully starred, and Metternich, who claims I'm beginning to glitter most vulgarly, will make even more fun of me."[17]

The Englishmen at headquarters were thoroughly shocked by the levity of the ceremony at which the Tsar got the Order of the Garter, and even more at the indecorous manner in which he proceeded to wear the most august and ancient of British orders—above his army boot, up around his thigh.

But, as Aberdeen observed at once, beneath the surface at headquarters "the ill will and spirit of intrigue" were increasing. "The evils of a divided command," he wrote, "are everywhere apparent," and Schwarzenberg was invested with "scarcely more than nominal authority."[18] The Tsar, pressed by his generals, still yearned for the high command, and Schwarzenberg had not forgiven the cruel accusations the Prussian King had hurled at him after Dresden.

The knotty problem of the future of the German-speaking lands, once they were freed from the yoke of the French, was already a source of dispute among the Allies. The Prussian patriot Baron Stein, who had been at the Tsar's headquarters since June of 1812 and was now in charge of the administration of occupied territories, proposed organizing the principalities and kingdoms into two Germanies, one of the North under Prussia, one in the South under Austria. But his plan entailed a seismic change in the traditional power balance of Central Europe to which Metternich could not agree.

To have Russia swallow up Poland, and Prussia swallow up Saxony was, Metternich felt, an unconscionable threat to the peace of Central Europe. As for the crown of the Holy Roman Empire, which Russia and Prussia offered to restore to the Habsburg Emperor Franz in exchange for their acquisitions, it was not at all an appealing prize in Metternich's estimation.

In spite of deep and troubling disagreements, Metternich was optimistic. "Things will soften down in time," he reassured Aberdeen.

One thing above all troubled Aberdeen: the fact that England's assent to Austria's peace negotiations in Prague had been kept secret from Metternich. Castlereagh had given Aberdeen permission to reveal that assent, but Cathcart had begged him to remain silent, and the Prussians had agreed. The alliance was none too steady as it was—and nobody knew what Metternich would say or do when and if he learned the truth.

3

In Prague Wilhelmine was absorbed heart and soul in the military and political affairs of the day. She had her own sources of news that flowed in daily. Her mother in Switzerland, her sister Dorothée in Paris, relatives and acquaintances in all the armies kept her posted. When she arrived in Prague she had brought Gentz the latest news from the eastern front and Blücher's army, and had informed Metternich that Bavaria was a plum ready for the plucking.

Her generous Courland hospitality meant that her apartment, like the hours in her day, was always crowded to overflowing. Sometimes Gentz, trying to work in neighboring rooms, found the comings and goings annoying. He could not understand how anyone could take such trouble for virtual strangers. He felt himself self-appointed to look after Metternich's interests, and Wilhelmine's friendships with other men he labeled "illegalities" that must be reported to Metternich at once. Besides old Prague acquaintances who congregated in her apartment, several newly arrived Englishmen were paying her court—including Frederick Lamb, third son of Lord

Melbourne, who had come to the Continent as a secretary to Aberdeen and was looking after English affairs in Prague.

There was also a handsome young Russian guards officer, Alexander Mihailovitsch Obreskoff, convalescing from not very serious wounds in Prague, and the dashing and flamboyant Charles Stewart, English ambassador to Prussia and Castlereagh's half brother, who had been wounded in the thigh at Kulm, and was recovering in Prague.

> [The Duchess, Gentz wrote] has so far turned the head of General Stewart—whom she saw for the first time day before yesterday—that he is now planning to stay 14 days longer in Prague. She has gone to such trouble for him that he could not do otherwise. She is dining with him this noon. . . . The only good thing about it is that Obreskoff is very unhappy because she is so much more occupied with Stewart.[19]

Louis Rohan, her first husband, hung about too, hoping Wilhelmine would use her influence with Metternich to get him a commission—preferably as a general or ADC in one of the headquarters. And Fontbrune wanted her to get a post for him too. She had entertained the Tsar, surely she could ask a few favors of him?

Prague wore a very different look now from the cheerful sunny streets of midsummer. Then they had been filled with strollers and sightseers, with fine carriages and bright uniforms. Now into the city limped long files of prisoners, grimy, tattered, often barefoot. And every day more wagonloads of wounded—Russians, Germans, Austrians, French—who were simply dumped unceremoniously at street corners in the hope that a compassionate householder would open a door to them.

Wilhelmine had been horrified at the lack of hospital facilities and set to work at once to do something about it. Already on September 12 she had written Metternich:

> For the love of God, have orders given for the wounded—they are dying in misery; people have to write to the war council to get even a tiny trifle—nobody here wants to take any responsibility for them— they have neither bed nor pallet nor coverlet nor nurses—they are not dying of hunger for we are feeding them. . . .[20]

He had replied at once:

> I shall take care of your hospitals. I've done everything I can to make twenty things run better that are not at all my concern. Those things you speak of will always take preference over everything else; you take an interest only in what is good.[21]

Wilhelmine, who could summon the energy to do anything that involved her brain and heart, immediately began organizing and equipping a hospital to care for several hundred wounded. Nor was she alone in the task. It was one of those moments in history when capable women who had had too little opportunity to make use of their talents came into their own. Gentz's friend Rahel Levin, the Berlin intellectual and admirer of Goethe, raised money from the rich Jewish communities of Berlin and Vienna for clothing, food, medicine, nurses for wounded Prussians. She organized a "Prussian Bureau" in Prague, set up huge kitchens to feed them, oversaw groups of women making lint and bandages, sewing socks and shirts; she herself looked after thirty to forty wounded every day.

Wilhelmine took all nationalities into her hospital, once made the mistake of putting French and Russians too close together:

> A short time ago a frightful noise scared all the attendants in one of the hospitals. They found wounded, cripples, amputees all fighting one another as if they were on a battlefield.[22]

She pressed all her friends into duty as nurses, including Madame Trogoff, who protested that her husband would die if he learned she had to bathe Cossacks, a picture that Metternich found wildly amusing:

> I told Trogoff this morning that his wife is going to see Russians in the costume of Adam—or dressed quite naked, as Marie said to me one day when she was three years old. He appeared to be very affected by it, and I beg you not to hide it from Madame.[23]

Metternich's letters were a delight to Wilhelmine, who looked forward to the courier each day from Teplitz. He asked her to send him Goethe's autobiography *Poetry and Truth,* which had appeared not long before, for he had nothing to read except army bulletins, dictionaries and an atlas. Would she buy or borrow it for him—"and I return books very exactly," he promised. Would she send him too a small reading lamp?—he always read a bit before dropping off to sleep. She ordered a lamp made for him in Prague, of silver, with a pierced silver shade, and sent him the Goethe book, and a velvet cap she herself had made him, and a package of bouillon tablets.

He sent her little gifts—imperial chocolate, which she loved, and for her *menus plaisirs,* an indiscreet letter written by Napoleon's marshal Berthier to his mistress, which had turned up in a bag of captured French mail and had already gone the rounds of headquarters.

Berthier was informing Madame Visconti that his wife appeared to be pregnant again, though he had been on leave only a few hours, and that his children were always beautiful because he concentrated his thoughts on his mistress in the moments of performing the connubial duties.

Wilhelmine asked Metternich for favors too; most of the favors were not for herself; she had fallen into the habit of promising too much to too many people. Could he do something about her promises to Fontbrune? Could he speak to Nesselrode about the payment of her mother's overdue income from Russia?—it was Nesselrode's father-in-law who was responsible for the delay. And there was a French captain in her hospital whose leg had been amputated at the thigh; he could never fight again; could he not be sent home to France?

Metternich did everything she asked. He spoke to the Tsar about her mother's income, and about a job for Fontbrune. If the young amputee was an Austrian prisoner, he would be sent home at once; if he were the prisoner of one of the other armies, Metternich would see what he could do.

In reply to the anguish Metternich had felt over Alfred's visit to her in Prague, she reminded him gently that he had known of her long liaison, that she had kept nothing from him, that he must accept Alfred in her life as if it were a marriage of long standing, just as she accepted the reality of Metternich's marriage:

> . . . there are bonds [she wrote] though not as indissoluble as those contracted before altars—this is the viewpoint with which you must envisage our situation.[24]

Oh yes, he replies, there are such bonds, and well does he know the distinction between the bonds of marriage and of love: "The heart needs no laws because it is stronger than all of them." But she should not cite those bonds as a source of consolation to him. He could not bear the thought of sharing her with anyone. Nor could he bear the thought that she might never return his love in the whole and intense way that he loved her. "Tell me that you love me and that a fatality presides at my destiny."[25]

Sometimes his imagination played with the thought of what life would have been like could he have married her.

The misfortune of their love, he believed, lay in its ill timing. They had simply come to know one another too late—they two, so well matched for one another, so closely linked by natural inclination, by natural bonds of feeling, intelligence, taste, understanding.

> My love, if heaven had favored me by belonging to you in a happier time, our life would have flowed in that kind of quietude that is the prime blessing of this world. You would have fulfilled all my desires— I would not have given you a single cause for pain. I am convinced I would have made you happy and this conviction fills my soul with pride. Your own is so fine, so pure—all the evils of life would have withered under our alliance; my dear, I would have been the happiest being on this earth![26]

One of the strange accidents of the moment brought both Wilhelmine's former husbands into Metternich's orbit. Louis Rohan he had known casually for years, and here he was, salon Bummler par excellence, longing to be touched by a magic wand, even Metternich's magic, and turned into someone important. And husband number two, the tall somber Russian Prince Wassily Troubetskoi, was on the Tsar's own staff in the Teplitz headquarters:

I can't tell you what a strange effect he has on me. I seem to see in him a crazy fool who bought a lottery ticket and carried off the grand prize. Scarcely does he have in his possession what would have made the happiness of any sane, reasonable, intelligent man than he squanders his fortune, and there he is a beggar again.[27]

In the Teplitz headquarters, meantime, plans were being made for large-scale operations against the French. It was evident they would soon be leaving Bohemia. Metternich had to see Wilhelmine before the campaign took him farther away from Prague.

Gentz borrowed rooms in an inconspicuous rear courtyard of the Fürstenberg Palace, not far from the Waldstein, and left directions with the watch at the city gate so that Metternich might preserve his incognito.

On September 20, a Monday, Metternich drove to Prague, sharing his carriage with Paul Esterházy and Giroux.

Again, as at Laun, the brief two days were a joyously happy reunion with her, hours that he counted "among the best in my life."

On Tuesday morning as soon as he was awake he sent Giroux with a tiny note across the street to Wilhelmine's apartment:

I am still here; I shall leave tonight after Louis' supper party. Please invite me for lunch, offer me dinner, let me come to you this morning around 10:30 or 11, let yourself be tormented and wearied by me, let me write you a great deal, and love me a little bit! These are my modest plans for the day which I love already since it promises chances of seeing you.[28]

The day finished with a merry supper party at Louis Rohan's that lasted until after midnight, a lucullan meal ending with an exquisite kirsch that Gentz termed "not only the most perfect kirsch the world has ever seen but the first of all earthly liqueurs." At one in the morning, Metternich, Paul and Giroux climbed into the carriage for the twelve-hour ride back to Teplitz. Waving them off, Wilhelmine laughed at the funny little low-slung inelegant carriage Metternich had bought for the campaign.

Still in a glow of pleasure Metternich wrote her the day after his return to headquarters:

Here I am again in the midst of cannon, disaster, mud, horror, far from all happiness, from everything I love. . . .

Have you been laughing for one small moment with all your heart as I saw you laughing only twenty-four hours ago? *Dieu, mon amie,* how clearly you are here before me, beautiful, good as you truly are, repaying me by a single look for twenty years of unhappiness. . . .[29]

Wilhelmine's letter after their September meeting in Prague was different in tone. She had been, she wrote, "in a mortal sadness," had had bad dreams the night before, which always seemed to her a presentiment of evil. "I have such a superstitious heart." And then the real anxiety broke through the lines of her letter:

> Don't you know where Windischgraetz is? Trogoff writes me nothing of it. To what corps does his regiment belong, and where is it right now? I beg you to inform me very exactly.[30]

At once Metternich's joyful spirits were crushed, his confidence and peace of mind vanished. "I think I have caught your sadness," he wrote her.

At the end of a long day's work he sat in his makeshift office at two in the morning, as he would often find himself doing in the months to come:

> Don't think, dear, that I will tax you for not having real feeling for me. . . . I never claimed to be loved; I never conceived that I could be —I've always been happy *to be able to love.*

He did think that Alfred's once flagging devotion to her had been sparked into new life by jealousy of Metternich's attentions:

> You are more to the lucky man (whom I don't envy, for that sentiment is beneath my heart) since I've loved you than you were before—I have myself forged the arms that are being used against me. . . .
> Don't worry about W. The armies are on the march, but there are no indications of a battle happening soon—This war could lead us to the Rhine without risking anything but fatigue.[31]

4

On September 27, the week after Metternich's visit to Prague, the Russian Guards gave a great festival in honor of the anniversary of the Tsar's coronation. All the Allied officers and ministers were invited to a banquet in an outdoor hall the Guard troops had built out of fir and evergreen.

The three sovereigns, in their dress uniforms and diamond-studded orders, sat side by side at the head table, surrounded by their leading generals and ministers. There was caviar in abundance; vodka and wine flowed; choruses from all three armies sang folk and marching songs. Even one small crisis—when the improvised kitchen caught fire and it looked for some moments as if the distinguished guests would have to flee—did not dampen the spirits. The wind changed in time and the banquet proceeded. Everyone ate and drank a great deal, talked and laughed and told stories in several languages, as pretty a scene of good spirits and brotherly understanding as possibly could have been staged on the boards of the Court Theater in Vienna.

And indeed the Guards' banquet did appear to mark a new phase of better feeling among the Allied leaders.

Schwarzenberg, who had written so bitterly to his wife of the feuding and infighting over the high command, wrote his dear Nani a day or so before the banquet:

I have won against Alexander. His confidence increases according to the success of our military efforts.[32]

Even more effusively had Metternich reassured his Laure—not, of course, without the thought of providing her with the proper information to scatter abroad in Viennese society: "We all live here like brothers despite what they are saying in Vienna. There is only one cabinet and I find myself at the head of it."[33]

In actual fact the banquet was something of a miracle, and Allied harmony had come dangerously close to shipwreck only a day or two before the festival.

Six weeks had passed since the courier from London had reached Allied headquarters shortly before the armistice ended, bringing word that the English Cabinet would agree to take part in peace negotiations. Instead of peace, war had been declared, battles had been fought, thousands had died—and Metternich, originator and designer of the peace attempt, had not yet been told of England's assent.

Aberdeen had wanted to inform Metternich of the truth from the day of his arrival. He found it embarrassing to be treated with such friendly frankness by the Austrian minister when so critical a diplomatic decision had deliberately been kept secret from him by his Allies. The Russian, Prussian and Swedish sovereigns and their ministers and aides all were in on the secret; sooner or later it would certainly come to Metternich's ears.

On September 25 Aberdeen finally informed Metternich. England had been willing to join negotiations in Prague, but the Castlereagh dispatch had been kept secret from him. Aberdeen was astonished at the composure with which Metternich received the news. He exhibited "some surprise," but there was no explosive scene; Metternich continued to be "as cordial and as confidential" as ever with the shy young Englishman. "I think this man must be honest," Aberdeen wrote Castlereagh, "yet it may be, after all, that he is only a most consummate actor."[34]

Sir Robert Wilson, an insider at both Russian and Prussian headquarters, as Aberdeen was not, discussed with the King of Prussia Metternich's anger and displeasure "at the concealment of England's acceptance of the Congress proposition. The King admitted it was done from a fear of its influencing the Austrians to protract negotiations."

The fact is [Wilson wrote] that Metternich is justly furious at this deceit; and it was a want of candour for which I fear he will one day or another pay the Allies in their own coin *with interest*.[35]

As Wilson discerned, Metternich's temperament was not the kind to burst into a noisy rage, as Napoleon or the Tsar would have done. Metternich's was the anger of ice, often suppressed for a long period, but hard, unyielding, unforgotten below the surface.

Bitterly must he have turned over in his mind in those last days of September how costly had been the termination of his Prague negotiations. In a single month the Allies counted some 150,000 casualties.

To have been so close perhaps to peace! The Russians and Prussians had made a joke of the Prague Congress, had declared that Napoleon would never negotiate. And Napoleon had said repeatedly that he would negotiate if the English would join in the congress. And England would have joined—

But all that was now too late. One could not change what had happened. Metternich made an enormous effort to carry on as before for the sake of the Alliance. Whatever scenes he had with the Tsar and the Prussian King, with Hardenberg and Nesselrode remained the best-kept secret of his life. In his *Memoirs* Metternich says nothing of the deception practiced on him in the closing days of the Congress of Prague—a failed peace congress that might have succeeded. Metternich's "will of iron for maintaining good harmony," of which Nesselrode wrote his wife, was bent but not broken.

In those days toward the close of September, while Metternich took his place at Schwarzenberg's side in the councils of war, so that Wilson called him "the real commander," the idea of peace was never out of Metternich's mind. For a long time—during the spring months and early summer of 1813—he had probably been the most unpopular man in Austria. But the dignity and firmness with which he had conducted the negotiations in the summer, his steadfastness in supporting Schwarzenberg, had won him a consensus in Austria. Wilson wrote at this time:

> Count Metternich does not conceal his choice for peace, nor do the Austrians. . . . Before the war he stood almost single; now he is sustained by the army and nation.[36]

But when Napoleon, in an effort to separate Austria from her Allies, offered to turn over to his father-in law the fortress of Zamość on the Galician frontier between Poland and Austria—a fortress still held by the French but under siege by the Russians—Metternich drafted the polite letter of refusal that went out to Dresden by special courier. "Your Majesty cannot doubt the wish I cherish for peace," he wrote in the Emperor's name, adding that the peace must be a lasting one, not one that led to new conflicts.[37]

Metternich, however, believed the Allies should listen to any genuine proposal Napoleon made that might lead to peace, that nothing could be lost by negotiation. He hoped another congress might be arranged—and soon. Aberdeen, reporting Metternich's sentiments to Castlereagh, wrote:

[Metternich] thought that we should never refuse to treat . . . that, as a good peace was the sole end of the war, it was indifferent by what means it was obtained.[38]

But the Prince Regent and Castlereagh, determined now to wage an all-out war against Napoleon and the French, did not want to listen to talk of peace. Aberdeen must urge Metternich to prosecute the war more vigorously, must do more to arouse a truly warlike spirit in Austria:

It appears [Castlereagh wrote in reply] as if [Metternich's] ears could hardly bear the sound of war, and that he is disposed rather to whisper than to din it into the ears of the nation.

I wish I could see the Austrian minister rely more on exertion and less upon negotiation.[39]

5

"The storm, my dear, is in the offing; it is growing larger and will soon explode," Metternich wrote Wilhelmine as the armies prepared to move.[40]

Metternich came to Prague on October 4 for a last visit, bringing gifts of chocolate and Russian caviar. He stayed again incognito in rooms in the Fürstenberg Palace, where she could visit him quite easily, and the October days were as sweet in his memory as the two stolen meetings in September:

the joy of having seen you again, of being able to tell you that I adore you—the joy above all of having found you again an angel of goodness —of having heard you give me the assurances that are engraved even more deeply in my heart than your image . . .[41]

She listened with eager absorption to all the latest political news, and learned with joy that her prophecy of early September had come true: Bavaria was all but won for the Coalition. Moreover, Metternich told her, there was a chance that both Denmark and Naples might swing to the Allied camp—despite the fact that Murat had led Napoleon's cavalry at the battle of Dresden.

His urgent political business in Prague in October included secret meetings with both the Danish ambassador, Count Bernstorff, and with the envoy Cariati, whom Caroline Murat had dispatched to him from Naples.

In Prague too he talked at length with Baron vom Stein about the future of the German-speaking lands, but they could reach no agreement. Stein had wanted to see written into the Treaty of Ried with Bavaria a clause that insured the future unification of Germany. Bavaria declined those terms, and Metternich agreed.

On the evening of October 5, when Wilhelmine had intended to come to his rooms "to bid him good night," she had to dispatch a servant to him with a tiny note of apology, for her maid Hannchen had chosen that moment to give birth, in the rooms in the Waldstein Palace, with Wilhelmine playing midwife. Next day Wilhelmine could inform him that both Hannchen and her little girl were doing well, and that she hoped to see him, on condition that even though he pardoned Stein from hanging, he would pronounce "an eternal anathema" against Stein's ideas and share her scorn "of those miserably sick Prussians."

On that last visit to Prague he went with Wilhelmine on her hospital rounds, walked through the rooms with her while she looked to see that all was in order, spoke with each of her patients in his own language. Metternich was amazed at what the women in Prague had done to provide care for the wounded and sick. He wrote Marie:

> There is no middle-class family which is not caring for sick and wounded at their own expense. Women of the first society are working in the hospitals. Countess Schlik, Countess Clam, Madame de Sagan have each founded and equipped whole hospitals to care for two to three hundred wounded, fed out of their own kitchens.[42]

He remembered her afterward as he watched her that day:

> . . . good, entirely good, compassionate, honoring yourself and your sex. If ever I am sick I will go to your hospital. I think your presence would cure a good part of the world.[43]

There were complications, to be sure, in the fervor with which Wilhelmine fulfilled her compassionate duties. For one thing, all the young officers in her care fell madly in love with her. One of her patients, the handsome young Russian officer Obreskoff, only slightly wounded and quite able to follow her about, bragged a bit loudly about the ministrations of his beautiful duchess. It came to Wilhelmine's ears that the officers at Russian headquarters in Teplitz were joking about Obreskoff's conquest of his lovely nurse, and it made her furious:

> I detest gossip. I never gossip about anyone, why should I be persecuted with such sour stupidities?[44]

She complained to Metternich, worrying lest such idle talk come to the Tsar's ears, whose good opinion she most devoutly courted. Metternich replied that he had warned her "not to protect young officers of the Guard, even if they are more severely wounded than your friend Obreskoff," for evil-minded people would always find a way to misinterpret her tender offices of mercy.[45]

When he bade her good-by on that Friday morning of October 8, 1813, it would be for an absence of many months. Army headquarters had already moved from Teplitz to Komotau; they were preparing to cross the Giant Mountains into Saxony again on the first lap of a long march that would take them across the breadth of Europe.

Bavaria had definitely joined the Coalition; he found the signed treaty awaiting him at headquarters and he could crow: "The conquest of Bavaria

is so completely my work that everyone who was involved in the affair—
all without exception—vowed the thing impossible!"[46] Aberdeen agreed that
Metternich should get full credit for that highly important event; at the
precise right moment, just when negotiations were slowing down and the
Bavarian minister Montgelas was applying delaying tactics—to see who
would win the next battle—Metternich sent word to his representative, Prince
Reuss, "not to protract the negotiations beyond 24 hours." The Bavarians
had signed.[47]

Many months later he looked back on the moment of his farewell to her
in Prague:

> When I think of the last moment I saw you. I came into Gentz's
> apartment. I told you that I would not see you again for some time—
> that we were going to cross the frontier—that we were preparing to
> take the offensive—What things and events since that time until the
> time when I shall press your hand again for the first time . . .[48]

XI

LEIPZIG:
BATTLE OF THE NATIONS

1

In the cold, wet days of early October, with the frosty breath of winter in the air, Napoleon could not make up his mind what to do.

His officers urged him to leave Saxony, to withdraw his army to the Rhine, make winter quarters near Mainz, where they would be among friends, where food would be plentiful, where one might even take leave now and again in the most blessed of all cities, Paris. His young recruits were weary from long marches on short rations. Men and horses had fallen sick. Typhus had taken a heavy toll. "The truth is," wrote his secretary, Fain, of those days, "the top generals wanted only peace, and would have bought it at any price."[1]

In France itself morale had never been lower. Would the long chain of wars never come to an end? It was true there had been few complaints while Napoleon was gaining victories; now the tale was different. A wagon-load of mail en route from France to Napoleon's army was captured by the Allies and published in the Austrian press. From Paris a mother wrote her son: "Two years in such a torment—it's beyond human strength." A general's wife wrote her husband: "*Mon cher ami*, think seriously of retiring. We need a little peace and we've never had any!" A wife recited the latest casualty lists: "If this goes on, everyone will be dead. Those who escape one campaign die in the next."[2]

At last, on October 7, Napoleon left Dresden with the King and Queen of Saxony, went first to Meissen, then to Düben, a few miles northwest of Leipzig. At first his generals thought the French Emperor was gathering his armies together to withdraw in safety to the Rhine. Instead, to their great chagrin, he began to talk of a grand new strategy. He would maneuver along the Elbe between Dresden and Magdeburg, using Magdeburg as the center of his operations; he had strong garrisons and plenty of supplies in the fortresses of Torgau and Wittenberg; he would retake Berlin; in the spring he would launch a new offensive—against Austria this time, for the Prussians and Russians would be finished. He had already ordered a new troop conscription in France.

In Düben, shut up in a little room in a moated castle, he remained from October 11 until the fourteenth sitting in silence most of the time on a sofa beside a large table on which his maps were spread out, with a heap of blank paper in front of him on which he doodled listlessly hour after hour. From time to time Berthier or Ney would come in and venture to argue about his plans. Once Berthier showed him a note he had got from Munich reporting with virtual certainty the defection of Bavaria. Napoleon waved it aside. Impossible! His generals redoubled their efforts, urging him to withdraw while there was yet time, before the rest of the Rhine Confederation had defected and taken arms against him.

Only when news came that Blücher was across the Elbe and moving down toward Leipzig from the north, while Schwarzenberg's vast Bohemian Army approached the city from the south, did Napoleon spring into action. Quickly he summoned his marshals to Leipzig; there was not a moment to lose. He would use his favorite old tactic of divide and conquer; he would meet his enemies separately while there was yet time, defeat them one by one, Schwarzenberg first, then Blücher.

A thunderbolt alone could save us [Napoleon said later on St. Helena]. Nothing was lost so long as I had the chance of a battle—a single victory could give us back the north as far as Danzig.[3]

He could not, simply could not, surrender his old dream of European conquest.

He issued orders for Augereau, Marmont, Murat, for Reynier and Bertrand. His staff was delighted to move into action. Leipzig was already on the road back to France!

It had been Blücher's idea to launch an immense pincer operation against the Grande Armée, closing in on it from the north, the northeast and the south. More than one reason pushed the Allies to decisive action. Winter was approaching; forage and food in eastern Bohemia and elsewhere were exhausted; it would be impossible to keep the armies encamped much longer in the Teplitz Valley. At the end of September great news had arrived: the Russian General Chernyshëv had taken Cassel, capital of Napoleon's kingdom of Westphalia, whose puppet King, Jérôme, Napoleon's brother, had fled. Most importantly, on the first of October, to the joy of Metternich and the Allied generals, Bennigsen reached Teplitz at the head of 60,000 reserve troops from the area of Breslau. Now the signal for the march into Saxony was given.

In the first week of October Schwarzenberg led his Bohemian Army across the mountains. Everywhere the French army fell back before their advance—fell back on Leipzig.

The great trade center of middle Europe, largest city in Saxony, Leipzig lay in a shallow marshy valley at the junction of three rivers, an old walled town whose fairs each year since the Middle Ages had drawn merchants from the whole known world.

Napoleon deployed his army now in a great circle around the city, with the heaviest concentration of forces on a low ridge five miles to the southeast to meet the main thrust of Schwarzenberg's army.

By the evening of October 15 Schwarzenberg's forces were in place in an immense half-circle facing inward toward the French, while Blücher's Prussians ringed in the French to the northwest. Bernadotte, who should have closed the ring on the northeast, had not yet arrived; he was disinclined to engage in battle if he could possibly avoid it. "The Crown Prince will cooperate or not, that remains to be seen," Schwarzenberg wrote to Nani on the eve of battle, adding that it was a sad truth fortune often favored the loudmouths of the world.[4]

Very early on the cold misty morning of October 16 a blast of Austrian cannon signaled the attack. The light snow that had already fallen in Saxony had changed again to dreary intermittent rain.

In the heroic paintings and lithographs of the battle of Leipzig that adorned the walls of homes and schoolrooms all over Central Europe in the early nineteenth century, like beguiling recruiting posters, the sun sparkles on gaudy uniforms, on polished boots, jeweled medals, flashing swords.

But eyewitnesses who wrote immediately after the battle remembered rather an immense spectacle of human insanity as a half million men grappled over a few square miles of muddy, bloody ground. Those immense masses of men who fought at Leipzig—far too many for either the naked eye or for the imagination to encompass—would have populated two cities the size of Vienna in 1813. There they were, 500,000 human beings engaged in slaughtering one another, men who, except for a crazy combination of circumstances—economic, political, psychological—who yet knows why?—might have been home, wherever home was, making shoes, measuring cloth, tilling fields, hoisting sails.

"I have seen many armies," wrote Napoleon's secretary, Fain, "but never so many under arms. It was a combat of giants. What could I see that day? Nothing but a tableau of vast carnage."[5]

Despite the disparity of numbers on the two opposing sides—more than 300,000 Allies pitted against 190,000 French—the battle was intense, ferocious and very close. All day long there were charges and countercharges. Advancing columns of men dissolved under murderous onslaughts of hurled lead and mortar. The tiny outlying villages—Gülden Gossa, Markkleeberg, Gross Pössna, where days before shepherds and plowmen had gone peacefully to bed, were wrested first by one side, then by the other. "Never did I see a more horrible battlefield," Schwarzenberg wrote a night or two later.[6]

The battle stopped when night fell on October 16. No one was victor. The still living, themselves half dead, stunned with exhaustion, deafened by cannon blasts, dragged themselves back to their camps. Each side counted some 20,000 lost on that first day.

In the total confusion of smoke, rain, infernal noise, mingling of troops on foot and on horse, there had been the usual accidents of identity on the battlefield. The Austrian General Merveldt, a man in his sixties and quite nearsighted—was leading a cavalry attack and thought he had Prussians beside him when he found himself in the midst of French cavalry, was unhorsed and taken prisoner.

The next day, October 17, a Sunday, there was a lull. Nobody fought. And on that Sunday Napoleon talked a long time with Merveldt about the possibility of an armistice.

The two men were not strangers. They had first met across the peace table at Leoben in 1797, when—according to Caulaincourt—Merveldt tried to lure the rising young Corsican into joining Austrian service. The two had met again at Campoformio, and again on the night of Austerlitz, when it was Merveldt who had scribbled a note to Napoleon asking for truce.

Now, eight years later, a stout man in a soiled uniform, his face lined with fatigue and discouragement, Napoleon sounded out Merveldt on the possibility of an armistice. It was Merveldt who broke the shattering news to Napoleon that Bavaria had indeed switched sides and joined the Allies. Napoleon was incredulous; he could not believe it until Merveldt swore on his word of honor. The next morning, Monday, October 18, Merveldt was sent back to the Austrian commander with Napoleon's offer of armistice.

The cannon of the Allies had already reopened the battle. "We will talk peace with him when he is back on the Rhine," Metternich wrote Laure that night.[7]

The silent hours of October 17 had given the Allies a priceless advantage. Crown Prince Bernadotte, who had deftly delayed his arrival—probably in the hope the battle would be over—now joined the ring of armies that had drawn a noose around the French. Moreover, Bennigsen and Colloredo had arrived with thousands of fresh troops. Napoleon had none.

The French had already drawn back closer to the city, so that the Allied sovereigns, with Metternich and their aides, watched the battle from a hill crest ridge near the village of Probstheida, where Napoleon's Guard had fought two days before. Gradually, by sheer force of numbers, the Allies drove the French in ever nearer the city walls. By early afternoon both Saxon and Württemberg troops who had been fighting for the French, went over to the Allies. As the afternoon wore on the French found their ammunition nearly exhausted, their supply and communications lines cut. Only one escape route still remained in French hands—the bridge over the Elster and the road to the west.

By nightfall the French had given up, swarmed pell-mell into the city of Leipzig. At eight that night, sitting on his folding camp chair, by the light of a bivouac fire, Napoleon dictated orders for retreat. By two in the morning the retreat had begun, all that remained of the army of children Napoleon had pulled together and drilled in midsummer on the fields outside Dresden —disheveled, weary, tattered remnants—hastening in wild confusion across the single precious bridge, in the wake of the French Emperor himself. Unluckily the bridge was blown up by mistake before more than two thirds of the fleeing army were across. Polish Marshal Poniatowski—who had enjoyed his marshal's baton for less than three days—drowned, along with many others, trying to swim the swollen Elster.

From his quarters in Rötha just south of Leipzig at eleven that night Metternich wrote Wilhelmine: "Alfred is well, my dear, and we have won the battle of the world."[8]

The next day Metternich rode with the sovereigns into the devastated city.

On the great open fields where the battle had been fought the dead lay everywhere, as far as the eye could see, in every kind of frightful and macabre mutilation—

half or quite naked [Humboldt wrote], stretched out face down, as Homer described them, gripping the earth with their teeth. In one place a dog ran about searching for his master.[9]

Two days later, on October 21, when Aberdeen crossed the battlefield at Metternich's side, he was stunned by the sight of that vast panorama of death:

For three or four miles the ground is covered with bodies of men and horses, many not dead. Wretched wounded unable to crawl, crying for water amidst heaps of putrefying bodies. Their screams are heard at an immense distance and still ring in my ears.[10]

Wounded and dead lay everywhere in the streets of Leipzig, where they had dragged themselves looking for help, or been abandoned. The horses of the monarchs entering in triumph had to pick their way carefully among the bodies. In the narrow streets of the old town wagons and carriages clattered past dead and dying, while Cossacks on horseback prodded hordes of French prisoners along "like a herd of cattle," wrote Humboldt, "a singular drama."

Humboldt saw a French soldier whose leg had been cut off trying to move with a stick of wood he had picked up. Where was he going? Anywhere. Nowhere. In St. Thomas Church hundreds of French wounded huddled untended, and before the church the dead were piled up "like an enormous heap of old clothes."[11]

2

Over Prague and Vienna in those days of mid-October lay the hush of immense anxiety and fear. Everyone knew a great battle was impending or in progress; everyone had someone—a husband, a brother, a father, a son— who would be in danger. And who could tell what would happen? People hardly dared hope for victory. Weight of numbers was on the Allied side, but when had gross numbers meant anything to the old magician Napoleon, who could pull success out of an empty hat, as he had at Bautzen and Lützen?

On October 17 Wilhelmine wrote Metternich, imploring him to send news. There had been no couriers for days; she was frightfully anxious despite her confidence "in God and you and in all you tell me."

To add to the suspense, a dispatch from Hardenberg reached Prague, written at the end of the first day's battle, October 16, when the outcome of Leipzig was still uncertain. After that—no word, nothing. People flocked to Gentz's rooms—he was known now as the Oracle of Prague—but he had nothing to tell anyone. He was annoyed and angry to be kept so long in suspense. He had had no word at all from Austrian headquarters; they might at least have confided the plan of battle to him! October 20 passed with no further news at all.

Somewhat testily Gentz wrote Pilat that evening:

> If the count has won a battle, then we shall have to worship his star just like the one that led the Kings of the East to Bethlehem.[12]

Of late Metternich had taken to talking a bit too Napoleonically about his precious star.

Later that evening of October 20, Wilhelmine sent a servant across to Gentz with a tiny note:

> I don't want to bother you, only tell me before you go to sleep what you make of this terrible silence.[13]

Gentz did not answer. For the love of God, he knew no more than she did! He went to bed instead.

An hour or so after midnight Metternich's courier Panoni pulled up before the Waldstein Palace and awoke Gentz with news of the great victory at Leipzig. Hurriedly he scribbled a note to Wilhelmine that silence was a happy state—almost as blessed as winning the battle of Leipzig! It was a "heavenly moment" for both of them:

> What happiness it is to be alive to enjoy such moments [Gentz wrote]. I stayed up the rest of the night, wrote my Extra, wrote countless letters telling the news, went to bed at 5 in the morning.[14]

... I believe now in Your Excellency as in the Delphic oracle, even when I don't quite get all you're saying. . . . The doubts of the duchess, always greater than mine, are beginning to melt like ice before the sun. Just between ourselves, the way you are now being worshiped is simply indescribable.[15]

If Gentz's words were sweet to Metternich's ears, Wilhelmine's were balm to his heart. She wrote to him as if Leipzig were his personal victory; she was happier, she declared, than she had ever been in her life.

In Vienna too everyone had waited in an agony of anxiety for news of the outcome of the battle. General Neipperg had been sent to carry official news of the victory to Vienna. He arrived on October 23, and the whole city went wild with rejoicing:

What a crowd! What shouting! [Marie wrote her father]. The poor man himself was so moved the tears coursed from his one eye. People threw themselves in his passage, kissed his spurs and his uniform. He made a little speech from Marshal Bellegarde's balcony, very touching and noble. He could barely speak for emotion.[16]

As for Laure, her joy "approached insanity," she wrote—an unusual state for cool and collected Laure:

God be praised and eternally blest for such good and excellent news! My room has not been empty since yesterday. Everyone attributes the whole glory of the success to you.[17]

Neipperg dined with Laure Metternich on the day of his arrival—with Lory Fuchs and Pauline Hohenzollern among the guests. Bottle after bottle of champagne was emptied drinking toasts, "yours at the head," Laure proudly wrote her husband. "We were at table until 8 o'clock"—a meal five hours long. It was a lovely day for Laure.

The victors of course had their rewards. There was another great shower of stars and orders. On the Leipzig battlefield Emperor Franz had pinned the Great Cross of Maria Theresia on Schwarzenberg's breast; only seven men in the empire wore that proudest symbol of courage.

Emperor Franz was not quite so quick about rewarding Metternich. Only after Schwarzenberg had prompted him, proposing that he do something nice and appropriate for "this faithful, clever servant of the state," did the Emperor call Metternich to him on the morning of October 27 and inform him he was making him a prince.[18] His father had been a prince since 1804, when the Emperor needed his potential vote in the Reichstag, but the title would not have passed to Metternich until his father's death.

The Emperor pre-dated the official citation back to October 20, "to bring it closer to the *great day*," Metternich informed Wilhelmine.

One morning in early November the solemn Hudelist climbed the stairs from the Chancellery offices in Vienna up to the Metternich apartments to announce that the whole family now wore an exalted new title. Not every day was a family turned into princes and princesses by the Emperor's magic wand. Hudelist reported the happy scene in a letter that was for him a remarkably emotional document:

> In a trice they were all thrown into the most joyful uproar. The Frau Fürstin—Madame Princess—was very excited, and her first thought was to call Victor to her, who appeared to take much pleasure in his new title. His elder sister Marie wept and could not speak through her sobs. The two younger children jumped happily about the room; such a scene would surely have been the greatest reward the father could have had, had he been able to witness it.[19]

The event provided Metternich with one of his favorite Giroux anecdotes. Years later he still loved to tell the story of how his valet appeared at his bedside the day after he had been made a prince, to inquire gravely and politely:

> Will Your Serene Highness put on the same suit Your Excellency wore yesterday?[20]

XII

✦

WINTRY PAUSE:
PEACE TRY IN FRANKFURT

*When then will men leave off murdering and mangling one
another? . . . Then I shall be with you and stay with you.*
—SCHWARZENBERG TO HIS WIFE,
NOVEMBER 18, 1813[1]

1

Miraculously, after Leipzig Napoleon himself escaped with a large part
of his army. Hastening across Saxony and Thuringia, scavenging food where
they could find it in unfriendly country, burning bridges behind them, sleeping with one eye open for pursuing Cossacks, the French struggled to reach
Erfurt, where Napoleon had stores of munitions, where the broken remnants
of his army could be hastily reformed and rearmed.

The Allies hoped to overtake and annihilate the remains of the now less
than Grand Army, but the pursuit was hopelessly bungled. Orders were misunderstood, commanders took wrong routes—and nobody hurried as fast as
the French, fleeing for their lives. At first only hours behind, soon the pur-
suers were a day, two days behind.

At the gates of Hanau, near Frankfurt, Napoleon found his way blocked
by his former ally Bavaria, with an army of 40,000 under Wrede. The French
blasted their way through in a bloody two-day battle. By early November
Napoleon was across the Rhine, by November 9, in Paris. Behind him strag-
gled some 56,000 exhausted men—perhaps a quarter of the fresh young
troops who had crossed the Rhine in spring to battle for whatever strange
reasons men do battle on foreign soil.

In Paris Napoleon at once stepped up conscription, calling up a new army of teen-aged boys, and a land army of older men. He had performed a miracle the year before in squeezing another army out of France; he would repeat the magic and have 500,000 men again under his eagles by spring!

Dogging the heels of the French on their headlong flight across Germany that autumn had been that other enemy more deadly than the Cossacks: typhus.

Along the roadways of Germany Napoleon's men had dropped in their tracks. They went to sleep in peasant huts and awoke too ill to stir. At night, wherever little troops of men huddled around campfires against the frost of late October, by morning six or seven or ten lay dead by the ashes of the burnt-out fire.

It was so the Allies came upon them—"every ten paces another corpse," Metternich wrote.

Nobody knew how the deadly typhus was contracted, or guessed that it spread through body lice; they noted only that it appeared wherever men crowded together in filth; the English commonly called it "jail fever" or "hospital fever." Rampant that autumn in the French army, it spread quickly to the civilian population, and presently appeared in the other armies as well.

In the isolated fortresses along the Elbe and the Oder, still garrisoned by French troops, some 80,000 in all—abandoned by Napoleon in his flight back to France—typhus took a terrible toll.

Louis Narbonne, former ambassador to Austria, that charming, frivolous leftover of the old Versailles court, with his great Bourbon nose and his talent for love and conversation, commanded the fort of Torgau. He had been sent there by Napoleon at the end of the Prague Congress as a kind of punishment for having, in the closing days of the congress, spoken too strongly for peace, and for having lost Austria as an ally.

It was a difficult post. Food was scarce for the garrison of 26,000; many of them, veterans of Dennewitz, were barefoot and in rags. Just before the Leipzig battle Napoleon had loaded 6,000 sick men from Dresden onto barges and shipped them down the Elbe to Torgau. The death toll from typhus, already high, soared at a fantastic rate.

Toward the middle of November Narbonne himself became ill. Dutifully he tried to make his rounds as commander, toppled off his horse one day and died of a fractured skull. His body was buried under the walls of Torgau; his horses had to be sold to pay for the funeral. When Torgau surrendered later that year only a pitiful garrison of perhaps 9,000 men remained—some 17,000 had died of typhus. Narbonne's old friend Captain Rohan-Chabot carried his heart back to Paris.

In the wake of Napoleon's army that October, and behind the pursuing armies of the Allies, followed the long caravan of carriages carrying ministers and diplomats, secretaries, servants, baggage, from Leipzig to Frankfurt, where the new headquarters were to be established.

Traveling was precarious and exhausting. Deeply rutted roads had turned stone-hard with frost; horses stumbled and carriages overturned. A regiment of Hungarian Guards had to precede the civilian group, to throw together bridges of rafts and boats over streams where there was no crossing, to level precarious ascents in the mountains and lay fascines across swamps. Sometimes the ministers slept in the grand rooms of a ducal palace; sometimes behind the village butcher shop. More than once several titled diplomats of assorted nationalities shared a single wretched room in a stinking inn filled to the brim with sick and dying French soldiers.

Most of the time Metternich, Aberdeen and Merveldt kept one another company, riding together the ten-hour daily stint on horseback, their carriages following, sharing the hazards of the journey and dining together at the end of the day. "In such good society one forgets the fatigues that are past," Aberdeen wrote.[2] For the stench and the danger of infection there was nothing except to wear "quantities of camphor," keep one's vinegar bottle close at hand to sniff, and at night burn sulphur powder to purify the sleeping rooms.

All along the roadsides lay the dead, stripped already of their clothing by the peasants, and soon after of their flesh by crows.

> I do not know [wrote Aberdeen] when I have felt more severely the wretchedness of mankind. . . . I pray God we may be near to a termination of these horrors. It is said that Bonaparte himself is inclined to peace; if this be really so we shall have no difficulty.[3]

Village after village they came upon, pillaged and burnt, not a cow, not a chicken, not a scrap of food left, women standing by the ruins weeping, children running merrily about as if their homes had not burned down before their eyes. The French were, of course, no better, no worse than other armies, but in their hunger and despair all discipline had broken down.

In a letter to his wife Metternich described a vivid little encounter:

> Yesterday walking beside my carriage on a sandy strip of road I chanced upon a pile of dead. Suddenly a body half raised itself from the heap and said, "Mon Dieu, Monsieur, don't you have a tiny bit of bread?"
>
> I asked if he were wounded. No, he had been sleeping for five days in a woods nearby with a broken arm. He had neither eaten nor drunk in five days.
>
> I return to my carriage, which had gone on a hundred or more paces up the road. I fetch bread and a bottle of wine. I come back. The man is dead.[4]

As they jogged along the wretched roads on horseback and sat together at an inn table by candlelight, Metternich, Aberdeen and Merveldt talked over the possibilities for peace. The French were all but out of Germany. Surely now the aim of the Coalition had been attained.

When Napoleon had sent Merveldt back to the Allied commander on the second day of the Leipzig battle with a request for an armistice, they had sent no reply. Now Metternich considered how best to frame a reply, and by what means to dispatch it.

In Weimar Metternich learned from the Duke that the former French ambassador to the ducal court, Baron St. Aignan, brother-in-law of Caulaincourt and like Caulaincourt eager to serve the cause of peace, had been taken prisoner by Austrian troops against all the rules of diplomatic immunity and was being sent to Prague. Metternich ordered him released and transported by the quickest means to Frankfurt, where he would make him a special emissary to Napoleon. The whole negotiation could be done quietly and without fanfare since St. Aignan would be journeying back to France in any case.

For all sorts of reasons peace seemed to be the first order of business.

The Austrian Army was in scarcely better case than the French. Schwarzenberg implored Metternich to use his influence to get shoes and warm clothing for his men. The paper money with which they had been paid would buy nothing; shopkeepers everywhere refused it.

Moreover, as Sir Robert Wilson urged, it was essential to make peace before the fragile Coalition split apart entirely.

Scarcely off the battlefield of Leipzig, with victory in their hands, the Allies had begun to dispute about the spoils. How the German-speaking countries liberated from Napoleon were to be administered during the interim before a final peace might well decide their destiny. Saxony would be one of the two bones of contention—Poland the other—over which the Allies would feud for the next months and years.

The old King of Saxony had waited in his palace in Leipzig for his fellow sovereigns to come and pay their respects. Metternich had planned to hold the Saxon King in Prague until the future peace congress decided the fate of Saxony; but Humboldt had outmaneuvered Metternich for control of the precious royal hostage, and the old King found himself whisked off to Berlin as a prisoner of war under the guard of the none too sympathetic Prussians.

Most undependable member of the shaky Coalition was Crown Prince Bernadotte of Sweden, who concerned himself very little with the general aims of the Allies but only with his own war aim—to add Norway to his Swedish dominions.

The meeting between the Austrian Emperor and Bernadotte in Leipzig had been cool, to say the least. Their paths had last crossed in Vienna in 1798, when Citizen Bernadotte, French envoy in Vienna, had hoisted the revolutionary tricolor from a balcony of the French embassy and drawn the wrath of a royalist mob. Since that day Bernadotte had risen to be a marshal under Napoleon, then got himself elected and adopted heir to the Swedish throne. The provincial lawyer's son had learned to be quite as autocratic as any monarch born to the purple.

The English delegation at headquarters, who agreed on little else, agreed on Bernadotte. It made them very nervous to be embraced by a man who pranced about, as Stewart said, "with a bottle of eau de cologne in one hand, a white handkerchief in the other, inundating lavishly everything around him with perfume."

England and Russia had agreed to hand over Norway to Bernadotte as a reward for his military support. Nobody, of course, asked the Norwegians what they wanted—no more than anyone would ask the Saxons, the Poles, the Italians or the Spanish. Metternich hoped to thwart Bernadotte on the question of Norway; he promised Wilson he could extricate England from "that most injudicious and impolitic engagement and present embarrassment," which he had considered as "unwise and inexpedient even at the time."[5]

Gradually the suspicion began to spread that Bernadotte not only wanted Norway but had designs on the French throne to replace Napoleon. Stewart's adjutant had heard Bernadotte remark some weeks earlier that "if anything happened to Buonoparte the French people would select him or Moreau as their chief." Now Moreau was dead.

To complicate matters further within the Coalition, the Tsar had made Stein administrator of all the occupied German-speaking countries. When Metternich protested that such a decision must be a matter of agreement among all the Allies, the Tsar replied loftily that "he had given his word to Stein, and it was impossible to break it without exposing himself to the reproach of weakness."[6]

All the way across Germany, from Leipzig to Frankfurt, Metternich and the Tsar argued over the fate of Germany, especially the harsh and autocratic policies of Stein in Saxony and the adjoining duchies.

In Weimar on October 25 there had been a three-hour quarrel between Metternich and the Tsar—"a terrible scene," Metternich described it to Laure.

In the end Metternich won two victories. The Tsar agreed to try peace negotiations through St. Aignan, and a more moderate plan for the occupied territories was drawn up.

One last little game of one-upsmanship was played out at the gates of Frankfurt over which of the sovereigns would be first to make a grand entry into the old coronation city of the Holy Roman Emperors, a matter of some political importance.

Emperor Franz had been the last Holy Roman Emperor to rule over that shadowy disjointed collection of states that Napoleon had rudely kicked apart when he formed the Rhine Confederation of German princes. Though neither Metternich nor Emperor Franz favored a restoration of the Holy Roman Empire, Metternich wanted to keep all his options open, keep a major voice for Austria in any decision on the future of Germany. But the

Tsar got there first, made a splendid entry into the city on November 5, surrounded by his guard of six-foot-tall Cossacks.

Not until the next day, in raw November weather, did Emperor Franz make his entry. If some of the cream had been skimmed off the celebration, still Frankfurt citizens were willing to stand shivering and cheering while he rode through the old Römerberg quarter, where he had ridden to his coronation twenty-one years before.[7]

2

"During the winter I shall make peace if God sustains me and if Napoleon is not entirely mad," Metternich had written to Wilhelmine.[8]

The chief war aim of the Allies had been accomplished. Napoleon had been driven out of Germany, back across the Rhine. Surely now all sides could agree on terms for a permanent peace in Europe. As for Napoleon, Metternich felt certain he could either persuade him to peace "or deprive him of the support of France."[9]

On the Monday after his arrival in Frankfurt, November 8, Metternich invited Baron St. Aignan to meet with him and discuss the peace proposal he would carry to Napoleon. In his luxurious quarters in the mansion of the banker Müller, Metternich first talked with St. Aignan alone, then called in Nesselrode and Aberdeen.

Nesselrode urged that they set Allied terms as high as possible, then reduce them if necessary during the negotiations. But Aberdeen insisted they should deal with forthright honesty from the start, state their terms as low as possible, and firmly adhere to them.

Castlereagh had notified Aberdeen a few days earlier that England would consent to a peace congress, provided that hostilities were not halted while negotiations were being conducted, and provided that the Allies and Napoleon reach an agreement beforehand on the bases for a permanent peace.

As the chief basis Metternich proposed that France accept as her "natural boundaries" the Rhine, the Alps and the Pyrenees. Those boundaries gave France more territory than she had possessed under her kings; it meant that Austria was willing to give up to France her old possession of the Austrian Netherlands, including the important seaport of Antwerp. They were boundaries Castlereagh had agreed to in his initial instructions to Aberdeen. In addition England would give up French overseas possessions she had conquered during the war. Germany, Spain, Holland and northern Italy would be made independent of French control.

St. Aignan took careful notes on their conversation. He showed his memorandum to all three men for their assent. A statement was added that England "was ready to make great sacrifices to obtain a peace in Europe," including freedom for commerce—a necessary economic guarantee for France.

Aberdeen amended the sentence to read that England would not abandon "a particle of what she felt belonged to her maritime code."[10]

St. Aignan doubted whether Napoleon would accept the bases, but he thought the French people, in their eagerness for peace, would be willing.

Metternich gave St. Aignan a personal note to carry to Caulaincourt. The terms offered, Metternich felt, were fair, but if Napoleon turned them down, he warned Caulaincourt, then new Allied military successes could enlarge their demands. He feared Napoleon would not yet make peace but would summon a new army instead. "I shall never be happier than to be mistaken," he wrote.[11]

Armed with his precious notes St. Aignan climbed into his carriage and started at once for Paris. Behind him Metternich, Aberdeen and Nesselrode talked far into the night.

To bring the full pressure of French public opinion to bear on Napoleon, Metternich proposed a powerful propaganda weapon—a manifesto to be published in France informing the French people of the generous bases on which the Allies were willing to talk peace, promising to preserve a France "great, strong and happy."

No man of his day understood better than Metternich the art of psychological warfare—or rather, peacefare. He was certain he could win the support of the French masses to a negotiated peace.

But Aberdeen was afraid such a proclamation would only anger Napoleon and even perhaps arouse resentment among the French. He and Nesselrode persuaded Metternich to postpone publishing the manifesto until they had a reply from Napoleon. That delay was doubtless a costly mistake; the manifesto, when it was finally published, was enormously effective.

3

The handsome, bustling, wealthy old imperial city of Frankfurt lavished hospitality on the Allied visitors during the six weeks of late autumn when the armies headquartered there.

Court receptions, galas, parades, banquets, and balls succeeded one another, quite as if another coronation were in progress. The rich merchants and bankers entertained in their opulent town houses; the burghers' wives outdid one another to attract to their dinner tables and tea parties some of the visiting royalty, or, at the very least, the handsomer officers of the armies with so much time on their hands. In Frankfurt were two emperors and three kings—the Prussian and Bavarian kings supposedly incognito, but the three-hundred-odd pounds of the King of Württemberg could scarcely be called invisible—uncountable grand dukes, dukes, princelings.

All the princes of the Rhine Confederation had been flocking to pay court to the victors of Leipzig—and to join the winning side before it was too late. Every day Metternich found his waiting rooms crowded with titled petitioners, coming to beg for territory lost under Napoleon—or begging to keep what they had got.

On the road to Frankfurt he had already arranged a treaty of alliance with Württemberg; by the end of November he had drawn up twenty-two treaties with small German territories, most of them agreeing to furnish a troop contingent to the Allied army.

The Rhine Confederation no longer existed.

He worked ordinarily as he did in Vienna, "from 9 in the morning until 3, and from 4 to 10"—but sometimes it was morning before he went to bed. "I am so swamped with work and conferences that I curse Frankfurt," he wrote Laure.

In spite of the burden of work, he found time to enjoy the social life of Frankfurt. Often he had guests for dinner; Wilson reported that Metternich "adds to the talents of a minister all the accomplishments of a liberal host, a gallant gentleman and *bel esprit,* so that his table and his soirees are very delightful points of rendezvous."[12] Late in the evening he often went to drink tea at the house of the banker Simon Moritz Bethmann, to whose handsome Holland-born wife the Tsar was paying gallant court, and who "talks French like a little Dutch cow," Metternich wrote Marie. If he stayed in his own quarters his salon would be filled in a twinkling with young officers, and he would go and come between salon and study.[13]

Now that the war seemed all but over, several ladies joined the company at headquarters in Frankfurt. The Tsar's two sisters, the Grand Duchesses Catherine and Marie, came, and Priscilla Burghersh, the pretty nineteen-year-old wife of the new English military commissioner, who was to supplant the popular Sir Robert Wilson at Schwarzenberg's headquarters. Lord Burghersh was an arrogant, self-important young man who had won his post through his Tory connections rather than by merit, but everyone liked his wife—"very amiable, a good child," Metternich described her—who had made up her mind to follow her husband, campaign or no campaign. In her luxurious pillowed carriage, with her mother's elderly French maid for company and a sheaf of scent bottles and sulphur powder to keep away infection, Priscilla Burghersh had driven intrepidly from Berlin to Frankfurt along roads strewn with the debris of war.

She provided an attractive excuse for a whole string of Frankfurt dinner parties at which she was more often than not "the only woman at table with from 15 to 30 men! I found it dreadful at first, but now I am quite used to it."[14]

To his wife and daughters Metternich sent gifts from Frankfurt, silk for dresses ("four dresses for grown-ups and one of the yellow for Clementine"), wrote them regularly, regaled Laure with political news carefully sifted for dissemination in her circle of society, and with amusingly naughty morsels of gossip.

At one magnificent ball in the parterre of a Frankfurt theater, not everyone was nimble enough to perform the new Viennese waltz, and several couples ended up sprawled on the dance floor, "including Count Paar and on top of him a fat Fräulein who fell so that everyone could see all her secrets revealed. Luckily a Prussian hussar tall as a treetop fell on top of her with his partner."[15]

Belatedly, just before he left Frankfurt, Metternich wrote Laure, "If I had foreseen that we should be in Frankfurt such a long time, I would have had you come with Marie and Victor."[16]

It appeared that, infallible as were Papa's political judgments, he could not foresee well enough to arrange this little domestic journey.

4

If he had not considered bringing Laure to Frankfurt, for a few hours, a few days, Metternich played with the idea of having Wilhelmine come.

"Prague bores me," she had written. "I would like to be nearer you." Prague was ever more distant from the political and military center. News was slower in coming. People were saying that the armies would surely winter over in Frankfurt. The grand duchesses had left Prague for Frankfurt; other ladies talked of going. Should she not come to Frankfurt, she asked Clemens. "If I can arrange something that is not absolutely compromising," he promised, then he would have her come nearer him.[17]

On the whole long journey, from Komotau to Leipzig, from Leipzig to Frankfurt, his brain and heart, he wrote, had been filled with her. *"Mon amie et l'Europe, l'Europe et mon amie!"* My love and Europe, Europe and my love. Wherever he found himself late in the evening, in the crowded inn rooms with half a dozen people sleeping around him, in his luxurious Frankfurt house with young aides-de-camp chatting and laughing and drinking their tea, he found moments to write her.

Nearly every day a letter goes off to Prague, small sheets written over in a fine clear hand, folded like the pages of a book and sealed in red wax with one or another device—most often a C, for his family crest would too readily be recognized. She too used a C seal—the initial of Catherine, her first given name, and of Courland.

Often late at night, by the light of a candle in the silver lamp she had sent from Prague, he would sit writing—first to Wilhelmine, then to Laure. "11 in the evening," the date lines read; or "midnight," or "2 o'clock in the morning," with Giroux snoring in the next room.

Everywhere he goes he sends her gifts. Metternich had a special talent for the delicate art of gift giving. She is delighted with the pretty things he sends to adorn her desk, the handsome writing desk he admired that her father had bought many years before from the estate of the Duc de Choiseul. He wants her to be reminded of him each time she sits down to write—a folding ruler and paper cutter of intricately carved India wood, an exquisite inkwell, a clock and thermometer enclosed in glass so that one could see the tiny works churn. She thanks him for the "new order on her writing desk":

> I even sacrificed for you a wretched very inconvenient inkwell that has made me angry for seven years every time my pen reached for it—but which I still regard with a fond pang as part of the cult I have for everything old—beginning with our most venerable social institutions right down to my wadded gown with holes in the elbows—that I find a thousand times more comfortable than any other—and which I only take off out of consideration for people who see me in this ridiculous dress—[18]

She does not hesitate to ask favors of Metternich. Will he please send from Frankfurt six pounds of good coarse tobacco, as many pounds of imported English tea, and a special kind of soap. He sends the tobacco and the tea, and a single pot of the soap—the only one in all Frankfurt—but he counsels her against using it, for it may harm the skin. The best thing for bathing, he advises her, is a good Naples soap such as men use for shaving; one must beat it to a lather with a cream whipper, rub it well into the skin during the bath, rinse it with clear fresh water, and *voilà!* one goes to bed perfectly clean.

Most of the time the favors she asks are for others. Louis Rohan is still pressing her to use her good offices with Metternich to get him a job with one of the army headquarters—any post, "so long as it isn't as cook or chaplain." Louis threatens to die if he gets no appointment, preferably in the headquarters of the Tsar or the King of Prussia. If Louis should die of chagrin, Wilhelmine asks Metternich whimsically, will she be an authentic widow?

She writes to ask him to get a pardon for an old man of seventy-eight, a French émigré named Henrici, who has been accused of spying for Napoleon in Prague and sentenced to exile. Metternich replies that "as a spy of seventy-eight is no longer very dangerous, I shall try to let him remain."[19]

And could he please, she begs, make the Russians treat their prisoners more humanely? The poor men are often obliged to march several hundred miles across Germany and Bohemia without food or water or sleep; in the streets of Prague they drop and die in their tracks. Most of them, she adds, are not French at all, but Italians and Germans from the left bank of the Rhine.[20]

One day, while the ministers were still in Leipzig, Metternich had walked into Hardenberg's quarters and been struck by the familiarity of the house and the room. Suddenly he remembered: it was the room in which he had met Wilhelmine's mother and her sister Jeanne ten years before, when he was a young minister at his first post. He had met Wilhelmine shortly afterward for the first time—at a moment when she was between husbands. They had never really become acquainted until long after. His brain was a tumult of memories and fantasies as he stood in that Leipzig room. He wrote her:

> Ten years passed before my eyes—I reviewed the past—the present— I trembled before the future! . . . My life belongs to you—but I love Wilhelmine a hundred times more than I have ever loved anyone.[21]

And indeed she had become for him far more than any other woman in his life ever had. She had become for him an alter ego, the apotheosis of his most romantic dreams and fantasies. He had created out of a woman of flesh and blood an ideal who would precisely meet all his needs. He was certain that he understood her completely, knew what was best for her, could make her happy—if she would but let him.

The exaltation of his love, his idealization of her into something other than an everyday human being, troubled Wilhelmine. She was disarmingly honest—most of all, with herself. Could he not, she begged, love her a little bit less?

> When I read you, dear Clemens, I always want to say to you, my dear, don't love me too much. . . . Love me as much as you can. Make of these contradictions what you like, dear Clemens.[22]

He replied quite grandly:

> Bon Dieu, how right you are to tell me as you have to love you a little bit less! My dear, you think everything is possible for me? No, I can defeat Napoleon and I cannot succeed in loving you a little bit less.[23]

He protests that his love for her is simple and natural, that he loves her truly for what she is, that his love is without the rage of passion.

But will he ever win that elusive heart of hers—win her for himself, completely, incontrovertibly? She must belong to him and to no one else—his friend, his mistress, his support, the vessel to hold his joy, his pain, his anger, his disappointment and hope. He had never known before a woman who combined beauty with such intelligence and charm. Now, in the maturity of his forties, he thinks he would hold to her for a long time. In the days to come, when the war is over and he is back in Vienna, she would be near at hand, part of his life every single day and as many nights as he desired her to be.

One of these days, when he has come that far with her, he will lay down the bases for their future relationship, as clearly and firmly as he has laid down the bases for peace with France. He deserves to win her—she is the prize Fate is holding in store for him to compensate for these months and years of anxiety and work and war.

In the Leipzig battle Alfred Windischgraetz had fought valiantly and had been decorated; Metternich had himself put Alfred's name on the list for citations. In the Frankfurt headquarters he meets Alfred nearly every day.

1. Clemens Lothar Wenzel von Metternich (1773–1859), Foreign Minister and Chancellor of Austria. Painted by François Pascal Gérard, Paris, 1810.

2. Princess Eleonore Metternich, born Countess Kaunitz, "Laure" to her husband and friends. Of Laure, whom he had married when he was twenty-one, Metternich wrote, "My wife is excellent, full of intelligence . . . She has never been pretty; she is lovable only to those who know her well. There is nothing in the world I would not do for her." Engraved after a painting by Friedrich Lieder.

3. Marie Metternich, eldest and favorite daughter of the Chancellor. "I always find myself again in her," he wrote his wife once. "If she were a boy, she would be a Cabinet minister by the time she was thirty." Engraved by J. Mecou.

4. Clementine Metternich, second daughter of the Chancellor, of whom he wrote, "Clementine is remarkably pretty; it must really be so, for when she goes out the people gather round her. I would rather she were a child of more common appearance, for such children grow like weeds." Watercolor by Moritz Michael Daffinger.

5. Marie, Clementine and Victor Metternich, the eldest Metternich children, about 1808. Unlike most aristocratic fathers in his day, Metternich enjoyed romping with his children. "If I had not been a Minister of State, I would have been a nursery governess," he wrote. Miniature by an unknown artist.

6. Austrian State Chancellery, Vienna, where Metternich worked and lived from the year 1809 until 1848. His own private apartments adjoined the offices of the Foreign Ministry on the second floor, while his wife and children lived in apartments on the floor above. In the conference rooms of the Chancellery in 1814–15 the men of the Vienna Congress decided the fate of Europe for a half century, and in the splendid representation rooms some of the most celebrated fetes of the Congress took place. Watercolor by Rudolf Alt.

Napoleon, sketched from life by A. L. Girodet at St. Cloud in 1812. He had returned from the disastrous Russian campaign, his wife Marie Louise wrote, "fatter than ever."

8. Caroline Bonaparte Murat, Queen of Naples. "Cromwell's head on the shoulder of a pretty woman," Talleyrand described Napoleon's intelligent, ambitious sister, whose friendship with Metternich survived even her brother's debacle.

9. When asked if it troubled her to pose in the nude for the sculptor Antonio Canova, Pauline Bonaparte, Princess Borghese, replied, "Oh not at all, there was a fire in the studio." Invited to call on Pauline Bonaparte one day, Laure Metternich and her children found the princess in complete deshabille. "She had herself dressed in front of us even to her undershirt and hose," Laure wrote her husband, "and the whole time sang only your praise."

10. Wilhelmine, Duchess of Sagan, painted by Giuseppe Grassi in 1800. "For some years," Metternich told her once, "Grassi has painted your look on all the faces that have posed for him."

11. The princesses of Courland as "The Four Graces," painted by Giuseppe Grassi about 1800. L. to r., Wilhelmine, Dorothée, Jeanne, Pauline.

12. Duchess Dorothea of Courland, mother of the four princesses. Painted by Anton Graff.

13. Wilhelmine's natural daughter (left) Adelaide Gustava Aspasia Armfelt, called "Vava" (1801–1881), with a foster sister in Sweden. When Metternich learned of the child's existence, he wrote Wilhelmine, "I feel rich now that I possess your secret—your child is mine—I love it like my own." Painted by Jean Baptiste Greuze.

14. The Castle of Sagan in Silesia (now Poland). The fief of Sagan comprised a territory of 120 square kilometers, a town of 7,000 people and 200 smaller villages. From a contemporary lithograph.

15. Palais Palm, Schenkenstrasse, Vienna. In the right wing of the eighteenth-century mansion the Duchess of Sagan had her town house; in the left wing, Princess Katharine Bagration.

16. Princess **Katharine Bagration,** widow of the Russian general who was mortally wounded at Borodino. Miniature by Jean Baptiste Isabey.

17. Friedrich von Gentz, journalist and secretary of the Vienna Congress. Engraved by C. F. Merckel after a painting by Friedrich Lieder.

18. Ratiborzitz, in eastern Bohemia, country house of the Duchess of Sagan. From a contemporary watercolor by Ernst Welker.

9. Tsar Alexander I of Russia. "It would
e difficult to have more intelligence than
sar Alexander," Napoleon wrote of him,
but there is a piece missing. I have never
managed to discover what it is."

0. Grand Duchess Catherine Pavlovna,
dear Katya," the Tsar's favorite sister,
ho followed him on the campaign of
813 to 1814. "I love you none the less
adly though you are a little mad yourself
ometimes," he wrote her. Miniature by
an Baptiste Isabey.

21. Prince Karl August von Hardenberg, Chancellor of Prussia.
Painted by Sir Thomas Lawrence.

22. Emperor Franz I of Austria.
Painted by Friedrich von Amerling.

23. Prince Alfred Windischgraetz, painted by Lampi in 1810.

24. Prince Karl Schwarzenberg, hand-picked by Metternich to command the Allied forces in the campaign of 1813 to 1814. Schwarzenberg is shown here wearing the Grand Cross of Maria Theresia, awarded him by the Emperor Franz on the field at Leipzig. Painted by François Pascal Gérard in Paris in 1814.

25. The battle of Dresden, August 26–27, 1813, was not nearly so tidy as depicted here by an unknown French engraver.

26. Schwarzenberg brings the news to the three Allied sovereigns that the battle for Leipzig was won, October 18, 1813. "Never did I see a more horrible battlefield," Schwarzenberg wrote his wife. From a contemporary lithograph.

27. Emperor Franz (center), accompanied by Tsar Alexander, the King of Prussia and Crown Prince Bernadotte of Sweden, enter the city of Leipzig the day after the decisive battle. From a contemporary lithograph.

28. Robert Stewart, Viscount Castlereagh, who looked when he arrived from England at Allied headquarters in January of 1814 "rather like an eighteenth-century prelate," Metternich thought. Painted by Sir Thomas Lawrence.

29. Talleyrand. Miniature by Derval.

30. Dorothée, Comtesse de Périgord, née Princess of Courland, at seventeen. In the background is the chateau of Valençay belonging to Talleyrand, her uncle by marriage.

31. The triumphant Tsar leads the Allied armies into Paris, March 31, 1814. Above the Arc de Triomphe are the horses of St. Mark's, Venice, which Metternich would eventually see returned to the Adriatic city, while on the skyline center appears the figure of Napoleon on the column in the Place Vendôme. Contemporary engraving.

32. A royalist crowd pulls down the figure of Napoleon from the Place Vendôme. Contemporary engraving.

33. Marie Louise. Painted by François Pascal Gérard.

34. Napoleon's son, the King of Rome.
Miniature by Karl Agricola.

Alfred is now promoted to colonel and appointed by the Emperor to command the 8th Cuirassier Regiment of Grand Duke Constantine—not an easy assignment, for the Tsar's younger brother is violent, ill-tempered, brutal.

Metternich does not yet dare propose that Wilhelmine break completely with Alfred. He is too fearful of her answer, still far from certain of her affection. She still speaks of the "friendship" between her and Metternich—an accursed word which he tells her he detests.

He is not yet *tu* to her. Just once, writing of her loyalty to Austria—"our second country"—Wilhelmine slips into *tutoiement*, using the intimate *thou*, which, Metternich cries out joyfully, "the usage of the heart has consecrated in every country to the language of true intimacy. I kissed that good letter; don't think I shall ever lose it!"[24]

But Wilhelmine is not ready to make promises. She can only write that she places her hope of unraveling the knots of her existence in God's hands. The expression holds Metternich's attention at once. Surely she means to break with Alfred? She must understand that no woman can have two lovers, even if she equates one with a husband of long standing:

> Do you think you can manage [he writes her] to keep alive two relationships like these, which without making you happy make my life miserable, which will end by troubling A[lfred]'s happiness—if his happiness—and I do not believe this—is exclusively attached to you? . . . Do you think you cannot untie a bond so badly put together? That depends only on you. Prepare all the people interested in it—A. and your sisters.[25]

But she cannot yet sever that tie, not now, when Alfred still faces possible death in battle.

But she does not want to lose the security of Metternich's love:

> I want absolutely that [the love] you have for me endures—I want to be able to count on it as on life. . . . I have made of your feeling for me an inseparable companion whom I am never without—which will lead me across pain and pleasure—to the last redoubtable moment that [love] will still know how to sweeten.[26]

Gentz had appointed himself a kind of unofficial watchdog over Wilhelmine while Metternich was away at the wars. He was relieved when the young Englishmen Lamb and Vernon had moved on to Vienna. Metternich had ordered Gentz to keep Wilhelmine informed of the latest military and political news arriving by diplomatic courier. But Gentz hated parting with this precious commodity—except at the right moment and on his own terms.

The months in Prague had been "heavenly months" for Gentz:

> My health excellent, my name had become great. I had plenty of money. I was stamped a great gentleman and highly honored in Prague.[27]

For drawing up the Austrian War Manifesto, the Tsar had given Gentz a diamond ring; it flashed and sparkled on the hand that gestured constantly as he talked, quite like the new engagement ring on the hand of a girl. The Austrian Emperor had finally conferred the title of *Hofrat*—Court Councillor —on Gentz, with the right of affixing a "von" to his name. But in the layered hierarchy of Vienna society, where it was unbearable to be simply "Mr. Gentz," Gentz had long ago assumed the aristocratic particle. He had to write Metternich and beseech him to keep the announcement of the title out of the Viennese press, since everyone thought he had got it years ago.

Wilhelmine could be impatient with Gentz's streak of old-maidishness, and irritated by his inquisitiveness into her personal life. In the middle of October she moved out of her rooms in the Waldstein to the apartment in the Fürstenberg Palace where Metternich had stayed on his visits to Prague. Certainly she had moved to escape Gentz's policing eye. On the whole, he reported to Metternich, the move was an advantage to him. "Our friendship is stronger than ever. . . . [but] I won't hear Trogoff and Louis and Obreskoff and Thesie and Zapary clacking and shrieking."[28]

Her "fatal tenderness for Alfred" vexed Gentz; why could she not scissor herself from that old attachment, devote herself wholly to Metternich, since that was what he wanted? Whenever word came that Alfred's corps was in an engagement with the enemy, she became silent, anxious, depressed. It was certainly not love, Gentz thought, no, not a shadow of it, "but the kind of feeling a very ordinary woman has for her husband." It angered him not only because her affection for Metternich should be exclusive, but

> because everything else in W. is truly in a great, noble, almost mas-
> culine style. . . . As soon as talk turns on this little creature, she be-
> comes weak, small and common. . . . I would give a lot if this person
> were not with the army. . . . In another situation she would be so
> fed up with him there would be no more question of him.[29]

Gentz continued to drop in on her each day. She enjoyed his company and his conversation; with him she could talk of Metternich, of the way the war was going, of the political future of Europe—that question that absorbed her more than any other.

"Since yesterday Gentz likes me a bit better," she wrote Metternich, "I have an excellent cook."[30]

One day in November, Gentz enters Wilhelmine's apartment to find her holding a letter in her hand. Her face is radiant; he must sit down, she tells him, make himself comfortable and listen. She holds in her hand a letter from Metternich, "a truly precious letter that in sweetness and depth of feeling surpassed any" she had ever had. She begins to read aloud hesitantly, as if she is skipping passages here and there.

It is indeed a beautiful letter, Gentz agrees.

"He must be pleased with me now," she tells Gentz, "and he has reason to be." To Metternich she writes, "You have conquered my heart as you have conquered the world."[31]

Gentz may not like Wilhelmine, or trust her wholeheartedly—he does not, by and large, trust any woman—but he knows how to write a letter to Metternich that will bring joy to his heart:

> I felt an aversion to her for years [Gentz wrote]; I have had to come a long way now to render her justice. She still does not possess for me what they call charm. My opinion of her therefore is as free, as pure, as certain as such an opinion can be.
>
> Her truly great qualities have won me irretrievably to her, bound me fast to her as only the most complete sympathy would be able to do. . . . The exceptional penetration of her mind, joined to an almost equally great (and with such a woman highly astonishing) clarity, I could almost say, transparency of soul, has been the thing which, next to her great beauty, has found a way to the heart. Since in this woman's whole being there is not a trace of sentimentality or affectation of any kind, and everything about her [is] true and genuine (I will bear witness to this before God and the whole world), consequently every relationship with her must soon assume a strong and regular course. I understand completely how, once one began to love her, one could not soon leave off.

Gentz reminds Metternich of one night during the preceding summer when they were walking late on the streets of Prague—"on the street by the bridge you were talking about this relationship with the tranquil confidence that knowledge of eventual success gives to a great virtuoso. . . ."

Gentz now assures Metternich of his victory in the realm of Wilhelmine's heart—"certainly one of the most delightful realms on earth."[32]

In Frankfurt Metternich had decided against Wilhelmine's coming. It would be too risky, too indiscreet—and they might soon be moving their headquarters yet farther away, to Freiburg.

It would be best for her to return to Vienna, he wrote. Couriers would be riding each day from headquarters to Vienna, so she could hear from him regularly. He would see her soon, he promised, "if God gives me life and strength!"

Gentz, meantime, begged Metternich to summon him to headquarters, where he could help with the chores of propaganda and editing:

> I would rather climb with you over crags and wade through marshes, fight my way through French and Cossacks than be separated from you.[33]

No reply came for days.

But when Metternich summoned Gentz at last to join him in Freiburg, Gentz was at once assailed by doubts. To exchange his warm nest in Prague, where he was cozy as a cat in his luxury apartments, with his perfect little household assembled to wait on him hand and foot, for the discomforts of traveling in midwinter, for who knew what wretched hardships awaiting him at headquarters?

But now there was no choice. On December 4 he started out gloomily on the two-week journey over the snowbound roads. Wilhelmine planned to leave almost at once for Vienna.

5

On November 25 the anxiously awaited reply to St. Aignan's peace mission reached Metternich from Paris. Napoleon agreed to a peace congress, proposed Mannheim as a meeting place, but he did not specifically accept the proposed bases, including a France confined within her natural boundaries of Rhine, Alps and Pyrenees.

Metternich's reply, dispatched at once, was peremptory. No negotiation could begin until France agreed to accept her "natural boundaries."

Meantime, in those last days of November, an important change in government occurred in Paris. Public opinion forced Napoleon to replace the war-minded Bassano as Minister of Foreign Affairs with peace-minded Caulaincourt.

Caulaincourt's first act in office was to send an instant reply to Metternich: yes, he was authorized to accept the bases the Allies proposed for peace negotiations.

Caulaincourt's response reached Metternich on December 5. The way seemed open at last for peace talks to begin.

> I think negotiations will soon reopen [Metternich wrote Laure on December 6]. Napoleon has already consented to retire on the basis of the Rhine, Alps and Pyrenees, to restore Germany, Spain, Italy and Holland. . . . I shall make peace for the world if it is makable, and it appears to be.[34]

In those first days of December 1813, Metternich's Manifesto to the French People was carried across the Rhine and circulated the length and breadth of France. Sending a copy to Laure, Metternich wrote, "I did it with much heart and fools will find it perhaps too moderate. Let them talk and let me make peace."[35]

Of its effectiveness Napoleon himself was the best witness. When the first copy found posted on a wall in Paris was brought to Napoleon by his Minister of Police, Napoleon said at once, "No one but Metternich can have concocted this document; talking of the Rhine, Alps and Pyrenees is a piece of cunning. It could only enter the head of a man who knows France as well as he does."[36]

A few months later Napoleon would tell Wessenberg that the Frankfurt Manifesto was in large part to blame for his downfall. "I nearly had a real quarrel with the French people on my hands—so I decided to accept the bases."[37]

Once again, tragically for Europe, with peace seemingly within grasp, hope for the war's end was shattered—this time by England and Prussia.

As Metternich had feared, the war aims of the victors enlarged with their victories.

Since Castlereagh had written his instructions to Aberdeen—which the latter had followed to the letter—the Dutch cities had revolted and thrown out their French officials, proposing to set up an independent state with a prince of the House of Orange at the head. England no longer looked favorably on a France extending as far north as Antwerp and the Rhine. French control of the important seaport and the mouth of the Scheldt threatened Britain's commercial interests on the Channel. Now the English Cabinet had second thoughts on the natural boundaries, and determined instead to reduce France to her "old boundaries"—that is, the territory she had possessed before the Revolution. England would marry the heiress to the throne, Princess Charlotte, to the heir of Holland, the Prince of Orange, so that England could safely and cozily straddle the Channel.

Increasingly England's Tory government wanted Napoleon overthrown —a possibility not envisioned in the war aims jointly agreed upon by the Allies—and replaced by the Bourbon Louis XVIII, brother of the last French King, who had been living in exile at Hartwell in England.

When the St. Aignan meetings had taken place in early November, Charles Stewart had been in the North at Bernadotte's headquarters. Though his assent had been obtained, the King of Prussia too had been absent from Frankfurt; his minister, Baron Hardenberg, had taken no direct part in the secret meetings, but he was kept fully informed. In the middle of November Stewart's secretary, George Jackson, managed to worm the details out of Hardenberg, and concerned lest a "premature" peace might be made, Jackson sent off an urgent warning to Stewart that "Austria and Russia, whose armies have suffered excessively . . . will be too happy to conclude a peace if anything like an honorable opportunity offers of giving up the contest."[38]

Stewart hotfooted it to Frankfurt. Soldier rather than diplomat, of a boisterous and unstable temperament, Castlereagh's half brother had his own ambitions to look after, was eager to impress both the Prince Regent and Castlereagh. In a series of explosive scenes he denounced the St. Aignan negotiations and Aberdeen's part in them, dashed off an alarmist dispatch to Castlereagh, declaring that the proposals compromised Britain's interests. Among other points he wanted to see the delivery of Norway to Bernadotte form part of the bases for a preliminary peace.

While quiet, studious Aberdeen attempted to defend his role in the peace move against the angry opposition of both Stewart and Cathcart, Caulaincourt's note accepting the proposed peace bases reached Metternich.

Clearly no negotiation with Napoleon could be attempted without full English backing, and the three English envoys were in violent disagreement. To Caulaincourt's note of acceptance Metternich could only reply lamely on December 10 that the Allies must now await word from England on their choice of peace delegate. Meantime, Austria, Russia and Prussia dispatched their own messenger to London to find out from the English Cabinet precisely what their views were on the peace, and to implore them to name a single delegate to act with authority in the negotiations.

By the time Pozzo di Borgo, a young Corsican serving on the Tsar's staff, sailed from a Dutch port and arrived in London, the Cabinet had decided that no less a person than Castlereagh, the British Foreign Secretary, should travel to the Continent and represent English interests at Allied headquarters.

And by the time Castlereagh left London on the day after Christmas, the Allied armies were already crossing the Rhine.

6

While the ministers in Frankfurt waited during the weeks of November for Napoleon's reply to the St. Aignan peace overtures, war councils had been meeting to decide on whether or not to make another military move.

The more peace-minded, including Austrian Generals Merveldt and Duka, argued that the Allied armies had reached their goal: Napoleon had been driven back across the Rhine. Why not wait now for the peace negotiations to begin? The King of Prussia opposed a winter campaign; the older Russian generals did not want to cross the Rhine. But Prussian Generals Blücher and Gneisenau, together with Humboldt, Stein and others—eager both for revenge on France and for the expansion of Prussia—argued for immediate invasion of France. The Prussian general staff proposed crossing the Rhine in the area of Coblenz, attacking France from the northeast at the point where Napoleon had a chain of heavily defended fortresses.

While Metternich and Schwarzenberg hoped peace could be made—and soon—they were uncertain whether Napoleon was ready to negotiate in good faith, and they feared above all the possibility that he might raise still another army. "We must not go to sleep," Schwarzenberg said. "As long as the Man lives, we can't think of any rest."[39] Schwarzenberg's invasion plan was more cautious than the Prussian, and oriented to Austria's strategic interests. The main army would invade France through Switzerland, thus protecting vital supply lines to Austria and affording a junction with the Austrian army of Italy.

The Austrian plan was accepted—or very nearly. There was one difficulty—and it was a critical one. Switzerland, while refusing to break off ties with France and continuing to provide a troop contingent for Napoleon's army, proclaimed herself neutral, and refused to permit the passage of Allied troops. And the Tsar steadfastly opposed the invasion of Switzerland by the Allied armies unless the Swiss themselves could be won over. He was strongly influenced in his stand by his old tutor, Fréderic de La Harpe, citizen of the liberal, French-controlled canton of Vaud, and by his sister's former governess, also Swiss, a certain Madame Morges.

While the English at headquarters tangled over the question of peace with Napoleon, Metternich and the Tsar throughout the month of December were locked in the dispute over Switzerland, a dispute so bitter that it threatened to wreck the Coalition once and for all.

Certainly an unresolved conflict between the two men had been simmering since late summer, when the Tsar had lost out in his struggle for the high command. And certainly Metternich was far from forgiving the Tsar's deception in the matter of England's consent to join the Prague negotiations. Both men were capable of using deceit and cunning to gain their ends; both were intensely proud, and each determined to control the inner machinery of power.

On the question of entering Switzerland the Tsar would not be moved.

When the Swiss Diet in Zurich sent a representative to Frankfurt to insist that their neutrality be respected, Metternich met the arguments with answers yet more cogent—threats and bribes. If Switzerland joined the Allied cause and permitted armies to cross her territory, she would recover lands she had lost to France; if Switzerland refused, "she would be abandoned at the time of the peace." In fact, the Allies would make use of "provinces torn from Switzerland to use as indemnities."[40]

But when the canton of Vaud a few days later sent their own delegation direct to the Tsar, he promised that Swiss neutrality would not be violated and gave his sister Marie permission to write her governess, Madame Morges, of his promise. Madame Morges and her friends—"*canaille* in the pay of the French police," Metternich called them—had copies of the letter made and circulated. A few days later, when a French spy was arrested and brought before Schwarzenberg, he was found to be carrying a copy of the letter—dangerous from the viewpoint of Allied military safety.[41]

When the Allies broke up their Frankfurt headquarters and moved south to the city of Freiburg just before Christmas, the Swiss question was far from settled. "I have furious quarrels with the Tsar," Metternich wrote. "He is more than ever against the whole Swiss operation."[42]

Schwarzenberg was relieved to be leaving Frankfurt; the area could no longer feed his troops and many had fallen ill. He hoped the peace negotiations could take place before another battle had to be fought. "I would have gone crazy in this place," he wrote his wife on the eve of his departure, "—that heaven knows—no mortal army ever has been commanded under such conditions."[43]

A few days after Schwarzenberg's departure for Freiburg, the Tsar and his suite left for Karlsruhe, where he and his sisters would visit their mother's relatives before the Tsar proceeded on to Freiburg.

Metternich wrote Laure that he was "going with the Tsar of Russia, who no longer leaves me, for literally I am as much his minister as our own."[44] It was pure propaganda intended for Laure to fire back at the Vienna *crieurs*, already circulating rumors of a rift in the Coalition. Far from traveling *with* the Tsar, Metternich carefully arranged his journey to avoid the Russian sovereign.[45]

Behind them in the Frankfurt area typhus spread quickly. "This dreadful fever," Aberdeen called it. "If it continues the mortality will be as great as if we suffered from the plague itself."[46]

CAMPAIGN IN FRANCE: 1814

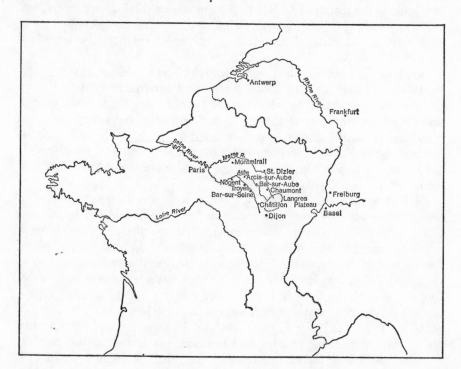

XIII

CHRISTMAS IN FREIBURG

*How can you ask who is Prince Metternich? I thought
everybody knew the fame of so great a person, who is,
and has been for years, the mainspring of all that passes on
the Continent. He is the Emperor of Austria's prime minister and reckoned the best and deepest diplomatist going.
He is wonderfully clever, and manages all the emperors,
kings and ministers, turning them round his little finger
and they are all afraid of him. He is uncommonly agreeable and good looking. . . .*
—PRISCILLA BURGHERSH TO HER SISTER EMILY[1]

1

The sleepy old university town of Freiburg, nestling on the edge of the
Black Forest in a valley surrounded by terraced hills, was jostled rudely
awake that December of 1813 as several hundred thousand Allied soldiers
poured through its streets and several hundred officers, ministers, diplomats,
secretaries and servants jostled one another for lodgings. "Full as an egg,"
Metternich described Freiburg; there was not a room or a bed to be had.

Young boys like Franz von Andlaw, son of Baden's Minister-President,
cheerfully tossed aside their Caesar's *Commentaries*, forgot their Latin verbs
to watch with awe and admiration the armies that pranced and paraded
through town: the dazzling Hungarian Grenadier Guards, plume-hatted hussars, and the first Cossacks ever seen in that part of the world. Excitedly
they could point out all the heroes of the recent battles—most astounding of
all, General Wrede astride a splendid charger, quite as if he had not been
given up for dead barely five weeks before and did not still carry a musket
ball in his stomach that his surgeons dared not try to remove!

If the schoolboys cheered the military heroes, the Freiburg ladies gaped at the female camp followers, straggling along in the wake of the armies, baggage on their backs like so many pack horses, decked out in bits and pieces of men's uniforms, boots if they could scrounge them, the Hungarian *cantinières* even riding astride horses like soldiers themselves! Freiburg would never be the same.[2]

All night the mountainsides around the town were alight with the flame of bivouac fires, smoke rising through the cold December air.

Metternich moved into the comfortable old mansion of his mother's family, the Kagenecks, where his mother had been born and spent her girlhood, where, in the same year as his own parents' wedding, Marie Antoinette had spent her last days as an Austrian archduchess before she journeyed across the border to become Queen of France. The Kagenecks were intermarried among all the titled families of the countryside, and Metternich found himself hugged and kissed by aunts, uncles and cousins of several degrees of kinship.

He went to work at once to prepare the way for a peaceful entry of Allied troops into Switzerland. "I am over my head in the Swiss question," he wrote Laure, adding, "I shall end up becoming a cow myself," which would bring a little dry smile to Laure's lips.[3]

Although the Swiss had refused to alter their official stance of neutrality, all the time leaving their troop contingent in Napoleon's army, they were by no means united on the question, and there was a powerful pro-Allied party within the country, especially among the old conservative faction in the North. Lebzeltern advised Metternich that the Allied entry could be successfully managed if the armies maintained perfect discipline, and if they paid the Swiss in cold hard cash for all their provisions.

By the Sunday after his arrival in Freiburg, on December 19, everything was arranged.

He had not even taken his friend Aberdeen into his confidence; Aberdeen thought Metternich had got the Tsar's prior approval. But the Tsar, who had said plainly "that he would consider the entrance into Switzerland as a declaration of war against himself" had not approved. Metternich intended to present the Russian ruler with a fait accompli. "I alone," he wrote Wilhelmine, "against the advice of my dear Tsar A., I risking a quarrel with him, a quarrel with Europe in case of failure—and nevertheless *daring* to take everything on me. Each hour, each minute counted—the world creaked on its hinges. . . ."[4]

It was on Tuesday, December 21, in the hours between midnight and morning that Austrian troops crossed the Rhine into Switzerland. If the Swiss Army leapt to arms to defend the borders of their country, all would be lost —and disaster would certainly follow. But all went smoothly.

The following day Metternich and Emperor Franz rode out of Freiburg to welcome the Tsar and escort him to his quarters. Care had been taken to arrange a fine military parade of the kind the Tsar loved. Crowds lined the streets, bands played, there was an air of holiday festivity everywhere.

The Tsar, however, was in no merry mood. The moment they met, the Russian ruler asked Metternich pointedly "whether there was any news."

Metternich answered that he would prefer to wait to answer that question until they reached the house where the Tsar was to live.

"I am not yet certain how Your Majesty will take what I have to tell you," Metternich began, once the two were inside the Tsar's study. "The Austrian army crossed the Rhine the night before last at several points between Schaffhausen and Basel."

Recalling the scene later in his *Memoirs* Metternich described the Tsar as having been "extremely agitated by the news." The truth was that the Tsar flew into a shouting tantrum. He was "outraged," he told his sisters, at Metternich, "and I told him so too, and anyone who cared to hear as well, for I cannot be indifferent to my reputation, and this behavior toward Switzerland sullies it." Metternich had "behaved abominably," the Tsar declared.

Only when the Russian sovereign had calmed down a bit did he ask Metternich how the armies had been received.

"Amid cheers for the Coalition, Your Majesty. The [Swiss] troops in a body have joined our flag, and the people come in crowds from all sides to bring provisions for the army, for which we pay in ready cash."

After a long moment the Tsar took Metternich's hand and said, "Success crowns the undertaking; it remains for success to justify what you have done. As one of the Allied monarchs I have nothing more to say to you, but as a man I declare to you that you have grieved me in a way you can never repair."[5]

The breach between the two men was indeed irreparable. Aberdeen declared that the Tsar "will never perfectly forgive Metternich for having put him in the wrong with respect to the Swiss operation."[6]

From a military standpoint the Swiss invasion was highly successful. Within days the Allied armies were crossing the Langres Plateau into the heart of France, meeting no resistance anywhere. Before Christmas Metternich could write Laure that the Allies had 180,000 men in France.

Yet the Swiss invasion was doubtless Metternich's gravest error of judgment during the campaign of 1813 to 1814. Not only was the invasion of a neutral country a clear breach of international law—however strained might be the definition of neutrality by Switzerland's participation in Napoleon's army—but the act completely destroyed the Tsar's trust in Metternich. It would be many months before any reconciliation between the two men took place.

In those dark days at the year's end in Freiburg Metternich carried a staggering burden of work. Again and again he spent the whole night at his desk. "For the ninth night," he wrote Laure, "I have not gone to bed before 5 or 6 in the morning, and I get up at 8 or 9. If this were to go on I could not hold out."[7]

He was so busy that Gentz, who had arrived in mid-December, could only find a chance to see him by coming to sit on his bed at eight in the morning.

Metternich was endeavoring to pry Napoleon's last allies loose and win them to the Allied cause—and, hopefully, bring peace a step closer. On the same Sunday, December 19, when he arranged the last details of the troop entry in Switzerland, he talked to ambassadors from Denmark and from Naples, and got their agreement to treaties of alliance. He was certain now they would have "a peace such as never was made." Naples was settled, Aberdeen informed Castlereagh. Murat "would vapour a good deal, but the Queen who rules everything" had sent word they would agree to Metternich's terms.[8]

The matter of Denmark proved to be more difficult. Norway, which had been part of Denmark for four hundred years, had been promised to Bernadotte by the Tsar and Castlereagh, to compensate for Finland, which Russia had taken, and as a reward for Bernadotte's military co-operation. Metternich was determined not to surrender the whole of Norway. But Bernadotte had taken matters into his own hands, marched into Holstein, forced a treaty on Denmark at swords' points. Just as Metternich had arranged a treaty with the Danish envoy permitting Denmark to keep most of Norway, word came that Bernadotte had arranged things to his own satisfaction—and with the full acquiescence of the Tsar. The whole of Norway would go to Sweden.

This time it was Metternich's turn to be enraged. The Bernadotte negotiations had been kept secret from him; he had been thoroughly gulled— "completely taken in by the Tsar and Loewenhielm. . . . I never saw Metternich really furious before," Aberdeen wrote on the last day of the year.[9]

The quarrel between Metternich and the Tsar, reflecting the bitter power struggle between Austria and Russia for control of the war's ends in Europe, was now in the open. "Everything which has been so long smothered is now bursting forth," Aberdeen noted. And Gentz wrote, "The *innerste Innere* [deepest interior] the common heart of the great Coalition is no longer intact."[10]

In the town of Freiburg, despite the banquets, troop parades and balls of the Christmas season, things were far from rosy. Prices had shot up. The colorful Cossacks, whose entry the Freiburgers had cheered, proved to be difficult guests. The troops of the Tsar's brother, Grand Duke Constantine, plundered the peaceful farms, set fire to villages, burned down the farm buildings on the estate of the Tsar's own host, Baron von Andlaw.

And by Christmas the dread disease typhus, gift of the armies to every place they passed through, began ominously to spread in Freiburg and through the duchy of Baden.

2

Metternich did not go to the banquets and balls that marked the year's end in Freiburg.

He had missed his family during the holidays; seven long months he had been away from home. He sent almanacs to Laure, and to Marie and Victor, a box of toys and bonbons for the younger children from Freiburg, and to Marie a pretty wallet "which smells of England," filled with ducats.

> I would have been very happy to spend the holidays with you, my dears [he wrote them], but heaven has decreed otherwise. God will reunite us by next year, and I shall be happy not to leave you again.[11]

He predicted peace by February or March, "That is my prophecy and you know I don't often make a mistake in any political calculation." A bit later he advanced his prophecy to April.

His family sent him a Christmas box too that reached him in Freiburg on December 22, full of *bêtises*, funny things to make him laugh.

It had not been a cheerful Christmas in Vienna with all the fathers and husbands away at war, and lonely for the Metternich family without dear Papa, around whom the whole world moved. When Laure asked Leontine if she still remembered Papa, the little girl replied very decidedly that she did.

Victor's tutor, Herr Schramm, had enlisted in the Army, and Victor had offered all his little store of kreutzer to help him buy a uniform and horse. Metternich wrote at once that Schramm was to come directly to him, he would outfit him, pay his wages as long as the war lasted, and find him a commission as second lieutenant.

Metternich's private study was kept locked in his absence, but Marie wrote her father:

> Sometimes when I come home I go through the little red salon and I amuse myself peeking through the keyhole into your study. I imagine to myself that you are sitting there writing at your desk, and this sweet fancy makes me more cheerful.[12]

Laure had been ill in November with a rheumatic fever that left her with a buzzing in the ears. Her health worried him:

> I hate it when you are ill and I am near you and I hate it even more when I am far away. Happily Staudenheimer is enough of a tyrant that I can count on him.[13]

She mustn't forget to give Dr. Staudenheimer a New Year's gift of a thousand or twelve hundred francs.

As always at the close of an old year and the beginning of a new one, Metternich was filled by what Humboldt called his "January thoughts." The year 1813 would remain for Metternich the turning point of his life, the year in which single-handed he had led Austria out of her wretched position as a Napoleonic satellite to the most influential rank in the councils of Europe. If he had not succeeded in avoiding war, as he hoped to do, he was certain that the war would be contained and shortened by his brilliant diplomacy. "Napoleon will think about this year," he wrote to Laure.[14]

He is busy with plans for the future, when the war is over and he is back home again. The Emperor, he confides to Laure, has promised him "everything—I should only ask for what I want!" Metternich has asked the Emperor to take an interest in his children, to promise to be their guardian in case of his own death. There were certain nice practical rewards in the offing as well:

> The Emperor will certainly give me a fine dotation [he wrote Laure], and then I shall see my old age approach with complete and certain security. The dotation will be worth a great deal, certainly more than the principality Napoleon offered me a while back.[15]

Laure is his incomparable partner, the manager of his household, to whom he entrusts as to a faithful steward the carrying out of all his little commands and wishes. She is to talk to old Count Zichy at some appropriate moment—Metternich has just done a favor for Zichy with the Emperor—and ask him on the quiet to keep his eye out for a fine estate for them—the estate of some family that has died out without heirs and has therefore reverted to the Crown—"which I can ask the Emperor for when all this is finished."[16]

And he has another idea in store to bring joy to Laure's heart—a house of their own in Baden. She had mentioned in one of her letters that the Eichelberg house is up for sale; she should send Ferdinand Palffy to inquire about it, pretending he wants it for himself, else the price would go sky-high. Metternich will go as high as 60,000 florins.

"It's a lot, but there is a bit of land." He will use his diamond-studded snuffboxes for the down payment—all except that one he got from Napoleon, "which I want you to have absolutely. The stones are too fine to be separated." Even if they have to borrow and pay interest, they'll be ahead in the end owning a place, "and I count your pleasure in being in Baden" as worth far more than anything else.[17]

Metternich is so certain of an early peace that he writes Laure to go through the rooms of the Chancellery with the decorator Moreau and get an estimate on the cost of redoing them. All the official buildings in Vienna have become run-down and shabby in the long years of war and occupation and bankruptcy. The lovely five-sided room in the Chancellery, the room with the fireplace, the grand salon and the two beyond—all should get new stucco ceilings, new wall coverings, new furniture and new marble fireplaces. "When the Emperor returns there will be great fetes and I shall give some very grand ones at the Chancellery."[18]

He has another Giroux story for Marie:

He comes into my bedroom yesterday. He opens the curtains, arranges everything for my toilette. He makes absolutely unbelievable noise, then he stands there in front of my bed and says, "It's really amazing the way you sleep with your eyes open."

"I am not sleeping, you imbecile!" I yell. I dedicate the story to Marie.[19]

3

Just before Christmas Wilhelmine had journeyed back from Prague to Vienna. She had waited extra weeks in Prague for a half-promised visit from Alfred. "I don't know what I want," she wrote Metternich, "but I know that I am tormented."[20] For a few days Metternich suffered all the demons of a jealous imagination—Alfred and Wilhelmine together in Prague! But as it turned out, Alfred had not been able to take leave.

From Vienna on Christmas Eve Wilhelmine wrote Metternich. She was suffering all the depression of a journey's end, the darkness of the season ("so that I cannot read or write before 11 in the morning"), the combined chill of an unlived-in house, where everything was in disorder, and of her unfriendly neighbor, Princess Bagration. Her sisters, she found, had become ardently pro-Prussian and insisted on arguing politics with her. Her little girls were sick, one with croup, the other they feared had measles. She herself had one of her wretched migraines—"my miserable head makes me suffer impossibly."[21]

All in all, Christmas was not a time of cheer.

Holidays are, besides, a time for families to be together, when ties of love and of blood are most poignant and most vulnerable, a time when more than any other moment parents' hearts dwell with absent children.

So it was that at Christmas Wilhelmine finally confided in Metternich the secret of her little illegitimate daughter, Gustava, whom she had given away in the folly and despair of youth.

Little Vava was now nearly thirteen, growing up in faraway Finland, where her father was governor and one of the Tsar's inner circle of officials.

Early in November Wilhelmine had begun to think of asking Metternich to intervene for her with the Tsar. Was it possible he could get back for her this only child of her body, of her first love, whom she longed with every fiber of her being to reclaim for her own, bring back into the circle of her life and affection?

In November Wilhelmine had written him that her mother was returning to Paris—a foolish and imprudent move that might cost the Duchess of Courland her Russian income just at the moment when Wilhelmine thought she had arranged matters with the Tsar.

In that direction [she wrote Metternich] I have a single matter, very different from the others—I repent not having discussed it with

you—I would like to know what you think of it, how you envisage
my position, if something can be done about it—if one should leave
everything as it is—it is an interest very dear, very painful, very delicate—but to which perhaps is attached the tranquillity of my old
age—[22]

She tells him no more, not yet. She must ponder it still longer. So carefully has the secret of her child been kept that no rumor of her existence
has ever reached the gossiping tongues of Central European society. Strangely
enough, a world that accepted certain levels of sexual freedom for women—
which, however, a woman of rank was expected to manage with taste and discretion—was far from accepting the fruit of that freedom.

Metternich replied to her tentative words:

Write me about that certain affair. I suppose it is a question of the
engagements you took toward that infamous Armfelt.[23]

Wilhelmine had foolishly promised a substantial income to Armfelt in that
time thirteen years earlier when she had loved him to distraction.

Hesitantly, fearfully, Wilhelmine confides in Metternich that it is not a
matter of money, but of something infinitely more precious to her—the
possession of her only child. She had, she tells him, begged her second husband, Prince Troubetskoi, to help her recover the child. He was a Russian
of position, close to the Tsar; he had advised Wilhelmine to forget the child.
Would Metternich too urge her to forget little Gustava, to abandon all hope
of regaining her?

Metternich wrote her at once:

I feel rich since I now possess your secret—your child is mine—I love
it like my own. I adopt her—she will remain my whole life the object
of my tenderest affection, of my most careful attention.[24]

Had he been married to her as Troubetskoi had been, how he would have
loved her child! *Eh bien,* my dear, he writes, does she finally begin to understand that she is not alone in the world, that he has become her other self,
that he can weep for her sorrow, smile at a gleam of happiness for her?
Gustava will be, he writes, "a great common bond between us."

I am happy for having joined my existence to yours by a tie that will
never again be broken. Not having the good fortune to be her father,
I shall be her teacher, her support for the rest of my life. If you leave
this world before me, you will know that she is in good hands—she too
will not be alone.

She is to ask her trustee and legal adviser, Count Wratislaw, for certain information and authorize him to correspond directly with Metternich on
Gustava's behalf.

He promises to put the question directly to Tsar Alexander. And Metternich adds a promise and a threat. *"I shall make the safety of Russia depend on it."*[25]

The days of early January 1814, when Wilhelmine confided the secret of her child to Metternich and begged his help, were the days that followed immediately after the quarrel between Metternich and the Tsar over Swiss neutrality. Hardly could there have been a less judicious moment to appeal to the Tsar for special favors.

Nevertheless, one day in January Metternich waited until the end of an important political conference, when things had not gone too badly, detained the Tsar, saying he had a special favor to ask him.

"I'll do anything you ask, provided you don't ask me to cut off someone's head without a trial," the Tsar replied, jauntily.

"It has nothing to do with killing," Metternich assured him, "rather with saving someone's life." He gave the Tsar no details; he himself must have full information first. He told him only that it was a favor the Tsar could grant and it concerned "an object sacred to me."

"I give you my word I'll do it," the Tsar replied at once. And Metternich told Wilhelmine, "Let me work; she will be ours."[26]

Never had Wilhelmine written more tenderly to Metternich than when she received his promise to help her:

> I would like to be with you, to throw myself into your arms and embrace you from the bottom of my heart, of this grateful heart, the best of men and the best of friends—I might perhaps in looking at you, in listening to you, in talking to you, explain what is happening in my soul. . . .
>
> A long time ago I put the care of my life into your hands—I do more today—yes, I confide in you what is dearest to me in this world. You will be her guide, protector, father. . . . Thanks to you I shall live happily and die in peace. I can scarcely see what I am writing for my tears—[27]

A little earlier Metternich had sent Wilhelmine a beautiful writing case ordered from London. Exquisitely made with golden locks and hinges, it enclosed seven compartments. She was to put his correspondence only in it; each compartment would hold a year's letters. "I am counting on seven years, as you see, and when they have passed I shall give you a new writing case." If she died before him, the case and the letters were to be returned to him. If he died before her, "which God grant and which is likely in the course of life," she was to bequeath the case to the person "in whom you have the greatest confidence."

Even his love letters Metternich destined for posterity.

He wanted the heir who received those letters to know that it was Wilhelmine's image that had sustained "a man called upon to influence the world's destiny." It was she who had given him the moral power to endure moments of greatest crisis:

. . . if humanity owes part of the salvation of its rights and well-being to me, I owe to this cherished being, Wilhelmine, the power to do good.[28]

Of his heart she could have no doubt.

If ever the world were lost [he wrote her] and you remained to me, I would need nothing more; but if I lose you, I would not know what to do with the world—except for the bit of earth they'd need to bury me.[29]

XIV

CAMPAIGN IN FRANCE

Peace will come like the guest whom you await, and only when, seized with impatience, you go running out looking for him, there he arrives. . . . I shall find him one of these days waiting before my door.
—METTERNICH TO LAURE, JANUARY 9, 1814

1

In the first week of January, while the Allied armies pushed deep into France, a carriage took its way out of Paris toward the east and on January 6 entered Lunéville, which had just been occupied by General Wrede and a Bavarian Army. Caulaincourt, Foreign Minister of France, had come to ask for a pass to travel on to Allied headquarters and open immediate negotiations for peace. Halted at the advance posts, he had to content himself with turning over letters, one addressed to Metternich and one to Emperor Franz from his daughter.

"The little man," Metternich wrote Laure that week, "is in a most frightful position. We shall have peace in February or March."[1]

Napoleon was ready to discuss a general peace, Caulaincourt's letter announced; he was sending his minister with full negotiating powers. Why, Napoleon asked, since he had accepted the bases the Allies had proposed at Frankfurt, had this long delay ensued?

In a warm personal letter to Metternich Caulaincourt congratulated him on his elevation to princedom, reminded him of their good relationship the previous summer when they two had wished so earnestly to make peace at Prague. "We want peace," he wrote now. "I hope Your Excellency will believe in the sincerity of this wish. . . ."[2]

Overjoyed with the proposal, optimistic now that peace could be arranged within days—weeks at the outside—Metternich replied that the Tsar was away from Freiburg at the moment, that they awaited Castlereagh's arrival from England. An official reply would be sent just as soon as it was possible.

With luck the whole thing could be brought to an end now without further battles. Writing Schwarzenberg the good news, he ordered him to "proceed—but prudently."[3]

Why not invite Caulaincourt to Freiburg and they could begin peace talks at once? But the Tsar objected. His troops were ready to enter France; besides, there was a kind of delayed justice in having those negotiations take place inside France.

A few days later the entire headquarters moved south from Freiburg to Basel to watch the Tsar's Cossack Guard cross the Rhine on January 13, the Russian New Year. In paralyzing cold and not in the best humor Metternich sat on horseback through the hours of the Russian troops' parade.

While Schwarzenberg's army crossed the broad plateau of Langres into eastern France, Blücher's Prussians invaded from the northeast. The two armies were to converge near the town of Langres and there wait for peace to be made. Metternich meantime wrote Caulaincourt that the Allies would meet him at the little town of Châtillon-sur-Seine, not far from Langres, and negotiations could begin as soon as Castlereagh arrived from England. "The world is saved," Metternich wrote Laure. "I busy myself only with details."[4]

But the Tsar had his own plans for the future, and they did not coincide with Metternich's. Chafing in Basel at Castlereagh's delay, he finally announced that he could wait no longer but was leaving at once to join his troops in France. Bidding good-by to his friend the King of Prussia that Sunday morning, January 16, the Tsar exploded a political bombshell. He did not intend to halt, he declared, "before he got to Paris and proclaimed Bernadotte Emperor of France."[5]

Though rumors had persisted of Bernadotte's ambition to secure the throne of France, until that moment the Allies had appeared to agree on a single war aim: to reduce French power outside the boundaries of France, but to maintain Napoleon on the throne. As an ally Bernadotte had been less than co-operative; he had not joined the strategic invasion-for-peace plan but had concentrated on wresting Norway from Denmark.

The idea of Bernadotte as Emperor of France threw all of headquarters into a turmoil. The Prussian King "was petrified with astonishment but asked [the Tsar] if he had not better wait for Castlereagh's arrival, who was expected daily. The Tsar said that he went on purpose to avoid him." This at least was Aberdeen's account, while Cathcart, writing Castlereagh urging him to make all haste, explained that the Tsar did not want to be overly hasty in making peace, but rather "to weigh well the question whether more should not previously be done by arms."[6]

Clearly the Coalition was in danger of splitting over that crucial question of war aims.

"I tell you that in less than fifteen days, at most in three weeks peace must be made or the Coalition will have to propose a new aim," Metternich told Schwarzenberg, ordering him "not to push military movements beyond what is strictly necessary. . . ."

> Don't expose yourself to a check but wait, saying nothing to anyone, for new directions before undertaking any new offensive operations, and these directions can only be given you according to the political position of affairs.[7]

Underlying the rift was once again the power struggle between Austria and Russia, and the personal duel between Metternich and the Tsar for leadership of the Coalition. Bernadotte on the throne of France would give his closest ally, the Tsar, far too much influence in western Europe.

Into the dissension-riven camp of the Allied ministers, clouded with distrust, suspicion, intrigue, Castlereagh arrived on the late afternoon of Tuesday, January 18. Spurred on by the urgent messages he found awaiting him in Frankfurt, he had driven all day and all night to reach Freiburg at two in the morning on that Tuesday. There Gentz waited up for him on Metternich's orders, indoctrinated him in the inner politics of the Coalition until five in the morning, scoured Freiburg for fresh horses and sent him at once on his way to Basel.

To the astonished eyes of the diplomats in Basel Castlereagh cut a strange figure. The headquarters group had been living out of campaign trunks for months and despite the best efforts of their valets they were a seedy-looking lot, "all of us," Humboldt wrote, "in awful uniforms, boots, no powder, shaggy locks like tattooed savages."[8]

Castlereagh had apparently designed his own costume for wartime traveling. Humboldt thought he looked "rather like a valet," but Metternich decided the effect was more that "of an eighteenth-century prelate . . . blue coat, red breeches, jockey boots, a fur cap with a gold band." One of Castlereagh's secretaries sported an even more singular outfit, a kind of hussar uniform "with a lace-covered dolman and a fur cape with silk laces, which looked as if he had put his undershirt on over his clothes." It would be some time, Humboldt decided, before Castlereagh would fit into the evening smoking sessions.

Handsome and grave, the English Foreign Secretary looked far older than his forty-four years. And while Metternich's cool exterior was the poise of the well-trained diplomat, Castlereagh's went to the heart of his psyche. Everyone described his personality in terms of arctic temperature—what John Croker called "that splendid summit of bright and polished frost."[9] A highly complex man, there was about Castlereagh a suggestion of tightly controlled violence under the icy surface, of some unresolved and tragic dilemma at the core of his personality.

Son of an Anglo-Irish peer, Castlereagh had begun his political career by helping to quell the bloody Irish rebellion of 1798, and to engineer, against the bitter resistance of the Irish, the union with Britain. Deeply influenced by Pitt, Castlereagh served as Secretary of War for some years, pursuing an aggressive though not particularly adroit role in the continental wars against Napoleon. Foreign Secretary since 1812, he had refused to allow the war with the United States to be resolved by mediation, and had the previous spring rejected Metternich's offer of Austrian mediation in the European war.

He spoke fractured French and no German. Nevertheless, to the troubled Coalition in January of 1814 Castlereagh brought a number of valuable assets—a keen intelligence, a fresh viewpoint, an open, frank way of dealing with issues—quite unlike Metternich's Venetian style that laid him open to frequent charges of duplicity.

The two men sized one another up shrewdly; they saw at once they could do business together. The following day and for the rest of that week Metternich and Castlereagh talked over the issues of the moment. Were there to be negotiations, and if so, what were to be the bases for a peace? And what about Bernadotte and the throne of France?

> Lord Castlereagh has everything [Metternich wrote Schwarzenberg that week]: amenity, shrewdness, moderation. He is agreeable to me in every way, and I am convinced I am equally so to him. We agreed on the stupidity of a Certain Person and I no longer worry about his digression.[10]

From far away in Vienna Wilhelmine discerned astutely that Metternich would not turn Castlereagh "round his little finger," as Priscilla Burghersh declared he turned the other ministers. "You were satisfied with Lord Aberdeen, and I do not believe you'll come quite so easily to the end of the other," she wrote.[11]

She was right. With Castlereagh the dynamics of leadership shifted. Desperately Metternich needed Castlereagh's support in resolving the split in the Coalition. He had to buy alliance with England at all costs; in a market with few options the price comes high. Metternich would retain leadership in the Coalition, but his diplomacy had to veer and his compromises to widen.

On the Sunday after Castlereagh's arrival, January 23, the English minister and Priscilla Burghersh dined early at Metternich's house in Basel and all three set out in late afternoon for Schwarzenberg's headquarters somewhere in France, Castlereagh in Metternich's swift little campaign carriage, Priscilla following with her maid in her big pillowed berline.

They had planned to leave Basel the previous day, but a courier from Naples had brought a draft of the proposed treaty of alliance with Joachim Murat, King of Naples. In return for Murat's allegiance to the Allied cause and a contribution of 30,000 troops, Austria guaranteed to maintain Murat on the throne of Naples, and even promised him an increase in territory at the expense of the Papal States. Metternich had sat up all night revising the treaty and only gone to bed at daybreak when his fingers were too stiff with cold to hold the pen.

He was in such a hurry to reach headquarters before the Tsar could carry out his plans that he and Castlereagh galloped at top speed and soon, somewhat ungallantly, left Priscilla Burghersh far behind, to ride through what she recalled as "the coldest night I ever felt."

If the French peasants in the villages greeted the passing carriage of the two foreign ministers with little interest, they did come running out to stare at Priscilla Burghersh—"*la princesse Anglaise*," they called her—wondering at sight of the vivacious blond girl in her furred traveling cloak, her face pressed to the frosty window of her carriage so as not to miss a single sight of this France she had never seen before.

The scene that winter of the final campaign—the campaign for peace as well as for war—was the long, low marshy stretch of land that lies between the rivers Seine and Marne like a crooked forefinger pointing toward Paris. To the invaders that winter of 1814 it was a dreary, anonymous landscape, crisscrossed by a network of streams and rivers, its scattered villages and peasant farms all but obliterated under a blanket of snow, the few roads— most barely more than a wagon track where two vehicles could just manage to pass—nearly all running in the direction of Paris.

Winter campaigns were rare in that day, and for good reason. Armies moved by foot and by horse; gun carriages and provision wagons often had to be dragged by main force through snow and ice, reduced now and again to a sea of mud by a sudden unexpected thaw. Over those wretched roads that winter would trudge the immense clutter of the armies, hundreds of thousands of feet booted or wrapped in rags. Behind them would trail the long snake of civilian carriages carrying the sovereigns and ministers and their staffs and servants, from one town to another as armies advanced and retreated.

Landmarks were few. Half the time neither army knew very precisely where the enemy was, and often not even where the rest of its own forces were. Couriers got lost or captured or killed. A sudden thaw or an unbridged river could separate armies, and in the low wooded hills a whole cavalry regiment could hide from sight.

Darkness fell early, swift as a curtain, the utter blackness of winter and poverty, when frugal peasants went to bed as soon as darkness came. Carriages then groped their way along barely visible tracks, lighted only by the gleam of a flickering tallow lantern.

Crossing France in the wake of the army Metternich and Castlereagh noted no resistance, no sign of an uprising to overthrow Napoleon, only apathy, discouragement, hatred of war. Deeply the peasants resented the folly and waste and disruption that took their able-bodied sons from the land, stole their last horse and cow—often burned their houses and barns to the ground. The retreating French army had already ransacked the countryside for food and forage; there was scarcely a handful of grain or a single scrawny chicken to be found. Bands of Cossacks roamed about, foraging freely; convoys were held up and robbed.

Though Priscilla Burghersh had seen the bleak poverty of Ireland, she was appalled by the misery of the French villages they passed through, "where," she wrote, "the number of beggars far surpasses Dublin."

Sharp-eyed Priscilla noted something else that had escaped the attention of her male comrades—"multitudes of miserable-looking women; one never sees a young man, and I am particularly struck with not seeing any babies whatever." In the towns they drove through Priscilla saw "all women and children, for of spare men there are none." Herds of begging women followed them in the streets wherever they went. "If you give money to one, the rest fall on her and then begins a regular fight."[12]

> They want peace and quiet [Metternich wrote Laure] and they seem to be saying to us, "But, Messieurs, we don't want your dear presence either." The French are so little accustomed to what is happening that their astonishment equals their apathy, and their hope is that this war will be the last in a long time. May God grant it![13]

Driving almost without pause, Metternich and Castlereagh reached Langres on Tuesday afternoon, January 25. They were only twenty-four hours from Paris.

2

On the same Sunday afternoon, January 23, when Metternich, Castlereagh and Priscilla Burghersh had set out on their long, cold journey across eastern France to Langres, Napoleon stage-managed a dramatic little scene in the Tuileries Palace in Paris.

Summoning several hundred officers of the Guard to the Salle des Maréchaux, he appeared before them, holding his wife, Marie Louise, by one hand, by the other, their little boy, the King of Rome, not quite three years old.

"Gentlemen," he declared, "the territory of France has been invaded. I am going to take my place at the head of my army. With the help of God and my brave soldiers I hope to throw the enemy back across the frontier.

"I entrust to you today what is dearest to me in this world. If the enemy approaches the capital, I entrust my wife and son to your courage!"

The officers crowded together in the room were deeply moved. Some broke ranks and ran forward weeping to kiss the Emperor's hand and swear lifelong loyalty.

Two days later, at four in the morning, Napoleon left Paris to join his army.

He had not expected the Allies to cross the Rhine and invade France in the dead of winter—a season when most armies in that day found comfortable quarters to wait out the weeks of inclement weather.

In December and January he had worked desperately to put together a new army, combing the regimental depots for men who had been exempted from service, calling up the class of 1815 a year early, ordering out the Home Guard, and a levee en masse on the eastern frontier, even summoning the young cadets from the military academy at Saint-Cyr.

But he was disastrously short of cavalry, his treasury was nearly empty. His people were sick to death of war. In barns and attics and woodlands thousands of deserters and draft-dodgers hid out. Aberdeen's Swiss landlord had reported after a trip to Paris that in France "the universal cry is for peace—the Declaration of the Allies [Metternich's manifesto] is everywhere, and has produced the most astonishing effect."

On December 19 Napoleon had addressed the Legislative Corps, informing them that negotiations were about to take place, that meantime he needed a new army to protect France and to win the best peace terms possible. He did not inform them that his first reply to the St. Aignan overtures had been couched in language so vague as nearly to wreck the possibility of peace talks. He demanded "fresh sacrifices" in the form of higher taxes, more troops. On New Year's Day at his public audience he had turned a ferocious diatribe on a committee of discontented deputies who had dared to demand guarantees of the personal liberties and political rights they had lost.

But Napoleon well knew that an underground movement of dissidents worked against him—among them such dangerous enemies as Talleyrand, his former Foreign Minister and still Vice Grand Elector, and Fouché, former Minister of Police.

In the last days of January Napoleon studied the map of eastern France, pinpointing the advance of the invading armies.

On January 25, with Bertrand beside him in his carriage, he drove out of Paris toward the east, reaching Châlons in time for dinner. Learning that Schwarzenberg was in Langres, moving slowly toward Troyes, and that Blücher was directing his army along the Marne toward St. Dizier, Napoleon ordered a ration of wine or brandy for all his troops; if no wine was available, they were to get champagne.

3

The weather was icy, bone-biting cold. Humboldt's ink froze in his inkwell. In Langres Metternich was quartered in the house of a Dr. Pistolet ("God keep me from having to call on his services!" he wrote Wilhelmine), where he worked half paralyzed with cold, for heat "only a wretched fireplace and 6 degrees above zero in my room." Wolves, he wrote Laure, had appeared in packs near the town, coming so close that an Austrian courier arriving by carriage had to chase them away with pistol shots and blows of the coachman's whip.[14]

While Caulaincourt chafed anxiously in the little town of Châtillon, waiting for word that negotiations would begin, in Langres, a few miles to the west, in Metternich's chilly quarters, the sovereigns and ministers of the Allied Coalition fought over whether there should be negotiations at all, or whether the armies should march on Paris and overthrow Napoleon.

Was the future to be decided by reason or by force?

A day or two before, Metternich had got a confidential letter from Caulaincourt written January 25, begging him to begin peace negotiations as soon as possible. He proposed an armistice, an offer which, he stipulated, must remain secret and if accepted must appear to have originated with the Allies—for the sake of Napoleon's pride, of course. Napoleon himself had suggested an armistice, but, angry at the delay in the negotiations, was ready to recall both the armistice offer and his plenipotentiary.[15]

Schwarzenberg, urged by the Tsar to press farther on into France, refused to advance until he had orders from Emperor Franz. Poorly clothed, badly fed, billeted anywhere that could be found—in barns or in open fields—troops by the hundreds were falling ill. In Schwarzenberg's army nearly 50,000 men were reported sick by February. There was danger too that the army could not be provisioned; Schwarzenberg lived in constant fear of a real famine in his huge army, which could mean a breakdown of all discipline. Langres, he pointed out in a memorandum to the Emperor, was the last military point at which they could reasonably stop and make peace with Napoleon. If they continued to penetrate deeper into France, Napoleon would be forced to fight with every last resource for his very existence, and then the Allies too would be forced "to fight with the same weapons."

Schwarzenberg favored making peace at once.

Here we should make peace, that is my advice [he wrote his wife]. Any push on to Paris is in the highest degree unmilitary. Our Emperor, Stadion, Metternich, even Castlereagh, are of my opinion, but the Tsar has another of his attacks of sublime foolishness. God help us in this crisis. Caulaincourt has been waiting for five days in Châtillon.[16]

The question to be decided by the Allied leaders in that last week of January 1814 was whether decisions reached at the council table through reason and persuasion should—or could—take precedence over solutions wrested on the battlefield by one side or the other.

Clearly each of the Allies, though paying lip service to the idea of a negotiated peace, had his own secret agenda and secret war aims. By framing a series of key questions which he circulated to the sovereigns and ministers that week, Metternich brought the issues into the open in a series of stormy conferences.

Did moderation, justice, love of peace still motivate them, as they had claimed throughout the earlier campaign? If their original war aims, enunciated in 1813, had been reached, were they ready to sign peace with France on the agreed-upon basis of her "natural" boundaries? If Napoleon refused peace, were they ready to present their proposals to the people of France? Do they want to give France a new sovereign, or do they consider the dynastic question as purely the internal affair of France? In case of the former, are they declaring only against Napoleon, or also against his heirs and in favor of the Bourbons?

And finally, Metternich asked, if the war aims of the powers had enlarged beyond those declared earlier, were they ready to enunciate them clearly to one another?[17]

A few conferences would make clear whether Napoleon would negotiate seriously or not. If he refused to make peace, then the war might have to be carried further. But the Allies would then have the task of redefining and agreeing upon new war aims.

When the ministers met on Friday evening, January 28, to discuss the issues he had raised, Metternich suggested at once that they accept Caulaincourt's armistice offer and begin to talk peace. Unless both sides laid down their arms while peace talks went on, the real decisions could be made by the armies, and military decisions would take precedence over political.

It was a crucial issue and one of immense import in the conduct of any war.

But the armistice proposal was voted down. The Russians and Prussians opposed it; so did Castlereagh, who insisted, "War should be conducted with vigor without regard to discussions for peace." If military operations continued, Castlereagh and Hardenberg agreed to negotiate.

The Tsar, on the advice of Stein and La Harpe, continued to oppose peace talks and press for a march on Paris. The debate that night was extremely bitter. Not until Metternich threatened to withdraw Austria from the Coalition if the peace talks were not to be held did the Tsar reluctantly give in. Very well, he would send a delegate to Châtillon.

So that much was settled: there was to be a peace congress. Metternich could send a message to Caulaincourt that "preliminary conferences for a general peace" would begin on February 3.

But the terms to be offered to France, threshed out in a long conference at Stadion's house, were far harsher than the bases offered at Frankfurt.

Metternich, who understood France and the aspirations of the French people better than any of the diplomats gathered at Langres, knew how deeply French national pride was bound up in the concept of "natural" boundaries, of a geographical and linguistic entity, defined by the first victories of the Revolutionary armies in 1792. Napoleon had taken his coronation oath on maintaining the integrity of those boundaries; whether he could or would break his oath added one more element of doubt to the negotiations.

But Castlereagh argued for what he called "the rights of war." The Allies were victors; they were occupying a large part of French soil; they had a right to demand more in January than they had asked in November. It was the same philosophy Napoleon had used: the right of the conqueror.

As Metternich had already learned in Basel, Castlereagh's instructions made Britain's return of former French colonies she had conquered contingent on the restriction of French maritime power and the absolute exclusion of France from any naval establishment on the Scheldt—above all, from control of the great port of Antwerp. The Channel was to be neutralized through an enlarged Holland, for the protection of British commercial interests. France must, therefore, be reduced to her "former" boundaries—that is, those she had had under her kings rather than the post-Revolution boundaries of Rhine, Alps and Pyrenees, which would have included the left bank of the Rhine and French-speaking Belgium.

Metternich had no choice except to give in. Yet to keep the promise he had made in the name of the Allies in his Manifesto to the French People, he asked that some generous concession be made to give France something more in territory than she had possessed under her kings.

Castlereagh's second demand was that all discussion of Britain's maritime interests—the definition of "freedom of the seas" in which she differed from such neutral nations as the United States—be excluded from the negotiations at Châtillon. Again it was an issue which Metternich well knew would make any peace talks with France far more difficult, for at the core of the long Anglo-French conflict lay the struggle of the two countries for commercial supremacy. Though Castlereagh insisted that England viewed her maritime code as conforming to the "law of nations"—that is, the accepted rules of international law—still he did not want France to have a voice in the interpretation of that code as it affected British interests.

Again Metternich agreed. A declaration to that effect would be made at the opening of negotiations. In exchange Castlereagh submitted a list of conquered colonies England was willing to return to France.[18]

Finally there was the question of the future of once occupied lands, now liberated from Napoleon's hegemony—the question that was to prove most difficult and most divisive of all.

According to the Treaty of Reichenbach, Prussia and Austria were to be restored to the territorial strength they had possessed in 1805, and the duchy of Warsaw was to be divided among Austria, Prussia and Russia. The Teplitz Treaty, however, left the fate of the duchy open "to amicable settlement"—which meant that Russia might obtain it all if she could in one way or another win the consent of her Allies.

The most worrisome question in Metternich's mind was how far the Tsar intended to increase the power of Russia at the war's end. Unlike Austria and Prussia, both of which had been shorn of territories during Napoleon's regime, Russia had made substantial gains.

There were well-founded rumors that the Tsar intended to keep Poland and to create a kingdom of Poland under the Crown of Russia.

Certainly the three partitions of Poland, which had totally destroyed Polish independence in the late eighteenth century, dividing the country among Russia, Prussia and Austria, had been a tragic and indefensible act of naked power politics. But the Tsar's proposal to set up a kingdom of Poland under the aegis of Russia seemed less a step toward true Polish independence than an extension of Russian power deep into Central Europe.

Closely allied to the question of Poland was Prussia's proposal to annex the independent kingdom of Saxony, Napoleon's ally up until the battle of Leipzig. The acquisition of Saxony by Prussia was closely geared to the Tsar's Polish plans, for if the Tsar refused to return the formerly Prussian part of Poland, then Prussia would insist on indemnification elsewhere—and to Prussia and Russia, Saxony was the logical answer.

Already in Freiburg and Basel the Allied ministers had wrestled with the knotty questions of Central Europe. Integral to Metternich's long-range plan was a strong middle European block led by Prussia and Austria, to balance a strong France in the West and an all too powerful Russia in the East. Russian designs on Poland threatened that three-way balance of power; Metternich was prepared to be generous and conciliatory to Prussia to protect Austria's eastern front—up to a point. But Prussian designs on Saxony could also upset the delicate equilibrium in Central Europe. Saxony and Austria had a long history of friendly neighborly relations. It could scarcely be in Austria's interest to exchange her small friendly neighbor to the north, bound by long ties of friendship and intermarriage between their ruling families, with a much enlarged Prussia, whose recent history had included the annexation by force of Austrian Silesia.

In the intricate labyrinth of Central European power politics Metternich moved with caution and finesse. He may have agreed in part to Hardenberg's plans for Saxony[19]; if so, his agreement was certainly contingent on some kind of total settlement that would protect Austria's interests.

As for the question of Poland, the Tsar refused to discuss it until the war was ended.

So the days of controversy in Langres produced a single victory for Metternich: there would be peace talks at Châtillon.

But there were no solutions to the complex problems of Central Europe. Nor had the future of France been resolved—whether Napoleon was to remain in power, or if not, what government was to supplant him.

On Castlereagh's secret agenda was a firm commitment to the Bourbons. Already during his first conversations with Metternich in Basel he had tried to win his support for a Bourbon restoration. He was sure he had succeeded in persuading the Austrian minister, he wrote Liverpool. But Castlereagh did not yet know Metternich, who listened courteously, smiled blandly and replied evasively, "There, you've put the questions well. Let us see what the French nation has to say about it."

Again and again Castlereagh would return to his pro-Bourbon arguments.

Each time Metternich replied quietly, "All this may be, but . . . I would not interfere in what belongs to France to regulate."[20]

Metternich continued to support firmly the Bonaparte dynasty, whether in the person of Napoleon, or a regency of Marie Louise for the son of Napoleon. This was the established government of France, the government with which the Allies had agreed to negotiate. It had the support of the French Army, and so far as they could discern in their advance through France, it still had the support of the French people.

Yet in Langres Metternich did begin to contemplate the end of Napoleon. If the Châtillon negotiations should fail, then it would be all-out war, a march on Paris, and the overthrow of Napoleon.

And Metternich reassured his Allies that Austria would not desert the alliance if the Napoleonic dynasty came to an end—even if the Emperor's daughter lost her throne. Austria would not interfere in any decision the French people made on their future government—nor would Austria support any dynasty which did not have a broad base of support within France—a clear warning to the Bourbon followers. Metternich did not believe the Bourbons had such a base, and he continued to doubt it up until very nearly the end of the campaign.[21]

Gloomily Emperor Franz acquiesced in the possibility that his son-in-law would be dethroned—and his daughter and grandson perhaps as well. It was a painful blow to him, as a father and as a monarch.

"The Emperor is ill today," Priscilla Burghersh wrote in early February, "and has got *une terrible migraine.* The fact is the poor man is completely miserable about his daughter whom he loves very much."[22]

"Don't abandon me, my dear friend," Schwarzenberg had written Metternich from the new site of army headquarters farther on at Chaumont. "You promised me at Frankfurt when I agreed to push military operations vigorously, that you would push peace negotiations. I have kept my word, but alas! how far behind me you've remained!"[23]

The reproach was undeserved. At one o'clock in the morning of January 30, having won the Tsar's reluctant consent to negotiate, Metternich could write jubilantly, "We've carried off the thing and they're going to negotiate. . . . I went so far as to threaten rupture and I carried the whole thing off."[24]

A few hours later he sent along to Schwarzenberg Caulaincourt's confidential armistice offer to be used if and when Schwarzenberg saw fit. If the situation became "dangerous," Metternich would consider accepting an armistice of fifteen days or three weeks. "If we were alone," he wrote, "we would undertake the thing today."[25]

It was Metternich who drew up the instructions under which the negotiators at Châtillon were to operate. "I have worked these last days in a way I cannot describe," he wrote Laure. "Will [the negotiations] succeed? The question is quite as problematical as the existence of Napoleon! As to the dynastic question [that is, the future government of France] all the cabinets agree to leave this question to the decision of God."[26]

As it turned out, the politicians were willing, when the time came, to lend a hand to God.

While Metternich worked feverishly in the last days of January to get the peace congress under way, Schwarzenberg was having grave problems in keeping the armies of the Allies under control.

Prussian Generals Blücher and Gneisenau—"the eccentrics," they were called—hot for revenge for the wrongs done Prussia, clamored for war to the death against Napoleon, and military action "to the last breath and the last horse."

Seventy-year-old Blücher, a stout, tough old soldier who had spent more than fifty years of his life in the Army and was about to win a final nickname of "Marshal Forward," made jokes about Schwarzenberg's cautious military strategy. Blücher had been quite mad in 1809, when he was convinced he was pregnant with an elephant, and that French agents had heated the floors of his house so he had to jump around on tiptoe. He had probably not entirely recovered. Now, secretly encouraged by the Tsar, who was in turn being prodded by Stein, Blücher ordered his Army of Silesia to move quickly toward Paris.

Angrily Schwarzenberg reported to Metternich that "this ridiculous madness" to visit the brothels of the Palais-Royale was endangering the whole Allied plan. He prayed the Tsar would not get another comeuppance as he had got at Lützen. Instead of protecting the right flank of the main Allied army, as he had been ordered to do, Blücher was scorning all rules of strategy, "running like a schoolboy," and forcing Schwarzenberg "to cut up my army to cover their rear."[27]

From Châlons, gathering reports of his couriers and scouts, Napoleon perceived a weakness in the Allied position and moved quickly toward Blücher. In Brienne, the town where, some thirty years before, a lonely Corsican boy had gone to military school at public expense, Napoleon routed the Prussians and very nearly captured Blücher himself.

Hastily Blücher sent to Schwarzenberg for reinforcements. Two corps were dispatched, with orders to Wrede to hasten to Blücher's aid as well.

In a blizzard on February 1, Blücher's forces fell on the French near the village of La Rothière and in a fierce battle soundly defeated them; Napoleon's army had been outnumbered two to one. "The Emperor [Napoleon] was always in the middle of the gunfire as if he wanted to get himself killed," Metternich wrote Laure.[28]

There was jubilation at Allied headquarters when news of the victory came. Charles Stewart described to a horrified Priscilla Burghersh how they "left the dead yesterday in heaps." He promised her there would be no more fighting, for "Buonoparte would not stay to be beat again but has run for it toward Paris." When Stewart went to congratulate Blücher, "the old boy invited us all to dine with him at the Palais-Royale on the 20th of February with all the mamselles."[29]

Many at headquarters believed the war was over.

4

While the Allies celebrated the victory at La Rothière and Napoleon gloomily assessed his defeat, the delegates met at Châtillon, southwest of Langres, for the opening of peace talks.

The composition of the Allied group hardly promised a conciliatory attitude. With the exception of Aberdeen they were not a peace-minded group of diplomats. Representing Russia was Count Razumowsky, "one of the fiercest, most implacable enemies of Napoleon," for Prussia, Humboldt, who had made up his mind "to second Razumowsky in everything." In fact the Tsar had secretly instructed Razumowsky to impede the progress of the Châtillon conferences as much as possible.[30]

Stadion, representing Austria, while too loyal to undermine the decisions of the Cabinet—that is, Metternich—detested Napoleon quite as cordially as Razumowsky. Of the Englishmen, Stewart and Cathcart had always advocated military solutions. Castlereagh at the moment was undecided. Only Aberdeen really hoped for a successful negotiation.

Caulaincourt, desperately eager to bring the war to an end, had been waiting more than three weeks to meet with the Allied plenipotentiaries. Of those Châtillon meetings he recalled:

> I was in a fever of despair; death was in my heart. . . . I confess that when I found myself face to face with some of the plenipotentiaries I had emotions that were akin to madness.[31]

Caulaincourt was determined, however, to succeed. When at the first brief meeting on February 5, after formalities had been taken care of and powers exchanged, Stadion read the declaration excluding maritime rights from any discussion at the meetings, to everyone's astonishment, Caulaincourt quietly accepted the exclusion.

When the delegates adjourned to Caulaincourt's house for dinner, Razumowsky began to talk of his lack of instructions from the Tsar, at first in a joking way, then suddenly, growing serious, he announced to his colleagues gathered around the French minister's table that "he would not take another single step before having instructions from his sovereign." Since all four Allied powers had clearly agreed to follow the common instructions drawn up by Metternich, everyone, even Humboldt, was shocked. In fact the whole congress was turning, in Stadion's words, "into a bad comedy."[32]

At the second meeting, on February 7, Stadion read aloud the Allied demands. France was to withdraw within her old boundaries and give up all influence outside her borders. Caulaincourt asked quite reasonably what compensations France might be granted were she to accept Allied terms, and whether peace might then be signed at once. The delegates equivocated.

Caulaincourt hesitated to take on himself the onus of settling on far more unfavorable terms than the bases that had been offered France at Frankfurt. He sent off a courier to Napoleon asking whether he should accept.

Meantime, Castlereagh, who was present only as an observer, created another complication. Having declared in the talks at Langres that England was ready to surrender all her conquests except Guadaloupe if France surrendered her continental conquests, he raised the question of whether England should not first demand to know precisely what were to be the arrangements made in Central Europe among Austria, Russia and Prussia, and what indemnity would be assigned the Bourbon King of Sicily for giving up Naples to Murat—the whole Pandora's box of complex questions that still remained to be solved.[33]

Each day the first week of February brought to Châtillon fresh news of successful Allied advances. Schwarzenberg was at Troyes with the main army, while advance bands of Cossacks were almost as far as Fontainebleau.

Napoleon, disheartened by the defeat at La Rothière, by the defection of French soldiers, by the despair of his marshals, sent a courier off to Châtillon giving Caulaincourt carte blanche to negotiate on the best terms he could get, in order to "save the capital and avoid a battle."[34]

On February 8 Caulaincourt wrote Metternich too, imploring him to come to Châtillon for at least three hours, bringing Nesselrode—"three hours that could end a struggle now without object and which is costing humanity so many tears." He, Caulaincourt, would not have come to Châtillon at all, he added, had he known he would not be dealing directly with Metternich. Astutely the French minister warned Metternich that an Allied march on Paris would bring in its wake a chain of events Austria would surely regret. Only by blocking a march on Paris could Metternich remain "master of events."[35]

The next day, February 9, at the third conference, Caulaincourt offered to concede on virtually everything. But before any discussion could begin, Razumowsky announced that by order of the Tsar all negotiation had been suspended for an indefinite period of time.

Caulaincourt was dumfounded. Looking around the table at the blank, stony faces of the delegates, he attempted to question them. Why was it suspended? It was the Tsar's wish. But how, he wanted to know, could "the simple desire of a single one of the four Allied courts . . . be a cause of suspending meetings indefinitely?" No one could or would reply.

With anguish in his heart Caulaincourt hurried back to his quarters and sent an express courier to Metternich asking whether, if France consented to withdraw within her old boundaries, she could obtain an immediate armistice.

While he waited anxiously for a reply, in Troyes in those days of mid-

February the Allies came close to splitting apart over the question of immediate peace or a march on Paris.

Metternich reached Troyes at six in the evening of February 9 and was almost at once summoned by the Tsar. He intended, the Tsar informed him bluntly, to march on Paris and summon an assembly of notable men who would choose the future ruler of France.

Marshaling all his arguments, Metternich tried in vain to sway· the Tsar. Such a march would necessitate more bloodshed, at least one more major battle. And would it produce a government representing the will of the French people? Metternich thought not. How could the French make a free choice with Napoleon still in control of the Army, with several hundred thousand foreign soldiers occupying France, and with a Russian military governor overseeing their assembly? Bernadotte, moreover, was poised and ready to enter France at the head of Wittgenstein's corps, Metternich had been told. But the Tsar would not be moved an inch.[36]

It was long after midnight when Metternich returned to his quarters, exhausted, and sat down to finish a letter to Wilhelmine he had begun three days earlier in Bar-sur-Aube:

> The questions are advancing fast; they are so peremptory that they can no longer remain undecided and I would even say unfinished for very long. How deeply I want [peace] this time, how much I need it—how much it is desirable for the world, needs no commentary. Everything wears out finally, my dear, and I am so much a part of this great Everything that what is applicable to Europe is also directly to me.[37]

In the next days Metternich again drew up a list of key questions for a vote by the Allied ministers. Should they grant the armistice Caulaincourt was requesting? How could they learn the views of the French nation on a change in their government? If Paris declared for the Bourbons but the French Army supported Napoleon, what should the Allies do? If they captured Paris, how did they propose to govern it?

At their first conference Hardenberg and Castlereagh cast their votes with Austria in favor of accepting Caulaincourt's overtures. Nesselrode too apparently agreed, but he could put nothing in writing, explaining that the Tsar opposed both an armistice and peace, and was still insisting on the march to Paris.[38]

Leaving the conference at three in the morning, Metternich wrote Wilhelmine, "This 13 will decide whether war is to continue or a peace such as has never been made."[39]

While the Allies debated over ending the war at once, Napoleon had decided to wait no longer but to take the action he understood best. Summoning up his old tough military bravado, he moved swiftly along the course of the Marne River in pursuit of Blücher. And Blücher, recklessly bent on getting to the capital, fell into the very trap Schwarzenberg had feared.

Within a day's march of Paris, Blücher had broken all the old military rules —including those agreed upon the previous summer at Trachenberg—and allowed his various army corps to scatter out across an area of many miles along the Marne, with wide gaps between them.

Moving with audacious speed, maneuvering his armies, as Stadion said, "like a sword in his hand," Napoleon put into brilliant performance his favorite tactic of "divide and conquer," fell upon Blücher's corps one by one and delivered a series of stinging defeats.

Sacken, Olsufiev, Kleist, Langeron and Yorck suffered heavy blows at Champaubert on February 10, at Montmirail on February 11 and at Vauchamps on February 14. Napoleon could send some 8,000 Russian and Prussian prisoners along with several thousand cannon and a sheaf of captured flags to be paraded through the streets of Paris to cheer the gloomy citizens.

Blücher managed to extract the rest of his army safely and to send to Schwarzenberg for help, but the Silesian Army was reeling. "Blücher's mistakes are being bitterly punished," Schwarzenberg wrote his wife. He had, he said, ordered Blücher to pull his staggering forces together while he— Schwarzenberg—would endeavor to repair the damage by drawing Napoleon away from Blücher toward the main army. Schwarzenberg sent part of his army across the Seine, ordering them to attack the French, so that "the enemy will let go of Blücher, but I confess to you that I continue this war with the greatest sorrow of heart. . . . I wish with all my heart God might give Alexander sharper wits. . . ."[40]

Furiously Metternich inveighed against the Tsar, Blücher and his generals: "imbeciles drunk with champagne," "a pack of brainless idiots who think talent is only found on the point of a sword."[41]

The internal dissension in the Coalition reached a boiling point on that February 13. Napoleon's chain of sudden victories made the need for a quick peace even more imperative. Austria, Prussia and England were ready to agree to an armistice and a reopening of the Châtillon negotiations. At the zero hour, when Nesselrode declared Russia would not abide by any majority vote, Metternich countered that he and his master would no longer submit to the "tyrannical methods" of the Tsar. If the Tsar refused to join the other Allies in negotiating peace, then the Austrian armies would withdraw and Austria would sign a separate peace.

Castlereagh was dispatched to confront the Tsar with the majority vote and to try to persuade him to join them in offering Napoleon an immediate armistice on condition that he surrender his fortresses and open peace negotiations on the basis of France's old boundaries. The Tsar's insistence on dictating peace terms from Paris, Castlereagh pointed out, was "full of hazard, at direct variance with the principles on which the Coalition was cemented, and might lead to disgrace and disunion."

The Tsar retorted that he did not believe Castlereagh represented either the views of his monarch, the Prince Regent, or those of the English Cabinet, or the public opinion of his own country.

It was a tense little scene. To Castlereagh's mortification the Tsar pulled out of his pocket a letter he had got from the Russian ambassador in London, Prince Lieven, reporting on a conversation he had just had with the Prince Regent. The Prince Regent had damned the Châtillon negotiations, declared himself in favor of all-out war, a march on Paris and the overthrow of Napoleon. Of the Tsar he had spoken glowingly as "the liberator of all, head of that august Coalition he was still guiding." And he had plumped firmly for a restoration of the Bourbons to the throne of France.

For once Castlereagh's polished frost cracked. Furious that Lieven's letter —undercutting all his patient and careful diplomacy of the last month—had already circulated among the ministers at headquarters without his knowledge and had even been copied and sent to Razumowsky at Châtillon, Castlereagh had an angry exchange with the Tsar. In typical understatement he described the scene as being "necessarily painful . . . [and having] a more controversial character than I could have wished."

In terms as frank as he dared, Castlereagh wrote Liverpool condemning the total lack of discretion on the part of the Prince Regent and the damaging effect it had had on his diplomacy at this most serious crisis in the Coalition. Though Castlereagh himself supported a Bourbon restoration, he felt England must refrain from mixing openly in what was an internal affair of the French.[42]

Metternich's views on the future government of France had not changed. He was ready to deal with Napoleon as the legitimate ruler. If Napoleon were killed or overthrown, a regency with Marie Louise was the next step in an orderly succession—provided that the people of France supported a regency. The succession, he had stated clearly in his memoir to Emperor Franz, was a matter for the French themselves to decide.

Castlereagh's arguments, like Metternich's, had failed to move the Tsar. He had Pozzo di Borgo draft a reply to the Coalition ministers. He admitted that his war aims had changed with military success; he now aimed at the overthrow of Napoleon.

Metternich made a last effort to produce a consensus, and to prevent military events from controlling the future of France. He drafted a new protocol, stating that in case of new victories in the field, no power should be permitted to reduce France's boundaries further than the agreed-upon boundaries of 1792. The Allies were not to interfere in the dynastic question. If there were strong agitation in France to crown one of the younger princes of the blood (the Duc d'Orléans or the Duc de Berry, as the Tsar had proposed), it would only be permitted after the renunciation of Louis XVIII, ensuring the principle of legitimacy. But meantime, they would continue to try to make a genuine peace with Napoleon either in Châtillon or in Paris. If Paris were captured, the Tsar might name a military governor for the capital, to be aided by an Austrian, a Prussian and a Russian.

Hardenberg and Castlereagh assented, and on the morning of February 14 Metternich took the protocol to the Tsar. Again a long and stormy session ensued. Once again Metternich had to threaten to withdraw Austria's forces from the war. At last, faced with Blücher's recent defeats and doubtful whether he could carry on the war alone, Alexander gave in. He would abandon his plan of a Paris assembly and reopen negotiations in Châtillon. Instead of an armistice there should be a "guaranteed preliminary peace."[43]

It had been, Metternich wrote Wilhelmine that night, "the hardest day of my life."[44]

And replying finally to Caulaincourt, he wrote, "It is not an easy thing to be minister of the Coalition. War, my dear Duke, is an ugly thing, especially when one wages it with 50,000 Cossacks."[45]

Metternich dispatched Paul Esterházy at once to Schwarzenberg to bring him the good news of an impending armistice. "Everything will be decided in a few hours," he wrote. "I warn you so that you can take your measure in consequence—that is to say, not provoke any considerable [attack] and neglect nothing useful." Another courier would be dispatched, he promised, "within a few hours and certainly still within the day." He was, he added, "dropping with diplomatic fatigue, which is almost as bad as that of war."[46]

But he was triumphant. "All my anxieties, my pains and cares, sleepless nights and work-loaded days, are richly rewarded," he wrote Hudelist. "Tsar Alexander has surrendered to us completely the direction of military affairs, and to me the political question." In a day or two, he added, they would hear from Châtillon that a preliminary peace had been signed.[47]

A few miles away, at army headquarters in the little town of Bray, Schwarzenberg found himself in a fearful quandary. With Metternich's letter in his hand, he did not know what to do. His forces were just crossing the Seine at Montereau to draw Napoleon's attack away from Blücher. What if the armistice were already signed? Should he send his troops into a costly battle with peace only hours away? To expose his troops to death for no reason whatever seemed to Schwarzenberg totally unconscionable.

By Thursday, February 17, the letter Metternich had promised had still not arrived. Schwarzenberg sent off a courier: "We are waiting most impatiently for news from Châtillon." To make the military situation worse, he had learned that the Russian General Wittgenstein, in distinct disobedience to Schwarzenberg's orders, had exposed his army unnecessarily and suffered a severe defeat at Napoleon's hands at Nangis.

The Tsar and the King of Prussia had meantime arrived in Bray to keep an eye on military operations. Fearful of engaging in a totally unnecessary, possibly major battle on the very eve of peace, Schwarzenberg proposed to the Tsar that they dispatch someone to Napoleon's chief of staff, Berthier, explaining that the sovereigns had authorized their ministers to sign a preliminary peace on the bases agreed upon with Caulaincourt.

Writing Metternich of his move, Schwarzenberg declared that the Tsar had approved of his armistice proposal; he had written the letter under the Tsar's eyes and with the full assent of the King of Prussia. Count Paar was on his way to Napoleon's headquarters; they would have an answer soon.[48]

If the victory of the Allies at La Rothière had changed their inclinations toward a moderate peace, so now Napoleon's victories had changed his mind too. He was on a winning streak; all his old arrogance and *machismo* returned. He sent a courier galloping off to Châtillon, withdrawing the carte blanche which he had sent Caulaincourt only days earlier. Caulaincourt was to sign nothing now:

> I gave you carte blanche to save Paris and to avoid a battle which was the final hope of the nation. Now the battle has taken place; Providence has blessed our arms. Sign nothing without my orders since I alone know the situation.[49]

And Caulaincourt was ordered not to treat on the basis of a France limited to her "former" boundaries.

The note Count Paar carried to Napoleon at almost the same time declaring that Schwarzenberg had halted his offensive against the French, proposing that the French now halt theirs, was received with contempt. Napoleon wrote his brother Joseph the following day, February 18:

> At the first defeat these wretches fall on their knees! Happily they did not allow [Count Paar] to be admitted. I shall reply in my own good time. I shall grant no armistice until they have cleared out of my territory.

And casually, almost as an afterthought, he added:

> If I had agreed to our "former" boundaries, I would have taken up arms within two years.[50]

At Troyes Metternich waited, just as anxiously as Schwarzenberg a few miles away at Bray, for good news from Châtillon that the expected preliminary peace had been signed.

Instead, on February 18, an army courier brought him Schwarzenberg's letter informing him that he had sent an armistice envoy to Napoleon. Metternich was filled with consternation. Schwarzenberg had completely misunderstood. It was never intended that he should act on his own, but to await final word from him. There was nothing to do except to go at once and settle things on the spot at army headquarters, disentangle as best he could the whole serious misunderstanding.

Sending a relay of horses ahead to a midpoint and taking along Paul Esterházy for company, Metternich jumped into his traveling carriage and set out in late afternoon of that bitter cold day, February 18, for army headquarters at Bray.[51]

"You know the route to Bray?" he asked the postilion.

"Like the back of my whip hand, Sire."

The two men in their greatcoats settled back in the carriage for a long ride. Whether they talked or not, Metternich does not tell us. He had plenty of grim and unhappy thoughts to brood on during the long winter journey. Not only were diplomatic and military affairs now knotted in a wretched tangle, but he had got the previous day from Vienna a letter from Wilhelmine that might well sever their relationship. He had not slept a wink the night before.

Buried in pessimistic thought, jogging over the frozen ruts of the road where armies had passed and repassed, Metternich noticed that it was taking an unconscionably long time to reach the town where fresh horses awaited them. Yet they could not be lost; Paul had been over the road to Bray twice that week, taking the crucial letter of February 14 to Schwarzenberg, and returning.

Night fell; the carriage with its flickering lantern burrowed through the blackness of a starless winter night. When they came at last to a town, Metternich halted the driver, pulled down a window, and shouted to a passerby.

"What place is this?"

"Villeneuve-l'Archevêque, monsieur."

"How much farther is Les Granges?"

The man looked astonished. "To Les Granges? Monsieur must be joking."

"Not at all. My relays are waiting for us at Les Granges."

The man scratched his head. "Well, I'll tell you, monsieur. There are two ways of getting to Les Granges. One way you've got twenty-seven leagues to go, the other way, twenty-five."

Was it possible—they were still hours away from Les Granges!

"Where the devil are we then?"

"Four leagues from Sens."

"From Sens! Good God!" They must have gone in the wrong direction —southwest instead of northwest—and the horses were dropping with fatigue. No choice but to sacrifice the rest of the night.

Metternich asked if any post-horses were to be had. He found some, and they continued on the road to Sens. Suddenly on the road they met several thousand Austrian soldiers in full retreat.

Everything was utter confusion. Nobody could tell him anything. At dawn they reached Sens, where Metternich asked the name of the commander, was informed it was General Moritz Liechtenstein, his wife's cousin.

Telling the story of his adventure afterward, Metternich remembered,

> Moritz thinks he is dreaming to see me arrive at the advance posts
> of the Austrian army—an army in full retreat. He is convinced I've got
> some important mission and am on the road for Paris.

Napoleon, Moritz informed Metternich, had attacked Schwarzenberg's army as they were crossing the Seine at Montereau. Schwarzenberg had ordered a retreat, was just now moving his headquarters back to the east, from Trainel to Troyes. There was not a moment to lose if Metternich wanted to intercept the marshal at Trainel.

But how to get to Trainel? The road out of Sens could no longer be traversed. It was completely blocked by thousands of men, horses, baggage, munitions wagons, all the impediments of a retreating army. The French were already close at hand. There was no way to reach Trainel except by cutting straight across open country, through fields and woods and across frozen streams—a hazardous course, for the enemy cavalry were certainly all over the countryside by now.

Nevertheless there was no choice. The two diplomats rested a few hours at Moritz's headquarters in Sens; then at midnight, with borrowed ordnance horses, for no carriage or saddle horses were to be had, the two began the cross-country drive. Twice the carriage turned over, and in the end they mounted the horses and Metternich ordered his carriage to follow. Moritz Liechtenstein had insisted on sending along an escort of ten men.

The night and the early morning were cold as the grave, with a wind that cut through to the marrow. Metternich was not dressed for riding; his long coat flapped about his legs, and the clumsy mount—used to pulling ammunition wagons but not to carrying a rider—was hardly a gentle horse to handle; more than once his horse stumbled over a broken tree trunk or a hump of frozen ground.

Through the day they pressed on, half frozen, not daring to stop.

Instead of the eight hours Metternich had calculated, it took them fourteen hours to reach Trainel, exhausted, stiff with cold and dropping with fatigue. The town was empty. Schwarzenberg had evacuated it an hour before. "Not a cat in the whole village," Metternich recalled, "not a guide. Not a single horse."

Their own horses were stumbling with exhaustion, but there was nothing to do but push on to Nogent. At Nogent the horses collapsed. Fresh horses were not to be had for prayers or love or money; instead, they found themselves foundering in the utter confusion of 60,000 soldiers, most on foot, in full retreat, swarming pell-mell back to Troyes.

At last by a stroke of luck Metternich met the Bavarian General Wrede, who detached seven artillery horses from one of his cannon, "and there I am afloat again!"

They threaded their way through the retreating army back to Les Granges, the town they had missed the previous day, where Metternich's own relay horses were expected to be waiting. His horses had disappeared without a trace; someone else had snatched them in passing.

> I had no choice but to stop a vehicle convoy. I made them detach an artillery wagon and here I am with four of the most infernal horses, who had already gone six leagues and had ten more to go. . . . So I am drawn along like a munitions wagon for another eight hours.

Early on Sunday morning of February 20, after a harrowing journey of forty hours, without food or sleep and "in the very cold of hell itself," Metternich was back in Troyes.

Schwarzenberg had already reached Troyes. When it was learned that he had not seen Metternich, all of headquarters was in a panic. Where was the Austrian Foreign Minister? Lost in that dangerous countryside, covered now by advancing French cavalry? Already a prisoner perhaps, a precious hostage whom Napoleon might hold—against the rules of diplomatic immunity—until he made his own terms?

Or had Metternich in reality—as some of the Russians, Prussians and even English suspected—not gone to see Schwarzenberg at all, but gone to make a deal with Napoleon? Or to Paris, perhaps, to steal a march on his Allies and arrange for a regency?

The search parties sent out to look for him returned empty-handed.

Everyone in my chancellery was in despair. The Emperor sent every hour to inquire. Wrbna was running around like a crazy man. The cavalry were out looking for me on all the roads.

In fact Metternich had been within a few miles of the main French Army and had certainly rather narrowly escaped capture. The danger he had run that night, and the close call he and Paul Esterházy had, would have certain important consequences only a few weeks hence.

XV

LADIES OF VIENNA:
A LONG-DISTANCE QUARREL

1

In Vienna it is Fasching again, the six traditionally merry weeks that precede Lent. But Fasching this year of 1814 is anything but cheerful; the carnival spirit has left town along with the men.

Peace that seemed so near one day has receded out of sight the next. Bad news circulates faster than good. When will this wretched, this terrible war be over?

Marie Metternich passes her seventeenth birthday in January, pretty, charming, eager Marie. She is ready for society, but there is no society ready for her. The Metternichs' old friend Lory Fuchs gives a tiny party for Marie—as always, more women than men. The Duchess of Sagan comes to kiss her and wish her years of happiness.

From Basel Metternich writes to this child who is so close to his heart:

> You are seventeen today; one needs no more than that. May God protect and keep you. You know I love you with all my heart; you've never given me a moment of sorrow. . . . I wish I could have been with you today, my dear child. Your eighteenth year I shall not pass far from you, I promise you that.[1]

When he was back in Vienna—which would be very soon, he predicted—he would go riding with her in the Prater, and Victor could follow on his pony. He had been away so long from home little Leontine must surely think her Papa is some mythological creature "like Neptune or Mercury."

Wherever he happens to be, wherever headquarters move, he manages to find gifts for them—sweet spice cakes from Basel (the children must be careful not to eat too many), scissors from Langres, where fine cutlery is made (both pairs will probably be mislaid by the time he gets home), and from Troyes, where a single *boutique de modes* still sells finery, he sends material for a white dress for Laure and a pink one for Marie.

Nearly always in his letters there is a Giroux story for Marie. How Giroux in the streets of Troyes meets a soldier who looks like a French deserter or a prisoner of war, and asks him, "Are you one of ours or one of yours?"

Another morning Giroux opens the shutters in Metternich's chamber. From his bed his master asks what kind of weather it is outside.

"Beautiful."

"Ah, then it is no longer cold?"

"No, it looks like spring has come."

"But from here it looks as if the day is quite gray."

"Yes, because it's snowing."

Gruffly Metternich tells his valet, "Go outside and find out if I have to wear a fur cape or a nankin suit!"[2]

In Vienna Laure gives little dinner parties, goes to such Fasching balls as there are. Shrewd observer of the social scene, Laure reports to her husband—not always without a touch of malice—the little events and contretemps of society in the capital. Princess Bagration, she wrote,

> has become really crazy. At Count Stackelberg's ball she led a Cossack dance. . . . People held their stomachs for laughing. She is a funny woman. One day she's dying, and the next she's dancing like a mad thing.

Another night Laure goes to the chambermaids' ball Princess Bagration gives for the maids, seamstresses and footmen in her friends' employ. Hidden behind a screen, Laure watches the servants, all in mask, frolicking until five in the morning. And at Mid-Lent Laure enjoys a lively party at Franz Palffy's, with *ombres chinois*, marionettes, dancing and supper—the mid-Lenten festivities a clear breach of liturgical rules. "I left after midnight," she tells her husband. "It was a great scandal to the archbishop."[3]

Metternich's picture is now on public sale at Artaria in the Kohlmarkt, between portraits of Schwarzenberg and of Wellington. Her father is quite a hero, Marie writes, adding, "Everybody is buying it, and a huge crowd of people are always standing in front of this window." It is not a terribly good likeness; there is a leer in the right eye and Metternich when he sees it declares, "Next time I have my portrait made it will be without any eyes at all." Not quite everyone is hurrying to buy his picture; Metternich still has plenty of enemies in Vienna.

The Vienna *crieurs* still carp that nothing is going right, that Napoleon should have been defeated long ago, had anyone but Metternich been in charge of affairs.

Rumors of a rift in the Coalition and of Napoleon's new victories provide more food for the *frondeurs*. Laure reports to her husband who are his real friends and who are his enemies. At a reception in the palace the

Empress Maria Ludovica is very cool to her. "She did not ask me once about you, and scarcely spoke to me at all."[4]

Gentz, returning to the capital at the end of January, describes for Metternich "a certain malicious intriguing secret bitter outwardly moderate party who talk only in half-words." They are saying, says Gentz, that "much to be sure has been done, but much more is actually lost. . . . In this sense I've heard the silly Princess Marie, the not so silly Princess Grassal-kowich talk. Also the Empress."[5]

Nor did news of Metternich's treaty with the Neapolitan Murats meet with the approval of the anti-Metternich cabal, who were shocked that Napoleon's sister and her husband might be left to occupy their Italian throne.

To complicate matters still further, Emperor Franz's old aunt, Queen Caroline—once Queen of Naples and now only of Sicily—appeared in Vienna in January, to be warmly greeted by the Empress and her friends as the rightful ruler of Naples.

The old Queen quarrels with everyone, Laure writes; people are saying she is not quite right in the head.

At a palace reception the old Queen asks Nani Schwarzenberg how many children she had.

"Three, Your Majesty," Nani replied.

"And how many does your husband have?"

Nani almost went to pieces and could not find a word to answer.

Laure, regaling her husband with this little scene, adds naughtily,

> I must admit *I* would have answered the Queen at once, "I don't know, Majesty, I've never asked him."[6]

Another time Laure wrote that the Empress had very graciously told Nani, when the latter had recovered from an illness, that she would like to call on her soon, if she would fix a day and an hour. Nani replied that she could not receive the Empress that week as she would be having her period.

> You can imagine that the Empress, who is not sweet-tempered and who has wit, is saying some pretty things—among others that Nani must take her for a lover. For the love of God don't say anything to Schwarzen-berg. You know he can't bear jokes about his wife.[7]

Laure did not quite like Nani Schwarzenberg. Perhaps she envied the little dark, eccentric woman, whose husband, field marshal and commander of all the Allied armies, had never looked at another woman since his marriage, went blissfully to sleep on her shoulder at the opera, refused to dance with another woman at the balls in Frankfurt and hurried home to sleep with his wife just as soon as his duties permitted him.

Laure wondered if her own domestic life might not be altered a bit once peace came. Wandering through the apartments in the Ballhaus, with Moreau's sketches for redecoration in her hand, the idea came to Laure that she might rearrange things, move her own rooms down to the second floor, the *nobel etage,* adjoining her husband's.

Sending off to her husband Moreau's plans and estimates, she added her tentative proposal. Metternich replied at once:

> If you go *down,* I shall go *up* for my private rooms, and keep the apartment below only for my work.

When Laure did not abandon her idea of moving closer to him, he wrote with a touch of ill humor:

> I don't know why you want to live downstairs. You'll be sorry certainly if you move. There's nothing more depressing than the rooms that look out on a corner of the Ballplatz.[8]

Whatever Laure suspects of her husband's feelings for the Duchess of Sagan, she knows above all she must keep a cool head.

Metternich for his part sees no particular complication involved in the life he plans for himself. Once the war is over and the crushing burden of work is lifted, his life will divide quite nicely into three parts, he writes Wilhelmine: "you, my children, and Laure."

He wants his wife and his mistress to be friends; he sees no reason why they should not be. When Wilhelmine dines at Laure's and finds her distant reserve difficult to penetrate ("I would like so much to please her even a little, but I don't think I shall ever succeed"), he urges Wilhelmine to make an effort to know Laure, to draw her out. Wilhelmine demurs; she is afraid Laure will think her the kind of woman

> who by her apparent intimacy with the wife tries to hide her real intimacy with the husband. I am incapable of that and that's why the possibility of arousing such a suspicion would be painful to me.[9]

But Metternich tells her:

> Get her used to seeing you. Laure is excellent, filled with intelligence and tact, but so unilateral that anyone who doesn't understand her is nothing for her—and in the end there is nothing for her except her children and me. She would give up her life at any hour of the day for us with the calm you observe in her—I would do the same for her.

He adds, "One can love one's wife very much and adore one's mistress without one of these feelings crossing the other."[10] To be sure, it requires a special kind of man to do so.

After her long sojourn in Prague Wilhelmine has again fallen into the pattern of Vienna society, receiving and returning calls, giving and going out to dinner parties, which, she complains, have become unbearably long, "for nobody knows what to do or become out of boredom." It is only out of despair, she writes Clemens, that she does any of these tedious things.

At the dinner parties the women have taken to arguing ferociously over

politics and the conduct of the war. One day Nani Schwarzenberg and
Fanny Kaunitz quarrel over Bernadotte—Fanny for, Nani against—the next
day they clash over Denmark—Nani against, Fanny for. A day or two later
Sophie Zichy and her sister-in-law Molly have at one another over some
military matter, which ends when Sophie calls Molly *une sotte* and all but
breaks up the party.[11]

As for the balls—and Wilhelmine does not think the moment appropriate
for such amusements—they too are unconscionably dull, with no one left who
can dance—old men only, "students, Englishmen, sensible people, the kind
who are good for nothing at a ball."

Nevertheless she takes pains dressing for Count Stackelberg's ball, not
to please anyone in particular—"no one here inspires the desire"—but, she
says lightly, "to maintain my reputation." One day perhaps, before too
long, she will be old, her beauty gone; she hopes a kind friend will tell her
so before she makes herself ridiculous. That day is still far enough off that
Wilhelmine can joke about it.

Meantime, at his ball Count Stackelberg makes her

> waltz like a lost soul—between ourselves I think he gives the balls for
> himself for he dances to exhaustion.[12]

For male society Wilhelmine is reduced to the young men at the English
embassy—the "worst" of them, George Charles Vernon, who had come out
from England the previous summer with Lord Aberdeen and was now
secretary of the embassy in Vienna, and the "best" of them, Frederick Lamb,
the English chargé d'affaires, whose reputation as a lady-killer had preceded
him. Not for nothing was he the son of the fascinating Lady Melbourne. She
thought, she wrote Metternich gaily, that she would be able to revenge her
whole sex on the devastating Lamb.

They dine with her almost daily:

> I see every day of my life the dangerous and cruel Lamb. He is the best
> boy in the world. . . . As for my Obreskoff I know nothing about him
> except that he left Prague about the same time I did to rejoin the
> army.[13]

Her three little foster daughters are now living with her again, with their
governess, and she sees to their lessons (she will make sure they receive a better education than she herself had), takes them to the ballet and the
theater and for rides in her carriage when the weather is fine. She shields
them carefully from any precocious view of society. She is affectionate,
strict. And full of fun: to the end of her life the eldest of the girls, Emilie
von Binzer, thirteen then in 1814, recalled how in the morning when they
would go to visit her room, their pretty Maman would suddenly leap out of
bed, perform the funniest dance in the world on the carpet in her night-
gown and bare feet, and just as suddenly, while the children shrieked with
laughter, leap back into bed and hide under the covers.[14]

The only balls she gave that Fasching season were for the children. At the first one a violin played for dancing, Laure brought the little Metternichs, and Wilhelmine reported that Laure quite melted:

> She must have thought me mad. I pressed her to my heart like a dear friend.

Perhaps, Wilhelmine wrote Clemens hopefully, one day Laure "will like me out of love for you."[15]

When she wrote Metternich of one of her parties where she had played games with the children, the thought, he said

> drove me crazy. God, how I would like to see you playing blindman's buff—how happy I would be to be able to watch you—if only for a single instant see you smile at me.[16]

Of Gustava Armfelt nothing more was heard at the moment. Wilhelmine had not yet got from Count Wratislaw the papers Metternich needed to pursue a change in guardianship. Metternich wrote of Gustava as "our child."

Metternich's letters continue to delight her. Arriving several times a week by courier they save her from total ennui and despondency—maladies, she agrees, no sensible person ought ever to suffer:

> You understand better than anyone else how to soften the pain of absence with the charm of your letters, but if you write beautifully you talk even better.[17]

When she reads now of his glory in the official *Austrian Observer*—dispatches Metternich may well have penned himself—she feels a special joy and pride, as when out walking at Ratiborzitz she sees the sun gleam down unexpectedly on a lovely secluded spot.

Writing him has become medicine for her:

> I know no other remedy than to seek refuge with you, dear Clemens. You are good for me in everything.[18]

Writing him she enters that other world—the world he inhabits, the world of action, of politics, where things are made to happen. "I find myself," she says simply.

One thing in her life continues to trouble him. Commodious and elegant as are her apartments in the right wing of the Palais Palm, so conveniently close to the Chancellery, it is highly awkward to have her living across the courtyard from Princess Bagration, who can watch all the comings and goings from her windows. That situation, he foresees, may lead to endless complications and gossip when he is back in Vienna.

He advises Wilhelmine to buy herself a town house, cost what it may.

Princess Bagration's wing in the Palais Palm is the center of the Russian colony in Vienna. It is important for Metternich—most of all now, amid the succession of crises with the Tsar—to keep on friendly terms with her. He still carries on a desultory correspondence with her, all the time agreeing with Laure that the Russian woman is certainly a bit mad, in fact "quite impossible."

Thus far he has managed everything adroitly, in fact so adroitly that Princess Bagration still lays claim to Metternich's affections. Only the previous autumn, when Countess Nesselrode visited Vienna, the latter wrote her husband in great vexation because every time she said something to Princess Bagration about her husband—Nesselrode—Bagration retaliated with something about "her" Metternich. It was quite shocking, Madame Nesselrode thought.[19]

Once in one of her letters to him Princess Bagration threatened Metternich with replacing him in her affections with someone else. Delighted, he wrote Wilhelmine that Bagration ". . . threatens me with what I would be so happy to see established—someone whom she likes very much and who in turn felt called upon to make her happy. Don't you know such a person?" Could they not, he proposed, make some kind of trade? If, for example, Alfred Windischgraetz could be induced to take over Bagration, it would solve all problems delightfully in a single switch. "But perhaps you yourself would not wish it!"[20] Wilhelmine did not reply to that half-asked question.

At Metternich's bidding Wilhelmine paid a call on her Russian neighbor when she returned from Prague,

> in spite of the fact that she announced loudly she would never make the first step in any kind of rapprochement. . . . I don't like her but I hold nothing against her—I believe that is true indifference.[21]

As yet Katharine Bagration knew nothing for sure of Wilhelmine's relationship to Metternich, but she was watchful and suspicious.

One day one of Wilhelmine's letters to Metternich, intended for the diplomatic pouch and sent to the Chancellery, was accidentally returned to the Palais Palm. The porter carried it back to the Chancellery, but Princess Bagration, hearing about it, had summoned Hoppé, who took care of such little matters at the Chancellery as Metternich's private mail, and interrogated him. Hoppé had lied valiantly.

Metternich, already worried about such a mischance, directed Wilhelmine to address her letters henceforth to his secret cover, "Captain Willaman."

A day or so after the letter incident Princess Bagration called on Wilhelmine just as the latter was preparing for a ball, stayed to help her dress and insisted on rouging her. "I confess to my shame I looked at it very closely—I did not trust very much the result it had on my charms—Otherwise we live in the best of relationships, without liking or hating one another—"[22]

Metternich continued to send Wilhelmine gifts, often the same gifts he chose for Laure and Marie—a knife and scissors from Langres, which superstitious Wilhelmine gave at once to Gentz. Sharp gifts cut friendships, she had always heard.

He sent her pastilles of Italian olive for scent, the whitest sand for drying the ink of her letters, a pretty clip to hold her letters in place ("Don't let Gentz carry it off!"), and from Troyes, a soft, loose *robe de chambre*. He begged her to wear it a great deal, "so that you become attached to it—the shopkeeper said the material laundered beautifully." He wanted the things he gave her to belong to her in an especially intimate way, to become part of her life—as he himself hoped to be:

> *Ma bonne amie,* when I cannot write you, I do not think less of you— and when I do not think of you, be sure I am asleep. I buy you these foolish things so you do not forget me.[23]

Wilhelmine wishes he would write to her in a more political vein, re-counting in detail everything that is happening at headquarters. But when Metternich sits down to write her, wherever headquarters happens to be, often long after midnight, with the candle on his desk burned to a stump, it rests him, he tells her, to forget politics, to write a love letter pure and simple, to dream on paper of the future they will enjoy together when he is back in Vienna.

For all his optimistic confidence in his powers in the world of diplomacy, he is not entirely sure of his ultimate success in this critical love of his life. His feelings veer between hope of winning her—in the complete possession he would insist upon—and doubt and despair. Could he, a man now in middle age, past the physical attractiveness of first youth, could he persuade her out of what was certainly a purely sexual passion for Alfred?

> I've never claimed to be able to please—in spite of what silly people of both sexes tell you [he wrote her]—and I make even less claim today than in the days when youth itself enhanced even the smallest advantage.

He did not want her to compare him in this way with Alfred:

> . . . I declare myself entirely outside of all comparison with the being who has attached you only in this respect.[24]

Alfred, he told her, had been the best of her lovers:

> . . . but A. is a child and less than a child compared to you. You, my dear, have one of the strongest souls for feeling and one of the weakest characters—and if the word character is a bit hard I'll give you the pleasure of replacing it by will.[25]

Perfect love between a man and a woman, he tells her, must be both intellectual and physical; such a love is "the highest invention of the Creator." Surely she must perceive—is Metternich's unspoken thought—

how infinitely superior on the intellectual plane he is to Alfred or to any of her previous lovers.

He—Metternich—would love her in ways she had never been loved. He would spoil her, care for her, cherish her as no one had ever cherished her.

> I love you a hundred times more than my life. My dear, I love you as one loves good health, as one feels the warm sun in spring, as one senses all that is sweetest and best in this world. There are so many things that cannot be said that one's words fail one no matter how rich languages are. . . .[26]

Whatever doubts occasionally assail Metternich's superb self-confidence, they are nothing to the self-doubt Wilhelmine feels when she contemplates herself and her life—"this sad self whom I like so little." Where does she belong in the world? Whither is she going? She simply does not know.

Most often when she is despondent the painful attacks of migraine come, often lasting for days.

From far away Metternich worries about her health, besieges her with good advice, does not think much of her physician, Dr. Santini, who is good for treating only one disease—venereal—"and God keep you from consulting him for that." He wants her to consult his own physician, Dr. Staudenheimer, who is excellent, filled with good sense, but a tyrant. Shrewdly Metternich diagnoses her chronic headaches as at least in part *hystérique*—what a later generation would call psychosomatic.[27]

But a tyrant-doctor is not what she wants. She consults instead the fashionable Dr. Koreff, formerly of Paris, who has a new magnetic cure and writes poetry as a sideline. He magnetizes her, and her headache disappears like magic, she writes Metternich, who replies that Koreff is no doubt something of a charlatan, but she may go to him, it will do her no harm. Dr. Koreff, like so many of the men who pass within Wilhelmine's orbit, is presently enchanted with her, and she begins to find anonymous poems addressed to her in her mail.

Metternich's kind of love—the passionate, romantic, idealizing love of a middle-aged Werther—troubles Wilhelmine. She would like their relationship to be an honest one—he declares that is precisely what he wants too—but their definitions remain worlds apart. Could he not love her as a flesh-and-blood woman, a human being rather than a goddess in a shrine?

> Just there where you hesitate to pronounce on my account, take as a rule, dear Clemens, that I am neither so good nor so bad as people think.

And she begs:

> My dear, you must love me not only with all the imperfections you know I have but even more with all those you don't know.[28]

As for the future, Wilhelmine builds no castles in the air on dreams and promises. The future frightens her. Her kind of life has no future one dares to contemplate. Now she is thirty-two, still in the full bloom of her beauty, still desirable—but after that, what then?

From Basel Metternich had written of the old Swiss couple in whose house he was quartered—Monsieur Bachofen "in a well-curled wig and the best-brushed suit in the world, Madame in a cap of finest lace." Devoted to one another, with four children and eighteen grandchildren, they continue to live a serene old age; only the war has brought them unhappiness.

Lightly Metternich suggests:

> I would be quite satisfied to be forevermore Monsieur if you would be willing to be Madame.[29]

Wilhelmine could not suppress a stab of pain when she read that letter. "Don't paint so well the picture of the happy household," she begs him. The image has filled her with envy and with regret.

She must remain forever an outsider to the tranquil world of the Madame Bachofens and the Laure Metternichs—of the women who married, who bore children, who were content to live in the shadow of a husband's work and commands.

"Never has it been my share, never can it be," she writes. That path remains forever barred to her. The mistakes of her youth have closed it once and for all. For a woman, Wilhelmine could plainly see, the path to happiness is

> very narrow—if one strays but a little one has lost it forever—

Men might think it just, but it was also cruel. Sorrowfully she wrote that day to Clemens:

> On the road I've taken one can find illusions of happiness but never happiness itself—[30]

2

While the diplomats were arguing about peace bases in the last days of January at the Langres headquarters, the staff officers assigned to the sovereigns, chafing with inactivity, amused themselves as best they could.

One night the Austrian officers gave a dinner for the Tsar's aides-de-camp and Guard officers. Langres was in champagne country, a good many bottles were consumed that night. Toasts were followed by reminiscences, tales of conquest on battlefield and in the bedroom.

Young Obreskoff won the biggest ovation with a deliciously titillating tale of lying wounded in Prague after the battle of Dresden and of being nursed back to health by the loveliest duchess in Central Europe. The duchess had not only tended his wounds but had been compassionate enough to satisfy certain needs which, he boasted, "had been very pressing despite his wounds." Flushed by the champagne and by the instant success of his story, he expatiated in detail on the delights of love in the duchess's luxurious apartment in Prague. Obreskoff ended by passing around a wallet he declared he had just got from her as a gift, together with an affectionate letter that had already made the rounds of his regiment.

Paul Esterházy was present at the Guards dinner. He carried the tale back to Metternich, a knife plunged straight into his friend's heart.

All the hounds of jealousy that had gnawed him in Frankfurt during the days when he thought Alfred was with her in Prague were nothing compared to what Metternich felt now. It could not be true. Obreskoff had to be lying; this young scoundrel deserved to be drawn and quartered. And yet—if it were true—

The hours he—Metternich—had spent with her in Laun, the October days in Prague when she had begun to love him: he carried those days and nights with him, like the silver-pierced lamp she had given him to read by, to light the darkness and loneliness of all the days and nights since. No, he could never doubt her. And yet—she had certainly had Obreskoff under her roof. He had warned her then, when he had visited her hospital in Prague and observed the ardent looks the young Russian cast on his benefactress. Before he—Metternich—had come to know her as he now knew her, he had often enough heard that she was a careless creature in her affections.

But the thought was unbearable. All the sweetness of his own memories returned to mock him. He could not eat, or sleep; his head throbbed with pain.

Always so successful in his conquests, managing his liaisons with ease and grace, he had never known the torments of sexual jealousy.

At two in the morning of Sunday, January 30, he sat at his writing table in bitter cold while the candle in the lamp flickered and Giroux snored in the next room. He wrote her:

> One of my reporters brought me this morning the news that Monsieur Obreskoff, who was in the most intimate relationship with you during his stay in Prague, received two or three days ago a purse or wallet that you sent him, together with a letter which he has shown to the entire Simanoffsky[sic] regiment!
>
> I warned you long before of what might happen. I do not believe a single word of it for I would rather die than doubt you—and to condemn you, would it not be dying?

But had she no idea what such a tale as this did to *him*, Metternich? To have the being whom he had long placed on the highest pinnacle, "who for me is *holy*," given over by her own careless behavior to the disgusting gossip of the guardroom, to the tongue of an odious young Obreskoff, who bragged "of possessing a prize for which I would lay down my life a hundred times." Obreskoff had boasted of tasting his pleasures "with much greater safety than we could in towns where armies have passed through"—

and this of the woman who during the months of our relationship—that has absorbed my entire existence—has refused to give me the pleasure of changing the *vous* into *toi* by I know not what kind of misunderstood delicacy.[31]

And now, final twist of the knife, he had just learned that Vienna was gossiping about a new affair Wilhelmine was said to be carrying on with the young Englishman Frederick Lamb.

Only the day before the Guards dinner incident, Laure had written her husband, not perhaps entirely without guile: "They are beginning to talk of a liaison between the duchess and the dangerous Lamb."

And Paul Esterházy read aloud a letter from his wife, repeating a like morsel of gossip: "Lamb has found a diversion . . . things are apparently arranged so they are living together."

It did not occur to Metternich that the bored ladies of Vienna society might resent the fact that the most presentable bachelors in town were paying court to Wilhelmine, and that if she were involved in a secret liaison with Lamb, she might not have discussed him with such frankness in her letters to Metternich. That very day had brought a letter from her in which she wrote in a lighthearted vein of her "four English Nelsons."

Devoured with jealousy and wounded male pride, Metternich assured her he believed none of the tales. Nevertheless he scolded her for her conduct, for her carelessness in leaving herself open to gossip, for the pain she was causing *him*.

Never had he written to her—or to any woman—with the violence he threatened in that letter:

> And do not excuse yourself; you yourself are the cause of it. If I were near you I would beat you. . . . as it is I can only beg you not to make of yourself and the imbecile Lamb a second vicious story. . . . They have promised me a copy of your letter for I will only believe in it when you tell me you had the imprudence to write this wretched fool, who boasts he left Prague the same day as you—after you waited until he was *completely healed*.[32]

He finished his letter, sealed it, climbed into bed. Still sleep would not come. Tormented and wretched, he lighted his lamp and, sitting down again at his desk, opened the letter to add a few more words. He scolded her again, offered her good advice, in the end offered to undertake her "moral cure" if she would place herself in his hands. His enemies might have smiled at the image of Metternich undertaking the "moral cure" of a beautiful woman.

Metternich's letter reached Wilhelmine in the first week of February. Angrier in her turn than she had perhaps ever been, she sat down and dashed off a blistering reply.

> Your letter of the 30th is of a kind to oblige me to reply at once. . . .
> I ought perhaps to leave myself time to reflect—it would be wise but this kind of wisdom is not in my power. . . .

I begin with Mr. Lamb, on whose count I shall make myself clear in a few words. If he loves me, I don't know it, as for me, I do not love him—I've given no basis by my conduct for any talk— If people have nothing better to do than to busy themselves with my liaison with him I congratulate them on it. There are others who envy me my courage, I pity them. If this explanation does not satisfy you, your Vienna reporters can supply more.

The other tale of Langres is of such elegance that it would pain me too much to enter into details of an accusation so disgusting—the only thing I'd like to see is not a *copy* of my letter but the *original*, which after having been seen by a whole regiment and a portion of the Allied armies should not be too precious an object to be available as proof— When this original is before my eyes then I shall perhaps enter into details—which are always superfluous when one is condemned before being heard.

She would, she concluded with chilling irony, always be grateful for the advice of a friend who had such concern for her well-being.

That does not prevent certain expressions merited or not from completely revolting my heart. . . . Pardon me if so careless a style as mine expresses badly what I wish to say.[33]

The letter icy with indignation bore neither salutation nor close. It reached Metternich on February 17 in Troyes, at the climax of that week of great crisis for the Coalition.

He did not sleep at all that night of February 17, only tossed and turned in utter misery. He got up in the night to write and ask her pardon. Next morning had come the fateful letter from Schwarzenberg that sent him off on the long and dangerous journey to Trainel.

Their letters of apology crossed.

He had almost at once regretted sending off the "terrible letter" of January 30. Perhaps his accusations had been unjust; certainly his letter had been intemperate. Besides—he simply loved her too much to care.

Wilhelmine too had regretted her hasty reply. More calmly she had written a bit later:

In a few days I shall have a certain reply to a certain letter—dear Clemens—I shall soon have no more pleasure in waiting for your news —one more letter that I await with impatience, then another which makes me tremble—then another—I already weep for it, and then others, to make my face bloom again—that is my calculation.[34]

Finally in March all was well again between them:

What a conversation this is [he wrote her] where a twenty-day interval intrudes between the saying and the answering—and that in 1814, when every day counts as a whole century, or very near it![35]

He had burned her letter of February 7, he wrote. "That did me good." He begged her to burn his "terrible letter." Neither one burned the other's letter.

Weeks before, he had asked her for a lock of her hair, and she had sent it in an affectionate letter, just before their quarrel, a light brown lock, tinged with gold—more blond than dark—tied with a white ribbon. That lock of hair remained long afterward, carefully kept with the packet of Wilhelmine's letters in the black box bound like a book, on a shelf in Metternich's study in the Chancellery.

She had begun at last to address him as *tu* in her letters, and on February 27, when their peace together was made, she wrote him:

> Love has everything in his power, has made you link my destiny to yours, as fate has attached your whole being to that of the universe.[36]

XVI

NAPOLEON'S SECOND LAST STAND

I am so much in love with peace that I renounce all glory and content myself with having led Napoleon to where he finds himself.
—METTERNICH TO LAURE, FEBRUARY 21, 1814

1

Metternich had lost his bid for an early peace, as he had lost his bid for a moderate one. The fate of France and the fate of Europe were again to be settled ineluctably on the battlefield, not at the council table. "It is dreadful to think that the advantages bought at so high a price are again abandoned to the chances of war," Wilhelmine wrote him on March 1.[1]

Just as the Allies had raised the price of peace when they won a victory, so now did Napoleon. In reply to Schwarzenberg's armistice overture Napoleon wrote his father-in-law that his recent victories made it possible again to demand a France restored to her "natural boundaries."

It was not a conciliatory reply, but Schwarzenberg sent his aide-de-camp, Wenzel Liechtenstein, with a reply that was moderate and pacific in tone. Liechtenstein caught up with Napoleon in the hamlet of Chatres, where the French Emperor had set up his headquarters in the hut of a charcoal burner.

The conversation that morning was a typically one-sided Napoleonic diatribe. Railing against the bad faith of the Allies, Napoleon spoke angrily of rumors that had reached him that the Allies intended to dethrone him and bring in a Bourbon replacement. Was it not true that the Duc d'Angoulême was at Wellington's headquarters in the south, the Comte d'Artois in Basel, about to wing his way into France in the wake of the Allies? What else could it mean but that the Allies supported the Bourbons?

In the end he agreed to send a general to Lusigny to talk armistice terms with Allies' representatives.

Wenzel Liechtenstein had hardly left the hut when Baron St. Aignan was shown in—that same St. Aignan, brother-in-law of Caulaincourt, who had carried the Frankfurt peace proposals to Paris the previous November. He came now in the name of a group of prominent Parisians, to plead the cause of peace.

The Privy Council in Paris, whom in a moment of dejection Napoleon had consulted as to whether or not to accept the Châtillon terms, had voted nearly unanimously to accept. Napoleon chose to ignore the council. St. Aignan, however, urged Napoleon to grasp the terms offered him, make whatever concessions were necessary.

Napoleon hardened at once.

"Sire," cried St. Aignan, "the peace will be good enough if it is prompt enough."

"It will come soon enough if it is shameful enough," retorted Napoleon, scowling again. He gave St. Aignan a curt dismissal.[2]

The armistice talks begun at Lusigny bogged down almost at once. And though the Châtillon Congress reopened formally on February 17, discussions quickly reached a stalemate. Metternich's draft for a preliminary peace was read aloud to Caulaincourt. When the French plenipotentiary raised questions about the future of the rest of Europe, most particularly about the fate of Saxony and Westphalia, Stadion replied coldly that France had no right to ask such questions, that the Allies would make their own arrangements. Caulaincourt forwarded the proposed terms to Napoleon and got no reply.

Spirits at headquarters were at a low point. Everyone, said one of the Englishmen at headquarters, was angry, anxious, or ill-humored; Priscilla Burghersh added, "uncertain, dilatory, and *entre nous* frightened."

Bitterly Schwarzenberg wrote his wife of the cost in human life that must inevitably follow the wrecked peace hopes:

> So streams of blood must flow to fight for that peace which they wanted to force on us a few days ago and which only failed because in the eyes of Frivolity [i.e., the Tsar] it could not be signed except in Paris. Ach, meine Nani, you cannot believe how my inmost heart is revolted at the thought of it![3]

The Tsar had attempted to withdraw all Russian reserves from Schwarzenberg's main army and join them to Blücher's forces for a drive on Paris. Instead, two corps were detached from Bernadotte's Army of the North and sent to support Blücher.

Never, in the long, anxious and difficult days since the beginning of the war had Metternich been more deeply depressed than he was in those days at the end of February and early March. All his usual buoyant optimism, his self-confidence, his faith in eventual success, had deserted him. He felt crushed by the burden of work, by the tragic prospect of a war that seemed to stretch ahead needlessly—and endlessly.

Never had he been so plainly near the end of his rope, close to total nervous exhaustion. The weeks of intense pressures, of head-splitting argument and quarrel over negotiations, of frustration over the failed peace efforts, had taken their toll.

Vienna was in great alarm over Napoleon's mid-February victories and even more over Schwarzenberg's retreat. And indeed Napoleon's troops were pushing Schwarzenberg's army farther and farther back. Troyes was abandoned; headquarters moved to Chaumont. Would they retreat as far as Langres, or, as some pessimists asserted, back to the Rhine? Again and again Metternich wrote to Laure of the propaganda line she must adhere to: Schwarzenberg was not retreating, he had merely retired, "better to concentrate his forces."[4]

The famine that Schwarzenberg had predicted and feared was a reality in the war zone. Long since, every farm, every village in Champagne had been scoured of any scrap of food. No bread was to be had in Troyes; dogs and people ate the dead horses in the streets. The discipline Schwarzenberg had tried so hard to maintain in order to win the French people over to the Allies was rapidly breaking down:

> The Cossacks [Priscilla Burghersh wrote] steal and pillage everything, but that is their métier; but Bavarians and Württembergers and I'm sorry to say some of the Austrians have done horrors.[5]

Even for the favored few, the ministers and staffs at headquarters, daily life had become increasingly wretched. After the last battles one stumbled everywhere over dead and dying, wounded and crippled.

The bitter cold of that memorably arctic winter penetrated even indoors—

> an infernal cold [Metternich described it] tempered only by smoke you could cut with a knife—not a door, not a window that closed—many corpses and much filth—pillage—cries of women and children—no cream because they've killed the cows—no bread because everything is eaten—and for compensation over my head in work.[6]

He was utterly exhausted, working twenty hours out of twenty-four, "nailed or handcuffed to my desk most of the night," writing instructions to the delegates at Châtillon, the minutes and memoranda of the long, futile ministerial conferences—none of his colleagues, Metternich wrote Laure, did any of the paperwork—dispatches, even propaganda pieces for the Vienna press. Often he had to drive twenty leagues in a day and then work through the night that followed. His family and friends would find him, he thought, "quite aged." For eight days he had "not slept three hours between one night and the next." Certainly, he added, nobody would ever accuse him "of having fomented and supported a war because"—and he mimicked the autocratic finality with which the Tsar silenced all dissenting opinions—"*tel est mon bon plaisir.*"[7]

Three times the previous night, he wrote Laure one midnight in February, he had been summoned to go to the Tsar's headquarters a half league away in the intense cold, returning finally only at quarter of six in the morning. He had fallen exhausted into bed; fifteen minutes later his servants rushed in to rouse him. The house next door was on fire and everyone must run out and wait for safety's sake in the street.

Most of the houses in Troyes were built of wood; people and animals bedded down in straw. A single drunken soldier, knocking over a single candle, could set the whole town in flames. "Fire is one of the charms of war. As there are troops by the hundreds in the houses and straw everywhere, fire catches like everything, so one hardly dares undress. . . ."

That letter, written to Laure by candlelight long after midnight, when the fire in the stove had gone out and the icy winter invaded the chamber, unlike Metternich's usual clear graceful script, is barely legible.

> Heaven will grant a peace soon, for I personally can do no more. It's a dog's trade, being a minister in a war camp.

The last sentence trails off into nothing as if the pen had dropped out of the hand that held it:

> *Adieu, mon amie.* I am going to bed for I am so very sleepy. *J'embrasse les enfans.*[8]

Although Castlereagh had gone along with the negotiations providing England got her basic demands, now he roundly condemned the armistice attempt and favored energetic prosecution of the war. Ever since the previous autumn he had been trying to bind the Allies together by a treaty that would prevent any of them from seeking a separate peace with Napoleon until the war was concluded. Castlereagh was far more willing than Metternich to stake his chances on the battlefield.

At a long conference in Metternich's quarters in Chaumont, lasting into the early hours of the morning of March 8, a treaty of alliance was hammered out, binding the Allies to carry on war against France with armies of at least 150,000, to maintain an alliance for twenty years after the war ended, supported by standing armies. The main war aims contained in the Châtillon peace terms were confirmed. In exchange for the Allies' "vigorous pursuit of the present war," England promised handsome subsidies to Russia, Prussia, Austria.

Metternich's pen put the treaty into final form, and though the main terms were doubtless Castlereagh's—he always referred to it as "my treaty"—one important clause was certainly Metternich's contribution. This was the clause promising that the signing powers would "concert together on the conclusion of a peace with France as to the means best adapted to guarantee to Europe and to themselves reciprocally the continuance of peace."

Such a collaboration of nations had been part of Metternich's design for peace the year before, in 1813, and he had mentioned "a concert of nations" in his Dresden talk with Napoleon.[9]

If the Chaumont Treaty prevented the complete rupture of the Coalition, it did not prevent ominous fissures from reappearing in that shaky edifice. Rumors had been floating around headquarters for some time that Schwarzenberg had secret orders from Emperor Franz not to fight while negotiations were in progress; Castlereagh had heard it from the Tsar. A few days after the Chaumont Treaty was signed, on Saturday evening, March 12, the good news came that Blücher had won a victory over the French at Laon. At midnight that night Metternich was summoned to the Tsar's quarters, where he found himself surrounded by Russian and Prussian officers, all in a glowering mood.

In what Metternich recalled as "one of the most painful scenes I've ever had," the Tsar demanded to know whether Schwarzenberg had been forbidden to fight and ordered instead to retreat to the Rhine. "I replied in such a way," Metternich wrote immediately after, "that he will never repeat that question to me."

The Emperor of Austria, awakened in his quarters, declared pointedly that he "did not meddle with the command of the army," and that he had given his full confidence to Schwarzenberg. The upshot of the angry confrontation was that the Tsar wrote Schwarzenberg his "hands were henceforth untied." Schwarzenberg, wounded to the quick, replied instantly that his hands never had been tied, that he had only acted according to his best military calculations. If his military conduct displeased the sovereigns, he alone was to blame. How delighted Napoleon would be, he added, to learn that such suspicions as these were dividing the Allied monarchs at so critical a moment.[10]

The issue that night—and during those crucial weeks of the campaign in France—was the meaning and purpose of war itself. To Schwarzenberg as to Metternich war was a last resort; they viewed it in terms of Vattel's Law of Nations, which prescribed that in peace nations should do each other as much good and in time of war as little harm as may be possible without injuring their own proper interests. Military considerations therefore should always be subservient to political and diplomatic aims. But against the old Law of Nations was posited the new theory of total war—that kind of massive warfare that had only just appeared in the last years, that had for its aim to reduce not only armies, but the enemy's resources, morale, population. It would be expounded by a young Prussian officer, Karl von Clausewitz, serving now with General Gneisenau, in his classic work *On War*. "Let us not hear of generals who conquer without bloodshed," he would write, directing his special contempt against Schwarzenberg, who fought an old-fashioned "restricted, shrivelled-up form of war."[11]

The responsibility Schwarzenberg felt for the lives of the 250,000 men under his command was a fearful one; he could not bring himself to spend those lives as recklessly as a cabinet might spend pounds sterling. War was indeed, as Clausewitz would write, "the province of uncertainty."

The problem of feeding that huge army had worsened, and Schwarzenberg worried increasingly about famine. Austria's supply lines were too long; fewer and fewer convoys were arriving from Switzerland. Horses pulling wagons loaded with the precious zwieback that was the army's mainstay food collapsed for lack of forage along the route, "where there is not enough to feed a mouse," Schwarzenberg wrote. Famished peasants swarmed on to the convoys. Blücher, on the other hand, had the granaries of France behind him, "while we have only poor Champagne that we have been sucking dry for three months. It's a miracle we are still alive."[12]

Morale in the army was as low as at headquarters. "Peace is the constant cry of every officer in this army," Lord Burghersh wrote.

Injured in the arm by a musket ball in late February, Schwarzenberg had still kept going. In the raw cold of early March he caught cold and a severe cough. Finally the bad weather, the tensions and anxieties, going without food or sleep, made him really ill and his doctor ordered him to bed.

Meantime, with Napoleon moving his army corps rapidly back and forth like a lightning chess player, the Allied ministers fled from one town to another, sometimes returning to Troyes or Chaumont or Bar-sur-Aube for a third or fourth time to find it even more devastated, more starved, more uninhabitable than the last time.

> I came here fast enough [Metternich wrote Wilhelmine from Bar-sur-Aube, late on the night of March 14]. The road is so filled with dead horses and with horrors that I'd like to have come here faster yet. The continual spectacle of destruction is frightful and it makes me sick at heart.
>
> Heaven did not make me for war or perhaps not entirely for it. If I were a general I would press so hard that I would finish very quickly so as not to have to begin again for a long time.
>
> My dear, with what refinement men go about destroying all the good things with which Providence has showered them![13]

The sights of war filled him with daily horror, as they did Aberdeen. He could not ignore it, as the imperturbable Castlereagh appeared to, who made virtually no mention of life in the war zone to his wife or colleagues. Nor could he accept it, as Humboldt did, as a necessity to which one must resign oneself.

> I detest war and everything about it: the murder, evils, vileness, pillage, corpses, amputees, dead horses—and even rape!
>
> Life at headquarters is a dog's life [he wrote bitterly]. There is no kind of privation to which one is not prey, and when the thing lasts months and years you understand how a person can't stand it any more. Dead and dying, all the blood spilled and the cripples you meet by the thousand are such a sad thing the glory itself is tarnished by it. . . .[14]

More than anything else, he felt worn out. "I have a tired soul," he wrote, and he longed for rest the way "a suffocating man longs for fresh air . . . When I am back home I won't leave my room for three months," he promised Laure.[15]

As always his public and his private lives were inextricably woven together. The letters he wrote Wilhelmine reflected the depth of his despondency, his loss of self-confidence:

> The world, dear W., rejoices loudly around me. I am in such a mel-
> ancholy mood that every expression of open joy strikes me down. My
> life needs just as many supports as yours does. Will I ever have them?
> . . . You will never love me much, my dear. I love you too much.[16]

2

"I am worried about Maman and my sister and I shall be very glad if I can have news of them—If I didn't do so many foolish things myself I could be surprised about other people's *sottises*—" Could Metternich, Wilhelmine wrote, find a way to get news of her mother and sister in Paris? It had been foolish of her mother to return to Paris, Wilhelmine thought. What would happen to her if the Allies laid seige to Paris? And what would happen to her youngest sister, Dorothée, married to a nephew of Talleyrand, Napoleon's former foreign minister?[17]

Metternich reassured her; he could and did get letters through the war zone to her mother in Paris. Caulaincourt had regular couriers going between Châtillon and Paris, and Metternich could presently forward letters of the Duchess of Courland back to Wilhelmine in Vienna. Caulaincourt could well afford the kindness; he had been the intermediary in bringing about Dorothée's unhappy marriage.

What a bad thing they had arranged for poor Dorothée, Metternich commented. "How unhappy I'd be if they had sent him into *my* bed." He had known Dorothée as a child in Dresden and in Berlin. He had seen her again after marriage, the thin, pale somber-eyed young wife in the last festive days of Empire Paris. "Dorothée with three children appears like a fantasy to me," he added.[18]

Inside Paris in the raw winter days of early 1814, there was deepening gloom despite Napoleon's string of mid-February victories. St. Aignan was right; it was peace that people wanted—nothing else would do. In moody silence and without cheers Parisians watched the columns of Russian and Prussian prisoners marched through the boulevards of the capital. With mounting anxiety they learned that stores of powder were being laid up and cannons sent to Paris. So Napoleon intended to fight in Paris itself.

In the shop windows a new picture of Napoleon's small son was offered for sale, a sentimental pose, the child on his knees, eyes lifted to heaven, with a legend reading, "I pray God for my father and for France." When Napoleon got the little picture from Marie Louise, he had at once ordered several thousand copies run off for public sale in late February. "If this little engraving could be produced within forty-eight hours and put on sale, it would have an excellent effect," he wrote.[19] People glanced in the shop windows, shrugged and passed by.

Few carriages were to be seen on the boulevards in those days; all the horses had been taken for the army. On the streets one saw mostly very old men and very young—and cripples, the armless and legless veterans of all the campaigns who could no longer be used in this one.

Through the weeks of February and early March the shrewdest man in France watched events carefully and bided his time. "That man is finished," Talleyrand had told Madame de La Tour du Pin a few months earlier. "He has lost his means; he's at the end of his rope."[20] But what next? —that was the question.

Charles Maurice de Talleyrand, son of an ancient noble family of France, had been born clubfooted, and as a result, destined from childhood for the priesthood and deprived of the honors and titles that would have come to him as eldest son.[21] His whole life was a rebellion against the vocation that had been forced on him.

A bishop before he was thirty through the helpful offices of one of his mistresses, Talleyrand, with his brains, his charm and wicked tongue, made no bones about enjoying all the pleasures of sophisticated Paris in the sunset days of the old regime, those times of which he himself said, "nobody could appreciate the pleasures of life who was not born before 1789." He had supported the Revolution in the beginning—France clearly needed reform— saved his neck in the Reign of Terror by fleeing first to England, then to America. In America he had managed to amass a small fortune, see a good bit of the country, make friends with Alexander Hamilton and William Cobbett. His memories of America became a bit cloudy with time, for he described it later to Fouché as blooming with date-bearing palm trees—though he never got further south than Philadelphia.

Returning to France in 1797 he literally fell into the post of Foreign Minister under the Directory, and rode swiftly upward on the coattails of the audacious young Corsican lieutenant who made himself First Consul, then Emperor of the French.

Certainly Talleyrand had an exceptionally strong instinct for self-survival; he had survived several shifts of government in France; he could face another with equanimity. Besides, his profession was diplomacy; change in government should not affect the practice of that profession.

Talleyrand had been in disfavor with Napoleon since his outspoken criticism of the Spanish adventure. There had been a certain famous scene in January of 1809 when the Emperor, having heard rumors of Talleyrand's dis-

affection, had hurried back from Spain to confront his Foreign Minister, and
to hurl at his head a barrage of barrack room execration. In a gathering of
ministers Napoleon had called Talleyrand a thief, a coward, a traitor, a cripple
and a cuckold, while the other members of the council listened white-faced.
Talleyrand, leaning against a mantel, remained expressionless and silent.
Shaking his fist in Talleyrand's face at the end of the tirade, Napoleon had
hurled a last insult: "You're nothing but shit in a silk stocking. *Merde dans
un bas de soie!*" Limping out afterward, Talleyrand had murmured, "What a
pity that such a great man should have such bad manners."

Punitively Napoleon had saddled the exiled Spanish princes and their
uncle and suite on Talleyrand's neck; they were quartered at his chateau of
Valençay in the Loire Valley, and he bore the full expenses of their stay.
Napoleon had stripped Talleyrand of his more lucrative offices—a mistake,
for it encouraged the Foreign Minister—if he needed encouragement—to look
for gratuities in other sources.

As early as the congress at Erfurt in the autumn of 1808 Talleyrand had
begun to betray Napoleon. In exchange for valuable information furnished
the Tsar during certain long tea-drinking evenings at the house of the Princess
of Thurn-und-Taxis Talleyrand demanded and got the hand of Princess
Dorothée of Courland for his nephew and heir, Edmond de Talleyrand-Périgord. Talleyrand had been directed to this little female treasure-house by none
other than Dorothée's real father, Count Batowski, who had been with
Talleyrand in Poland in 1806.

It had indeed been an unfortunate marriage into which sixteen-year-old
Dorothée had been forced, against her will, by the collusion of her mother
and the Tsar.

Edmond, good-looking, shallow, with a taste for gambling for high stakes
—especially with his wife's huge fortune at his command—found his pleasures outside the ménage in rue de la Grange-Batelière. The two had nothing
in common except the three children begotten during his brief visits at home;
during most of their marriage—which was perhaps the best thing that could
be said for it—Edmond had been away at war, and since the previous autumn, a prisoner of the Allies at Berlin. Dorothée—too thin and sallow to be
thought pretty when she had first come to Paris—had matured in five years to
a strikingly beautiful young woman. Slender still, with ivory-pale skin, huge
eyes of a blue so dark and heavily lashed that they appeared to be black—
"*yeux bleus d'enfer*," Sainte Beuve would describe them—the graceful dark
head held poised and proud, the strong character of the aquiline nose:
Dorothée looked, as Rémusat remarked, like a beautiful bird of prey.

But it was the fine machinery of her brain, and the charm and intelligence of her conversation that put Dorothée at once on a level with the most
sophisticated and fascinating women in Paris, the women of Talleyrand's
circle who had spent a lifetime tuning the fine instruments of their small
talk.

Wilhelmine's mother, the Duchess of Courland, had accompanied her youngest daughter to Paris in 1809, had at once fallen in love with the city and with the old intriguer Talleyrand.

A tender autumnal affair linked the sixty-year-old, worldly-wise Talleyrand with the Duchess Dorothea, in her forties still a woman of great personal charm and an ageless porcelain loveliness. She had turned from an ardent Bonapartist into an equally ardent Talleyrandist, was recognized queen of the seraglio over which Talleyrand reigned as *prince enchanteur*.

Now, since his quarrel with Napoleon, all but retired from public life, Talleyrand had kept only his membership in the Council of Regency and the nominal office of Vice Grand Elector.

The previous autumn, after Leipzig, Napoleon—desperately in need of a skilled diplomat to win the best deal he could from his adversaries—tried to persuade Talleyrand to return as Minister of Foreign Affairs. Talleyrand steadfastly refused.

Incomparably shrewd, witty, worldly, the epitome of Molière's *"grand seigneur, méchant homme,"* with his tallow-pale wrinkled face, the pale blue eyes with their look of disdain and the faint secret smile on his lips, as if his greatest treasure was a single joke he refused to share with the world, Talleyrand waited that winter of 1814 for events to unfold.

For all his cynical worldliness Talleyrand was deeply loyal to his family and his few intimate friends; he was also astonishingly sentimental. In those weeks of crisis, while the Allied armies fought through the last campaign, within two days' march of Paris, Talleyrand found time each morning to dash off in his "wretched tiny handwriting" an affectionate note to the Duchess of Courland:

> I love you, *chère amie*, with my whole soul, in hard times as in gentler times. I press you to my heart. Adieu.

> In these times one loves those one loves more than ever; that is what I tell myself when I awake thinking of you, *chère amie*.[22]

A creature of the night, Talleyrand really came alive after dark. He made late dining—at five or after—the elegant hour. In the morning, on the other hand, he had to grope his way carefully into the day, breakfasting near noon with his fifteen-year-old ward, Charlotte—probably his natural daughter—perched on his bed chattering away while he looked at letters and the latest army bulletins, his valet Courtiade brushing and powdering his hair, and bathing the crippled foot in eau de Barèges.

If he did not dine at home in the splendid mansion in the Rue St. Florentin overlooking the Place de la Concorde, he would most likely dine with the Duchess of Courland in her town house in the Rue Drouot.

> I shall dine quietly with you [he wrote her]. The heart and the soul are at ease in your little salon. Adieu, I love you with all my soul.[23]

Nearly every day he stopped at Dorothée's house to visit with her and her children.

In the early evening he was careful to make a judicious appearance at court, limping into the Tuileries salons just long enough to be seen, to exchange a few polite words with the Empress Marie Louise, to banter with a few acquaintances and play a hand or two at the gaming tables.

Later in the evening Talleyrand held his own private court in the beautiful reception room of his mansion with its rococo painted ceilings and the light of a thousand candles, "the theater," Vitrolles called it, "in which this great comedian sparkled." Seated on a sofa, swinging his crippled foot, he would reassure and entertain his little circle of ladies, passing along the news he had garnered that day:

> The Bulletin tomorrow will tell us what we are expected to believe.
> . . . It won't agree with the modest truth probably, but they count us
> for nothing and we must be content with what they tell us.[24]

On the premises of the Talleyrand mansion but not in evidence at the soirees was the ex-bishop's wife, née Catherine Grand, whom Talleyrand had married as casually as he had doffed his bishop's mitre, in a fit of bravado in 1804. Catherine had aged from the pretty, lush playgirl of the 1790's into a rouged and blowsy middle age. The capacious roof of their common house with its labyrinth of staircases, corridors and separate apartments, was the only thing Talleyrand and his improbable wife now shared. She had lately been having an affair with the Duke of San Carlos, member of the little Spanish court exiled at Valençay, and once, during one of his violent scenes, Napoleon had flung at Talleyrand: "And your wife—you never told me that San Carlos was your wife's lover!" To which Talleyrand replied evenly with the unction of the perfect courtier, "Truly, Sire, I never thought this tale could reflect on Your Majesty's honor or on my own."

Sundays Talleyrand still went meticulously to Mass in the Tuileries chapel, where he could pick up the latest rumors at court. It was after Mass on January 16, 1814, that a last scene between Napoleon and Talleyrand took place. The Emperor tried to engage Talleyrand to represent France at Châtillon. Talleyrand declined. Napoleon grumbled about the failure of the treaty with Spain; Talleyrand replied politely, "As I predicted"—at which Napoleon flew into a rage and threatened to put his former Foreign Minister behind bars. The bystanders were certain Talleyrand's end had come, but Bassano could not be found, Napoleon's temper subsided, and next day Talleyrand wrote the Duchess of Courland that the "storm was over," but one must take precautions.

Talleyrand did not hold out much hope for the Châtillon negotiations:

> . . . bad people remain bad [he wrote the duchess]. When you make
> mistakes of the brain it's forgivable; when you sin by the heart there
> are no remedies and therefore no excuses. Burn this note.[25]

In February the army came and took his carriage horses, impounded the cows from his country house at St. Brice outside Paris that had supplied cream for his table and milk for Dorothée's young children.

When news came that Blücher was within twenty-four hours of Paris and the Austrians were at Troyes, Talleyrand packed off the women of the family—his ward Charlotte, Dorothée and her children, his wife, Catherine, a diverse assortment of elderly marquises, with maids, governesses and nurses —to his château of Rosny, some forty miles northwest of Paris. The Duchess of Courland followed reluctantly.

After the departure of the women from his life, Talleyrand was more acutely depressed than he had ever been. "Uncertainty is the one thing the mind cannot cope with when one is no longer young," he wrote. What to do?

Around the middle of February—just when Napoleon was launching the brilliant series of victories—an old friend of Talleyrand's, Emmerich-Joseph, Duc de Dalberg, came to see him.

German-born Dalberg, whose uncle, the former Bishop of Erfurt, and more lately Prince Primate of Frankfurt, was an old friend of the Courland family—it was he who had taken charge of Jeanne and returned her to her family after the escapade with the Italian violinist in 1799—had, like Talleyrand, been a member of Napoleon's government and had turned against him. Dalberg had thrown his lot in with the royalists who were plotting a Bourbon restoration; he hoped to win Talleyrand's support as well. Talleyrand declined to commit himself. But he had some advice to offer Dalberg.

"Look," he said, "they are negotiating with the man they should be destroying. He will be cleverer than they. He will sign a peace—then what will become of us?"

A peace signed with Napoleon would be no peace at all, Talleyrand thought. Could Dalberg find a man of daring to penetrate the war zone, get to the Allied leaders and warn them that the Châtillon negotiations would be fruitless, advise them to march straight for Paris?[26]

Dalberg knew just the man for the mission. An ardent young royalist of his acquaintance, Baron de Vitrolles, was eager to make the perilous journey through the war zone to the Comte d'Artois, and bring him news of the royalist group waiting inside France. Vitrolles at once agreed to the dangerous mission Dalberg proposed: to find the Allied leaders and speak for the Bourbon cause, hopefully without being shot as a traitor by the French along the way, or as a spy by the Allies.

He needed the most persuasive credentials. Talleyrand not only refused to put anything in writing, but at no time did he even see or speak with Vitrolles, though Dalberg assured Vitrolles that they had Talleyrand's support.

"You don't know this monkey," Dalberg said with a wry grin. "He would not risk burning the end of his paw even if the chestnuts in the fire were all for him."

If Talleyrand gave Vitrolles no direct support, it may well be that the Duchess of Courland served as intermediary. Vitrolles like Dalberg knew the duchess well; he had lived in the 1790's in an émigré colony close to her *Schloss* in Saxony.

It was Dalberg in the end who furnished the only credentials that Vitrolles carried: a carnelian seal engraved with the Dalberg arms, and two words written in invisible ink inside Vitrolles' wallet—the first names of two Viennese women with whom he and Stadion had romped many years before. "That," said Dalberg, "should get you in to see Stadion." Dalberg added a scrawled sentence on a scrap of paper to be presented to Nesselrode. But he had one word of warning to Vitrolles. "Be careful of Metternich." The Austrian minister, said Dalberg, was not to be trusted.

At dawn on March 6, disguised as a Swiss merchant named Vincent on his way to visit his estates in the country, Vitrolles mounted the diligence for Lyon.[27]

3

Vitrolles proved to be an astute and audacious emissary. At Auxerre he talked himself into seeing the commander of the Austrian troops, Moritz Liechtenstein, who sent him on to Châtillon.

At Stadion's quarters he sent in a note that a traveler just arrived from Paris had important information to impart. Admitted at once, Vitrolles produced his wallet, passed the paper written in invisible ink across a candle flame and handed it to Stadion, who exclaimed, grinning: "Only Dalberg could have written those words!"[28]

They lunched together the following day, March 9. Vitrolles spoke glowingly of Bourbon hopes and Stadion for his part described frankly to Vitrolles the difficulties the Coalition had been facing—the quarrels precipitated by the sovereigns' presence at army headquarters, the enmity between Blücher and Schwarzenberg, an enmity that had been encouraged and fostered by the Tsar and the Prussian King:

> "It isn't in the presence of an enemy like the Great Captain that one plays such games [Stadion said]. So [Napoleon] has beaten Blücher's corps with double blows and forced our army to retreat as far as Langres. The Prussian marshal, not bothering over our retreat, has pushed on toward Paris. You may have heard the noise of his cannon.[28]

Vitrolles hoped to hear from Stadion that the Châtillon negotiations were failing, for successful negotiations would spell the doom of the Bourbon hopes. He was not disappointed. Yet even though the Châtillon Congress was collapsing, the Allies had nowhere seen support for the Bourbons, nor for any other party except Napoleon's. They had waited more than ten days at Langres, Stadion told him, hoping to learn from some source what the French people really wanted.

If Vitrolles hoped to further the Bourbon cause, Stadion advised, he should go to headquarters at Troyes and talk with Metternich. "The true direction of affairs is in Metternich's hands. . . . He is the bond of this great association."

"But I was warned against Metternich by Dalberg," Vitrolles protested. Stadion replied, "I am Dalberg's friend as much as you can be, and I am not considered a blind partisan of Monsieur de Metternich. . . . At this moment Monsieur de Metternich is the link that unites the sovereigns. He is at this moment as much the minister of the Tsar as of the Emperor of Austria."

A day or so later Vitrolles presented himself at Metternich's quarters in Troyes. It was noon; the Austrian minister had spent all night in conference, he explained, then in writing instructions and dispatches. He had caught only a few hours' sleep after daybreak. He was, nevertheless, delighted "to talk to people who know France better than we do."

Vitrolles produced his credentials. With Metternich was a tiny man in a Russian diplomatic uniform, who was introduced as Count Nesselrode. Together the two men stood at a window, scrutinizing the emblem on the carnelian seal and the scribbled note, while Vitrolles waited. "I do not know the Dalberg arms," Vitrolles heard Nesselrode say, "but this is certainly the escutcheon of the Empire."

Suddenly Metternich appeared to make up his mind, turned with a decisive movement and waved Vitrolles into a chair.

"It really doesn't matter to us, Monsieur, whether you are the person you claim to be or not—we are rather inclined to think you are. But even if you were sent by Bonaparte or Savary, we could say exactly the same things to you.

"Today everything is out in the open. Our intentions are declared. We would be happy to have them made public."

In a frank and friendly way Metternich appeared to be laying his cards on the table. The whole aim of the Coalition, he declared, was simply to restore equilibrium to Europe and independence to the countries that had suffered under Napoleon's yoke. These aims, he went on to say, had just been signed into permanence at Chaumont by a new treaty.

For ten minutes or more Metternich walked back and forth the length of the room, gesticulating now and then to emphasize a point, while he enlarged on the Allies' desire to bring a long-lasting peace to Europe.

Adroitly and purposefully Metternich had turned the Vitrolles meeting into his own use. He did not know who this mysterious "Monsieur Vincent" was, whether he was a spy for Napoleon and his Minister of Police, whether he really represented the royalists—or any other group of dissidents. Metternich was sending his own message back to all of them.

"What do they want in France?" Metternich demanded, stopping in front of Vitrolles.

And the latter replied—quite as if he had been appointed to speak for the whole French nation: "To be freed of the military dictatorship of Napoleon. There will be no peace with Bonaparte, and no France at all without the Bourbon."

Metternich and Nesselrode looked at one another in complete astonishment. "But we have been crossing this France," Metternich interposed. "We have been living in the middle of it for nearly two months, and we've seen nothing of what you describe—no nostalgia for old times, no discontent with the Emperor. . . . In any case, what have we to do with a question that concerns the internal government of France? The law of nations, universally recognized, forbids us from intervening in domestic affairs."

For reply Vitrolles launched a tirade against the despotism of Napoleon, the waste and carnage of the battlefields.

Each day for several days Vitrolles returned to converse with Metternich, usually at noon, in a high-ceilinged, well-lighted gallery of the house:

> [Metternich] wanted to see and he did not fear being seen [Vitrolles recalled]. His simple, easy, clear diction was not lacking in grace. His face was handsome and pleasant, his figure noble and even elegant; his manners engaging, natural and seductive.

Vitrolles gives us a vivid glimpse into Metternich's "portable chancellery," the tiny Foreign Office-on-the-move buzzing with activity, everyone scurrying about, writing and editing news and dispatches for home consumption.

Each day Metternich led the discussion skillfully through various channels, explaining the complexities that faced the Allies, insisting that Austria would not support a regency of Marie Louise if the French people voiced strong support for the Bourbons.

Vitrolles sensed that Metternich was more violently opposed to war itself than were his fellow ministers. The devastation of the war in France made Metternich shudder, but "far from thinking as others did that these were just reprisals, he wanted at any cost to stop the destruction."

On Vitrolles' main demand, however—that the Allies break off their negotiations with Napoleon and throw their support to the Bourbons—Metternich remained politely evasive.

Shrewdly Vitrolles analyzed Metternich's political temperament:

> He [Metternich] understood how to wait for events to unfold and took them as they happened rather than trying to bring them about. His brain, essentially practical and full of common sense, never got lost in theories, in imagining possible things. . . . He was sufficiently master of himself not to permit himself to be turned away from his aims, and his aims were to maintain what existed and to accommodate the interests of his country to them.[29]

Finding that his discussions with Metternich were leading nowhere, Vitrolles wangled interviews with the Tsar and with Castlereagh. The Tsar shocked Vitrolles by naming as possibilities for the French throne only Bernadotte and Napoleon's stepson, Eugène de Beauharnais, and finally suggesting that "maybe a wisely organized republic would be most agreeable to the French mentality."

Most impressed by Vitrolles and most encouraging to him was Castlereagh, who wrote to Liverpool in highly flattering terms of Vitrolles' judgment and of his backers.

So far as Châtillon was concerned, Vitrolles was to get his wish. Castlereagh was anxious to end the negotiations, which he now felt only impeded the war effort. "They enervate the temper of the army," he wrote.

Only Metternich and Caulaincourt made a genuine effort to keep the avenues of negotiation open.

Caulaincourt had sent on for Napoleon's approval the newest draft of a peace proposal which the Allies had agreed upon at Troyes. No reply came. On February 28, while Caulaincourt pled for more time, the Allied delegates told him firmly that they must fix a deadline for Napoleon's reply.

"I think ten days will be enough," said Caulaincourt.

"I think eight will suffice," Cathcart retorted.[30]

With "this devil of a Châtillon" grinding to a halt, the delegates filled their days and nights with whatever amusement they could find. Humboldt wrote sonnets, Cathcart pored over an etymological Greek dictionary in French, and Priscilla Burghersh pronounced herself "just out of my wits with delight" at Byron's *The Corsair*, which she had borrowed from Charles Stewart. Writing home she described the delegates "spending their lives giving great dinners to each other and gorging so effectually that two or three have fallen ill from the effects of their intemperance."

Priscilla's husband rode over from Schwarzenberg's headquarters to spend a day with her on her twenty-first birthday on March 13. Dear Lord Cathcart found a troupe of unemployed French comedians to put on two little plays for her, and Monsieur de Caulaincourt dispatched a courier to Paris to bring back the best perfumes for her, though of course she did not wish to put herself under any kind of obligation to a Frenchman.

The weather had turned warm and springlike. Priscilla rode out into the countryside, wrote her sister Emily to order a summer riding-habit for her:

> You know I like a very short waist behind, and I think the sleeves look better put in with a very few small plaits on the shoulders. . . . I should wish it light French grey. . . . and a man's riding hat of shepherd's straw.[31]

Meantime, by March 10, the day fixed for the deadline for Napoleon's reply to the peace terms, no word had come to Châtillon from French headquarters. Caulaincourt pled for more time, complaining that several days had been lost when the Allies had stopped his courier and taken the dispatches. The Allies gave him three more days. But on Priscilla's birthday no reply had come.

On Friday, March 18, Stadion read to the assembled group the official protocol signed by the Allied ministers announcing that Châtillon was dissolved.

Only on March 16 had Napoleon sent a counter-project for peace, again insisting on France's "natural boundaries." By the time it arrived Châtillon had been pronounced finished, and his proposals were in any case unacceptable.

So Metternich's last peace effort in the last stage of the war collapsed.

Why had Châtillon failed? It had failed because it was not a true negotiation, not a bargaining table at all; what the Allies had presented to France was an ultimatum. It failed because the majority of the Allies—and Napoleon himself—did not clearly *will* peace. Both hoped to gain more through force. And it failed most importantly because hostilities were not suspended during the term of the negotiation, because there was no armistice, so that in effect the military controlled the process of decision making. Napoleon hardened his demands when he was winning; the Allies hardened theirs when they were ahead.

Napoleon called Châtillon "a put-up game arranged between Metternich and Castlereagh to make the British parliament grant subsidies." The enemy, he said, wanted only to pillage and to overthrow France, while Metternich and Castlereagh—curious accusation—wanted "to stir up revolutions" in France.[32]

Even at the end of Châtillon the two men, Metternich and Caulaincourt, who had tried earnestly since the previous summer to bring the conflict to an end did not give up hope, and both tried to keep the channels of negotiation open.

Dalberg would boast months later at the Vienna Congress that a letter existed which Metternich wrote Caulaincourt at this time conjuring him to put all his strength to work to maintain Napoleon on the throne of France. That letter would be used to blackmail a pension for Dalberg's uncle.[33]

It may have been the last letter Metternich addressed to Caulaincourt, urging him to go in person to Napoleon and if he could get his agreement to the Allies' proposals to return at once:

> Affairs are taking a turn for the worse, Monsieur le Duc. On the day when you are completely decided for peace, with the indispensable sacrifices, come to make it, but not to be the interpreter of inadmissible plans. . . .
>
> It still depends on your master to make peace. In a little while affairs will perhaps no longer depend on him.[34]

Caulaincourt left Châtillon at six in the morning of March 21 with an orderly of Emperor Franz to escort him to the French advance posts at Joigny.

But when he reached Napoleon at St. Dizier on the night of March 23, events were already tumbling pell-mell toward a final denouement. The voice of a single reasonable and well-intentioned man was lost in the dissonance and confusion of that final closing act.

While Caulaincourt hurried toward Napoleon's headquarters, the ministers in Troyes were forced to scramble to safety as both armies moved toward battle. Metternich sent Vitrolles a message on Saturday morning, March 19, informing him that they were evacuating Troyes and seeking a safer spot at Bar-sur-Seine. It was not a retreat, he assured Vitrolles. Metternich and Castlereagh were going on horseback; Vitrolles might ride in Metternich's carriage with his secretary, Baron Binder.

Vitrolles describes vividly that hasty departure—one of many that had been repeated again and again in the course of the campaign as the fighting got too hot and close for comfort.

In the streets outside the ministers' quarters there were shouts, disorder, confusion, as dozens of servants and orderlies hurried about to load the hundred and fifty or so vehicles with trunks, campaign desks, document cases, kitchen equipment, all the traveling paraphernalia of the sovereigns and ministers, while a crowd in a motley assortment of strange costumes and the uniforms of several nations, jockeyed for position in the convoy. Finally came the procession out of town, the two-mile-long snake of vehicles moving at a snail's pace along the road southeast to Bar-sur-Seine.

At noon the convoy halted at Vandoeuvre for lunch, the ministers' vehicles pulling into the courtyard of the castle, devastated by armies that had occupied it one after the other. Everybody in the caravan tumbled out and began to lunch on whatever they had brought along. Vitrolles had brought nothing. He hurried into the village to scare up a bite. Nothing. Most of the houses had been pillaged and stood deserted. Here and there where a family still lived, they had not a crust of bread. One large house looked promising, but several people from the convoy had already converged on it, and the first arrivals had eaten up everything in sight. Vitrolles got a cup of bouillon.

Returning still hungry to the courtyard of the château, he saw in the middle of the confusion of carriages some servants laying rough planks over sawhorses, while the Prussian Chancellor, Baron Hardenberg, gave directions for the spreading of a beautiful cold picnic from the royal Prussian kitchen wagons. Nobody objected when Vitrolles sat down and joined in, making short work of the salmis of partridge, fried chicken and champagne—all delicacies but no necessities, said Vitrolles. Castlereagh, in a great floating white cape, stood on tiptoe to eat from a plate he had set on the gun rack on top of a campaign vehicle.

No one was cheerful. Everyone knew that a decisive battle was taking place not far away.

In the middle of lunch an Austrian officer galloped up, and after a brief conversation Metternich announced a cheering piece of news. General

Bubna had just sent word that Marshal Augereau had abandoned Lyon, and the Austrian army was occupying the second largest city in France. Spirits lifted. Everyone climbed back into carriages or saddles, and the caravan got under way again.

During the ride that day Baron Binder confided to Vitrolles that Metternich was softening on the Bourbons.

The negotiations at Châtillon had been broken off that day, March 19. Choices were growing narrower and the ministers were looking for alternatives.

That night, Saturday, March 19, in Bar-sur-Seine Metternich invited Vitrolles to come at ten o'clock and join the ministers' usual evening meeting in his quarters.

It was a cold Saturday night; the group of men sat in a half-circle warming themselves around a fire burning in an open grate. Only Baron Binder sat apart, at the big campaign desk, jotting down minutes of the conversation.

If the Bourbons came to power, one of the diplomats asked Vitrolles, just which able men in France could they hope to rally to their government? Could they call on such a man as Talleyrand, for example?

"And why not Monsieur de Talleyrand?" asked Vitrolles. "You can consider him as entirely attached to the [Bourbon] cause—" There was a minute pause, then he added—"At least in his heart."

Everyone in the room—most of whom had had dealings with Talleyrand's suavely evasive political stands—burst out laughing. "Ah, yes indeed, in his heart!"

"Well, messieurs, in his mind, if you wish."

The evening ended merrily. Everyone began to talk nostalgically of Paris and of old friends there. Vitrolles amused the group by reciting satirical *Noëls*—sharp verses making fun of Napoleon—that had passed from mouth to mouth the previous winter.[35]

If we are to believe Baron Binder, Metternich's secretary during the campaign, who shared his tiny billets wherever they happened to be and worked with him day and night, the Austrian minister continued to favor a regency until nearly the end of March.[36]

It may be that the night of March 19 marked his reluctant and still tentative switch to support of the Bourbons—contingent on how events unfolded.

The diplomats disbanded early that night. At eleven o'clock everyone had left and Metternich sat alone at his desk writing Wilhelmine. She was to warn Gentz that there would soon be a conflict between his principles and the turn of events, for Gentz fiercely opposed a restoration of the Bourbons. "If we could go back to 1789," Gentz had written, "then possibly the Bourbons might return, but Europe in the year 1814—that I could only wish for if I were Russian." Wilhelmine was to tell Gentz, "His principles are and will remain eternally mine," but the application of principles becomes problematical "when one deals with an adverse party who knows no other principle than not to profess any. If you see Gentz tell him he has to be *with us* to judge political events."[37]

Next day Vitrolles, encouraged by the tentative backing of the Allied ministers, left for Nancy to see Monsieur, the French king's brother.

Metternich had surrendered to the course of events. "I am for what happens," he wrote.[38]

4

After his defeat at Blücher's hands at Laon, Napoleon crossed the Aube River to attack what he thought was the last corps of Schwarzenberg's retreating army. He might even, he boasted, drive them back to the Rhine; he would certainly prevent their junction with the army of Blücher.

But it was not an isolated Austrian detachment that Napoleon attacked on March 19 but the entire main army of Schwarzenberg. And Napoleon was caught in an irreparable military blunder, with the river Aube at his back and the only bridge destroyed. Greatly outnumbered, the French retreated into the town, fighting from house to house and from street to street, defending every foot of ground, but inexorably driven back to the river.

Napoleon himself fought desperately, perhaps suicidally. Twice his horse was shot out from under him. Even his Guard troops, the precious unspendable capital hoarded in every battle, were ordered out.

His engineers threw together a bridge that Sunday night of March 20, and the survivors of the deadly battle scrambled across, leaving behind among the ruined houses of Arcis, in the fields and on the riverbank, more than four thousand dead on the French side—as many of the Allies.

It was a decisive battle.

Days before, Napoleon had written his brother Joseph that his troops were cracking under the strain of long marches, day in and day out, with little food, little or no rest. "The Young Guard is melting away like snow," he wrote. "The Old Guard holds on. My Guard cavalry too is melting away."

While he pondered his limited choice, the Allied generals asked themselves, what next? Should they pursue Napoleon wherever he was, deliver a final defeat? Or should they march straight for Paris?

By a great stroke of luck a French army courier fell into Allied hands; in the pouch was a letter from Napoleon to his wife in Paris, detailing his plan "to drive the enemy's army farther from Paris and get my own army back to my fortresses. I shall be at St. Dizier this evening. Adieu, my dear, a kiss for my son."[39]

At a final Allied war council on the night of March 25, the Tsar won out. The main armies would march to Paris while two divisions would be sent in pursuit of Napoleon to delude him into thinking he had succeeded in his ruse.

In those final days of war, the ministers and diplomats, within a few miles of the fighting along the Aube, fled from one town to another. Sometimes they found no houses left standing and had to sleep in their carriages. Food was scarce, and Metternich sent all his extra staff, his secretaries and aides, back to Vesoul. To reduce the size of the great awkward convoy of carriages and wagons that could clog an important highway at some critical moment, Emperor Franz sent all his extra carriage horses back to Vienna. Metternich parted even with the fine Cossack horse that Hetman Platov had given him, writing Laure to make sure the groom took extra care to exercise it.

At Bar-sur-Aube, where they paused for a day on Wednesday, March 23, Hardenberg invited the other ministers to dine with him. All of them came except Nesselrode, who excused himself saying he must go in search of the Tsar at army headquarters some distance away.

Late that night a courier brought news that Napoleon's army, moving quickly toward St. Dizier, had passed between the diplomats at Bar-sur-Aube and the main Allied army, severing all communication between them. The ministers were in grave danger. Nobody went to bed at all, and at daybreak they hurriedly left on horseback for Châtillon, only to find that town too threatened by French troops. They moved hastily on, southeast toward the city of Dijon, out of the combat zone.

Metternich was in a dilemma. Schwarzenberg had urged the Austrian Emperor to take refuge during the last days of fighting in the safety of Dijon, but the last thing Metternich wanted to do was to separate himself from the Tsar at this crucial juncture. It would be more than a little awkward, however, if the Austrian Emperor and his Foreign Minister fell into Napoleon's hands at the moment of final denouement.

Recollecting his narrow escape on the road to Trainel on the night of February 20, Metternich followed the Emperor and the other diplomats to Dijon. Only Nesselrode, who had rejoined the Tsar, would be part of the climax of the campaign.

As it turned out, their escape had been a narrow one, for that same night after their departure from Bar-sur-Aube, "Buonoparte slept in the very bed the Emperor Francis had left that morning."

In Dijon the ministers were joined by the Châtillon diplomats—Aberdeen, Stadion and Razumowsky—who with Priscilla Burghersh had left Châtillon two days earlier in a convoy of twelve carriages with an escort of hussars and Cossacks, bound for headquarters. They too had barely escaped falling into the hands of Napoleon's army. They had got as far as Chaumont, where they found

> the tocsin ringing and the whole town in an uproar. A corps of 16,000 French were within a few miles of town, some 2,000 armed peasants even nearer, and in the other direction some 2,000 Austrians.[40]

They bivouacked that night with the Austrian troops around a great campfire, Priscilla crouching in the open air "surrounded by several thousand sol-

diers and horses." A few hours later French troops were camping on the
same spot.

On Friday afternoon, March 25, the whole convoy of diplomats reached
the peaceful, prosperous town of Dijon, feeling as if they had been transported by magic out of the horrors of the combat zone, the daily sight of
starving and wounded, dying and dead, into a place where food was plentiful, where people slept in beds, where shops were still filled with beautiful
things. "I almost hugged the first oxen I saw," Metternich wrote Laure, as
well as "a rooster, 12 chickens, and an old peasant woman spinning on the
doorsill of her house."[41]

On that same afternoon, near the little town of Fère-Champenoise some
hundred miles to the north, the main army of Schwarzenberg fought a savage
battle with the forces of Mortier and Marmont. At the end of the day the
road to Paris lay open to the Allies.

5

In Paris in the last days of March Talleyrand made ready to flee if necessary. He sent clothes and a chest of money and valuables to Rosny.

On March 24 the Duchess of Courland came back from Rosny "to warm
herself" in Paris, bringing Charlotte along, as Talleyrand had asked her. An
invading army would be far easier to put up with, she thought, than fifty
quarreling women shut up in an icy château in the country.

Talleyrand was delighted. "Adieu, my angel, we are dining together—but
I shall see you before dinner," he wrote her. "*Mon Dieu,* how I love you!"
"My day begins as I like it to, a note for you, and Charlotte breakfasting on
my bed."[42]

In mid-March news had been smuggled into Paris that the Duke of Wellington had captured Bordeaux, and that the Duc d'Angoulême, nephew of the
exiled French pretender, Louis XVIII, had entered Bordeaux amid cheers of
the populace.

Astutely Talleyrand assessed the situation. If Napoleon made peace with
the Allies at once, then Bordeaux was unimportant; he could still salvage
his throne. But if Napoleon failed to make peace with the Allies at once,
then Bordeaux became very significant. "Burn this letter, please," he had
written the duchess. He knew he was under surveillance, and that some of
his letters had been scrutinized by the police. The duchess saved the letter.

Did Talleyrand during February and March of 1814 plot to restore the
Bourbons? He maintained a close relationship with the royalist group in
Paris, and had encouraged Vitrolles' mission. But it had been indirect and
meager encouragement; he had not even seen Vitrolles. His friendship with
the royalists cost nothing and kept his options open.

Talleyrand's thoughts appeared to parallel Metternich's very closely during the tense days of March. By allowing the Châtillon negotiations to collapse, Napoleon had lost his throne. But there was still a chance for a regency, and if Napoleon were removed from the scene, the army would certainly opt for a regency for his son. Almost until the end of March both Talleyrand in Paris and Metternich in provincial France assessed the Bourbon cause as weak—no power base, minimal popular support. Talleyrand hoped—as Metternich began to hope during the latter days of the campaign —that Napoleon would be killed. He alone stood in opposition to peace. The situation, now so confused and cloudy, would clarify at once.

"If the Emperor were killed," Talleyrand wrote the duchess on March 17 —and to no one else but this dearest, most trusted confidante would Talleyrand have dared express his thoughts so openly—"we would have the King of Rome and the regency of his mother. . . . The Emperor's brothers would certainly be an obstacle, but this obstacle could easily be disposed of—they could be forced to leave France."[43]

Three days later he wrote her again in the same vein. "If the Emperor were dead, the regency would satisfy everyone because a council would be named that would please all opinions."[44] And who would be the head of the council, and the Empress's closest adviser? Who else?

That Talleyrand had the regency in mind and, as always, was thinking ahead, is clear from a little palace intrigue he carried through in those perilous days. Dorothée was one of the *dames d'honneur*—honorary ladies-in-waiting chosen from women of high rank—who took turns serving the Empress. While Dorothée was still in Rosny Talleyrand adroitly managed to have her named for official service duties to Marie Louise beginning on April 1—precisely the time he figured for Napoleon's debacle. If Napoleon either were killed or toppled from power by revolt or by the Allied capture of Paris, then clever little Dorothée would be one of two or three women closest to the person of Marie Louise during a critical period. It was one of the nice little guarantees for which Talleyrand had such exceptional foresight.[45]

In Paris people waited gloomily and fatalistically. Hard money had disappeared. Rich women, such as the wives of Napoleon's marshals, sewed their diamonds into their corset linings and kept their carriages in readiness. If the Cossacks and the Prussians reached Paris first, it might well go up in flames as Moscow had.

Earlier he had reassured the Duchess of Courland that so long as the Empress remained in the capital, they need not prepare to flee:

> As long as she is here Paris is safer than any other place; if she leaves one
> must be ready to leave at once.[46]

On Monday, March 28, the Council of Regency met in the Tuileries for the last time. The Empress presided, and around her were gathered the men Napoleon had chosen to guide her—his brother Joseph at their head, Cambacérès, Lacépède, Clarke, Savary, Champagny—and Talleyrand.

The question to be decided was whether the Empress and the King of

Rome should, with the Allied armies nearing Paris, take flight? Or should they stay, meet the Allies, face out whatever happened?

One by one the Empress asked her council to speak.

Talleyrand argued that if she remained with her son in Paris and calmly awaited the arrival of the Allies, she could throw herself into her father's arms, greet the Tsar and the Prussian King as Regent of France. They would find it exceedingly difficult to dislodge her; there would be no break in the government.

Marie Louise nodded in agreement. Without any intellectual pretensions, Marie Louise was not a stupid woman. Like her father she had a *fond* of shrewd common sense and an exceptional instinct for survival. But she had been bred up from infancy—as were females in general, and most of all, royal females—to docility and passive obedience.

A vote was taken. The majority of the council agreed that the Empress should remain in Paris.

Then Napoleon's older brother Joseph unfolded the last letter he had got from the Emperor. Written on March 16, it commanded:

> If the enemy were to advance on Paris in such force that all resistance becomes impossible, see that the Regent and my son, together with all the court officials, are sent off in the direction of the Loire. Do not become separated from my son, and remember that I would rather see him drowned in the Seine than fall into the enemy's hands.[47]

Never had Napoleon encouraged anyone under him—neither his brothers nor his marshals nor his wife—to make any real decisions for themselves. They were expected to follow orders—his orders.

A silence followed as Joseph folded the letter and returned it to his pocket. Reluctantly the council agreed that the Empress, her son and the major part of the government should leave Paris.

Getting into his carriage at midnight after the long council meeting on that fateful Monday evening, Talleyrand shrugged. "So that's the end of that. They had a good hand and they threw it away."

Marie Louise wrote her husband that night—the last time she would write to him from Paris:

> I am sure it will have a dreadful effect on the people of Paris. . . . I entrust myself to Providence, convinced that no good will come of this.[48]

The following morning in a dreary rain the long line of carriages took its way out of the Tuileries, "like a funeral procession," one of the courtiers wrote later, bound for the château of Rambouillet southwest of Paris—ten big green traveling berlines with the Empress, the child and their suites, then the coronation coaches covered with canvas against the weather, and finally wagons loaded with crown jewels, plate, silver-gilt service, and thirty-two barrels filled with the gold of the Treasury.

In the exodus were members of the Regency Council—all except Talleyrand. His mind was made up. He would stake his cards on the next act.

6

For thirteen critical days—from March 25 to April 7—Metternich, Castlereagh, Hardenberg, together with Emperor Franz and the diplomats from Châtillon, were trapped in Dijon without any knowledge of or participation in the final events of the war. Only some hundred and sixty miles southeast of Paris, they were four days' journey and a whole world away in the confusion of the last days of the campaign. Cut off from the Allied armies by Napoleon's last march, they might as well have been on the moon, or, as Priscilla Burghersh wrote, "in America."

In his *Memoirs* Metternich passed lightly and quickly over the Dijon stay. To the end of his life it must have rankled deeply that he had missed the climax of the whole campaign, had not entered Paris on that sunny Thursday, March 31, or had any hand in the critical decisions hammered out in the days immediately following. "I considered for a long time whether I should run the risk of attempting to reach headquarters myself," he wrote. But the dispatch of all their extra horses to Vienna in the scramble from one spot to another in those last days had left all of them without the relays that were essential for a journey of more than four hours.[49]

Though they did not know of the fall of Paris until nearly two weeks after the event, one piece of news reached Dijon very soon after the arrival of the ministers: that the Duke of Wellington had captured Bordeaux, and that the Duc d'Angoulême, nephew of Louis XVIII, had been warmly welcomed by a pro-royalist populace. Castlereagh was jubilant—for Castlereagh. That night he gave a dinner party to his fellow diplomats and raised a toast to the mayor of Bordeaux and to the Bourbons.

Whatever were Metternich's feelings about the Bourbon restoration and the loss of the last wisp of hope for a regency, he wasted no time on regrets, but set to work at once to maneuver events insofar as possible to Austria's advantage. He dispatched Count Bombelles, a French émigré in Austrian service, to try to arrange that Emperor Franz make his entry into the French capital side by side with the brother of the presumptive king. "He will install the new rather than the old monarch," Metternich explained to Laure.[50]

But a restored Bourbon did not need the father-in-law of the deposed Emperor riding beside him into his own capital, and Bombelles was turned down on his mission.

Meantime, a totally unexpected traveler arrived on Metternich's doorstep in Dijon, as if to dramatize the dangers from which they had narrowly escaped. It was Wessenberg, Metternich's emissary to England, in a deplorable state, unshaven, disheveled, half-clothed in borrowed rags.[51] He had crossed the Channel from England to Holland and Germany, thence across the Rhine into occupied France. But in the war zone, on his way to Allied headquarters, he and his party had been attacked by a band of several hundred French peasants, partisans of Napoleon, and stripped of everything he owned—in Castlereagh's words, "produced for Buonoparte's inspection, I believe without a fig leaf, there being none to be found." The whole group had been loaded into a gun wagon and driven through a long cold night to Napoleon's headquarters at St. Dizier. Caulaincourt had recognized Wessenberg in the band of prisoners, brought him into the peasant house where Napoleon was staying and invited him to sit down to a hot breakfast.

"Never," Wessenberg remembered long after, "will I forget that delicious stew with white beans that the great hero of the nineteenth century offered me." Over breakfast Napoleon had given Wessenberg messages to take back to the Allies.

"Tell your Emperor from me that I am ready to make peace," Napoleon declared at once. Wessenberg would be free to leave because "your court never arrested my diplomats, while Russia and Prussia have." He excused the shabby treatment of Wessenberg and his party as a reprisal for the behavior of Russian and Prussian troops in France.

Napoleon knew that his chance for survival hung by a slender thread. He would accept whatever terms the Allies proposed; he would give up Germany, Italy, Switzerland, Spain; he would prefer to see Holland a republic rather than a kingdom.

"I wanted France left with the same boundaries I found when I mounted the throne. I do not maintain that I am not forced to make peace on more unfavorable bases, for an end to the thing must finally be made. I insisted on keeping Antwerp, for without this harbor France can have no fleet again. I am ready to renounce all colonies, if through this sacrifice France can keep the mouth of the Scheldt. England could not insist on the cession of Antwerp if Austria did not support it."

He was ready, Napoleon told Wessenberg, to leave the whole peace up to Austria.

"If the Austrian doesn't save me—I am lost! Don't think I have any illusions. I know my own position perfectly!"

He brooded still about his mistake in marrying an Austrian archduchess. "Better if I had married a Russian princess," he told Wessenberg. But he added quickly, "My wife is an incomparable woman." He was thinking now finally in terms of a regency. He was growing tired, he admitted, and "near the age when one likes peace and quiet."

Napoleon had words of warning for Wessenberg to carry back to Metternich. "Austria may one day have need of me," he declared. Austria must beware of Russia and Prussia. "They are the ones who will reap the biggest profit from the Coalition."

In Caulaincourt's carriage Wessenberg followed the French Emperor to

Doulevant, where he dined with Napoleon's marshals, and was given a horse and an escort through the war zone.

Writing Laure from Dijon of Wessenberg's adventure and of Napoleon's last-minute peace offer, Metternich spoke not without bitterness:

> If he had known it as well fifteen days ago he would have made peace! The last army is destroyed, negotiations are broken off—and the Bourbons are proclaimed in one of the first cities of the empire!
>
> How many ways he still had until now to stay in office, to remain at the head of the most beautiful country in the world, to live and to be happy in caring for the happiness of 25 million men! . . . And now he has risked everything. He is fleeing. His life becomes a gamble in the middle of all these passions and hates.
>
> . . . We are in a moment of extreme crisis. The great scaffolding will probably collapse soon. I cannot imagine what is happening in Paris at this hour.[52]

Locked away in Dijon in those spring days, the Allied diplomats amused themselves as best they could. The weather was mild; they strolled in the town, dined together, enjoyed the theater.

Released from the terrible tensions and the exhausting grind of the last weeks, Metternich's thoughts could turn at last to the private world of his family and to Wilhelmine.

Laure had written him of Marie's illness; suddenly he realized that for a long time he had had no letters at all from Marie. Was her illness more serious than Laure led him to believe, and were they hiding it from him?

In acute anxiety he wrote his wife about this beloved child:

> God keep her, I do certainly love her as much as you do. I can regard Marie as my own child for it is impossible to have a greater identity of interests than we two—I always find myself again in her. If she were a boy she would be a cabinet minister by the time she was thirty.[53]

Metternich was quartered in Dijon with a young widow and her two children, a little girl and boy who amused and delighted him. As always he had a way with children. "They are charming and spend all their time in my room. We are the best of friends. . . . I'd like to bring these two little cabbages home with me," he wrote Marie. "They would get along beautifully with Leontine." He admired "a very short little dress with pantalette to match" that the little French girl wore, and had it copied for his own Leontine.[54]

As for Wilhelmine, the cool tone of her last letters had cast Metternich again into a state of despondent pessimism. Would she ever love him, really love him? he wondered. Tormented again by doubts he wrote, "My dear, I need other things than your letters! And what letters! Why don't you write me as you have sometimes written?"

He dreamed on paper of the moments when he would be back in Vienna, sitting beside her, would talk to her, "tell you how much I love you."

> My good W., will those moments ever come? You have told me so often—why then does my heart, this painful voice inside me, always cast doubt on what ought to offer none if only I believed your word? . . . Of everything in the world what I believe least is that anyone could love me.[55]

On the road to Dijon the diplomatic party had overtaken a courier who was carrying a thick packet of papers for Metternich; they were the legal documents pertaining to the custody of Gustava and to the fortune Wilhelmine had settled on the child. Now in Dijon in the first moments of leisure he had had in a long time, Metternich examined the papers and wrote her that very night:

> Poor W! In what hands you found yourself! A[rmfelt] is the worst scoundrel on earth; never have I seen such a tissue of deceit, such calculated cunning, and I use the word—swindling.[56]

Armfelt, he told her, had got everything she had paid out for the child, "and Gustava has nothing, not a sou." None of the money could be recovered, but he promised, "You shall have Gustava and you shall make her fortune." The child belonged rightfully to her, "because children always belong by preference to the mother. She belongs to you because you alone are charged with her support—because all divine and human laws intend it to be so."

He, Metternich, intended to see that Armfelt would be forced to account for all the money and forced to surrender their child. "I will act," he promised, "and I'll make W[ratislaw] act directly on A[rmfelt], and I on my side will work on your handsome A[lexander]."[57]

The recovering of her child would be a powerful bond joining them. Already Metternich called little Gustava "our child," and her recovery he regarded as "an affair I would not surrender for all the treasures of this world."

Profoundly moved by Metternich's diligence in this dearest issue of her life, Wilhelmine replied. If only she could have her child back! If only she need never hear of "that man" again! Gustava would not have a great fortune during her mother's lifetime, but after Wilhelmine's death "there will be enough for her." And the proud mother added, "She showed promise of being very beautiful, very good, even very bright; with all that one makes one's way in the world."[58]

A few days earlier Metternich had written her, "If fate places me in Paris, I shall think of ways of having you make the trip." Now in Dijon he began to dream of seeing her again, perhaps very soon, in the Paris he loved above any city in the world:

> I shall write you as soon as I am in Paris. If your mother is there— if we stay a while there—will you come? *Mon Dieu,* how fine all that would be if—[59]

7

On the same Tuesday, March 29, that Wessenberg appeared on Metternich's doorstep in Dijon, bringing Napoleon's last-minute acquiescence to a peace, the Allied armies, pushing up the Marne Valley, fought a last engagement and reached the suburb of Bondy. Presently they lay spread out in a vast encampment on the heights of Montmartre, whence they could look down on the spires and the gleaming rooftops of the city of Paris.

On that same Tuesday, March 29, Napoleon got news of the defeat at Fère-Champenoise. He knew then that the Allies must be approaching Paris. He ordered his army about-face and hastened to Troyes. That evening, with Caulaincourt and a small staff, he left the army, climbed into a post coach bound for Paris, rode the rest of the night and next day, and an hour before midnight on Wednesday, March 30, reached a relay station called the Cour de France, the last post stop before Paris. There he learned that Paris had already capitulated.

"Four hours too late!" he cried. In his desperation Napoleon began to run up the road toward Paris, as if single-handed he would recapture the city.

In the early hours of that Wednesday morning, March 30, a delegation of officials from the city of Paris drove out to Bondy to beg the Tsar not to bombard the city.

While the city officials talked with the Tsar another emissary arrived, red-eyed, exhausted from a long chain of sleepless nights. It was Caulaincourt, come in the desperate hope of last-minute negotiations. Nesselrode was sent to tell him he was on a fool's errand; Châtillon had been the place to negotiate. The Tsar was polite but firm; they were no longer treating with Napoleon.

Meantime, Count Paar and Count Orlov had been sent into Paris to talk with Marmont and ask the marshals to lay down their arms. Early that Wednesday morning the city of Paris surrendered.

Talleyrand, who had the prescience to be in the right place at the right time, was at Marmont's palace that day in time to send Count Orlov back to the Tsar with his deepest respects.

That morning of Thursday, March 31, was certainly the golden hour in the life of Tsar Alexander.

Preceded by tall Cossacks of the Black Sea Guard, beside him the King of Prussia and Field Marshal Schwarzenberg, he rode into the city of Paris, followed by Russian cavalry, by his officers and their staffs, by column after column of Russian, Prussian and Austrian infantry all decked out in their best uniforms. Through the working-class suburbs, where they got few cheers, down the Boulevard des Italiens, past the Madeleine to the Place de la Concorde and the Champs Élysées, where they were greeted by shouts of "*Vive le Tsar!" "Vive notre libérateur!"* and, most heartfelt of all, *"Vive la paix!"* the victorious Allies marched.

Even while the parade progressed through the streets of Paris, Talleyrand, with a little group of Bourbon supporters he had summoned to his house—Dalberg, the Abbé de Pradt, Baron Louis—conferred with Nesselrode on what was to be done next. Together they drew up a manifesto for the Tsar's signature, declaring that the Allies would no longer treat with Napoleon or with any member of his family. The door for the Bourbon restoration was wide open.[60]

A last odd chance contributed a fragment to the future of France. In the last days of fighting there had been considerable confusion among the Allied troops, who, speaking a half dozen languages and not recognizing one another's uniforms, had shot at one another all too frequently instead of at the French. An order had gone out that all Allied troops were to wear a piece of white cloth on the left shoulder. Troops had raided thrifty housewives' stores of sheets and shirts, to tear up for the protective symbol. When they entered Paris still wearing their white shoulder bands, people lining the streets stared in astonishment. The Allied armies were wearing the Bourbon symbol! Placards had already been posted here and there by ardent royalists appealing to Parisians to shout *"Vive le Roi! Vive Louis XVIII!"* Now, seeing Allied soldiers with their emblematic white cloth, Parisians concluded the restoration had already been decided. They sighed, shrugged. So the Bourbons would be back. So be it. So long as it meant peace.[61]

While the Tsar rode his gray horse through the streets of Paris accepting the cheers of the watching throngs, someone passed a note to one of his aides warning him that the Élysée Palace, where the Russian sovereign was to have been quartered, had been mined. The Tsar went instead directly to Talleyrand's house in the Rue St. Florentin. Obligingly Talleyrand moved out of the beautiful rooms on the second floor and took up quarters in the entresol.

"What does France want?" the Tsar demanded of Talleyrand at their first meeting. "We must get the opinion of France!"

Talleyrand opened the door of the salon and summoned in his royalist friends—Dalberg, De Pradt, Baron Louis, kept waiting for just such a moment. "France wants the Bourbons!" they declared in unison.

That night thousands of candles blazed in the windows of Talleyrand's house. Horses trotted up to the main door between the two crouching stone lions; spurred boots of Russian and Prussian officers clattered up and down the grand staircase. Far into the night the Tsar sat up talking with Talleyrand, the Prussian King a silent witness. Schwarzenberg also, it appears, said little. He had no instructions for making crucial political decisions; he hoped against hope that Metternich would arrive at any moment. There would certainly, he thought, be one last bloody battle before Napoleon gave up. As for the Bourbons, they were, he wrote Nani, "completely odious."[62]

Later on Talleyrand wrote of those hours:

> I never plotted in my life except at those times when I had the majority of France for my accomplices and where I was looking for the salvation of the country. Napoleon never had a dangerous conspirator against him except himself.[63]

In that Talleyrand was certainly right.

XVII

◆

REUNION IN PARIS

*You see I was not wrong when I told you months ago that
by April we shall have peace.*
—METTERNICH TO LAURE, APRIL 13, 1814

Nothing is so difficult as the fifth act of a tragedy.
—METTERNICH TO WILHELMINE, FEBRUARY 16, 1814

1

News of the fall of Paris did not reach the ministers stranded in Dijon
until April 4, the Monday of Holy Week, when an English courier brought a
letter to Priscilla Burghersh from her husband, followed shortly after by
Schwarzenberg's messenger, Count Széchenyi. Széchenyi brought a copy of
the Tsar's proclamation as well, that promised "not to treat with Napoleon
nor any member of his family." "A wretched piece," Metternich called it.
Never had he felt so frustrated, so defeated. "If I had been with him," he
wrote Laure, "I would not have allowed it."[1]

So it was the Tsar who had won in the end, who had ridden into Paris
like a liberating knight—*un rêve chevalier*, the French were calling him—
and it was the Tsar who was making the crucial decisions on the future of
France: the Tsar, that is, with the help of Talleyrand.

Schwarzenberg's letter warned Metternich that the roads were still too
dangerous to travel. Napoleon had not surrendered; his army lay somewhere
between Paris and Dijon—nobody quite knew where. Another battle certainly
remained to be fought, probably near Fontainebleau, Schwarzenberg thought.
Detached troops of French cavalry still controlled many towns, and bands of
armed peasants, such as those who had captured Wessenberg, roamed about
freely. One could not think of traveling without well-armed escort parties,
safe-conduct passes, and plenty of relay horses sent on ahead.

Priscilla Burghersh, however, who had shrewdly bought extra horses in Châtillon, set off for Paris two days after her husband's letter came, quite cross that she had not been "in at the death," as she put it. Castlereagh was annoyed with her for departing alone; she had been left in his charge, and he did not like ladies taking matters into their own hands.

In later years Priscilla loved to boast of how she had beat the Allied ministers to Paris at the end of the war. As a matter of fact, however, their warnings had turned out to be only too true. A troop of French cavalry seized her carriage along the way and brought her before their commander. Only Priscilla's tearful pleas that she was a defenseless woman trying to rejoin her husband melted the French officer's heart, and she was permitted to continue her journey.[2]

In something less than grand style Metternich, Castlereagh and Hardenberg rattled into Paris on the evening of Easter Sunday, April 10, squeezed into a public post coach, jammed to the roof with passengers and baggage. It had taken three days and three nights to make the journey.

Hardly taking time to change his travel-rumpled clothes, Metternich hurried to Talleyrand's house in the Rue St. Florentin. His news of Paris was already nearly a week old—and in that critical week any single day could have changed the future of France.

The drama that Easter evening in the Talleyrand mansion was, Metternich recalled later, "the most remarkable scene of my public life."[3] The Bonapartes were being liquidated; the most important men of new royalist France and a handful from the old were gathered to haggle over the price.

Just a week earlier, on Palm Sunday, Napoleon had reviewed his Guard in Fontainebleau, haranguing them with all his old military bombast:

> Soldiers! the enemy has taken possession of Paris. We must turn him
> out. The cowards will pay for this fresh outrage. Let us swear to conquer
> or to die![4]

But Napoleon's marshals had little stomach for conquering now, and even less for dying. Eager for peace, they urged Napoleon to abdicate in favor of a regency for his son.

For a few hours a regency again rose as a distinct possibility. Caulaincourt and the three marshals—Ney, Macdonald and Marmont—had called on the Tsar, offering to exchange Napoleon's abdication for a regency for his son.

"I'm no supporter of the Bourbons," the Tsar told the marshals. "I don't know them. I shall lay your proposals before my Allies and give them my support. I too am in a hurry to make an end to it all."[5]

So in those critical hours the Tsar wavered. The Prussian King could be counted on to follow where the Tsar led. And although Schwarzenberg had given Caulaincourt an icy reception earlier, the Austrian commander did in fact—as Napoleon had discerned—favor a regency over a Bourbon restoration. "Those weaklings," he called the Bourbons scathingly, "who eke out a miserable living from the capital of a Louis XIV or an Henri IV.''[6] But Schwarzenberg, with no instructions to guide him through those fast-eddying political waters, stung still with memories of the recriminations heaped on him when he had asked for the February armistice, postponed any decisive move, waited anxiously for Metternich's arrival.

While the Tsar talked with Napoleon's emissaries, downstairs in Talleyrand's offices, Vitrolles, chafing to be sent off to Nancy and lead the Comte d'Artois back in triumph to Paris, waited the signal from Talleyrand. "The Tsar can behave in an unexpected way," Talleyrand cautioned Vitrolles. "Not for nothing is one the son of Paul I.''[7]

Persuasively Talleyrand argued against a regency. As long as Napoleon remains alive, he reminded the Tsar, Napoleon and Austria would be the real power behind any regency for his son.

But the real blow to the marshals' hope for a regency came when Marmont's Sixth Corps went over prematurely to the Austrian Army on Monday night, sharply undercutting Napoleon's bargaining power.

Talleyrand and the royalists won out. During the final days of that Holy Week, while Metternich, Castlereagh and Hardenberg were bumping over the road from Dijon in a drizzling early April rain, the powers in Paris united to rid France of the Bonapartes. On Wednesday Napoleon signed a conditional act of abdication, and on the same day a rump Senate, with Talleyrand in the chair, voted to summon Louis XVIII to the throne of France. Vitrolles left for Nancy at once. It would be some weeks before Louis XVIII, suffering from a bad attack of gout, could make it to Paris from his exile in England. Meantime, his heir and younger brother, the Comte d'Artois, would represent him in Paris.

What to do with Napoleon? The Tsar that week, scanning a map of Europe for a likely spot, put his finger on Elba.

In Fontainebleau Napoleon waited for the abdication treaty to be drawn up, restlessly turning over in his mind plans for recouping his fortune. For three days his emissaries had been in Paris, wrangling over the terms with Nesselrode, and with the men of the French Provisional Government who must agree to pay the promised pensions.

Just before Metternich reached Paris Napoleon had sent an aide-de-camp to Caulaincourt in Paris, asking that his Act of Abdication be withdrawn. He had been talking to his generals of a grandiose scheme for rallying all his scattered forces behind the Loire and marching to join the Army of Italy. A core of his old government was with the Empress Marie Louise at Orléans; even now his Minister of War was issuing orders for a new troop levy. His army would be loyal to him, Napoleon declared, even if his marshals were not.

So that when Metternich arrived in the Talleyrand mansion on the evening of Easter Sunday, the Bourbon restoration was a fait accompli; the question was how to be rid of Napoleon quickly and effectively. The Tsar presented Metternich immediately with a paper detailing the terms of Napoleon's abdication and urged him to sign it at once. In an adjoining room of the mansion Napoleon's deputies, Caulaincourt and the three marshals, waited anxiously. They feared, as did the Tsar, that even at this zero hour Napoleon might change his mind and leap into some sudden action.

But Metternich, glancing over the terms, at once protested the choice of Elba. "This treaty . . . will bring us back on the field of battle in less than two years!"[8] Elba belonged to the grand duchy of Tuscany and was supposed to revert to Emperor Franz's brother, the former grand duke. Besides, Elba was far too close to Italy and France to guarantee a safe exile.

"But if the Emperor Napoleon gives us his word of honor as a soldier and a sovereign," the Tsar argued, "we may not question it without insulting him."

"Even so," Metternich replied, "I do not feel authorized to make such a decision without consulting the Emperor."

"But that is impossible," the Tsar cried heatedly. "We've postponed signing the treaty for three days waiting for you and Lord Castlereagh. If the act is not signed tonight, hostilities can begin again tomorrow and God knows what will happen then. Napoleon already knows that the King of Prussia and I have approved. I cannot take back my word."

Castlereagh and Schwarzenberg were summoned. Both expressed concern at the choice of Elba.

There were other problems. Napoleon had demanded that Tuscany be given to Marie Louise and her son, and this provision had formed part of the original draft of the treaty. But Metternich pointed out at once that Tuscany could not be given to the Austrian Emperor's daughter for the simple reason that Tuscany belonged to her father's brother.

Castlereagh raised objections to certain promises of title for Napoleon's family. Hour after hour, clause by clause, the diplomats wrangled over the terms. Napoleon's deputies paced back and forth and listened to the clock strike the hours.

Not until midnight were all the terms finally agreed upon and the last clause initialed. Elba remained Napoleon's portion, while Metternich had got agreement on the duchies of Parma, Piacenza and Guastalla for Marie Louise and her son.

The days that had passed since Marie Louise had fled from Paris on her husband's order, first to Rambouillet, then to Blois, then further yet to Orléans, had been days of desperate anxiety, of wretchedness and humiliation. One day she had been Empress of a country of forty million, petted, praised, flattered by an admiring court. Next day she was a bewildered refugee with hardly more than the clothes on her back.

Letters from Napoleon in Fontainebleau had not told her what to do nor summoned her to join him. Never in her twenty-three years of life had she been asked to decide anything more critical than the color of a dress or the shape of a bonnet.

An emissary of the French Provisional Government, sent to Orléans to reclaim the imperial treasure, had seized everything of value in sight, including the pearl necklace Marie Louise was wearing that day, which had been a gift from her husband.

The wildest rumors flew about the little court, throwing everyone into a panic. It was said that the Russian General Chernyshëv with a troop of Cossacks was close by, planning to kidnap the little King of Rome. The people about her besieged her with advice, most of it contradictory.

Meantime, thinking that her father had entered Paris with the Tsar and the King of Prussia, she directed plea after poignant plea to him. She did not know where to turn; she wanted only "to throw herself into his arms with her little son."9

Ironically it had been Napoleon's last military coup, severing Allied communications lines between Dijon and Paris, that had prevented Marie Louise's letters from reaching her father. In Fontainebleau Napoleon, railing against the perfidy of the "hollow-hearted" Austrians, especially his father-in-law, did not choose to recall that until March 19 he might have concluded peace and kept his throne—and even after that, had he abdicated in time, might have established a regency.

The first news Emperor Franz got of his daughter was a dispatch of Schwarzenberg informing him that the Tsar had sent two emissaries to Orléans "to conduct Empress Marie Louise to Fontainebleau to her husband."10

Emperor Franz had been furious. He had not, he fumed, expected his Allies to make decisions about his daughter without consulting him. "From that moment on in which she is separated from her husband, she belongs entirely to her illustrious father, and it is he who can and must take her under his protection." He had commanded Metternich to take charge of Marie Louise and her son until he himself got to Paris.11

Letters from Marie Louise to her father were waiting in Paris when Metternich arrived. He read them and sent them on to her father. He wrote Marie Louise begging her to be calm, to have no fear and to have confidence in him. "All I want is to be able to live somewhere in peace," she had written, "and to be able to bring up my son. God knows I shall tell him never to have any ambition." Metternich replied that it might be best for her to return to Austria with her child for the present, then she might choose "among the places where Emperor Napoleon will be and your own establishment."12

The following day Metternich sent Paul Esterházy and Wenzel Liechtenstein on the somewhat delicate errand of moving Marie Louise and her child to Rambouillet—closer to Paris and off the direct route Napoleon would have to pass in journeying to Elba. Paul and Wenzel were to use whatever means necessary to persuade her to make the move, and at once.

The two men were back in Paris a day later, their mission accomplished.

The move may not have been accomplished quite so smoothly as Metternich pretended in the account he wrote. Paul and Wenzel dined with the Burghershes the night they returned from Rambouillet, and Priscilla learned that Marie Louise had

> cried very much but consented to leave Buonoparte, for which I think she is a monster, for she certainly pretended love for him, and he always behaved very well to her. She said she would not see him before he goes, for that if she saw him and he asked her to come with him, she knew she could not refuse him; but that to obey her father, and for the sake of her child, she agreed to go to Vienna.[13]

Years later, living in Italy, Priscilla Burghersh was to become a warm friend of Marie Louise and to hold a quite different view of her. When she knew her she found her to be "a most lovable person, affectionate, generous almost to excess, and possessing much common sense, which was, however, marred by her extreme diffidence and distrust of herself. . . . Her own instincts, had she had the courage to follow them, would have guided her far more rightly."[14]

When her father got to Paris shortly after, he drove almost at once to Rambouillet to see his daughter. Metternich did not accompany him but a few days later he visited her.

> She is perfect [he reported to Wilhelmine] and like her father—of gold with the appearance of brass. Your handsome Tsar went to see her too and he was enchanted with her. Do you know what he loves best in the world right now? The Bonapartes! He would give them the impossible if he could.[15]

Already the Tsar regretted his part in restoring the Bourbons. He would regret it even more in the weeks that followed. Just like the volatile Tsar, Metternich thought. While the regency still had a chance, the Tsar failed to support it; now it was too late. "The King of Rome—Prince of Parma," Metternich wrote Laure, "is very handsome. He is as like his mother as two drops of water and has nothing of his father. He is a very good child and altogether nice."[16]

On April 23 Marie Louise climbed into her carriage in Rambouillet and set off for Vienna.

The decision to separate Marie Louise from Napoleon was not a sudden decision, cruelly and heartlessly arrived at. It was rather a series of small decisions, goaded by chance events, by political expediency, by her father's love and concern—not least of all, by Marie Louise's pleas, confused as they were by her own uncertainty about where to go, what direction to take.

But more than anything else, the decisive factor was the position of all women in a patriarchal society—and royal women above all—who belonged legally and socially not to themselves, but first to their fathers, then to their husbands—and if their husbands for some reason failed, back again to their fathers. Not for nothing did Emperor Franz use that word "belong."

It was at once apparent to Metternich how much the two-week halt in Dijon had cost him. He had fatally lost control of the inner circle of power. Events had taken place without him, while the Tsar occupied front stage center and Talleyrand in the wings had directed the action.

Everywhere the Tsar was acclaimed as "Europe's liberator"; in a broadside sold and sung on the streets of Paris he was hailed as "king of kings." Everyone credited the Tsar with Napoleon's defeat, with the bringing of peace. "Europe and victory seemed personified in the Tsar," Vitrolles recalled of those heady days. Schwarzenberg could not help resenting deeply that all the glory of the military victories had gone to the Tsar, while he had had the difficult job of leading the armies under that contentious divided command. He—Schwarzenberg—had won the decisive victories at Leipzig and at Fère-Champenoise, but it was the "vain, weak but cunning Tsar" who was preening himself as a great soldier and victor.

Austrian prestige had sunk very low—both in France and abroad. The men in the new Provisional Government—all royalists—knew perfectly well that Metternich had supported the negotiations with Napoleon longer than any of the Allies—indeed as late as March 15. Talleyrand and his friends suspected and feared that Austria might still support a regency. Dalberg in particular remained an outspoken enemy of Metternich.

Never had Metternich needed to move more adroitly, more cautiously, more swiftly to recoup his position and Austrian prestige than in those first difficult days in Paris.

He was above all a political realist and the Bourbons were political reality. He needed to allay the suspicions of the Provisional Government and prevent the violence of a Bonapartist uprising, first by disposing of Napoleon, then by removing Marie Louise and her child lest they serve as a Bonapartist rallying point.

With Schwarzenberg Metternich worked out details for Napoleon's journey to Elba, and a few days after Marie Louise's departure Napoleon left Fontainebleau, with an escort of Allied officers.

Of Napoleon's farewell to his Guard Metternich wrote his wife:

> He kept up a good countenance up to the last moment. Then he wept very bitterly! The hour of his departure was fixed for 11. General Bertrand came to warn him it was already 11. [Napoleon] asked him brusquely since when he [Bertrand] had acquired the habit of fixing another hour than *his* appointed time. He remained until noon. Then he called his people and descended the grand staircase of the castle.
>
> In the Great Courtyard the remaining grenadiers of the Old Guard were drawn up in formation. He lost his countenance at that and wept a great deal. He mounted into his carriage and the soldiers shouted for a last time, "*Vive l'Empereur!*"[17]

Laure and Marie would shed tears over that final scene of the departure of *le petit homme* from Paris. What a sad fate for a great misled man! Had she been in his place, Marie wrote her father, she would have fled to America, fed on the fruit of the cocoa tree, hunted wild animals in the woods and pondered her vanished glory. "Thank God I am Marie von Metternich who needs no such consolation."[18]

2

The thing that most astonished Metternich was the utter quiet of Paris. "Everything is calm," he wrote Laure, "the most profound silence reigns," quite as if there had not been bitter fighting at the very gates of the city only weeks before, and a revolutionary change of regime.

When he awoke in his luxurious bedroom in the Sébastiani mansion and opened the shutters in the morning to gaze out over the gardens of the Élysée Bourbon Palace and the beautiful city gleaming in the sunshine of early spring, "I think I am dreaming when I am no longer dreaming."[19]

To Metternich, who loved Paris above any city in the world, it had that spring of 1814 an air of glittering unreality.

On the streets one heard half a dozen languages. Placards in Russian were stuck up on walls. In the Bois de Boulogne Cossacks bivouacked, their horses tied to trees while the riders sat cross-legged on the ground, mending a tunic or cooking their dinner over a fire, as peacefully as if they were on the steppes of the Caucasus. Officers of all nations in medal-bedecked uniforms dashed in and out of the loges of the theaters. Young conscripts from East Prussia, from Styria and from Hungary stared in wonder at the shop-windows, while the *filles* who loitered invitingly near the gambling rooms and brothels of the Palais-Royal called out jolly invitations.

Everywhere there was an air of gala pleasure and of celebration. To Parisians it was resignation to the inevitable, thankfulness for war's end. Now one could live, arrange one's life, taste all the postponed joys.

Everything was most "extraordinary," Metternich wrote:

> The boulevards are filled with people—elegant people, hussars, ladies in mask, Cossacks, cabriolets, army vehicles, all of it mingling—everybody knowing everybody else and greeting one another cordially. Marshals with white cockade, the Comte d'Artois in uniform of the National Guard, people crying "*Vive le Roi*" under the windows of the Emperor Napoleon —*mon amie* [he wrote Wilhelmine] one must never swear allegiance to anything—except to what I feel for you.[20]

Émigrés—like Louis Rohan, Bombelles, Trogoff—who had lived abroad for years, gazed in amazement now at the spacious, open neoclassical city, with its splendid new boulevards laid out by Napoleon's architects, the Italian arcades inscribed with Napoleon's victories, and all the monuments meant to remind the French perpetually of his military glories—the Madeleine, the trimphal arch of the Carrousel crowned by the bronze horses taken from St. Mark's in Venice. "Paris makes a singular effect of grandeur and of luxury when one sees it," Metternich wrote Laure. Along the Champs Élysées the chestnut trees budded and bloomed, and in the fine squares near the Étoile and St. Antoine new fountains splashed and murmured. There were new quays along the south side of the Seine—and two new bridges named for Jena and Austerlitz, the former so rankling in the ears of Prussian soldiers that they threatened to blow it up.

Visitors swarmed to the galleries to see the great art collections—filched, to be sure, from all over Europe, and just now one of the bones of contention dividing the peacemakers. Aberdeen, when not engaged in conference, spent most of his time in the Louvre. "Were it not for the inexhaustible stores of art collected here, Paris would be intolerable," he wrote home. He urged that the splendid collections be left in France, "principally as a lover of art, for they would infallibly be destroyed by a journey into Italy."[21]

Everywhere the monogram and eagles of Napoleon were being effaced. The figure of Napoleon topping the column in the Place Vendôme was dragged down; a group of citizens called on the Tsar to ask if he would like his effigy put in Napoleon's place. The Tsar declined with becoming modesty, saying with a smile, "It's too high for me to mount; I'd be afraid of falling off." A new drop curtain with a crown encircled by golden fleur-de-lys replaced the old curtain with Napoleonic emblems in the Théâtre-Français. French state prisoners were released. Priests who had declined to pray for Napoleon were set free.

> There is [wrote Metternich] no longer a trace of Napoleon. One speaks of him as of a regime of the 14th century; all the eagles have disappeared; not one of the innumerable N's. Everywhere the royal arms in all the shops; all the theaters—nothing but white cockades. All the lackeys, all the coachmen, all the postillions [wear] fleur-de-lys.[22]

Indeed, it seemed almost indecent the way the French had abandoned Napoleon. At the theater "they shout *Vive le Roi* at every occasion with all their might, just as they used to shout *Vive* good King Henri, Great Louis, the King, liberty, the Convention, the Directoire, the First Consul, Napoleon, Down with the Tyrant. . . ."[23]

Yet although Metternich assured Wilhelmine that "the reign of Napoleon has disappeared like smoke," nevertheless Paris—and France—continued to be haunted by the ghost of a great man, not yet dead.

In the drawing rooms of restoration Paris, Bonapartists and royalists skirmished with well-sharpened verbal swords.

One night in Talleyrand's salon Pozzo di Borgo, an ardent royalist, engaged in heated debate with Charles Flahaut over Napoleon's last campaign. Flahaut defended it as Napoleon's most masterly, outnumbered as he was, one to four, while Pozzo claimed the march on St. Dizier was sheer madness and had sealed the fate of Paris.

"He ought to have known the people were against him," said Pozzo.

"To be sure," snapped Flahaut, "he did think that Paris would stand by him. He did not reckon on treachery."

Talleyrand sat nearby, swinging his crippled foot, a cool little smile on his face.[24]

Napoleon's journey to Elba had not gone too smoothly. In Provence, where royalist sentiment ran high, the party was attacked by a furious mob who nearly lynched Napoleon. "Poor Napoleon," Metternich wrote Marie, more compassionately than he had written three weeks before, "was nearly hanged between Avignon and Aix, stormed by angry people who built a gallows and put a dummy of Napoleon in the noose."[25]

At the gates of Aix another threatening crowd had gathered. A young Austrian officer, Major Clam-Martinitz, rode on ahead and tried to calm the mob and send them back inside the walls of the town, while Napoleon put on an Austrian uniform of General Koller, entered the general's carriage and circled the road outside town.

Returning from Elba toward the end of May, General Koller brought a number of personal messages to Metternich from Napoleon. "Having done him such harm, I can now afford to do him good since he is not to be feared, and he begs me to see that his pension is paid him very exactly," Metternich wrote his wife. But the pension was not paid regularly, and there was nothing Metternich could do about it.

One day on Elba Napoleon had remarked to Koller, "I am fair. Prince Metternich behaved like a skillful minister. He is the only statesman who has appeared in Europe since the Revolution. He has destroyed me systematically and I helped him with my mistakes. . . . We shall see," added Napoleon, "whether Metternich can remain in power and whether his appetite will increase in the eating."[26]

With Napoleon out of the way, the new French monarch, Louis le Désiré, a large, flabby pear-shaped man whose gouty feet could endure nothing heavier than velvet booties, set out from his exile at Hartwell in England.

In London there was a gala celebration to send him on his way. The Prince Regent, who had contributed so much to setting the Bourbon back on his throne, knelt ponderously and fastened the Order of the Garter around the fat bulbous knee of his brother-monarch. A naughty Whig versifier scribbled of the event:

> And France's hope and Britain's heir
> Were, truth, a most congenial pair;
> Two round tun-bellied thriving rakes,
> Like oxen fed on linseed cakes.

The Tsar and Talleyrand drove to Compiègne to greet the returning monarch. The King had flattering things to say to Talleyrand at their meeting, though it was soon clear he did not trust the minister in the least. The

Tsar was received with notable coolness, almost disdain. Though the King had stood to receive Napoleon's marshals coming to kiss his hand, he remained seated to receive the Tsar and almost at once asked whether the royal gold plate and the Gobelins in the Louvre had been properly looked after in his absence. When dinner was announced, the monarch sprang nimbly to his feet and despite his bulk, hurried out, leaving the Tsar nonplussed, to follow into the dining room.

As the Tsar remarked later to Nesselrode, "You would think *he* had restored a throne to *me*."

Louis le Désiré rode into Paris on May 3, with the surviving daughter of Marie Antoinette, the Duchesse d'Angoulême, dressed in white in the carriage beside him, and all the church bells pealing. Great pains had been taken by the police to avoid "accidents"—such as assassination. Regulations forbade flowerpots on windowsills, no carriages were allowed in the streets, nobody could climb on the ledges of buildings, and there were to be no firecrackers.

Metternich and Schwarzenberg—neither one an early or ardent Bourbon supporter—watched the entry from a window in the Rue Montmartre. There was little enthusiasm among the spectators, indeed not even many smiles; Metternich noted:

> [The entry] made a most painful impression on me. A contrast prevailed between the gloomy countenances of the Imperial Guard who preceded and followed the royal carriage and that of the King beaming with studied affability—which seemed to reflect the general feeling of the country.[27]

The most dramatic moment of the day was the one in which the intrepid female aeronaut Madame Blanchard set loose her balloon just as the King entered. Slowly the huge silvery globe floated upward, caught for one perilous moment on a statue of Henri IV, then freed itself, floated up over the rooftops and spires of Paris, where the balloonist released a whole flight of white doves to wing their way across the sky as a symbol of the longed-for peace.

It was for peace the people of France had opted—not for the Bourbons. Of all the watchers that day, Metternich most clearly perhaps recognized that truth.

Paying his formal call on the restored King in the Tuileries a few days later, Metternich could not help remarking, "In this same room, sitting at this same writing table, surrounded by this same furniture, I passed many hours with Napoleon . . . Your Majesty seems to be quite at home here."

"It must be allowed," the King replied with a smile, "that Napoleon was a very good tenant. He made everything most comfortable."[28]

Talleyrand—encouraged by the Tsar—had planned a considerable measure of control over the monarchy through a written constitution, modeled closely after the first French constitution of 1791, and guaranteeing a number of popular liberties. Metternich, who admired the English system, described it to Emperor Franz as "similar to the English, but with some sensible modifications." He approved of the original plan, called it "above all a very constitutional monarchy," and did not appear to be in the least disturbed, as some English were, by the democratic composition of the upper house.[29] ("Such a House of Lords!" wrote Castlereagh's assistant Edward Cooke— "without family, property, character.")

"If the Bourbons are wise," Napoleon had remarked to Caulaincourt, "they will change only the sheets on my bed; they will give employment to the men whom I have trained."[30]

But Louis XVIII rid himself of the more liberal men who had helped form the government and surrounded himself with ultra-royalists. The Parisians who had been quick to don white cockades were presently punning, "*Les anglais ont nourri un cochon; les français l'ont acheté pour dix-huit louis, mais il ne vaut pas un napoléon.*"[31]

3

Every day the ministers met in Metternich's quarters in the Sébastiani palace, working from noon until evening, sometimes far into the night, on the peace.

The terms agreed upon for Châtillon were to form the basis of the permanent peace with France. But there were problems, and there were disagreements. Prussia and England to some extent wished to impose harsher peace terms on France than did either Austria or Russia. The Tsar was determined to be magnanimous toward the French, and Metternich—frustrated ever since Frankfurt in his desire for a fair and non-punitive peace—opposed the imposition of war indemnities. Castlereagh found Metternich's moderation at times "inconvenient."

With enormous doggedness and skill Talleyrand bargained for France's future, fought to retain Flanders with its great seaport of Antwerp and its fleet of French merchant ships locked up in the harbor, which the English proposed turning over to Holland. England also wished to hang on to a number of conquered French colonies—notably Mauritius, Tobago, the Cape of Good Hope, Malta and the Saintes.

Most thorny, however, were the problems that revolved around the reorganization of the rest of Europe—especially the kingdom of Saxony, which Prussia wanted, and Poland, which Russia wanted.

Hardenberg proposed a compromise solution that would give all of Saxony to Prussia, but the formerly Austrian part of Poland back to Austria. The Tsar bluntly refused. In fact he now demanded a larger portion of Poland than he had outlined before. Even Humboldt remarked on the "arbitrariness of the Russians who wished absolutely to control all of Poland." The Tsar's views had hardened. He was, after all, Europe's liberator. Besides, his armies were occupying Poland.

Metternich had calculated that a peace could be completed in three weeks. "Then a congress will be convoked in Vienna," he wrote Wilhelmine, "where arrangements for the rest of Europe will be treated, and this task will not last beyond three more weeks. The world will be pacified by the first of July."[32]

Talleyrand had been more realistic. "What took twenty years to destroy," he said, "can't be rebuilt in thirty days."

Metternich was far too busy for the pleasures of Paris, he wrote Wilhelmine. "Paris doesn't exist for me. I have seen nobody, I have been only once to the theater, and I am in conference from morning to evening, or more often, till morning."[33]

He did, however, manage to steal time for a few pleasures.

The day after his arrival, on Easter Monday, at a magnificent dinner party at Talleyrand's, he had seen Wilhelmine's young sister, Dorothée, slender, poised, exquisite, at Talleyrand's side, receiving guests of all nationalities. The evening had given him his first glimpse of the new Paris—"Tsar A., with a large suite, French marshals wearing the white cockade, your mother *tout royaliste*—in a word, *mon amie*, a vast great beautiful house of fools!"[34]

The Duchess of Courland and Dorothée had been close to all the momentous happenings in Paris in the early days of the Allied occupation, had dined with the Tsar several times. To the duchess had been given one of the delicate political maneuvers sometimes left to women to perform—to initiate a possible marriage between the Duc de Berry, nephew of the French King, and the Tsar's sister, Grand Duchess Anna—a marriage the Bourbons hoped would cement a solid future relationship with Russia.

One night the Duchess of Courland gave a "very beautiful ball," of which Metternich wrote Wilhelmine:

> Your handsome Emperor was there. He danced as always. That's all he does passably well for the rest is not worth much.[35]

Metternich was fond of her mother and thought she was even prettier since she had turned royalist. "She is astonishing for her age, and nobody could be surprised to find himself in love with her."[36]

Another evening Metternich found time to take the Emperor Franz and his adjutant Count Wrbna on a sightseeing tour of Paris night life, including the naughty and well-advertised delectations of the Palais-Royale.

Nearly always one ended one's evenings at Talleyrand's where everyone who was anyone was sure to be seen, and the conversation was better than anywhere in the civilized world. Usually now, for the Tsar's sake, Talleyrand's soirees ended in dancing.

Madame de Staël, back from England, where she had lived in exile during Napoleon's reigme, held court again in her house in the Rue du Bac, and Talleyrand gave a nice little dinner party to welcome back his one-time mistress. Metternich was not included. He did not like Madame de Staël and rebuked his wife rather crossly that spring for reading one of her novels:

There are microscopic little beings in the water who are in continual movement. Madame de Staël, who is not microscopic, resembles their nature in the rest.[37]

One celebrity who enchanted Metternich was the Duke of Wellington, fresh from his victories in Spain. His appearance in a Paris theater the night of his arrival almost caused a riot. The entire pit rose to shout, "Vive Wellington!" Metternich and the hero of Vitoria got along famously; Metternich could write his wife that Wellington was "Austrian in his soul."[38]

It was to honor Wellington that Charles Stewart gave a ball for four hundred guests on May 4. A small contretemps marred the splendor of the occasion. While most of the guests waited in line to shake Wellington's hand, Grand Duke Constantine stepped up to the orchestra leader and asked him to play a waltz. The grand duke and his partner had just taken a few whirling steps on the floor, when Charles Stewart with Wellington's niece, Priscilla Burghersh, on his arm—and probably the worse for drink—gestured the orchestra to stop playing and ordered a quadrille.

The orchestra leader stopped, uncertain what to do. A glance at the face of the glowering grand duke, poised in midstep on the dance floor, and he hastily proceeded with the waltz.

Charles Stewart demanded loudly, "Who dares insist on having this waltz played?"

"I did," replied the grand duke, scowling.

"I give the orders in my house, monseigneur," Stewart snapped, and commanded the conductor, "Play the quadrille."

The grand duke left the floor in a fury and stomped out, followed by all the Russians at the party.[39]

If Castlereagh and the Tsar had their problems at the conference table, their brothers did not contribute to the smooth progress of diplomacy.

4

Every day more wives were arriving in Paris to share the festival atmosphere of peace. Nesselrode's wife had been waiting in Basel along with other Russian wives, and Nesselrode sent for her at once. They had not been married long, and Nesselrode was like a bridegroom. She was to direct her carriage straight to the Élysée Bourbon, where he would be waiting to embrace her in the apartment that had once belonged to the little King of Rome.

Emily Castlereagh had come down from The Hague, and was giving little *soupers* in the Castlereagh quarters, chiefly for the English. "They say she is good," Schwarzenberg wrote to Nani, "but her outward appearance is not prepossessing; she is very fat and dresses so *young*, so *tight*, so *naked*, that I wish she were not good, for it annoys me that she is ridiculous."[40] The Castlereaghs were a strange married pair, no doubt about that.

Several ladies were coming from Vienna. Leopoldine Liechtenstein, wife of General Moritz Liechtenstein, was coming to join her husband.

Wistfully Laure wrote Clemens: should she come to Paris?

She adored Paris; in no place did she feel so well as in that lovely sparkling city. The years she had spent there as the ambassador's wife had been perhaps the happiest of her life. To be with Clemens after nearly a year of separation, to be part of the excitement of great events unfolding, to enjoy the dinners and balls and receptions, taking her place very near the top of every table as wife of the Austrian minister, the real leader of the Coalition, he had often assured her—Laure would have gloried, quietly to be sure, but nonetheless gloried in all that.

But Metternich had no intention of bringing Laure to Paris.

> *Mon Dieu, ma bonne amie* [he replied to her proposal] how happy I'd
> be to have you here with me. I do not have the time to have you come,
> for I hope our stay will not be beyond the 10th or 13th of May.[41]

What in the world would he do with her, working as he was all day and often far into the night? Besides, he had other plans in mind.

And he needed her at home in Vienna to manage all the important preparations already under way for the great peace festival he planned when the Allied sovereigns came for a visit to Vienna.

To salve his conscience at not bringing Laure to Paris, Metternich promised to send her pretty new clothes from the great couturier LeRoi, who already had her measurements and who had designed all the gowns for the ladies of Napoleon's court. He ordered her a redingote just like the one Marie Louise had been wearing the day he called on her at Rambouillet, "which I find charming," and he sent material to have it copied for Marie as well. The new hats were outrageous but one must be in fashion, and he asked the Duchess of Courland and Julie Récamier to choose hats for Laure and Marie.

So Laure had to resign herself to awaiting her husband's return. She sent him a list of things to buy for her in Paris, and suggested he place the cook Chandellier, who had been with Metternich all during the campaign, in several good Paris kitchens, such as that of Monsieur de Talleyrand, to polish up his culinary accomplishments.

> When will you send me some of your purchases [she wrote]? Some bon-
> nets and hats would do no harm. The time is coming when one could
> need them.[42]

Her husband would be home by early June, along with the Emperor Franz and the victorious army. She could look forward to the important place Clemens would have in that celebration.

> Most people [Laure wrote her husband] think the Emperor will have to
> give you at least a duchy and even this wouldn't be enough for the serv-
> ices you have rendered. Will you not be made Chancellor of Court and
> State, as my grandfather was?[43]

Of course it was precisely what Metternich wanted above all else—to be the Prince Kaunitz of his century.

To heap one disappointment on another Laure learned presently that Clemens was to go to England instead of coming directly home from Paris, and he would not have any part in the grand celebrations when the Emperor and the army returned.

Sadly she wrote her husband:

> I wish our fetes were over, and all these good sovereigns who have been out of their countries so long would return without stopping to visit you.[44]

Wilhelmine too wanted to come to Paris. Metternich was torn. He wanted desperately to see her, to meet her on such enchanted neutral ground as Paris, where so much more anonymity and freedom might be theirs than in Vienna. If only he could have her to himself!

But Alfred Windischgraetz was here in Paris; at the receptions and balls and sovereigns' entries Metternich's path crossed Alfred's almost daily. If she were to see Alfred again, before he, Clemens, had really won her? "You know, my dear, what torments me to death."

On the other hand the armies of Schwarzenberg were preparing to march home to Vienna. Alfred would be leaving with his regiment. If he were to reach Vienna before Metternich? "I shall die of fear if that happens. If you were away things would be easier; I shall have seen you meanwhile—twenty things would arrange themselves more naturally—*for it is you I fear!*"[45] He underlined the crucial words.

Alfred had distinguished himself brilliantly during the campaign in France. In February, leading the O'Reilly Light Horse Regiment, he had covered General Nostitz's retreat, holding off more than four thousand French cavalry with fewer than six hundred men of his own. At Fère-Champenoise, mounted on the splendid horse Opposition which he had bought after Leipzig from the booty of captured French generals, Windischgraetz had led a courageous attack to dislodge Marmont. The Tsar had personally presented Alfred with the Russian sword of honor, while Emperor Franz bestowed on him the highest of all Austrian military decorations, the Cross of Maria Theresia.

The dashing young cavalry colonel in his well-cut uniforms, flashing his new decorations, cut a splendid figure in the military parades and in the Paris drawing rooms. No, Alfred was not a rival to be lightly dismissed.

Soon Metternich intended to press her to make a final, irrevocable choice between them. But he could not, simply could not, gamble on losing her. The promise must be exacted from her at the precise, right moment.

He knew that his faithful letters, filled with love and amusing banter and political news, together with subtle and not so subtle reminders of his high position among the world's political movers, those letters written two or three times a week during all the months of the campaign, had done much to win her. From Alfred she had heard nothing for weeks. Perhaps, she thought, the miserable Obreskoff gossip had reached Alfred's ears too. "I have right on my side," she wrote Clemens, "for the least I can claim is not to be condemned without being heard."[46] If only she would break off all correspondence with Alfred—not because he had not written, but because she loved Metternich more. "The day when that happens will be the happiest day of my life!"[47]

It was willpower she lacked, Metternich decided, the lovable weakness of very feminine women. ". . . pure will is what I need, and I miss that so very much in you."[48]

When Alfred Windischgraetz in Paris brought him a letter and asked him to forward it to Wilhelmine by diplomatic pouch, he did so, adding a note of his own:

> My dear, you tell me your choice is made; it is on that I count. There is
> my guarantee—and I shall not torment myself because you ask it of me
> *for your sake.*[49]

He decided therefore that she should come to Paris. She must come at once, he wrote for her, for the peacemaking would be finished before long. She should persuade her sister Pauline to come with her, and they should travel by way of Frankfurt, which was the safest route. She could use her mother as an excuse for her journey, and the sea baths her doctor had prescribed. "If you cannot be sure of coming before May 15, do not come. . . . *Mon amie,* you know you are the first and last of my thoughts, that I love only you."[50]

But hardly had he written her, urging her to come, when a new complication arose to worry him.

Already in January the Prince Regent had invited his hero, the Tsar, to come for a visit to England when the war ended. The Tsar had accepted, and even sent his sister, Grand Duchess Catherine to pave the way—which Catherine was proceeding to do, in her own inimitable and prickly way. Castlereagh, intent on good relations among all the Allies, urged that the other sovereigns be invited as well, "diluting the libation to Russia." The Tsar, he thought, "ought to be grouped." Somewhat reluctantly the Prince Regent extended the invitation. The Prussian King promptly accepted, but Emperor Franz—fully aware of the depth of anti-Austrian sentiment in England—feared that as father-in-law of the hated "Boney" he would be cold-shouldered. He decided to send Metternich in his place. The sovereigns, generals and ministers would go to London just as soon as the Paris peace was signed.

Peace might be signed in a matter of days—and Metternich would be leaving Paris for England. He wrote in haste to Wilhelmine, telling her if she had not left by the time his letter came, not to leave at all. Her letter, telling him she would soon be on her way, crossed his.

So she would come after all. Would it be for the best or not?—he could not tell.

This rendezvous happens like so many other things in my life. I regret
much having given it to you—I am on the height of joy because of it.[51]

Metternich took immediate steps. Alfred was sent to Turin as the personal
emissary of Emperor Franz to the King of Sardinia. "The choice is the
Emperor's, not mine," Metternich assured Wilhelmine. But the move was so
swift, the timing so exactly coinciding with Metternich's plans, it is difficult
to believe he did not engineer the perfect solution to his amatory problem.

So Alfred would not be in Paris when Wilhelmine arrived in May, and
Metternich would have her to himself.

"What a sad thing are absence and great distances!" he had written her
not long after his arrival in Paris. "They put between hearts such intervals
that nothing can fill."[52]

On Friday, April 29, just after Alfred's departure, a courier brought a dispatch bag full of letters from Vienna to Metternich's office in the Hôtel Sébastiani.

Among the letters in the bundle was a brief note from Gentz, enclosing a
report from the Vienna Secret Police. Glancing over the closely written pages
Metternich's eyes were suddenly riveted by the name of the Duchess of Sagan:

> Life is very tenacious. How am I not dead at the very moment my eyes
> fell on that fatal report?

Gentz had written:

> I would like to unburden my heart of a great deal to Your Serene High-
> ness. I will not do so today . . . in part because what the enclosure con-
> tains is of such great importance that I dare not mix anything else with
> it.[53]

He begged Metternich not to let the duchess know that it was he who had
sent on the report.

The police dossier began with a long account of an affair Pauline Hohenzollern had been having with a Baron Türkheim, who had sent his wife off
to Graz for convenience's sake, and of an affair Caroline Humboldt was
said to be having with the popular magnetizing physician, Dr. Koreff.

It did not surprise him to find the name of Wilhelmine's sister figuring in
police reports. Pauline's indiscreet tongue had already got her named there
more than once.

> I take an interest in Pauline, because I have long regarded her as a sick
> person. She is mad. But, *mon amie*, why was it reserved for me to find you
> named in this report with all the details of a liaison with Lamb?[54]

Unable to take his eyes off the pages, Metternich absorbed each detail
laconically set down by some anonymous police secretary in a dusty little

office in a Vienna *Gasse*. "They cite your pleasure parties, your meetings in an unworthy society with odious connections."

It was true then, the bits of gossip he had been hearing all spring! Once again Metternich plummeted down into the tormenting whirlpool of sexual jealousy. All the time she had been writing him affectionate letters, all the time he had been feeding on the sweet hope of her promises, and the memories of the days and nights in Laun and Prague, *she* had been casually lovemaking with some young imbecile from the English embassy.

Over and over he read the report, fascinated and sick at heart. He had to write her, of course; he simply could not help himself. The following day, as soon as he could put his thoughts together, he wrote:

> Among the government papers brought me by yesterday's courier was a police report which came to me as usual. Among other things the report bears on a question not ordinarily in the province of the police but which becomes so as soon as affairs of a secret nature tend toward scandal and to attract the attention of the public.

It did not occur to him to question the veracity of the police reports. "Don't say they are false," he wrote. "I answer for their exactitude. They come from persons thoroughly experienced in surveillance—persons of the diplomatic corps." This was not quite true, as Metternich must have known, for the police swept in information from all kinds of questionable sources— from bribed porters and chambermaids, from informers paid to report drawing room and backstairs gossip, with no attempt made to sift truth from malicious rumor.

Nor did it occur to Metternich to question the orders that sent the Secret Police ransacking people's private lives. Since the time of Empress Maria Theresia, who had hoped to impose puritanical morals on the casual Viennese, a vice squad had functioned in the capital, prying into the lives of its citizens, a source of amusement, annoyance and certainly not of reform. More than once Metternich himself had figured in the reports—as when he was a regular guest at certain wild gambling parties at Alfred Windischgraetz's in 1810—and he would appear again until he had made himself fully master of the internal security system.

Whether the report was true or not made no difference. What was real was the torment into which he was plunged. Never had he suffered such exquisite pain.

The spoiled child, the darling of the Paris and Vienna salons, the easy charmer of ladies all his life—no one had ever really hurt him. Not his mother certainly, nor his wife Laure. He had made love times without number, with a light touch, giving pleasure and contriving wherever he could to avoid pain. What had he done then to merit this—this disaster, this disillusionment, this appalling grief? In the wonderful scale of balances in the universe, one surely won in this life what one deserved, measured out as exactly as the grains in a potion the apothecary prepared. How then had he fallen into this terrible trap, this net of suffering from which he was unable to free himself?

> *Mon amie*, how and where to begin this letter? How speak to you without hurting you—and how not to speak to you? Not in the state of soul I am in today could I dissemble—and, *mon amie*, have I ever been able to dissemble with you? I shall tell you everything—everything. If my heart be broken, it matters little—but let me speak truly to you—that you see up to the last moment of my life of what fate my heart proved worthy.

He did not ask her whether the report was true or not; perhaps now he preferred not to know.

> Never answer the question—I do not want to find you at fault. It may be that you do not love me—I know it—but never tell me a falsehood.

He promised not to reproach her, but he could not refrain from dropping just a coal or two of fire on her head:

> May Heaven grant you all the tranquillity of which you have deprived me for the remainder of my life. May this thought not torment you.

He would not, he said, break off relations with her. "I shall write you— when I have the strength for it." It did not occur to him that *she* might break off relations with him when that accusing letter reached her.

Whatever happens, he promises to remain her true friend, "the only friend you have ever had." He will continue to work to secure custody of Gustava for her. Well does he know that the child is Wilhelmine's most vulnerable spot.

> I shall do everything, everything in the world for you. This matter is the most essential of my life here below. *One day you will render me justice.* That is the sole and the last hope that remains to me. This thought is the first and the last of my sad days.

Poor Metternich! He could not get out of his head the conviction that love was meted out as a reward for good conduct, like the medals that followed a victorious battle.

He no longer counted on her trip to Paris.

Once more, quite literally, he broke down under the intensity and pain of emotional turmoil. Only two weeks earlier he had written discerningly of himself:

> With me everything is on the inside, everything takes a violent turn inside me, everything seizes me by the heart and nobody suspects. My life is a singular compound of strong feeling and of cold appearance—the first kills me, the second does not save me.[55]

Now the mask of self-control was shattered. He had lost all his tranquillity, all his self-confidence. He could neither eat nor sleep; his head ached wretchedly. He hardly knew what he was writing. "I haven't two ideas to put together. I have only suffering. . . . I want only the end of my existence—I want it with an inexpressible ardor. Wilhelmine, I don't deserve to be so cruelly grieved by you—you don't deserve to be so injured by yourself!"

The first letter he wrote and sent her on Saturday, April 30. Gradually the pain dulled a bit. Was it possible, he wondered, that the Lamb episode was only the fabric of Vienna gossip, or at most a momentary caprice, a moment of weakness on her part, that had no importance for her at all? Still she ought not have forgotten *him*, Metternich, not even for a moment. "How in forgetting yourself could you not think one single instant of the death you prepared for me?"

He wrote her again, a calmer letter. He blamed himself for the suffering he was enduring:

> The fault is not yours. . . . I had for the first time in my life surrendered myself. I am punished for it by the loss of this life which I thought I could fill with happiness and pleasure.

In the middle of his anguished letter he remembered to tell her that he had taken care of the commissions she had sent him in a recent letter, asking her mother to order gowns for her for the coming victory cele- brations. Lightheartedly she had described "court gowns in blue or rose," ball gowns, and blouses, and would dear Clemens lend her mother money if she did not have enough to cover the purchases?

He had instructed the Duchess of Courland to order Wilhelmine's dresses. "I shall advance all she wants—you will reimburse me when you wish—don't worry about that. I do not need it and it will remain a bit of happiness for me."

He ended his letter:

> Adieu, I am very well. I have just spent three days between my bed and my desk. My heart can stop beating and I am still not allowed to stir from my work. There will be another world without pain, without work, with- out such frightful suffering—and Heaven will place me there after so very many griefs here below. Adieu.

How Gentz came into possession of that report, why it was he who sent it on to Metternich, remains unknown. Had Metternich asked him to examine police records? Had Hudelist or another assistant in the Chan- cellery come across the report and given it to Gentz to send?

Had Metternich himself prepared that cup of poison by setting the police on Wilhelmine's trail? It is impossible to know for sure. After the Obreskoff incident in January, after the hints Laure and others had sent him of a liaison between Wilhelmine and Lamb, he may well have in- structed the police to watch the two. Perhaps he thought he could not bear *not to know* the truth about her. He learned now that it was worse to know, or to think he knew—though even now he realized he did not really know—and so he garnered the usual harvest of suspicious lovers who set a watch on the life of a beloved.

Metternich's two letters with their reproaches of infidelity never reached Wilhelmine.

On May 7—just before that particular courier arrived—she and Pauline and her maid Hannchen climbed into Wilhelmine's commodious traveling berline and started off in the highest of spirits on the nine-day journey to Paris.

Wilhelmine had tried, as Metternich had suggested, to persuade Gentz to go along as escort, for the roads were not yet safe for ladies traveling alone. Like Laure, Gentz longed to be in Paris at this historic moment, garnering up rumor and gossip for a thousand future dinner parties. But Metternich had not written Gentz a line for weeks, nor invited him to come to Paris. Gentz sulked, in the end refused to go, declaring he must take the waters of Baden instead for his rheumatic ills. So it was Frederick Lamb who was pressed into service to escort the ladies as far as Munich.

Instead of any of the letters of rancor or indignation or self-defense Metternich might have got from Wilhelmine had his letters reached her in time, he got a charming note informing him that she would be in Paris almost as soon as her letter, that she would go on to London if he still planned to go, that she was overflowing with excitement and delight at the notion of traveling again. "I'm already so impatient to be there, what shall I be when I am in the carriage?" She would stay at Maman's, if no other arrangements had been made for her—she was thinking of how cleverly he had arranged accommodations in Laun and in Prague so they could be together, but discreetly—"you will do what you think best. See you soon, dear Clemens!"[56]

Almost at the same moment came a letter from Laure to her husband, reporting dryly the latest titillating bit of gossip:

> The Princesses of Courland took leave of me yesterday. They hope to arrive for your birthday, an attention which should flatter you.
>
> They say but I don't vouch for the fact, that the Duchess of Sagan has left with Monsieur Lamb, who is accompanying her to Munich.[57]

"I should love to sign the peace on my birthday," Metternich had written Laure. "That deed would be worth so much more than my forty-one years."[58]

On May 15, Metternich's forty-first birthday, he did not get as a gift the completed Paris peace. But toward evening of that day Wilhelmine's traveling coach drew up before her mother's house in the Rue Drouot, and that same evening he embraced her for the first time since their parting seven months before in Prague.

What words did the two exchange? What explanations took place? There is no clue. Only Talleyrand in his *billet-doux* to the Duchess of Courland next morning wrote:

I congratulate you on the arrival of your lovely daughters. They tell me they were a bit tired but are well. I saw someone who saw them last night.[59]

That someone would have been Metternich.

A few days later the third Courland princess, Jeanne Acerenza, reached Paris, and for the first time in many years the mother and four daughters were reunited.

Unhappily a tragedy marred the family's pleasure at being together again. Just before Wilhelmine and Pauline reached Paris, Dorothée's little three-year-old daughter died of complications following measles, and Wilhelmine found her youngest sister and her mother grief-stricken over the child's death.

Metternich, who was always fond of children, had admired the pretty little girl and blamed her death on the incompetence of a doctor who had failed to diagnose her illness:

Poor Dorothée [Metternich wrote his wife] lost day before yesterday a charming little girl. . . . [Dr.] Gall, who was called in at the last moment, claims she was the victim of the doctor's stupidity who did not recognize her illness and took a lung infection for measles. Since Gall is now treating the other children they have hope of saving them. It is certain the doctors here have become even greater imbeciles than before and they will not change.[60]

Dorothée's husband, who had been away at war during most of the child's short little life, was back in Paris, but he was small comfort to the young mother in this first wrenching grief of her life. It was to her uncle, Talleyrand, that Dorothée turned for sympathy and sensitive understanding during those days. Immersed though he was in settling the future of France, Talleyrand found time nearly every day to drop by Dorothée's house and try to cheer her.

The week after the arrival of Wilhelmine and Pauline, he wrote their mother, "What your beautiful princesses most have is a resemblance to you, my dear." He added then as an afterthought, "Dorothée has the prettiest face anyone could have."[61]

In the last two weeks of May the sun shone brilliantly on the boulevards. The chestnut trees bloomed in the Bois. In the elegant restaurants and cafés—in Frascati's, the Cercle des Étrangers and in the candlelighted Café des Aveugles, where an orchestra of blind musicians played after dark—thousands of foreigners laughed and drank and ate and talked. Parisian ladies in their chic audacious frocks and deep-crowned enormous hats turned to stare at the English ladies in their modestly cut dresses and prim little bonnets.

It's raining English here [Metternich wrote Laure]—five to six hundred a day, and the prostitutes of the Palais-Royale cry, "Long live the little

hats!" You should see the unbelievable appearance and costumes of some
of these English women.[62]

More than twelve thousand English tourists were in Paris by early June.

The English ladies were as shocked by the sophisticated manners of continental society as they were by Paris hats. Priscilla Burghersh, who thought
the hats "outrageous" and "refused to put one of these horrors on my head,"
was vexed to find the singer Grassini and Talleyrand's wife—both ladies of
the most dubious morals—sitting near her in Notre Dame at the Requiem
Mass for Louis XVI. Quite haughtily Priscilla delivered her judgment of
Parisian society: "not only naughty to an excess, but so vulgar, such *mauvais
ton.*"[63]

One night at a supper party at Lady Castlereagh's, all heads turned to
stare at the appearance of an exquisite dark-eyed fair-haired woman. Louis
Rohan remarked to his hostess, "That was once my wife." It was Wilhelmine.

Lady Castlereagh, shocked to find she had entertained a divorcée, said
to her niece after the guests had gone, "Emma, I am afraid we live in very
bad company."

Young Emma Sophia shrugged and commented in a letter home, "Too
true, but we could not help ourselves and we got used to it."[64]

A week after Wilhelmine's arrival Metternich wrote Laure—to reassure
her no doubt:

> The Princesses are busy seeing everything and Monsieur de Talleyrand
> has seized hold of them. I've only seen them three times since their
> arrival for the simple reason that I see only ministers and pass my life
> in conferences. I shall bless heaven when I've finished here.[65]

In fact he and Wilhelmine met somewhere nearly every day; somehow
he stole time from his conferences to be with her. Before she came he had
bought a whole array of charming gifts—*bêtises*—for her in the Paris shops;
when he had an hour or two he took her around the boutiques and ateliers
he knew so well—to Biennais, and Thomire, to le petit Dunkerque, with its
beguiling array of luxury wares, and to the *confiseur* le Fidèle Berger, for
bonbons to carry home to the children.

Wilhelmine helped him choose gowns for Laure at the house of the great
couturier LeRoi; two trunks of dresses were dispatched to Vienna to outfit
Laure and Marie for the celebrations that were to greet the return of
Emperor Franz from the wars. Clemens would bring his ladies more
gowns when he returned himself, and an especially beautiful ball gown he
had chosen for his darling Marie.

Wilhelmine had brought him reassuring news of his daughter's health;
Marie had indeed been more seriously ill than they had written, but she
would soon be completely well.

They talked a great deal of politics and the process of peacemaking.
And they talked of themselves and their future together. No doubt Metter-

nich talked too much. He had a habit of explaining, discussing, probing, everything that had happened or was to happen between them.

Two weeks had passed since he had read the police report; he had had time to repair his equilibrium at least in part.

As to *l'affaire Lamb*—no, Wilhelmine would not admit to being in the wrong. She was mistress of her life, she needed to answer to no one—she would live as she pleased. She did not inquire, she said, into his private life. He had in fact been seeing Laure Junot nearly every day—if we are to believe Laure's own memoirs.

Yes, of course she loved him, Metternich. Had she not written him that her decision was made? He must be satisfied with that! No, she would not promise to give up Alfred; she must at least see him again first. What, after all, was he—Metternich—offering her in exchange for the promise he wanted to exact of single-hearted love and fidelity? Only the dubious security of a long liaison. She herself might wish to marry again, she said wistfully one day; it was hard for a woman to live outside marriage. No, she would give no binding promises—at least not for now.

In the bundles of letters exchanged between Metternich and Wilhelmine are several dozen tiny notes from those May days in Paris, in Wilhelmine's small, quick hand, breaking an engagement, asking a favor for a friend, setting a time when he might see her. She is sitting for her portrait in Isabey's studio at one; she will expect Metternich at the studio at two. She adds rather crossly, "Paris is odious to me, and I don't know if I will like London any better."[66]

There were certainly scenes between the two—scenes that bored and wearied her.

A few days after Wilhelmine's arrival in Paris a bundle of letters from Vienna came by ministry courier to the Hôtel Sébastiani. Among them were the two letters Metternich had written her on the Lamb affair—those fatal letters which had reached Vienna after Wilhelmine's departure, which —had they come in time—would most probably have canceled her journey, very likely ended their affair.

Instead of destroying the letters, Metternich sent them on to her on May 23 with a note that was tender, even poetic, and showed how completely he had forgiven her—whatever there was to forgive:

> I would have preferred not to send you this one, but I do so because you want to have the complete collection. My letters are like me—they are good and bad, they wear the imprint of happiness and of pain. Perhaps they have even more in common with me for giving you more vexation than joy—but certainly one day when you reach the limits of your life, when all illusion disappears and the true remains exactly that —when you recall your most beautiful years and during that recollection you leaf through my letters—all of them, the good ones and those which are not good, will prove to you that I loved you more than my life, more

than you have ever been loved, more than you will ever be. You will think then of the old friend who perhaps will no longer exist, who will be dead, with your name on his lips, your image in his heart.

Bon jour, bonne amie, I will see you at 4 o'clock.[67]

5

At five on the afternoon of May 31 all the church bells of Paris rang lustily, salvos of artillery were fired, and the next day heralds appeared in the principal squares and at the gates of the city to read the proclamation that peace had been signed.

Not quite so generous as Metternich had originally envisioned it, the peace was nonetheless exceptionally moderate. Metternich could write with pride to Laure:

> People will be satisfied with it—the conditions are superb, at the same time they furnish a great and beautiful proof of the moderation of the powers. We could have destroyed France—have made her pay dearly for the evils she has brought to Europe for twenty years; we preferred a state of things which does not leave causes for well-founded discontent. But it will happen of this peace as of all human things. It will be found too harsh in France and too soft beyond their frontiers.[68]

France was restored to her old boundaries of 1792, with a few enclaves added to round out her borders. Holland and Switzerland were to be independent, with Flanders added to Holland. Italy would again be composed of "sovereign states," with Lombardy and Venetia going to Austria. England had got virtually everything she had wanted—the Bourbons back in power, a commercially weakened France, a free hand in maritime questions, the formerly French islands of Mauritius and Tobago, plus the Cape of Good Hope.

France was to pay no indemnities for the losses suffered by other countries at the hands of her armies. The Allied occupation troops would leave France at once. And France would keep most of the art works looted from all Europe—a matter of special pride and concern to Frenchmen.

The published version of the treaty invited all the powers who had taken part in the war to come to a congress in Vienna. A secret clause placed the settlement of all the undecided issues—including the knotty questions revolving around Central Europe—in the hands of the four great powers—Austria, Russia, England, Prussia.

During his weeks in Paris Metternich had envisioned and designed the congress that would take place in Vienna after the sovereigns' visit to London was over. He intended that the major questions left dangling would be settled in London with the help of Castlereagh. The congress would merely meet to ratify the decisions.

Emperor Franz would be delighted to leave much of the entertaining to his sociable and imaginative minister. Metternich planned to give a great peace festival at his villa on the Rennweg in late June, just when the gardens were at their best. The French decorator Moreau, who was already doing the Chancellery, had been ordered to "plan it on a grand scale for the court will pay for it." Perhaps large tents set up on the lawns between the conservatories?

Letter after letter had gone off to Laure during May giving her most minute instructions for the redecorating. His bedroom and salon in the villa were to be repapered; his study looking onto the garden should be turned into a library lined with open mahogany bookshelves deep enough to hold quarto volumes. He had been spending a good deal of spare time in Paris bookshops.

He would bring materials for upholstering from Paris "for they are incomparably better than at home." He would bring sconces for the large salon and many beautiful things for both their Chancellery apartments and for the villa—furniture by the cabinetmaker Jacob in the very latest Empire style, gold and silver from Biennais, porcelain and Thomire bronzes. His purchases in the end filled several transport wagons.

He had personally chosen and hired the best dancers in the Paris ballet to perform at the congress. "Desprieux has made me a ballet program and I think the contract will be signed today with Aumer, Bigottini, Gosselin and Antonia."

At Talleyrand's suggestion he had engaged Isabey, former court painter to Napoleon, to come to Vienna and help design the festivals. "I will lodge him for a time with us," he wrote Laure. "You know it was he who always directed the festivals here [in Paris]."[69]

The Vienna Congress was to be both a culmination and a beginning. It was the culmination of his dream to end war—that "political dream" of which he had written Floret in November of 1812—to end the domination of Europe by military force, to celebrate a new era of peace for Europe.

Everyone made ready at last to leave Paris.

Emperor Franz climbed into his carriage and set off on the road back to Vienna—a year to the day from that famous June 1 when he and Metternich had galloped out of the city to Bohemia on the first stage of the journey that had brought them finally to Paris and a Europe at peace.

Schwarzenberg rode with his troops back to Bohemia. Metternich had wanted the Allied commander-in-chief to go with him to London, but Schwarzenberg steadfastly refused. He would not wait to be back at his beloved Castle Orlik with Nani in his arms.

The Tsar and the King of Prussia were on their way to London.

On Saturday, May 28, there had been a last spectacular review of the Allied troops in the Bois de Boulogne. All the armies had been drawn up in a single line six miles long. The three Allied sovereigns, followed by princes, generals and Napoleon's marshals, galloped at full speed the length of the parade line, while cheers of the soldiers in several tongues passed from one set of throats to another.

Metternich left Paris for London on Friday, June 3, weary but in the best of spirits. Everything, he felt optimistically, was now going his way— in love as in politics.

Emperor Franz wanted him to stay on forever as his chief minister. Sending Laure those precise instructions on refurnishing their Chancellery apartments, he had added, "I've decided to furnish these rooms well, because I have more chances than I might wish for to spend a good many years in that building."[70]

As for Wilhelmine, he had won her, he thought, or very nearly. The last hours with her had been happier; there would be more hours in London. Her last note from Paris was, to be sure, a trifle cool:

> I have had enough *explications* with you, *mon ami*—and I am grateful to you for the way you've explained yourself—so the last moment of my stay here is the best. I shall see you in England. I shall be calm and serene and you will be pleased with me. Adieu, dear Clemens, *à revoir* in England, may God watch over you.[71]

On her last day but one in Paris Metternich sent her a golden bracelet engraved inside with a date that was memorable to them both—perhaps the date of their meeting in Laun. With it went a tiny note, playfully lettered backwards so that she must hold it to her mirror to read. Would she please write answers in the spaces provided and return the answers to him?

Requests	*Replies*
1. Give me a *pledge of will* in London.	
2. Always wear my bracelet.	
3. Take off A's bracelet forever.	
4. Take it off to put it on again.	
5. Tell me when our relations will be entirely re-established.	
6. Wear the little medallion.	

> What have you answered?
> Many good things!
> Do you tell me yes _____
> no _____
> yes _____[72]

She did not reply—at least not at once. That evening, just before her departure, she wrote Alfred Windischgraetz a last deeply tender letter. She offered him his freedom if that were best for him, but it must be he who decided. She could not, she simply could not, make up her mind to part with Alfred forever.

XVIII

POLITICAL COMEDY IN LONDON

Heaven inspired this trip to London. I don't know what would have happened if I had not been here. Now only good will come of it.
—METTERNICH TO LAURE, JUNE 19, 1814

1

Metternich crossed the Channel on a beautiful Sunday in early June, a summer Sunday of blue skies, white-flecked sea and a brisk wind that carried the Prince Regent's frigate *Nymph* to Dover in less than five hours.

A throng had been waiting all week in Dover to greet the visiting sovereigns. But the Tsar was delayed in Boulogne waiting for the King of Prussia, and Metternich, reaching England twenty-four hours before the Tsar, fell heir to at least part of the joyous welcome. "At Dover I was received like the sovereigns with all possible honors," he told Laure.[1] It was political capital he needed, and he would put it to work effectively.

After twenty-two years of war, of tightening their belts and paying more for bread and beer, the English were ripe for a good celebration. They were prepared to give a thunderous welcome to the Allied monarchs—especially the Tsar—who had finally handcuffed that devil Boney to the little island of Elba.

Austria's prestige in England in early June of 1814 was as low as Russia's was high. The English could neither forget nor forgive the Napoleonic marriage, and they suspected quite rightly that Austria would have preferred a regency with the King of Rome as France's future ruler. Emperor Franz had declined the Prince Regent's invitation, to avoid, as Aberdeen wrote, "the risk of mortification incompatible with the dignity of his situation."[2]

So it was Metternich who was to stand in for his sovereign. Never perhaps in his life would he exercise more adroitly his charm, grace and polished affability than in the weeks in England that June.

The Tsar, on the other hand, went about almost perversely alienating his host, the Prince Regent, and the government—to say nothing of the patient exuberant crowds who followed wherever he went.

Unluckily the Tsar and the Prussian King had a rough Channel crossing, the Tsar was seasick all the way, so that he was in something less than dazzling high spirits when he stepped off the boat. Eluding the crowds he secluded himself in a private house overnight. Though the ladies of London would fight and swoon for a glimpse of the fair-haired Russian sovereign, a seventeen-year-old English girl, Muzzy Capel, who was waiting with her family in Dover to take a boat to the Continent, got a close look at the Tsar and was not in the least impressed. "I was near enough to touch them," she reported to her grandmother, "and think Alexander not the least handsome—horridly Pink and Puddinglike." He looked, she thought, rather like their dentist.[3]

Next day, June 7, the Tsar and the Prussian King declined the splendid state carriages the Prince Regent had dispatched for his guests, secreted themselves in the closed carriage of the Russian ambassador, Prince Lieven, and rode into London incognito by a back road.

All along the seventy-mile route between Dover and London streets and house fronts had been ordered scrubbed, painted and embellished in their honor. Everywhere immense crowds had gathered. Near London grandstands had been erected and thousands of tickets sold at exorbitant prices for a view of the visiting monarchs. Only late in the day did the news spread that the spectacle for which everyone had waited was already over, without ever having taken place at all. "Those extraordinary crowds," Metternich could report to Emperor Franz, "expressed their disappointment loudly."[4]

The Prince Regent, waiting to welcome the Tsar to the guest apartments in St. James's Palace, learned that the Tsar had gone straight to his sister Catherine's rooms in the Pulteney Hotel in Piccadilly, where he announced he would be staying during his London sojourn.

Grand Duchess Catherine, the Tsar's "delicious lunatic" sister, had been in London since the end of March. She had already succeeded in undermining English-Russian relations at the top level and in planting seeds of prejudice against the Prince Regent in her susceptible brother's mind.

The British royal family at that moment in history was in a highly delicate position. King George III had declined into madness. The Prince Regent, a haughty fifty-year-old monument to a lifetime of greed and self-indulgence, was living apart from his wife, Princess Caroline, whom he loathed cordially, while both fought a devious ongoing battle to control their only daughter, the throne-heiress Princess Charlotte, and to hustle British public opinion. The morganatic wife, Mrs. Fitzherbert, with whom the Regent had lived openly during a good part of his conjugal life, had been followed by a succession of mistresses, of whom Lady Hertford was the current favorite. But by the year 1814 the Prince Regent was treading on very thin ice. His enemies, the Whigs, and a large segment of the public supported the cause of his estranged wife, Princess Caroline. More than once of late he had been pelted with mud and stones when he appeared on the streets of London.

The one really popular member of the royal family was the eighteen-year-old Princess Charlotte, the unlucky pawn of her parents' ongoing feud. It was her marriage to the Prince of Orange, heir to the newly independent country of Holland, that Castlereagh had painstakingly arranged the previous winter on his way to Allied headquarters. That cross-Channel marriage, it was hoped, would insure English influence in Holland and serve British commercial interests admirably.

Into the troubled domestic waters of the English royal family Catherine had steered that spring like an imperious little tugboat. Having, as Princess Lieven described her, "an excessive thirst for authority and a very high opinion of herself," the widowed Catherine was engaged in a tour of matrimonial prospects, which included the Prince Regent (if he could rid himself of his unwanted wife), and two of his brothers, the Dukes of Clarence and Cumberland. The latter two she crossed off at once. "He sniffed around the pot," she reported of the Duke of Cumberland. "I made believe not to understand him." The Duke of Clarence, coarse of tongue and a pincher of bottoms, who had had ten children by an actress, got even shorter shrift. "This I know for certain—that I shall not become Mrs. Clarence," Catherine announced by letter to her brother.[5]

She and the Prince Regent had taken an instant dislike to one another. On the day of her arrival in London, the Prince had gone ostentatiously to call on her, having announced his visit ahead of time, at the Pulteney Hotel. Catherine kept him waiting half an hour, then appeared not quite dressed and visibly flustered. "Your Grand Duchess is not good looking," he muttered to the Lievens as he took his departure. "Your Prince is ill-bred," Catherine snapped in return.[6]

That night at dinner in Catherine's honor at Carlton House the Regent had compounded Catherine's dislike by ogling the décolletage of her low-cut black gown and prophesying jovially that she would not long be a widow.

"She answered," reported Princess Lieven, "by an astonished silence and looks full of haughtiness."

When the orchestra struck up a tune, Catherine instantly asked the musicians to halt because music made her violently sick. "The Queen and the Regent were cross about it, the evening was spoiled. The Duchess was much delighted," said Princess Lieven. "From that evening she and the Regent hated each other mutually."[7]

To her brother Alexander Catherine described the Regent scathingly as—

a man visibly used up by dissipation, and disgusting rather. His much-boasted affability is the most licentious, I may even say obscene, strain I ever listened to. You know I am far from being puritanical or prudish, but I vow to you that with him and his brothers I have often had not only to get stiffly on my stiffs, but not know what to do with eyes and ears. A brazen way of looking where eyes should never go, that one must be made I know not how to stand.[8]

Catherine was doubtless right. The First Gentleman of Europe, as the Tory press called him, was no gentleman. But the Tsar's forthcoming visit was a political event of considerable importance to the future relationship of England and Russia. Tactless and mischievous, Catherine proceeded to muddy the political waters. Ostentatiously she befriended the Regent's sworn enemies in the opposing party. She made friends with Princess Charlotte—whom she described to her brother as looking "like a young rascal dressed as a girl," planted seeds of defiance in the princess's mind against her prospective marriage—chiefly because Catherine wanted to preserve the Prince of Orange as a possible suitor for herself or her sister. She went so far as to declare she was going to call on the Regent's estranged wife, Princess Caroline, and was only dissuaded when Prince Lieven, the Russian ambassador, threatened to resign his post if she did so. For several weeks thereafter, Catherine refused to speak a word to the unlucky diplomat, though seated regularly next to him at official dinners.

Carefully indoctrinated by his sister's letters, the Tsar arrived in London on June 7, drove straight to the Pulteney Hotel to embrace Catherine, while the Regent waited fuming in the beautiful apartment in the palace that had been decorated and furnished especially for the Tsar's visit.

The Regent sent word that he would call on the Tsar at once at his hotel. The Tsar waited several hours, but his host did not appear. Late in the afternoon a message arrived from Carlton House for Prince Lieven, explaining that the Regent had been "threatened with annoyance" if he appeared in the streets; he dared not drive to Piccadilly for fear of being hissed and mobbed and pelted with eggs—humiliating avowal for a sovereign. The Tsar drove at once to Carlton House, hailed and cheered by crowds along the way, and talked briefly with the Prince Regent. "A poor prince," he remarked to Prince Lieven as they drove away.[9]

The Tsar had declined the Prince Regent's invitation to dine with him that night, preferring to dine tête-à-tête with Catherine at the Pulteney. But Metternich dined that evening with the Prince Regent, and stayed till three in the morning, exercising all his considerable charm. He had met the Prince Regent some twenty years before, during his youthful sojourn in England. Now he won his way wholly into the prince's graces.

The next day, June 8, he and the Austrian ambassador, Count Merveldt, repaired to Carlton House at noon to hang about the portly neck of the Regent the Order of the Golden Fleece in diamonds—the first English sovereign since Henry VIII to wear the distinguished order. The Regent was enchanted, according to Prince Lieven, and rarely went out without his Fleece.[10]

Metternich had troubled to explore other little fancies of the Prince Regent's, and he had arranged another superb gift for a prince who had everything: the command of an Austrian hussar regiment. The Regent adored things military, fancied himself a commanding soldierly figure, spent hours having an elegant white Austrian dress uniform, glittering with gold braid and epaulettes, tailored to encompass his immense corseted bulk. The bestowing of an honorary military command, common among continental nations, was unheard-of in England, and had required a special negotiation between Metternich and Castlereagh, and considerable discussion in the Cabinet. The Regent was enchanted, told Metternich over and over that it was the most delightful present he had ever got in his life.[11]

Every day the foreign guests faced a day filled with official entertainment. There were formal dinners and assemblies at Carlton House, private dinners and routs at the great English houses. There was a day's excursion to the Ascot races, and a river trip by royal barge down the Thames to Woolwich, where a champagne lunch was served, and Colonel Congreve, the famous artillery expert, entertained with a display of his inventions—rockets and shells that, reported Metternich, "only the opening of hell could imitate. . . . More than 1,000 boats went down the river at once," he wrote to Laure. "The whole population of London was on the quays and bridges."[12]

Everywhere enormous crowds were on hand to view the visitors from across the Channel. Traffic jammed for blocks along the London thoroughfares whenever one of the low-slung dark green French carriages appeared in which one or another of the foreign guests was riding.

> I was nearly killed the night of the 10th to the 11th [Metternich wrote Laure]. I left the Prince Regent's at midnight. The crowd recognized me; they threw themselves on my carriage with wild cries of "Hurrah! Prince Metternich forever!" The crowd wants to *touch* even more than to see. They want to *sheck hands* [sic]; I had 300 hands thrust into my carriage; the coachman was thrown down off his seat and I had to flee inside my house so as not to be suffocated with *love*. . . . One is always tempted to cry, "For the love of God love me a little bit less!"[13]

The Prussian generals were especially popular with the English crowd. Again and again General Blücher had his horses detached from his carriage while a mob pulled the vehicle to his hotel, or else lifted the old soldier out bodily and carried him on their shoulders. Tickets were sold for standing room inside the entrance and along the staircase of the Pulteney Hotel for admiring ladies who wanted to view the Tsar. The private parties were as jammed as the London streets, with three or four hundred people crowding into a single room at the great receptions.

At the gala opera performance on the night of June 11, such a crush assailed the doors that the ticket-takers were mobbed and two thousand people pushed in without paying. Fortunately the guests of honor had been dining late that evening at Lord Liverpool's, and reached the theater after the crowd was inside. But when they entered their boxes, the stage performance came to a dead halt while the immense audience rose, shrieked, yelled, clapped, finally subsided to sing "God Save the King."

The little high comedy duel between the Russian imperial visitors and their royal English host continued unabated. The Tsar and his sister boycotted as much of the official program as they dared, went off sightseeing together, arrived late at official functions, and sometimes not at all.

Invited to a dinner party at the Prince Regent's one night, the Tsar kept the whole party waiting while he talked at the Pulteney Hotel with Lord Grey and other leaders of the Opposition. The Prince Regent sent several times to the Pulteney to see if the Tsar had left. The Russian sovereign did not arrive until half-past eleven, excusing himself by remarking to the shocked company that he had been occupied talking to the Whig leader.

At a palace assembly the Prince Regent led his current mistress, Lady Hertford, up to the Tsar to present her. The Tsar was engaged in examining with a spyglass an especially fetching lady at the opposite end of the ballroom. "This is Lady Hertford," said the Regent. The Tsar bowed coldly and returned to his spyglass. The Regent, knowing the Tsar was quite deaf, thought he had not understood her name and repeated it quite loudly, "This is Lady Hertford." The Tsar merely bowed. Of Lady Hertford he remarked to Princess Lieven in tones loud enough for the Regent to hear, "She looks mighty old."

To complicate matters further, the Tsar paid marked attention to the Regent's discarded mistress, Lady Jersey, who now thoroughly hated the Prince Regent.

Grand Duchess Catherine continued to do her share to aggravate matters yet further. At a dinner party at the house of Britain's Prime Minister, Lord Liverpool, the Prince Regent was seated between Catherine and Princess Lieven, who reported the following dialogue.

> *Catherine:* Why then, Your Highness, do you keep your daughter under lock and key? Why does she go nowhere with you?
> *Regent:* My daughter is too young, Madame, to go into the world.
> *Catherine:* She is not too young for you to have fixed on a husband for her.
> *Regent:* She will not marry for two years.
> *Catherine:* When she does marry, I do hope she will manage to make up to herself for her present prison.

Regent: When she is married, Madame, she will do as her husband
pleases. For the present she does as I wish.

Catherine turned to the Regent, gazed at him fixedly with her shrewd
eyes and in a voice as sweet as a Borgia potion, replied, "Your Highness is
right. Between husband and wife there can be only one will."

The Regent turned purple and remarked loudly to Princess Lieven,
"This is intolerable!"[14] The following night he arrived at Lady Salisbury's
rout thoroughly drunk.

In the middle of the London sojourn the leading guests were treated
to a two-day jaunt to Oxford, where at an exceedingly long and tedious
ceremony, with several dozen Latin discourses and several dozen English
odes—including one written by Coleridge on the fall of Napoleon—they were
given honorary degrees. The Tsar and his sister made no pretense of enjoying the academic ritual. Shown about Oxford the Tsar declared he
disliked Gothic architecture, while Catherine threw confusion into the program by calling a peremptory halt to a voluntary by the famous organist Dr.
Crotch, vowing again that music made her sick to her stomach. As soon
as the degrees had been presented, the imperial pair jumped into a carriage
and went off sightseeing to Blenheim Palace, drove back to London that
night in an open landau through a thunderstorm to dance until dawn at
Lady Jersey's ball, a circumstance which the Oxford excursion had been
expressly planned to prevent.

Metternich, on the other hand, was charmed by the medieval university
town. If the long-winded academic ceremony bored him, he had the grace
to be amused too, writing his family that he felt quite like the doctor in
Le Malade Imaginaire, emerging from the experience "at least ten times
more *savant* than a few hours ago."[15]

Lunching at Christ Church after the ceremony he and Blücher flirted
with an exquisite English peeress sitting opposite them, "the prettiest
young person I've ever seen." While a regimental band played allemandes
in their honor, Blücher leaned his old red Prussian face across the table to
declare his passion to the young lady. " '*Moi—si pas avoir 70 ans et pas
avoir femme, vous marierai femme à moi.*' *Milady lui a répondu,* '*Moi
comprendra pas.*' " Metternich collapsed in gales of laughter.[16]

Metternich rode back from Oxford to London with the Prince Regent,
expressing his delight over the Oxford visit and everything English.

On the Saturday following the Oxford visit, the lord mayor and the
dignitaries of the City of London tendered a banquet at the Guildhall to
the foreign celebrities. The event caused the popularity of the Russian
imperial pair to drop yet a few degrees further.

Ordinarily ladies did not attend such affairs and Catherine had not
been invited, but she announced her intention of accompanying her brother,
and Princess Lieven was hastily invited to make another lady at the head
table.

As the distinguished guests entered and made their way through a throng to the raised dais where they were to be seated, the Regent, walking behind the Tsar with Princess Lieven on his arm, had to stop and wait, quite red with annoyance, while the Tsar paused several times to talk with some member of the Opposition.

The guests had barely been seated when the Italian singers hired for the occasion began their program. Catherine leaned over the Prince Regent to warn Princess Lieven in Russian. "If the music goes on I'm going to be sick." The Princess translated for the Regent, who ordered the music halted in mid-note to the bewilderment and irritation of the listening audience.

When the orchestra was observed putting away their instruments, several people approached the Regent to protest in dismayed undertones. "This won't do in England," he agreed, and turning to Princess Lieven asked her to beg the grand duchess if the orchestra might not at least play "God Save the King." Catherine replied haughtily, "As if that was not music!"

An audible murmur of displeasure was heard from the throng of banqueters, and presently an anonymous note was passed up to the dais to Princess Lieven. "If your Duchess does not allow the music, we won't answer for the royal table," the note threatened. Princess Lieven passed the note to Catherine, who shrugged, "Well, let them bawl then!"

In the end "God Save the King" was sung, but the relations between the Russian visitors and their English hosts were irreparably shattered. Lord Liverpool remarked sharply to Princess Lieven as the banquet ended, "If people don't know how to behave, they would do better to stay home. Your Duchess has chosen against all usage to go to a men's dinner."

The whole series of contretemps at the Guildhall luncheon had amused Metternich, who, Princess Lieven reported,

> turned it to account out of hand. Glancing calmly over this lively scene he easily did some high policy while greatly diverting himself. He made capital of the Regent's foibles with the [Grand] Duchess, all of whose confidences went to him, and in return laughed at the Tsar to the Regent, which was a sure way of pleasing him. He got complete hold of that Prince's mind, ministered to all his vain leanings, which were carried to an incredible extent for a Sovereign.[17]

Catherine's humor during the English visit had, meantime, been made yet worse by a hurdle put in the way of her favored matrimonial project. Though she was still looking over the field, she had given great encouragement to the quiet, earnest suit of Emperor Franz's brother Archduke Karl, victor of the only battle Napoleon lost in mid-career, at Aspern. The Russian Orthodox Church, however, frowned on the marriage of two brothers to two sisters, and Karl's brother, Joseph, Palatine of Hungary, had been married to Catherine's elder sister. The Tsar himself would not object to the marriage, but their mother, Dowager Tsarina Maria Fëdorowna—the one person in the world to whose will Catherine bowed—had the deciding voice. In London during the sovereigns' visit, Catherine got a letter from her mother forbidding her to marry Karl. "The Duchess," reported Princess Lieven, "shut herself up for several days to give way to a great attack of despair."[18]

But Catherine was made of tough fiber, and she did not intend to give in easily. She summoned Metternich to the Pulteney Hotel and begged him to ask the Austrian Emperor to write a persuasive letter to her mother. If Emperor Franz declared that he strongly favored his brother's marriage to Catherine, the political possibilities inherent in the match might sway her mother.

Metternich did write Emperor Franz, enclosing for good measure a copy of a love letter that his agents had intercepted from Catherine to Karl. Metternich thought the marriage desirable "in the present situation of affairs." Catherine was, he added, very *decided* on the marriage.[19]

Perhaps as a result of his sympathetic role in helping her marriage plans along, Catherine had begun to give more and more of her confidence to Metternich. She was, Princess Lieven reported with some anxiety, imparting to Metternich "more than sly hints as to the political frame of mind of the Tsar at a moment . . . when, as I knew, such hints were of genuine importance to the cabinet of Vienna. Prince Lieven tried to alert the Tsar to his sister's indiscreet revelation to Metternich, but the Tsar appeared not even to hear."[20]

To Emperor Franz Metternich could report in mid-June that Russia was losing ground while Austria was garnering a harvest of goodwill in England.[21]

2

Amid the heady and exhausting social whirl of that London sojourn the diplomats endeavored to make progress on all the unsolved questions of Europe's future.

"I shall try to complete everything here that can be well done, and to leave open everything that could be compromising," Metternich had promised Hudelist, adding that the congress when it met in Vienna "will be less to negotiate than to ratify."[22]

"We made peace with France in Paris; we shall make that of Europe in London," he wrote to Laure.[23]

What he hoped to accomplish in London above all was to break the impasse on the Saxony-Poland question. In Paris the adulation that surrounded the Tsar, and the pressure from Poles living in France, had not only hardened the Tsar's resolution to create a kingdom of Poland, but had increased his territorial demands.

If he could, Metternich calculated, detach Prussia from her close alliance with the Tsar into an alignment with Austria, then persuade Castlereagh to step in as mediator of the final disputes, all might be smoothly arranged before the Vienna meetings.

But everything conspired to prevent such a resolution during the London stay. Neither Prussia nor Russia showed the slightest sign of relenting in their demands. Prussia was demanding not only all of Saxony but the left bank of the Rhine and the fortress of Mainz—which Metternich intended to use to indemnify Bavaria in exchange for the return of the Austrian territories Napoleon had given to Bavaria. No, the complicated questions of Central Europe showed no sign of being settled.

Moreover, Castlereagh declined to act as mediator at this point.

And though the ministers had begun by setting themselves a daily conference schedule as in Paris, the social interruptions of that celebrated London season soon made any regularity in their meetings impossible.

To complicate matters further, personal antagonisms, old and new, continued to obstruct the course of diplomatic business. Hardenberg could scarcely have found the air of Carlton House very congenial. In London, years before, he had been forced to leave the diplomatic service of his native Hanover when his first wife became entangled in a scandalous liaison with the Prince Regent—then Prince of Wales. Why the King of Prussia was in an ill humor no one could say, but Creevey described him as "sulky as a bear." Castlereagh had arranged for the Prince of Orange to come to London to hasten his betrothal to Princess Charlotte. But the prince got very drunk at a dinner at Carlton House and Charlotte, encouraged by Catherine, declared she would not marry him. The Tsar and his sister continued to infuriate the Prince Regent. Creevey reported, "All agree that Prinny will die or go mad; he is worn out with fuss, fatigue and rage."[24]

Meantime, there had been another shift in allegiances, one of the slight wind changes that an intuitive diplomat like Metternich was quick to detect. Even before the sovereigns' departure from Paris the Tsar's friendship for Talleyrand had chilled noticeably. The Bourbon government was becoming increasingly reactionary, and the Tsar blamed Talleyrand, who had talked him into supporting the restoration as the only possible solution. The Tsar left Paris without saying good-by to Talleyrand, who wrote the Tsar in London, pleading with him to permit their mutual friend the Duchess of Courland to intercede and heal the rift between them.[25] The Tsar apparently did not respond.

In the end Castlereagh and Metternich agreed to postpone further discussion of the crucial unsettled questions until the meetings in Vienna.

3

To Wilhelmine London was deeply disappointing.

In Paris she and her sisters had been invited everywhere. Her mother's close friendship with Talleyrand and the Tsar had assured her daughters a warm reception wherever they went. With her strong predilection for everything English, and her memories of gay months in England in 1802, Wilhelmine had looked forward to being part of the celebrations attending the sovereigns' visit.

But nothing turned out as she had planned. During the long separation of the island kingdom from the Continent the two parts of Europe had gone their separate ways, she wrote, and "the comparison is not to this country's advantage." She thought the sovereigns would not like it in England—in which she was right.[26]

And despite the apparent laxity of Regency society, rigid ground rules governed the social scene in England. Divorce was a nearly fatal barrier to social acceptance, and to be invited to Carlton House or to be included in any of the official parties, a lady must have been presented at a Drawing Room of the old Queen, consort of George III.

As for the private parties, a woman of wit and charm might never be noticed at all. The assemblies were jammed with strangers to whom the hostess paid scant attention. At the dinner parties, just as the conversation became interesting the ladies had to rise and leave the table, and sit fanning themselves in boredom in a drawing room, while the gentlemen talked politics over madeira and port well laced with brandy for as long as three or four hours.[27]

It was all frightfully tedious.

Metternich, on the wing from one engagement to another, instructed her to call on Countess Merveldt, wife of the Austrian ambassador, and arrange to be presented at court. But when Wilhelmine and her sisters Pauline and Jeanne went to call, they were told that Madame Merveldt was out. And though they left their cards, and Wilhelmine wrote a note with their request, Madame Merveldt did not reply. Apparently she did not approve of Wilhelmine—least of all of her intimacy with the Austrian Foreign Minister.

Meantime, the precious days of the festival season slipped by. Wilhelmine fretted. She was, she said, the most *contrariée* person in the world. She could have asked the wife of the Prussian ambassador to arrange things, for Wilhelmine's Sagan estates were among the largest in all Prussia. Or she could, she wrote Clemens, drop a word in the Tsar's ear, and certainly *his* ambassador's wife, Princess Lieven, would be happy to arrange her presentation at court.[28] One night at a dinner party at Charles Stewart's she sat near Princess Dorothea Lieven, who took in the Duchess of Sagan from head to toe and decided at once she did not like her.

What was especially vexing to Wilhelmine was that, after finding her friends so solicitous in Paris, "taking a bit of care of me, I find myself very isolated here, and the arm of a man is almost indispensable. One cannot get along without it."[29]

But in London, as Metternich hurried from conference to luncheon to audience to dinner party, Wilhelmine scarcely glimpsed him at all. He admonished her, "Share my happiness, *mon amie*, but do not irritate it."[30] If they met it was usually at the very end of the day, at one of the big routs where throngs of ladies pressed about the handsome personable Austrian minister, eager to be introduced. "The English ladies," he reported to his wife, "are of a rare beauty, but dressed to scare you. . . . I haven't been to a rout without having three or four hundred ladies asking to be presented."[31]

But Wilhelmine in London was bored and cross and out of sorts, and her notes to him had a petulant tone. She and her sisters planned to go to the Ascot races on the day the sovereigns were to be there, but at the last moment they could find no horses for hire and had to stay in London. Metternich was not much help! "Where are you dining? Try to come for a moment and see me," she wrote. Or, more peremptorily: "Even if you leave the Prince's after midnight, we'll be waiting for you at the Duchess's. Don't fail to come." Or: "We expect you for dinner, dear C., although I don't believe in it, for you will surely find some other engagement during the course of the day." Or: "I hope to see you at dinner and that you will be nice to me, for I found and kept the book the Duchess lent you yesterday and which you very gaily left in the carriage."[32]

"The Duchess" was an old friend, the Duchess of Somerset, to whose country house Wilhelmine and her sisters went for a few days. And though the royal dinner parties were at first closed to her, through Frederick Lamb's introductions she had invitations to Melbourne House, where she met his sister Emilie and his madcap sister-in-law, Caroline Lamb, and to other great Whig houses. At Lady Lansdowne's she met the poet Byron and could tell him of her admiration for *The Corsair*, which George Vernon had given her. Though Metternich shunned most Whig houses so as not to offend the Prince Regent, he appeared at Lady Lansdowne's, in company with General Koller, who entertained the guests with an account of his journey to Elba with Napoleon.

In the loneliness of her first days in London, feeling herself more a stranger than she had felt anywhere for many years, Wilhelmine thought increasingly of Alfred. The nostalgia for her old love was still deep and powerful. She had written him from Paris offering him his freedom but now she wrote him a long tender letter filled with memories:

> Just a year ago today, dear Alfred, we were drinking tea together in Czaslau, where I found myself happy beside you in the most wretched room in the world—and one where I could have wished to spend my whole life if only you were staying there with me. I was sad just then. The war was about to begin again, and I did not know if I would be seeing you any more. Now I would give the whole world to find myself back there again beside you, so good, so perfect for me. I have no more courage, no more strength. I spent all my courage when I wrote you just before leaving Paris.[33]

No, she was not yet ready to surrender Alfred completely, though she tells him again, "You are completely free, dear Alfred, to make the choice that is best for you." She adds that she will be back in Vienna by July 8, she thinks. "Just four weeks from now and I shall see you again." She hopes that he will be the very first person she sees when she returns home. Perhaps he might even drive out to meet her at Purkersdorf, the first post stop outside Vienna, as he had so many times ridden to meet her traveling carriage in days past.

She must certainly see him again before she made any decision. Certainly she had not made up her mind nor her heart; she was deeply torn.

There was Clemens, whose ardent love she no longer doubted, with his brilliant gifts, his charm, his formidable place in the political world. But simply to be his mistress for a few years—was that enough?

Wilhelmine had hoped that in London Metternich could devote himself to her, with the peace treaty out of the way and the Austrian emperor far away in Vienna. In those few leisurely weeks their intimacy might flower into what, through the long months of their separation she had hoped it would be—the safe harbor or some deep and lasting relationship. But in London she and Metternich had no long, idyllic hours together.

She wanted to remarry some day. A woman alone—without marriage—there was no place for her in the world. She envied the stability of the well married, she whose position in society would always be equivocal.

Did Wilhelmine during their London sojourn drop the word "marriage" ever so lightly, tentatively, to Metternich? Did she calculate the possibility of his one day divorcing his wife, Laure, to marry her? Perhaps. Certainly she made clear her dissatisfaction with the position in which she found herself, that ambiguous position of *amie*, that carried with it no name, no honor, no real sovereignty.

Could Clemens not see how humiliating it was to be cut by the Austrian ambassador's wife, who is afraid she will be compromised by introducing a divorced woman at court?

If she dropped even a delicate glimmer that marriage might be a possibility, Metternich certainly evaded it. He loved her more than he had ever loved any woman. He wanted to possess her completely—beautiful, yielding, untroublesome, giving her intelligent counsel and comfort, making no other demands than his devotion—given at the times he could spare. And if Wilhelmine were to bear him a child—or children—he would be overjoyed to welcome that child. Already he spoke to her fondly of "our children," including little Vava Armfelt in that circle of future affection.

In a light flirting exchange he had once written her that he could never marry her while Louis Rohan was alive. But it was more than Louis Rohan and the Catholic laws of marriage that stood in the way of their legal union. If Wilhelmine was heady champagne, Laure and the children were the good fare of everyday life. Never, never in the world could he do without them. He spoke of her frankly and freely to Wilhelmine; he wanted the two women to like one another; why should they not be friends? Laure was nearly the deepest tie of his life—that marriage of *partis* that had set his feet firmly on the ladder of success in the world of international diplomacy. It was the prestige and title of Laure's grandfather that Metternich most coveted: to be the heir of Kaunitz, the State Chancellor of Austria, the Kaunitz of the nineteenth century.

If Wilhelmine pointed out during those London days that her position was an impossible one, if indeed she introduced the question of marriage, it was Metternich who made the first demand. He insisted on a crucial decision from her, a proof of her love: fidelity. "Give me *a pledge of will* in London," he had written her in his last note in Paris. He wanted her to make the decision to break with Alfred once and for all.

But Wilhelmine did not have the strength for that.

On June 24 a shattering letter from Alfred reached her in London. He had returned to Vienna from his mission in Italy, burning up the roads from Turin in his eagerness to see her and to share with her the joy of the victory festivals that accompanied Emperor Franz's return to his capital. But in Vienna he had found her gone in a cloud of rumor and gossip—tales of a liaison with Lamb, more tales of a compromising journey to meet Metternich in Paris and another journey with him to London. Furiously Alfred wrote, accusing her of infidelity, of fearing to meet him—Alfred—face to face, even of avoiding the victory fetes because she had not really wanted victory. He announced that he would not see her again, that their relationship was at an end.

She replied at once, defending herself. She had no fear of gossip, "such as I know people are amused to make about me." Her conduct merited no reproach. Though she had had no letter from him in more than a month, she had counted on seeing him in Paris—it was one of her reasons for going there. How could she know he would be sent to Turin? "The witness of my own conscience sustains me in this moment—and will help me perhaps pass over the painful impression produced by injustice and ingratitude combined in the one person who perhaps less than any other should cause me such grief."[34] Her heart breaks at the thought of losing him. She will be in Vienna in fifteen days.

No, she cannot give Metternich an answer, a pledge of will—not yet, not until she has seen Alfred.

On June 20 an icily formal third-person note from Countess Merveldt informed Madame la Duchesse de Sagan that the Queen would hold no more Drawing Rooms until after the sovereigns' departure. She sent it at once to Metternich:

> How can one go to dine at the Prince Regent's, never having been presented to him and not knowing a single living soul there. It's up to you to arrange all that or I shall believe you don't love me at all, and I on my side shall love you a great deal less.[35]

Metternich intervened with Madame Merveldt. Wilhelmine curtsied to the old Queen of England at the last Drawing Room of the season. The

Prince Regent was enchanted with her, and she was at once invited to all the final palace parties for the sovereigns.

4

The Tsar announced quite suddenly in the last days of the London sojourn that he would not go directly to Vienna for the long-awaited Congress, as everyone was expecting, but would return to Russia first. He had been away from his homeland too long—he had pressing business to attend to.

For a time there was anxiety over whether the planned Congress would ever meet, but the Tsar gave his word that he would be in Vienna in September. Writing Laure of the new postponement of the Congress until October 1, Metternich instructed her, "If anyone speaks to you of the delay in the arrival of the sovereigns in Vienna, leave no doubt that they will come *for sure* before September 27."[36]

The last act of the comedy was played out in Portsmouth, whither the sovereigns had been invited to view naval maneuvers. It was a reprise of Act I. Again crowds waited along the entire route through Surrey and Hampshire to see the sovereigns. Again the Tsar, the King of Prussia and Grand Duchess Catherine journeyed by back roads, arriving in Portsmouth unobserved and too late in the evening to attend the splendid banquet that was given in their honor at Government House. Small wonder that the visit closed as it had opened, in an atmosphere of chill.

Catherine, however, managed to enliven the Portsmouth visit by falling passionately in love with Crown Prince Wilhelm of Württemberg, whom she had met a few days before at a garden party in Chiswick. The affair had one small drawback, though not enough to disengage Catherine's impetuous and imperious affections: the prince was already married to the Bavarian Princess Charlotte, and both families were Catholic.

Metternich had intended to view the fleet and had been invited to ride to Portsmouth and back with the Prince Regent. In the end, however, he declined, and stayed in London to finish the most pressing of his business.

As his visit in London drew near an end, his letters to Laure breathed a deep and heartfelt homesickness.

> I can't tell you the kind of joy I shall feel to find myself with you again. There is still a long road for me to travel—it will seem doubly long after thirteen months of absence. May God keep you till we see one another again.[37]

He was sending Pilat on ahead to Vienna to announce his arrival very soon and to bring them gifts. The portfolio in Russian leather was for Marie, the book bound in red for Victor. For the whole family's pleasure there would be two new English carriages, a landaulet and a *birotiti* that rides just four.

More than anything else he was bone-weary. He had not slept "four hours consecutively since my arrival here. . . . *Too much is too much.* I shall be so happy not to leave you any more, my dears, that this thought alone sustains me." He was glad for the postponement of the Congress. It meant he would "have the good fortune to rest for a few weeks." If there was no room for him in the apartment Laure had rented in Baden, she was to see Count Wrbna and arrange a *Hofquartier*—quarters the Emperor had at his disposal for his staff.

Laure too was at the end of her rope. "According to your plans you are leaving London perhaps at this very hour. I desire it with all my heart, for I am absolutely at the end of my patience, and I find at least as much as you that too much is too much."[38]

On a fine moon-bright night Metternich, with Humboldt, Binder and Wenzel Liechtenstein for company, sailed back to Boulogne. It was a night without wind and a sea of glass so that the crossing took eighteen hours, and Wilhelmine, who had left London before him, waited all day at her mother's house in Paris. When he came next day for dinner, Wilhelmine had gone on an excursion to Malmaison.

There were reproaches and apologies and counter-reproaches ("I don't know whether to write you or not, not knowing whether you are good or bad to me") but at the very end of the second brief stay in Paris, they had finally good quiet hours to talk together without quarrel or misunderstanding. Perhaps Alfred's angry letter had finally forced her to come to terms with her feelings.

During their last untroubled hours together, Metternich reminded her of the decision she must make, a definite and final choice, between him and all others. He for his part promised fidelity, demanded hers in return. He would not see her again, he said, until she had made a final choice.

He left Paris July 7, having talked with Talleyrand and King Louis XVIII again, to return to Vienna by way of Karlsruhe, where he was to meet the Tsar, and Stuttgart and Munich, to see the ministers of Württemberg and Bavaria. Wilhelmine had planned to leave Paris with her mother and sisters—who were traveling to the Bohemian spas again—on the following Sunday, but the portrait for which she was sitting to Napoleon's court painter Gérard, was not quite finished.

> Seeing you for once reasonably satisfied did me a great deal of good. I hope to find you again just the same and that you will continue to be. . . . Adieu, dear Clemens, I count for always on your friendship, your attachment, and your interest. . . .[39]

She said nothing of his passion.

Metternich traveled home by swift stages, dozing through the night in his traveling carriage, so as not to waste time.

Stopping in Munich he wrote her a tender letter, which she found a day or two later when she crossed the customs barrier at Lambach:

> It is a very long time since I talked to you and I am too full of you to be able to get along without you easily.

My dear, I have certainly felt during this journey what some good hours are worth. I left you happy with yourself and I was therefore happy with myself. *Thank you for the last 36 hours of our stay in Paris.* They gave me new strength, they proved to me that a few hours can make one forget whole epochs of privation and of suffering—I did not need them to know how much I love you! You, you do know how much, I need not repeat it to you.

The hours that will decide my future relations with you and therefore my whole future are about to sound. I await them with confidence. You have restored that confidence, and I am never halfway about anything. Don't forget, my dear, what I told you and what you agreed to. It is up to you to tell me: *mon ami*, I am yours. I can do nothing more about it. My role is finished. My fate is no longer in my hands. I do not regret having placed it in yours.[40]

He would neither come to her in Vienna, nor write to her, nor would he make any effort to see her. When she had made up her mind, she must come to *him*. That would be the sign of her decision, of her complete surrender.

—————◆—————

XIX

INTERLUDE IN BADEN

*I swear to you my faculties have fallen like those of a
courier at the end of the road. I am dropping from fatigue.*
        —METTERNICH TO LAURE

It was a joyful reunion Metternich had with his family when his carriage
drove up to their door in Baden on Tuesday, July 19. There were kisses and
hugs and tears of joy—at least Marie and her father wept; her mother, as
Marie said, shed tears only at the theater. He was delighted to see the children well grown and blooming with health, even Marie, whose long illness
that spring had shadowed all his pleasure.

He had brought presents for everyone—a ball gown from Paris for Marie,
a gold watch for Victor, who had placed first—*primae eminenter*—in all his
examinations at the Schotten Gymnasium. And the stories *cher Papa* had
to tell, an endless fund of tales of all the people and the happenings during
"the long, the terrible absence" of thirteen months. "I shall have to give you
a summary of more than a year," he had written Laure. "This year will
appear to me more and more as the most memorable year of my life."[1]

He had missed his share in the victory celebrations of June, but his
friends tried to make up for it, and Count Palffy arranged a festive serenade
in the square outside the Chancellery the night after Metternich's return.
Everyone who was anyone from the Emperor on down came to hear the
cantata which Count Kinsky had especially composed for the occasion. It
sang extravagant praise to

> this statesman who, untroubled by the cry of the impatient masses, with
> wise care long delayed the decision of taking arms. . . . Hail to thee,
> great prince . . . whose prudence guided the royal hand, until it led us
> to deliverance, us and our brothers.[2]

The day following the serenade, Thursday, was Victor's name day, and all the Metternichs' friends helped celebrate the happy occasion and Clemens' return. It was an exciting week.

Every day packages arrived from Paris and London—gifts for Laure and the children, beautiful things for their apartments in town and for their garden villa.

One day a gift came that surprised even Metternich and completely enchanted the children. In London an Austrian sea captain had come to see the Foreign Minister to ask a favor of some kind. In gratitude he sent Metternich his own parrot.

> I've been looking for one for a long time, and I don't know how this good man was able to guess one of my secret thoughts. They claim my bird speaks English and Spanish. The only word I've heard him say thus far is "Floret"—which is not a great deal in two languages.[3]

Before the summer was over everyone in Baden had made acquaintance with the Metternich parrot that hung in their open window and chattered incoherently but in the friendliest fashion to every passerby.

In the charming little spa of Baden in the Vienna Woods, just two hours' pleasant carriage ride out of the city, Metternich had hoped to enjoy lazy days and weeks of complete rest after the terrible strain of the year before. "I think you will find me much aged," he had written Laure. "I need six months' rest as I need my daily bread!"[4] But in the Chancellery in Vienna his desk was heaped with unfinished business—dispatches from envoys all over Europe, notes and reports and letters to be answered. Though foreign affairs were his department, nevertheless Austria's domestic problems intruded into his sphere as well—especially the thorny question of money. Work—work—endless work. At least part of every week he would have to spend in town in the Chancellery.

It would certainly not be a summer of real leisure—not yet.

On the days he worked in town, he would often drive out from the Chancellery through the Kärntner Gate to their country house on the Rennweg to see how work was progressing on the redecorating that was being done in preparation for the Congress festivals. It was almost the most peaceful place on earth that summer. Late roses bloomed, the fountains splashed, the sound of workmen's voices and hammers echoed across the gardens, the graveled paths white in the hot July sun. He would wander through the empty rooms, his little study that looked out on the gardens newly painted a sunny yellow, the library as he had ordered it with bookshelves to the ceiling, his bedroom a cool blue, all summer freshness, the enormous new ballroom wing, "as big as the whole house," Marie described it, and the long light gallery where sculpture was to be placed. Utter summer solitude.

He did not see Wilhelmine.

Gentz had swallowed his pique at Metternich's neglect of him all spring, and had driven up the Danube as far as Melk to meet the Foreign Minister on his return—more than anything else, of course, to be first to sieve out all the news there was to hear. He had had the glory and the pleasure of climbing into Metternich's traveling carriage and riding the two days with him back to Vienna, of hearing the latest political news, of the last interview with Talleyrand in Paris and with the Tsar at Karlsruhe, and of receiving all Metternich's confidences on Wilhelmine. In return he discussed her attachment to Lamb; it was clearly his duty to keep Metternich informed. Gentz was struck by the intensity and the anguish of Metternich's feelings; he had thought surely by now Metternich would have seen the light—he would have broken with Wilhelmine—the worst would be over.

Wilhelmine arrived back in Vienna on July 22, the Friday after Metternich's return. One of her terrible migraines had attacked her during the journey, and she had had to spend two days in bed with a fever in Wels.

She was astonished to find no sign of Metternich awaiting her in the Palais Palm. She had grown so accustomed to his attentions that she was quite taken aback. There was no note, there were no flowers, none of the little *bêtises* with which he enjoyed surprising her.

He would surely call on Saturday morning around eleven—"our hour," he called it, when they would drink chocolate together, and he would tell her the latest news and his program for the day.

Metternich did not come on Saturday, nor did he send his valet or footman with a word of welcome. It was quite vexing—and somehow ominous.

In her trunks she had brought back numerous purchases of Clemens' from Paris. On that Saturday she sent a large box of dresses and bonnets to the Chancellery apartments with a note:

> Here are the things that belong to you, dear Clemens, and that you confided to me. The first three pieces—that is, those on top, are the ones you intended for Marie. Laure's dress is not there, since I feared they would be severe at the customs and I did not have the courage to take anything brand new along with me. I put it with other things in a package that I took the liberty of addressing to you. If—as it appears—the few words [I wrote you] from Paris as well as those from Wels remain without reply, I dare not complain, having often been less than prompt myself, but what I might perhaps complain about is your absolute lack of desire to see me—I would take that on myself as my fault if I did not have to tell myself that I have absolutely no *right*—I am in a position that is not easy or agreeable.[5]

She closed her note with a cool *"Bon jour."* It was well to remind him how difficult and ambiguous her position really was. The note remained without reply.

Wilhelmine was truly astonished and not a little annoyed. Dear Clemens, was he going to prove stubborn now after all? Was he really going to mean what he said—to insist that *she* accept *his* bases, as if she were the cabinet minister of a defeated country?

She was surprised to find how much she missed him, that it grieved and pained her not to find him waiting as she had expected him to be.

Vienna was in the summer doldrums. Her mother and her sisters had parted with her halfway on the journey home, going to Bohemia. When she sent a lackey around to Alfred's house, she learned that he too had gone, to Tachau, to his Bohemian estates. Vienna was utterly deserted. Even the house of her unfriendly neighbor, Princess Bagration, stood empty. There was hardly a soul in the streets. Not a carriage crossed the courtyard of the Palais Palm, hardly a horse's hoof clattered over the hot afternoon pavement of Schenkenstrasse. Everyone, she learned from her servants, was out of the city, most in Baden.

Very well, then, she would go to Baden. She intended to spend the month of August there and she must look for a house to lease. She drove to Baden late Saturday, and on Sunday morning—a gloomy, rainy Sunday, to depress one's spirits if they were not already depressed—Gentz appeared at her lodging just as she was about to pay a call on her English friend Madame Cadogan, and offered his carriage. Climbing in after her Gentz began at once to berate her on her behavior toward Metternich. Did she not know she was adding to the griefs of a man who already bore the welfare of all Europe on his shoulders? He lectured her on the gratitude she should feel to be chosen the friend of a man in such a position.

Never had Wilhelmine been more angry. His gratuitous advice was something she did not need, busybody that he was! She had learned from Metternich in Paris that Gentz had been the source of the reports of her affair with Lamb. Furiously she accused him of talebearing, of slander, ordered the carriage to halt, descended without saying good-by. Late that day she drove back to Vienna in the pouring rain. She had at least learned that Clemens was in Vienna and would not return to Baden until Tuesday. She had her own arsenal of weapons.

Gentz, brooding over the frailties of womankind in general and of this damned woman in particular (how could His Serene Highness have allowed himself to be so totally ensnared in her power?), went back to his Baden apartment and wrote "a very energetic letter . . . on her conduct toward Metternich and me." He sent one of his servants to deliver the letter personally to the duchess wherever he had to go to find her.[6]

To Metternich in Vienna he addressed a yet longer letter:

> W. has begun a separate war with me, in which I must as best I can protect my skin. I do not know for sure if she has returned this evening to Vienna. In any case she will find a letter from me there, which she perhaps scarcely expected. From this little episode in the story of her utter faithlessness without parallel, I am duty-bound to divulge all the detailed circumstances to Your Serene Highness.[7]

His conversation with W., he wrote, had left the saddest impression on him. He cannot put down in writing all the details, but he is certain the Prince's own observations and conclusions "cannot diverge far from my own." He will await Metternich's return to Baden "to pour out his heart" to him.

In his diary Gentz recorded of those summer days in Baden:

> With the arrival of the Duchess of Sagan our stay became very stormy. . . . I had to pay dearly for the honor of being the confidant and intermediary of Metternich in his relationship.[8]

Clumsy, blundering Gentz: he was hardly the diplomat for delicate missions of love and of confidence.

On Monday, July 25, the sun shone on a cool, golden, rainwashed world. "Superb weather," Gentz commented briefly in his diary.

That day—the day after her futile excursion to Baden—Wilhelmine rose earlier than was her custom, wrote a tiny note, folded it into the shape of a cap and sealed it with her Courland ring:

> As you insist, dear Clemens, that it must be I who ask to see you, please name the hour at which I may find you at home.[9]

To Metternich, whose inner life was composed of anniversaries of days that had precious secret meanings, that date, July 25, was one of the most significant in the calendar of his love affair with Wilhelmine. "The first day of my life," he called it later.

Though they had parted in Paris only eighteen days before, already their separation seemed like an agonizing chain of days and weeks. After the first joyful pleasure of his homecoming there had come swiftly a sense of letdown, of black depression, as if the whole of his life had suddenly been emptied of meaning at the very moment when he should be enjoying its pleasure to the full.

He loved her far too deeply to abandon hope of possessing her. She had been his guiding star through the terrible crises of the past year; she had been his blessed fortune. His dream of her had carried him to the pinnacle of success—he might even say—of greatness.

It had required all his strength of will to stay away from her, to send no footman to inquire for the moment of her return, to leave her letters without reply—though in his mind he had written long answers through every waking hour. Brooding at his desk in the Chancellery, he had been sick for the sound of her voice, for a glimpse of her as he had last seen her in Paris, radiant and loving, bidding him good-by.

She came to him at once that Monday morning. That day and that night they spent together—perhaps in Metternich's apartment in the Chancellery, perhaps in the Palais Palm. Perhaps they drove out to the garden villa on the Rennweg, to make love in the echoing rooms and walk together in the sun-drenched gardens, among the cool clipped hedges and spraying fountains.

Wilhelmine gave him that day the promise he wanted. Yes, she loved him, she would belong to him alone. For six months, he said, let us see. He for his part promised to leave off tormenting her, fretting her with imagined wounds, and with fits of jealousy. He promised to trust her.

Next day he bade her good-by at the Palais Palm to return first to the Chancellery, then drive out to Baden. Wilhelmine sat down at once and put her promise in writing. Dashing off the note on a torn half-sheet of note-paper, as if she would set down her thoughts at once while the memory of their blissful hours was still fresh with her, she sent it off with a footman to catch Metternich as he stepped into his carriage for Baden.

> Yes, *mon ami*, my device will be surrender and complete confidence in the best of men—and I know in advance that I shall find happiness and peace of mind along this road— Already I feel a great sense of peace in wandering no longer on that sea of self-doubt, and in seeing your happiness, dear Clemens—I have so often been torn in my soul at mak-ing you unhappy— Now I shall begin to work seriously on my physical and moral well-being— I am going to rest my soul and body, and then begin a new life, with the absolute certainty of happiness— Believe me, it is more necessary for me than you think—in all the time that is before us there will also be time to talk little by little of that—you will see that I am, or better said, have been, crazy-mad and deeply unhappy, deeply tormented, I think I would have died of it before long—
>
>   Here is Laure's dress—*Bon voyage, mon Ami*, don't be too kind at Neustadt—*Au revoir bientôt*—[10]

Reading her letter in the carriage back to Baden, Metternich felt a joy he had never before known. Everything, everything he had most wanted in the world was now his. Fame, power and this most desirable of women. She would belong to him as he wanted her to belong; the terrible rending jealousies and griefs of the past year were over. He had her word.

Everything was falling into place for him. He could begin to savor the fruit of his important political victories—and set his mind on planning the next ones.

Did he sense that Wilhelmine's note was, for all its sincerity, not a love letter? Perhaps it did not matter; her promise was enough. He was certain he could win her love.

In Baden Metternich dropped in on Gentz, listened with amusement to Gentz's tale of his encounter with Wilhelmine on the previous Sunday. When Gentz waved in his face the "truly insolent" letter he had got from her in re-ply to the "very energetic" letter he had written her, Metternich laughed at him, and then soothed his ruffled feeling by inviting him for dinner. Floret came to dine too; they made a fine pair—the silent Floret and garrulous Gentz.

Later that evening in great good humor Metternich went along with Gentz to Princess Bagration's house. He had not seen his former mistress since his return from the campaign; it was not a bad idea to mend a fence here and there. He sat down for an hour to play a hand of *l'hombre* with

Gentz, Madame Feketé and Xavier Fuchs, but his head was in the clouds, he could not concentrate. He gave Floret his hand, walked home early and alone through the lovely moonlit night.

The following day Gentz dined again with the Metternichs *en famille*. Dinner was later than usual, for Metternich had had to drive that morning early to Neustadt to talk with Napoleon's eldest sister, Elisa Bacciochi.[11] Elisa wanted Metternich's permission to come to the Vienna Congress and plead for the restoration to her of her former grand duchy of Tuscany, or if not Tuscany, at the very least, Lucca. Why not? she argued. Her sister Caroline and her husband were still comfortably ensconced in their kingdom of Naples. Metternich replied in vague terms, promised Elisa nothing.

In Baden at dinner he could amuse them with a story of how Elisa's young lover, Lucchesini, had appeared at Metternich's *hôtel* in Paris to ask that Princess Elisa's lingerie, which had been confiscated at Florence, be returned to her "because she has only six chemises."[12]

Metternich returned to town after dinner that day, and during the weekend that followed he spent every moment he could spare with Wilhelmine. It was the last weekend of July, and already the fetes were beginning that would make the following months unforgettable in Vienna and in Europe. There was a general exodus that weekend from Baden into the city, where on Saturday night, July 30, the Empress Maria Ludovica gave a ball in the Hofburg.

Before the ball the Metternichs entertained at a large dinner party in the Chancellery, elegantly redecorated now and graced by the new Empire furniture, the silks and bronzes and bibelots the Foreign Minister had brought from Paris.

"Verbal exchange, passably disagreeable with the duchess [of Sagan] after dinner," Gentz notes tersely in his diary.[13] No doubt Wilhelmine suggested to Gentz that he would do well to stay out of her private life from that moment on.

Gentz with his voluble and indiscreet tongue had been seeing altogether too much of Princess Bagration, of whose excellent cook and generous table he took a bachelor's advantage. Whatever Gentz had relayed to Princess Bagration that week in Baden—and she was still insanely jealous of Wilhelmine—the gossip had been relayed back to Wilhelmine.

On Saturday night, the Empress's ball and the Metternichs' dinner party; on Sunday night an exhibition of fireworks—and on Monday night everyone in Viennese society appeared at the Theater auf der Wieden to see the opening performance of the Paris ballet, the dancers Metternich had himself arranged to perform for the Vienna festivals.

Gentz did not go to the ballet, but late in the evening, after the performance was over, Countess Fuchs suddenly appeared on his doorstep, begging him to go at once to Princess Bagration's apartment in the Palais Palm, where Metternich had announced he was calling. There was no party that night at Bagration's and Metternich had found her quite alone. Gentz's brief entry in his diary gives us no clue to Countess Fuchs's concern. Certainly Gentz's indiscreet babbling had involved both Metternich and Wilhelmine.

Did Metternich go to Princess Bagration to tell her the truth at last, break off their relationship? Probably not, for frankness was not Metternich's way of dealing in diplomacy or in love. Carrying a name greatly honored in Russia and distantly related to the Tsar, Katharine Bagration was bound to play an influential role, socially and politically, in the coming Congress. He needed her continuing friendship at this crucial political juncture.

> I got there at 11 o'clock [Gentz tells us]. I spent two hours with her and Metternich in a remarkable (political) conversation which I shall not very soon forget. Afterwards I walked with Metternich through the streets, busy with a quite different affair, until 3 o'clock in the morning sounded.[14]

The "quite different affair" was certainly Wilhelmine. And Gentz was scarcely the confidant to quiet troubled waters. He could not bear to refrain from repeating any choice morsel of gossip.

A few days later Wilhelmine could take amusing revenge on Gentz. She had managed to lease a spacious double apartment in the Maison Eichelberg in Baden, the same house the Metternichs had tried to buy the preceding winter. She moved in with servants, cook and the invaluable Countess Trogoff on Thursday of that week, August 4. That very day, before her trunks were even unpacked, she gave a spur-of-the-moment dinner party. Having run into Gentz at the Metternichs' house in the morning, she invited him to come along.

Among the guests at her dinner table that day was a certain Count Coronini, a comparative newcomer to Baden. Gentz, as was his wont, gossiped rather freely, alluding in unflattering terms to the morals of a pair of sisters, "the Demoiselles H.," who lived in the neighborhood. After Count Coronini's departure Gentz learned to his discomfiture that the count was engaged to one of the demoiselles whose virtue Gentz had called into question.

Later that evening, while Gentz played his usual card game at Madame Feketé's, a messenger delivered a note from Count Coronini challenging him to a duel the following morning. Poor Gentz, who barely knew one end of a pistol from the other, was so shaken he could not concentrate on his cards, his game was spoiled and he lost heavily. He went home early to toss and turn in a sweat of terror and despair.

At six in the morning Coronini's messenger returned. Was it to be swords or pistols? The count awaited a reply. Frantically Gentz sent a servant off to fetch his friend Count Schulenburg, who had been at the dinner party. What in God's name was he to do? Eventually Schulenburg himself appeared, took pity on Gentz and confessed the duel was all a joke Wilhelmine and her dinner guests had cooked up.[15]

Life in Baden took its leisurely course that summer. One got up early and examined the skies for signs of rain ("I think like Laure that we shall have a beautiful day, dear Clemens, and will be at the Fuchs' at the appointed hour," Wilhelmine writes.) One breakfasted alfresco, walked in the sunshine on the promenade, bathed and sipped the waters to heal one's rheumatic ailments; nearly everyone in that day suffered a rheumatic pain somewhere. In Baden, unlike most spas, ladies and gentlemen could bathe together, encased in voluminous bathing shirts, neck-deep in the warm sulphurous pools. Afterward they retired by sex into separate rooms to soak in steaming tubs.

Life was both more casual and more intimate than in Vienna. There were long walks in the country, into the beautiful Helena Valley, and to climb the comfortable little mountains thereabouts. There were excursions in open carriages to admire more distant mountain landscapes and ruined castles. There were dinner parties in someone's garden, with musicians playing behind the shrubbery, and in the evening ladies had their soirees just as in Vienna, where one dropped by to drink tea, play a hand of cards, often for perilously high stakes. At the dances at the Casino that summer there was no dearth of young army officers for dance partners.

The Metternich house that summer was always filled with people—old close friends like Clemens' pretty cousin, Flora Wrbna, of whom he was very fond; Wenzel Liechtenstein; Philipp von Neumann, one of Metternich's most trusted aides—rumor had it that Neumann was old Prince Metternich's natural son and therefore Clemens' half brother—Princess Jean Liechtenstein; and old Prince Esterházy, Paul's father, and dozens of other visitors who dropped by to pay their respects and to hear Metternich's tales of the campaign.

Nearly every day Metternich and Wilhelmine met somewhere. Sometimes he saw her on the promenade with Hannchen, on her way to the baths, where, more energetic than most of the ladies, Wilhelmine was learning to swim. Or they met on an excursion, such as the one to Count Dietrichstein's castle of Morkenstein, where a long lucullan dinner was served to the guests in the garden. Another day Wilhelmine sent Hannchen into the city to bring her little girls, Emilie, Marie and Clara, out for a holiday in Baden and a family dinner party. "I count on your children," she wrote to Clemens. "Mine have already come and I promised them this party. . . . We shall be only 18 at dinner."[16]

When Metternich went in to town to work in the Chancellery, two or three days of every week, Wilhelmine often came into town too. Whether in Baden or in Vienna he tried to see her each day in the late morning, when, fresh from sleep, she drank her breakfast chocolate, her hair loose, wearing the soft morning dress he had bought her in Dijon. "Wear it often so that you will become accustomed to it," he had written. Eleven o'clock was consecrated in their private vocabulary as "our hour."

It was their time for talking politics as well as making love. She was his sounding board; as he talked to her his ideas clarified, and she reinforced his confidence. Often he brought official letters and dispatches to show her, and sometimes she suggested changing a word or a phrase. She would, he told her, be his secret adviser.

Both were avid readers; often he sent her a beautifully bound book for her collection, or one on which he wanted her opinion. Sometimes, meeting in Vienna, they unpacked together a newly arrived purchase from Paris or London, and she helped him put it in place in the Chancellery apartments. He could rely on her fastidious taste. Once in Baden that summer he sent his people to scour the countryside for some rare delicacy—he does not name it—for which she had expressed a wish. Was it a kind of field lettuce, or asparagus or wild strawberries? "Here is what I have been able to get," he writes her. "I send it to you and pray Heaven it does not disappoint your pleasure."[17]

Where was Laure in all this? There is no clue, no letter, no note, to reveal her feelings. She is simply there, at the luncheon and dinner parties cited in Gentz's diary, playing the wife of the great man. She and Wilhelmine exchanged friendly invitations. Laure, so shrewd, so perceptive, must have divined in a hundred ways what was her husband's relationship to Wilhelmine, but she gave no sign. She was happy to have him back, after the long months of absence, his old cheerful, affectionate and amusing self. She was delighted to have their household buzz again with excitement and activity. Besides, when one has no choice, sharing too must do.

That summer day succeeded day of perfect golden weather. Yet from time to time sudden thunderstorms deluged a picnic party or a country walk or an outdoor dance in the casino.

And sometimes lightning flashed momentarily through their relationship as it did through the Baden skies. It was difficult for Metternich not to be jealous when he watched Wilhelmine at a soiree, surrounded by admiring men, when she forgot to write him a promised note, or when he went to call at her house late in the evening, and a servant told him Madame la Duchesse had already retired. Only a few days after the joyous reconciliation on July 25 Wilhelmine wrote him from Vienna that she hoped to see him in Baden

> in a good humor for you know perfectly well I don't at all like your sulky look. After you left me my bad humor seized me again, and I was tempted twenty times to go away to Ratiborzitz. It seems as if only there can I find peace.[18]

Most of the summer their relationship was tender and smooth; the storms Gentz mentions in his diary were between him and Wilhelmine.

However much Metternich longed for a total holiday that summer, for lazy tranquil days without conferences or papers to peruse or petitioners to see, a complete rest in which to compose his mind and soul, it was not to be—not then on the eve of a great congress.

On August 10 Cariati and Rocca Romana, envoys of the Murats in Naples—last of the Bonaparte family in power—arrived in Baden and dined with Metternich that night. The three at once launched into a discussion of how to preserve their throne for the Murats, whom both the English Government and the French King wanted to turn out of their kingdom. A few days later Castlereagh en route to Vienna would stop long enough in Paris to affirm with Talleyrand their common aim of ousting Napoleon's sister and brother-in-law in favor of the former Bourbon ruler. But Metternich had bound Austria by treaty to support the Murats at a crucial point the previous winter when the Murats' support was sorely needed in the battle against Napoleon. He was not ready to abandon them in favor of the weak and dissolute Bourbon King Ferdinand even though the latter was uncle-by-marriage to Emperor Franz, and even though his consort, old Queen Caroline, born a Habsburg archduchess, was lobbying vehemently in Vienna for her husband's restoration.

Besides all the political business to which he must give his attention that summer, Metternich had to take charge to a large degree in the planning of the Congress. The logistics and protocol of housing and entertaining so many kings, princes and ambassadors would tax the imperial household to the utmost. When questions arose, the court marshal and everyone else concerned came to Metternich.

Toward mid-August he had to leave the pleasures of Baden for a trip up the Danube to confer with Emperor Franz at Castle Persenbeug, where he was staying.

The journey was doubly painful, he wrote Wilhelmine, "because I am leaving you; and then because I hate traveling and then because I shall have enormously huge work for two days near the Emperor, and then finally as in the first place, because I will be spending 4 days far from *mon amie*.[19]

Before his departure he left a note for Gentz telling him that Wilhelmine had quite forgiven him—that is, Gentz—and was ready to be friends with him again—"which interests me only mildly," Gentz confided somewhat sourly to his diary.[20]

But he did go to call on her in Metternich's absence. She received him in friendly fashion, he wrote, adding one of his sententious Latin quotations, "*sed haeret lateri letalis arundo*"—but still the deadly arrow clings to the brick. He noted that he had found Windischgraetz with the duchess. Alfred was certainly the deadly arrow.[21]

Metternich knew that Windischgraetz was in Baden; he himself had seen him the preceding week. But he did not mention Alfred in his letters; he had promised to trust her, and he meant to keep his promise.

From Persenbeug he wrote her telling her that his soul was still in

Baden. Emperor Franz had inquired whether the Duchess of Sagan would be in Vienna for sure for the Congress festivals. *"I consider her one of the most essential ingredients of the Congress!"* the Emperor told Metternich.

Metternich added, "I would have embraced him if I hadn't feared to make him suspect that such warmth might have a less political motive. . . . We now speak of you only as *She*."[22] Certainly Metternich's liaison with Wilhelmine was no secret, and no doubt the Austrian Emperor hoped the affair would not interfere in his Foreign Minister's conduct of critical international problems.

The Emperor kept him an extra day and night in Persenbeug. Would Wilhelmine please let Hoppé in the Chancellery know whether she would be in Vienna or in Baden the morning of his return?

> If you are in Baden the 17 I shall come to you at the hour you awaken, and so I shall be seeing you *at our hour*. Why is it not already sounding?
> . . . *Adieu, bonne amie.* Au revoir until next Wednesday and loving you the rest of the week and all weeks! Don't forget me *completely*.[23]

She left a tiny note at the Chancellery telling him she would be in Baden the morning of his return. "I have thought about you very often," she reassured him.[24]

In Baden on that Wednesday morning he embraced her after the five days' absence, and he could recount to her all the important political decisions that had been reached during the days in Persenbeug.

In her salon in those August days young men gathered. Alfred was often there and Wenzel Liechtenstein and Fontbrune; so too was Frederick Lamb, sometimes other young Englishmen. Metternich tried to restrain his jealousy.

Baden was gossiping, Humboldt wrote his wife, that "three claimants are dividing the kingdom." It may well have been true.

On the very day of Metternich's return from Persenbeug, August 17, 1814, Frederick Lamb wrote a long report in cipher for Castlereagh. The report details the most important—and most confidential—matters engaging Metternich's attention at the moment, including those he had discussed with the Austrian Emperor at Persenbeug in the days just previous.

In the report Castlereagh was enjoined never to mention that the information had been communicated by Lamb, nor to mention it to the Austrian ambassador, Count Merveldt. In conclusion Lamb explained:

> Your Lordship will think this letter strangely put together but the Information such as it is may be depended upon as coming from a source equally certain and Secret and which might be of great use in matters of more Importance.[25]

It is the only report Lamb sent from Vienna that contains any information of value. He could only have obtained it—and that very day—from Wilhelmine.

The chief purpose of Metternich's trip to Persenbeug is at once made clear:

> On the 11 August P. Metternich received a courier from Paris from Louis XVIII himself stating the existence of a Conspiracy to assassinate the Emperor of Austria on the 1st of October. The Conspirators are chiefly Italians who have taken refuge in England where the conspiracy has been organized. Three Persons concerned in it have since been arrested under pretext of having false passports. . . .
> The prime minister [sic] says he has told it to only two persons here.

The two persons Lamb mentions must surely have been—besides the Austrian Emperor himself—Baron Hager, chief of the Austrian police, and Wilhelmine.

The existence of such a plot to murder the Austrian Emperor on the day the Congress of Vienna was to open no doubt explains the extraordinary precautions the Austrian police began to take to enlarge their surveillance, to increase the number of paid informers, to arrest suspicious persons —both in the capital and in the Italian lands they were soon to annex. Lamb adds that two agents have been sent from Vienna—"one to Milan one to England to mix with the Persons engaged to learn further details of the conspiracy."

Besides the assassination plot—a matter of great enough moment in itself to occupy the young English chargé d'affaires, obviously pleased with himself to be sending off important dispatches in cipher—he reported the imminent appointment of Stadion as Minister of Finance before Stadion himself knew of it. "He does not yet know it but is to learn it today by a letter from the Emperor of Austria ordering him at the same time to keep it secret for the present."

Lamb reported furthermore that Metternich "is negotiating with the wife of Murat to induce her husband to obtain some indemnity by resigning his Kingdom rather than risk the being turned out." Moreover, it appeared almost certain that Grand Duchess Catherine would marry the Crown Prince of Württemberg, since letters "of the most passionate love" had been intercepted and were in Metternich's hands.

A less important matter, but one that would satisfy Castlereagh's curiosity, was the identity of a certain Wifeman (probably Lamb's error for Willaman), about whom Castlereagh had inquired of Aberdeen the previous October. It is, explained Lamb, "the secret address of the prime minister himself." And indeed, Captain Willaman was the secret cover name Metternich had given Wilhelmine the previous autumn.

Lamb's cipher report, with its bagful of prizes, missed Castlereagh, who left London for the Continent on August 16; no doubt the message caught up with him somewhere along his route, perhaps before he reached Paris to discuss with Talleyrand and Louis XVIII their common aim of ousting the Murats from Naples.

Why had Wilhelmine betrayed Metternich's confidence and given all these precious details to Lamb? There is no evidence that she had done so before; his previous reports were bland to the point of boredom. Perhaps, with her strong pro-English bias and her certainty that Metternich and Castlereagh were working hand in hand—as Metternich himself had written and told her repeatedly—she did not consider it betrayal, but merely a passing-along of useful information. Perhaps too, being a woman engrossed in politics and denied any role, Wilhelmine could not help making use of such power as she had at her command.

As August wore on, Baden swarmed like an ant heap. Congress visitors were already arriving; one could not find for love or money even "a tiny hole" to rent, according to Humboldt, who arrived from a visit with his family in Switzerland to confer on the future of Germany before the Congress opened. He had been told he would find instructions from Berlin awaiting him in Vienna, but the days passed, no instructions came, and there were no conferences. "Society is more blank, empty, monotonous than ever," he complained. He wanted to steer clear of the rivalry of the two northern ladies—the Duchess of Sagan and Princess Bagration—both of whom had invited him to stay with them. He had chosen to move into Princess Bagration's house, although he was being careful not to neglect the duchess. "Gentz has not had the same wisdom. He sailed far out on the stormy sea and has not entirely but very nearly alienated the one."

As to Metternich, Humboldt complained, he "is in Baden and so removed from affairs, lives so much in society, that you can imagine it is nearly impossible to arrive at an orderly discussion."[26] It was not quite true, especially not on August 14, when Humboldt's letter was written, for on that day Metternich was in Persenbeug working very hard indeed. When he returned he had not only the question of Germany to discuss but an interminable tangle of other complex problems demanding resolution.

Among them were Austria's finances—and the burning question of the coming Congress: the fate of Poland.

Just after his return from Persenbeug Metternich dispatched General Koller to St. Petersburg to sound out the Tsar's intentions on Poland— "whether, if he still persists in the idea, he plans to effect it through secret machinations, or whether he is willing to present it through the Congress."[27]

Koller's interview with the Tsar in early September did not foreshadow smooth sailing for the Congress.

"Are you going to behave yourselves at the coming Congress?" the Tsar demanded of Koller. "You [Austrians] are not going to make any stupid proposals there?"

Koller replied that Austria intended to behave very well.

"Ah yes," the Tsar went on, "as far as your Emperor is concerned, I'm convinced we shall be in agreement at once, but Metternich will treat me in a hostile fashion; it's he who wants to keep everything for Austria and for a few others and will let nothing come to us Russians. He will do us more harm than any Austrian minister ever has. I think he would like to take away from us what we already have."

"Your Majesty's preconceived opinion against Prince Metternich is without basis," Koller objected. But the Tsar, tapping him affectionately on the shoulder, told Koller he was good for nothing since he had gone to Elba and had fallen, on his return, under Metternich's spell.

"In any case," the Tsar concluded, "I am still hopeful that all will go well and that I can come to an understanding with the prince."

At the end of their conversation, when Koller remarked that the Poles did not seem to care for the Russians, the Tsar rejoined, "Nor any more do the Italians love you Austrians. The Venetians are supposed to be saying that they went through purgatory under Napoleon only to find themselves now in hell under Austria."

Koller had also been instructed to find out about Grand Duchess Catherine's marital plans if he could.

From the spa of Franzensbad in Bohemia that summer Catherine had been writing letters "of the most passionate love," as Lamb had described them, to the Prince Royal of Württemberg, giving him advice and encouragement on getting rid of his wife as quickly as possible. The prince had already dispatched his wife, Princess Charlotte, back to the Bavarian royal family—which did little to warm relations between Bavaria and Württemberg. Some of Catherine's letters had been intercepted by the Austrian Secret Police.

To complicate matters further, Archduke Karl, the Austrian Emperor's brother, whose suit Catherine had warmly encouraged, and who was still in love with her, was in Franzensbad to continue his wooing. Having led him to believe he was the favored contender for her heart, Catherine was now finding his presence so uncomfortable that her fainting fits returned the moment he appeared. Countess Nesselrode was shocked by the whole affair and thought the abrupt termination of Archduke Karl's marriage hopes was the crowning blow "to the position we are in with Austria . . . and to give more weight to all the evil rumors going about."[28]

The lovely month of August ended in a series of thunderstorms, followed in early September by hard driving rain and unseasonable cold. The houses in Baden were unheated, everyone was chilled to the bone, an epidemic of feverish grippe was rampant, and a good many Baden visitors packed up and moved back to town. Princess Bagration became ill and moved to her town house in the Palais Palm. Gentz, finding his fingers too stiff with cold to write one day, went to Bagration's, where he found the princess's young friend and companion Aurore de Marassé packing up the last of the mistress's belongings. Aurore stoked up a stove and heated a room for Gentz to work in, and he took Aurore home with him for dinner. Then Gentz too became ill, had to send to Dr. Koreff to prescribe some powders, and had the pleasure of being deluged with visitors.

Metternich had leased a house in Baden through September, and he was determined to make summer last until the month's end. He was still very weary; he knew the weeks ahead would be full and difficult ones. He wanted a few weeks more of sunshine and leisure.

More and more often when he went to see Wilhelmine he found her salon full of visitors, not only in the afternoon and evening, but sometimes in the morning as well. She would dash off a little note to him:

> I have people coming for lunch, dear C., and I know they will encroach on your hour. I shall send a word later on to tell you when I can see you.

Or:

> I very much fear, dear Clemens, that I cannot find a moment in the whole day to see you, unless you prefer to find me in company, for this morning I haven't an instant to myself, then my bath, and here I am back for dinner at 5, this evening I am receiving—*Bon soir*, I have not thought about you any less in all the 24 hours except those when I have slept deeply.

Or:

> Madame Clam comes to breakfast this morning for the last time. I warn you because it will upset *our hour. Bon jour, mon ami*, I love you with all my heart.[29]

Did her affectionate words really reassure him when he found her in a circle of admirers? Though he tried not to importune her with doubts and jealousy, he wished she would no longer see Alfred Windischgraetz, cut herself free, really free of this young man she had once loved so deeply.

But Alfred, meantime, filled with contrition for the cruel letter he had written her in London, pled with her to renew their liaison. No, she would not break her promise to Metternich. When Alfred wrote a tender, pleading letter she replied with one that was intended to sever their affair. She reminded him of the painful history of their love, the impossibility of their building an enduring relationship, and her steadfast resolution to break off.

> You could not love me [she reproached him] when my whole life hung on you, when I tried to banish the truth from myself, when I still preserved the illusion that I could finally win love with love. My life is not strong enough to walk again through such bitter suffering, and that would be my lot if I gave in to you again.

Had he—Alfred—not declared from the beginning that he could never marry her, that theirs was a love without future? During those four years he had often neglected her, more than once for another woman.

> Not for a moment [she continued] did your heart speak loudly enough to overcome the voice of reason. I would have loved you always and would never have thought there could be another existence for me than to live

for you and through you. . . . And now farewell, my Alfred, that you will always be for I have bought it dearly. My tears hinder me from writing— You must guess at my scrawl. Farewell—and be always good to me.[30]

She would prove to Clemens that she could shut that door on her past, that she did have willpower and that she was capable of steering her own life. As if to bolster that fragile will, she had a note from Metternich inviting her on an outing and reminding her to bring the letters that pertained to Gustava Armfelt's custody.

She did not join the outing; the day after she had written Alfred she was ill with one of her incapacitating migraines, but she sent the letters off to him that day:

Here, dear Clemens, are the letters in question. . . . God grant that this affair move forward—I shall have no moment of peace before it is finished.[31]

General Koller, returning from his mission to Russia during that first week in September, had brought news of Armfelt's death in St. Petersburg on August 19. During the last weeks of Armfelt's life, the Tsar had visited the sick man often, talking with him about the future of Finland and of Europe; no doubt too the Tsar had discussed with Armfelt the delicate matter of the child, informing him of the new efforts Wilhelmine was making through Metternich to regain custody of Gustava. Armfelt's wife and the girl herself had come to St. Petersburg to be with the dying man, and the Tsar had talked with fourteen-year-old Vava.

With the natural father dead, Metternich told Wilhelmine, her chances of regaining her child were immensely enhanced. He would move on the matter at once, he promised.

A few days later, on Thursday, September 15, when Metternich drove from Baden to Vienna to begin the business of the Congress, he left her a kind of farewell letter—farewell to an era in their lives. With his acute sensitivities to time and place, to the inner meaning of time-related events, he felt an anxious prescience that the departure from Baden might bring a change in their relationship. Despite Gentz's description of the summer as a stormy one, and despite the clouds that had darkened their relationship from time to time, the Baden weeks had been on the whole serene and happy. It would soon be two months, he reminded her, since "the first day of my life," that golden day when she had given him her promise.

It is with a very heavy heart, my dear, that I think of the possibility of leaving Baden.

The two months' sojourn here has decided the destiny of my life. Inseparable from yours I shall share joy and sorrow with my love; I have vexed and tormented you but my heart has never wronged you; I have had moments of happiness—they came to me from you.[32]

Once more, like a lawyer summoning the arguments in his brief, Metternich argued the case for himself. He had given her proof of an attachment and a confidence without limit, of a *soberness* of sentiment—he underlined the word—without equal. He believed in her promises; she belonged to him "with the greatest strength of your being—*by your will.*"

> In giving me back to life, you have given me back the strength I had lost; I shall no longer use it except for your peace and happiness. I had much need of this return of strength in one of the most difficult moments of my life. My head, my dear, is filled to the brim. I am like the general who is disposing his army and his terrain for a decisive battle. My love will not abandon me at this moment.

XX

—◆—

EUROPE COMES TO A CONGRESS

When I got to Vienna yesterday I found all Europe as-
sembled in my antechamber.
—METTERNICH TO LAURE, SEPTEMBER 19, 1814

1

The weather had turned fair again by mid-September, and fair it would remain during the whole of that memorable autumn of 1814, sunny, mild and sweet as the grapes that ripened on the terraced hillsides outside the city of Vienna. As late as December people went walking on the walls as if it were midsummer, and in the gardens of Schönbrunn the buds began to push forth unseasonably on the rosebushes.

When Metternich collected his papers and moved back to the city from Baden on Sunday, September 18, he found workmen hastily putting finishing touches on the Chancellery rooms. Overnight Vienna had changed from the dozing, half-empty town of summer to a city thronged with traveling carriages and bustling crowds, and everywhere an air of excitement and festival.

Important visitors had already arrived for the preliminary meetings. Metternich had hoped to hold those meetings in Baden so that he could enjoy a last few days of sunshine. But, as he wrote Laure, "Madame Nesselrode is pregnant; she is afraid of having a miscarriage," so the negotiators were to stay in Vienna. He had been with Castlereagh when stout Lady Castlereagh burst in crying, "*Mon Dieu*—what a fine city! What shops! We almost broke our necks looking."

"Note," Metternich wrote Laure, "that Milady had only crossed Mariahilferstrasse and Kohlmarkt to descend at the Auge Gottes. . . . It does not take much sometimes to please weak mortals!"[1]

That first busy crowded Sunday would be a foretaste of Metternich's life for the next week and months. His calendar was full, his waiting room crowded with people—among them Chancellor Hardenberg, newly created a prince, General Wrede, a delegation of knights of the Order of Malta and a delegation of senators from the German cities, together with a miscellaneous assortment of petitioners that included, he wrote Wilhelmine that night,

> 3 old ladies and one young and pretty one who had come to offer me what either is not worth a sou or what all the treasures of the world could not pay for, saying she was in a fearful hurry to get a passport so she could rejoin her *Maman* in Paris.

He had sent the beauty and her treasure "to the devil," put off the deputies, and "talked with the Chancellor *in your sense* and having your instructions in mind." As to what Wilhelmine's instructions on Prussia business were, there is not a clue.[2]

On his way out of Baden that morning he had spent an hour or two with her, an unusually blissful meeting. "I could have sweeter moments than this happy morning—I shall never have more blessed ones." She had, he wrote, "lifted the last obstacle" between them, apparently reaffirmed the promise she had given him in July.[3]

Although the Alfred affair was ostensibly at an end, Alfred had continued to importune her, to haunt her salon in Baden, to Metternich's intense distress. Now she had finally agreed to put an end to the meetings with Alfred. "My dear, you have given me back my life," Metternich wrote her. "You gave me a word that consoles me for all my past troubles."[4]

That Sunday evening Castlereagh, Nesselrode and Hardenberg met for several hours with Metternich in his study in the Chancellery, laying plans for the Congress. The meeting had apparently gone smoothly, for Metternich reported to Wilhelmine that he had "produced and got accepted my work of last night"—his draft of a plan for organizing the business of the Congress.

Everything—in his private as well as his public life—was going according to his wishes. When the ministers' conference broke up at midnight he had gone on to an enormous soiree at Princess Bagration's. He was in great good humor and of course had an amusing story for her. When Münster pointed to Henriette Crenneville, a very plain lady of their acquaintance who had married late in life, and said to Metternich, "She must have carried on pretty hard all her life," Metternich "forgot to tell him no, and silence in diplomacy always means affirmation." So poor Henriette "who carefully hung on to the flower of her maidenhood right up to the age of 40—she who has never given herself to any embraces but Crenneville's, will now have the reputation in Hanover of being one of the most dissolute women in Austria!"[5]

2

No international gathering of such scope as the Congress of Vienna had ever been held in the history of Europe. No precedent existed for handling the intricate questions of procedure, of organization, of decisions on agenda and credentials.

Vattel, who had defined congresses as "assemblies of plenipotentiaries appointed to find out means of conciliation, to discuss and adjust the reciprocal pretensions of the contending parties," had not spelled out how those conciliations and adjustments were to be reached in a meeting of two hundred delegates and in the face of conflicting claims of stubborn and ambitious sovereigns whose pretensions would surely be fiercely defended.

The design of the Congress was Metternich's. It had taken shape in his mind as early as the spring of 1813, when he had proposed peace to France, Russia and England and had won Napoleon's tentative assent to such a congress. The abortive Congress of Prague, the unborn Congress of Mannheim, the miscarried Congress of Châtillon had been conceived as dress rehearsals for the final international Congress that would settle the affairs of Europe. It had been Metternich who had proposed Vienna as a meeting place for the sovereigns as soon as the Battle of Leipzig was won, and it had been he who had written into the Peace of Paris the invitation to "all powers engaged on either side in the present war" to send delegates to Vienna.

As for the organization of Congress business, he had already formed a plan the previous June in London. The four Allied ministers would meet in September in Vienna before the arrival of the sovereigns and other delegates and work out a plan of operation. When Congress opened a committee of seven directors would be chosen, with the four ministers comprising, needless to say, a majority voice. The Central Committee would submit a plan of organization and arrangements for the approval of the Congress, and since the four would already have worked everything out ahead of time, the business of the Congress would move smoothly and quickly to an early conclusion. This at least was Metternich's optimistic plan, which he confided in a letter to Emperor Franz, warning him to plan his summer so that he could be close to Vienna from mid-September on, stealing a march on the other sovereigns by being at hand for the preliminary meetings.[6]

When the four Allied ministers met for their second conference on that Sunday, September 18, Metternich had his draft plan ready.[7] Castlereagh went a step further than Metternich in proposing that the four ministers keep the decision making in their own hands. It would be awkward, he pointed out, to permit Congress to choose a committee, for it would embroil them at once in the tricky question of credentials. At Châtillon the four powers had already arrogated for themselves the right of representing Europe; far simpler now if they simply designated themselves *the* Central Committee, with the possible addition of France and Spain. But Prussia and Russia objected strenuously to the inclusion of France and Spain. Both Castlereagh and Humboldt tried their hands at drafting plans for procedure. In the end Metternich's plan was adopted in substance. The Central Committee of Four would make major decisions, especially on questions of territory, with a separate committee representing the six larger German states handling the problems relating to the reorganization of Germany. France and Spain would serve as consulting members—that is, they would be presented with *faits accomplis* and permitted to voice objections.

By the following Thursday the four had agreed to sign a protocol embodying the plan. Cautiously Castlereagh protected himself by adding an extra paragraph: he would not, he said, necessarily be bound by a vote of the majority.[8]

So far everything had gone beautifully.

Wilhelmine had moved back to town and was installed again in her apartments in the Palais Palm, where Metternich could see her every day, and where her drawing room could be an invaluable political arena for him. "I haven't seen you in two days," he had written her on Wednesday, "and I have a hundred things to tell you. The world turns very fast on its hinges in times like these."[9] On that Thursday night, when the four ministers had reached their first important agreement, Wilhelmine entertained at a large soiree, "dull at first," Gentz observed in his diary, "but later on a very lively discussion about England."[10] At the soiree that night both Metternich and Gentz talked with Serra Capriola, Sicilian minister to Russia, who had just arrived from St. Petersburg. It may have been from him that Metternich learned of the opposition in St. Petersburg to the Tsar's plans for a future Polish kingdom under the Russian Crown. So much the better if the Tsar's own officials were protesting it! Surely the worrisome matter of Poland's future—the first and most critical issue on the Congress agenda—could be settled with dispatch if the Tsar behaved sensibly.

To both Laure and Wilhelmine Metternich predicted that the Congress would last four—at most six—weeks. By early November everything would be over. His prophecy was off by more than seven months.

The following day, Friday, September 23, Talleyrand's big traveling coach lumbered into the courtyard of the Kaunitz Palace in Johannesgasse, where the French delegation was to have its headquarters.

Talleyrand arrived with a carefully selected staff: Dalberg, "to broadcast those of my secrets which I wish everyone to know"; an able diplomatic assistant, La Besnardière; his secretary, Perrey; the musician Neukomm; and his superb chef Carême to provide the most exquisite cuisine in Vienna.

"I don't need secretaries so much as saucepans," he had told the French King. Other staff members, including the Marquis de la Tour du Pin, had already preceded him to Vienna, and the French King would send a few weeks later the ultra-royalist Alexis de Noailles. "If one must be spied upon," commented Talleyrand, "at least it is better to choose the spy one-self."

Most important of all he had brought along Dorothée to be his companion and hostess during the weeks of the Congress. "By her wit and her tact," he wrote later in his *Memoirs*, "she attracted and pleased people and was very useful to me."[11]

Talleyrand had discerned that Dorothée desperately needed distraction from the grief of her child's death and from the boredom and vexation of her unhappy marriage. He was not yet in love with Dorothée, but he had certainly grown fond of her; he was delighted to have a pretty young woman to sit on his bed in the morning and talk to him during the ritual of his levee, who would take letters at his dictation in odd moments, who would preside with poise and charm at his dinner table and sit beside him on the sofa during the late evening hours when he received guests.

Dorothée would also be an important political asset, and it was on this Talleyrand counted above all. Not only did she possess a cool, keen, analytical intelligence, not unlike his own, but she had friendships and connections with most of the important men of Central Europe. She had nearly been betrothed to Prince Adam Czartoryski, the Prussian royal princes were her childhood playmates. The Radziwills, the Reusses and dozens of other princely families were old friends of her family. Perhaps most importantly, her sister Wilhelmine was hostess of Vienna's leading political salon and the intimate friend of the Austrian Foreign Minister.

Talleyrand would need all of Dorothée's charm and connections, for the French delegation was to endure an unpleasant isolation during the early weeks of the Congress, and France was not to be taken back into the society of nations until after a chilly initiation period.

Defeated France could not expect to wangle any bonuses out of the Congress—no more territory, no more colonies than the Peace of Paris had granted. Talleyrand would tell the Allied ministers, "I am perhaps the only one who asks nothing. . . . I want nothing, but I bring you a great deal." His disclaimer was not precisely true or he would not have been in Vienna at all: Bourbon France needed desperately to regain lost prestige, and one of Talleyrand's main objects was to restore the King's Bourbon relatives on the thrones of Spain, Parma and Naples. The fifty closely written pages of instructions Talleyrand himself had drawn up spelled out in detail the objects of his embassy: near the top of the list was the prevention of Prussia's acquisition of Saxony and Russia's acquisition of Poland.[12]

Talleyrand quickly learned that the four former Allies had been meeting regularly at conferences from which he had been excluded. He courted the political "outs"—men like Stadion, who had been shunted out of diplomacy into finance, and Starhemberg—to learn what he could, and waited, anxious and irritable in the Palais Kaunitz for some moment to present itself when he could penetrate into that intimate little enclave of power, the Central Committee of the Congress.

3

At daybreak on September 25 a blast of cannon startled the Viennese out of their Sunday slumbers to announce that the Tsar of Russia had just left the border town of Nikolsburg and would in two or three hours be approaching Vienna.

Metternich sent a note around to Wilhelmine to explain what the cannon thunder meant. "It proves that nobody has any common sense any more, for never did anyone wake up a whole city with cannon shots to inform them that a sovereign is still forty leagues away." He would call for her at half past ten that morning to show her the place reserved for her in the inner court of the Hofburg. She replied with a sleepy little note: "My eyes are still quite shut. Your note just woke me up!"[13]

Emperor Franz rode across the Danube to meet the Tsar and the Prussian King, embraced them affectionately. Grand Duchess Catherine, who had come with her brother, tactfully made herself inconspicuous that day, got into another carriage and rode into the city incognito. The Tsarina Elizabeth—with whom the Tsar never traveled or lived if he could avoid it—had been visiting her family in Baden; she would arrive in Vienna separately a few days later.

The three monarchs on horseback led a parade through streets lined with troops, first to the Prater, then to the imperial palace.

The whole city wore an air of holiday and of festivity. Church bells rang, bands played, crowds filled the streets and hung out of the windows as the parade passed. The sun sparkled on gold braid and diamond-studded orders, and on the gems that dangled from the hat and boots of Prince Esterházy in his jewel-covered Hungarian magnate's uniform as he rode at the head of the Emperor's guard troops.

Five of the six monarchs who were to be present at the Congress—only the Bavarian King had not yet arrived—lunched together that Sunday.

They were hardly a prepossessing lot in appearance. Anna Eynard, wife of one of the Geneva delegates, described Austria's Emperor: "You have to know he is Emperor to believe it for he looks only a quarter of an ordinary man, and as if, if you blew hard, you'd blow him to the ground." The King of Denmark was skinny and cadaverous, with whitish eyebrows and lashes and pale skin marred by a perpetual rash. The King of Württemberg was so enormously fat that a hole had to be cut in his dining table to accommodate his immense girth and a specially built carriage provided for his excursions. "An arsenal of a face," said the witty Prince de Ligne of the solemn, stone-visaged King of Prussia. Only Tsar Alexander, despite his growing plumpness, still had an appearance of youth and grace, especially when he danced—which was to occupy a large part of his time during the early weeks of the Congress.

None of the monarchs attended any of the diplomatic conferences, but they busied themselves behind the scenes making and unmaking decisions, to the ministers' consternation.

Even that first day the royal elbow-rubbing did not go particularly smoothly. Norway, which had belonged to the Danish Crown for five hundred years, had been handed over to Sweden by the Tsar as a reward for Bernadotte's support in the war—against the bitter protests of the Norwegians themselves. The Tsar was visibly embarrassed to meet the King of Denmark that Sunday, and their first interview did nothing to heal the breach.

Affably the Tsar announced he would guarantee all the Danish King's conquests in Germany as recompense. The King of Denmark replied that nothing could repay him for the loss of Norway, and that he did not propose to traffic in men.[14]

Barely was the royal luncheon over when the Tsar sent for Metternich. The two men, on whom more than on any others hung the fate of the whole Congress, took careful measure of one another and exchanged the suavest amenities.

In a note scribbled off to Wilhelmine at half past three that afternoon, Metternich described the encounter:

> Instead of being with *mon amie* I have had my first skirmish with the Tsar. I saw that he wanted to reconnoiter the terrain. As a good captain I did not hesitate to allow myself to be reconnoitered, and the result of the Tsar's attempt is that he knows nothing of what I want, and I see clearly what he wants. I've put my advance guards in position and I can sleep peacefully—the army corps will not be surprised.

He would, he told her, be dining with the sovereigns late in the afternoon at Razumowsky's. It was to be a very Russian day; it would be in fact a Russian week. Later on that evening the royal guests were to attend a gala performance of a comedy and a ballet. Where was her box at the theater so he could find her? And what was she planning to do after the theater? Would she be at Princess Bagration's *grand souper* in the Tsar's honor? And finally would she reply to one tiny word: *mine?* He could not hear often enough her word of reassurance—that she belonged to him and to him alone.[15]

4

From the beginning Metternich had envisioned the Congress of Vienna not merely as a concert of powers meeting to put back together a Europe splintered by war and conquest but as a glittering Peace Festival to mark the beginning of a new era.

Accordingly the arrival of the Tsar and the King of Prussia signaled the

opening of a magnificent program of public and semi-public fetes, to celebrate the peace, to divert the Congress guests, and to restore the luster of Austria's public image, tarnished by lost wars and the Napoleonic association.

Certainly neither Metternich nor anyone else had imagined the size of
the throng that would gather in Vienna in the sunny days of autumn to be
participants or onlookers at the Congress. The idea of an international meeting to shape a new world on principles of moderation and justice had captured the imagination of Europe. In the intoxicating air of victory and of
peace—the first real peace Europe had known in twenty-five years—everyone
was ready for a holiday.

From every corner of Europe, in every kind of vehicle, in stately berlines
with armorial bearings, in public post coaches jammed to the roof, from
boats on the Danube, a hundred thousand visitors poured into Vienna—
half again as many as the city's total population. No fewer than two hundred fifteen heads of princely families came, with their relatives and servants,
their ministers, statesmen, diplomats, aides and secretaries by the hundred.
The new kingdoms Napoleon had created were represented, and the little
princes he had obliterated by "mediatizing" them. The Pope sent delegates
to win back his states and Napoleon's marshals sent theirs to hang on hopefully to their dotations. Besides official and semi-official delegations there
were hundreds of self-appointed claimants and pleaders for special causes,
from the Jews of the German cities hoping for civil rights, to the book-pub-
lishing industry hoping for international copyright laws.

Who indeed did not come to Vienna in those weeks? There were place-
seekers, artists, writers, inventors, philosophers, actors and actresses, dancers,
acrobats, prostitutes, pickpockets, swindlers, reformers burning with a cause,
political dreamers with constitutions in their pockets—all congregating on
Vienna to see or to be seen, to bribe or make money, to have an old kingdom restored, or to acquire a new one.

All the reigning soverigns with their families and servants were put up at
the Hofburg, a feat of housekeeping that taxed that imperial establishment
to the utmost. Every night forty banquet tables were laid in the palace; each
morning hundreds of stoves were stoked, hot and cold water carried to the
rooms, chamber pots emptied, meals brought, linen washed.

The Amalia Wing, a handsome suite of rooms in rococo style that faced
across Ballhaus Square to the Chancellery, had been assigned to the Tsar,
while the Austrian Empress moved out of her charming rooms in the Schwei-
zerhof Wing to make way for the King of Prussia. The court marshal and his
assistants had worked long head-splitting hours all summer to arrange living
quarters suitable to the rank of hundreds of guests, and to iron out all the
complexities of protocol.

The many thousand other visitors, including diplomats and government
officials, put up where rooms could be found. Before long Viennese families
were jamming themselves into a single room and renting out the rest of their

dwellings for what the traffic would bear. Even unheated garret rooms and quarters in distant suburbs were fetching fancy prices.

With the aid of a Festivals Committee headed by Isabey and Moreau, the Emperor and Empress hosted day after day, night after night, receptions, balls, hunting parties, gala theatricals, musicales, military exhibitions. In all the theaters boxes were reserved for royalty and top officials. Solely to amuse the guests some 20,000 elite grenadiers and 60,000 infantrymen, all outfitted in new uniforms, were kept in readiness for maneuvers. Fourteen hundred horses and several hundred new carriages, dark green with the Habsburg coat of arms, and manned by coachmen in new yellow livery, were kept in readiness to carry the Emperor's guests wherever they might wish to go at any hour of the day or night.

Besides the imperial festivals there were parties every night in private houses. The Metternichs entertained on Monday nights, the Castlereaghs on Tuesday nights, Karl and Julie Zichy on Saturdays. All the ladies of Vienna society had their Evenings where one dropped in to drink tea, play cards or dance, exchange the latest morsel of gossip and rub shoulders with who-knew-what international celebrity. Of Molly Zichy's recherché parties, it was said by one wit it was not enough to be a king to be invited, one must also be elegant.

The political work of the Congress was by no means separate from the Congress festivals but was rather imbedded in them. The parties were a second arena of diplomacy where the discussions of the conference table often continued in a casual and informal setting. Important talk could continue around a dinner table, or in a corner of a salon where teacups tinkled and fans swished. Opinions might be elaborated and arguments marshaled under the palm trees in a conservatory with the lilting measures of the latest waltz floating in from a nearby dance floor. More than once crucial documents were exchanged and read under the light of a candelabrum in the corner of a crowded ballroom. And since the sovereigns appeared at many of the festivals as private persons, it was quite possible to approach and talk with them informally, foregoing all the complications of appointment and protocol.

The festivals provided a marvelous seedbed for intrigue, gossip and rumor. Everyone watched the leading performers and tried to guess what was going on behind the scenes. Did this or that minister look cheerful or troubled? Did the Tsar speak to Metternich or avoid him? Was Hardenberg really ill or was he only avoiding a decision?

One element of Emperor Franz's generous and lavish hospitality did not contribute to the good fellowship of the peace celebration: this was the espionage activity of the Austrian police.

Baron Hager had been working all summer to expand his police force and to recruit professional and non-professional assistance for his espionage network. The discovery in August of the plot by Italian nationalists to assassinate

Emperor Franz on the day the Congress opened had certainly panicked the authorities and tightened security measures.

Emperor Franz was, moreover, responsible for the safety of all his guests, and the presence of the ruling sovereigns, together with thousands of strangers of all nationalities and all political hues and purposes was enough to increase the nervousness and apprehension in upper government circles.

Early in their conferences in September, perhaps at Castlereagh's suggestion, the ministers had considered policing the Congress through a special force under direction of the Central Committee, but the idea was dropped and all security measures were left in the hands of the hosts.[16]

All the most distinguished guests and many of the undistinguished were regularly tailed by police agents night and day. Letters were intercepted, copied and resealed. The public writing bureaus in the city, where stenographers and translators worked for hire, were manned by police employees. Porters, coachmen, chambermaids and couriers were bribed to report conversations and movements of prominent people, and a whole subsection of the Police Bureau functioned to handle the *chiffons*—scraps of paper salvaged from wastebaskets and stoves.

Wherever they could the police placed informers in the houses of important foreigners. A police agent worked as porter for the Spanish ambassador, Labrador, and another as valet to Baron Stein, reporting to Hager that he hoped "we will now procure all the information we want." Despite the great precautions Talleyrand and Castlereagh took to prevent leakage of information in their own households (Talleyrand's house, the police reported early, "was like a locked fortress in which he lives alone with his trusted servants"), nevertheless, the police managed to gain entrée, to gather *chiffons* and intercept letters, including a delicious series of *billets-doux* between Dalberg and a married lady, a distant relation of his. Some of Castlereagh's servants were bribed, and after the minister's departure, the police endeavored to place the same agents in the household of his half brother, Charles Stewart.

Since police were not permitted to penetrate the Hofburg, and as the imperial palace had far too many doors to be able to post an effective watch on the comings and goings of royal guests, Hager asked permission of the court marshal, Prince Trauttmansdorff, to use regular palace servants to report the movements of the important guests—a job the Hofburg servants apparently did not want to undertake.

Not only were servants often in the pay of the police, but men and women in the upper echelons of society who had entree to some of the great houses worked for pay as informers. The Abbé Giuseppe Carpani, poet and musician, supplemented his scanty income by reporting what people said and did.

There was no careful sifting of the information gathered; everything went helter-skelter into the bulging office files. Most of what was reported had no political significance, and some of it was purely malicious. "The King of

Prussia went out in the evening in civilian clothes with a round hat pulled down over his eyes, he had not come back at ten o'clock." "Every morning they bring to Tsar Alexander a big piece of pure ice with which he washes his face and hands." "Lord Castlereagh, dissatisfied with the fourteen-room apartment he had at the Auge Gottes, has moved to the first floor of Minoritenplatz No. 30, where he will have twenty-two rooms." "They say the King of Württemberg inspires a mad terror among his ministers and his suite." "The Poles report there is a secret staircase to the Tsar's apartments by which he can go up and down without being observed."

While the Austrian police spied on foreign visitors, an international network functioned as well, reporting to the various embassies. Talleyrand maintained his own excellent sources of information; the Prussians and Russians had theirs.

The whole police system in Austria was just saved from being intolerable by its lack of efficiency. Emperor Franz, to whom the reports were brought daily, probably found them diverting reading, but during the Congress epoch the Austrian police failed to uncover anything of real political significance.

Yet notable too is the fact that during the months of the Congress all the strangers in the city, from the Tsar of Russia on down, walked about freely in the city without bodyguard or special precaution, mingled in crowds at the balls and public festivals even during periods of the bitterest political controversy, without any mishap, not so much as a jewel robbery.

5

Wilhelmine had resumed her role as an important political hostess, and her salon promised to be the most cosmopolitan of any during the Congress. It was common knowledge now that she ruled undisputed queen of Metternich's heart; the presence of the Austrian Foreign Minister at her parties was a foregone conclusion. Her sister Dorothée and Talleyrand brought the French embassy group into her drawing room. "Talleyrand spends all his evenings at Madame de Sagan's, where he flatters himself he can ferret out Metternich's secrets," an assiduous police agent reported.[17] Though the Castlereaghs continued to shun her as a divorcée, the young Englishmen from the embassy, Frederick Lamb and his friends, and presently Castlereagh's half brother, Charles Stewart, congregated in her drawing room.

Her family connections with Prussia were of the closest, and her Sagan estates, liberated finally from French occupation, lay in Prussian Silesia. For her generous contributions of money and troops and a military hospital during the late campaign, the King of Prussia would bestow on her the Order of Louise, the highest honor a woman could receive. At nearly all her soirees appeared Prince August of Prussia, younger brother of that Prussian hero, Prince Louis Ferdinand, who had once courted her ardently. Among the younger princes of Germany she and Dorothée could count several who had

danced attendance on the beautiful Courland princesses at one time or another.

But most important of all to her was her friendship with the Tsar—
"*your* Emperor," Metternich continued to call him ironically. There were
pressing practical reasons for maintaining that friendship at all costs—not
only for the Russian income still owing her mother and herself, but, most important of all, her chief hope for winning custody of her child.

So far as it lay in her power, Wilhelmine would strive to continue the
gracious acquaintance that had begun so auspiciously the previous summer
at Ratiborzitz, and had continued in Paris, where the Tsar had shown her
the warm consideration due the daughter of his dear friend the Duchess of
Courland, and the flattering attention an Emperor might naturally bestow
on an exceptionally beautiful and charming woman. Surely she might hope
that he would honor her house with his visits during the Congress.

She had been among the chosen few of Vienna's top aristocracy to greet
the Tsar in the inner courtyard of the Hofburg on the day of his arrival.
When they had met at one of the festival events during the first days of the
Russian sovereign's visit, he had escorted her home in his carriage.

But Vienna was not Ratiborzitz. The Tsar was vexed and conflicted
that this lovely woman and former subject was the intimate friend of his
bitterest enemy to whom she might well be reporting every word, every gesture. The Tsar was perfectly aware from the day of his arrival that Vienna
did not receive him with the open arms and uncritical adulation that Paris
had. He well knew that eyes watched and ears listened in the beautiful rococo
suite in the Amalia Wing, that the honor guard of Austrian officers attached to
his service certainly reported to Metternich.

What he needed in Vienna was friendly ground where he could meet and
talk with people in complete privacy and safety. Where could he find such
security save in the house of Princess Bagration, a distant relative of his and
widow of one of his most gallant generals? She knew everyone in Vienna,
was long established as a leading hostess. So it was to Princess Bagration's
house and not to Wilhelmine's that the Tsar turned in the early weeks of the
Congress.

Her house was at once dubbed by Congress wits "Russian headquarters,"
while Wilhelmine's was called "Austrian" or "ministerial headquarters." It was
endlessly amusing to Congress gossips that the rival hostesses maintained
their rival salons in opposite wings of the very same mansion.

6

Congress, it had been announced, would open officially on October 1,
and for the Congress to open it was essential that the pivotal questions of
Poland and Saxony be resolved.

Optimistically Metternich hoped to find the Tsar more yielding on the
critical issue of Poland. For if the Tsar agreed to return to Prussia the por-

tions of Poland it had previously controlled, then Prussia would no longer demand Saxony to restore it to pre-1806 power, and all the pieces of the German puzzle would fall into place.

But the Tsar had written firmly into his instructions to Nesselrode that the duchy of Warsaw was his "by right of conquest." Austria had won northern Italy; England had got commercial supremacy and control of the Channel. "It is only fair that my subjects be indemnified for so many sacrifices," the Tsar added. At the very first ministerial meeting Nesselrode had accordingly announced that Russia would demand the entire duchy of Warsaw; nobody had bothered to argue with him.[18]

But when Castlereagh and Metternich approached the Tsar one after the other that week of his arrival and tried to persuade him to modify his plans for Poland, they found him stubbornly unmovable.

"They wanted to make us an Asiatic power; Poland will make us European," one of the Tsar's ministers boasted to Talleyrand that week. It was precisely why Austria felt threatened and resolved to resist to the utmost the extension of Russian power into Central Europe.

When Metternich talked with the Tsar on Wednesday evening, September 28, marshaling all his most persuasive tactics, he got precisely nowhere.

In a mood of depression his footsteps turned down the street toward Wilhelmine's. He needed to talk to her, get her opinion, be cheered up. But a servant came to the door to inform him that Madame la Duchesse was ill and seeing no one. He could only leave a note for her. "If the love of my heart grants me another night I shall be repaid for the pains of a lifetime." He would see her tomorrow "at my hour." The tiny note that came in reply promised that she would be quite alone the next day and waiting to see him at eleven. Until then she would be thinking of him.[19]

Talleyrand too tried his skill at persuading the Tsar that week. "Sooner war than renounce what I occupy!" the Tsar informed him. When the Tsar referred to the Saxons as "those who betrayed the cause of Europe," Talleyrand rejoined, "Sire, that is a question of dates"—a nice little needle to remind the Russian sovereign that he, the Tsar, as well as the King of Saxony, had once been an ally of Napoleon.[20]

The four ministers of the Central Committee had, meantime, decided to invite Talleyrand and the minister of Spain to ratify the protocol they had drawn up on the handling of Congress business.

On Friday morning, September 30, Talleyrand was still in bed—which he did not ordinarily leave until noon or after—when a note was brought in, signed by Metternich, inviting him to attend a preliminary conference that afternoon. The minister of Spain, Monsieur de Labrador, the note added, had also been invited. [21]

It was precisely the wedge Talleyrand needed. His valet Courtiade was hastily summoned to bathe and coif his master in record time, so that he could confer with Labrador before the two presented themselves at the Chancellery just before two o'clock on that momentous Friday afternoon.

They found the other ministers already seated around a long polished table, with Castlereagh presiding at one end, and Gentz at the other end taking notes. A chair between Castlereagh and Metternich was empty; Talleyrand sat down.

His first remarks revealed at once that he intended to be neither conciliatory nor obsequious in his role as envoy of defeated France. Looking around the table he pointed to Humboldt and Gentz and demanded, "Why have I alone been invited from the embassy of His Majesty the King of France?"

"Because we wanted to include in the preliminary conferences only the heads of cabinets."

"But Monsieur de Labrador is not a cabinet head, yet he has been invited?"

"That is because the Secretary of State for Spain has not yet arrived in Vienna."

Talleyrand cast his cool, supercilious glance over the table and gestured again. "But over there beyond Prince Hardenberg I notice Monsieur de Humboldt, who is also not a Secretary of State."

"That is an exception made necessary by Prince Hardenberg's infirmity, of which you know."

Talleyrand leaned back in his chair. The ghost of a smile flickered over his lips as he swung his crippled foot. "Ah yes, well, if it is a question of infirmities, each of us has his own and each has the right to make use of them."

A murmur of discussion followed. All right then, everyone would agree to that. Henceforth each Secretary of State might bring along one of his assisting plenipotentiaries.

It appeared then that Count Palmella, the Portuguese ambassador, had been informed of the meeting but had been told that Portugal was not to be included in the conferences. Lord Castlereagh read aloud to the assembled group the strong letter of protest Palmella had drafted, arguing that all eight powers who had signed the Peace of Paris ought to share in the committee making decisions for the Congress. Talleyrand and Labrador supported the position of Portugal, but it was decided to postpone a final decision on the inclusion of Portugal and Sweden until after the Swedish plenipotentiary had arrived.

"The object of today's meeting," Castlereagh informed the two newcomers, "is to acquaint you with what the four powers have accomplished since our arrival here. You have the protocol," he added, turning to Metternich.

The protocol, signed by the ministers of the four big powers, justified their retaining in their own hands the power over redistribution of territories, since those arrangements were inevitably bound up with treaties they had made with one another as Allies against Napoleon.

Talleyrand cast his eye over the paper, fell on the word "Allies," and demanded sharply, "Who are these Allies? Are we still at Chaumont? At Laon?

Wasn't peace signed in Paris? Has there been any war since then, and if so, with whom?"

The other ministers protested quickly that they had intended no slight to France. They had simply used their habitual old expression for the sake of brevity.

"Whatever the price of brevity," Talleyrand interrupted, "it must not be bought at the cost of precision."

He picked up the protocol and began to read again. He noted that it was intended to provide bases for the territorial decisions, but that those bases were drawn from agreements at Kalisch, at Reichenbach, at Teplitz. He laid the paper down, looked slowly around the group and said, "I do not understand. There are only two dates for me: May 30, when a congress was stipulated, and October 1, when it is supposed to meet. Everything between those dates is foreign and does not exist for me."

Once more a little flurry of discussion followed. The upshot was that the four ministers declared the protocol had little importance for them and they would withdraw it.

Now Metternich produced a second piece of writing; it was the draft proposal of a declaration on opening the Congress, of which he had sketched the original and Gentz had produced the final version.

But Talleyrand perceived at once that even though France and Spain were admitted to membership on the main decision-making committee, and even though they might be able to agree together, they could always be outvoted by the other four powers.

"You are proposing to end where I think we must begin," he objected. "You propose that the power to make decisions be given to a committee of six. But the whole Congress ought to be assembled to decide who is to have that power. Of course ministers with no responsibility to anyone but themselves can adopt such measures, but Lord Castlereagh and I"—Talleyrand looked meaningfully at the English minister to intimate that they were true allies since only they represented constitutional monarchies—"we are in a different position."

Castlereagh replied that he agreed with Talleyrand in principle, but that to submit difficult questions to an assembled congress would delay matters interminably.

In the lively discussion that followed someone mentioned the name of the King of Naples—meaning Joachim Murat.

Talleyrand demanded at once, "Of what King of Naples are we speaking? We do not know this man in question."

"We are speaking of King Joachim Murat," replied Humboldt. "The powers recognized him by a treaty and guaranteed his boundaries."

Talleyrand, whose instructions included the ousting of Napoleon's brother-in-law and the restoration of the Bourbon Ferdinand to the throne of Naples, replied coldly, "Those who guaranteed his boundaries ought not to have done so, and consequently they have not succeeded in doing so."

Bringing the discussion back to the question of convoking the Congress, Talleyrand repeated that certainly any difficulties in summoning the Congress could be overcome. He had discerned and seized on a valuable bludgeon to force open the inner doors of the power structure: he would threaten to call together the whole Congress and put the issue to them.

The atmosphere in the room was tense. Hardenberg remarked shortly that perhaps the difficulties could be overcome, but he did not want to see little princes like those of Leyen and Liechtenstein meddling in the great territorial questions. Hastily Castlereagh proposed adjournment.

Only Metternich appeared not in the least disturbed by Talleyrand's contentious tone. He invited Gentz to ride out to the Rennweg villa with him and look over the preparations they were making for his peace fete. They walked together in the gardens for an hour or so and dined together afterward in the Chancellery. In his diary that night Gentz noted:

> The intervention [of Talleyrand and Labrador] has furiously upset and torn apart our plans. They protested against the form we had adopted, they scolded us roundly for two hours. . . . The Prince [Metternich] does not feel as I do all there is of embarrassment and even of dreadfulness in our position![22]

7

That Friday evening, September 30, the Emperor and Empress gave a gala reception for visiting dignitaries. There were hundreds of gate-crashers; a huge crowd mobbed the main staircases and reception rooms of the palace, all dressed to the nines and pushing in to be presented to the imperial couple. In the main reception room the press was so terrible that one could only "stand without stirring and let the sweat pour off one's face," Humboldt recalled. He envied Count Münster, who had broken a rib in a carriage accident the day before and stayed home "in his beautiful lonely bed outside all the disturbance."[23]

After the *cercle* in the palace many of the guests repaired to a party at the Duchess of Sagan's. Metternich and Gentz were there, Dorothée and Talleyrand and Dalberg, Prince August of Prussia, the two Reuss princes and a hundred or so more.

The Tsar, however, whom Wilhelmine had invited, did not come. Instead, he had sent Chernyshëv, one of his aides, with a note declining her invitation while to Katharine Bagration he sent word that he would call on her after the *cercle*.

Closing the door to callers on the excuse that she was indisposed, Princess Bagration received the Tsar that evening—in negligee, according to the police informant, who reported that they chatted in her boudoir for three hours. There had been one amusing little incident. As the princess led the Tsar through her salon, the monarch raised his eyebrows at sight of a man's hat lying on the sofa. The princess went into peals of laughter. "It's nothing—

just the hat of my decorator, Moreau. He forgot it when he left. He's doing the house for tomorrow's ball."

Next day all Vienna buzzed with the titillating morsel that the Tsar had spent several hours tête-à-tête in the late evening with Princess Bagration. What had gone on in the left wing of the Palais Palm on Friday night? What in the world had they talked about? Gossip speculated—but there were no hard facts. Katharine Bagration's old friend Fontbrune, who, it so happened, was a houseguest in Wilhelmine's commodious apartment across the court-yard (the ladies had a way of sharing friends if not friendship, it appeared), called on Princess Bagration promptly on Saturday morning to try to pry out of her everything that had happened. But Katharine Bagration was not to be wheedled; she dropped an intriguing little hint or two, but she told him nothing.

She did confide in one person—on an oath of deepest secrecy—her young friend and companion Aurore de Marassé, the pretty émigrée who lived in a garret room in the Palais Palm. Eventually Aurore told someone, who told someone else, and presently everyone in Vienna had heard an account of the Tsar's visit. It appeared that the Tsar had questioned the princess closely about her liaison with Metternich. When had it broken up, and why? Did she still have his letters? He would like to see them. Was Metternich really infatuated with the Duchess of Sagan?

The princess reported the Tsar as saying, "They tried to throw Sagan at my head this week, even putting her tête-à-tête in a carriage with me." But it had done no good, the princess added gratuitously, "His Majesty enjoys beauty but he must also have esprit."

Of Katharine Bagration's past romance with the Austrian diplomat the Tsar had declared scathingly, "Metternich never loved you or Sagan. He is an ice-cold man, believe me; he loves nobody!"[24]

When the Tsar drove away at midnight that Friday, the courtyard of the Palais Palm was still filled with carriages of guests at Wilhelmine's soiree. Metternich was one of the last to leave. Indeed, he may not have left at all.

The next day, Saturday, October 1, the doors of the Chancellery were closed to visitors. There was no conference, and Gentz did not come for his usual morning talk with Metternich. Apparently Metternich spent that night after the soiree with Wilhelmine and returned to the Chancellery early Saturday afternoon. That day, October 1, remained a vivid, cherished memory. "The 25 July and the 1 October . . . live in my heart—they will live there forever," he wrote Wilhelmine a few days later, calling October 1 "the greatest happiness of my life."[25]

On Saturday night, October 1, Princess Bagration gave a brilliant ball for two hundred. The Tsar appeared just after ten, having attended a gala performance at the Burgtheater. He was his gayest, most gracious self, danced the first dance with his hostess, the second with Wilhelmine. At one point he drew Hardenberg into a window niche, but since it was necessary to shout in the Chancellor's ear, the two retired into the princess's boudoir, where they talked for a time. Surprisingly the Tsar was not seen to speak much with Adam Czartoryski, who had arrived in Vienna that day, nor, less surprisingly, did he speak with Metternich. Gentz, however, recorded the golden words in his diary that night: "The Emperor spoke to me." At midnight the guests sat down to what Gentz described as a "magnificent supper." Not until daybreak did the last carriages rumble out of the courtyard; the Tsar himself had danced until four in the morning.

Though the opening of the Congress had been indefinitely postponed, the program of festivals went on as planned, and the long weekend of October 1 was filled to the brim with entertainment.

The Tsar had danced till dawn at Princess Bagration's, but he managed to appear bright and early Sunday morning with the other sovereigns, in dress uniform and glittering with his jeweled orders, at a religious-military fete outside the city walls on the glacis. Infantry and cavalry paraded for the monarchs and then, forming a huge double square, heard Mass sung before a canopied altar outdoors in the sunshine.

That Sunday night of October 2 the Austrian sovereigns gave their first palace ball, a masked *redoute* to which everyone came in domino or in character costume. Tickets had been given out for the affair, but the canny doortenders had sold and resold the same tickets so many times that it was estimated twelve thousand people jammed into the palace—several thousand uninvited. It was also true that some three thousand of Their Majesties' silver teaspoons bearing the imperial crest disappeared in the enormous crush around the floating buffets and refreshment stands that night.

It was certainly a wildly gay affair. The English thought it shocking and immoral that the Empress would give a ball on Sunday, which the Castlereaghs observed quite properly with an Anglican service and hymns. Everyone else came to dance and eat and drink at the ball—and to gossip and make love and talk politics. All languages, all nationalities mingled in the bewildering medley of costumes and conversations.

A young Frenchman, Comte de La Garde-Chambonas, writing his memoirs of the Congress many years later, still recalled vividly the carnival atmosphere of that first great ball:

> The continuous music, the mystery of the disguises, the intrigues with which I was surrounded, the general incognito, the unbridled gaiety, the combination of circumstances and of seductions, in a word the magic of the whole vast tableau, turned my head; older and stronger heads than mine found it equally irresistible.[26]

All ages mingled at the Congress balls, and every ball opened with a polonaise or two, a kind of stately ritual dance stepped to music. The young deplored the polonaise as hopelessly dull, but everyone, even the old and frail, could join in the long procession of couples moving to music through the rooms of the palace. There were other dances as well—*russes* and allemandes and reels and *tempêtes,* and even the minuet was briefly revived at the Congress, but hardly anyone knew how to dance it any more, only a few decrepit émigrés.

For the young and liberated there was only one dance, the enchanting waltz, which Austria had invented out of the centuries-old turning dances. Certainly the most bewitching, self-intoxicating dance ever devised, the waltz had captivated all Austria during the Napoleonic Wars, and after the Congress would spread through the rest of Europe. It required a spacious ballroom, great energy and grace—and many people would continue to condemn its inebriating rhythms as immoral—but it was the waltz that wore out thousands of slippers night after night in that autumn and winter of 1814.

Somewhat extravagantly La Garde-Chambonas described the waltzing at the Congress balls:

> You should have seen those ravishing women, all sparkling with flowers and diamonds, carried away by the irresistible harmonies, leaning back into the arms of their partners, looking like brilliant meteors; . . . . the shimmering silks and light gauzes of their gowns floating and swaying in graceful undulations; . . . . the look of ecstatic happiness on their charming faces when fatigue forced them to leave the aerial regions in which they had been whirling to come back and ask new strength of the earth.[27]

Even the Castlereaghs succumbed and began to take lessons in waltzing. Lady Castlereagh became the most indefatigable of dancers, and a caller one morning at the Castlereagh apartments in the Minoritenplatz found the English Foreign Secretary gravely humming waltz rhythms while he practiced moving about with a chair for a partner.

Metternich and Wilhelmine were both at the masked redoute that Sunday night, but they missed each other—easy to do in that enormous crowd.

They met the next day, on Monday, October 3, at the elegant dinner party Count Razumowsky gave in honor of the Tsar at his sumptuous newly completed palace. Everyone was shown through the palace and the splendidly laid-out gardens; everyone admired the fine collection of paintings and sculpture, and the latest, most up-to-date equipment the palace boasted, including a new-fangled heating system carried by underground pipes.

That Monday the meeting of the Central Committee adjourned early in the Chancellery, for the Metternichs were giving the first of their weekly supper parties.

Their closer circle of friends were invited to come every Monday night during the season. Distinguished guests got special invitations, and others Metternich wanted to include were invited for a particular Monday night.

That morning Wilhelmine had sent him a hurried note asking whether her sister Dorothée might come to his reception. "She has scruples since she has not got an invitation." Metternich replied at once that Talleyrand and Dorothée could consider themselves invited "once for always." As for the Starhembergs, who had become friends of Talleyrand, no, he did not wish them invited. He well knew that Louis Starhemberg was not one of his supporters. "I am not very close to the Starhembergs," he explained, and he had already invited thirty of the most elegant women in Vienna to adorn his Monday nights. If Wilhelmine very much wished them included, he would of course do so.[28]

All Metternich's orders for redecorating the state apartments in the Chancellery had been faithfully carried out. The wallpapers and silk coverings and the handsome bronzes he had brought from Paris were in place. Fires burned in the new marble fireplaces on that cool October night. Servants in brand new livery—the braid and buttons for which he had brought from London—passed champagne and ices. There was music and dancing; late in the evening supper was served. The ladies were seated at small tables and the gentlemen fetched delicacies for them from the exquisitely furnished buffets.

Laure Metternich in one of her new LeRoi gowns moved among her guests, quietly pleasant, sharply observant, seeing that everything went smoothly, that every lady was waited on, that every gentleman had a chance to talk, catching here and there a snatch of conversation that would be worth garnering for her husband's delectation next day. Clemens, slender and elegant in court dress as he is painted in his Congress portraits, played the great host to perfection, dropping a pleasantry here, an anecdote there, charming the ladies, severing a political discussion that threatened to become too serious.

At his first Monday nights, Metternich personally saw to it that his guests were introduced to one another; only later, when the Monday supper parties became too crowded, he could no longer do so.

As Foreign Minister Metternich was Austria's official host and the flair and grace with which he carried out those duties—though his political enemies would make capital out of his "frivolity"—were highly important for Austria's public relations. Emperor Franz, a shy man and not fond of partying, shunned those official chores as much as possible; he was delighted to have his Foreign Minister stand in for him.

Anna Eynard, the pretty wife of one of the Geneva delegates, recalled her first meeting with Metternich at one of the large Congress fetes. She happened to be wearing around her neck a double strand of finely cut rock crystals:

> During a moment when no one danced I saw Prince Metternich approach me. He stood a moment before me not knowing how to begin. Then he asked me what my necklaces were made of, said he had seen nothing like them and found them charming. While I replied that they were jewels of our mountains, he sat down beside me. I was astonished

at his politeness, even more when he pointed to Gabriel and said, "Do me the pleasure, you and your husband, of coming to dance at my house next Monday." I accepted.[29]

8

Though the Congress had not officially opened on that Saturday, October 1, the political drama behind the scenes continued to unfold.

After the contentious meeting at which Talleyrand had challenged the four erstwhile Allies, he addressed a formal note of protest to them, insisting that all eight powers who had signed the Peace of Paris be included in the Central Committee of the Congress. To fortify his case he sent an account of the Friday meeting to the five smaller powers—Portugal, Sweden, Bavaria, Württemberg and Baden—asking them to support his demand for a Committee of Eight. If the four big powers thought they could shut France out of their deliberations, he—Talleyrand—could play politics too; he would organize a block of excluded powers and force his will on the four former Allies.

On Sunday afternoon, before the palace redoute, the "four friends," as Gentz now called the little enclave of ministers, Metternich, Castlereagh, Nesselrode and Hardenberg, met in Metternich's study, and he read aloud Talleyrand's note. "They want to break us apart!" exclaimed Nesselrode. "They won't succeed." Humboldt called the note "a firebrand thrown among us."[30]

The four agreed that they would take no official notice of Talleyrand's note nor reply to it in writing, but only by word of mouth. Very well, if he demanded it, they would enlarge the proposed Committee of Six to a Committee of Eight. It would not really change things in the least: they four would continue to make the decisions.

Accordingly, on Tuesday, October 4, the day after the Metternichs' supper party, a planned meeting of the Committee of Six was again postponed, and instead the "four friends" met in the afternoon around Prince Hardenberg's dinner table. When the other guests, including several Prussian generals, had departed, the four ministers talked over their problems and put the finishing touches on a rewritten protocol for handling Congress business.

That Tuesday evening Wilhelmine was again hostess at a large soiree. Here and there among the tinkle of teacups and glasses, of laughter and conversation in half a dozen languages, a little knot of men talked in low voices in a corner of the room about the issues of the Congress. Sometime during the evening Metternich handed Talleyrand a revised draft of the proposal for handling Congress business. Castlereagh had rewritten the original draft, but the substance remained unchanged. So did Talleyrand's mind.[31]

That evening the Tsar drove into the courtyard of the Palais Palm, intending to call on Princess Bagration. But he found the courtyard filled with the carriages of Wilhelmine's guests and assuming that his Russian friend was entertaining, he drove away without alighting, as one of the police informants reported.

The following day, Wednesday, October 5, the twice-postponed meeting of all six powers—the "four friends" plus Talleyrand and Labrador—finally took place.

Talleyrand arrived at the conference room a few minutes early. He had been looking for an ally to break through the wall of isolation that separated him from the inner enclave. He had marked his man. It was Gentz, who had been chosen to act as secretary for the ministers' meetings, Gentz, with his boundless appetite for flattery and fine food, both of which Talleyrand would know perfectly how to supply. Before the others arrived Talleyrand talked with Gentz, overwhelming him with charm.

It turned out that both had been invited to dine that day at Alfred Windischgraetz's; they would talk further at Alfred's after the conference was over, Talleyrand promised. And would Gentz come to dine the following day at the Palais Kaunitz? Gentz could and would. "He is entering into league with me," Gentz noted that night with satisfaction. "He treats me with the greatest distinction."[32]

The conference of the six that Wednesday was even more explosive than the first meeting had been. "Very stormy and very memorable," Gentz reported.

The rewritten Congress protocol Talleyrand flatly rejected. The four powers could not arrogate to themselves the right to speak for all Europe unless Europe consented to give it to them.

Once more he produced his bludgeon. Unless all powers, big and little, were represented on the Central Committee, he, Talleyrand, would simply withdraw and insist on the opening of a general session of the Congress, with all unsettled issues left to the whole assembly.

Such a solution would be no solution, the four ministers well knew. The fate of Poland and Saxony, of boundaries between Bavaria and Prussia, of territorial compensations and exchanges and a hundred delicate matters that required the most refined bargaining, could scarcely be solved efficiently and amicably in a huge open meeting with neither agenda nor platform.

"We cannot wait to settle things for the opening of the Congress," Nesselrode interposed. "His Majesty the Tsar intends to depart by October 25."

Talleyrand shrugged and replied in a tone of indifference. "I'm sorry to hear it, for he will not be here to see the end of things."

"But how," Metternich asked, "can we possibly assemble a Congress when none of the business to be transacted by that Congress is ready?"

"*Eh bien,*" Talleyrand replied affably, to show, he said later, that he was not moved by any wish to make difficulties, "I am willing to agree to everything that accords with principles I cannot abandon. Since nothing is ready yet for the opening of the Congress, since you wish to postpone it, let it be delayed for fifteen days or for three weeks. I consent but on two conditions only: one, that you decide at once on a fixed day to convoke it, and, second, that you settle in the note of convocation on the rules by which delegates are to be admitted to the Congress."

And what rules did Talleyrand propose for admitting delegates? Quickly he scribbled down his plan and passed the note around. Foreheads creased in frowns, questions were asked, objections raised. Nothing was settled. The conference was again adjourned.

Moving slowly because of his crippled foot, Talleyrand was the last to leave the conference room. Castlereagh lingered behind and joined the French minister at the top of the flight of marble stairs. Taking Talleyrand by the arm, he began to talk to him persuasively, trying to make him see things the way the "four friends" saw them. Castlereagh even held out the most delicate of bribes, "making me understand," Talleyrand reported to the French King, "that certain affairs that most interest my court could be arranged to my satisfaction."

Talleyrand replied, "It isn't at all a question of certain particular objects, but rather of the law which ought to serve to rule us all. . . . We must answer to the wishes of Europe. How can we answer to Europe if we have not honored those rights, the loss of which caused all our troubles? The present time is one that scarcely occurs once in the course of centuries. A finer occasion will never be offered us. Why not put ourselves in a position of answering to it?"

"Ah yes," Castlereagh murmured in a kind of embarrassment at this reminder of the Law of Nations, "but there are difficulties that you do not know."[33]

Talleyrand had won his point—at least it appeared so. A meeting of the eight powers, including not only Talleyrand and Labrador but Loewenhielm and Palmella, the delegates of Sweden and Portugal, was called for Saturday evening, October 8.

Metternich's note to Talleyrand added that if the latter wished to arrive a bit earlier than the others that evening, he would find a way "to inform him of very important things."[34]

The "four friends," meantime, met at the Chancellery that afternoon to lay their plans for the evening meeting and to approve the draft of a note Metternich and Gentz had drawn up convoking the Congress.

Promptly at seven that night Talleyrand arrived at the Chancellery and was at once shown into Metternich's study. The scene that ensued was an adroit little verbal sparring match between the two most skilled diplomats in Europe.

"I've drafted a note convoking the Congress which differs a bit from yours," Metternich began, "but I hope you will be pleased with it."

Talleyrand asked to see it.

"I do not have it yet," Metternich replied. "Gentz has carried it off to put on some finishing touches."

"Probably," Talleyrand observed caustically, "it is being communicated to your 'Allies.'"

"Let us not speak any longer of 'Allies,'" Metternich replied. "There are no more 'Allies.'"

"But there are people here who ought to be Allies," Talleyrand cut in quickly, "in the sense that even if not concerting together, they should be thinking alike and wishing for the same things!" He paused a moment, looked meaningfully at the Austrian minister and went on, "How do you have the courage to put Russia like a belt around your most important possessions, Hungary and Bohemia?" It was, of course, precisely Metternich's deepest political anxiety—that Russia's encroachment in Europe through the seizure of Poland would give her a frontier along most of Hungary and Bohemia.

"And how can you," Talleyrand pursued relentlessly, "endure that the patrimony of your former good neighbor, with whose family an archduchess is married, be turned over to your natural enemy? It seems strange that we French oppose [the sacrifice of Saxony] while you do not seem to want us to!"

Metternich evaded the thrust to reply cautiously, "You have no confidence in me."

"You've given me no reason to have any." Talleyrand began to cite instances in which he claimed Metternich had failed to keep his word, adding, "And then how have confidence in a man who is all mystery toward those who are most disposed to take his part? As for me I make no mysteries and I need none. That's the advantage of those who negotiate only with principles."

Talleyrand the actor came to the fore again. Seizing a paper and pen that lay on the table he handed them to Metternich. "Here, write down if you please that France asks for nothing and that France will even refuse to accept anything!"

Talleyrand intended to parlay France's weakness into a strength; it was one of the few weapons at his command and he would make good use of it. He could see himself appearing before the whole Congress as the only envoy equipped to mediate all conflicts, since France, stripped of power and unable to claim anything, could at least argue that she alone had no self-interest involved.

Metternich interjected swiftly, "But you have the business of Naples, which you are clearly making your affair."

"No more mine than everybody's. For me it is only a matter of principle. I insist that he who has a right to be in Naples must be in Naples! Never will I agree to see all of Saxony handed over to Prussia, nor all of Luxembourg nor Mainz, for that matter. Nor will I agree to having Russia acquire forty-four million subjects beyond her frontier."

Metternich took Talleyrand's hand, assuring him warmly, "We're not so far apart as you think. I can promise you Prussia will get neither Luxembourg or Mainz. We don't want to see Russia enlarged any more than you do. As for Saxony we shall do everything in our power to keep at least part of it."

Someone knocked just then on the study door to inform Metternich that the other ministers were assembling in the conference room. Complacently Talleyrand reported next day to the French King, "It was only to sound out Metternich's feelings on these various matters that I talked to him as I did."

That evening Metternich opened the first meeting of the Committee of Eight by reading his proposed draft convoking the Congress for November 1. His draft was worded in such a way as not to exclude the delegates of King Joachim Murat.

Talleyrand's draft was next read; clearly it excluded the Murat delegation from the Congress and other envoys who could not claim to represent "legitimate" monarchs.

Hardenberg and Humboldt at once declared they voted in favor of Metternich's draft, which did not "prejudge anything while Talleyrand's prejudges a great deal." Nesselrode agreed with the Prussians, while the Swedish delegate, Count Loewenhielm, sitting at the table for the first time, nodded sagely and agreed that one should never prejudge anything.

Talleyrand interposed, "Very well then, but if we are announcing the postponement of the Congress until November 1, let us add the words 'and it will be organized according to the Law of Nations.'"

At these words, Talleyrand recollected later, pandemonium broke out at the conference table.

Hardenberg leapt to his feet, pounded with both fists on the table and shouted "almost threateningly and very loudly as deaf people do," "*Non, Monsieur, le droit public?* the Law of Nations? That's no good! Who is saying we shall act according to the Law of Nations? That goes without saying!"

Coolly Talleyrand replied, "If it goes without saying, then it will go all the better for saying it."

Excitedly Humboldt cried, "What is the Law of Nations doing in here anyhow?"

"It brought you here," Talleyrand replied evenly.

Everyone began to talk and argue at once.

Castlereagh led Talleyrand to a corner of the room and asked point-blank whether, if they ceded this point to him, he would promise to be less difficult and more co-operative. Talleyrand promptly countered, "If I become less difficult, will you promise to support me on Naples? And get Austria to do so as well?" Castlereagh agreed. "I'll speak to Metternich about it," he promised.

Gentz in the meantime had been arguing with Metternich about Talleyrand's proposal. "How can one refuse to speak of the Law of Nations in a public act of the kind we are drawing up?"

When the delegates sat down in their places at the table again, Metternich put the question to a voice vote. Talleyrand had won; it was agreed that the phrase, "*le droit public,*" the Law of Nations—public justice, should be inserted in the protocol.

When the meeting broke up at eleven that night, Gentz, gathering up his papers, declared, "This evening, gentlemen, belongs to the history of the Congress. I am not going to be the one to write it because my duty will prevent me, but this evening will certainly be found there."[35]

Gentz was right. The debate that night in the conference room of the Ballhaus was one of historic significance. Whatever had been his reasons— and they had not been pure idealism—Talleyrand had reminded the Congress makers and reminded them cogently, of the great body of international law in which most of them had been trained as young men.

Were the affairs of Europe to be settled according to the highest thinking of the Enlightenment on problems of international order, according to the rational code laid down by Vattel in his *Law of Nations?* Or were they to be decided as Napoleon, the military mind, had decided them, by arbitrary conquest and superior force?

To be sure, even the highest dicta of international law set the rights of property over the rights of human beings. To be sure, the little group of men leading the Congress, all born into a world of wealth and privilege, would restore as much as possible the old world they had known. Yet very dimly that night, in the recesses of the conference room, hovered the ghosts of great voiceless populations while the debate raged over *le droit des gens,* the right of peoples. And the ghosts of those voiceless populations would not quite be lost in the debates over territory. At the Vienna Congress, for the first time at any great international gathering, certain rights of human beings —the abolition of the slave trade, civil rights for German Jews (Jewish men, that is, for women's rights were not yet even debated)—would be considered and argued. And the value of territory would be weighed not in terms of square hectares but of human souls.

XXI

"SIX WEEKS OF HELL"

I find myself again in charge of this whole immense task, and if there is anything fine in the fact there is hardly anything good for me in it. I am going to have four to six weeks of hell!
—METTERNICH TO LAURE, SEPTEMBER 19, 1814

1

"Nothing but visits and return visits. Eating, fireworks, public illuminations. For the last eight or ten days I haven't been able to work at all. What a life!" Archduke Johann wrote in his diary.[1] Some of the ministers, squeezing conferences in between dinner parties and balls, might have echoed his words.

Day after day the social calendar was filled with delights; week after week that October and November the Empress's Festivals Committee presented the Congress guests with a fantastic menu of diversions.

There were concerts of the finest music—five hundred voices sang Handel's *Samson* in the Riding Hall—and of extraordinary novelty—a hundred pianos played under the composer Salieri's direction.

There were gala performances of opera and drama. The sensation of the season was the Paris dancer Bigottini in the tragic ballet *Nina, La Folle d'Amour*, which she mimed so movingly that strong men wept openly while "more sensitive men were carried fainting from their boxes," and Nesselrode forbade his wife to see it for fear of the effect on her delicate condition.

There were falcon hunts in medieval style at the imperial country palace of Laxenburg; there were boar hunts and *grandes battues* in which beaters drove hordes of game into a clearing and each monarch could kill to his heart's content, having four pages assigned to keep his guns loaded. There were artillery maneuvers and military parades and exhibitions of cavalry. There were so many dinner parties that Gentz's invitations sometimes overlapped and he would find himself downing two banquets, one immediately after the other.

All Vienna flocked out to the gardens of Augarten Palace for the People's Festival on October 6, given in honor of the veterans of the late wars. Military bands, acrobats, folk dancers and horse races entertained the crowds. As a grand climax the famous aeronaut Kraskowitz made a balloon ascension, rising majestically in his airy bubble to unfurl the flags of all nations over the city. Four thousand of his Majesty's old soldiers feasted at tables set under huge tents, and the crowds were so great that ladies had their sleeves and skirts torn off.

In the evening a hundred thousand colored lamps lighted the gardens. A fireworks exhibition by the pyrotechnical artist Stuwer painted the flags of the nations in rockets and showers of stars, and people danced all night in the open air.

To walk in the streets of Vienna was entertainment in itself. There, among the uniforms of all the armies and the latest frocks and bonnets, one might meet celebrities from all Europe taking the air, a long queue of smart green-and-white court caleches carrying the Emperor's royal guests out to Schönbrunn, or the Castlereaghs' English carriage driven by a coachman in powdered wig and three-cornered hat and mounted by two lackeys armed with long bamboo poles to prod a way for the vehicle through the dense crowds.

Every night there was at least one ball. Red-eyed dressmakers and seamstresses worked feverishly to stitch up new ball gowns, costumes for masquerades, elaborate dresses with trains for presentation at court. Dancing masters worked overtime teaching rhythms to the slow-footed; hairdressers rushed from one great house to another with curling irons and combs and a growing store of gossip. A pair of witty Viennese journalists created the character of Herr Eipeldauer, a Bohemian rustic come to gawk at the sights; into his mouth they put naïve—and pungent—comments on the Congress. "Because Congress is going to have a heap of dirty laundry to wash, soap's already gone up, and because of the great enlightenment they're going to bring us, so has the price of candles."[2]

Whether the Congress would be a political success remained to be seen, but a social success it was from the beginning. In spite of his eighty years the Prince de Ligne went to all the balls, dropping his witticisms that quickly made the rounds of Congress society. "All Europe is in Vienna," he remarked at the first redoute. "It's a royal rout; *le Congrès ne marche pas—il danse*." Everyone, he said a bit later, had come to claim something at the Congress. As for himself he would have only one claim to submit—for a new hat; he had quite worn out his old one, tipping it to every sovereign he met on a street corner.[3]

The visiting royalty certainly appeared to be enjoying themselves, wandering about the city like ordinary people, appearing at the masquerades incognito. The Tsar declared he had never in all his travels and campaigns had so much fun as in Austria, while of the Russian sovereign the Viennese said he had caught dancing-fever in its most virulent form.

It was, all in all, hardly to be wondered that an atmosphere of carnival reigned in the city, that when Congress visitors sat down years later, gray-headed men and women, to write their memoirs, they remembered Vienna as a glittering, whirling music-lifted ballroom, unlike any other place in the world.

The festivals that autumn had their own internal rhythm and intensity, rising to a crescendo in October and November as political tensions and struggles behind the scenes reached their painful climax, continuing subdued to *lento* in Advent season and rising again *con brio* in carnival.

But all among the rhythms and harmonies there were decided notes of dissonance.

Castlereagh's half brother, Charles Stewart, appeared at more than one fete quite drunk and was reported by the police to have engaged in a nasty fight with a local *Fiaker* driver, out of which he emerged second best.

The Prince Royal of Bavaria and the Crown Prince of Württemberg quarreled one night at the house of the Princess of Thurn and Taxis over a game of blindman's buff. The Württemberg prince accused the Bavarian of moving his eye bandage so he could capture the beautiful Countess Julie Zichy; words were exchanged and the Bavarian prince challenged the other to a duel with pistols in the Prater. Only the intervention of Prince Wrede, sent by the Bavarian king, halted the angry affair. Under the surface of the quarrel lay the tensions between the two countries, not only over territorial rivalry but over the recent action of the Prince Royal of Württemberg in sending back his Bavarian wife, Princess Charlotte, to her royal father in Munich like a rejected parcel, while he applied to the Pope for an annulment so he could marry Grand Duchess Catherine.

The romance of Catherine and the Württemberger had left wounded feelings in the Austrian imperial family as well. Catherine had overtly encouraged the suit of Archduke Karl, then dropped him coolly without explanation when she fell in love with the Prince Royal.

Meantime, against the backdrop of whirling dancers and the light rhythms of the waltz, the official hostess of the Congress, twenty-seven-year-old Empress Maria Ludovica, mortally ill, guided her Festivals Committee, night after night stepped through the ritual polonaise on the arm of the gross King of Württemberg, greeted hundreds of guests at the great banquets and receptions, and fainted in the arms of her ladies-in-waiting on the way back to her apartment when the evening ended. "The poor woman with her pale consumptive face and her frail bent form is killing herself every day," wrote Anna Eynard feelingly in her diary.[4]

2

While the world waited for the Congress of Europe to begin, Metternich found himself in those weeks of October and November embroiled in a double crisis that threatened to bring both his personal and his political life to shipwreck.

The Poland-Saxony question was approaching a climax. On Sunday, October 9, Hardenberg sent to Metternich and Castlereagh a formal memorandum demanding the whole of Saxony with its two and a half million inhabitants for Prussia, together with the city of Mainz on the Rhine. Small wonder that Hardenberg had objected loudly at the previous evening's conference to the inclusion of the Law of Nations in the declaration on the opening of the Congress.

Castlereagh had England's reply ready almost at once. England, he wrote, would agree to the absorption of Saxony by Prussia, provided that Saxony was not to be a recompense to Prussia for losing her Polish possessions to Russia. To such a trade-off England would not assent.[5]

Metternich could not decide. Castlereagh urged him to give in to Prussia on the question of Saxony so that Prussia would support them in resisting the Tsar on Poland. But Metternich himself opposed the annihilation of Saxony as an independent kingdom. The Austrian Emperor, the Cabinet, public opinion, all protested against the injustice of sacrificing a once friendly monarch—and worse yet, the grave danger of so great an aggrandizement of Prussia.

Yet how else to win Prussian support in thwarting the Tsar's plans for a Russian-dominated kingdom of Poland?

For ten days Metternich brooded over the Prussian demand, while he weighed all the political eventualities, tried to foresee and to assess every contingent gambit on the chessboard.

As ill luck would have it, while he tried to reach a decision on that critical issue—on which depended a whole array of other decisions—he was living through one of the most shattering emotional experiences of his lifetime.

What had happened between Metternich and Wilhelmine in those early days of October? Everything—and nothing.

Since that star-marked October 1, which he remembered as a day of "the greatest happiness in my life," the whole tide of their love affair had changed. Though he saw her nearly every day, at a dinner or supper party, at a soiree or a ball, more and more seldom did she give him an opportunity to see her alone. Even when he left his busy office and hurried to Schenkenstrasse at the consecrated hour of eleven in the morning, he would find visitors in her salon—among them, nearly always, Alfred Windischgraetz. He had not, after all, vanished from her life.

That "fatal tenderness" for Alfred! Once again Alfred seemed omnipresent, at her dinner table, at her elbow when she poured tea for visitors in the evening, dancing with her at the great balls, holding her fan and fetching her supper. As colonel of that distinguished regiment of cuirassiers whose renown went back to the Thirty Years War, rechristened now for its titular commander, Grand Duke Constantine, Alfred rode at all the military fetes and maneuvers, handsome and dashing in his parade uniforms, one of the most admired cavalry officers in the Allied armies.

With the antennae of a sensitive lover Metternich was at once aware of a subtle change in that triangular relationship.

He would not at first allow himself to believe anything was irretrievably amiss. She had given him her word; he had promised not to provoke her with jealousy and accusations. Gentz, with his sardonic and suspicious temperament, looking for "illegalities" to prove her faithlessness, was scarcely the friend to allay Metternich's wretchedness.

On Wednesday afternoon, October 5, Alfred had given a lively little dinner party. Talleyrand and Gentz were there, the two sisters Wilhelmine and Dorothée, Wenzel Liechtenstein and a half dozen others. Talleyrand reported to the King of France "a very long and serious conversation" he had had with Gentz after dinner. "Gentz appeared to regret I had not arrived in Vienna sooner. Affairs, with which he seems very dissatisfied, might have taken a different turn. . . ."[6]

Apparently something else had happened at that dinner party, something between Alfred and Wilhelmine, that made perfectly clear at least to some present that the liaison between the two had been renewed. It may have been an indiscreet gesture of affection, a word or a look; it may have been the manner in which Wilhelmine presided as hostess at Alfred's dinner table quite as if she belonged there. In any case either Gentz or Wenzel, or perhaps both, reported straight back to Metternich.

Despite his promise, Metternich importuned her for reassurance, begged for explanations, which irritated and bored her.

Sunday night the Emperor and Empress gave a magnificent *bal paré* in the palace. The beautiful double-arcaded Riding Hall had been transformed into a glittering ice palace of crystal and silver, with silver-shot hangings and immense mirrors over the windows, reflecting the dazzle of ten thousand candles in the crystal chandeliers.

Women had been asked to come in gowns of white, pale blue or rose, gentlemen to wear uniform, or blue or black tailcoats with white or blue breeches. Both men and women blazed with jewels. There was no naïve modesty in that day about exhibiting gems on one's person. Tiaras and bracelets, jeweled belts and orders appeared, many of them worn for the first time since the Revolution, when they had been carried precariously from one country to another, hidden in the carriages of families fleeing to exile. The most precious gems in the imperial treasury had been brought out to adorn the pale thin neck and arms of the Austrian Empress, while the Tsarina Elizabeth glittered with the celebrated jewels of Catherine the Great.

During the intermezzo at the ball that night, twenty-four of the most beautiful women of the court, costumed to represent the four elements, appeared and moved gracefully around the arena to music—the daughters of Air in blue gauze with zephyr wings, the daughters of Fire in flame-colored silk with torches, the daughters of Water in blue-green with crowns of coral and pearls and seashells. Wilhelmine appeared among the daughters of Earth, in brown velvet with diamonds, carrying on her head a golden basket filled with jeweled fruit.

Never had she appeared more alluring to Metternich—never more distant.

Already Vienna society gossiped of the renewal of the old ties between her and Alfred, and of Metternich's lost amour.

A little later he would recall to her that painful period in their relationship:

> . . . Each day, far from enlarging my claims, saw them diminish. Unhappiness exhausted my physical strength to the point of making my friends fall silent. I had to vanquish my affections to the point of finding a bit of pleasure in the brief space your other relationships allowed you to allot me, without any other favor than what any person admitted to your company might share. I would not ask you any longer for love. I deceived myself to the point of thinking I could live without it. . . .[7]

There had been no intimacy between them since October 1, the day, he had written her in a moment of joy, "that gave me back much of my strength." He did not accuse her outright of infidelity; he had promised not to doubt her, but he suffered again the most excruciating torment of jealousy.

The day after the *bal paré*, on Monday afternoon, October 10, he and Hardenberg and Humboldt dined with the Saxon envoy, Count Schulenburg. Metternich broached the idea of some compromise plan on Saxony—if for example, Prussia would be satisfied with a portion of Saxony, and the rest could be saved as an independent kingdom. But the Prussians showed no sign of diminishing their demands, and Metternich could only promise Schulenburg privately that he was "falling back on time and was arming himself with patience."

Later that evening the German Committee met at Metternich's—with Hardenberg, Humboldt, Wessenberg and Gentz, but nothing could really be decided about the rest of Germany until the matter of Saxony was settled.

The meeting adjourned early for the Metternichs' Monday night supper-dance for two hundred fifty guests. Not until long after midnight did the last of the long queue of carriages rumble away over the cobblestones of the Ballhaus Square.

He had tried in vain to talk to Wilhelmine alone for a few moments, but she had eluded him. It was on Alfred's arm she had gone to her carriage.

Metternich was utterly devastated. At this moment when he most needed all his faculties, a clear mind, perfect composure and self-confidence, he was shattered by the pain of losing the woman he had loved above any other in his life.

Instead of going to bed at the end of that exhausting, eighteen-hour day, Metternich bowed over his desk by the light of a candle in a room grown cold, writing Wilhelmine a letter freighted with anguish. How did one handle heroically a lost engagement on the field of love and still keep one's pride intact? He would withdraw, he wrote her, for the sake of *her* honor. The world would never forgive her for appearing to have two lovers:

> Of all faults that is the only one the world will not pardon; the world must not accuse you of what is not true. W. is doing everything possible to publicize relations that lose their invidious character the day they are exclusively joined. You encourage both his actions and appearances.[8]

He would not admit the possibility that she had deceived him, but the attitude between them had utterly changed. This immense sacrifice he would make for her sake. "I love *your honor* a hundred times more than *your life*."

He would not, could not break with her:

> In me you will find the friend of your life: I take on myself the role of rejected suitor. . . . My attentions will cease. No complaint will escape my mouth. I shall punish all evil jokes at your expense. Between you and me you alone are everything!

How could he give her up—he, a mature man, profoundly in love as he had never been in his life, with a sexual passion he had felt for no other woman, joined to admiration and pleasure in her intellectual gifts, in her insights and political acumen, sharper at times even than his own, more valuable at this moment to him than ever? "You have surely been loved," he wrote, "and you will be loved again, but you will never be more loved, and you have never been more loved, than by me."

His strength was quite broken; she had borne it all away. He concluded his letter:

> Let my heart break now as much as it wishes, let my life itself cease, I shall not have been called to live for my beloved but I shall redress her honor and I shall die content.[9]

There was not much of the night left when he had finished and in those few hours he tossed and turned sleeplessly.

At nine o'clock in the morning Gentz was on his doorstep wanting to talk about Saxony. "Important conversation," Gentz noted that night in his diary. "Resolution brought about by Prince Hardenberg's letter. I declare that he [Metternich] will not yield on Mainz, etc., and in case of necessity he will draw closer to France."[10]

As soon as Gentz had gone, Metternich hurried to Wilhelmine's carrying his letter with him. Again he found her with friends, and though he stayed long beyond his usual visit, he had only a few moments alone with her. In those moments she broached with him the question of Gustava Armfelt. Could he not press the Tsar further on it? As soon as Congress was over, the Tsar would be leaving, so it must be done soon.

At one o'clock on that Tuesday, two Swiss gentlemen from Geneva, Jean-Gabriel Eynard, a banker, and Pictet de Rochemont, a professional diplomat, appeared at the Chancellery for an appointment with Metternich.

The prince was not in, they were told. Gradually the anteroom filled with petitioners: Cardinal Consalvi, the papal legate, in red stockings and *calotte*, important-looking gentlemen with morocco *portefeuilles*, their breasts gleaming with stars, and humbler petitioners armed with the patience of habitual waiting. "In Paris I spent five to six days on end waiting like this without ever getting in to see anyone," De Rochemont murmured to Eynard.[11]

When Metternich arrived finally at half past two, the cardinal was the first to be ushered into the inner office, where he remained nearly an hour; then Humboldt, who had burst in in a great hurry, took priority over those waiting since one o'clock. At four Eynard, still waiting for his one o'clock appointment, approached a valet de chambre who guarded the door of the inner sanctum, to ask whether there was any hope of being received that day.

The valet replied, "Monsieur le Prince was invited to dine at Countess Zichy's at half past three. It is late already and he has not yet begun to dress."

The Swiss remarked that they would rather go away now than wait longer and be dismissed with the crowd. Perhaps at this juncture a golden coin changed hands discreetly, for the valet suddenly took a fatherly interest in them and said optimistically, "Since you've waited so long already, stay another moment, perhaps he will receive you." And so it turned out: the instant Humboldt left, the friendly valet called them to enter. Eynard noted in his diary that night:

> The minister received us very well. It would be impossible to have more charming manners than Metternich.

They discussed the problems of Geneva and of Switzerland, especially of Geneva's need for a bit of territory that had been given to France in order to join her effectively to the rest of Switzerland.

Metternich, Eynard also noted in his diary that night, appeared "overwhelmed with exhaustion." His face was drawn, his eyelids drooped; despite his beautiful manners he could barely suppress yawns in their presence.

His weariness was hardly astonishing. For days on end he had got along on little sleep; the previous night he had scarcely slept at all.

A brief note in reply to his long letter of renunciation had come from Wilhelmine. It was more concerned with the matter of Vava Armfelt than with the possibility that he might no longer be her lover:

> I have given your letter to W—— What can I find to tell you again. I can only thank you again and ask you to speak to Brassier; a word from you will decide him much more surely. Bonjour, good and dear friend—and then—[12]

Wilhelmine's trustee and legal adviser, Count Wratislaw of Prague, who knew the history of the Armfelt entanglement and had all the documents pertaining to the case, was in Vienna. In these two weeks of October, Metternich—despite the crisis in his love affair—continued to work on a plan for regaining custody of the child.

He had promised to win her daughter for her; he would do his best to keep that promise. Did it appear to him now that if anything could win her heart back to him, it would be the gift of her child?

3

Promptly at nine o'clock on Wednesday morning, Gentz was waiting to talk with Metternich while Giroux coiffed and dressed him for the day. Again it was the burning issue of Saxony that Gentz had come to talk about.

Castlereagh had hired Gentz to translate into French the English reply to Hardenberg's demand for Saxony. Gentz was appalled at the reasoning behind Castlereagh's note that agreed to the surrender. He had translated it, he wrote, "with a feeling of shame. It is difficult to believe that men with reputations to lose could put their names to such miserable reasoning."[13]

Castlereagh argued that the sacrifice of Saxony would serve a dual purpose: a greatly enlarged Prussia would make north Germany safe from the encroachments of either France or Russia—and, most importantly for English commercial interests, it would protect the Low Countries against France.

Besides strengthening Prussia, the destruction of Saxony was clearly intended as a punitive measure against the King of Saxony for maintaining until Leipzig his alliance with Napoleon.

> I do not know [Castlereagh wrote] if there is in Germany another example of a political immorality of like character. I know none that is equally shocking.
> If ever a sovereign placed himself in a situation of having to be sacrificed for the tranquillity of Europe, I believe it is the King of Saxony.[14]

There was a third reason for England to support Prussia's demand, though it was not a reason Castlereagh would convey openly to Metternich. In Paris Wellington discussed it frankly with Jaucourt: "A powerful Prussia is a useful rival of Austria. . . ."[15]

Certainly Castlereagh had been strongly encouraged and supported in his decision both by his aide Cooke and by his brother Stewart, who had spent many weeks during the previous campaign at Prussian general headquarters and had been completely won over by the Prussian expansionist group.

But Castlereagh's arguments for destroying an independent nation would hardly accord with the Law of Nations. As it turned out, his move was a grave error in political judgment and presently most of Europe, including his own Tory Cabinet, would object in no uncertain terms.

When Gentz tried to press Metternich that Wednesday for his stand on

Saxony, Metternich replied vaguely that he was still pondering it, had reached no decision. To Gentz's vexation Metternich's mind kept wandering to other matters—especially to his star-crossed love affair.

If Metternich was evasive, Talleyrand was an ally on whom he could count. From the Chancellery Gentz hastened to the Kaunitz Palace to inform Talleyrand of the contents of Castlereagh's letter.

The preservation of Saxony was one of the first points Talleyrand had listed in his own instructions; he was prepared to battle it through to the end. He urged Gentz to argue it out with Metternich, though Gentz declared that Metternich these days was barely listening to him.

Back went Gentz to the Chancellery, maneuvered an invitation to dinner for himself and Wessenberg. As soon as dinner was over he broached the Saxony question "in the most energetic language [Metternich] has ever heard from me." No more the timorous Gentz, overshadowed by Metternich's brilliant personality. No, that night it was Metternich who had little to say, while Gentz, secretary of the Congress, argued with vehemence and power. Austria must defend the independence of Saxony! If force and conquest are to decide the disposition of territory, then we have returned to the principles of Napoleon. That Wednesday Gentz recorded as "one of the most crucial in the history of my public life; it will perhaps be the finest of my life."[16]

While the three men sat talking of Saxony, a footman brought a note in Wilhelmine's hand proposing that Metternich come to the Palais Palm that evening. Her sister Jeanne had returned to Vienna; could he—Metternich—grant a passport so their half brother, Schwedhof, might come? She added, "Brassier has come. I have things to talk over with you."[17] Those "things" were the matter of Gustava Armfelt. Brassier, an old friend from Sagan who was the steward of her sister Pauline's Silesian estates, had come to Vienna to aid her on the matter of her child. Metternich had proposed that Brassier be sent to St. Petersburg and perhaps also to Madame Armfelt in Sweden.

But tonight Metternich would not see her; complete exhaustion overwhelmed him. As soon as his dinner guests had left, he sent off a note declining her invitation:

> I shall not go to you tonight, *mon amie*. I am a little more calm and I shall try to sleep. I think I shall succeed by not moving, and you know better than anyone what sleep does for one. I have an absolutely imperious need for it, and if you think about me after midnight, hope that I am not thinking.
>
> I shall see W[ratislaw?] tomorrow. I shall tell him all my thoughts and I hope he will approve. As soon as we are agreed we shall begin the question with Brassier. If you have an hour free tomorrow morning I shall go to you. I shall give you an account of my work and you will approve it or discard it as you judge it suitable and useful. You know that in many ways I trust your ideas more than my own and that in many ways I like to see the latter approved—yours. In the present case I defy anyone

to do better than I. I could defend it against everyone; I adore it because it is entirely mine, because it is placed outside all vulgar expectation, and because my life will never appear long enough to prove to you that one being exists in the world who does not limit his claims to sharing your happiness alone.[18]

While Metternich postponed his own decision on Saxony that week, "falling back on time," as he had told Schulenburg, he hoped for some significant turn of events to point his direction. He urged Castlereagh to talk to the Tsar, to sound him out on his Polish plans again. If the Tsar showed signs of relenting his demands, then he—Metternich—could take a harder line on Prussia; he could insist on salvaging at least a portion of Saxony. He would be less in need of Prussia's total support.

Castlereagh therefore agreed to ask the Tsar for an audience, which the Tsar granted in a roundabout way by going to pay a formal call on Lady Castlereagh on Thursday afternoon, October 13, then staying on to discuss Poland with Castlereagh for an hour and a half. Both men produced all their arguments on the disposition of Poland, but the discussion ended in a stalemate. Far from softening in his plans to make a kingdom of Poland under the Russian Crown, the Tsar had hardened his stand, and he defended his plans, "both political and territorial, with much warmth and tenacity." The question of Poland, the Tsar concluded flatly, could end in only one way, since the Russian Army was in occupation and he had no intention of withdrawing his troops.

Castlereagh was bitterly disappointed. He had expected that his mediation on the problems of Saxony and Poland would produce instant results. It had not done so, and the Poland problem at least seemed far from solution. In his memorandum to the Tsar he reiterated all his arguments, proposing that if the Tsar conceived it his moral duty to establish a Polish monarchy, "let them be rendered again really independent as a nation instead of making two-thirds of them a mere formidable military instrument in the hands of a single Power." All Europe would applaud the re-establishment of a truly independent nation of Poland, and it "would be cheerfully acquiesced in by both Austria and Prussia."

If, however, the Tsar continued to adhere to his own plan, Castlereagh warned, "it is impossible that any plan for the reconstruction of Europe can be brought forward, or that the present Congress can be assembled to discuss any such arrangement."[19]

The Tsar did not reply.

To Castlereagh it now appeared more urgent than ever that Austria buy the support of Prussia by sacrificing Saxony. The following day, Friday, October 14, Castlereagh persuaded Gentz to support the provisional occupation of Saxony by Prussia.[20] Let the cat then hold the mouse—but just for the moment.

Hastening back to the Chancellery to report, Gentz could get Metternich to talk of nothing except "alas!—the unhappy liaison with Windischgraetz, which appears to interest him more even than the affairs of the world."[21]

Again and again in the next days Gentz would fume to his diary about Metternich's absorption in his disastrous love affair.

Worse yet, Metternich had assigned him—Gentz—to iron out the details of the Gustava Armfelt case. On Friday morning early, at the hour he usually appeared at the Chancellery, Gentz stayed home to discuss the case with Wratislaw. The duchess's bastard against the future of Europe!

And very late that Friday night, when he appeared at Wilhelmine's soiree, and Talleyrand showed him the sharp letter of protest he had addressed to the Committee of Eight against Prussian annexation of Saxony, Metternich took no part in the discussion apparently. He was busy showing Wilhelmine costume engravings he had brought for her to choose from to wear at his masked ball in early November, and discussing Handel's oratorio to be given in the Riding Hall on Sunday.[22]

Whatever reply Metternich might be shaping in his head to the Hardenberg memorandum, when Gentz talked to him on Saturday morning, Metternich appeared ready to give in:

> The effect of my great efforts of last Wednesday is effaced [wrote Gentz]; he wants to yield and he will yield. Saxony is lost.[23]

So Gentz informed both Hardenberg and Castlereagh, and though nothing had yet been put in writing, the rumor that Austria would surrender Saxony flew from one end of Vienna to the other.

That same Saturday morning, October 15, while Metternich breakfasted with his family, a servant brought him a letter bearing Wilhelmine's seal:

> When I saw that it was long I went downstairs to my rooms, shut myself in and read it. My dear, I could not reread it for one must be able to see to read—and one does not see with one's eyes filled with tears! What did I feel! I felt, I wept—that is all I know. I shall reread this letter which contains so many good things. . . .[24]

She had finally written a reply to his long letter of the Monday before:

> Mon ami, I have read and reread your letter. I understand you in everything except the relations that are to follow the new direction you want to take.[25]

His generosity and his sacrifices touched her deeply, but she did not really understand his exalted way of loving. As for herself, she felt fragmented "by the whirlwind in which we live and the much greater whirlwind in which I myself am tossed." She thought she was at heart the same person, but calm reason that should have put all the pieces together had disappeared.

She promised to "give a different direction to W.'s conduct—at least to neutralize by my own what there is in him opposed to my peace of mind."

She would soon put a distance between Alfred and herself. She would go to Ratiborzitz as soon as the Congress was over. "A greater separation and a longer absence will put an end to my torments and to the uncertainties of this world." She asked only two things of him: that he take care of himself, "if it is true that I am so dear to you." The second was to judge her with indulgence "until that time when I tell you myself I am no longer this person sick in heart and soul that I am now." She had broken her promise to him, but she could not help herself:

> Adieu, dear Clemens—pardon me for the wrong I do you. God knows it is despite myself and believe that nobody is more truly attached to you and devoted to you than I.

She denied nothing; clearly the old passion for Alfred had reasserted itself.

She said nothing of her "honor," that ambiguous article for which Metternich claimed to be sacrificing himself. What did they mean, these funny men, talking about a woman's "honor," when what they really meant was some sort of stamp permitting themselves exclusive possession of her body? All these rules they had set up around so simple a matter as loving a man or men?

He wrote asking her to set an hour the following day when he might see her. The famous Peace Ball at his villa was to be given the following Tuesday, and she had asked about the arrangement of the supper tables so that she might sit facing the table where the sovereigns were to sit. He enclosed a plan of the supper room; she might mark the table she wished:

> Among the dreadful bizarreries of my position at the moment [he wrote her] are the incongruous occupations I must perform. To be far away from everything—far from business, far from pleasures that are only torments if your heart is not sharing them—far far away from everything—that is what I need. I long for such a place as a person sick with fever longs for a refreshing drink! Such a place with you would be heaven—without you it would still have some charm for me! My beloved one, I am very ill and God [. . .] my hope. If the world offers me no more happiness, my soul released from all that crushes it at this moment will look for reward on high! I shall love you always—and the day when you follow me you will find me calm, serene, happy. On high there will be only happiness between us.[26]

The four "friends" met briefly that Saturday, and when the conference was over Metternich went to dine at Wilhelmine's.

"Political conversation with Metternich and Talleyrand," Gentz noted succinctly that night. That intimate dinner party, apparently so casually arranged, had probably been at Talleyrand's instigation. Present were Metternich's closest men friends—Gentz, Floret, Wenzel Liechtenstein—together with Wilhelmine and Dorothée. Windischgraetz was conspicuously absent.[27]

Talleyrand had already learned all the details of Castlereagh's unsuccessful conversation with the Tsar on Thursday. He knew that Metternich still hesitated on Saxony, had not yet put anything into writing. If Gentz had failed that week in his arguments with Metternich, then perhaps he, Talleyrand, could succeed. That Saturday Talleyrand marshaled all his forces to persuade Metternich to resist the Prussian demands.

If Prussia, he pointed out, were allowed to swallow up Saxony and to dominate all Germany with a military monarchy, "very dangerous to her neighbors," a revolution in Germany might follow—not a revolution of the middle and lower classes as in France, but a nationalist revolution led by the mediatized princes, who wanted to restore Germany to an empire made up of over a hundred small independent bits and pieces.

Austria, he urged, ought to be prepared to use force or the threat of force to bring Prussia and Russia to terms. Bavaria had already offered an army of 50,000 to help Austria defend the integrity of Saxony, and Württemberg had offered 10,000.[28]

Metternich, in reply, asked quietly whether France too would be willing to join such a war?

It had probably been Gentz a few days earlier who quipped to Dalberg when the latter spoke hotly of the need for force, "You [French] look to me like dogs who bark very readily but who do not bite, and we don't want to bite alone!"[29]

Congress had not yet opened officially; already the specter of war hovered over the negotiations.

The day after the dinner party at Wilhelmine's Talleyrand would write the King of France asking for special instructions permitting him to promise Austria the military aid of France; he would use it only "in the case of evident and extreme necessity."[30]

But farthest from Metternich's mind was the idea of going to war; there were many ways the threads could be woven—one did not snap them apart.

At some point after Wilhelmine's dinner party that day, Saturday, October 15, Metternich talked with the Tsar and again discussed Poland with him. According to Charles Stewart, the Tsar told him a day or two later that he repeated to Metternich his intention to keep the whole of Poland, and Metternich had made no objection. "I am afraid," Stewart added, "that Prince Metternich is not acting with that straightforward policy which becomes him at so critical a juncture."[31]

Poland was not the only subject on Metternich's mind that afternoon. He had talked "in depth" with the Tsar, he wrote Wilhelmine next day, on the subject "of our little one." The Tsar had seen and talked both with Madame Armfelt and with Gustava at the time of Armfelt's death in August. The child had told him she wanted to stay with her adopted mother, the only mother she had known. He, the Tsar, would put no obstacle in the way, but clearly he felt the child's wishes should be considered. It would be absolutely necessary, Metternich thought, for Brassier to go to St. Petersburg.[32]

October 18, the day of Metternich's Peace Festival, was a day as beautiful and as mild as summer.

From early morning troops and holiday crowds filled the streets on their way out to the Prater. If the sovereigns in their luxurious quarters in the Hofburg thought they might sleep a bit later that morning, they were sorely mistaken, for just after daybreak Grand Duke Constantine led his regiment of cuirassiers, in which Alfred Windischgraetz served as colonel, through the courtyards of the palace with all trumpets blasting, a right that regiment had exercised since the Thirty Years War. Bells rang, bands played military marches, cavalry clattered over cobbles, and the ladies of the court in open carriages drove out to be seated in velvet-colored armchairs on the reviewing green.

Metternich had planned it originally as a celebration of peace without a hint of the military in it. Writing to Laure earlier on arrangements for the fete at their villa, he had firmly specified that he would have

. . . nothing military because we [want] no more soldiers but everything pacific. My soiree must breathe 20 years of peace.[33]

Yet almost at the last moment Emperor Franz ordered Schwarzenberg and Langenau to arrange a grand military exhibition in the Prater that day, the first anniversary of the battle of Leipzig. Schwarzenberg grumbled a bit to his wife that he was in a "furious turmoil" to prepare it on such short notice.[34] It may be that the turn of political events, the increasing tensions of the Saxony-Poland quarrel, had induced the Emperor to rattle the sword a bit. Let his difficult allies, especially Russia, be reminded that Austria had an army in readiness.

The troops paraded, then formed a great double square around an open pavilion where an altar had been set up, the columns of the pavilion decorated with banners and trophies of the late campaigns. The Archbishop of Vienna said Mass, and at the moment of the consecration of the host, an immense salvo of artillery boomed out, the whole assembly—emperors, kings, generals, troops and citizens—fell on their knees, to rise at the end of the service and sing in German the "Hymn to Peace." Afterward some twenty thousand veterans dined as guests of the Emperor at long tables set up on the green. The high-ranking guests withdrew to the nearby palace of Prince Razumowsky to be wined and dined. "A splendid unforgettable day," the novelist Karoline Pichler called it.

If the military had dominated the day's festivities, the famous ball at the Metternich villa that night did indeed have only peace as its theme. Ladies had been asked to wear the symbolic colors of peace, white or blue, and they came in gowns embroidered in gold or silver, wearing wreaths of olive or oak in their hair and wound in their tiaras.

The ballroom addition built on especially for the festival, in the form of a great domed pavilion supported by a circle of pillars, was so spacious, Eynard observed, that it was not crowded even with eighteen hundred guests, yet it could not have accommodated a hundred more.

As soon as the royal guests had arrived and everyone gathered in the gardens, a balloon rose releasing into the night sky rockets and showers of stars that formed the arms of the sovereigns and gave the signal for the elaborate festival program to begin.[35]

With the sovereigns leading the way, the throng of guests strolled through the gardens, where along the way little spectacles had been arranged —a ballet before a miniature temple of Apollo, a *tableau mouvant* before a temple of Minerva, vocal and instrumental music from performers hidden in the shrubbery and behind the hedges.

At the climax of the program the guests, seated in a large open amphitheater facing a stretch of lawn, watched a pantomime in fireworks of a city under siege, and at the end a symbolic pageant of the nations meeting in concord before an altar of peace.

Everyone marveled at the brilliance of the lighting of the villa and gardens —outdoors, colorful *feux de Bengale*; indoors, the ballroom, according to one guest, looking like the palace of the princess in the tale of Aladdin's lamp, "white as snow and lighted as if by the sun at noon."

Eynard declared it outshone any fete he had attended in the Tuileries in the heyday of Napoleon.[36] No expense had been spared to make the festival memorable; the Emperor was paying the cost.

Metternich had taken great precaution against the danger of fire, and there were no draperies anywhere. A single candle falling from a single candelabrum could turn a crowded ballroom into a holocaust, as the Metternichs well knew from their memories of the terrible fire at the Austrian embassy in Paris in 1810, when Schwarzenberg's sister-in-law had lost her life.

The ball began with the inevitable polonaise, but this was succeeded by lively Russian dances in the Tsar's honor, and by a long series of waltzes.

At midnight the guests flocked down the broad flights of stairs that led from the ballroom to the supper rooms, where ladies sat at little tables, each decorated differently with flowers and favors, the gentlemen fetching them delicacies from the loaded buffets. The sovereigns sat on a raised dais in the center of the room, except for the Tsar and the King of Prussia, who preferred to "float" and attend to the wishes of the lovelier ladies.

Many guests remembered the Metternich Peace Ball as the most beautiful of all the Congress fetes.

Even the traffic jam at the end of the evening, when hundreds of carriages coming to call for guests became hopelessly snarled in the narrow roadway, brought a merry finale to the evening. As Countess Bernstorff recollected:

> The crush for carriages was so great that we had to wait hours for them.
> . . . I shall never forget the original and beautiful appearance of
> the scene. [Imagine] a flight of stairs almost as high as a house, carpeted

in red, canopied with Turkish tents and lighted by bright pitch torches, on which camped a large part of the company, wrapped in cloaks . . . I waited until early dawn for the arrival of my carriage.[37]

Chatting, laughing, humming the latest waltzes, the last of the guests crowded together on the carpeted stairs, watching the beautiful starlit night change to daybreak.

Whatever the party had been for his guests, and however flawlessly he had played his role of host, Metternich was in the depths of despondency next morning when Gentz called at the Chancellery. Metternich and Laure were at breakfast, Laure a silent and sympathetic reflection of her husband's misery.

"Sad morning after," Gentz noted. "Very black scene."[38]

Toward the end of the ball and unnoticed by most of the guests had occurred an unpleasant little scene between Metternich and the Tsar, which the Austrian Emperor's brother, Archduke Johann, noted later in his diary.[39]

The Tsar, standing in a circle of listeners, had said sarcastically to Metternich, "You diplomats make decisions and then we soldiers have to let ourselves be shot up into cripples for you."

When the Tsar noticed that Archduke Johann was listening, he repeated the remark. "I was silent," Archduke Johann wrote, "because others stood nearby, but finally I said that it was unfortunately true, and that the great sovereigns (*die Herren*) only regarded us as tools for their whims and counted blood for little. A pity that I could not speak to this sovereign alone; I would have made other observations to him."

The Tsar's remark, intended to offend Metternich, had of course reached its mark. No charge could have wounded and infuriated Metternich more, nor could any accusation have been more patently unjust. It was he who had offered to mediate peace in 1813, who had held out longest against war, who had arranged the St. Aignan mission and the Châtillon Congress, while the Tsar had destroyed the chance for an earlier peace at the Prague Congress by keeping secret England's acquiescence to negotiation, and later by insisting on the march to Paris.

Yet as host and minister Metternich had to bite his lip and remain silent.

The Tsar had made other slighting remarks during the evening that had already been carried back to Metternich's ears. To Marie Thérèse Esterházy the Tsar had commented that while the fete was beautiful and the ballroom splendid, there was "always diplomacy in such things and he did not like what was deceitful."

To old Princess Metternich, Clemens' mother, the Tsar had remarked caustically, "I don't trust any man who has never been a soldier."[40]

Certainly the personal animosity between the two men had grown increasingly bitter, while a peaceful settlement of the Congress issues seemed increasingly remote.

But if the quarrel with the Tsar deepened Metternich's despondency, his love affair plunged him into black despair.

Everything between him and Wilhelmine had changed. There were scenes, confrontations between them that often ended for her in a torrent of tears. Though he had promised not to reproach her, whenever he found himself alone with her, he besieged her with arguments and accusations—as if a broken affair could be reasoned back together again. He heaped recriminations on her head—then begged her for an hour in which to ask her pardon.

At his ball the night before she had kept herself surrounded by a circle of admirers. "I hoped not only to see you but to say a few words to you during the evening," he wrote her that Wednesday morning. "As that could not be, I had to renounce it." He had begun a long reply to her last letter, but he would not be able to bring it to her until the next day, "seeing that the kind of life one leads now resembles nothing on earth."[41]

He would do anything for her—anything. At the moment he was trying to dislodge Princess Bagration from the Palais Palm, a move that could have dangerous consequences.

Even though their relationship was in a state of crisis, he could still win her instant attention by speaking of Gustava. And as if to prove the generosity and disinterest of his love for her, he would continue to work to win the child back. That Wednesday he enclosed in his note a letter and a plan of action for recovering Gustava:

> Just now they brought me the enclosed letter—read it and tell me what you think. The plan attached is the one I did not at all wish to support. Tell me too when Wratislaw could discuss it with you as well as with me.[42]

Like nearly all his letters to Wilhelmine, the note was written in French. But he had added a last line in German: "This affair is bringing me to my grave, it can go as it will."

All of them dined that day at Talleyrand's—Wilhelmine, Dorothée, Gentz, the Stackelbergs and the Metternichs—Laure too, who was not always included in dinner invitations. At some point Metternich, Wilhelmine and Gentz arranged certain important negotiations concerning Gustava for the following day.

The next morning, October 20, Wratislaw appeared very early at Gentz's apartments to discuss "affairs of the Duchess of Sagan," Gentz notes tersely. Gentz went immediately to the Chancellery to report to Metternich and to discuss "relations with her"; from the Chancellery he went on to Schenkenstrasse. "To the duchess's at 11 o'clock for one of the most remarkable negotiations!" The exclamation point is Gentz's, and it is an especially maddening one. Not a clue does he give us to those mysterious negotiations; all has been discreetly erased from the diary.[43]

Certain it is that Wilhelmine reached a decision that Thursday to try one last avenue of her own—direct intervention with the Tsar. She was prepared to do anything, even to buy the child back if Madame Armfelt could be bought.

Time was growing short. The following Sunday the Tsar and the King of Prussia were to travel to Hungary as guests of the Emperor Franz. The Tsar had expressed a wish to visit the tomb of his elder sister, Alexandra, who had married Archduke Stephen, Palatine of Hungary, and had died in Budapest; they would be absent from Vienna for a week.

When the Tsar returned it would be nearly the end of October. Congress was to open November 1 and everything would certainly be finished by mid-November. No, Wilhelmine thought, there was no time to be lost. Only the powerful Tsar could reach out his hand and restore Gustava to her real mother.

On that evening of Thursday, October 20, Count Stackelberg gave a ball in honor of the Tsar and Tsarina, an intimate affair to which only the sovereigns, the top aristocracy and the diplomatic corps were invited.

During the evening, as Metternich stood talking to a group not far away, the Tsar approached Wilhelmine; she curtsied deeply and asked if His Imperial Majesty would grant her an audience. She had a favor to ask him.

The Tsar replied charmingly, "My dear Wilhelmine, there is no question of an audience. Of course *I* shall come to see *you!* Only name the day and the hour—shall it be tomorrow at eleven?"[44]

He nodded coolly to Metternich and passed on.

Nothing could have wounded Metternich more profoundly than Wilhelmine's overture to the Tsar. Just at that moment, as the Saxony-Poland affair approached its climax, did she not understand that what she did and said was bound to be misinterpreted by the world at large?

More cruel yet, at this moment when the ties of their liaison were severing, when he walked a sharp knife-edge of pain, for her to ask favors of the man with whom he was engaged in deadly combat was to hand his enemy one more weapon against him. And she had set the hour of their meeting at eleven in the morning, the hour that had for long been consecrated to their love. She, who knew him so well, who understood better than anyone the precarious diplomatic campaign he was waging—it was sheer betrayal!

Metternich had read all the police reports, he knew what gossip was saying of his broken love affair. From those police reports he knew too of the Tsar's strange, almost pathological interest in Metternich's relationships with women.

Metternich left the Stackelberg ball at once that night and drove home. The fine autumn weather had broken at last, and a chilly rain had begun to fall.

Giroux was in bed; in the study the hearth was cold, the candles extinguished except for the night lamp. As he had on so many nights in the winter before, Metternich sat at his desk in the numbingly lonely hours before daybreak to write her once more—not a love letter this time, but one of the most painful letters of his life. In later years, when he had to write letters announcing the death of persons very dear to him, those letters would be less grieving than the one he wrote at four in the morning on October 21, 1814.

A few hours later, at ten o'clock in the morning, Gentz found Metternich at his desk again. While they talked together that gloomy day, one of the dark green carriages reserved for the Austrian Emperor's guests drove into the courtyard of the Palais Palm.

Everything was cheerful in Wilhelmine's pretty drawing room, candles and fire lighted against the chill of the morning, and breakfast for two laid on a table by the fire. Never had the Tsar been more charming. Of course he would help her recover her child if it lay in his power to do so, he promised. As for her mother's income and her own, he would send Nesselrode to her in the next days to get the precise details. Nesselrode's father-in-law, Count Gourieff, was the Tsar's Minister of Finance; he would be told to attend to the matter at once.

Is it possible that the Tsar proposed to Wilhelmine that she have nothing more to do with Metternich? So gossip reported of the Tsar's visit. Interestingly enough, no hint of Wilhelmine's natural child, the real purpose of the Tsar's visit, ever reached the ears of Vienna society or of the scores of police informants looking for evidence of scandal. According to Rosenkrantz, the Tsar told Wilhelmine he had wanted to visit her earlier if he could have been certain not to meet that *Scribe*, as he called Metternich witheringly.[45]

They talked together until half past one, when the Tsar had to leave to keep an appointment. Wilhelmine drove at once to Talleyrand's to tell Dorothée the details of her meeting.

Metternich had not yet sent off the long, painful letter he had written in the early hours of that morning of October 21. Perhaps he postponed sending it as one postpones a visit to the surgeon when the symptoms are alarmingly certain. It may be that an undated note to Wilhelmine belongs to that day. It begins, "A relationship, a dream, the fairest of my life has vanished. Another still endures, until this too will perhaps be shattered by you." He asks for an hour to see her and closes the note, "In the end it is all the same —I have no more feeling for grief and suffering."[46]

Late in the afternoon, when she returned from the visit to her sister, Wilhelmine sent him a tiny note, "The Tsar was at my house and behaved very well, at least with words." Could Clemens come the following day after eleven, since they were to go to watch maneuvers earlier? She added:

My dear Clemens, I still have a very heavy heart. Soon you will not find fault with me for weeping too little—[47]

He avoided her Friday night soiree. If he went to her in person the following day, Saturday, "after eleven," as she had suggested, to deliver the fatal letter severing their relationship, he did not stay long, for he kept a twelve o'clock appointment in the Chancellery.

In the afternoon, when Gentz and Nesselrode appeared to dine with him, he could inform Gentz bleakly "of his definite rupture with the duchess, which is today an event of the first magnitude!"[48]

He had promised not to reproach her, but he could not help reminding her of "the frightful pain of which you alone are the cause." He wrote:

> *Mon amie*, I am punished for having surrendered to my heart what should never have been given over to it completely. I am punished for having entrusted my existence to a charm only too seductive. You have brought me more pain than the whole universe could ever repay me for. You have broken all the resources of my soul. You have compromised my existence at a moment when the fate of my life is bound up with questions that decide the future of whole generations—[49]

Magnanimously, he informed her, he would forgive her everything. "You would have behaved differently had your heart served you better." Why had she not loved him as he deserved to be loved? He had risked everything for her sake:

> My life itself has not appeared to me too dear. I put everything I had, my life, my confidence, my whole future, all my hope: I put everything in the balance. I have never risked the least part of *your existence*.

Clearly, as he had warned her so often before, it was her willpower that was weak. Had she kept her promise, given up Alfred, surely she would have come to love him as she ought to have loved him—Clemens Metternich, the most important man in Austria, perhaps in Europe!

> You tell me that the whirlwind drags you along—but the whirlwind in which you find yourself is one of your own choosing. . . . Your will it-self has become uncertain—you prove to me that you have no more will.

Even in this terrible moment of divorcing himself from her forever, "this moment which resembles death . . . where the world is without color and life without charm," even now he had advice to offer her: never carry on a liaison with two men at one time!

> I shall make a last immense effort—it tears apart my very soul. What does it matter after what you tell me—I shall pronounce my own sen-tence: our relationship no longer exists!

It may be that he added the last tender paragraph to the letter some hours later, when he was no longer so distraught as he had been in those early morning hours after the Stackelberg ball:

> You will always remain the person most dear to my heart. . . . If you need a friend, a father, a support, you will find it in me.

So it was over, finished, this great love that had absorbed him for two critical years of his life! And yet how could it be over, when for all those months that love had filled the empty spaces of his life and his mind, had given color and radiance to his inner and outer life, to his present, to his dream of the future? The surgery could not be quick and clean. He would see her wherever he went; their paths would cross at dinner parties, at soirees, at balls. Vienna was a small town, after all, and they moved in the same circles.

Nor could he stop probing the wounds in their terminally sick relationship, begging her for answers where there were none to give.

No, it was far from over—not yet. Years later, many years later, he could still remember the taste of that love, sweeter than honey, more bitter than blood on the tongue.

4

On that same critical Saturday, October 22, the day Metternich sent Wilhelmine the letter terminating their relationship, he put together the final draft of his reply to Prussia on Saxony. Perhaps he had been shaping it on paper all week; certainly it was a letter nearly as difficult to write as the letter of rupture to Wilhelmine. Knowing Gentz's bitter opposition to the step he was taking, Metternich had not asked his help nor taken Gentz fully into his confidence.[50]

Impatiently Castlereagh had been pressing Metternich to put into writing his assent to the surrender of Saxony. "I have not been able yet to bring Prince Metternich to give an answer to Prince Hardenberg's letter," Castlereagh wrote Liverpool on October 20. Stewart was vexed that Metternich "paralyzes the decided part he might take," and Cooke complained to Liverpool that Metternich "will never play a great, straightforward game except by necessity. I have tried to force Metternich to act by goading his employees." The delay was making Castlereagh "rather fidgety."[51]

Though Metternich's memorandum acquiesced to Prussia's acquisition of Saxony, it was a provisional assent, and far different in tone and argument from that of Castlereagh.[52]

Stressing the close ties that bound Austria and Prussia as joint leaders of the German-speaking peoples of Europe, and urging the danger that Russia's Polish plans held for both Austria and Prussia, Metternich pressed Prussia hard to reconsider her plans for incorporating the whole of Saxony, to weigh again the unhappy results that were bound to follow such a course —above all, the loss of confidence of other German countries in Austro-Prussian leadership.

At least some of the "disagreeable consequences that will inevitably follow the total absorption of Saxony" into the Prussian monarchy could be avoided, in Metternich's view, if Prussia would agree to preserve at least a portion of Saxony—that portion neighboring on the frontier of Bohemia.

If nothing would persuade Prussia to abandon her plan to acquire the whole of Saxony—supported, Metternich pointed out, by the British Government and by Russia—then Austria too would be obliged to assent, but that assent could only be given subject to several important provisos. First, Prussia must make no other demands in Germany—give up all hope of acquiring Mainz or other lands along the Rhine. Second, the acquisition of Saxony must be joined to the settlement of all other territorial arrangements in Germany; it could not be isolated from the total arrangement of a future Germany, satisfying to all. Third and most important proviso: Prussia must support Austria absolutely on the question of Poland.

Metternich's surrender on the question of Saxony, therefore, was a far more limited agreement than Castlereagh's had been, and it would be withdrawn if Prussia did not support Austria in blocking the Tsar's plans for Poland.

At the end of his memorandum Metternich once more urged Prussia to consider preserving at least *"un noyau"*—a kernel or core—of the kingdom of Saxony.

When he left the Chancellery that Saturday night for a ball at the Zichys', Metternich carried in his pocket the draft of the memorandum on Saxony, one of the critical documents in the history of the Congress.

The Tsar appeared to be in an especially gay and carefree mood, choosing all the prettiest women for his partners. Countess Bernstorff remembered that when the Tsar danced opposite her that night in a *tempête*, he gave her at each pause an unusually deep, low bow, the compliment that belonged to old dance usage and was hardly ever seen any more.

What Talleyrand noticed at the Zichy ball was that the political climate had undergone a sea change in a single week. Suddenly he found himself warmly received by people who had all but ignored him until now. As the Saxony problem approached a decision, public opinion had been swinging steadily to the side Talleyrand represented: resistance to the demands of Prussia. Even the archdukes, the Emperor's brothers, paid him the most flattering attention.

Metternich too must have sensed the atmosphere, a deepening chill toward him on the part of the Austrian court and officialdom. Everywhere the rumor had spread that he intended to sacrifice Saxony.

At the ball he cornered Castlereagh and showed him the draft of his memorandum.

Glancing over Metternich's paper, Castlereagh's first thought was that Prussia would be disappointed not to be given Mainz as well as Saxony. But the next day, Sunday, October 23, when the three ministers met at Castlereagh's house, Hardenberg agreed "to proceed at once to act in concert with Austria and England on the Polish question," while Metternich still pressed Hardenberg to modify his stand on Saxony. [53]

The three then worked out a plan of procedure for forcing the Tsar to abandon his plans for Poland. They would propose to settle the issue "amicably and confidentially" with him, reducing their proposals "within the narrowest possible limits." But if the Tsar refused a friendly compromise, then they were prepared to use against him the very cudgel with which Talley-

rand had threatened them three weeks before. If they could not come to an
agreement on Poland, it would be necessary to summon the whole Congress,
and under the eyes of Europe the question of Poland would be publicly argued and settled.

If the fate of Poland were to be thrown into the lap of an assembled Congress, the matter would be initiated through a note signed jointly by Metternich and Hardenberg offering Russia three options.

The first choice would be to re-establish a completely independent nation
of Poland under an independent sovereign, such as had existed before the
first partition of 1772, with Austria, Russia and Prussia surrendering the
Polish lands they had acquired at that partition.

If the Tsar refused the first option as entailing too great sacrifices for
Russia, then as a second choice Prussia and Austria would agree to establish an independent kingdom of Poland as it had existed in 1791, "when it
gave itself a free constitution under Poniatowski." It would be a smaller
Poland, and Russia would retain only the portion annexed in 1772.

The first two choices were certainly red herrings, which neither Metternich nor Hardenberg would have wished as a solution, but they were designed to show the Tsar how far they were willing to go to force him to the
third option. If he refused the first two options, then the two powers would
agree to a new partition in which Austria and Prussia would receive fair
shares.

The Tsar was to be informed that while it would be painful to the other
three powers to use an assembled Congress to settle so difficult an issue, they
would not hesitate to ask the whole gathering of delegates to decide what to
do about so dangerous a threat to their mutual safety as the Tsar's proposed
Polish plan, and "by so alarming an infraction" of existing treaties.

Such was the plan of attack the three ministers reached in their secret
meeting at Castlereagh's that Sunday afternoon, October 23.[54]

Eager as they were to force a quick solution of the Poland impasse so
that the other affairs of the Congress could be settled, the Tsar, it appeared
at once, was no less determined to conclude that critical business before he
departed for Hungary on Monday. He had already summoned Talleyrand
to appear for an audience at six o'clock that Sunday evening before the
palace ball.

"Let us talk business," the Tsar began as soon as Talleyrand appeared.
"At Paris you were in favor of a kingdom of Poland. Why have you changed
your mind?"[55]

"My opinion, Sire, has not changed. At Paris it was a question of estab-
lishing a whole and independent Poland. I wanted it then and I want it
today. But now it is a question of something quite different—of a large
piece of Poland attached to the Russian crown. Limits must be fixed here
that give safety to Austria and Prussia."

"They need not worry," replied the Tsar. He added quickly, "Besides, I have 200,000 men in the duchy of Warsaw. Let anybody try to chase me out! I gave Saxony to Prussia. Austria consents to it."

"I don't know whether Austria consents to it," Talleyrand replied evenly. "I can hardly believe it—it is so contrary to her interests. But in any case how could the consent of Austria make Prussia the rightful owner of something that belongs to the King of Saxony?"

"If the King of Saxony does not abdicate, he will be taken to Russia. He will die there. Another king has already died there," said the Tsar, referring to Poland's last King Stanislas.

"Your Majesty will permit me to refuse to believe this Congress was summoned to witness such an outrage."

"An outrage? Didn't Stanislas go to Russia and die? Why won't the King of Saxony go? For me there is no difference!"

Talleyrand could scarcely contain his indignation. He reminded the Tsar of the treaties among the Allies, and of the Law of Nations.

"What have I got to do with your parchments and treaties?" the Tsar demanded angrily. "You talk about principles. Your Law of Nations is nothing to me! For me there is one thing above everything—my word! I gave my word and I shall keep it. I promised Saxony to the King of Prussia at the moment when we joined forces."

"Your Majesty promised the King of Prussia some nine or ten million souls. Your Majesty can give them without destroying Saxony." Producing a map from his pocket, Talleyrand unfolded it and pointed to a portion of Saxony that might be sacrificed without destroying the whole country.

"The King of Saxony is a traitor," the Tsar declared shortly.

"Sire," Talleyrand replied, with the authority of the recent convert to monarchical principles, "the word traitor can never apply to a king!" Talleyrand must have enjoyed reporting that retort to the French King.

The Tsar was silent for a moment. Then he concluded with finality, "The King of Prussia is to be King of Prussia and of Saxony. I shall be Tsar of Russia and King of Poland. Whatever support France gives me on these points will be the measure of what I will show to the interests of France." With an abrupt gesture he indicated that the audience was at an end.

All the ministers met at the palace ball that Sunday night—even Castlereagh, who no longer considered Sunday dancing so offensive. Talleyrand had just cornered Castlereagh in an alcove off the ballroom when the Tsar caught sight of them, drew Castlereagh into an adjoining room and harangued him for twenty minutes on the question of Poland, though with somewhat greater courtesy than he had Talleyrand an hour or so earlier.

Talleyrand was not at all displeased to observe Castlereagh's discomfiture when he emerged from the one-sided interview with the Tsar. Even a Russian cloud had a silver lining! Thanks to the Tsar's intransigeance, the English plan of isolating France was failing, Talleyrand informed his King. Talleyrand had certain plans of his own that could perhaps now come quickly to fruition!

Bluntly Talleyrand informed Castlereagh that he and Metternich alone were to blame for the autocratic power the Tsar was able to exercise. "If you two had supported my proposal to call Congress together, none of this would have happened. If the Tsar had been placed face to face with Congress from the first day, and therefore facing the wishes of all Europe, he would never have dared use the language he used today."[56]

Castlereagh retorted to Talleyrand with his own brand of blackmail. If France chose to make Saxony their primary point, and Poland only second- ary—which could effectively scuttle the plan the three ministers had made at their secret meeting that day for settling Poland—it "would not only de- stroy [France's] friendly relations with England, but would lead to imme- diate hostilities, and its obvious and first effect must be to compel England to sign a peace with Murat." That was a threat which could not fail to move Talleyrand. If, on the other hand, France promised to co-operate with the three on Poland, Castlereagh promised, and if their efforts succeeded, then it would be much easier to urge Prussia to modify her demands on Saxony.

The Tsar had laid down the law on Poland to both Talleyrand and Castlereagh. On Monday morning, October 24, it was Metternich's turn to be summoned by the Tsar.

Crossing the square from the Chancellery to the little courtyard that leads into the Amalia Wing of the palace, Metternich must have marshaled his ar- guments swiftly and with care. He could not present the Tsar with the ulti- matum contained in the memorandum of the previous day, for it had not yet been approved by the monarchs involved. Yet he must be prepared to take a strong stand without giving away that secret agreement.

Abruptly the Tsar began, "I intend to create an independent state of Poland. I want your agreement before I leave for Hungary today."

"Your Majesty," Metternich replied smoothly, "if it is a question of creat- ing an independent Poland, Austria too can create one."

The Tsar flushed. Not only were Metternich's words disagreeable, he de- clared, but they were downright "indecent." He had made up his mind. The future of Poland was settled.

Metternich declared, "But it is impossible. Your Majesty's plan is con- trary to the treaties we signed at Reichenbach and at Teplitz. It would make it difficult if not impossible to establish a balance of power."

Alexander slapped his sword and replied, "I know no other balance than this one!"

When Metternich continued to offer carefully reasoned objections to the Polish plan, pointing out how many of the complex arrangements of the Congress were contingent on it, the Tsar grew angrier. He had made im- mense sacrifices to win the war. He would defend his right to Poland with

400,000 soldiers! He was certain, moreover, that His Majesty, the Austrian Emperor, agreed with him, the Tsar, and that the Austrian public did so too. Only Monsieur de Metternich dared take such a "tone of revolt" against the Tsar of all the Russias!

During the two-hour debate the Tsar lost his self-control completely, according to Talleyrand, and abused Metternich "with an arrogance and a violence of language which would have been astonishing had he used it with one of his servants."

In vivid accounts of the scene that circulated in Vienna that week, Metternich had kept miraculous rein on his self-control, replying to one threatening tirade: "How am I to reply to Your Majesty, since you are a sovereign and not like me only a minister?"

At the end of the scene, certainly one of the stormiest and most violent in the entire course of the Congress, Metternich told Alexander he would ask his master to name another minister than him to handle the affairs of the Congress.

Although he had managed to maintain his composure throughout, Metternich left the Tsar's rooms ashen-white, "in a state of mind persons close to him say they have never before seen him in."[57]

According to Gentz, Metternich told his friends "he neither would nor could ever again see the Tsar in private." Gentz added, "He has kept his word; with the exception of one explanation which the honor of the prince rendered inevitable, he has never again set foot inside the Tsar's door."[58]

Metternich reported the turbulent scene in writing to Emperor Franz, who had already left for Hungary. "It brought to mind," he wrote, "many earlier scenes I had with Emperor Napoleon, both in content and in expression."[59] If Metternich offered his resignation, as he said he would in the heat of the moment, the Emperor brushed it aside.

Not until a few days had passed could Metternich speak lightly of the encounter, saying the Tsar had flown into such a tantrum that he—Metternich—had not known if he would leave the Tsar's suite by the door or by the window. He told Rosenkrantz, "The Tsar will end up mad like his father."[60]

5

That October weekend, when the political drama of Poland and Saxony erupted in the violent scene with the Tsar, it was Wilhelmine's turn to explain and defend her side in the shattered liaison.

At the Zichy ball on Saturday night, October 22—that fatal Saturday when Metternich had sent off his letter breaking with Wilhelmine and his memorandum on Saxony to Hardenberg—he had seen Wilhelmine for a few moments, long enough to ask if she had read his letter. When would he have her reply? He must know what there was to know. She must explain herself so that he could come to terms with the catastrophe. It was impossible to end the affair smoothly, impossible to sever the painful links between them unlesss he could grasp somehow the real reasons why he had failed.

Very well, Wilhelmine said, she would give her reply. As he had written his long letter of rupture in the early morning hours after the Stackelberg ball, so Wilhelmine returned home from the Zichy ball, and in the early hours of Sunday morning penned her reply. Seldom did Wilhelmine bother to date her letters, but this letter is carefully dated "Nuit de 22–23 Octobre."

> For eight days now I've written you volumes in reply to the letter you gave me last Monday, but nothing satisfies you, and I must now answer for the last time and speak to you clearly on our position.[61]

She began writing in a mood of vexation and anger; if he could not understand, then she must make the whole affair completely clear! He was behaving as if the fault were entirely on her side when she had done her best to make the affair succeed. He had accused her of lacking willpower. Didn't he understand—willpower had nothing to do with loving or not loving?

She reminded him that she had at one time in the past—in the spring of 1810—been strongly attracted to him; it had been he who had rejected her:

> Later on you loved me—at the time I believed neither in the genuineness nor the strength of that feeling. I was involved in a love affair I cherished, but which at the same time became a torment to me. I did not feel my love was truly reciprocated; the fear of unhappiness, perhaps of an eternal separation, tied that bond yet more strongly, but the reconciliation was only for a moment, the memory of my torments returned, with it the firm determination to tear out of my heart a sentiment so inadequately returned—

She had tried, she said, to sever the unhappy liaison with Alfred, and she had turned to Metternich in the hope that she would succeed in loving him as deeply as he wanted to be loved. It simply had not happened.

> In marriage [she wrote] friendship supported by duty is doubtless enough. In a liaison one must find something to silence duty. I did all in my power. I succeeded in giving you all the justice you deserved. I saw in you the first of men and doubtless the one who loved me best. But beyond the enthusiasm of friendship all remained calm within me. Even this misfortune could have been met—if instead of so much passion I had found in you more art. You will surely understand that this is only a regret and not a reproach.

Bitter blows that letter of Wilhelmine's rained on Metternich's pride! No man more than Metternich enjoyed claiming mastery of the arts of love. He had written Wilhelmine as he had written and would write to other women, "No one loves better than I when I love truly.'" But Wilhelmine, the one woman he had wanted to win above all others, he had failed to win. Clearly the sexual relationship that had lifted him to the height of ecstasy had left her somewhere on the plains below. Less passion and more art, she had written. To this sensual and experienced woman Metternich had been a less accomplished lover than he thought himself to be. He would never, never forgive her for that.

And so she joined him in writing a finis to their relationship:

> . . . I am finally come by means of all the unhappiness and griefs with which one can be overwhelmed at once to the conviction that we cannot be happy together, and to the sad necessity of pronouncing an end. . . .

She made no mention, as she had not in her former letters, of his sacrifice for the sake of her honor. That curious article, as Wilhelmine well knew, belonged to the male book of rules—women had had nothing to do with the writing of it. If it salved his pride to think this was the reason for their parting, very well, let him think so.

If her letter had begun in a mood of irritation at his persistent questioning, she had grown calmer in the writing. Wistfully she pointed out the difference between the essential capacity each of them had for happinessss:

> You have always been happy, and you find yourself today deceived in the most powerful of all your hopes. I have the habit of unhappiness—I thought I was entering the harbor—now I see myself far away again, back in the same place from which one could say I had never departed.

In the end she offered him again what he had turned down so bitterly months before—her friendship:

> My dear Clemens, may God protect you—I should have been too happy perhaps if I might have been the means by which He repaid you for so many virtues and for so much grief. When you are more calm, please let your best friend tell you how much she cherishes you—[62]

Wilhelmine's letter was certainly not a full explanation of the reasons for their parting. Her relationship with Alfred had been broken by repeated quarrels and ruptures, and now in its fifth year could hardly have exercised the command over her senses that it had once had. The last time she had broken with Alfred, she had determined to make the rupture final. She had given Metternich her solemn promise on July 25; she had given him some kind of engagement, perhaps a promise of final closure with Alfred, on September 18. Yet within two weeks she had broken her word and renewed the relationship with Alfred.

And to Metternich, not to Alfred, was tied all hope of her continuing involvement and influence in the political arena that absorbed her so intensely.

During the weeks of the Congress her salon had been recognized as a pivotal spot for political exchange, and her judgment and opinion sought by men in important positions. Karl von Nostitz, whose comments were so often malicious, wrote warmly of Wilhelmine:

It would have depended only on this remarkable woman to acquire a great influence on serious affairs through her superior intelligence; her judgment was authoritative but she did not misuse it.[63]

And the Prussian diplomat Varnhagen von Ense recalled:

The Duchess of Sagan formed as always the focus of a lively circle that was enhanced in distinction and importance [during the Congress]. The enchanting personality of this beautiful woman, as kind as she was spirited, operated with victorious power, and it depended only on her to win influence on great decisions. That she did not nourish ambition in such a capacity but willingly and lightly limited herself to the most proper sphere of women only increased the charm of her winning character.[64]

Why then at this crucial juncture during the Congress did Wilhelmine choose to renew the ties with Alfred and give up the liaison with Metternich? It was certainly not on emotional grounds alone. What is clear from the correspondence between her and Metternich is that she longed for a stable marriage; life was too difficult for a woman without it. Perhaps, as some biographers have suggested, she hoped at one time that Metternich might consider divorce. There is no direct evidence, however, that they had ever discussed it. What does appear likely is that Alfred finally held out to her a hope of their eventually marrying.

In one of his letters to her at this time Metternich wrote, "You ended by entrenching yourself in the conviction that only in the ties of marriage would you find the happiness you searched for in vain." He went on to warn her:

Marriage is the one state that will never be right for you. It is not with an independence of soul like yours that duty can become the means of peace. Ties? You will break them all.[65]

She had once, in a letter to Metternich, equated her relationship with Alfred to a marriage of long standing; perhaps she thought now that this relationship in which she had so long and deep an emotional investment might be transmuted in the end, as her sisters predicted, into marriage.

In the evening of that Monday when he had quarreled with the Tsar, Metternich again had to act out, despite the political and emotional turmoil in which he was plunged, the part of gracious host at his weekly supper party.

The story of the morning's stormy interview was already all over town. Metternich drew Gentz aside to give him the full story of "'his famous and sad conversation with the Tsar.'"[66]

People were whispering too of the ruptured love affair between Metternich and the Duchess of Sagan, which had followed, everyone said, on the heels of the Tsar's visit to Wilhelmine the previous Friday. Gossip drew the natural conclusion: the Tsar had supplanted Metternich in the duchess's affections. "Sagan wrote a four-page letter of farewell to Metternich," a police report noted that week—information of sufficient accuracy to indicate that someone's servant was talking. Each day Metternich could read in the police reports everything people were saying about him, a task of self-flagellation he did not deny himself.[67]

He had certainly heard the rumor that the Tsar had, during his visit with Wilhelmine, insisted as the price of winning his help, that she break with Metternich completely. Metternich was inclined to believe it was true; he remarked that weekend to Wenzel Liechtenstein that Wilhelmine "had sacrificed him to the Tsar."[68]

Even on that tumultuous Monday he found moments to write her, begging for time to talk in private. "You have had the power to kill me—I told you it would be so." He could not talk to her at balls or in society, and he needed at least to know the truth about what she had promised the Tsar.

> I could not imagine a day when I would feel a wrong toward you. . . .
> For the rest do not fear my conversation. I shall not make you spend a single moment for which I have to reproach myself later. At least a hundred years have passed in three times 24 hours; I am no longer the man I was the day before yesterday. None of the torments I have made you feel any longer hold true. The old friend is dead and you have thrown his ashes to the wind. My soul remains to me—I have no longer any heart—and that alone was what you once had to fear.[69]

At his *grand souper* Monday night he tried to talk to her, but she turned away impatiently. Yes, she would give him time to see her—that was all.

Briefly and coolly she wrote him later that night:

> If the hour of midday is agreeable to you, I shall await you—if not, mark another more convenient for you. I am not afraid of you despite what you tell me, that you have no more heart, and that contrary to your thought, this evening it was precisely this heart that I feared the least.
> But everything is so completely changed in us that it is not at all surprising that our thoughts and our feelings no longer meet in anything, and that we find ourselves in a situation more than strange to one another. I begin to believe that we never did know one another. We were both pursuing phantoms. You saw in me a model of perfection, I saw in you all there is of beauty and of intellectual grandeur, something well above honor. By a natural consequence of our illusions you find it good to make me descend in your imagination as low as I was once placed high. I with more calm shall decide only after our conversation—but I am tempted to believe you a man like all the others—Pardon my sincerity.[70]

If their meeting that Tuesday noon began hardly more pleasantly than his dialogue with the Tsar the day before, with mutual accusations, still it ended more calmly, with apologies and something of their old intimacy.

When she wrote him later that day, she addressed him again as *tu;*

she denied vehemently that she had promised the Tsar she would give up Metternich's friendship. "To sacrifice someone to anyone whatsoever and for any consideration in the world is so little like me, is so far from my soul that I would prefer a thousand times to die—and on this occasion to whom will I sacrifice my best friend, and for what?"

She had always, she added,

> at heart . . . been of good faith with you—I have regarded our relations as of necessity being eternal— My weakness and unfortunate circumstances that I could neither foresee nor overcome made it impossible for me to establish them at once as they should have been in all their details, but never did I think they were less solid.

She counted on his friendship; she knew that she needed his guidance; her life, she found, was still in confusion.

> My heart remains completely the same toward you—while all is changed in you nothing is in me. . . . In the end, dear Clemens, you are good— you would never become a stranger—you will remain interested in my fate—you do not want to be either my friend or my brother but I shall always be your best friend—I shall never hesitate to address myself to you with confidence and trust. May God bless you.[71]

They continued to see one another that last week of October at dinner parties and at balls. He was not at her soiree on Friday evening, October 28; had he been there he would have admired how adroitly she handled a touchy little scene.

Charles Stewart was among the guests. He had perhaps drunk a bit too much, for suddenly, in a booming voice that carried through the whole room, filled with guests of all nationalities, he cried, "Well, Duchess, what do you think of Alexander? I think he's a fool, an ambitious impostor! That's my opinion. What do you say?"

A hush fell on the room; conversation came to a halt. Heads turned, ears pricked up. Everyone in the room knew the gossip that had gone the rounds that week: that Wilhelmine had broken with Metternich, that she might perhaps be *liée* with the Tsar.

Wilhelmine stood still for a long moment. Then, a bright smile on her face, she replied, "I think, milord, you are inclined to take the bit in your teeth like that horse you gave my sister Dorothée this morning that nearly broke her neck in the Prater."

With a good-humored tap of her fan on his epauletted shoulder, a tiny gesture of reprimand, she moved swiftly across the room to greet a new arrival.[72]

Though both she and Clemens had written letters declaring their relationship at an end, the affair was not so easily terminated. Metternich continued to brood over the history of their liaison; he plunged back into his memories as if he would finally touch the bottom of that black and bitter pool. He was still torn between the slenderest of hopes and a despair to which he could not reconcile himself. While the beloved still lives, walks, breathes, there must be hope that she—or he—will eventually return one's love. He had to ransack the past, prove he was not at fault, apply the rules of reason once again to the more or less irrational.

When he replied to her letter it was again the confession of a man deeply in love, who could not bring himself to abandon hope, who tried desperately to understand why he had lost her.

> All the unhappiness of your life [he wrote her] comes from one source alone—you have never learned to resist the temptation of the passions; you have always followed your first impulses. You knew almost at once that you folllowed a false path—but you looked for the remedy in the evil itself. You, a being so privileged by nature, you who emerged from the hands of the Creator beautiful, noble, pure, good—endowed with all the qualities of mind and of heart—you without intense passions but susceptible of quick impressions, you have spent the most beautiful of lives the way a wastrel spends an immense fortune, without real pleasure, without giving the world the faintest idea of what that life might have become![73]

What that life might have become! What might have been the life of so intelligent, so gifted a woman as Wilhelmine, had she been permitted to make full use of those gifts in the larger world?

Though he admired Wilhelmine more deeply than he had ever admired a woman before, and though intuitively he appreciated the richness and breadth of her intellect, it did not occur to Metternich that the real tragedy of her life was the narrowness of the sphere society marked out even for its most highly endowed women. He perceived her life only as a series of sexual mishaps.

As for him, he had risked everything for her sake:

> I made a sum of my frail existence; I put my entire fortune on a single head; I chose that head not in a vague impulse but after long thought.
>
> My friends trembled. I never shared their fears. All of them foretold an inevitable denouement; I had confidence in the great qualities of your soul, and in the strength and purity of my love. I would have died twenty times rather than risk a single chance of your existence. . . . At any hour of the day I would have given my life for you. . . .
>
> To tell you what is happening within me is impossible. Everything can be described except nothing. I tell myself that I still feel, but I do not know what. I am everything and nothing. I look for some rule of conduct in the history of my life—I find none. In the human heart? Would a second example of my love be found there? Needs? I have no more. Future? I know none. Memories? They are all frightful.
>
> I live; some rest, much calm—a great need to feel no more in life, to be tormented no longer. No more love, no more involvement, no more

trouble, days without a morrow. After that, nothing but good for you, all happiness on your side, all the blessings of heaven on your head, no reproach on my part, the hope that my memory will never be a stranger to you and that it will be mingled with no regret.[74]

When Wilhelmine replied the following day, she mixed *tu* and *vous* in her letter, as if she were not yet certain what this new phase in their relationship required. His letter had touched her deeply. Yes, she would come to him for advice though she did not know what to ask:

> . . . for I do not know where to begin—At my age, when tranquillity should be succeeding the storms of life, when life ought to be settled, I find myself in all the uncertainties of a fifteen-year-old, without the privilege permitted to youth, and without the time still before it— You see I have no illusions about myself, *mon ami*.[75]

She did not want to go through life as he had described her, acting out all her impulses like a self-willed child. But how to change? Desperately she needed some weeks of solitude and peace to put herself together again. She thought of fleeing to Ratiborzitz, but when could she leave Vienna? She could not go away while Dorothée was still here. Won't this Congress ever come to an end?

And she does miss him, his supportive presence, one person she could count on:

> You know that I always loved seeing you, but I waited for the moment with calm, since one day counts for so little in life. Only now I feel the need of it, as one comes to value youth and health and all the good things in life only when they have escaped us.

She knows she has no claim on his time any longer; her company cannot be very agreeable to him just now.

> Adieu, *mon ami*. Tell me very frankly if I would not do better to write you less often and if the way I talk about us does not displease you—

He wrote back almost at once:

> What would I not have given in the moments that present themselves to my imagination like so many dreams if I had received a line like those you wrote me yesterday! My heart is dry and withered; it experiences a sense of pleasure that you were not angry at the recitation of its long anguish. I come back to the only words that describe my state of soul: I am no longer of this world.
>
> You want to talk to me, my dear Wilhelmine. I shall go to you tomorrow morning. You will set the hour this evening if I see you or you will write me if I do not see you. One happiness remains to me, that of perhaps being useful to you. *Bon soir*.[76]

There was no signature. He was above all enormously weary.

6

In those days of late October and early November Metternich's reputation sank to a dangerous low. He had few real friends and supporters. Head of a great international conclave, he was the target of barbs from his own countrymen and from all nationalities among the visitors as well. The rumor that Austria was about to sacrifice Saxony to Prussia aroused the Viennese public to alarm and to anger.

The police reports were full of bitter attacks on the Foreign Minister, and of prophecies that he would soon be forced to resign. The eyes of the Emperor would soon be opened, his enemies predicted. "Even in 1809 the situation of the monarchy was less precarious than it is today."[77]

Worried about the dilemma in which he found himself and the Gordian knot of the Poland-Saxony problem, Metternich called a conference of leading Austrian officials on October 28, to ask their advice and no doubt to share some of the terrible onus of responsibility. All of them—Stadion, Schwarzenberg, Duka, Wessenberg—urged him not to surrender on Poland and Saxony. Even Schwarzenberg no longer supported Metternich's policy; the meeting, he wrote his wife, was only Metternich's attempt "to hang the bell around our necks."[78]

A powerful group among the Austrian aristocracy favored deposing Metternich and replacing him with Stadion. The same group who in 1809 had urged continuing the war against Napoleon, who had quarreled with Metternich's appeasement of Napoleon and with his long attempts to mediate a European peace, now clamored again for a change in ministry.

Why had he not settled the business of Poland and Saxony months before, when he might have driven a harder bargain—at Prague, for instance, where he had the upper hand? Or during the campaign in France? Or at least at the Peace of Paris? "Your Metternich should have spoken up strongly and firmly at Paris," the Tsar's aide Anstett declared.

A police informer reported the current *Salon Klatsch:*

> Russia will have Poland, Prussia will keep Saxony; the sovereigns will leave Vienna. Congress will be dissolved and Austria will go to war with Russia —that's what we hear at the Starhembergs and the Stadions.[79]

The mediatized German princes—former rulers of small independent German states which Napoleon had wiped out to form the Confederation of the Rhine—had come to the Congress hoping to win back their former princedoms. But Metternich had already settled on a middle-of-the-road solution for the future of Germany: it was to be a loose federation made up of larger states under the leadership of Austria and Prussia. The mediatized princes at the Congress, therefore, enlisted themselves in the ranks of Metternich's enemies, and tried, "with all the means in their power to provoke a ministerial crisis and to lead Count Stadion back to power because they know he is committed to their cause."

The Prussians too predicted that "Metternich will resign his portfolio." Humboldt was reported as saying that Metternich's position was "shakier than ever; he could not remain, Congress would end without accomplishing anything." "Public opinion," wrote another police informer, "does not favor Metternich, whom Louis XVIII and Russia would like to see replaced by Stadion." The Saxon Count Senfft von Pilsach remarked, "They'll go back to Stadion; at least he is an honest man."

"The enemies of Metternich feel sure of success," was the consensus in late October.[80]

Even within his own Chancellery Metternich found little loyal support. Wessenberg, it was reported, "though highly esteemed and protected by Metternich and very deep in his confidence, also supports Stadion." Both Hudelist and Hoppé criticized their chief openly. Gentz, Metternich's confidant in both his political affairs and in his love, could not in the least understand the minister's emotional state during those weeks. How could this clever Ulysses of a minister have allowed himself to be so enmeshed in the coils of a Circe that he forgot who and where he was, neglected his work, evaded decisions? Bitterly Gentz talked of Metternich to Talleyrand, to Rosenkrantz, to Humboldt and others, helping them forge weapons that were useful in their day-to-day politicking.[81]

The old criticisms of Metternich—that he was frivolous, indolent, a womanizer and a diplomatic playboy—were revived and leveled against him with renewed acrimony. Only two days after his arrival in Vienna, before he could possibly have formed any true judgment of Metternich's Congress work, Talleyrand, in a letter to the French King, was attacking Metternich's "inconceivable frivolity."

The English too blamed the impasse of Congress on Metternich. Castlereagh had complained the previous spring of Metternich's "temporizing"; he complained in autumn of Metternich's lack of energy and decisiveness.

Edward Cooke, Castlereagh's chief of staff, whose correspondence with Liverpool was more gossipy than Castlereagh's, wrote that Metternich was "most intolerably loose and giddy with women."

The Russians too were saying that Metternich was "laughable with regard to his womanizing," while the Prussians jibed about the Austrian minister

> crazy with love, wounded pride and vanity, idling away all his forenoons
> —not rising until ten, then running to the Duchess of Sagan and spend-
> ing the rest of the morning sighing at her feet, having barely time to re-
> ceive 3 of the 40 persons who wait to speak to him, making Hudelist and
> Gentz wait. . . .[82]

It is quite obvious from what source the Prussians got their information.

Were the charges leveled at Metternich true? Was he during those critical weeks of the Congress "inconceivably frivolous," lazy in his work habits? And—even more important—did his personal life, the emotional crisis he was living through with his shattered love affair seriously impair his work as minister and affect his powers of judgment?

As to the first question, Metternich was carrying a far more staggering work load during the days of the Congress than any of his fellow ministers, whose tasks were strictly delimited to the issues that concerned their individual countries. Metternich, on the other hand, not only bore chief responsibility for the entire mass of Congress problems but he was performing both the duties of Foreign Minister and those of Prime Minister of Austria as well—without the title. He had to attend to Austria's internal machinery, to concern himself with questions of domestic economy, finances, even of the Army.

As minister-host at the Congress, he carried a major share of Austrian hospitality and representation. He was the person sought out by innumerable foreign visitors of all rank, all nationalities, who had some claim, some problem, some quarrel to be resolved at the Congress.

While he did continue to operate in the light-handed style of the eighteenth-century diplomat, Metternich could hardly be accused of laziness during the months of the Congress. Gentz himself is the best witness to the long hours Metternich kept. Gentz attended few of the fetes; day after day, as he recorded in his diary, he would appear at nine or ten in the morning at the Chancellery for a long conversation with Metternich on the day's affairs. Metternich was nearly always there to meet him, even though he had frequently spent a large part of the night at a fete, returning to the Chancellery in the small hours of the morning to finish his correspondence just before daybreak.

Compared to the other diplomats at the Congress, Metternich was an early riser. Talleyrand was seldom out of bed before noon. When Jean-Gabriel Eynard appeared at the Palais Kaunitz for a noontime appointment, he had to cool his heels for nearly an hour in an antechamber, through which passed a whole procession of footmen on their way to Talleyrand's bedchamber, armed with basins, bottles and brushes.

Although Castlereagh's biographers stress his rigorous work habits, when Eynard went to call on Castlereagh at noon one day in October, he was informed that the English minister was not yet out of bed. When he asked to speak to one of Castlereagh's secretaries, the butler informed him that they were all out hunting.

Certainly with the night-long balls and the fun-filled calendar of those Congress days, it is miraculous that the diplomats accomplished as much business as they did. Metternich worked as hard as, probably harder than, anyone else.

Despite all the criticism leveled at him that autumn, he had one supporter who remained stubbornly loyal: Emperor Franz. The Austrian Emperor had no faith in any of the possible alternatives, and he had a shrewd intuition that in the long run Metternich would best serve the monarchy. Learning from the police reports at the end of October that Metternich's liaison with the Duchess of Sagan was at an end, Emperor Franz no doubt breathed a sigh of relief. Now perhaps his Foreign Minister could devote his whole mind to business.

As to the second question—whether Metternich's personal life affected his political decisions in those crucial days—the answer must be that it most certainly had. Through painful days, sleepless nights, anguished weeks, exchanging long tormented, probing letters with Wilhelmine, he had lost for a time that integration of mind and personality so absolutely necessary in the operation of the complex machine he was directing. "You have compromised my existence," he accused her, "at a moment when the fate of my life is bound up with questions that decide the future of whole generations.[83]

That shattered love affair with Wilhelmine was the first serious failure Metternich had ever experienced; nothing in his favored life had prepared him for failure. His self-confidence, his leadership, his decision-making powers were all severely damaged.

It had been no ordinary love affair; it had in no way resembled the lighthearted liasons that had in the past added an arpeggio of charm and decoration to the ordinary melody of his daily life. Partly because Wilhelmine was a remarkable woman, whose gifts of intellect and personality closely matched his own, partly too perhaps because winning her love had presented a greater challenge to his ego than had any affair in the past, his involvement with her was far deeper, more sexually absorbing than any love in his life. She had not rejected him, but he had failed to win her on the terms he had demanded; it was a debacle enormously wounding to a sensitive, self-centered, highly complex nature like Metternich's. Never would he love another woman as he had loved Wilhelmine.

Certainly for a time in October and November, he lost full control of his faculties, of his powers of concentration and of judgment. He had yielded in the end to Castlereagh's persuasion on Saxony, against all his diplomatic instincts and with a most reluctant assent wrung from the Emperor Franz.

It was one of the gravest errors Metternich had ever made. Had he reversed his arguments in the memorandum of October 22 to Hardenberg, and insisted on the preservation of at least a portion of Saxony, the crisis of the Congress might have ended weeks sooner.

Suffering from exhaustion, sleeplessness, depression, profound psychic shock, he was in truth a sick man, perhaps as close as he ever came to emotional crack-up.

> As to my health [he wrote Wilhelmine on November 1], there is no question of it any longer! I am completely ill, my body attacked, my soul has not protected it for a long time. I am still needed for a few

weeks more; those weeks will bring to an end the most painful years of my life, and if they finish my life, the world will lose only the sad remnants of an existence which I myself deserved to lose.[84]

Metternich's supporters blamed Wilhelmine bitterly. "His friends and defenders affirm that all these difficulties would never have happened if from the month of August the police had sent both Bagration and Sagan away."[85]

Toward the end of that year, 1814, Gentz would, in talking with the King of Denmark and condemning Metternich's failure of leadership, assert that Metternich "had not had his head about him for the past several weeks, so much had the thwarted love affair with the Duchess of Sagan absorbed him, and it was for that reason that affairs had not moved ahead and had been so badly handled."[86]

—————◆—————

XXII

CHANGING ALLIANCES

The Congress is a bad play whose author is being hissed.
—BARON LINDEN, NOVEMBER 4, 1814

1

Was there to be a Congress or was there not to be?

"People are awaiting the declaration of November 1 and the opening of Congress with feverish impatience," an anonymous informer reported to the police in the last week of October.[1]

A public, "greedy for spectacle," Metternich recalled later, "had taken into its head that the meetings of the plenipotentiaries at the Congress would be held in the great ballroom of the imperial palace, that the public would be admitted to the galleries that run around it."[2]

Certainly, people thought, the splendid, precedent-breaking international Congress would open with fanfare and pageantry, with parades and bands and sovereigns on horseback, and from the opening day, November 1, the world would be able to watch and listen to the debates that were to settle the destiny of the continent.

But could a Congress open with the big questions still unresolved? How could the knotty problems of Saxony and Poland be thrown into an open arena of three hundred assorted delegates, all representing different interests? What to do? The four "friends" met until after midnight on Saturday, October 29. "I talked a great deal," boasted Gentz. "I killed the idea of a Congress."[3] He could hardly have killed what had not yet come to life.

It turned out that on November 1, in place of the splendor and pageantry of a parliamentary opening, a quiet little announcement appeared in

35. The Tsar and his sister Catherine are warmly welcomed at the Billingsgate Fish Market in London, June 1814. The contemporary cartoon bears the caption: "Russian Condescension or the Blessings of Universal Peace."

36. Vienna welcomes the returning Emperor Franz in June 1814. Painted by Johann Peter Krafft.

37. The Kurpark of the little spa Baden-bei-Wien. Engraved by C. Berger.

38. Wilhelmine. From a pastel sketch by Sir Thomas Lawrence.

39. The jewelled, morocco-bound letter-box that held the correspondence of Wilhelmine to Alfred Windischgraetz between 1810 and 1816. Windischgraetz family tradition holds that Wilhelmine gave the box to Alfred, and that it is her miniature set in the cover. The picture does not resemble Wilhelmine, however, and may have been a later replacement.

40. The Metternich villa in Rennweg. Here during the summer of 1814 Metternich carefully supervised the construction and decoration of the immense ballroom where hundreds of distinguished guests at the Congress were to dance. He himself designed the gardens where he liked to breakfast and dine *en famille*. Lithograph by Eduard Gurk.

41. Emperor Franz welcomes Tsar Alexander and King Friedrich Wilhelm of Prussia to Vienna on September 25, 1814, a Sunday that marked the unofficial opening of the Vienna Congress. Watercolor by Johann Nepomuk Höchle.

42. Jean Baptiste Isabey's famous painting of the Vienna Congress. The artist sketched each of the participants separately and then combined them into a single scene, choosing the moment in early February 1815, when Metternich introduces the Duke of Wellington as Castlereagh's replacement. Left to right, standing: Wellington, Lobo da Silveira, Saldanha da Gama, Loewenhjelm, Noailles, Metternich, La Tour du Pin, Nesselrode, Dalberg, Razumowsky, Stewart, Clancarty, Wacken, Gentz, Humboldt, Cathcart. Seated, left to right: Hardenberg, Palmella, Castlereagh, Wessenberg, Labrador, Talleyrand, Stackelberg.

43. Empress Maria Ludovica. As the official hostess of the Congress, the mortally ill Empress appeared night after night at banquets and balls. "The poor woman with her pale consumptive face and her frail bent form is killing herself every day," one visitor wrote in her diary. Miniature by Jean Baptiste Isabey.

44. Countess Flora Wrbna, Metternich's cousin and one of his closest friends.

45. Countess Julie Zichy, "the heavenly beauty" of the Congress, who died tragically in childbirth a year later. Drawing by Philipp Veit.

46. Emily, Viscountess Castlereagh.
Painted by Sir Thomas Lawrence.

47. Emilia Bigottini, premiere danseuse
of the ballet troupe Metternich brought
from Paris to entertain the Congress.
Her performance in "Nina, the Girl
Made Mad by Love," was so moving
that "more sensitive men were carried
fainting from their boxes." Miniature
by Jean Baptiste Isabey.

48. On the city walls near the Imperial Palace in Vienna.

49. Ball in the Imperial Riding School in Vienna, 1814. Painted by Johann Nepomuk Höchle.

50. Military festival in the Prater in Vienna on the first anniversary of the battle of Leipzig, October 18, 1814. Emperor Franz, flanked by the King of Prussia and the Tsar, review the troops. Lithograph by Franz Wolf after a drawing by Johann Nepomuk Höchle.

51. The famous Carousel, a re-enactment of a medieval tournament at the Imperial Riding School performed before the Vienna Congress guests, November 23, 1814.

52. Imperial sleighing party in Vienna, January 22, 1815.

53. Napoleon returns to France from Elba in March 1815. This contemporary lithograph celebrates the moment when, at the gates of Grenoble, Napoleon steps forth and calls to the royalist troops drawn up to defend the city: "If there is one among you who would kill his general, his emperor, he may do so!"

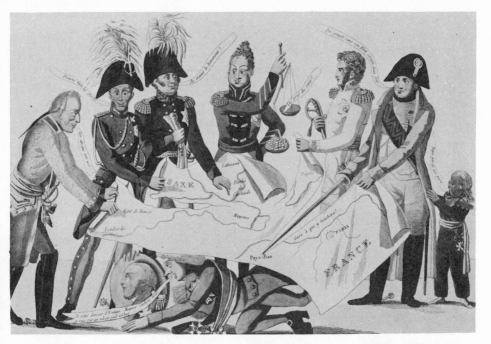

54. "Cutting Up the Cake of Kings." A French cartoonist views the quarrels of the Congress and Napoleon's return. The Tsar has seized Poland; the King of Prussia is tearing out Saxony; Austria-Metternich grabs Italy, while Castlereagh has exacted a heavy price in gold for England. Meantime, Napoleon returns to proclaim, "He counts twice who counts without his host," and sends Talleyrand to hide under the table.

55. Napoleon flees from the battle of Waterloo, on June 18, 1815, losing his hat and cloak. "*Ja, mein Gott*," said the Viennese, "he doesn't need a hat when he's gone and lost his head." Contemporary Austrian engraving.

56. A Whig cartoon views the second restoration of Louis XVIII, with the French king trying in vain to wash the stains of Bonapartism out of France, while Napoleon looks on complacently from St. Helena. Contemporary British cartoon.

57. Count Karl Clam-Martinitz. Engraved by Kriehuber.

58. Sir Charles Stewart, Castlereagh's half-brother and English ambassador to Vienna.

59. Metternich, painted by Sir Thomas Lawrence. Of this famous Congress portrait of Metternich, Lawrence painted at least three versions, including one for the Waterloo Gallery at Windsor Castle. The original and probably best was the one retained by the Metternich family.

60. Wilhelmine, Duchess of Sagan, 1818. Painted by Johann Ender.

61. Metternich, 1819. Bust by Bertel Thorwaldsen.

62. Metternich, with two of his grandchildren, shows visitors through the sculpture gallery of the Rennweg villa in Vienna.

63. Wilhelmine's writing desk, a gem of eighteenth-century French cabinetmaking, had been originally owned by the Duc de Choiseul, ambassador of France at the court of Vienna, then acquired by the Duke of Courland. Wilhelmine used it all her life; after her death, Metternich's wife bought it for her husband at an auction.

the court gazette: plenipotentiaries might deposit their credentials for examination with a special committee at the Chancellery.

The monarchs were safely back from the excursion to Hungary, and on Sunday night, October 30, there was another masked redoute in the palace. The royal guests in domino mingled with the crowd, carrying on flirtations with pretty costumed strangers and enjoying all the pleasures of *lèse majesté*. The Tsar was observed talking for a long time with a person in mask and black domino, while Bigottini, the ballerina, in a pink domino "pressed close" to him. Only the glacial King of Prussia, "walked about alone."

It was probably at the masked redoute that night that a fairly open attempt was made to bribe Metternich, ostensibly in the name of the Tsar. According to the account Cooke wrote to Liverpool, an unidentified person approached Metternich and handed him a paper promising that "a person of the highest distinction" who had quarreled with him—Metternich—was prepared now to reward him well if the minister would cease to oppose his views.

The reward would take two forms: first, "a million in ready money"—100,000 English pounds, Cooke translated—and second, "a woman of rank whom Metternich wanted to get." The anonymous note had concluded: "Your Highness will understand."[4]

The reference could only have been to Wilhelmine. Did the Tsar believe that he could persuade or bribe Wilhelmine to renew her liaison with Metternich, perhaps by the promise of her child and the Courland family revenues?

On the journey to Hungary the Tsar had complained bitterly of Metternich to Emperor Franz and urged him to appoint another minister. "Your Metternich will make us fall out with one another," he had warned his host, adding that Metternich was the only "obstacle to harmony." But Emperor Franz had defended his minister firmly. Metternich represented his own views, he declared, adding that he thought it best if sovereigns did not interfere but left matters of business in the hands of their ministers.[5]

Since other means had not worked, the Tsar apparently decided to change his tactics. If threats failed, he would try what honey and gold would do. Though Cooke's account is the only one we have of the bribery attempt, there are other clues that the Tsar tried a different kind of persuasion on Metternich. Stein noted in his diary that week that the Tsar was "attempting to restore good relations with Metternich through the Duchess of Sagan."[6]

Metternich had not taken the bait offered in the bribery note, though he regretted afterward that he had not held on to the evidence:

> When the paper was first shown him [Cooke wrote] Metternich was unprepared and off his guard, tossed it aside, pretended not to understand. The next day he sorely repented his folly in losing such an opportunity to get the Tsar in his power.[7]

So crude in attempt by a sovereign to bribe another nation's Foreign Minister might seem hardly plausible, had we not documentation of Alexander's earlier effort in the summer of 1813 to bribe Metternich into war. To Emperor Franz Metternich wrote asking to see him in person to recount to him "the various steps the Russian Emperor has taken in the course of the day to win me by every art."[8]

The night following the palace redoute, on Monday, October 31, Count Razumowsky gave a ball in honor of the Tsar's return from Hungary. He was too busy to attend, Metternich wrote Wilhelmine, but he begged her to avoid speaking to the Tsar of him or of her relations with him:

> Let him talk, and refuse any kind of proposition he may make to you for or against me. If he speaks to you of nothing, this rule of conduct falls of itself for you will not go in search of it.

He asked this favor of her

> because I have strong reasons for it. I shall tell them to you the first hour you can give me and which I on my side can find free.

And he reminded her again:

> Never forget that our relations so pure and simple on my side ought never have lent themselves to complications of the kind to which the ridiculous conduct of certain personages has led.[9]

Wilhelmine went to the Razumowsky ball, and reported reassuringly to Metternich the following day:

> The Tsar said little to me yesterday but following your advice I cut him off short at once—I shall ask you, dear Clemens, to give me more exact instructions one of these days since I wish to do only what you want. *Bon jour, mon ami.* How are you and when shall I see you?[10]

He replied at once, thanking her. She would be, he wrote her,

> quite astonished at what I tell you; as for me I am no longer astonished at anything especially when it concerns that man. If you had followed a somewhat different path, how much pain and embarrassment you would have spared yourself and me. As to my portion of that grief, it is all the same, but I do not forgive you yours.[11]

If the Congress could not open until the dilemma of Poland and Saxony was resolved, then resolved it must be—and soon.

All that first week of November, behind the scenes of the festivals, negotiations continued.

Immediately after his return from Hungary the Tsar had replied to Castlereagh's memorandum on Poland. The reply had actually been written by Czartoryski and Anstett during the Tsar's absence; it defended the Tsar from the charge of breaking the treaties of Reichenbach and Teplitz on the ground that circumstances had changed, and that the fortunes of war gave him the right to Poland. To which Castlereagh retorted in a note brought to the Tsar by Stewart "that the Powers fought for the liberties of Europe and not for the extension of their dominions." The Tsar had at first refused to receive Stewart; their conversation ended with mutual sword rattling and talk of war.[12]

Metternich, nevertheless, was sanguine that the unraveling of the Poland-Saxony dilemma was at hand.

Even the majority of the Tsar's own advisers, among them Nesselrode and Stein, opposed the Tsar's Polish plans. On Saturday of that week, November 5, when Stein went to see the Tsar, the Russian sovereign accused Stein of not backing him on his plans. "You've ranged yourself with my enemies," he declared irritably. "I had not expected that." He had carried on a dangerous war, risked his life, given his Allies what they wanted, and now found "his most reasonable demands opposed." He complained that everyone, even his friends, were against him.[13]

He asked Stein to use his influence "to lead Hardenberg to deal alone with Russia in this case and not to make common cause with Austria against him." Then he added an astonishing statement—Austria had proposed, he told Stein, to concede everything in Polish affairs if he—the Tsar—kept Saxony from Prussia.[14]

Recording the conversation in his diary, Stein made no comment. He must have known that the Tsar was fabricating that accusation in order to split Prussia and Austria.

Metternich, meantime, was himself treading on quicksand. When Talleyrand buttonholed him after the meeting of the Committee of Eight on November 2, demanding to know on what terms Austria and England were buying the support of Prussia—was it, for example, with an offer of the whole of Saxony? Metternich replied not so, they planned to offer Prussia only a fourth part of Saxony.[15]

It was almost—though not quite—an outright lie. Metternich already realized his mistake in acceding to Castlereagh's persuasion. Sentiment in Austria, in government and army circles and among the general public, was rising vehemently in favor of Saxony, and Metternich knew he would have to backtrack. But how to keep Prussia in line until the Polish question was settled? The situation was very tricky indeed.

The Tsar, however, fully aware of the English-Austrian-Prussian combination at work against him, held one trump card, which he now proceeded to play.

On Sunday, November 6, he invited the King of Prussia to dine alone with him in his suite in the palace. As the dinner of the two royal friends drew to an end, Alexander led the conversation around to the question of his Polish plans.

Surely his closest ally, his comrade-in-arms, who had stood beside him during all the difficult weeks of the last campaign, who had ridden triumphantly into Paris at his side on that glorious day last March, surely his old and dear friend would not desert him on an issue of such critical importance. Long ago in Berlin they had vowed eternal brotherhood before the tomb of Friedrich Wilhelm's Hohenzollern ancestors. They were nearly the same age. Both might expect to reign for many years, to bring their two nations a long period of peace. "It was sweet to him to think that he would be witness for a long time of the happiness that their peoples owed to the intimate friendship of the monarchs."

"I have always linked my own glory to the reestablishment of a kingdom of Poland," the Tsar went on. "It was a vow I gave my Polish friends when I was still young. Shall I have to face the grief today of finding among my opponents my dearest friend, the only prince on whose lofty sentiments I believed I could count?"

With tears in his eyes Friedrich Wilhelm protested his loyalty. He would support Alexander on the Polish issue as on everything else; he could be counted on until death!

Only that morning Hardenberg had talked earnestly with the Prussian King, persuading him to give his assent to the Polish plans the three ministers had drawn up to present to the Tsar.

"It is not enough," the Tsar pointed out, "that you support me in this. Your ministers must agree to support me too!"

"But of course my ministers will support what I choose to support!" the King declared.

Then perhaps Friedrich Wilhelm would be kind enough to summon Chancellor Hardenberg, so that he could be witness to the Russo-Prussian entente?

When Hardenberg appeared, the Tsar triumphantly repeated the conversation he had just had with the King of Prussia and the promise that had been exacted.

In vain Hardenberg tried to urge the importance of compromise on the question of Poland, of weighing the arguments on the other side.

"But those are the arguments of Monsieur Metternich!" the Tsar interrupted angrily.

Did Hardenberg know, the Tsar went on, that Metternich had already offered to betray him, Hardenberg, that he had proposed to the Tsar that he would yield on Poland if the Tsar would oppose the Prussian acquisition of Saxony?

Hardenberg, shocked, though unbelieving, could find nothing to reply.

"You see how ministers will act!" the Tsar remarked, turning to the Prussian King. "But we are friends and we must take the business from the diplomats."

"Certainly," agreed Friedrich Wilhelm. Of course he would align himself on the side of his friend, and Hardenberg must do likewise.

In vain Hardenberg objected to so high-handed a manner of settling international problems—issues that could bring a whole continent again to war.

Angrily now the Tsar demanded to know whether the Chancellor intended to obey his King's orders or not. "And these orders," the Tsar added, "are absolute."

Bluntly Friedrich Wilhelm ordered Hardenberg to cease making common cause with Austria and England.

The old diplomat bowed and withdrew.[16]

Gentz told the Danish King afterward that "the Tsar had berated Prince Hardenberg in the most violent manner, so that the latter had gone away affected to the point where they feared for his sanity."[17]

Hardenberg recounted the humiliating scene in a letter next day to Metternich and Castlereagh, assuring them that, though he had had to yield at the moment, he "still asserts his determination to act with Austria." Indiscreetly Hardenberg argued that it would be best for his fellow ministers to go along with the Tsar's wishes since they were certain to lead to the Russian sovereign's ruin, would weaken rather than strengthen his empire.[18]

The Prussian Chancellor did not inform Metternich that the Tsar had accused him—Metternich—of betraying his Prussian Ally, but he told someone else—perhaps Castlereagh—and it came to Metternich's ears, probably at Stewart's ball on Monday night.

In a letter to Hardenberg written late that night Metternich angrily denied the Tsar's accusation:

> I've just learned, my dear Prince, that the Tsar of Russia in the course of the conversation that you had with him and with the King said, Austria had declared or insinuated it would be more accommodating in the Polish affair if the Tsar Alexander succeeded in rescuing Saxony.
> I deny not only the fact but I am also ready to maintain the opposite in the presence of the Tsar himself.

The Tsar, Metternich countered, was only trying to split Austria and Prussia.[19]

If Metternich's reputation had fallen and bitter criticism of his policies increased rather than diminished, the Tsar's reputation had fallen even lower. News of the scene in the palace on Sunday with the Prussian King and Hardenberg spread quickly through the city.

"Animosity against the Russians, especially the Tsar, is at its height," Rosenkrantz wrote the next day.[20]

The Tsar's erstwhile Prussian friends complained bitterly. Hardenberg, said Cooke, had called the Tsar "the most perfidious, treacherous, usurping character, and infinitely more dangerous than Buonoparte." Humboldt told Frau von Eskeles, the banker's wife, that the Tsar was "deceitful and capricious; one couldn't be careful enough with him." All the diplomatic corps, noted one police informer, "agree that Tsar Alexander would have done better for his own interest to stay home."[21]

If Metternich had critics within his own inner circle of the Chancellery staff, so did the Tsar. Stackelberg told Bernstorff that "they are making no progress because his master is so stubborn." Razumowsky and Stein were critical. Pozzo di Borgo shook his head over the Tsar's ambition. Anstett no longer believed the Congress could have "a happy issue"; he tried to resign his post, "but the Tsar paid no attention, only swamped him with more work than ever." In the Tsar's opinion Nesselrode had become a tool of Metternich; he was no longer consulted on business of any importance. Increasingly the Tsar turned to Czartoryski and to the smooth, shrewd Corfiote, Capo d'Istria.[22]

Even the ladies who had in the beginning been beguiled by the Tsar's attentions cooled considerably. When the Tsar remarked jovially to pretty Countess Széchenyi at a ball, "Madame, I note your husband is not present; may I have the pleasure of occupying his place temporarily?" the countess retorted, "Does Your Majesty take me for a province?"

Rosenkrantz, the Danish diplomat, reported that week that the court quartermaster had found a letter in which a plan was detailed for poisoning the Tsar with the aid of a cook in the Hofburg kitchens. Rumor had it that the Russian monarch would either move into Count Razumowsky's palace for safety or return to St. Petersburg.[23]

As if the Tsar did not have troubles enough, his family were not aiding his public image in the least.

His brother, Grand Duke Constantine, had made himself thoroughly disliked by a series of cruel and childish pranks. His chief passion was for things military. He loved to call up the Austrian regiment of which he was honorary commander at any hour of the day or night, no matter what the weather, and put it through difficult maneuvers. He thought nothing of summoning Alfred Windischgraetz, the regiment's colonel, wherever he might be, to lead the cavalry through intricate parade movements. One day in late October, when Windischgraetz was host at a dinner party, a message was brought in that the grand duke wished him to assemble the regiment at once. Alfred sent word that he could not come until his guests had departed. He took his time to arrive at the parade ground. When he appeared the fuming Constantine greeted him: "You're putting on airs and acting like a great lord!" To which Alfred replied with icy hauteur, "Sire, we do not need to play the *grand seigneur*, since we already are."[24]

A few days later, the regiment was again ordered to maneuver for the grand duke's pleasure. This time Constantine shouted orders which the men either did not know or could not understand. The regiment was thrown into utter confusion, some riders going one way, some another, while Constantine, growing furious, shouted louder and louder and began to beat about with his staff at anyone within range.

At this Windischgraetz intervened and declared with carefully chosen words that he could not permit such mishandling of his troops. Constantine,

already in an ugly mood, leaned over in the saddle and hit Alfred a resound-
ing crack on the head.

Windischgraetz, as commander, had his sword in his hand; with great
self-possession he returned it to the sheath, turned to a young lieutenant
riding beside him and requested that he take over command. Then he
went at once to his commanding general and reported the affair, sending his
second to the grand duke's quarters to challenge him, as a dynastic equal,
to a duel.

Such a scandal the Tsar hardly needed at the moment. He ordered his
brother to apologize to Windischgraetz and to leave the city at once—for
Warsaw.[25]

2

Metternich was plunged into such deep depression at the new impasse
in negotiations that, walking with Gentz on the walls on Tuesday morning,
November 8, he told Gentz it would be impossible to continue the present
situation much longer. "He is," Gentz wrote, "in a state of crisis!"[26]

So tense was the mood of the city that Congress-watchers were certain
Metternich would have to cancel his masked ball planned for that night.

But Metternich's fete was not canceled. Everyone came—even the Tsar
and the King of Prussia, quite as if nothing at all had happened, as if the
political weather remained as clear, mild and cloudless as those fine autumn
days of Austrian old wives' summer. Despite the anxieties and the hostility
in the air—or perhaps because it provided an escape valve for everyone's
pent-up tensions—the Metternichs' masked ball of November 8 was one of
the gayest and liveliest of all Congress fetes. "The most magical fete," Bertuch described it.

The entire decor of the Rennweg garden villa had been changed from
the pale blue and white of the October Peace Ball to the exuberant colors
of a Venetian masquerade. Ladies had been asked to wear national costumes, gentlemen to wear red or white dominos if they did not choose national costumes, and everyone was to be masked. Champagne flowed liber-
ally. Under the "freedom of the mask" all protocol was abolished. Any one
could approach anyone, talk to anyone, dance with anyone, never knowing
if it were an emperor or a queen—or even a chambermaid, for Metternich
sent Wilhelmine tickets for Hannchen and for her girls, Emilie, Marie and
Clara, proposing that mistress and maid switch masks at midnight, "if that
would amuse you."[27]

"Wildest gaiety," was the report when everyone changed one mask for
another at midnight.

Wilhelmine and Dorothée had chosen the colorful costumes of Carin-
thia; Countess Bernstorff wore the dirndl of the Salzkammergut; Lulu von
Thürheim and her sisters, the bright dress of Transylvanian peasant girls.

Among the prettiest costumes by common consent were Anna Eynard's Swiss dress, which she had finished sewing only an hour before the ball began, and the Danish ladies in full red skirts fringed with gold, their hair woven with scarlet and golden cords. Most amusing was stout Lady Castlereagh, whose outfit was not precisely ethnic; most people thought she had dressed as a vestal virgin; certainly she had wound her husband's august Order of the Garter in her somewhat eccentric coiffure.

Fifteen hundred guests shared supper, and so that ceremony would not interfere with the spirit of the evening, the sovereigns were seated this time in a separate room, while in the spacious downstairs hall ladies were grouped at small tables. Not to be banished, the Tsar and Prussian King table-hopped among the ladies, begging delicacies from the plates of the prettiest women.

After supper dancing became even gayer, with *tempêtes* played in ever faster time, until only the youngest and nimblest dancers were left on the floor—among them Prince Eugène de Beauharnais and Anna Eynard, both of them laughing so hard "we could hardly perform the steps."

Next a polonaise was played—but not the usual sober and solemn two-step procession of couples. Many of the dancers were already quite tipsy, and winding their way through the rooms of the villa, the head of the dancing queue crossed the tail, the dancers became wildly and hopelessly entangled, partners were lost in the melee, and the King of Denmark "laughed so hard he could barely stand up, Lady Castlereagh almost as much."[28]

At the end, as daybreak appeared, the orchestra played a last delightful old-fashioned dance customary at all Metternich parties, "Mon Grandpère," which those who still possessed head and feet danced in a comically stiff way to delight the onlookers.

Even Gentz, usually sour on such frivolity, did not go home until four in the morning, pronouncing it "the most beautiful fete that has ever been seen."[29]

3

The collapse of his political plans only deepened the pit of depression into which emotional catastrophe had already plunged Metternich.

He lived during those days in a landscape of gray dejection. Life was drained of all color and taste. He was listless and tired, forgetful of details. He could not sleep.

> I am writing to you at an hour which has very often been consecrated to you when I was still in the other world [he wrote Wilhelmine]. This hour has seen me given over twenty times to the most frightful suffering. I know that the dead are no longer able to calculate time and space. A thousand years or one minute, the world or one tiny corner of the earth, everything mingles together, it is all the same.[30]

And he confessed to Wilhelmine:

> I have so completely filled the emptiness with everything that can keep me busy even if only in material ways that I need some kind of calculation so that I don't miss real duties, or at least duties I've created for myself.[31]

If only they might have parted forever, made a clean break, never had to see one another again! But instead their paths crossed nearly every day. In the glittering framework of festivals that continued through the November days, he met her everywhere, at the theater, at dinner parties and soirees. At the balls he would see her, wearing one or another of the gowns he had helped her choose in Paris, the rose tulle over blue satin that General Chernyshëv admired, with a coronet of sapphires in her hair, or the deep green velvet and the famous emerald circlet on her forehead that set off so admirably her fine dark eyes.

He must bow and greet her smiling, kiss her hand or cheek, as if they were still flirting friends, while a stab of uncontrollable pain set his heart pounding again. She was almost never out of his mind.

To uproot a passion that has grown into the very marrow of the soul's bones: that is not a matter of days or of weeks.

He had to see her, he could not help it, and he would write asking her to set a time, "whatever day you will be pleased to indicate for me," adding, not without a touch of irony:

> Despite Europe and the congress I certainly dispose more freely of my moments than you do, and after having been for so long an active torment for you I can claim to have become a point of repose for your thoughts. You will no longer have to write that I torment you to death, and that only one person does not behave so and that one person is not I.[32]

On the rare occasions when he sees her alone the confidences pour out of him, as before; he needs her so desperately:

> What I had to say about myself[today] I got from the soul; what I had to say to you weighs no more on my mind. . . .[33]

Wilhelmine still asked him for favors. It embarrassed her a bit to do so, "despite your manner, which continues to be so perfect toward me." At the end of a note asking for extra tickets to his ball she scribbled two questions that shattered in a single instant the fragile wall he had begun to build between them:

> Are you really persuaded [she wrote] that I've given you up without the slightest restriction? Can nothing lead you back?[34]

He sent the tickets off at once, promised to reply to her questions as soon as he had an hour to spare:

... not by a yes or no but with all the simplicity of my heart. You will find me again exactly as you have known me, or as you would have known me if you had attached a greater value to a being who gave himself as never anyone has done—to a being who ceased to exist for anything except his love.[35]

Alarmed at the note of anguish she had not intended to arouse, and by the promise of a long letter full of details—certainly fuller than she wished to hear—Wilhelmine wrote hastily:

I only asked you for a yes or no. Please give me only such a terse reply as that. All the explanation will only make me quarrel with myself again. If that does not suit you, please leave me without reply and regard my questions as not being asked.[36]

Her note came too late; his long letter, in which the floodgates of his grief again released a torrent of words, crossed hers:

No, to the first question. To the second, nothing, nothing will ever lead me back into a position such as that I have just left. No more complications, no more sharing, nothing more that degrades, nothing more of what kills the most noble part of our being! I broke a liaison that was criminal for me, for you, for the two beings I am not called upon to respect, but I shall not even aid in deceiving my enemies—I shall never again permit myself to be the accomplice of *une amie*—and I give you this name after all that has passed. . . .

   Do you ask me if this being endowed with so many good qualities, so little created for the precipice that is leading her down into an abyss from which one does not return—this being whom I have loved a hundred times more than my life, and the liaison with whom appears to my shattered soul like a sweet dream followed only too soon by a frightful awakening— Do you ask if this being will ever extend her hand and join to my existence a single idea of happiness? Consult yourself on this act and do not consult me. . . .[37]

Clearly he had not yet given up hope, not quite. There is more, much more in the same vein. If she has a moment to give him the next day or the day after, he will come to see her. Some things are better spoken than written.

Had his been a grief that the world recognized, the death of a wife or child perhaps, he need not have hidden his feelings so carefully behind the pale mask that was his face, and those around him would have conspired to protect and cheer him.

He had only Gentz to confide in, who listened without understanding and went home and scribbled in his diary:

November 6. Long discussion with him on his affairs of heart.
November 11. Long conversation with Metternich, always more on that damned woman than on business.

A few days later Gentz heard the other side of the tale:

Sunday 13. From 3 to 4 a very curious conversation with the Duchess of Sagan on her fatal history with Metternich.[38]

It was almost precisely a year since Gentz had written Metternich effusively from Prague of Wilhelmine's great qualities of mind and soul, and how "once one began to love her, one could not soon leave off."

In the Metternich household the climate was bleak. Husband and wife barely exchanged a word with one another. He would tell Laure nothing, but she knew of course. They had been married for nearly twenty years; like most wives she knew her husband through and through—there had been plenty of time and occasion for painstaking study.

She had borne with his love affairs from the first liaison with Princess Bagration, her own painful initiation into the world of jealousy and anguish. She had come to accept marriage on his terms, as did most wives in that day; there was simply no choice. She had learned to avert her eyes from his flirtations, knowing that eventually he would be back, that she and their children were the solid anchorage of his life. Always before now he had entered those *affaires de coeur* so lightly, emerged unscarred.

Laure sensed that this affair with the Duchess of Sagan was different. Never had she seen him so tormented, so devastated by a kind of storm she could not recognize. His rosy optimism had left him. He was silent, withdrawn, unapproachable. Even to the children he paid little attention, he who had always been so devoted and charming a father.

Yet their public life went on as before. Guests saw her at her husband's side receiving at the Monday evening supper-balls, at the great fetes in the garden villa, a plain woman without visible charm, whom people were inclined to overlook as they turned to talk to the scintillating minister. Laure is accorded barely a mention in the dozens of memoirs written of the Congress.

Only to Marie, his darling Marie, did Metternich give any attention during the autumn weeks that he would look back on as his personal hell. To enter society at the Vienna Congress—an incredible debut for a pretty seventeen-year-old! In a whirl of parties, new gowns and admirers, Marie barely noticed the troubled atmosphere at home.

A thoroughly nice child, with unaffected good manners, and a touch of dear Papa's dry humor in her conversation, Marie was a decided success. The old princesses and countesses, arbiters of Vienna society, who sat whispering behind their fans in the alcoves around the ballroom, thoroughly approved of Marie and began to cogitate suitable matches for her. Dinner partners of all ages found her charming. Her dance programs were always filled —even the Tsar of Russia never failed to dance at least one dance with Marie during the evening.

Gentz, writing to the hospodar of Wallachia, described how at one of the Metternichs' Monday night supper parties, he had opened the door of a little salon to find Marie seated at the piano gaily playing a waltz, while a single couple, the stern-looking King of Prussia and an unidentified partner, waltzed all by themselves round and round the piano.[39]

In the daily police reports Metternich could read what people were saying of his love affairs—most of it untrue. A lady who had engaged Metternich in conversation at a masked ball, "under the mask," reported he had confessed his undying love for Caroline Bonaparte, and that it was for this reason that he could not abandon his alliance with Murat."[40]

Gossip was not kind to Wilhelmine. One informer told the police that she had written to a friend, "A Minister of Foreign Affairs who has lost the confidence of foreign powers can hardly keep his post." Another agent reported that at the Crennevilles' one night

> Princess Bagration, Sagan, Talleyrand and Rechberg all joined in making fun of Metternich. Sagan and Bagration went so far that the police ought to expel them.[41]

Bertuch, the Weimar publisher, who of course knew none of the principals and related only what he had picked up at the second level of society, wrote in mid-November:

> Sagan is busy between Metternich and Alexander. She sharpens and fires her arrows. Doesn't that have some connection with the little Périgord [i.e., Dorothée]?[42]

A story current then and later reported that Metternich had spent the night of November 10 to 11 with the Duchess of Sagan, oversleeping and missing an important morning meeting of the German Committee, through which carelessness Austria lost a large piece of territory to Bavaria. But on November 10 their affair was many weeks over; Wilhelmine herself was at the great *redoute parée* in the Riding Hall the night of November 10, and Metternich's only lapse at the meeting of the German Committee on November 9 was to scribble off a few lines to her telling her he was about "to draft a good article of the German constitution."[43]

Another more troubling tale carried in the police files involved the young Hungarian-born wife of Count Karl Zichy, both of whom were among the closest and most dependably loyal of Metternich's friends. Julie Zichy, whose cameo beauty, childlike sweetness and candor had brought her the respectful homage of the Prussian King, was of blameless reputation, and devoutly religious. According to a story repeated in early November, the Tsar informed Julie one night at a ball that Metternich had boasted Julie was according him her favors, at which Julie burst into a torrent of tears and refused to listen to Metternich's protests of innocence. If the tale had any truth in it, it would have wounded Metternich deeply and further embittered his relations with the Tsar.[44]

4

Metternich's *Lieblingsidee*, his cherished plan to carve an axis for the wheel of Europe out of an Austro-Prussian entente, had collapsed. The dinner scene in the Tsar's apartments on November 6, when Alexander had bound the loyalty of the Prussian King firmly to Russia, wrenched apart the delicate fabric of power relationships Metternich had been weaving since the previous May. Where to turn next?

Public opinion in Austria had been increasingly outspoken against Prussia's annihilation of Saxony. Now, in mid-November, to intensify widespread bitterness over the direction of the negotiations, news filtered into Vienna that Prince Repnin, Russian military governor of Saxony, had turned over the reins of occupation to Prussia. People were shocked to read in Repnin's printed circular that the transfer had been made with the agreement of Austria and of England. Both Castlereagh and Metternich protested loudly that their consent had been purely provisional and disavowed the Repnin circular. But it was too late; the damage was done.

Next came the ominous news that the Tsar's brother, Grand Duke Constantine, was in Warsaw taking over command of the Russian army of occupation in Poland, as if the new kingdom of Poland were well under way.

Certainly negotiations had been badly bungled, so far as both Metternich and Castlereagh were concerned.

Castlereagh, arriving in Vienna in September expecting to play a heroic role and settle the complicated problems of Central Europe in a matter of days or perhaps weeks, had criticized Metternich's "lack of vigor," his tendency to procrastinate, the weakness of Austria's financial structure and her army.[45]

A greatly-enlarged Prussia was part of Castlereagh's master-plan for containing France, and the Saxon King's support of Napoleon was reason enough to abandon the Saxon monarchy to Prussia. Castlereagh like Metternich considered the settlement of Poland the paramount issue. The plan had failed. Replying to Castlereagh's second memorandum, the Tsar had rapped him sharply on the wrist. "A mediator," the Tsar informed him, "is only useful in a discussion if he tries to conciliate; otherwise he had better leave the parties concerned alone." "Schoolboy's diplomacy," Talleyrand termed Castlereagh's procedures.[46]

Though the English public had been kept in the dark about the happenings in Vienna, and even the Opposition only gradually were lifting voices to protest "the monstrous proceedings of the robbers at Vienna," still there were already rumblings of disapproval within the Tory Cabinet itself against Castlereagh's policies. There was strong feeling that Castlereagh had gone too far.

It took two to three weeks for a dispatch to leave Vienna, cross France, reach London, and another two to three weeks for a reply. When Castlereagh sat down finally in a state of dejection on November 11 and wrote Liverpool attempting to explain and to gloss over his failure, laying blame on the autocracy of the Tsar, already dispatches were on the way to him, written in London before the end of October, ordering him to slow down on the question of Poland. While Castlereagh was asking for "the Prince Regent's gracious approbation" and "the concurrence of my colleagues in the government," he was shortly to receive notice that if his negotiations on Poland had not been brought to a satisfactory conclusion "we should withdraw ourselves from the question altogether."[47]

Liverpool's dispatch of October 28 enclosed a strongly worded memorandum from Chancellor of the Exchequer Vansittart pointing out the danger to Britain if the Tsar became sufficiently irritated to bring the question of maritime law—that delicate and critical question which Castlereagh had so adroitly maneuvered to have omitted from any joint peace talks among the Allies—before the Vienna Congress.

There were other dangers in the line Castlereagh was pursuing, his fellow cabinet ministers pointed out. The war with America—being fought over the question of maritime law, among other things—showed no signs of ending. The English and American commissioners meeting in Ghent were no nearer to settlement of conflicting issues than were the plenipotentiaries in Vienna. If the Tsar and possibly other powers were to support the cause of the Americans, it might seriously embarrass Britain's chances of getting the best possible deal in Ghent. If Castlereagh antagonized the Tsar, Russia might decide to intervene in the war on the side of America; there was, Liverpool pointed out, a sizable party in Russia supporting the Americans already. The American war was costing England far too much; let Castlereagh take no chances of adding any further expense![48]

The nervous Cabinet in London might have trembled even further had they overheard what Anstett was suggesting as a possible trump card for the Tsar to play. If England continued to press the Tsar to give up his Polish conquests, Anstett thought, let the Tsar agree to do so—provided that England surrendered all she had conquered since the Peace of Amiens, and return the Low Countries to Austria.[49] It would mean the sacrifice of all those canny protective devices Britain had built up for the development of a great commercial empire. No, such a risk would certainly be out of the question!

There was nothing Castlereagh could do now except to withdraw from an overt and active role in the negotiations. He would remain only, as Metternich put it, a *point d'appui* to Austria.

Metternich was now, to all extents and purposes, isolated. If Castlereagh felt the dejection of failure, Metternich's despondency was yet lower. The only faintly bright spot in the tenor of political events was that Prussia's defection nullified the provisional offer of all of Saxony contained in Metternich's unfortunate October 22 memorandum. Metternich could now begin to insist, with or without Castlereagh's approval, that at least a portion of Saxony be preserved.

If anyone besides the Tsar could rejoice at the collapse of the Austro-Prussian understanding, it was Talleyrand. France the Outsider might just possibly become once more France the Insider. Already Talleyrand pondered combinations that might bring France into the inner circles of power as someone's partner. France, England, Spain and Holland perhaps? For mutual aid and support? But Castlereagh remained cool. "A limited man," Talleyrand wrote home to Paris. "No imagination and absolutely no daring." No one could accuse Talleyrand of lacking either ingredient.

If either Metternich or Castlereagh was tempted at times during the crisis month of November to make use of France as a partner, the secret reports both were receiving from Paris of the dangerous internal situation in France gave them pause. How count on an ally threatened by civil war? Bonapartist sentiment had been increasing, in direct proportion to resentment against the Bourbons. Plots to overthrow the King's government were widely rumored, even a conspiracy to kill the King and members of his family. In the army there was a surge of nostalgic sentiment for Bonaparte. Ah, the fine days of France's glory, when the army was marching forth to conquer all Europe—perhaps Asia as well! One Guard regiment had burned their eagles, gathered up the ashes, each soldier swallowing a part of them while he drank a goblet of wine to Bonaparte's health.[50]

From Italy came a flood of ominous rumors. There were suspicious visitors going back and forth between the Italian mainland and Elba, rumors of Bonapartist plots in Tuscany. The French consul in Leghorn wrote Talleyrand in November that Napoleon had plans to leave Elba, "and as soon as he appears at the head of his Guard in Italy, more than 50,000 men will rise up and follow his banner and thousands of French soldiers will join them."[51]

If Metternich and Castlereagh were in a state of gloom, so too was Talleyrand. Had he guessed wrong, Talleyrand must have wondered in those anxious November days? Had he played the wrong card in this international whist game, betting on the Bourbons, risking his life and his career on a throw of the dice that day the Allies marched into Paris last March?

In the loneliness and isolation of his position, he depended increasingly on Dorothée for companionship. At his dinner parties she piloted the conversation with nimbleness and tact. At his soirees, sparsely attended and chiefly by second-string diplomats of second-rate powers or by Austrian "outs," Dorothée played hostess with composure and charm. At the balls her exotic looks drew eyes and admirers. Talleyrand recognized, moreover, in Dorothée's a brain that was kindred to his own—a subtle, intricate brain, crisscrossed with byways and passages. She would make a perfect political partner.

Sitting on his bed mornings while he breakfasted and read aloud important dispatches and letters, they consulted together about the answers, laid plans for the day's events. Often he dictated important messages to her; they would work together, revising again and again, until the precise nuance in the phrasing had been found.

Certainly already, though he might tell himself otherwise, Talleyrand viewed with uneasiness, perhaps with dismay, the admirers her beauty was attracting, especially a certain attentive young Austrian, Count Karl Clam-Martinitz, favorite aide of Prince Schwarzenberg, who was already deeply in love with Dorothée.

Dorothée herself was blooming in her new independence, finding herself as a person with her own interests and tastes and talents—for the first time in her life free of mother, governess, husband. Vienna opened up a new world for her, as she would write later.

5

People talked of the Congress ending abruptly, a lesson in futility. Far worse, people were talking of war.

Prussia continued to demand all of Saxony, while Bavaria announced it would enter into no agreement on the future of Germany unless the kingdom of Saxony were preserved. The smaller German states agreed. Hardenberg had a stormy interview with Wrede, during which the Prussian Chancellor threatened to go to war. When Castlereagh intervened and tried to persuade Wrede to accept Prussia's demand, Wrede expressed himself shocked that Castlereagh could propose "so immoral a step."

The Tsar clung stubbornly to his plans for Poland; for once he would not, Stein noted in his diary, even listen to his sister Catherine, who argued against it. He told her that "his honor had been engaged." Anstett called the rupture of the Congress "almost probable," thought that "war will follow in five to six months."[52]

Throughout November the rumblings of war grew louder. In response to Constantine's appearance in Poland to take charge of the Russian army there, Austria was said to have ordered part of her army to the Galician border.

Stein wrote early in November that Hardenberg had consulted him "on whether it was wise to advocate a war now." Stein advised against it. "Peace is needed in order to calm everything and to bring security," he told him.[53]

Within the French embassy in the Kaunitz Palace they talked gloomily of war. Dalberg complained about Austria keeping "so large an army on foot without wishing to use it; a campaign would produce more results than all the notes of Prince Metternich."[54]

Talleyrand wrote home before the end of October to ask how far he could go in threatening force, and the French King replied that much as he wished for several years of calm to heal the wounds of the country, "I wish above all to preserve intact the honor of France."[55]

Talleyrand quoted Castlereagh as declaring, if the Tsar won't stop at the Vistula, "we must force him to it by war, that England can furnish few troops because of the war in America but she will furnish subsidies." Austrian official opinion was "very warlike," but Metternich and Schwarzenberg refused to discuss the possibility.[56]

The Viennese public, meantime, grumbled about prices, which had risen astronomically in the last weeks. It was said that the cost of entertaining Emperor Franz's guests was at least 100,000 gulden a day. From the pen of Herr Eipeldauer came a steel-tipped comment:

> Now, hallelujah and God be praised, the massacring with people has been stopped for the nonce. Now has begun a great war with the geese, ducklings, capons, pheasants, oxen, calves, lambs, wild pigs, stags, deer, and snipe, and there's been published a terrible conscription in the animal kingdom. . . . But the sellers of meat, of fowl and of game get a much higher price for an animal carcass than for a human body, which in all of these wars never came to much more than six to seven kreutzers, when a capon or a turkey comes to three to five gulden. Imagine what a stag or a wild boar's life will fetch![57]

The weather that November remained incredibly lovely. Despite the political gloom, people dined, walked, rode, hunted, talked, danced as tirelessly as ever. They strolled along the Graben and on the walls. In the Prater people gathered as in summer to watch the elegant carriages of the English visitors trot smartly along the main *Allee*, and the English women—otherwise not noted for their attention to fashion—canter along the bridle paths in chic habits with long black veils floating gracefully behind.

One could walk in the gardens at Schönbrunn Palace, and if one were lucky stare at the little son of Napoleon, out for an airing with his governess. No longer King of Rome but renamed now Duke of Parma, he was to inherit the Italian duchy after his mother—providing, of course, that Talleyrand and the Bourbon forces did not insist on divesting Napoleon's kin of everything and giving Parma to the Bourbon Queen of Etruria. The King of France had sent all the little boy's toys from the Tuileries to Schönbrunn, including the tiny carriage drawn by sheep.

The Eynards went to see the child several times for they had been in Paris at the time of his birth, in March of 1811. Anna Eynard had suffered a miscarriage just then, that nearly cost her life and prevented her from ever bearing a child of her own. With a pang she watched the little son of Napoleon, precisely the age her own child would have been—"a lively beautiful boy," Eynard described him, "very pale, big blue eyes, long curly blond hair, in a hussar uniform red with gold."[58]

Even amid prophecies of the doom of the Congress, there was a great flurry of cheery talk and preparation for one of the most famous of the festivals, the Carousel, that was to take place on November 23 in the Spanish Riding Hall adjoining the imperial palace.

Twenty-four of the most skilled riders of the Austro-Hungarian aristocracy dressed as knights, would re-enact a medieval tournament, giving an exhibition of high style horsemanship, while twenty-four of the most beautiful women of the court set—among them, Wilhelmine and her sister Dorothée— were to appear as Ladies of the Tournament.

The exhibition had already been postponed once, because the Austrian Emperor caught a chill out hunting. Then the Tsar became ill and took to his bed for several days. Stories varied about the cause; certainly he had fainted while dancing at a public dance at the Mehlgrubsaal on November 17. Some said he had been kicked in the shin by Lady Castlereagh during a fast waltz. Castlereagh said the Tsar's illness had been brought on by over-fatigue and exertion in the "hottest rooms"—all the rooms in Vienna were too warm for the cool-blooded English. The Tsar had in fact danced through thirty nights in a row, and might well have dropped from fatigue.

In the end the Carousel was not postponed, but an extra performance would be given later expressly for the Tsar's benefit.

The day of the Carousel, November 23, was also Clemens Metternich's name day.

On the eve of that day Wilhelmine wrote wishing him a *bonne fête* and sending him a handsome candlestick she had long ago promised him:

> It is to replace the one that stands on your writing table; the only thing
> I ask is that you forbid your people to decorate it with those hideous
> green leaves.[59]

He was pleased with her remembrance and thanked her: "Any proof what-soever that you think of me is worth more than anything that comes to me from anywhere else."

Since childhood, he wrote her, he had always looked forward to his name day with a joy mingled with fear of disappointment. He had built "castles in Spain" looking forward to this name day of 1814, and if his reason had prophesied that St. Clemens' Day would find him "in the most frightful soli-tude," Eh bien, dear W, everything has betrayed me except my heart.[60] She would of course be too busy preparing for the great Carousel that evening to be able to see him during the day, but perhaps the following day?

Certainly Metternich did not spend his name day in "the most frightful solitude." Gentz was on hand at ten in the morning to greet him with his usual obsequious compliments—no matter what he might be saying behind his back. Karl and Julie Zichy gave a dinner party to which Clemens' family and dearest friends were invited—his parents, Laure and Marie, Flora Wrbna and her husband, Lory and Xavier Fuchs, Floret, Mercy, Gentz and a few others. Whatever may have been the contretemps involving Julie Zichy ear-lier in the month, it had certainly blown over. The Zichys continued to be his warmest friends.

After dinner everyone went home to rest and dress for the Carousel. Tickets for the event were in such demand that they had of course been counterfeited, and a special police guard was on hand to scrutinize admission cards.

The double gallery of the Riding Hall was crowded with spectators in brilliant evening dress and uniforms.

Promptly at eight the herald-at-arms trumpeted the entrance of the Ladies of the Tournament, veiled from head to foot. When a second trumpet ruffle announced the entrance of the sovereigns, the Ladies, standing on the balcony at one end of the hall, threw back their veils, revealing elaborate gowns in French Renaissance style in black, crimson, green and blue velvet, encrusted from head to toe with jewels that shimmered in the light of the ten thousand candles. Applause drowned out the trumpet blasts. It may well have been the most ostentatious display of jewels ever seen in Central Europe.

Dorothée's long tunic of black velvet with slashed sleeves over white satin bodice and underskirt, was held open with huge diamond clasps. Wilhelmine wore emerald green velvet, the low-cut vest studded with diamonds, on her head a Renaissance cap of green velvet sewn with gems.

In that day when fine horsemanship was the most admired of manly skills, the twenty-four young knights on their black Hungarian horses—among them Alfred Windischgraetz—put on a spectacular demonstration, riding with lances full tilt to spear a row of rings suspended in front of the imperial boxes, tilting with short javelins at Saracens' heads on railings around the arena, cutting loose apples suspended by ribbons from the ceiling while riding at full gallop, then splitting the apples in midair with scimitars. There was a simulated knightly battle, and finally an exhibition of the pirouettes, turns, leaps and gambols that were part of the skills of *haute dressage* riding.

When the tournament was over everyone adjourned to the ballroom, where tables were laid for supper, and companies of minstrels strolled among the guests playing the harp and singing ballads. The Ladies of the Tournament opened the ball that followed with a series of quadrilles.

The Carousel was the talk of the city for days after. The police reports were filled with allusions to the extravagance of the ladies' jewels. "The Prussians tell me," one agent noted, " 'My God, we could fight three campaigns with that money!' " A Florentine banker who had appraised the largest and finest gems in Europe declared he could not begin to assess the value of the jewels worn that night.

The Prince de Ligne entertained a dinner party that week with stories of how the ladies had borrowed jewels from all their friends and relatives and got them so mixed up "nobody could tell one from another." The Duchess of Sagan, lending her diamond coronet to a friend, "broke it into a thousand pieces so that her friend could arrange it to suit her."[61]

Whether De Ligne's anecdote was true or not, Wilhelmine was certainly generous in lending her jewels, had written Metternich to ask whether Laure preferred to borrow her sapphires or her emeralds for the evening.

It was also true that even very wealthy women were becoming alarmed at the enormous costs of the continuing festivities. "Ladies cannot manage on their ordinary budgets," a police informer reported, "and husbands are already reduced to adding another sizable deficit to their accounts." The bankers of Vienna were doing a rush business in exchange and in loans. Wilhelmine that month asked Metternich if he could help her sell some of her emeralds. "I will sell them with much pleasure," she wrote. "I prefer to pay my debts."[62]

Interestingly enough, the crime rate in Vienna was so low that with a hundred thousand strangers in the city and millions in jewels flaunted quite publicly nearly every evening, there is no mention in the bulging police reports of a single jewel theft.

Two days after the Carousel, on November 25, was Wilhelmine's name day, and though as a Protestant she did not ordinarily celebrate St. Catherine's day, she was pleased that Metternich remembered it and sent her a charming leather portfolio monogrammed in gilt. No, he wrote her, he would not come to see her that day:

> Alone I shall not find you; in company I will not see you, and for me it is better to be far from everything that in the long run brings me to the grave.[63]

The Advent season was beginning, the tempo of the festivals would slacken, and official entertainment at least was to continue in a subdued key. When Wilhelmine wrote to ask if there was to be a supper and ball at his house on the following Monday evening, he explained:

> We cannot dance in Catholic houses, but Catholics may dance in houses that do not believe in the Pope. Thus the Stackelbergs, the Razumowskys, the Bagrations can destroy us without our being able to reciprocate.

He wished that he might have a few good friends at his house for the evening, but how could he?

> Everyone bores me, and you—I cannot have you in a small committee. I cannot invite you without inviting your lover, and I cannot invite him without making myself miserable. So I give up the idea of pleasant evenings—this is a small sacrifice for the man who bears each day the sacrifice of his life.[64]

6

Since the Tsar had been taken ill on November 17, and remained bedridden in his rooms in the Hofburg, no progress had been possible on the negotiations.

He saw almost no one—only his closest aides, including Stein, his sisters and the Tsarina.

Something happened to the Tsar during those days of his illness—a tiny event, a spark that set fire to tinder long waiting in the recesses of his psyche.

One of the Tsarina's ladies-in-waiting, a young Rumanian woman, Mademoiselle Roxandre Sturdza, had been in correspondence for some time with a woman preacher from the Baltic region, a religious mystic and member of the Pietist sect named Julie von Krüdener.

Through Mademoiselle Sturdza, Julie von Krüdener had been aiming her literary missiles at the Tsar, and now she had scored. The Tsarina brought her letters and read them aloud to her husband. In one Madame Krüdener had written:

> You wish to speak to me of all the deep and striking beauties in the soul of the Tsar. . . . I have great things to say to him for I have suffered much on his account. The Lord alone can prepare his heart to hear them. May the Almighty direct and bless him who is called to so high a mission![65]

Alexander had long suspected he had been chosen for a divine mission; now in his rooms, his Bible open before him, he thought about this inspired woman and her enigmatic message. What was he to do? What path should he take? In the next weeks Mademoiselle Sturdza frequently read him Madame Krüdener's letters full of mystical passages and prophecies.

When Hardenberg was finally admitted to see the Tsar on the evening of November 23, he found the Russian sovereign "very conciliatory in his language," and quite willing to leave the negotiations on Poland in Hardenberg's hands.

The proposal that Hardenberg and Metternich worked out appeared to be a reasonable compromise. Prussia would get the city of Thorn, with the Warthe River as a defensible frontier. Austria would get Cracow, the circle of Zamość and the Nida River frontier. In exchange Russia would have the rest of Poland to organize as a kingdom according to the Tsar's wishes.

The old Prussian Chancellor was elated at the Tsar's expressions of goodwill, and dropped an encouraging note to Metternich the following day signed, "Wholly yours heart and soul." Everything looked hopeful. "His Majesty has promised to inform me of his counter-proposals at the earliest moment."[66]

But when the Russian reply to the Hardenberg-Metternich proposal was handed to the Prussian Chancellor on November 27, it contained no real compromise on any of the issues at conflict. Though the note spoke of the new sacrifices the Tsar was prepared to make, he refused to give up any Polish territory to provide river boundaries for Prussia and Austria. His sole sacrifice would be to make neutral cities of Thorn and Cracow. At the same time he insisted that Saxony was indivisible, and must be turned over *in toto* to Prussia.

Affairs were again at an impasse.

On November 28, the first day the Tsar was up and about again, Metternich went to talk with him and tried to persuade him to agree to the compromise proposal. In vain. Writing Wilhelmine late that Monday night after his fruitless meeting, he told her:

> I've had a very troublesome day. Tomorrow will bring us no less of a trial. This evening I was with Tsar A. for several hours. A few— very few moments—will decide great questions. Much lies on my soul —and I carry an immense burden like the wanderer in the wilderness; not the pressure of a hand—not a rewarding look—not a word of sympathy falls to my lot . . . 1814 is truly a dreadful year.[67]

In the last days of November the long spell of fine weather broke and a cold rain fell.

Now finally, his nerves stretched to a breaking point, it was Metternich who took to his bed, ill again apparently with one of his "rheumatic-catarrhal" afflictions.

Never had things looked blacker and bleaker than in those days at November's end.

7

Though all the sovereigns put on cheerful smiles for their appearances in public and continued to polonaise through the balls that followed the two final performances of the Carousel, it was clear from the gossip of servants and aides that the royal house party in the Hofburg had turned somewhat sour.

The King of Württemberg declared crossly that he had made up his mind to go home as soon as possible—Metternich was accomplishing nothing at his Congress. There were recurrent rumors that the Tsar would depart, leaving Anstett and Nesselrode "to bury the Congress."

When Emperor Franz went to congratulate the Tsar on recovering from his illness, he urged his fellow monarch to take a more conciliatory view of Poland and Saxony. After all, he pointed out, the King of Saxony had been bound by treaty only to Austria, so that only he, the Austrian Emperor, could be offended by the King's broken promise. If he was ready to pardon the old King for joining Napoleon, surely it was not up to other monarchs to punish him?

The Tsar replied somewhat brusquely that he had promised Saxony to his friend the King of Prussia; let Emperor Franz address his complaint to Friedrich Wilhelm.

But when Emperor Franz approached the Prussian monarch during one of the informal royal gatherings that preceded the palace dinner hour, he was rudely rebuffed with a remark spoken loudly enough for the whole company to overhear, "Let's not discuss it any more!" The Austrian Emperor was offended and complained to the Danish King about "having to live every day with sovereigns like the Tsar and the King of Prussia who behave so rudely to him."[68]

To complicate the negotiations still further, Hardenberg, who had agreed at least verbally with Metternich that a part of Saxony should be preserved, now, backed by the Tsar's insistence on Prussia receiving all of Saxony, withdrew his assent. In a note written to Metternich on December 2, Hardenberg proposed that the King of Saxony be given some bits and pieces of German-speaking territory along the Rhine.

Negotiations had again, as Castlereagh put it with his characteristic understatement, taken on "an embarrassing complexion."[69]

Everyone had the glooms. Castlereagh and Count Münster blamed the Tsar. Count Schulenburg blamed Metternich, who had permitted the provisional occupation of Saxony by Prussia. Gentz "did not hide his despair and did not spare Prince Metternich." Gentz had no constructive ideas to offer, however. Austria, he thought, would have to yield on Poland. He himself was advising Metternich "to declare that Austria would meddle no more in others' affairs, neither in regard to Saxony nor otherwise," but wash her hands of everyone and everything. Congress could then be dissolved "without causing an immediate rupture . . . which would be a scandal."

Emperor Franz was vexed at Castlereagh, who refused to promise British support when Metternich asked him, and replied that "he finds himself without instructions in this respect."[70]

Pessimistically Castlereagh wrote back to London on December 5 for instructions in case war broke out. Things might take a turn for the better, he told Liverpool, or they might end in a stalemate, but on the whole he thought it most likely affairs would end in war, "if we cannot agree upon some general system . . . as Europe is more extensively armed than at any former period."

Should Britain be prepared to enter the fray at once, since she was sure to be dragged in sooner or later? Or should she take the role, in conjunction with France, of armed mediation?[71]

On the same day Castlereagh sent off his dispatch, Metternich tried again to reach a direct understanding with the Tsar. The two men—hiding their bitter personal enmity now with cool and distant courtesy—exchanged "subtleties and stratagems," but neither persuaded the other to move an inch.

That night, the night of December 6, two events of note took place in Vienna.

The Tsar gave an extravagant ball in the Razumowsky palace in honor of his sister Catherine's name day. No expense had been spared to make it one of the most magnificent and memorable of Congress fetes, as if the Tsar would prove he could outshine Metternich even in party-giving.

When the usual polonaise wound its way through the palace, the dancers were awed by the magnificence of the rooms—rooms transformed into Arabian tents with silken hangings and invisible lamps, marble halls decorated with the finest bronzes and antique sculpture, painting galleries hung with gems of the Italian and French Renaissance, a mahogany-paneled library with a hanging staircase that led to a gallery filled with rare manuscripts and books, glass houses where flowers from all the continents had been brought to a profusion of bloom.

All sorts of delicacies for supper, including tiny fresh cucumbers, hearts of lettuce and sweet cherries from the greenhouses of Tsarskoe Selo outside St. Petersburg, were served on the Tsar's own precious porcelain and plate, all brought across Central Europe some fifteen hundred miles by sleigh and carriage, to serve the Tsar's guests that night in December.

Even while the throng of guests lingered over the lavish feast, a courier galloped up to the door of Castlereagh's house in Minoritenplatz, carrying a dispatch from England that had been three weeks on the way.

In reply to Castlereagh's letter of October 24, which had transmitted Metternich's October 22 memorandum to Prussia—so long did it take for messages to go and come between Vienna and London—Liverpool had written most forthrightly against Castlereagh's original plan of sacrificing Saxony. The English Government did not, of course, yet know that the plan had collapsed. "I ought to apprise you that there is a strong feeling in this country respecting Saxony," Liverpool wrote, enjoining him—and using Metternich's own words to do so—"that a *noyau* at least should be preserved. . . ." The English Cabinet disavowed Castlereagh's original policy, and supported Metternich's desire to preserve at least part of Saxony.[72]

Castlereagh immediately informed Metternich of his new instructions. Next morning, when Wrede appeared at the Chancellery, Metternich could jubilantly hand him Castlereagh's note.

For Metternich—no matter what came afterward, and things were to continue in a tangle through December—that dispatch of December 6 was a godsend and marked a turning point in his conduct of negotiations. It was a signal to resume leadership of the inner councils where he had faltered so badly in October. Where Castlereagh had refused support a few days earlier, he rallied now again to Metternich's side.

When Rosenkrantz made his daily round of official visits, news of the English courier had preceded him. Count Schulenburg of Saxony was elated. At the Austrian Chancellery everyone was wreathed in smiles. Saxony would yet be saved! Metternich's father, the old prince, told Rosenkrantz that day "with extreme satisfaction" that at the very moment

> when his son was about to give an important reply to Prince Hardenberg, a courier arrived for him from London which put him at his ease, and that he had not lost an instant in sending a reply.[73]

Emperor Franz cheerfully informed the Danish King that the London dispatch had ordered Castlereagh to support Austria in everything, that he had been blamed for acting differently. Rumor exaggerated the content of the dispatch, and presently people quoted it as saying that Castlereagh was to offer Austria "all the subsidies they wanted" in case of a rupture, and if necessary the Prince Regent would renounce the "300,000 souls promised him for his kingdom of Hanover by the treaty of Kalisch."[74]

Talleyrand was delighted to learn of the dispatch, declaring it was the first day since he got to Vienna when he could breathe easily. His criticism of Metternich vanished, and he wrote him at once "a beautiful letter."

Buoyed now by English support for the preservation of a portion of Saxony, Metternich prepared his careful reply to Hardenberg. Austria could no longer, he wrote, agree to the incorporation of the whole of Saxony into Prussia. He proposed instead that Prussia accept indemnification elsewhere, and he appended a list of population figures, showing how other fragments of German lands could make up her population deficit, so that she would need only 330,000 Saxons to restore her former size.

The note was brought to Hardenberg on December 11, and it precipitated at once what was the most violent of all the diplomatic explosions at that long and stormy Congress.

Hardenberg, Humboldt and the other Prussians were furious. Preferring to forget that Austrian assent to the absorption of Saxony, as couched in Metternich's note of October 22, had been wholly contingent on Prussia's support of the Austrian position on Poland—which the King of Prussia himself had forbidden on November 6—they declared that Austria was breaking her promise. Besides, they had conquered Saxony—it was theirs by right of conquest!

Hardenberg went at once to the Tsar, taking with him the confidential correspondence that had passed between himself and Metternich, including the memorandum of October 22. It was a grave breach of diplomatic decorum, "a very blamable indiscretion on the part of the Prussians," Castlereagh called it. "The exhibition of these secret papers," Castlereagh wrote, "were accompanied with an insinuation that Austria now broke faith with Prussia upon the point of Saxony, in consequence of Prussia *refusing* to enter into a hostile alliance against Russia."[75]

But it was the note Metternich had written in anger to Hardenberg on the night of November 7, denying any "deal" with the Tsar on the Saxony question—and in effect calling the Tsar a liar—that particularly infuriated the Russian sovereign.[76]

The Tsar stormed in to Emperor Franz, threw the correspondence on the table, declaring he intended to challenge Metternich to a duel.

Emperor Franz tried to soothe Alexander. A duel, he pointed out, would be a strange example to give the world just as the leading powers were endeavoring to prove that differences of opinion might be settled peaceably. The Tsar was unmoved; his honor had been impugned; the matter could only be settled with swords. "His Majesty," Metternich recalled later, "told me that he had most vigorously urged the Emperor [Alexander] to have a third explanation with me before giving the challenge, to which Alexander at last agreed."

Scarcely had Metternich returned to his apartments when Count Ozarowsky, one of the Tsar's adjutants, was announced.

"I am charged by His Imperial Majesty to call upon you to declare to the
Prussian Chancellor that you were mistaken in what you told him of your
conversation with Tsar Alexander."

"Please inform your imperial master," Metternich replied coolly—this is
of course his own account—"that I shall never recall one word of that conversation, the correctness of which I am certain. If, however, Prince Hardenberg misunderstood me and therefore repeated my words incorrectly, I shall
be ready to remove the mistake."

Count Ozarowsky retired.

A few moments later the Tsar sent word that he would not appear at the
fete at Metternich's house that night.

By some unlucky chance that autumn, whenever the political situation was at its very worst, when Metternich stood on the brink of a perilous
fall—each crisis seemingly more serious than the one that had preceded it—
he was always giving some great festival at which he must appear before the
public, like an actor going on stage in a state of critical illness—to preside, as
Humboldt said, "like a master of ceremonies."

That Monday night, December 12, the Metternichs were entertaining at
a large reception and supper to which all the sovereigns had been bidden.
The Tsar did not come, but his sisters, the two grand duchesses, appeared,
quite as if nothing had happened.

"Great political storms," Gentz noted in his diary that night of December 12. "Crisis in the Congress." "The horizon is black, black," Eynard
wrote in his diary right after the Metternich reception, while Bertuch wrote
in *his* journal, "Congress is in such a state everyone expects war in four or
five days if things are not settled."[77]

Certainly Bertuch had reason to be anxious.

Stein, who some days before had urged the Tsar to peace and conciliation on the question of Poland, now became very warlike on the question
of Saxony, called Metternich's counter-proposal to Hardenberg "pernicious
and objectionable," and recommended to the Tsar that he plan for departure
and moving of troops.[78]

In order to clear himself of the clouds left by Hardenberg's indiscreet exhibition of correspondence, Metternich brought the Tsar copies of his own
letters.

As Castlereagh wrote, "The only really objectionable letters were Hardenberg's. . . . Metternich's are perfectly fair diplomatic papers, avowing in
very proper terms the objections of his Court to the Russian views."[79]

Metternich's interview with the Tsar was nearly as violent as a duel,
though less bloody. Listeners at the keyhole reported they heard voices raised
in anger, that the Tsar had stamped his foot more than once. The Tsar's
aides reported that Metternich's ordinarily pale face was crimson when he

left, that he remarked to one of them, "It's terribly hot in the Tsar's rooms. One can hardly bear it."[80]

The only paper of Hardenberg's which Metternich showed the Tsar was the memorandum of November 7, that had followed the disagreeable dinner meeting with the Tsar and the Prussian King on November 6. As Stein described it, Hardenberg had "presented the reasons why it was wiser to make concessions now and make preparations for the future so as to be in a position to oppose the action of Russia against Europe." It convicted Hardenberg clearly of the very sin he had imputed to Metternich—collusion against Russia.

"[Metternich] turned this over," Stein reported, "with the remark that he possessed other writings of the Chancellor of which he could make no use because they were the secrets of a third party."

The Tsar was utterly confused. Caught in a lie himself, and finding his accusations against Metternich now turned against his ally Hardenberg, he was between two fires. The Tsar ended up reproaching Metternich for writing a letter about a sovereign which was "*de peu convenable*"—not very proper. This remark, Talleyrand agreed, not without irony, had some basis.[81]

In the end, says Stein, the Tsar turned over all the papers to Emperor Franz, declaring he would no longer deal with a man "so untrustworthy as Metternich." No more than Metternich could the Tsar admit he had been in the wrong.

The situation was awkward, for the two met nearly every day.

> Alexander, who went a great deal into society [Metternich recalled], liked especially certain more intimate circles, which I too used to visit. Thus hardly a day passed without my meeting him.

Not only did their paths cross at the large receptions and dinners and balls but often at the house of the young Zichys, who were favorites with both men:

> We did not take any notice of each other [Metternich recalled]. The peculiarity of this conduct before the crowd of spectators who at that time frequented the salons of Vienna was gradually effaced by custom. The public grew used to the idea that the Tsar was out of humor with me.[82]

This time Metternich did offer to tender his resignation, but Emperor Franz refused to accept it. He knew better than to let Metternich go. Who in the world could replace him?

That "diplomatic explosion" of mid-December was the climax of more than a year of growing personal animosity between the two men. "The dispute," Metternich wrote, "caused no interruption in the important discussions of the Congress. . . . The conferences went on as if no difficulties at all had been raised."

This was not quite true. The Tsar refused to deal with Metternich and declared he himself would act as mediator. He would talk directly with Emperor Franz and if they could reach an agreement, then he would appoint Razumowsky and Stackelberg to complete negotiations.

8

During the Advent season, as Metternich predicted, a series of quieter pleasures took the place of the nightly balls, opening with an all-Beethoven concert on November 29 at which the beautiful Seventh Symphony was played for the first time, directed by the composer. It was unfortunately all but drowned out by the military bombast of his "Battle of Vitoria," complete with drums, guns, cannon fire, "God Save the King" and "Rule Britannia."

People went to visit Isabey's studio across the Danube Canal to look at his portraits of Congress celebrities. He was painting each of the minister plenipotentiaries of the Congress separately; he would then assemble them around a table, all smiling and affable as if a very pleasant discussion had just taken place among them. In actual fact those twenty-three men never sat together in conference in all the weeks of the Congress. It was Isabey who helped invent the Congress legend.

People flocked that autumn too to hear the flamboyant priest and romantic poet Zacharias Werner preach fiery sermons on carnal sin, about which he could speak from intimate personal experience. Before his conversion to Catholicism in Vienna in 1809, Werner—as one biographer described him, oozing "religiosity and lechery from every pore"—lurched across Europe, leaving a trail of scandal, and seduced serving girls in his wake.

Wild-eyed, with ragged beard and hair and dirty surplice, the self-proclaimed mystic Werner might be seen trailing along Kärntnerstrasse or in the pulpits of the best churches, ready at the drop of one of his large, soiled, blue-checked handkerchiefs to recite an erotic poem about the orgasmic rhythms of the Rhine waterfalls and the Jupiter-like yearnings of a Swiss bull toward a cow, or to preach a sermon mingling sexuality with religious rapture. His sermons, preached to packed churches, were a sensation of the Congress.

At the Franciscan Church on December 8, before a huge crowd, he preached a famous sermon on "that tiny piece of flesh, that abomination, the most dangerous appurtenance on a man's body." Gentlemen blanched, ladies blushed, riveting their eyes on their prayer books.

Werner, his huge piercing eyes gleaming with lubricity, bore down hard with graphic descriptions of sin and its consequences.

At the climax of his sermon he leaned over the pulpit to scream at his listeners: "Shall I name you that tiny piece of flesh?" Paralyzed silence. Smelling salts issued out of reticules. He leaned out farther, sweat glistening on his face, his voice raised to a hoarse shout. "Shall I *show* you that tiny piece of flesh?"

Horrified silence. Not a whisper, not a rustle of the page of a prayer book.

This crazy incredible preacher: everything they said of him was true! He was capable of *anything!*

Werner's voice dropped and a sly smile slid over his face. "Ladies and gentlemen, behold the source of our sins!" And he stuck out—his tongue.[83]

All Metternich's ladies were begging to be introduced to Werner. The very week after the notorious sermon on "The Tongue," the charismatic presence in the seedy surplice appeared at the Metternich dinner table, along with writer Friedrich Schlegel, Gentz, Flora Wrbna, Theresa Jablonowska, Lory Fuchs and Julie Zichy. After dinner Werner read aloud, with sonorous melo-dramatic effects, the first act of his long-winded new tragedy, *Cunigunda.*

Certainly far more entertaining than the formal banquets that took place each day in the palace were the informal dinners at the Metternichs', the Zichys' and at Gentz's, where the most amusing of Congress visitors—dancers, actresses, writers, artists—sat elbow to elbow with diplomats and duchesses.

In Gentz's tiny salon-turned-dining-room, guests sat so tightly squeezed in they could barely move their chairs, and the doors had to be removed so the servants could hand in the dishes to the table. But the conversation sparkled and ricocheted; Rahel Varnhagen might be there, Countess Bern-storff, Humboldt, a Reuss prince and often a German-born American from Philadelphia named Erich Bollmann, who was the sole American to attend the Congress of Vienna.

Ghost stories were all the rage just then. One day, around Gentz's din-ner table, ghost stories were told. Another day, after dinner at the Zichys', when the Tsar confessed to a fondness for tales of the supernatural, all the lights were extinguished except for a single flickering candle, the guests sat on the floor in the salon telling the most hair-raising tales in their repertoire. Just as Prince Radziwill had recounted a chilling story of a ghost that haunted a Polish manor house, the door to the Zichys' salon creaked slowly open with no hand on it at all, then creaked slowly shut again. Ladies screamed, gentlemen leapt to their feet. Count Zichy laughed, lighted the candles again and showed how he had worked the door with a thread from where he sat across the room.

In the wake of the successful Carousel, performed three times to overflow crowds, Isabey and Moreau organized a French comedy troupe which gave the first of a series of amateur theatricals on December 9 in the imperial palace.

Marie Metternich and Aurore de Marassé had parts in a one-act comedy *Le Pascha de Suresne,* while Wilhelmine had been chosen to represent Marie of Burgundy in one of a series of *tableaux vivants* depicting paintings by con-temporary artists then on exhibition in Vienna.

She sought Metternich's help; she needed to see the original painting, "The Meeting of Maxmilian of Habsburg with Marie of Burgundy," by Anton Petter, but the exhibition was by invitation only. He sent her a ticket at once, reminding her:

> You did not wish to share the throne with me, my dear W., but you rule
> none the less in my domains. It depends only on you whenever you wish
> to see the exposition of pictures.[84]

She wrote a bit later to ask if she might borrow his Golden Fleece for her
costume? He replied he did not think it appropriate, for no woman, not
even Marie of Burgundy, had ever worn the order. If the painter had painted
it into his picture, then one must quarrel with him! She might go to talk
with Petter, or she might wear the chain alone without the pendant Fleece,
and so she did decide to wear it, with a crucifix in place of the lamb.

Metternich himself enjoyed charades and amateur theatricals. During
that week in December when the important dispatch from England about
Saxony reached Vienna, while Hardenberg was pressing him hard for a reply to the Prussians' demand, he took a hand in the amateur theater,
helped make up the ladies, arranged the lighting, ordered the posters. He
was bitterly criticized for leaving a meeting of ministers to direct a rehearsal
of his daughter and her friends in an adjoining room.

> Couldn't you [Wilhelmine pleaded in another note] be there to direct
> us and to explain things, for it is not at all the forte of Fischer.[85]

Of course, he replied, she would always find him ready on the day of battle:

> I shall be there to place you properly and especially to arrange the light-
> ing on you. If I had to limit myself to my own light alone you would
> never leave the shadow that has taken possession for so long of my soul
> and of my whole being![86]

The *tableaux* were charmingly staged in the rococo white-and-gold ballroom of the Hofburg with an improvised stage, and boxed orange trees in
blossom scenting the room. When the audience were seated, all the candles
in the silver torchères were extinguished except those on the stage. Harps and
French horns played a delicate musical accompaniment.

Anna Eynard was astonished to see the Tsar and the King of Prussia
mount the stage during the interval and peep through a hole in the curtain
like a pair of curious children.

A few days before Christmas a particularly imaginative performance was
given by the group. When the curtain rose on the lighted stage, the painter
Teniers was seen in his Brussels studio, leafing through a portfolio of paintings, while at the back of the stage a group of dancers moved through the
rhythms of a *danse champêtre*. As Teniers lifted out each drawing and held it
up to the audience, a group detached themselves from among the dancers,
moved to the front of the stage and posed in the outlines of the painting.
Dorothée and Marie Metternich again took part, but Wilhelmine was ill on
December 20 and had to excuse herself from the performance.

There had been a difficulty or two with the production. For one thing,
handsome young Count Wrbna, who was to play Apollo in the finale, re-

fused to shave off his hussar moustaches even to play a Greek god, until the Empress Maria Ludovica had a private talk with him and he was persuaded to make the sacrifice for the success of the production. Another problem had been to find a suitable lady willing to pose as Venus. Princess Bagration had at first accepted, then had second thoughts and withdrew her offer. Finally a certain Mademoiselle de Wilhelm agreed to play Venus, provided that Isabey posed her in a rear view only, with sufficiently discreet and elegant drapery.

Of that December 20 production Gentz told Count Bernstorff crossly that Metternich had left the Prussian reply to Austria's note lying on his desk for half a day unread "because he was busy correcting the song sheets for one of the fetes."[87]

The *tableaux vivants* given that winter during the Congress were a great success, were widely imitated, and became a popular drawing room amusement all over Europe.

There was a distraction of a different mode in the death and funeral of the eighty-year-old Prince de Ligne. He had caught cold waiting on the ramparts for a lady who did not keep her rendezvous; he had made his cold worse by going out the next night without his cloak to see some ladies to their carriages after a ball. Dying of pneumonia, he could still joke to a friend that he would contribute a nice distraction to the Congress festivals by providing a field marshal's funeral.

Anna Eynard, who had been as charmed by the old courtier as almost everyone else had been, burst into tears that beautiful December day when the funeral cortege passed, the prince's old battered plumed hat atop the coffin, and slowly following, his favorite horse, the stirrups reversed:

> I can't tell you [she wrote that night] what a heart-breaking sight it was, this horse without a rider, walking slowly, head bent down, covered with a funeral cloth.[88]

The brief spell of cold ended, and once again fine autumn weather lingered on into December. In the gardens of Schönbrunn leaves appeared on the rosebushes as if April had unseasonably leapt into being. "Most delicious weather," Gentz noted, "a complete springtime has descended on the city."[89]

Gradually the gloom of the Congress began to lift. There was a feeling in the air that the crisis would in some way be resolved.

There were subtle signs that winds were shifting into new directions; there was growing rapprochement between Austria and France. Castlereagh noted that Metternich and Talleyrand were growing overtly more friendly. "The personal intercourse between these ministers has been considerably augmented within these few days." Cooke thought that "if Austria goes on and succeeds in her overtures with France, and a tone of pacific authority is taken, it is not improbable that Prussia will compromise." He believed Metternich's mind was already made up to an alliance with France, "and I shall not be surprised if he makes a direct overture, without consulting Lord Castlereagh, in case Talleyrand is favorable upon his overture as to Saxony."[90]

In order to clarify and reach an agreement with Prussia on population figures, Metternich suggested a commission to verify statistics, and Castlereagh put the idea into a proposal. When he brought his plan to Talleyrand for approval, Talleyrand suggested "a little convention" between France, Austria and England "to recognize the rights of the King of Saxony." Castlereagh was startled and drew back. He was not ready yet to put anything into writing.[91]

It was evident that, despite the quarrel with the Tsar, Metternich had regained leadership of the negotiations. Once again he worked extremely hard to put together a plan, reweaving the complex and delicate strands of conflicting interests into a new and possible pattern.

Not only had the dispatch from Liverpool underlining the need to save at least some of Saxony given Metternich new courage, but later dispatches from London had put a quick end to Castlereagh's query about using force. The Prince Regent through Bathurst, Secretary of War, had replied to Castlereagh's solicitation of His Majesty's "gracious approbation" with a sharp reply. Under no circumstances could another war be considered "for any of the objects which have been hitherto under discussion at Vienna."[92]

But though he had clear knowledge now of the stand of the Prince Regent and the English Cabinet, Metternich still had to force from Castlereagh an open pronouncement of his new views on Saxony.

When the Committee of Six met on December 29 in Metternich's study —"a very unpleasant" meeting—Hardenberg still insisted on Prussia's claim to all of Saxony. Castlereagh remained silent, and Metternich had to goad him into speaking on the critical issue. "I ask Lord Castlereagh to clarify this situation in a positive manner. We must now know his intentions and I beg him to tell us if he has orders to oppose the invasion of Saxony, and if he approves it."

Castlereagh appeared very disconcerted by Metternich's challenge. He could not, however, retreat, and he replied in a somewhat embarrassed tone that he "could not recognize the occupation of Saxony and its union with Prussia."

At Castlereagh's words, Hardenberg flew into a temper, turned on the English minister shouting, "You're defecting from the agreement you made with Prussia on October 22. You consented then that we should take possession of Saxony!"

Castlereagh was visibly flustered. He did not speak for a moment, then replied hesitantly, "But you have not spoken of this affair since October 22. If you had asked me, you would have known then that I have become opposed to the plan."[93]

If Eynard's report of the conference "on best authority" is true, then Castlereagh's was an odd rejoinder. Little else had been talked of during November and December except Saxony and Poland. Castlereagh had been the main figure in an important conference with Prussian and Russian ministers on December 15, yet apparently he had not spoken of his shift of opinion or of his new orders.

Hardenberg became even more angry. "I thought I could trust your word," he cried. "If you received orders to the contrary, you should have warned me!" He got up and stamped out of the room.

Despite the thunder and lightning of the Hardenberg scene that day, Eynard noted that the conference had been a constructive one. The cards were finally on the table; England's support of Saxony was openly affirmed. Opinions of Metternich were changing. There would still be rumors afloat that he had been asked to resign, that Stadion would get his portfolio. Nevertheless among Congress-watchers were many who thought his conduct had been *fort adroit*, and that Castlereagh had cut "a very sad figure."[94]

At the conference two days later, on December 31, the Prussians were even more truculent in their demand for Saxony. Hardenberg declared bluntly that Prussia would consider the refusal of Prussia's right to all of Saxony "tantamount to a declaration of war."

That threat was not an empty one. Humboldt, writing his wife, did not believe they could get the whole of Saxony "as I shall continue to insist on, without a war, or urgent danger of war."[95]

It was an ominous note on which to end the year 1814. The Prussian chief of staff had arrived in Vienna; Prussia was said to be organizing her Army in the field.

The Prussian threat finally moved Castlereagh. Fearing some "bold and desperate coup" on the part of Prussia, he agreed to join a defensive alliance with Austria and France.

As for Metternich, it was evident that he had regained his self-assurance and his powers of action.

He had passed through the deep crisis in his personal life that had threatened for a time, in October and November, to destroy him, and to bring his career to collapse.

He still loved Wilhelmine, still nourished in the recesses of his mind a seed of hope that he would one day possess her wholly as he longed to possess her. But he had passed through the lowest depth of his despair, through the fire of resignation; he had emerged, if not intact, at least again in control of his life. He could meet her now at dinner parties, at balls, could talk to her, write to her, with a semblance of calm and increasingly rare spasms of anguish.

The day before Christmas he sent her a little bottle of English lemon salts, soothing for her migraines.

Little gifts preserve friendships [he wrote her]; at least that is what

our fathers taught us. . . . *Mon amie*, something tells me I am your only friend—and this thought exerts a powerful charm for me, strong

enough not to make illusions out of everything I've suffered for so long.
. . . *Bon soir*, devote a good thought to me, and tell me you are mine!
I shall see you tomorrow evening.[96]

On the Tsar's thirty-fifth birthday, December 24, there were special services in the Greek Church, a banquet and gala concert in the palace, for which
Emperor Franz put on a Russian uniform in his guest's honor. On Christmas
day there was another fine Beethoven concert, and in the evening, to celebrate the end of Advent, an intimate little *Kammerball* in the palace.

But it was not in the imperial palace but in the house of Berlin-born
Fanny Arnstein that the first Christmas tree seen in Vienna was unveiled that
Christmas of 1814. Before a crowd of Prussian visitors, including Hardenberg,
Prince Radziwill, "and all the converted and circumcised relatives of the
host and hostess," the huge pine tree, lighted with tiny candles, decorated
and laden with gifts for everyone, glittered in Fanny's salon on Christmas
Eve.

The day after Christmas the Metternichs' Monday night supper balls resumed again.

But Gentz's charges of frivolity against Metternich would become increasingly rare; Metternich did not go to the great Razumowsky ball on
December 30, or perhaps even to the Zichys' charming New Year's Eve ball.

> *Mon amie* [he wrote Wilhelmine on December 28], I've had a very
> hard day! I've had an enormous amount of work, business affairs, politi-
> cal torments. I've worked like a [convict?] on a chain, and I am very
> tired. . . . *Bon soir, mon amie*, I am going to bed, and I need sleep des-
> perately.[97]

He got no reply to that note. He wrote her again next day, December 29,
the day of the explosive political conference, taxing her for giving him no
sign of life:

> What are you doing—what are you thinking—Nothing perhaps but let
> me know it! Is it kind of you to leave a friend far far away from you, from
> all contact, from everything he needs to live by?[98]

Would there be a moment when he could come and speak to her that evening? Everyone will be at the Razumowsky ball—everyone except him. "Certainly I shall not go," he told her—not to a ball where the Tsar would be
the sunlike center of the universe. If she had no time that evening, perhaps
she could give him an hour next day, but he must be back at the Chancellery
by noon for a very important conference that concerned "the safety of the
world." He could not afford to be one moment late.

"Write me a word," he begged, "I am quite sad, and I certainly need
all my strength at this moment!"

A tiny scrawled note, barely legible, came in reply. It was so dark in her
house she could hardly see to read. She had been "so very ill," that no, she
simply could not see him, not now.[99]

He was not quite cured, not yet. A spasm of his old passionate desire came over him; it seemed to him absolutely imperative that he see her, talk to her once more before that year 1814 came to an end.

He wrote again pleadingly the following day, Friday, December 30, begging her to let him see her once more before the end of "this cruel year."

> *Mon amie,* I have had a good many moments of weakness since fate attached me to you, but I've never had more *concentrated* weakness than that which makes me attach such special importance to the moments that are bringing this cruel year to an end and to those that are beginning a new one.[100]

If she were still his friend, surely she would handle gently this feeling he still had for her. If she was not his friend, then better that she tell him frankly and openly. He begs only for a little of her time; it is so very important to him. Even if she is ill she need not speak. If he can only be near her for a moment or two at this time that marks the end of an era and the beginning of a new one. "My dear, are they so very great, my claims?"

But the tiny scribbled note that came in reply was adamant:

> *Cher ami,* I cannot see you now; it is quite impossible, I am sick as a dog —but you will ask later if and when I could see you.[101]

At daybreak on the last day of that year, 1814, all Vienna was awakened from its slumbers by the sound of night watchmen's cries and the alarm drum of the fire guard.

Count Razumowsky's palace was on fire!

Volunteer fire-watchers pulled pump wagons through the streets, where soldiers from the barracks, summoned to help, hurried, buttoning their uniforms as they ran.

No such fire had been seen before in the memory of the hundreds who crowded about to watch the flames sweeping through the opulent palace, from which the dancers of the ball the night before had barely departed. It was as if one final splendid spectacle had been improvised for the entertainment of the Congress before the old year had finished.

Emperor Franz, who, it was said, never missed witnessing a fire if he could help it, even when the house of one of his poorest subjects in the city burned down, arrived on horseback. People saw him dismount, walk to the tree under which Count Razumowsky sat weeping and try to cheer him. Smoke and flames poured out of the windows; firemen threw rare sculpture, fine paintings, antique furniture, out of the windows into the mud and debris below.

For the first time people began to feel a certain sympathy for the millionaire aristocrat who dabbled in diplomacy, whom Anna Eynard called "the most haughty and impolite man in the world," and who had earned for himself the nickname of "Count Tout-fier" (All-proud).

It had been the extreme *luxe* and comfort of the brand-new palace that had set it in flame. The marvelous heating system of pipes laid in floors and walls—the only such system in all of Vienna—had set fire to the wooden floor structure, had, in fact, almost burned the count himself alive in his bed.

On that last day of the year, before he set out for his round of evening calls, Gentz happily totaled up the year's gross intake of gifts and bribes. He had got a handsome present from Castlereagh—certainly for more than mere translations. From Talleyrand he had got a princely 24,000 florins—in all, he wrote, "extraordinary benefices of 48,000 florins," so that "all segments of my economy were flourishing."[102]

He stopped by for a time on New Year's Eve to drink a toast with Wilhelmine and her circle of intimate family and friends—Jeanne and Borel, Dorothée and her adoring lover, Clam, the princesses' half brother, Schwedhof, and Alfred.

Compunctious perhaps at putting Metternich off that day, Wilhelmine had written him a long letter, a recapitulation of her state of heart and of what had happened between them. She is still attached to "bonds that have lost their charms for me," yet she cannot bring herself to loosen them. She has not had the strength "to follow the path that might perhaps have led to happiness."

> I would pity you more, *mon ami*, if I did not pity myself even more . . . you will always remain my friend, my heart tells me, count on mine— I am ill—I have an erysipelas in the right foot—I shall not be able to go out for several days. That will give us time to prepare ourselves to see one another again. Adieu, dear Clemens, may God bless you and give you all the happiness my heart wishes you and that it has not been able to show you.[103]

The reply Metternich wrote her at once that afternoon of December 31 appears to have been written under some tremendous strain. The bitter letter is barely legible; words are scratched out here and there, many scarcely decipherable:

> I am not replying to your letter. It is not addressed to me. You thought you were writing to a lover; for a long time I have no longer been that. It is not addressed to a friend, for the first title that friendship has a right to claim is confidence.
> What are you breaking off? What does not exist. My dear, do you know what this letter proves? That you do not know me, that you know me as little as I know you well. . . .
> I shall prove to you all the rest of my life that I am the best friend you have on earth—the most ready to hold out my hand to you, my hand of which you have so much need, to keep you from losing yourself, you who have strayed farther than human being has ever strayed.
> Three months ago you betrayed the lover in me; today the friend will

pardon you for everything he can pardon you. . . . Think of me with the greatest calm. . . . All I suffer, all you have made me suffer, all is pardoned with this day that terminates the year that is the most frightful year of my life, because it has been made so by the being to whom I vowed everything the Creator can bestow of good, simple, true feeling in the heart of a man! For a long time I have counted only on the reward of a better world than this one here below.

Take care of your illness; rest calmly and let me know if I may see you tomorrow at noon. I do not want the first day of the new year 1815 to pass without seeing you.[104]

As it turned out, that letter to Schenkenstrasse was not the last message Wilhelmine had from him before that fateful year 1814 came to an end.

During the evening a jeweler's servant delivered a package to the Chancellery: it was the New Year's gift Metternich had ordered for her many weeks before, during the brief golden weeks of early autumn when, deeply in love, he had imagined he would share with her the first moments of the new year. He had designed the jeweled bracelet himself; it was to replace the one she had long worn that Alfred had given her.

The pretty trinket glittered in his hand. He packed it again in its silken nest and sent it to her with a note:

I intended the gift for you; it burns my hand. You can throw it away as well as I; whether you keep it depends on you—its value is not your concern, let it be mine. . . .

In that romantic age, stones, like flowers, spoke their own vocabulary of love. He had had four gems set in the golden bracelet: a diamond, symbol of love; an emerald, his birthstone; an amethyst, hers; a ruby, symbol of fidelity in love.

Each gem was engraved on the reverse side with a Gothic letter G, signifying, he wrote, the words he had hoped to say to her that night when he himself fastened the bracelet on her wrist: *Gott gebe Gnade, Glück, Gedeihen*—God grant you grace, happiness, prosperity. On the back of the golden bracelet was engraved the year, "15."

Now let the poor man pray for you, and obtain by prayers from heaven all that he himself may not bestow on you!

May the year 1815 be for you the first of a long series of happier years, full of peace, of undisturbed pleasures! In times to come when you feel forlorn, think of me, my soul will always come to meet you with the same affection and the same love. May your life be long and good. Let it turn to mine if ever you need a friend and a support; may my memory darken none of your moments—all sacrifices have already been made.

Even as a rejected lover Clemens Metternich could be persistent—and disturbing. He added in that note written at eleven at night and sent so that the bracelet would reach her just at the hour of midnight:

If ever some cause, some forbearance should hinder you not only from wearing my gift but from *wearing it always*, then return it to me at once. If you do not wear it and it is still with you, then I will tell myself that you do not lay a value even on my wishes for you.

Now good night, and sleep better than I shall.[105]

It may be that Metternich dressed in evening clothes and went to the New Year's Eve ball at the Zichys', where La Garde says he saw him among the crowd. If so, he would have heard, as midnight sounded, the toast that Countess Paar proposed to the Tsar: "May I be the first, Sire, to offer so great a sovereign all wishes for the New Year. May I also beg Your Majesty in the name of all Europe for a general peace and for the union of all peoples."

To which the Tsar replied graciously that he joined in the same hope, adding, "No sacrifice will be too great for me to consolidate a peace that is the first need of humanity."[106]

But La Garde's memory was faulty; he put many people in places where they were not. It may be that Metternich went nowhere, but sat at his desk in the Chancellery while the church bells rang in the New Year.

Of Laure on that New Year's Eve of 1814 we hear nothing. It may be that she was at the Zichys' too, unnoticeable as always.

Or it may be that she lay awake in the chamber on the third floor of the Chancellery, listening for a familiar footstep that did not come.

Two years later, writing to Laure from a journey in Italy, Metternich would call to mind how that year 1814 had ended for both of them. They had not spoken to one another for days; their relations, he recalled, "had passed in contemplation."[107]

Nevertheless there had been one night during that month of December, perhaps in some moment of great weariness, of intolerable loneliness or pain, when Clemens Metternich had sought out his wife's bed to find what consolation he could in her familiar embrace.

By the end of January Laure Metternich knew she was again with child.

XXIII

A NEW YEAR BEGINS;
AN OLD ACTOR REAPPEARS

1

Snow fell all night on the last night of the year, and in the morning the baroque angels on the roofs of palaces and churches stood knee-deep in snow. It seemed a double good omen that New Year's Day of 1815 fell on a Sunday, and that fresh snow covered the world, as if all the scars and shabbiness, the quarrels and violence of an old world and an old year were effectively buried from sight.

Early that morning a courier's carriage, mud-spattered, ice-covered, pulled up to the door of Castlereagh's house in Minoritenplatz. He had been on the roads since Christmas Eve, carrying to Vienna from Ghent the good news that England had ended the war with America and peace had been signed.

Peace with America! The news spread through the city. People on foot, cheerfully greeting one another on their New Year's calls, thronged to Castlereagh's to congratulate him.

> It has produced the greatest possible sensation here [Castlereagh wrote
> Liverpool]; and will, I have no doubt, enter largely into the calculations
> of our opponents. It is a most auspicious and seasonable event. I wish
> you joy of being released from the millstone of an American war![1]

For the first time in many years no war was being fought anywhere in the Western Hemisphere.

Only a year before, all Europe had still been at war, and on New Year's Day the armies were poised on the Rhine to begin that last deadly assault against France. How much had happened in a year! Napoleon had been conquered and sent to exile. The Allies had marched triumphantly into Paris, had written a generous peace. An era had died. Not everything, to be sure, was settled as yet—but surely now a splendid new era was beginning. "A golden age," Castlereagh called it expansively to his guests that night. The cynical Cooke wondered whether that would mean more subsidies for England to pay.

Wars might be finished for the moment, but the age seemed something less than golden to closer observers. The price of bread in England, Russia and elsewhere had gone up. "We understand the dearness of every article in St. Petersburg is oppressive and there are great discontents."

In Austria's Italian provinces nationalists conspired against the Austrian regime; on the night of December 28 police arrested another covey of plotters.

At a soiree at Wilhelmine's the first week in January Dorothée revealed that a conspiracy against the Bourbons had been uncovered in Paris and several generals placed under arrest.

As soon as the news from Ghent arrived, Castlereagh had sent word to Talleyrand and Metternich. The three met that New Year's Sunday in the best of spirits to review the English text of their secret treaty of alliance, which Castlereagh himself had drafted the day before. Goaded finally by Hardenberg's threat of war in the stormy conferences of December 29 and 31, Castlereagh had agreed to join with France and Austria in a defensive alliance, each to come to the aid of the other if attacked.

Yet even while they wrote their treaty, the danger that had prompted it began to recede. On that same New Year's Day the Prussian Cabinet met with the Minister of War, General Grolman, to decide how far they should go in backing their claim to all of Saxony. As far as war, for example, as Hardenberg had threatened, as Humboldt predicted might be necessary?

The news of the American peace had arrived in the nick of time, according to Cooke. Grolman exercised some timely persuasion, and "the project of immediate war was abandoned." They would give in on Saxony— how far was not yet decided.[2]

That night everyone appeared at the formal ball in the palace in uniforms, orders, ball gowns and jewels. Emperor Franz was ill with a cold, but the Empress greeted guests, seated with her ladies at one end of the long reception room, while Prince Schwarzenberg, taking the Emperor's place, led the opening polonaise, round and round the long room and out into the palace, through antechambers where guards in spangled military best stood at attention, through card rooms where the players looked up a moment from whist to smile at the dancers, through distant rooms where the music could barely be heard, back finally into the candle-glittering ballroom.

Talleyrand was observed that night to be wreathed in smiles. "This peace with America is a fine thing for England," he told Eynard, and suggested to the Swiss D'Ivernois, something of an expert in international finance, that he look into Austria's currency troubles. "Austria is the boulevard of Europe,"

Talleyrand declared, "and everyone must be interested in seeing that the court of Vienna is in a state of prosperity."[3]

A few days later, when the secret treaty was signed, Talleyrand could write the French King the best news he had yet been able to impart. "Now, Sire, the Coalition is dissolved—and forever."[4]

In any case, the treaty itself was chiefly important for bringing France back to a place among the summit powers. At the insistence of Castlereagh and Metternich, Talleyrand was now at last admitted to the inner council, so that it became a Committee of Five—or, as Humboldt termed it, the real Congress of Vienna. The committee had agreed that in one way or another the King of Saxony must be induced to agree formally to whatever arrangements were made for Saxony. France would be needed, Metternich had argued, to persuade the King to sign away any of his lands.

Though the Treaty of Alliance was presumably highly secret, rumors of such an alliance spread quickly through Vienna. Already on January 7, three days after its signing, when Castlereagh had an audience with the Tsar, the latter had heard some talk of it and questioned Castlereagh closely. The leak may have been through any one of the three chancelleries, but it was very likely through the unreliable Hoppé in the Austrian. Without denying the existence of a treaty, Castlereagh reassured the Tsar that if Russia "acted on pacifick principles he would have nothing to fear from those Powers."[5]

Undoubtedly anxiety about such an alliance persuaded both the Tsar and the King of Prussia into a more conciliatory attitude on Saxony.

As for the three newly bonded allies, they did not remain allies in any real sense of the word. They did not even concert their efforts on Saxony until after a bitter wrangle in the last weeks of January that ended in a rift between Castlereagh on the one hand, and Metternich and Emperor Franz on the other, Talleyrand siding with Austria but unwilling to jeopardize France's *arriviste* position in the new power structure.

Metternich's original memorandum, written in early January in reply to Hardenberg's demand for the whole of Saxony, proposed to save for the Saxon King a country of a million and a half inhabitants, retaining its chief cities and fortresses. He admitted he had erred in his first tactic in October; he was prepared to backtrack and begin again.

But Metternich needed the backing of both his allies on his proposal, which Talleyrand agreed was a "very good" one.

Castlereagh, however, refused to agree to the new Metternich proposal. Determined still to build a powerful Prussia in the North as a bulwark against both France and Russia—and also apparently against preponderant Austrian power inside Germany—Castlereagh urged ceding a much larger portion of Saxony to Prussia, including her chief cities and fortresses.

Castlereagh's knowledge of the geography and military topography of Central Europe was exceedingly weak; according to police reports he did not even know where Leipzig was and was "surprised to find it in Saxony."[6]

Through those mid-weeks of January the debates raged over Saxony, and bitterly the Austrian Emperor complained to his friend the King of Denmark that Castlereagh "was abandoning them" on the question of Saxony. Metternich, Talleyrand and Wrede spent hours endeavoring to win Castlereagh to their plan.

Schwarzenberg begged Metternich to remain absolutely firm on his plan for Saxony. "A cession such as the one Castlereagh proposes would make a joke of the principle of saving Saxony." Since Austria had lost on Poland, she must remain firm now on Saxony. "It concerns our very safety," Schwarzenberg pointed out.[7] Prussian occupation of the larger part of Saxony and the fortresses of Torgau and Erfurt would constitute a real danger to Austria. Castlereagh waved away the argument: "A mere question of details," he called it.[8]

Austria went so far as to offer to give up the 400,000 inhabitants she was to receive in the Tarnopol region of Poland if the Tsar would turn over an equivalent number of Polish "souls" to Prussia and thereby preserve more of Saxony. The Tsar declined. He had, he said, nearly completed his arrangements in Poland, and he did not wish to change his plans.

Once more rumor spread that Metternich would be forced to resign his post to Stadion. The Congress was again at a standstill. In drawing rooms and on street corners people asked one another, "What is Metternich doing? Why has he not replied to Hardenberg? Is he spending his days making love and his nights in the ballroom?" In the police reports that month informers reported new criticism of the Austrian minister in overheard conversations. "He is doing nothing. He drags us from one week to another." "He stops and we stop." "He intrigues in the ear of one and the other. He confuses and gets confused."[9]

Some Congress-watchers thought everything would move faster if Castlereagh went home. Eynard declared that Wellington, who was soon to replace Castlereagh, would certainly have a better knowledge of geography.

Still others, such as the Bavarian Wrede, thought it was high time for the military to take over and solve these insoluble questions by force of arms. "A vigorous offensive," Wrede declared, "and Prussia would be crushed and after two battles won Russia would be thrown back behind the Niemen. Norway could return to Denmark, Finland to Sweden."[10]

On January 24 Castlereagh sent brusque word to Metternich that if Austria refused to accede to his own—Castlereagh's—plan for Saxony, then England would withdraw from negotiations altogether.

Castlereagh was invited to talk personally with Emperor Franz the next day.

It was not an agreeable encounter, though Castlereagh did not so report it to his home office. To all of Emperor Franz's suggestions for a compromise on their differences—that Prussia might be given additional "souls" in Poland if Torgau could be left to Saxony, and that the three important Saxon cities which Prussia demanded be turned over to the latter but with their

fortresses dismantled—Castlereagh replied with a cool and stubborn "no."
He remained "unshakable in his opinion that Prussia must be great and
powerful, "insisting absolutely, according to Rosenkrantz, "that the King of
Prussia get Wittenberg, Torgau and Erfurt."[11]

Metternich concluded from this final failure that Castlereagh must have
had strong orders from his Cabinet to support Prussia in her demands, and
that further resistance would be futile. Castlereagh, however, had had no
such orders—only Liverpool's somewhat laconic communication of November 18 proposing that "a kernel" at least of Saxony be saved. In England,
Liverpool wrote, nobody was giving much thought to the concerns of the
Congress. "Very few persons give themselves any anxiety about what is passing at Vienna, except in as far as it is connected with expense."[12]

Discouraged, Metternich wrote Schwarzenberg on January 27, "I have
argued more these last days than in the whole course of my life." He had
not even been able to save Torgau, "for England declares against us. . . .
We shall save the rest of Saxony."[13]

Metternich had no choice but to redraft his memorandum, which was
finally sent to Hardenberg on Sunday, January 29. Emperor Franz made perfectly clear that the offer represented Austria's final concession on Saxony.
Prussia was to get 850,000 Saxons and the larger part of the territory of the
old kingdom, including the fortresses on the Elbe—intact. The King of
Saxony would keep the other half, a country of 1,200,000, with the cities of
Leipzig and Dresden.

Would Prussia accept?

Certainly the two allies Metternich and Castlereagh felt no warmth for
one another as January came to an end. Castlereagh told Talleyrand that he
regarded "as desirable a change of ministry in Austria, where the ministry
is very weak—not to say more."[14]

What Metternich and Emperor Franz said to one another of Castlereagh
is not on record.

2

While the inner council of the Congress fought out the last act of the
drama of the dismemberment of Saxony, Vienna was enjoying the gayest,
most exuberant carnival season in the history of the city.

The moment Advent season was over, everyone plunged at once into a
new round of merrymaking—*tableaux vivants*, concerts, theatricals, dinner
parties, supper parties, soirees, balls of every description. "It was," wrote
Countess Bernstorff, "as if we had just returned from the country and
longed for the diversion we had long missed." People grew so used to going
to another ball each evening that they began to arrive later and later, and the
dancing would hardly be under way before midnight and seldom end before
daybreak.

There were children's balls where little girls wore their hair put up like grown ladies, gowns of silk and tulle, with a bouquet on the left and a little fan, and all the important guests of the Congress came to watch and join the fun. The Stackelbergs gave such a ball and so did the Zichys, and Laure took the three younger Metternich children. At the Karl Schwarzenbergs' children's ball, the Tsar danced with all the little girls. Later, when the children had been taken home by their mothers and nurses, the grown-ups carried on the ball.

The Metternichs entertained several times during Fasching, giving a spectacular fancy dress ball at their garden villa on January 9, another on January 23, and finally a brilliant Mardi Gras ball on the eve of Lent. Though the trees were winter-bare and snow lay deep on the ground, the country house was lighted as in summer and filled with fresh flowers, and the guests entered from their carriages up the long flight of carpeted, canopied stairs between rows of liveried servants holding flaming torches.

Metternich hoped to heal the rift with the Tsar, who had not spoken to him since the day of their quarrel in mid-December. He asked the archduke palatine, the Tsar's brother-in-law, to find out whether the Tsar would come to the ball on January 9. The Tsar replied that he would come if he were invited. He was invited, but he did not go; neither did the Tsarina nor his sisters. Moreover the Tsar told someone who told someone else that rather than dance at Prince Metternich's house he would prefer to fight him with pistols. But the Tsar's quarrel with the Austrian Foreign Minister began to turn to the latter's advantage. People were now saying that Metternich had behaved correctly to defend his master's interests, and that the Tsar was a cheat and a swindler.[15]

The King of Prussia came alone; he was not cheerful, he did not dance or talk to the ladies, and it was apparent that he appeared merely from duty. As he stood in the background, leaning against a wall, Eynard mistook him for a footman and nearly asked him to fetch a glass of champagne.

Talleyrand, on the other hand, enjoyed the fete thoroughly. He looked radiant, obviously took full credit for saving Saxony. He took credit too for restoring France to a place among the summit powers, and he was about to celebrate his own baptism among the faithful monarchists of Europe. He invited the entire Congress to attend a funeral service in St. Stephen's Cathedral on January 21 in memory of the guillotined Louis XVI, exactly twenty-two years after his execution in Paris. Talleyrand billed it as a "solemn and expiatory service" to mark the anniversary of "a day of horror and eternal mourning."[16]

The lugubrious ceremony took place at the height of the carnival season; there is no evidence that it dampened any spirits. Isabey and Moreau had designed the immense black-draped catafalque in the middle of St. Stephen's Cathedral, with plaster figures at the corners representing France "crushed with sorrow," Europe "shedding tears," Religion "holding the testament of Louis XVI," and Hope "lifting her eyes to heaven."

The aged Archbishop of Vienna officiated, and a French priest living in

Vienna delivered a solemn and tedious oration which Talleyrand himself had penned, while his house musician Neukomm composed the funeral music.

Everyone, or nearly everyone, of importance came; one could hardly afford to stay away without being accused of revolutionary sentiments. The ladies of the aristocracy attended, veiled in black from head to foot, shivering in the icy church even under their furs. The Tsar expressed himself with some frankness. If the funeral obsequies for Louis XVI being held in Paris that day were highly "impolitic," in view of the mood of the country, the services in Vienna were a "clumsy and undignified imitation."[17]

Talleyrand invited "all the great personages of the Congress . . . and many others" back to his palais for a splendid banquet, at which his chef Carême outdid himself. Later in the evening he received several hundred more guests at a *cercle* at which he held forth on the "eminent, edifying and imposing" character of the morning's ceremony. "To hear him talk," Eynard remarked, "you would have thought he had always been the most faithful servant of Louis XVI."[18]

Ever since the New Year's Eve snow the streets of the city had been filled with sleighs and sledges; even the public hackney coaches had their wheels replaced with runners. Instead of the rattling of thousands of wheels over the cobblestones, one heard the swishing of runners and the tinkling of hundreds of sleigh bells.

The day after the funeral service for the guillotined French king, one of the most celebrated fetes of the Vienna Congress took place—the imperial sleighing party.

It had been Metternich's idea to give a sleighing party for the Emperor's distinguished guests, and on Sunday, January 22, thirty-two magnificent sleighs, upholstered in emerald and sapphire velvet, embroidered and fringed with gold, golden sphinxes fixed to the axles and ostrich plumes nodding on the horses' heads, waited in the courtyard of the Hofburg to carry the leading guests out to Schönbrunn Palace.

A sledge, drawn by six horses, bore a full orchestra of trumpeters and timbaliers; next followed the imperial sleighs, each with a gentleman holding the reins and a lady beside him in furred cloak and jeweled headdress— "and a notable quantity of rouge," Dr. Bright, an English visitor, noted disapprovingly. Emperor Franz drove the first sleigh with the Tsarina Elizabeth beside him, in a pelisse of green velvet lined with ermine, on her head a velvet toque on which nodded an aigrette of diamonds. The Tsar had invited Princess Gabrielle Auersperg as his companion, and the King of Prussia, Julie Zichy. After the sleighs bearing the sovereigns came twenty-four pages in medieval costume, then a squadron of His Imperial Majesty's Hungarian Guard, then a long procession of sleighs bearing court notables and important guests, finally a sledge bearing a full orchestra garbed as Turks.

The trumpeters were about to give the signal to depart when a great berline lumbered into the courtyard, blocking the way and startling the horses. A pair of equerries rode hastily over to the berline to ask the driver to leave. The carriage did not budge, only moved a few feet nearer to the circle of sleighs.

Count Trauttmansdorff, the Emperor's Master of the Horse, sent an aide over to the berline, who, thinking it was a simple coachman sitting on the box, ordered him to leave the square at once.

Everyone now asked everyone else, "Who is this insolent fool who dares intrude on the pleasures of the sovereigns?"

It was none other than Charles Stewart, Castlereagh's half brother and the English ambassador to Austria, who had taken the driver's place with a pair of his secretaries beside him and his sister-in-law inside the carriage.

"What a scandal!" people said. "He must be drunk again!"

To the aide's peremptory order, Stewart replied, with a crack of the whip, that he was the ambassador of Great Britain and he intended to remain.

A second message from Trauttmansdorff arrived.

Stewart moved the berline a few yards but continued to block the courtyard. Finally Count Trauttmansdorff himself approached Stewart's carriage to deliver the Emperor's wishes with courtesy.

Plaintively Stewart demanded, "But where can I go then so we can see everything?"

"My lord, you must see where you can, but right now you must move. These are the orders of the Emperor."[19]

Reluctantly the great berline moved out of the courtyard and through the archway onto the bastion, and the sleighing party could begin, riding first through all the streets and squares of the Inner City, then the hour's drive out to Schönbrunn. Around the frozen lake outside the palace the carriages formed a half-circle to watch two pretty Dutch skaters dressed as milkmaids waltz on the ice, and a young attaché from the British embassy perform intricate figures, ending up tracing the monograms of each of the empresses and queens. Finally everyone went inside the palace to watch a performance of *Cinderella*, have supper, dance and return to the city through a whirl of falling snowflakes by the light of torches fastened to the sleighs.

On the walls people crowded to look down on the magical sight of the sleighing party at night, "marked like a river of fire by the flames of the moving torches."

The day ended with a masked ball in the Hofburg, open to the public. The English physician, Dr. Bright, shocked that so much merriment could take place on Sunday, found himself enjoying the Sabbath-breaking as much as anyone:

> After watching the sleighing party return I went to a little card party, afterward to one of the masked balls at the Redoute, where I laughed with great princes and flirted with masked ladies till a late hour . . . and thus

concluded a Sabbath in the capital and court of this most Christian and Catholic country.[20]

The sleigh ride, however, was not an unqualified success. Once more police informers swept up the aftermath. The King of Prussia had grumbled to the Tsar about Metternich's "putting them on show for his Viennese."

As for Viennese, they grumbled too, though perhaps with better reason. On January 1 the taxes on Austrian wages had gone up 50 per cent. Watching the splendid gilded sleighs drive by, the elegant gowns and jewels and furred lap robes, bystanders remarked, "There they go, riding off on our fifty per cent! Every day we have to pay more for their keep!"

The foreign guests had long overstayed their visit, and Austrians were murmuring, "They're buying up our gold. They're gobbling us up, making fun of our people. We ought to drive them to the devil."[21]

3

Talleyrand gave several sumptuous dinner parties during those weeks of carnival that surpassed in magnificence even the famous banquets he had given under Napoleon's Empire.

Talleyrand dinners were like nothing else in Europe, and it was little wonder if Gentz broke other engagements when Talleyrand invited him at the last moment—or even, as happened more than once, managed to put down a second dinner at Talleyrand's even though he had dined somewhere else just before.

Talleyrand dined later than was customary in Vienna, usually at five; in winter the light of a hundred candles gleamed on vermeil, on flowers and bonbons arranged along the great table, on the extravagant and fanciful desserts used as table decorations, architectural masterpieces made of nougat, *biscuit*, spun sugar and whipped cream, shaped into a fairy castle, a Persian pavilion, a triumphal arch or a Chinese temple. As an eager apprentice of the great pastrycook Bailly, Carême had laid the foundation of his reputation as Europe's greatest chef by studying architectural books at night and by day transposing the designs into sweet and extravagant fantasies for the table of First Consul Napoleon, for Cambacérès and for Talleyrand.

January, according to Carême, was the best month for dining, and the menus Carême preserved from the days of the Congress describe banquets that required three full kitchens and a small army of servants to prepare and serve.

The moment the guests sat down at table, liveried servants bore in great silver tureens of soups—at least eight different kinds—followed by eight or ten varieties of fish, as many as fifty delicately composed *entremets*, which were uncovered and passed with great ceremony. Carême, writing fondly and poetically of his career, recalled how those dishes "diffused throughout the dining room the suave perfumed odors of fine cuisine." There would be roast larded plover, *poulets à la reine,* stuffed red partridge, pullets with watercress, pheasant garnished with ortolan (a tiny bird highly cherished by gourmets) and woodcock, followed by a dozen or more roasts, a dozen "flying platters" of tiny sweet soufflés, apricot, orange, apple, chocolate; by parmesan fondus and jellied fruit, and finally the cutting of the elaborate set pieces of desserts.

The arrival of the Duke of Wellington on February 1 to take Castlereagh's place in the very last stages of the Congress—for Castlereagh was needed in England, and desperately, to defend the Tory government—was the signal for such a sumptuous banquet at Talleyrand's. Sixty guests— "all the distinguished men in Vienna," according to Gentz—and such distinguished women as Dorothée, Wilhelmine and their sister Jeanne—sat down to one of Carême's virtuoso productions.

The following day, February 5, a Sunday, Metternich entertained at another great dinner for Wellington, with several hundred more invited for the reception afterward. And on Tuesday, February 7, the Metternichs gave their Mardi Gras ball to mark the end of Fasching, when dancing came to a halt again and the more frivolous kinds of entertaining ceased for Lent. It was a grand masquerade, the last time the Congress guests from emperors and kings on down, put on mask and fancy dress to forget for a few merry hours who and what they were.

The next day, Ash Wednesday, February 8, was Wilhelmine's thirty-fourth birthday.

Metternich had scarcely seen her in January, and only on public occasions, at banquets or at balls. During those weeks while he wrestled with the final solution of the Saxony issue, he had made an effort to tear out of his heart the last roots of his passion for her. He did not ask her if he might come in the late morning for a consoling hour of conversation; he avoided her soirees, declined her invitations to dinner.

In response to her New Year's Eve letter he had written on January 3 one of those revealing letters that seem so astonishingly candid for a man of Metternich's temperament:

> I was your lover for two years. I loved you—I ended by adoring you. You ceased even wishing me well the day when I began to love you—natural enough course of human affairs! I was not disheartened; I did not ask you for love at all but only for some certainty—either refusal or hope. You did not cease giving me [hope]; you nourished that feeling in me that you saw as more than imperious; you encouraged it even while you saw it exhaust those faculties of which my honor demanded the full use. I was no longer a child. My conduct had to be ruled by my will alone. Called to lead twenty million men, I should have known how to conduct myself. I do not reproach myself in spite of the feeling that you observe [I have] for my mistakes; I would be worth nothing if I did not know how to love; yes, I do know how.[22]

That letter with its abrupt ending was his last attempt to explain the period of madness out of which he had just emerged.

Only at the very end of January, when she asked his help in drafting a letter and memoir to the Tsar—apparently in the matter of the money owed her mother—he sent it to her promptly with a little note that spoke to her with the formal *vous*. "You know that I shall always be the most zealous business manager you could have, and certainly the most reliable."[23]

He broke the silence between them on her birthday, sending a pair of delicate little vases fashioned from lava to adorn her writing desk. He had taken such pleasure in furnishing that desk with exquisite appurtenances in the long months of his absence from her that he did not want, he wrote, "to lose this right."

He wanted his wishes "to be the first to reach you on that very day which I certainly celebrate with more feeling than anyone else in the world!" And he reminded her again of what might have been, had fate disposed otherwise of their destinies:

> I would have renounced my life to live yours; I had formed dreams of which none has been realized; I had given you all I possessed, more perhaps than any man has ever given before me—more, much more than I even knew I possessed of the faculty to love— In two years of torment, of pain, of grief, I lived through more than twenty years of [the kind of] gentle life such as falls to the great majority of human beings!

Nevertheless his wishes for her happiness remain the same. He promises her friendship, the most loyal she will ever have. His own life, he says, is ended. "I am no longer good for anything." All his strength, all the resources of his soul are used up. "There may be in this world an immeasurable sum of happiness, but no more will be found on my road."[24]

She wrote thanking him warmly for "the prettiest gift in the world."[25] She invited him to come to see her that day; of course he did not go; it was too painful to him to see her with Alfred and perhaps other admirers around her. Alfred Windischgraetz was giving a birthday dinner for her; there would be a gala soiree at her sister Jeanne's.

Thirty-four years old. "One's life is usually fixed by your age; yours is not," he had written her—words that must have cost her a pang. Wilhelmine, who always arranged special fetes to celebrate her sisters' birthdays, did not care very much to celebrate her own. She did not need the reminder in his letter that she was growing older, and did not yet have her life's course fixed in any way.

In that day, when women's life expectancy was so much shorter, thirty-four for a woman was middle age—and it was for youth and beauty that women like Wilhelmine were valued. At the Congress festivities a bouquet of younger women, debutantes and pretty young wives—Marie Metternich, Selina Meade, Julie Zichy, Aurore de Marassé, her own sister Dorothée

—were the new belles of the day, "queens of love," La Garde-Chambonas called them. Moreover Wilhelmine had enemies; in the police reports she was accused of intrigue; her name was linked with Bagration's as a pair of Prussian-Russian agents—certainly untrue in Wilhelmine's case. An anonymous informer in January spoke of their "scandalous conduct," declared they were "promoted and guided by Humboldt," thought the police should expel them both.[26] To be a woman actively engaged in politics was a dangerous occupation without the powerful protection of a man like Metternich.

What was she then to do with her life? Should she remarry, she wondered, and whom?

"I am ruining myself with husbands," she is said to have remarked to Lory Fuchs during the days of the Congress. But the remark was probably apocryphal. She had had only two husbands, after all, and the second had been divorced nearly ten years before. It was true that Louis Rohan, her first, continued to cling to her like a charming impoverished relative one cannot possibly turn out.

"Marriage is the one state that will never be right for you," Metternich had written her. "It is not with an independence of soul like yours that duty can become the means of peace."[27]

Yet if she did not choose to marry, but remained independent, how could she survive even in the easygoing society of Vienna, with the eyes of the police always on her? What other choice did she have for security, for a position in the world?

Her mirror was still kind to her—that much was true. The women of her family were celebrated for their long-lasting beauty, and she might expect to draw for many more years, as her mother had, the admiring glances of men. But what then?

4

On the evening of Ash Wednesday, while Gentz played *l'hombre* at Wilhelmine's birthday party, the long, fierce wrangle over possession of Saxony came to an end.

At a meeting in Metternich's study in the Chancellery, Prussia accepted the proposed arrangement. Until almost the very end the King of Prussia had fought for possession of Leipzig. But at the last moment the Tsar had offered to give Prussia the city of Thorn in Poland as a consolation prize, and the King consented. The more populous half of Saxony, 1,200,000 in population, including the cities of Dresden and Leipzig, was to remain an independent kingdom. The remainder, larger in extent of territory but smaller in population—some 800,000—would go to Prussia, together with Thorn and some additional bits and pieces found elsewhere in Germany.

The King of Saxony was to be released from confinement in Berlin and brought to Pressburg on the Hungarian border not far from Vienna, so that a formal consent to the partition of his kingdom could be wrung from him.

It would look better to have his signature on the pact—else the world might accuse the gentlemen of the Congress of disposing napoleonically of other people's possessions.

Castlereagh, writing to Liverpool, took full credit for winding up the Saxony affair. Talleyrand, writing to the King of France, took full credit for the same. In essence the settlement represented Metternich's compromise proposal of January 29.

"The Prussians," Rosenkrantz reported, "were so angry that all of Saxony was not given them that when the news reached Berlin, people broke the windows in Hardenberg's house."[28]

Although, as Humboldt pointed out, Prussia had got "all military points in Saxony and Thuringia without exception," the Prussian Cabinet was far from satisfied and considered the arrangement merely temporary. Consolingly Humboldt wrote his patriotic Caroline:

> . . . the first war that comes must increase Prussia's possessions at the point where they are still incomplete. . . . Each and every Prussian must consider himself as a warrior reserved for that time, but must also make himself worthy during the interval of peace to fight for this cause. I look forward to this sort of a future with conviction.[29]

Castlereagh, writing Liverpool, added a parallel thought:

> We have become more European and by spring we can have a very nice army on the continent.[30]

It was not precisely a pacific vision of the future.

The snows of January melted, and by mid-February there was again warm sunshine and mild air that smelled of fresh earth and violets and an early spring. "Magnificent weather. Spring temperature; finest sun in the world; winter such as I've never seen," Gentz wrote in his diary. And a few days later: "The most superb summer weather we have ever had in winter has continued without interruption."

An air of great good cheer prevailed in Vienna. Things were settled at last. Conflict and quarrels and war—it was all so tedious! Now at last one could draw a deep breath and plan for the pleasures that lay ahead in a peaceful world.

Dancing had ceased with Lent, but again the inventive Viennese devised all kinds of games and entertainment to divert the guests.

There were declamations and orations and poetry readings for the more serious. There were amateur theatricals in which talented Dorothée played the lead, and Marie Metternich and Aurore de Marassé took part again. "There is nothing that Dorothée attempts that she does not do well," Talleyrand wrote her mother in Paris, adding that Dorothée acted quite as ably as the celebrated Mademoiselle Mars.

The succession of grand dinner parties continued, and if Chef Carême found the meatless cooking of Lent a trial, he managed nevertheless to produce a concert of delicacies out of fish and aquatic birds and the delicate little shellfish caught in the Danube.

One night at a party the Tsar bet Flora Wrbna that he could dress faster than she. A few days later, at Julie Zichy's house, both were put into separate rooms in street clothes, with witnesses to attest to the fairness of the contest. Within five minutes the Tsar appeared in the salon in a dress uniform with every order in place. But Flora was already waiting for him, smiling, dressed in a ball gown of the old regime, her hair powdered and even a tiny black beauty patch fixed to her left cheekbone. The Tsar agreed that she had won hands down and presented her with a fine set of books.

He was less good-humored, however, when he lost another contest a week or so later.

To fill in the evenings empty of balls, hostesses had contrived a series of lotteries, where guests contributed rich prizes that were later distributed by lot.

At Princess Marie Esterházy's lottery party one night, the Tsar and the King of Prussia brought magnificent gifts that were to go, by collusion of the hostess, to their favored ladies of the moment—Gabrielle Auersperg and Julie Zichy.

Marie Metternich innocently foiled the plot by drawing a straw out of turn, and consequently winning the most splendid of prizes, a jewel case the Tsar had brought for Princess Auersperg. The Tsar did not hide his vexation, and everyone at the party was amused. But to make matters worse, the prize Gabrielle had brought and intended for the Tsar was mistakenly won by a young aide-de-camp of the Prussian King, who refused to surrender it on the Tsar's invitation, declaring he had won it fair and square.

It was one of those delicious revelations of human foibles that amused Talleyrand so much he took the trouble of recounting the whole evening in a letter to the French King.[31]

Toward the end of February Talleyrand made a sentimental journey to Pressburg to see his very old friend, the mistress of his youth, Madame de Brionne.

Forty years before, when he had been a dashing gay blade of a cleric, he had frequented the salon of this great beauty and hostess of pre-Revolutionary Paris.

Now ill and in her eighties, for many years an exile, she had received the last rites and was waiting for death as she had once waited for a young dandy to step out of his carriage at her door.

She had never forgiven Talleyrand for abandoning his class and joining first the revolutionaries and then the upstart Napoleon. But now she asked to see him.

In Pressburg this most sophisticated and cynical of all men in Europe knelt at her feet.

"So there you are once more," she said. "I always believed that I should see you again. I've disapproved of you but I have never ceased for one moment to love you."

He could not bear the scene, he wrote the King of France, and he left her house to go outside and weep.[32] She died a few days later.

Nearly every evening Wilhelmine held open house. Her sister Pauline had returned from her Silesian estates on the first of March, so that the four Courland sisters were again united.

That first week of March in the lovely weather of early spring, there was a carriage excursion through the Prater and out into the countryside and the Vienna Woods. A procession of court barouches, smart little open vehicles with golden spokes and armorial bearings, each holding one couple, drove through the city, down the long *Allee* of the Prater and out into the country, to return for a banquet at the Augarten Palace and the premiere performance of *Agnes Sorel* with the famous actress Caroline Seidel. It was to be one of the last of the gay Congress parties.

The end of the Congress was approaching and people were already leaving Vienna. The King of Württemberg had left the day after Christmas. The Eynards were gone.

The Castlereaghs had left in mid-February. Castlereagh had got the agreement of Portugal and Spain to end the traffic in black slaves—with a sufficient time interval permitted the plantation owners in the colonies to stock their estates. And he had got Gentz to draft a declaration to be attached to the final act of the Congress, that all the signers would agree to take arms against any disturber of the peace. Gentz called it "one of the most beautiful pieces of my life." For that little task—and for other chores the precise nature of which remains unknown—Castlereagh handed Gentz a princely tip of a thousand English pounds.

The Tsar and the King of Prussia announced they would leave Vienna together in the middle of March. The Tsar wished to be back in St. Petersburg to celebrate Russian Easter among his people.

5

On the morning of Tuesday, March 7, Giroux awoke his master at the unseasonably early hour of six to hand him a dispatch marked "Urgent," which had just arrived from Genoa.

Sleepily Metternich waved him away. He was exhausted. The Committee of Five had argued until nearly three in the morning over the business of Murat, and he was understandably cross to have Giroux interrupt his slumbers when he had specifically been ordered to leave his master undisturbed until eight. He closed his eyes again but for a some reason sleep would not come. At half past seven he reached out resignedly for the dispatch and broke the seal.

The words leapt out of the page at him.

The message was precisely six lines long, an express dispatch from the Austrian consul-general in Genoa, informing him that Napoleon had disappeared from the island of Elba. Nobody knew where he had gone.

Metternich rang for Giroux and jumped out of bed. No leisurely levee this morning with perfumed massage and the ministrations of the curling iron. He was dressed in minutes and hurrying across the square to the palace to inform Emperor Franz, who sent him at once to break the news to the Tsar and the King of Prussia. Vividly in his *Memoirs*, Metternich recalled the drama of that morning call:

> It was the first time in nearly three months that I had presented myself to the [Tsar]. He received me at once. I told him the news of the great event. . . . Emperor Alexander expressed himself with calmness and dignity. We did not require much time to deliberate about the measures that had to be taken.

They would call a meeting of the ministers at once. Then the Tsar said to Metternich gravely, "We have still to adjust a personal difference. We are both Christians, and our sacred law commands us to forgive offenses. Let us embrace and let everything be forgotten."

Metternich replied that he nothing to forgive, "but only to forget painful occurrences." According to justice, His Imperial Majesty must agree that he too had nothing to forgive.

"The Tsar embraced me and dismissed me with the request that I would be his friend once more." From that moment on, Metternich recalled, "no mention was ever made of our former disagreement."[33]

Talleyrand was enjoying his usual leisurely breakfast in bed that Tuesday morning, with Dorothée in negligee sitting at the foot sipping chocolate and chattering about a dress rehearsal at Marie Metternich's of a comedy in which both young women were to perform that evening at the imperial palace.

A servant knocked on the chamber door to deliver a note that had just arrived for Talleyrand from the Chancellery.

"It's probably about the time of our meeting today," Talleyrand remarked indolently, handing the folded note over to his niece to open.

Dorothée glanced at the note; her eyes widened.

"Napoleon has escaped from Elba!" she cried. "Oh, Uncle, what about my rehearsal?"

The rehearsal, Talleyrand assured her, would take place. But he, like Metternich, dispensing with the ritual of his levee, threw on his clothes and was the first of the ministers to enter Metternich's study promptly at ten. Metternich handed him the dispatch from Genoa, and later he recalled the laconic conversation that took place between them.

> *Talleyrand:* Do you know where Napoleon is going?
> *Metternich:* The dispatch says nothing about it.

Talleyrand: He will disembark somewhere on the coast of Italy and throw
  himself on Switzerland.
Metternich: He will go straight to Paris.[34]

Everything was at once all business. There were conferences with Schwarzenberg. Adjutants were sent off in all directions to order the armies that
were on the verge of demobilization back to duty, and to urge the Austrian
Army already on its way to Italy to move forward with all possible speed.

Wellington alerted the English troops in the Low Countries to hold
themselves ready to oppose Napoleon. Orders went out to the Russian troops
in Poland, to the Prussian troops on the Rhine.

The news of Napoleon's flight from Elba was not at once bruited abroad
but remained during the first hours a rather well-kept secret.

According to Stewart, Metternich wanted to keep the matter quiet until
next morning "so as not to throw a sudden gloom" over the performances
in the Court Theater that night.

Gentz, calling at the Chancellery that morning, was told nothing. Only
later in the day, after soaking his rheumatic limbs in the warm waters of the
Diana Baths, he ran into Humboldt, who gave him the dramatic piece of
news.

That night the cream of the Congress gathered in the palace to watch
the amateur players perform a gentle little comedy of Kotzebue called *Old
Love Affairs* and a *tableau mouvant* and ballet in which Dorothée, Marie
Metternich, Selina Meade, Flora Wrbna and Gabrielle Auersperg were performing.

The sovereigns were in the audience, the orchestra struck up the opening
music. The curtain was about to part, when suddenly the news spread. Napoleon had escaped and no one knew where he was going! The *tableaux*
were all but forgotten in the excitement.

"The faces of the sovereigns," said Rosenkrantz, "were very long."

The Tsar called on the King of Denmark next day, and as he left the
King's study remarked to Rosenkrantz and Bernstorff, "Well, the bird has
flown!"

"We'll have to catch him," Rosenkrantz replied.

"Yes, and we can't make our measures too vigorous! We can ease them
later if we have to."[35]

The Tsar, who had placed Napoleon on Elba and had drawn up the
Treaty of Fontainebleau, had changed his view. The men of the Vienna
Congress who had fought through long, wearying months to hammer out
some kind of agreement on all the conflicting issues, to put together a new
production on the stage of Europe, did not intend now to see their hard
work ruined by the unexpected appearance of an actor who had been
fired from the set.

At the French embassy they tried to put on a cheerful countenance. "It will turn out to be a lucky thing for us all. Napoleon will be caught right away and we won't have to worry about him this time."

Some blamed the Treaty of Fontainebleau, which had been too lenient and had not even required of Napoleon that he remain on Elba. The truth was, of course, that Napoleon's pension had not been paid by the Bourbon government, and as Rosenkrantz remarked of the French, "They are acting as if they had put a dangerous man in prison, refused him bread and then left the door open."[36]

The next night, Wednesday, March 8, Metternich, Talleyrand and Wellington climbed into a carriage and galloped off to Pressburg to persuade the old King of Saxony to sacrifice half his country. The work of the Congress must be brought to an end as quickly as possible now.

But the seventy-four-year-old King's consent was not wrung out of him as easily as they had hoped. He received each of the ministers separately, to each flatly refused the partition of his country. On Friday he and his Prime Minister, Count Einsiedel, met with all three, and mustered all their most powerful arguments against the cession. In vain the ministers pointed out that the King had really no choice. On Saturday as they prepared to leave, Einsiedel handed each a note containing the King's refusal to give away his land and his people.

The Duke of Wellington was furious; he told Humboldt, "He must be answered sharply. He must be treated so meanly that he will feel himself blacker than my boots."[37]

Back in Vienna on Sunday the ministers decided to proceed exactly as if the King of Saxony had consented. Prussia was to take full possession of their part of Saxony and continue to occupy the other half provisionally. Meantime, they would prepare a reply to Einsiedel's note "in which the conduct of His Majesty since 1806 would be recorded."

For nearly two months the old King held out; not until May 20 did he set his signature on the document that abandoned half his country to Prussia. It was scarcely a voluntary cession.

Talleyrand, his life and career once again in jeopardy, drafted a harsh declaration for the powers to sign in which Napoleon was branded "a bandit" and "a brigand." Gentz drafted another, somewhat milder version, declaring that Napoleon had placed himself "outside the law" and was consequently subject to "public vengeance." At the end of a stormy meeting the Committee of Five voted to adopt Gentz's after Metternich had changed many expressions which he found "too strong."[38] The Declaration of the Allies was to have been printed and circulated in France as a support to Louis XVIII and a warning to Bonapartists, but it missed fire, arriving too late to be published in the *Moniteur* under the King.

As Napoleon stepped onto French soil he had declared, "The Congress is dissolved." But his timing was off; he was both too late and too early. Had he arrived in the midst of the Saxony-Poland crisis in November or December, when war among the Allies was imminent, who knows what his return might have precipitated? Had he waited another month or two until Congress had finished, the sovereigns departed and the armies demobilized, his might again have been a different second act.

◆

XXIV

VIENNA'S HUNDRED DAYS

1

On March 7, the day the news of Napoleon's escape from Elba reached Vienna, the little company of troops with the ex-Emperor at their head had reached Grenoble. Knowing it would be dangerous to cross Provence, where royalist sentiment was high, Napoleon had chosen instead the more difficult and dangerous route through the Maritime Alps. He had had to abandon his few cannon, which could not be pushed through the snow-deep mountain passes. At the gates of Grenoble the royalist troops drawn up to defend the city refused to load their guns and shouting "*Vive l'Empereur!*" went over to Napoleon. On Friday, March 10, the royalist troops at Lyon under the King's own brother, the Comte d'Artois, defected to Napoleon. The count and his cousin the Duc d'Orléans left hastily for Paris.

Only Marshal Ney, commanding 6,000 troops, blocked the road to Paris. Ney had promised Louis XVIII that he would bring Napoleon to Paris "in an iron cage"; there had been a good many royalist jokes about how to dispose of such an unwieldy bird. But when Ney read the proclamation Napoleon had dashed off on the day he landed in the Gulf of Juan, the marshal sighed, "Nobody writes like that any more! The King should write like that!"

> Soldiers [the proclamation read]! In my exile I have heard your voices! I have surmounted all obstacles and all perils to come here. Victory will march in double time! The eagle, bearing the national colors, will fly from steeple to steeple as far as the towers of Notre Dame![1]

A note from Napoleon informed Ney that the tricolor was flying everywhere in France, that Louis XVIII was leaving Paris, that England and Austria supported him. Surely Ney did not wish to see French blood spilt? In a dramatic little scene Napoleon and Ney met and embraced. Ney's 6,000 troops brought Napoleon's army to nearly 20,000. By Palm Sunday Napoleon's old servants were hastily readying the castle of Fontainebleau for their master's return.

When news of Ney's defection reached Paris, a placard was hung on the Vendôme column:

Napoleon to Louis XVIII: Mon frère, you needn't bother to send me any more soldiers. I have enough.[2]

Whatever the Allied ministers thought in the first days after news of the flight from Elba reached Vienna, no one believed Napoleon would reach Paris alive. He would certainly be lynched by a royalist mob such as had threatened his life on the way to Elba. Or he would be shot by a trigger-happy guard on the outskirts of some town, or taken prisoner by the huge, well-equipped royalist army of which Talleyrand had boasted all winter.

It was in that spirit the Declaration of March 13 had been written and signed.

When a few days later Metternich got news that Napoleon had reached Grenoble and that the French Army was flocking to his colors, Wellington demanded at a conference of the ministers, "What shall we do if he gets to Paris and subdues all of France?" There was silence for a moment, then Humboldt cried, "What we did in 1813 and what we have just now promised! No peace and no armistice with Napoleon!"[3]

That night, Friday, March 17, a military committee met at Wellington's. Wellington would leave as soon as possible for the Low Countries to take command of a combined Anglo-Dutch-Hanoverian army assembled there. The Allies, he hoped, would march their armies as soon as possible to the Rhine. The sovereigns again would accompany the armies; this move, Rosenkrantz noted, was the idea of the Tsar, who distrusted Metternich and "thought this would be the only way of assuring the support of Emperor Franz."[4]

Metternich dined that day at Gentz's with all four Courland princesses —the party "a bit disturbed," Gentz reported, "by the bad news from France." Everyone turned up at Wilhelmine's soiree that evening to exchange anxieties and to learn from Metternich if there were any fresh news from France. "General consternation," Gentz summarized.[5]

It was the first time in many weeks that Metternich appeared at one of Wilhelmine's Friday evenings. She was delighted, she wrote him next day, that he had "at last broken the chains that kept you away from my house." If only now they might be able "to enjoy peacefully the charms of a friendship and of an agreeable relationship. . . . All that may be only an illusion," she added, "but what in our days is real?"[6]

It was surely unreal, a nightmare, that Napoleon was back to disturb the hard-bought peace of Europe!

Only two or three days earlier Metternich had written her a last letter of reproach. Even then, in the middle of March, with their love affair many months over, he could not quite bear to let her go. "My whole life, all my moral faculties, everything I ever possessed of power to feel has belonged to you," he told her.

He described himself "like a man who sees cast up on the shore the wreck of the vessel carrying his whole fortune. . . . I have wept much, I have sought help from my friends and I have not found it." His life was without charm or pleasure or beauty. "I find myself," he wrote her poetically, "*sans feu ni lieu*"—like a homeless creature without a fire to warm himself or a place to lie down in comfort.[7]

It was the last such letter he wrote her.

In the weeks that followed, absorbed in the final act of the Napoleonic drama, the last dregs of his unhappy love were transmuted into friendship. He began again to see her nearly every day, casually, as they had once met in the period of their old acquaintance. Her presence no longer disturbed him—at least not so painfully as in the months just past.

Once more he turned to her to talk over his political views and to send her the latest news of Napoleon. Even before Napoleon reached Paris Metternich believed the fall of the Bourbons was inevitable. There would be some kind of revolution and he did not shrink from exploring the alternatives. "Civil war alone can do good," he wrote Wilhelmine that week, "and the Bourbons appear to me morally sick the way aged bodies are; the doctor says the sick man may be saved if nature makes an effort and if he has enough strength to survive the fever. *Bon jour*."[8]

When the painter Isabey, who had designed some of the most brilliant of the Congress festivals, departed that week for France and called at the Chancellery to take leave of his patron, Metternich told him gaily, "Hurry up, Isabey, you'll reach Paris before the Emperor!"[9]

In Strasbourg on his journey homeward Isabey found that the postillions had donned their green vests again with the eagle buttons and tricolor ribbons on their hats. A story had it that Napoleon, going into exile the previous year, had promised he would return when the violets bloomed again. Now at every inn along the way people were toasting the health of Père La Violette, who had kept his promise and was back in France with the violets.

2

So began the memorable Holy Week of 1815.

In Vienna theaters were closed; one might go to concerts or to hear sermons or declamations. Everyone was in any case too anxious and too excited that year to notice the deprivation. Rumors flew about the city. Outside Metternich's office people gathered in the anterooms to pick up chance shreds of news. His salon in the evening was thronged with visitors.

On Palm Sunday, March 19, at the end of a long ministerial conference, Metternich, Wellington and Talleyrand dined at Wilhelmine's, with her sisters, Gentz, Louis Rohan and aides from the French and British embassies.

The following day Metternich had a piece of cheerful news for Wilhelmine, which if it was not precisely political was at least pleasantly economic.

Wilhelmine had spent lavishly playing her part as a leading hostess at the Congress, entertaining extravagantly, housing a small flock of live-in guests in her commodious wing of the Palais Palm, appearing at all the festivals elegantly gowned and jeweled. Careless with money, perennially short of cash, she found herself now, as the Congress drew to an end, in severe financial straits.

Just before news of Napoleon's escape reached Vienna, Wilhelmine had written Metternich offering to sell him a set of her jewels he had once admired. "Once you indicated to me a wish to buy my sapphires in preference to my emeralds." She had had her superb emeralds mounted in new settings—a necklace, pendant earrings and a delicate circlet for her hair from which hung suspended on the forehead a single enormous emerald drop. "If you want [the sapphires] still, set a price that is agreeable to you." He could subtract the debt she still owed him, send her at once "some hundreds of ducats," and pay the rest at his convenience.[10]

She sent him the sapphire necklace, wrapped in a length of silk, together with the appraisal of the invaluable Hoppé. "I would like to be able to touch a thousand ducats soon," she reminded him the day before Palm Sunday.

On Monday he replied that he had a buyer for her necklace, and could she dine with him next day?

> My dear C. [she scribbled hastily in return], I am sorry but I am dining at Stewart's. Sell my sapphires although they cost me more—I wear them so little that it is better—[11]

Late that night—or rather at one the following morning—he could write her that her sapphires had been sold for 3,000 ducats, that Madame de Montesquiou, governess to the little King of Rome, had carried them off "on the wing." He added the latest bit of news of Napoleon's progress toward Paris, though she would no doubt have heard it already. She would have her lovely ducats by the following Saturday.[12]

Wilhelmine's necklace, it turned out, had played its own small role in the drama of Napoleon's return.

To no one had the news of Napoleon's flight brought more anxiety and confusion than to Marie Louise, waiting in Schönbrunn Palace through the months of the Congress for the men in power to decide her destiny. The news had been broken to her on the morning of March 8 by Madame Montesquiou. Marie Louise had burst into tears, rushed into her bedroom, where she could be heard sobbing loudly all the way out in the anteroom.

When she went to talk with her father, he had expressed anger at Napoleon's audacious adventure, promised her he would not allow her to return to France unless Napoleon's plans succeeded—which was unlikely—and only if they could absolutely count on Napoleon's peaceful intentions.

Marie Louise made clear at once that she wanted under no circumstances to return to France. At Metternich's suggestion she wrote a dutiful letter to her father, certainly drafted by Wessenberg and intended to be passed around the ministerial conference table, to allay the suspicion that Austria might intend to use Marie Louise to regain influence in France. "I entrust our fate to your hands and to your fatherly protection," Marie Louise had written. "We shall know no other will than yours."[13]

She ordered her suite to change from the Napoleonic uniforms they had been wearing into imperial Austrian livery. The arms of Napoleon were painted off her carriages.

The months of the Congress had not been happy ones for Marie Louise, neither wife nor widow, reduced in rank from Empress of the most important nation in Europe to that of archduchess, like her young unmarried sisters. She had taken no part in the Congress festivities; it would have appeared unseemly. Not yet twenty-three years old, she had lived as a virtual recluse in Schönbrunn Palace, with her child and her all-French staff. She had not danced nor masked nor frolicked; once or twice she had been allowed to watch a fete through a little window in an upper gallery of her father's palace.

All during those weeks since her return from France she had been under double surveillance. Her father's Secret Police reported every move she made, examined every letter that passed in or out of Schönbrunn. Within her palace apartments the persons closest to her—her secretary, Méneval, her reader, young Madame Harault, her son's governess, Madame Montesquiou, were loyal not to her but to her husband.

And what did she really feel for that stern authoritarian husband of hers, who could frighten even his generals with his fits of insensate rage? He had treated her fondly to be sure, like a child, to be pampered, but whose obedience must be instant and absolute. Certainly whatever affection she felt for him was strongly tinctured by fear.

Since her return to Vienna that affection had surely been put to the harshest of tests. The question had been raised in ecclesiastical circles as to whether her marriage was legal or not, in view of Napoleon's dubious divorce, and whether there were grounds for annulment.

She had certainly heard whispered the report of the Prussian General Knesebeck, who had accompanied Napoleon to Elba, that the ex-Emperor treated himself each day on that journey for a venereal disease.

And while Austrian clerics cast doubts on the legality of her marriage, the

French historiographer Flassan circulated a rumor that her own child was not Napoleon's at all but a substitute. There had been, said Flassan, no official witness to the birth. The doctor had had to use forceps, which—as everyone knew—could not possibly have produced so robust and beautiful a child as the little King of Rome.[14]

Little wonder that Marie Louise lived for the moment when she could leave Vienna for Parma, where she hoped to live for the first time in her life freed of constant surveillance, freed of a dominating father and an even more dominating husband. She hoped to have only new faces around her —men and women whose first loyalty would be to her. She intended to rule wisely, to choose her staff entirely from natives of Parma. Already her father had angered her by naming two men to important posts in her suite without consulting her at all.[15]

It had required the greatest skill on Metternich's part to win Parma for the Emperor's daughter, against the bitter opposition of Talleyrand and the delegates of Bourbon Spain, determined to give nothing to a relative of Napoleon and to turn over Parma to the Bourbon Queen of Etruria.

In the end Metternich had bypassed regular diplomatic channels, gone over Talleyrand's head and treated directly with the King of France. He had prevailed on Castlereagh to bargain with the King for Parma on his way through Paris. Baron Vincent, Austrian ambassador in Paris, had followed up Castlereagh's call by an audience with the French King on March 2, "a secret and direct mission."[16]

Louis XVIII was not above enjoying this bit of behind-the-scenes diplomacy, maneuvered over his cunning ambassador's head. He had stipulated only that the sovereignty of Parma, which had come to the Bourbons through Elizabeth Farnese, must return to the Bourbon family when Marie Louise died. He hoped to win in exchange Austria's abandonment of Joachim Murat in favor of the Bourbon Ferdinand IV for the throne of Naples. Metternich put nothing in writing.

The King sent instructions to the French embassy in Vienna. Talleyrand was furious: Metternich had outwitted him on Parma.

The joyful news that Parma was won, that she might leave Vienna soon to take up an independent life in her own little duchy, had reached Marie Louise in the first week of March 1815. Almost at once came news of Napoleon's landing in Fréjus.

Small wonder that she wept. Once again she was to be plunged into turmoil and uncertainty over her fate. Would they let her have Parma, these men of the Congress, when her husband had broken the Treaty of Fontainebleau? She was not ambitious; she did not want to be Empress or Regent. What she wanted with all her heart was infinitely more precious: the right to personal independence, the right to make choices, for good or ill, in her own life.

To only two or three persons that spring could Marie Louise turn with trust. One was her old governess, Countess Colloredo, who visited her almost every day and found her growing each day "more sad." Another was Wessenberg, appointed by Metternich to represent her interests at the Congress, who was to be for her whole life a loyal and disinterested friend. And finally there was Count Adam Neipperg, the dashing one-eyed general, who had been apppointed to guard her the previous summer at Aix and with whom she had fallen deeply in love. Years later Wessenberg wrote of Neipperg: "Neipperg gave her sympathy when the whole world had deserted her, and she learned to love him from gratitude."[17]

She did not trust Metternich. Had he not arranged her marriage—which might have been in the interests of Austria and of her father, but certainly had not been arrranged with regard to *her* interests?

In those March days of 1815, as Vienna waited anxiously for news from France, rumors spread through the city of all kinds of Bonapartist plots.

Anatole Montesquiou, a former officer of Napoleon, had arrived in Vienna in February to visit his mother, the governess of the little King of Rome. Ostensibly he had brought financial reports from the royalist government in Paris to the French embassy in Vienna; he also carried secret letters to the French members of Marie Louise's suite and quite probably a letter from Napoleon. The two Montesquious, mother and son, were hoping ardently for Napoleon's return to the throne of France, the police reported, and mother and son "were alarmed at the attitude of Marie Louise."[18]

At the French embassy there was near panic. The royalist cause would be enormously endangered if Napoleon succeeded in bringing his wife and child back to France, re-establishing his dynasty on a firm footing. Dalberg and others were certain that Anatole Montesquiou had come to Vienna "with the plan of abducting the little prince." Talleyrand complained loudly that Metternich was inexcusably dilatory in taking action against the Montesquious.

On the Monday of Holy Week, March 20, which happened also to be the little boy's fourth birthday, wild rumors flew about that attempts had been made in the night to abduct the child and that at least forty persons had been arrested. Emperor Franz assured the King of Denmark that no such attempt had been made, that he had merely had the child, accompanied by his mother, his nurse and his governess, driven into the city the night before and lodged close to his own apartments in the Hofburg. The move had been made "at the insistence of the French embassy."[19]

That same Monday, March 20, the Emperor sent Count Wrbna with a letter dismissing the child's governess in as gracious terms as he could muster:

> Madame la Comtesse de Montesquiou, the circumstances of the day leaving me no alternative but to effect certain changes in the personnel entrusted with the education of my grandson, I do not wish to miss this opportunity of expressing to you my gratitude for the services you have

rendered him since he was born. Pray accept my expression of this sentiment and the token of remembrance which I have asked my Grand
Chamberlain to give you on my behalf.

Your affectionate: Franz[20]

The token of remembrance was a beautiful sapphire necklace. At first
Madame de Montesquiou indignantly refused to accept it—or so she wrote
later in her *Memoirs*. Wrbna replied "that one could not refuse a present
from the Emperor." He apologized for not giving her the necklace in a jewel
case, explaining that it had been chosen in too great a hurry.[21]

Madame de Montesquiou, of course, had kept the sapphires, and Metternich had solved two problems in a neat sleight of hand. He had lost out on
only one count: Emperor Franz, a cautious man with money, had bargained
him down two hundred ducats on Wilhelmine's sapphire necklace.

Both Montesquious were denied passports to return to France for the
present. Nor is it impossible that both actually were involved in a plot to abduct the child and return him to France. A circle of ardent Bonapartists—
among them Fouché—had continued to support a regency in place of the
Bourbons. In his *Memoirs*, Fouché wrote that the abduction of the child
"had been attempted and had nearly succeeded."[22]

On Thursday of Holy Week, March 23, a letter arrived for Marie Louise
from Napoleon, written at Lyon and routed circuitously through Count
Bubna in Genoa. "Be quick, come back to me with my son!" he had written.
"I hope I can embrace you before the end of March."[23] As always in his
letters to his wife, their child was "*my* son." On rare occasions he referred to
the boy as "your son"; never was he "our son."

The note was barely legible—it was passed about among the ministers—
scrawled, said Humboldt "in a paw whose awfulness you can't imagine."
Bubna would have done better, Humboldt added, to have had Napoleon's
officer arrested and to have refused to accept the letter. But Bubna, along
with others—whom Humboldt refrained from mentioning—"had once dipped
deep in this slime—one could expect no better of them."[24]

Metternich had promised to send Wilhelmine news the moment it came
and he wrote her this latest, predicting that a battle would probably be
fought near Fontainebleau which would decide the fate of Bonaparte and
of Paris:

> I have told you from the beginning that Bonaparte will be in Paris about
> March 21. He will either be there or he is dead. I go my own way, let
> people talk, shout, bawl, and I am not afraid of the result for I foresee
> it.[25]

His calculation was off by a few hours.

There was no fresh news on Good Friday, but toward midnight that
night a mud-spattered traveling carriage pulled into the courtyard of the
Kaunitz Palace and out stepped the Duchess of Courland, exhausted from

a five-day flight across Europe. She had fled Paris the previous Sunday with Napoleon only hours from the capital and the King and his government preparing to run.

It was scarcely cheerful news to greet the Easter weekend, but Talleyrand put on a brave front and had Chef Carême outdo himself with a magnificent dinner on Easter Eve, all five Courland ladies, mother and daughters, present to sparkle and charm.

The atmosphere of the Talleyrand mansion that Easter was certainly not without tension.

If the King left Paris, what would become of his government, of his embassy in Vienna, of the long hard work Talleyrand had put into the Congress? He had written the King urging him not to flee Paris unless absolutely necessary, and then to go no farther than a town in the North of France, taking with him both chambers of the government and as much of the army as he could induce to accompany him. But would he have the sense to do so? He had made so many blunders already! And had he—Talleyrand—made an irreparable blunder himself that day at the end of March 1814 when he had put all his bets on Louis XVIII and the Bourbons?

And there were certain other tensions that had nothing to do with the political situation. Though Talleyrand had welcomed the Duchess of Courland warmly, for he was truly fond of her, still her arrival at just that moment had not been without certain complications.

She had surely discerned at once what she had already divined from the distance of Paris. Talleyrand was no longer the kindly old uncle looking out for a young niece's welfare. He was deeply in love with Dorothée—and in love with all the intensity of an aging man's final passion. All the fires so carefully banked by the experience and the wisdom of a lifetime were flaring again in a last wild bonfire.

In Dorothée her mother noted at once the new bloom that excitement and happiness and self-fulfillment had given to her beauty. She was surrounded by men who admired and loved her—not only Talleyrand but young Count Clam and the polished and worldly Count Alexis Noailles as well. "The great man is at least kept in the family," Wilhelmine quipped that month to a friend.[26]

Dorothée herself, who would harbor all her life profound resentment against her mother for forcing her into a wretched marriage, was not a little angry at her mother for leaving Dorothée's two small sons behind her in Paris when she fled. Tante Elisa too would write that month reproaching the duchess. "I tremble knowing them in the power of this bloodthirsty tyrant . . . this monster with his band of brigands."[27]

So it was not altogether a happy reunion that week in the Kaunitz Palace. The duchess made the best of it. If she was, as Madame de Boigne wrote, "dying with jealousy" of her youngest daughter, she was also genuinely devoted to Talleyrand. She would do her best in those anxious days to give him sympathy and support. Her last love affair might be over, but she could still steep herself in the pleasures of politics. And if her mirror told her she was no longer young, she could still draw admiring glances. Her former son-in-law, Louis Rohan, seeing her one evening in a black gown of devastating Parisian cut, remarked that she "outshone in elegance every other lady present."[28]

3

Easter Monday, March 27, was a day as mild and fair as June. People walked on the walls in the sunshine. In the tavern gardens in the Prater musicians played; along the *allées* cantered sleek Hungarian horses and chic little landaus in which ladies in summer dresses and parasols looked, as La Garde-Chambonas wrote romantically, "like so many bouquets of flowers." In white gowns and diamonds, in uniforms and jeweled orders, the more distinguished Congress guests appeared at St. Stephen's for Easter Monday services, following the procession on foot back to the imperial palace.

Despite rumors current in the city that Napoleon had reached Paris, there was a masked redoute in the palace that evening, and all the sovereigns enjoyed themselves immensely. The King of Denmark spent the whole night at the ball, Rosenkrantz noted disapprovingly in his journal, while the King of Prussia was observed "surrounded by *filles de joye*."[29]

On Tuesday, carried partway by the newfangled semaphore telegraph, came the sobering news that Napoleon was indeed back in Paris. A full week before he had been borne into the Tuileries on the shoulders of a cheering, shouting mob, his eyes half closed, drunk with the taste of his triumph.

The King had exited hours before—no one knew where, Talleyrand least of all.

Everything was suddenly changed. Napoleon had become a perplexing reality, and the future a confusing labyrinth of possibilities and probabilities.

In Paris a witty broadsheet described the political *bouleversements* of the three preceding weeks:

> The Tiger has broken out of his den,
> The Ogre has been three days at sea,
> The Wretch has landed at Fréjus,
> The Buzzard has reached Antibes,
> The Invader has arrived in Grenoble,
> The General has entered Lyons,
> Napoleon slept at Fontainebleau last night,
> The Emperor will proceed to the Tuileries today,
> His Imperial Majesty will address his loyal subjects tomorrow.

The Allies' Declaration had been addressed against the Tiger. The question now was what to do about the Emperor whom they had defeated and deposed a year before at enormous cost in blood and money.

On Tuesday night, March 28, everyone gathered at Wilhelmine's, where

Wellington "bade a tender adieu to the whole society." All the ladies kissed him and promised to meet him soon in Paris. He was to leave the following morning for the Low Countries to take command of the army there.[30]

Little eight-year-old Marie Wilson, Wilhelmine's foster daughter, could not take her eyes off the great duke in his magnificent red-and-gold uniform. Creeping up behind him, she gently stroked his epaulettes. The duke, annoyed at first with the child, then pleased, sent her a gold medal with his portrait.

Wellington had grown fond of Wilhelmine. He exhorted Stewart, now English ambassador in Vienna, to look out for her in what might be troubled times ahead if the war lasted. "Help her, Charles, if she needs any help. For my sake don't lose sight of her." Stewart would not forget his promise.[31]

For Wellington, staunch Tory with his monolithic military mind, there was one immediate course of action: defense of Britain's Channel interests and the restoration of the Bourbons. The Prussians too had no difficulty making their decision. As Gentz pointed out, the Prussians were chiefly interested in protecting their newly acquired lands on the left bank of the Rhine and in Saxony. Already during Holy Week, Caroline Humboldt noted everything in Berlin had taken on a warlike look. Cannon and munitions wagons lumbered through the streets, and well-disciplined regiments were on the march. "The military is unbelievably happy," she wrote her husband, "and all see this happening as the great crisis needed to cleanse and unite Germany. God grant that it be so!"[32]

The Allies, meantime, had renewed the Treaty of Chaumont, pledging to guarantee one another's territory against invasion. Talleyrand had not at first been invited to sign, but the following week all the signatories of the Treaty of Paris were permitted to subscribe.

But despite the Declaration of March 13 and despite the renewed Treaty of Chaumont, there was by no means unanimity among the Allies. Everyone was blaming everyone else for Napoleon's escape and for the exasperating fix in which they now found themselves.

Dalberg blamed Austria and "the diplomatic coquetry of Metternich and the sentimental politics of Alexander." Royalist France, he pointed out, had been trying to remove Napoleon to some safer exile than Elba. Humboldt recollected that Austria had been content to fight Napoleon, "but had not taken the slightest part in his downfall." Worse yet it had been an Austrian, Count Clam, who had saved Napoleon's life in Provence—a great misfortune. And *where*, asked Humboldt pointedly, had Napoleon got so much money?[33]

Others, the Duke of Serra Capriola for one, believed Metternich already regretted signing the truculent Declaration; if it had not been signed the very day it was, Metternich would not have consented to it twenty-four hours later, the duke told Rosenkrantz.[34]

As for the Tsar, though he had assured Talleyrand he would support the King of France "up to his last man and his last ecu"—this at least was what Talleyrand reported to the King—he spoke rather differently when he called on Marie Louise a week later. "If the nation wants Napoleon or a regency, I shall not hesitate to propose recognizing it. One cannot oppose a whole nation."[35]

And Emperor Franz, bidding good-by to Prince August of Prussia the day before Easter, had remarked, "Well, if the French want that Napoleon, I think we must leave it up to them."[36]

Metternich himself was cheerful enough in those spring days to prepare a delicious April fool's joke on Gentz, who had been suffering "agitation and insomnia" for fear Napoleon might take dire revenge on him for authoring the Declaration. Metternich composed a thundering broadside, which he had printed up over Napoleon's signature, promising a reward of ten thousand ducats to anyone who would deliver Friedrich von Gentz, dead or alive, or simply produce proofs of his murder.

The broadside was delivered to Gentz's bedside on April 1, along with his morning coffee. According to Countess Bernstorff, Gentz was "paralyzed" with fright, could hardly down his usual large pastry pie for breakfast. Later that day, however, at Prince Wrede's dinner party, Gentz declared grumpily to Clemens and Laure Metternich that the sheet had not fooled him for a moment, he had known all the time it was only an April *poisson*.[37]

4

"I can promise Your Majesty," Talleyrand wrote gloomily to the French King, "that it is an extremely difficult thing to make so many people march toward the same end. I put all my efforts into preventing any of them from straying."[38]

He had not precisely succeeded.

Talleyrand in those weeks of late March and April was in a state bordering on despair.

At the very moment when by sheer skill, intelligence and persistence he had managed to bring France back into the summit council of Europe— amazing feat to have accomplished in the space of four months—when, through maneuver and bargaining and persuasion he had won major diplomatic victories for the King of France, Napoleon's triumphant return to Paris had reduced his brilliant diplomatic feat to a heap of ashes.

In Lyon Napoleon had issued a decree granting amnesty to all Frenchmen who had worked for the Bourbon regime—except Talleyrand, Dalberg, Jaucourt and Marmont. All Talleyrand's property in France—the fine mansion in the Rue St. Florentin, the chateau of Valençay in the Loire Valley, Rosny and St. Brice—were confiscated. His young ward Charlotte and her husband had fled with the King to Ghent.

Worst of all, the bankers of Vienna had suspended Talleyrand's credit, leaving him virtually stranded without a sou to support his expensive ménage in the Palais Kaunitz. He had been promised large bribes by various countries—Ferdinand of Naples and the King of Saxony, among others—but it would be months before he could collect. Meanwhile, he turned to England. Lord Stewart would lend him 100,000 livres—if he could get the approval of the Foreign Office. But even with the most drastically reduced household expenses, 100,000 livres would barely carry a spendthrift ambassador through four months. No purgatory could have been more cruel for Talleyrand than the prospect of semipoverty. "Il ne faut jamais être pauvre diable," he said more than once.

He had other worries too. Had the fleeing Bourbon court left his letters behind—some of them filled with the bitterest criticism of Metternich and of Castlereagh, whose help he desperately needed now—letters that could be compromising indeed if Napoleon made use of them, as he certainly would?

And though he assured and reassured the King that the French embassy enjoyed the same prestige as before, it was not of course true. Once more the four Allies were meeting and concerting their plans without him.

For many anxious days Talleyrand had no word at all from his exiled government. Again and again he addressed letters to the King, reminding him that lack of direct news "is extremely painful and is very harmful to affairs here." How could he keep the Allies in line supporting a Bourbon second restoration if nobody even knew where the King was?

When a letter came at last, written by the King from Ostend, and Talleyrand brought it to a meeting of the ministers the response was a series of polite but pointed questions.

"Ostend?" murmured Metternich. "Ah yes, the King has chosen a seaport. So much safer in case one must flee again to England!"

And if the King still had loyal troops about him, why had he not remained in France, somewhere in the North, at Lille perhaps?

But the King admitted frankly to Talleyrand "the total defection of troops. . . . Bonaparte has the armed forces on his side. . . . All hearts belong to me."

The hearts on the King's side, however, were useless, it appeared, "without foreign aid," for which he was pleading. "It's necessary for the Allied armies to enter France and as soon as possible. Every instant of delay takes power away from me."[39]

The King's plea did not move Metternich and the Tsar quite as quickly as Talleyrand might wish. So the King needed Allied troops to restore him to the throne a second time? But what did the people of France really want?

Writing Talleyrand on April 10, Jaucourt from the Foreign-Office-in-exile was willing to bet ten to one that Napoleon would fall. He would not place any bet that the Bourbons would return.

But if not the Bourbons, then who should or would rule France? Even if the Allied armies were to depose Napoleon—a matter that was by no means a certainty—who could replace him?

Once again Metternich made his way cautiously through the uncharted country of alternatives. He must not lose the support of his Allies, nor risk the sacrifice of his Congress accomplishments—the months of brain-breaking work that had gone into the arrangements to assure a peaceful Europe. It was more important than ever now to dispatch the rest of the Congress business.

But Metternich was not committing himself prematurely in any direction. The task he set himself was to discover what alternatives to Napoleon would win the support of the French people, and how such a change might be accomplished with a minimum of bloodshed.

Napoleon, meantime, bent every effort to persuading the Congress powers that he was interested only in "a crusade for the happiness of mankind," that he intended to govern France constitutionally, and that he would rule in peace.

During April and early May Napoleon sent message after message to Vienna, while Metternich sent his own discreet inquiries back to Paris to sound out other possibilities.

Napoleon's first messenger, young Charles Flahaut, one of his most loyal partisans and Talleyrand's natural son, never reached Vienna. Halted at the Württemberg frontier, his dispatches and letters—including notes from Napoleon to Marie Louise and her father and from Caulaincourt, newly appointed Minister of Foreign Affairs, to the various embassies—were taken and he was sent back to Paris. The letters eventually reached Vienna.

The next emissary, an old friend of Talleyrand's, Casimir Montrond— "le beau Montrond" to society—was more successful. He reached Vienna on April 3, stayed three weeks in Talleyrand's house, his ostensible mission to win over Austria and the Tsar to the cause of Napoleon and to detach Talleyrand from his allegiance to the Bourbons. "Talleyrand is still the man," Napoleon remarked, "who knows the most about this century, the cabinets and the people. He left me; I myself left him rather abruptly. We were not always of the same opinion; it happened more than once that he gave me good ones."[40]

If Talleyrand would, Napoleon's message ran, behave "like a Frenchman and render me a few services," his property would be restored to him and he would be granted an income of 200,000 livres a year. Montrond brought letters too from Napoleon to Marie Louise and to Prince Eugène, and verbal messages to Metternich and Nesselrode.

In all likelihood Montrond was also the secret emissary of Fouché, bearing instructions to feel out the Allies on alternatives to Napoleon. Would they support a regency? Would they support the Duc d'Orléans? Montrond himself was known to hold Orleanist sympathies.

When Montrond asked Talleyrand point-blank, "What about the Duc d'Orléans?" Talleyrand replied cautiously, "That door is not yet open, but if it ever came to the point of opening, I would see no necessity for slamming it shut." Asked about a regency, the shrewd old diplomat replied yet more obliquely. If Montrond would go to visit Dorothée in her apartments, he would find her with her friends rehearsing plays. "But one does not play any of Voltaire's tragedies, least of all *The Orphan of China.*"

"Would you then," Montrond asked finally, "support a war against France?"

Talleyrand handed Montrond the Allies' Declaration. "Such a war would not be against France, only against the man of Elba," he replied, adding, "You are coming too late. Europe has made her decision. I too."

With Metternich Montrond had no better luck. "Has Austria completely abandoned the ideas she had for France in 1814?" Montrond asked.

"You mean the regency? No, we don't want that at all." At least that is what Metternich is *said* to have said. When Montrond returned to Paris toward the end of April he brought no encouraging news for Napoleon.[41] To Fouché he could confide that the Congress powers did not insist on Louis XVIII. France might choose any ruler—except Napoleon.

Another old friend of Talleyrand, Alexandre Dufresne de St. Léon, presently arrived from Paris, armed with threats for Talleyrand, bribes for Metternich. If Austria would again join the system of Napoleon, Metternich could win ten million francs. On the other hand, if Talleyrand did *not* return to France at once and pledge loyalty to the new government, he would be tried for treason by the highest court in France. Neither tactic worked; Dufresne was ordered to leave Austria.

A third emissary, Belgian-born Baron de Stassart, brought letters to Vienna from Napoleon, "very sensible and moderate in tone," asking for his wife and child, and a letter from Caulaincourt to Metternich pleading for their return. Metternich carried the letters still sealed to the ministers' conference, where they were passed from hand to hand. Napoleon's letter, Humboldt reported, was "very cunningly written," pleading with his father-in-law not to separate wife from husband nor little child from his father. Metternich wished to write sympathetically to Caulaincourt on the question of "the tender family relationships," but Humboldt, Stewart and Razumowsky protested vehemently, fearful that Metternich might be laying secret grounds for a regency. [42]

Napoleon no longer tried to win over Talleyrand. Countess Romer, arriving a few days later from Paris, quoted Napoleon: "I've made two mistakes with Talleyrand—first, when I did not take his good advice, and second, because I did not have him hanged when I did not follow his ideas."[43]

If Emperor Franz and Metternich became convinced that their Allies would not tolerate Napoleon, they continued to weigh the possibility of a regency.

Just before returning to Vienna in early April, the Austrian ambassador, Baron Vincent, had a long conversation with Caulaincourt, again Napoleon's Foreign Minister, at the house of their mutual friend Madame Souza, mother of Charles Flahaut. The powers would never permit Napoleon to remain on the throne, Vincent told Caulaincourt, but "Napoleon's son did not suffer the same repugnance."

Throughout the previous winter Metternich had kept in touch with Fouché, former Minister of Police under Napoleon, and through him had been apprised of rising Bonapartist sentiment in France. People were so unhappy with the Bourbon regime, Fouché had written, "that if the Emperor's son appeared in Strasbourg mounted on an ass and led by a peasant, the first regiment he met would bring him to Paris."[44]

Now back in power again as Napoleon's Minister of Police, Fouché was not averse to carrying on his own little intrigues behind the Emperor's back. He continued to support a regency for Napoleon's son as the best solution for France's future, intending no doubt to keep his own hand firmly on the reins of government.

In early April Emperor Franz shocked his friend the King of Denmark when he confided that Metternich had been talking with an emissary of Fouché. That unnamed agent was probably Bresson de Valensole, who had been official representative of the interests of the French marshals at the Congress. Metternich invited Bresson to a conference with the Tsar, Talleyrand and Nesselrode—one of the little incidents Talleyrand neglected to report to the King. Bresson was sent to France with a message for Fouché: if Napoleon would leave France, then the Allies would accept either the restoration of Louis XVIII, another Bourbon—the Duc d'Orléans—"or even a regency during the minority of young Napoleon."

Both Metternich and Talleyrand were exceedingly cautious, it appeared —more so than the Tsar. Rosenkrantz, who learned of the secret Bresson mission from General Waltersdorff, who got it from Count Wintzingerode, reported that Talleyrand remained silent when another Bourbon was discussed, while "as to a regency neither he nor Prince Metternich uttered a word."[45]

But Marie Louise fought against returning to France under any conditions; she was determined not to be made a second time a victim of political manipulation. She told the Tsar when he came to call on her that at no price would she return to France. A few days later she repeated her refusal, adding that she would rather end her days in a convent than go back to Napoleon.

"It is not pleasant to see myself treated as a child," she told Wessenberg. "So I am obliging in matters of secondary importance in order to offer resistance in big matters, for if they wanted to persuade me to degrade myself by returning to this hateful country of France under any conditions whatsoever, I shall show that I can be firm, and a woman, if it is necessary, will be able to oppose all the cabinets and all of Europe."[46]

At least Metternich and the Tsar were finally in agreement: neither was eager to support a second restoration of Louis XVIII. When the Allied ministers tried to draft a manifesto to the French people that would persuade Napoleon's supporters to desert him and force an abdication, the project ended in bitter wrangling over the question of succession. Gentz, once one of Napoleon's stoutest antagonists and author of the original Allied Declaration, now strongly opposed going to war against Napoleon and called the whole project of the manifesto "useless, improper, unpolitical and indecent." Clancarty, who had succeeded Wellington as England's representative, damned the first draft of the manifesto as "entirely Jacobin," while Talleyrand was furious with Metternich for applying his favorite delaying tactics. The ministers of Spain and Portugal refused to sign the so-called Second Declaration, while Stewart, once he had signed, had qualms and tried to withdraw his signature.[47]

In the end the famous manifesto shrank to a mere report published in the Vienna *Gazette* in May. Replying to Clancarty's query, the English Cabinet refused to ratify any second declaration, declaring they would not interfere in the right of the French people to choose their own government —aided, to be sure, by the troops of the Duke of Wellington.

It was clear that once more the powers of Europe were about to launch another war without in the least agreeing on their war aims.

While the ministers wrangled over the manifesto, Metternich made one last attempt to find an alternative to Napoleon who would be acceptable to the French and so prevent a war that seemed all but inevitable.

With his natural taste for intrigue he must have thoroughly enjoyed the little conspiratorial adventure on which he now embarked, complete with secret agents, invisible ink, code names and passwords, false covers and fake messages to throw the enemy off the scent.

To Fouché in Paris Metternich sent an agent with a letter in invisible ink in his own handwriting but without signature, asking Fouché to send a trustworthy person to Basel to meet an emissary from Vienna. An agent of the Viennese banking house of Arnstein and Eskeles, a man named Franz Christian Koekh, who had legitimate business in Paris, carried the precious letter.[48]

Koekh was able to deliver the letter to Fouché, but he was observed by a police officer who reported at once to Napoleon. The Emperor had Koekh arrested and questioned him personally. Furious with Fouché and eager to foil any plot that existed between him and Metternich, Napoleon sent off his own secretary, Fleury de Chaboulon, to Basel, armed with the code name and password. Fouché, meantime, warned of Koekh's arrest and the grave danger he himself was in, hastened to Napoleon and produced the incriminating letter with profuse apologies. He had been so "overwhelmed with public affairs" that he had totally forgotten to show the Emperor the letter that had come from Metternich. Crossly Napoleon accepted Fouché's excuses; he could not afford to hang him without good reason.

In Basel meantime, Metternich's emissary, Baron von Ottenfels, waited several days before a Frenchman finally appeared at his inn, produced the correct password and launched a long and flowery panegyric on Napoleon.

Ottenfels interrupted him to say that if such was the only communication that had been entrusted him, then he, Ottenfels, had nothing to say and would leave at once. Fleury lowered his tone. Napoleon, he insisted, was a changed man. "He is now a man of peace. The new constitution will guarantee the restriction of his ruling powers."

"Past experience," Ottenfels observed, "proves that Napoleon has no more respect for constitutions than he has for treaties with foreign powers."

"His Highness Prince Metternich should consider," said Fleury, "that it is no very easy thing to overthrow Napoleon. . . . He will not scruple to burn and destroy Paris from top to bottom rather than surrender the capital." Fleury paused a moment, then added, "But in the end we will never let things reach that point. Think anything of us you want but before things go that far we shall abandon him to save the nation and peace."

When the two men reached the crux of their dialogue—possible alternatives to Napoleon—Fleury asked, "Wouldn't your court see with pleasure the establishment of the regency of Her Majesty, Empress Marie Louise?"

Ottenfels, carefully instructed by Metternich, replied that there were bound to be difficulties in a long minority and "too much danger of trouble and factions. . . . However, if the [French] nation really wishes it, we will not refuse it. . . . The most natural solution," Ottenfels continued, "would be the re-establishment of Louis XVIII." If this were the choice of the French, the Allies would permit him to re-enter France only under new stipulations, such as ridding himself of the ultra-royalist émigré group who had surrounded him before.

"The Bourbon party is lost!" Fleury interrupted him sharply. "The return of the Bourbons can never enter into consideration!"

"And what of the Duc d'Orléans?" Ottenfels asked. "If the Allies could persuade the King to surrender his rights to the younger line?"

"Fouché," said Fleury, speaking as if he came as the delegate of the Police Minister, "has nothing against the Duc d'Orléans, but also nothing in his favor. One would have to create a party, which is not an easy thing to do."

Fleury rose to leave. "Do the Allied powers really feel so strongly against a regency in France as you've just told me? Remember that in the past year the majority of the French people have pronounced in favor of it. A regency would be the surest way of giving the nation a constitution that conformed to its wishes and in keeping with the times."

Ottenfels repeated, "The regency at the moment enters only in the third line of consideration. But if the French absolutely want it, the powers would not refuse."

The two men departed for their respective capitals promising to meet again in Basel with new instructions.

Metternich was delighted with the Basel meeting. Ottenfels recalled later, "When I repeated to him Fleury's words, 'We shall never let things go that far; we shall abandon him,' the Prince was unable to restrain his joy. He jumped up and actually leaped in the air, exclaiming, 'Didn't I tell you it would happen that way?' "[49]

Ottenfels' mission appeared to confirm what Metternich had already sensed. The French did not, in the end, want to wage war to maintain Napoleon in power; the preferred alternative would be a regency.

With Ottenfels' report in hand, Metternich met again with the Tsar and Nesselrode to prepare instructions for a second Basel meeting. Fleury would get the same message that had been sent Fouché via Bresson: the Allies would not tolerate Napoleon, but once he was removed from the throne the march of the armies could be halted. They would not refuse to recognize a regency if that was what the French nation chose.

Metternich, however, prepared his own separate set of instructions for Ottenfels that differed in certain important respects from the set written jointly with the Tsar. Metternich's instructions supported more firmly the cause of Louis XVIII, and made perfectly clear that in no case would the Austrian Emperor permit Marie Louise or her son to return to France while Napoleon remained on the throne. If a regency still had the support of Fouché, then he must inform the Austrian Government more precisely "what forms would be given this government."

Certainly by May 9, when the new instructions were written, both Marie Louise's strong objections to returning to France, and the fear that a regency could lead to civil war had influenced Emperor Franz's consideration of a regency.

Ottenfels' second trip to Basel was in any case fruitless.

The two letters Fleury brought signed by Fouché had clearly been written at Napoleon's dictation. Fleury again launched into a panegyric on Napoleon, on the impossibility of overthrowing him, on his desire to rule in peace. Napoleon had become, Fleury said, "fat and heavy. He sleeps a great deal. He only wants to be peaceful and happy. No one can guarantee peace like Napoleon."

There was no discussion of alternatives, and Ottenfels returned empty-handed to Vienna on May 16. The attempt to force Napoleon to abdicate through an internal conspiracy had failed.

5

In the soft weather of May—"divine weather: the most beautiful spring I've ever seen," Gentz called it—Vienna's hundred thousand visitors took their departure. The million candles that had glowed in the ballrooms were snuffed out. The violins that had played a thousand waltzes were stilled for the moment. Dancing slippers and masks, ball gowns and dominos were packed away. Every day the roads out of the city were thronged with departing carriages and with regiments on the march.

Summer came early that year; there was a general exodus from the city to houses in the country.

The Metternichs moved out to the garden villa on the Rennweg, and there in mid-May the family celebrated Clemens' forty-second birthday. The intimate dinner party was to have been outdoors among the blooming flowers and playing fountains, but a thunderstorm broke at the last moment and they dined inside instead, very merrily, with Flora Wrbna, Gentz, Nesselrode, Wessenberg and Hudelist gathered with Laure and the children to toast Clemens' health.

With his acute sensitivity to anniversaries he must have thought poignantly of his last birthday, when he had met Wilhelmine in Paris after their long separation. She was not invited to his birthday party this year, though they were again friends, dined together often at his house or hers, joked again and exchanged political confidences. Once again he shared with her his treasury of news and plans, as at a dinner party of which Gentz wrote furiously and jealously:

> As usual when he is in the company of the Duchess of Sagan he barely hears me. The whole whorish Courland crew was there, consequently no mind for other people. Metternich has in the last 8 days initiated those females into every political secret; what they know is unbelievable.[50]

Yet under the tranquil surface of the restored friendship remained a hard bitter kernel of frustration and wounded pride. Metternich would never quite come to terms with that failed love, never really understand how or why she had eluded him.

Most of the parties that month were farewell parties. Stackelberg gave a fork breakfast for Grand Duchess Catherine at his country place, and Molly Zichy gave a wild party for the Tsar where "they did such crazy things" it was the talk of the neighboring villages for weeks after. Molly's sister-in-law, Julie, expecting her fourth child, had moved with her family out to their summer house in the Jägerzeile; she entertained more modestly for the King of Prussia with two picnics, one in the Prater and one in Augarten.

Gentz, shopping for a country place of his own, found a charming house in the suburb of Weinhaus, which he leased on the spot, "happy as a child with the thought of moving out there as soon as this wretched Congress is over."

Everyone paid good-by calls on everyone else and settled accounts of one kind or another. Servants in the palace compared notes on the tips they got from departing royal guests. For the diplomats and court officials there were pleasant rewards as well. Lord Clancarty had sensibly proposed that only the four Allied ministers exchange gifts, but there was in fact a veritable rain of jeweled snuffboxes—some of them filled with golden ducats—and another shower of orders and titles and even of estates. Gentz came off particularly well. Every day during the last weeks of the Congress he could calculate another addition to his swelling exchequer as departing and de-

parted guests paid him for services rendered. One gift that sent him into ec-
stasies was a handsome English carriage delivered to his door from an unnamed benefactor—was it perhaps Castlereagh?

There were romantic accounts to be settled as well.

Gossip reported that Princess Bagration had been having an affair with
the Prince Royal of Württemberg, Grand Duchess Catherine's somewhat
unenthusiastic fiancé, and on the day the prince left for the army a police informer observed Bagration driving with him as far as the first post stop at
Purkersdorf, where there had been "tender adieus."[51]

Some of the royal guests repaid the pleasures of their Congress visit
with appropriate monetary mementos: the King of Denmark and Prince
Leopold of Sicily settled pensions on their Viennese amours, while the ballerina Bigottini extracted from Franz Palffy a generous income for life for
herself and the child he acknowledged.

But if butchers and bakers, hairdressers and goldsmiths had reaped a
golden harvest from the Congress, most Viennese found themselves much
poorer than before. Paper money had dropped to scarcely more than half
its former value, while the cost of food, drink, firewood and housing had
continued to rise alarmingly. Professors at the university were forced to
moonlight on extra jobs to maintain their families, and students, it was reported, were often too hungry to study.[52]

Even the rich had overspent during that long carnival season. Instead of
carriages with coats of arms, a swarm of creditors waited outside Princess
Bagration's door. Already in February it had been rumored that her famous
chef, Monsieur Bretton, had gone on strike, refusing to advance the princess any more money for food until she paid his wages. In June most of her
valuables were impounded and her creditors put watchmen on the door to
make sure nothing else went out to the pawnbroker's, while the princess sent
message after urgent message to her rich stepfather in St. Petersburg imploring him to come to her rescue.

Certainly the most staggering bills were those of Emperor Franz, who
had hosted a palace full of guests for some nine months. Talleyrand thought
it had cost the monarch as much as 100,000 gulden a day. Count Wurm-
brand, official Master of Ceremonies, publicly denied that figure, claiming
the whole enormous house party—including fetes, banquets, livery, stables
and all—had come to no more than 8,500,000 gulden.[53]

The Tsar and the King of Prussia left on May 26, the Prussian King
going first to pay a visit to Berlin, the Tsar traveling directly to Allied
army headquarters in Heilbronn. The Tsar's last days in Vienna had been
particularly enjoyable and carefree. He had been seen several times in small
wine taverns in the suburbs, tasting wine and joining in all the fun. One
night someone saw him in one of the taverns laying bets with friends as to
which one could make the most horrible face. The Tsar had only praise
now for the Austrians, "among whom," he declared, "one could mingle in-

cognito without having anything to fear." Riding at the head of his regiment as far as the outer barriers of the city, he remarked, "If I were not the Tsar of Russia, I would have no other ambition than to be a general in Austria."[54]

Emperor Franz left for Heilbronn the day after the Tsar, on May 27. The Empress went with him, hoping perhaps to spur her husband's uncertain marital ardor. But she was back in Vienna almost at once, ill and racked by such terrible coughing that her doctors forbade her to talk.

"Dear Grandpapa, you won't hurt Papa, will you?" Napoleon's small son asked Emperor Franz on the eve of his departure.[55]

No longer apparently worried about kidnapping, or perhaps no longer moved by pressure from the French embassy, the Emperor permitted the child to move back to Schönbrunn with his mother.

Marie Louise too talked with her father the day before his departure. Once more she made her wishes perfectly clear. Never again under any circumstances, she told him, would she return to France. She wanted her independence, and Parma for herself and her child.

She had, meantime, talked with Metternich and the Tsar, and it appeared that at last the path was assured for her chosen future. On May 31 Metternich and Nesselrode signed a secret agreement, granting Parma and Piacenza to Marie Louise, with the succession to go to her son—which had been expressly forbidden by the French King. Neither England nor France was informed of the secret treaty.

Overjoyed, Marie Louise wrote a warm letter of thanks to Wessenberg, who had pursued her claims through the labyrinthine negotiations of the spring. "I will bring you a gift for Nesselrode tomorrow," she wrote Wessenberg, "and will do my best to draft a really charming letter for the Tsar." And would Wessenberg please advise her

> whether the letter to the great prince [i.e., Metternich] should be accompanied by a gift? The customs of the Congress are completely unknown to me. Do you think a present of 10,000 francs is fine enough for Nesselrode?[56]

A few weeks later the police docket revealed that Marie Louise had sent Metternich a snuffbox covered with diamonds worth at least 36,000 francs, "a token of her gratitude for the duchies of Parma, Plaisance (the French form of "Piacenza") and Guastalla."[57]

"Vienna is becoming a desert," Wilhelmine wrote Alfred toward the end of May. "Everyone is leaving."

Alfred himself had left in April with his regiment. Princess Bagration had not, after all, been dislodged from the Palais Palm, and so it was Wilhelmine who moved, leasing, after Alfred's departure, part of the Windischgraetz palace.

She was going nowhere, she wrote him, except to her sisters' soirees, "which are not at all gay," least of all the evenings at Talleyrand's. Not too kindly she added, "My mother thinks only of that old cripple who is taking it into his head to play the fool at 62 years old, and so I am dying of boredom in the middle of this." She would leave soon for Ratiborzitz, and Dorothée, who planned to visit Berlin for the first time in six years, was to accompany her. It would be much more fun with Dorothée than with Hannchen, whom she loved dearly of course, but who was not a lively conversationalist for four days in a carriage.

There was a coolness, a casualness now in her letters to Alfred. It was he who complained that he did not hear from her often enough, and when he returned to Vienna on a brief visit he left again cross and unhappy. Dear good Alfred. "How stubborn you are," she wrote him, "taking another road than that of a Christian." He must know that no one would ever be more sincerely devoted to him than his *ancienne amie*.[58]

The long, stormy relationship that had broken and mended so many times in the course of four years was at last coming to an end. And, as almost always happens, it did not end for both at once. She could write the word "farewell" without tears. But Alfred, who had fought so long against surrendering to that passion, who had grieved her time and again by his neglect and his infidelity, it was Alfred who could not accept the end of their liaison.

If Metternich still carried scars of his love for Wilhelmine, the deepest love perhaps of his life, Wilhelmine too had regrets. She would reproach Alfred for having persuaded her back into a dying liaison. "I should have broken off relations with you; instead I sacrificed everything for you."[59]

The Metternich affair had indeed been star-crossed from the beginning. Had Clemens loved her earlier, she reminded him more than once, in 1810, when she was already half in love with him? Or had he only waited until the Alfred liaison had spent itself—? Half of love, as both these experienced lovers knew, was in the timing. They two, Clemens and Wilhelmine, so well matched in a hundred ways, might they not have had the deep and lasting relationship both were seeking? "Tell me that you love me and that a fatality presides at our destiny," he wrote her once.

Wilhelmine was not, however, quite so lonely and bored in May and June of 1815 as she described herself in her letters to Alfred. Nearly every day she and her sister Pauline rode in the Prater, Wilhelmine on a beautiful horse, " a real perfection," which she had just bought from Lord Stewart. Alfred, a connoisseur of fine horses, would be delighted, she wrote, with this beauty.

In late February it had happened that she had to turn down several invitations from Stewart. On March 7, the very day news of Napoleon's flight from Elba reached Vienna, she had sat down, conscience-stricken, and addressed a little note in French to Charles Stewart:

Every time when I should have had the pleasure of dining with you, My-lord, I've had such bad luck that to break the chain I propose you come to my house at 6 o'clock on Thursday, March 9, for a very small dinner party.[60]

Castlereagh's younger half brother, tall, blue-eyed, with his soldierly good looks and his chivalrous manners, had been an interesting figure in Vienna society that winter. He loved to ride and hunt, had brought his pack of sixty prize foxhounds to Austria. His wine cellar was first-rate, his table lavish.

There was, to be sure, something unpredictable about Stewart. He had a hot temper that could explode over a trifle. He drank heavily—common enough trait among officers of that day, who spent months and years in garrison. Stewart's escapades had appeared more than once in the reports of Baron Hager's police informers. There had been a fist fight with a *Fiaker* coachman in the autumn, and the incident of the Emperor's sleigh ride. After Castlereagh's departure there were tales of wild parties in the English embassy in Minoritenplatz; the straitlaced Genevan doctor Carro called it a bordello. And one day in April passersby had stared to see the English ambassador riding along the Graben, teetering unsteadily in the saddle, his horse's head covered with lilies of the valley.

Stewart was a physical type—forthright, outspoken, uncomplicated, as different as possible from Metternich. And Stewart was a widower—free of all ties.

For Wilhelmine it was as difficult to live without the intimate friendship of a man as it was for Metternich to endure life without an *amie*. Frederick Lamb had returned to England with Castlereagh. Alfred was away at the wars. In the last days of May it was with Stewart that Wilhelmine was seen riding along the main *allée* of the Prater on her fine horse, under the blooming pink chestnut trees. Or they might be seen driving out of town together in one of Stewart's elegant carriages, toward Nussdorf or Mödling or Laxenburg, Wilhelmine dazzling and fresh in the prettiest of summer muslins and a deep-crowned Paris bonnet with curving plumes. Sometimes they drove as far as Semmering to spend the night in a charming inn she knew high up on the mountainside.

A police informer reported on May 28 that "Lord S. often disappears from his house around 1 or 2 in the morning to go to Sagan's, whence he does not return until 5 or 6." On June 2 one of the informers noted, "Lord Stewart, who intends to leave for headquarters on the 5, spends the whole night at Sagan's. Arrives before midnight, does not leave until nearly half past five in the morning." Or a bit later: "Lord S. got a letter from Sagan at midnight—he went to her at once and did not return until 5 in the morning."[61]

Not until Congress came officially to an end in mid-June and Stewart too departed for army headquarters did Wilhelmine leave Vienna, and then not for Ratiborzitz after all but for nearby Baden, where she would be sure to get news as quickly as possible.

Dorothée had left the first week in June for Berlin; she would live again for a few days in her own palace on Unter den Linden, visit childhood friends, and their aunt, Elisa von der Recke. Dorothée had not yet made up her mind which of her admirers she really loved. For a time in late spring it was Noailles. When Talleyrand had sent Noailles on an errand to the French King in Ghent, Dorothée was "in despair," her sister wrote, adding, "I don't believe it will last long." Now Dorothée began to think it was perhaps the faithful Clam after all. ⁶²

Talleyrand too lingered in Vienna, unable to make up his mind to leave. The King had written repeatedly from Ghent asking, then commanding Talleyrand to leave Vienna and join him at once. "I am extremely anxious, especially in the present circumstances, to have you here with me." All the issues that most concerned France at the Congress—Saxony, Poland, Parma, Naples, had been settled, yet still Talleyrand procrastinated. "It does not matter who signs the treaty," the King wrote again. Still Talleyrand did not leave. The English ambassador at the King's court-in-exile remarked that no doubt Talleyrand preferred "an agreeable and comfortable position to any others."⁶³ Certainly Talleyrand was not eager to play his last card on the uncertainty of Louis XVIII's restoration.

6

Congress was at last coming to an end. "Busy and stormy period such as I've never experienced," Gentz noted of those final days when he was too busy even to write in his journal.⁶⁴ Instead of the three to six weeks Metternich had envisioned in early autumn, it had required a full nine months to argue through the complex questions that had confronted the first congress of its kind ever held in the world.

They had redrawn the map of Europe. And if the map they drew was a faulty one that would have to be modified time and again, if it gave scarcely a nod to the national aspirations of peoples in Europe, still it must be remembered that in 1815 the voice of national groups was hardly more than a whisper, plebiscites were unknown and the democratic processes scarcely put in practice anywhere in domestic affairs, much less on an international level. Even the United States and England were governed not by a majority of consenting adults but by small oligarchies of white male property owners. So it can hardly be astonishing that the ministers of the great powers, all monarchies, out of their imperfect—and diverging—visions of the future created a Europe from the fabric of tradition crossed with expediency.

Once the difficult questions of Poland and Saxony had been decided in early February, the other pieces of the puzzle fell into place.

In territory and population Prussia—thanks to Castlereagh—gained more than any other power: not only two fifths of Saxony but most of the left bank of the Rhine, the fortresses on the Elbe, the Duchy of Westphalia, Swedish

Pomerania and part of Luxembourg. Prussia, with a powerful military tradition, would dominate north Europe in the nineteenth century.

Decisions on the future of Italy were hastened by Napoleon's return from Elba. Austria had already got Lombardy and Venetia by the Peace of Paris, partly to compensate for giving up the old Austrian Netherlands. An early Congress decision—and one bitterly condemned by English liberals—gave Genoa to the King of Sardinia. Tuscany and Modena would revert to heirs of their former rulers, Tuscany to Emperor Franz's brother, the grand duke, and Modena to Empress Maria Ludovica's brother, grandson of the old duke.

The question of the government of the kingdom of Naples had lingered on, unresolved through March. It had in fact been Metternich's intent from the beginning to exclude the Murat-Naples issue from Congress entirely, despite the desire of Talleyrand and Castlereagh to overturn the treaty of January 1814 and oust Murat in favor of the Bourbon King Ferdinand of Naples. Though he was certainly pressed hard to abandon Murat, especially after securing the acquiescence of King Louis XVIII to Marie Louise's possession of Parma, Metternich put nothing in writing and continued to wait for events to unfold. His friendly correspondence with Caroline Murat continued.

It was the hotheaded and headstrong Joachim Murat who finally forced the issue. Against his wife's pleas he marched his troops into northern Italy, joining Napoleon's cause. Austria recalled her ambassador and declared war against Murat. On May 18 the Austrian army defeated Murat at Tolentino. The ultra-reactionary Ferdinand IV returned as ruler of Naples.

The last Congress issue to be hammered out was the future of Germany. The original plan for a federation of German states, drafted in the early weeks of the Congress, foundered on the Saxony-Poland quarrel and the resulting division between Austria and Prussia. In the end Metternich and Wessenberg produced a plan joining the thirty-eight German states in a loose confederation under a Diet at which Austria was to preside. The Diet would draft a set of laws; under one of the articles of the proposal each of the sovereigns was to grant his subjects a constitution.

The solution was a deep disappointment to German nationalists such as Stein and Humboldt, as well as to Austrian imperialists, among them Stadion and Schwarzenberg, who had hoped for the revival of an empire under Habsburg leadership.

Yet it is doubtful whether a more powerful union could have been forged among the German-speaking countries in 1815. The German kings created by Napoleon and the small princes fought fiercely for their sovereignty. Feelings of particularism were still stronger than those of nationalism: people felt themselves to be Bavarians and Prussians and Saxons before they felt themselves to be Germans. The mutiny of Saxon troops against the Prussian army command in May was but one evidence of the strong bond of loyalty that still existed between subject and King. Metternich's loose German confederation was a beginning.

Besides questions of boundaries and new constitutions for Germany and Switzerland, the Congress had resolved such intricate questions as the use of international waterways and rules of international protocol. Questions of diplomatic precedence had produced for three hundred years recurrent quarrels, duels, even rupture of formal relationships at international gatherings. Emperor Franz had to deal with that prickly question from the beginning of the Congress, with a palaceful of royal guests rubbing shoulders daily. It was wisely decided that the monarchs would enter the dining room and take their place at formal affairs by order of age, with the King of Württemberg as the eldest taking precedence. The Congress accepted the principle of seniority—the date an ambassador arrives at a mission—as the permanent rule for governing international protocol.

More important, crucial questions of human rights appeared on the Congress agenda, and if none was forthrightly resolved, two did appear as recommendations in the final act. The traffic in slaves was condemned rather than abolished. Civil rights for Jewish men in German cities were confirmed where they already obtained and a recommendation was included that they be extended. Both Metternich and Hardenberg had favored extension of full civil rights to Jews, but other delegates on the German Committee—notably the Hanoverian—had resisted.

The fact that questions of human rights were debated at an international gathering was an important first in history.

And though the voices of the Congress had often been angry, passionate, vituperative, and hands more than once had been dangerously close to swords, in the end the voice of persuasion and of reason had won out. The most important accomplishment of the Vienna Congress was just that: a powerful demonstration that grave international problems could be resolved through diplomacy rather than through arms.

On Friday evening, June 9, in the great reception hall of the palace, the final act of the Congress was read aloud to a gathering of delegates—the only time in fact that the Congress delegates had ever officially gathered together. A court gala followed, with Metternich playing host in the absence of Emperor Franz.

Now at the end of the Congress there was nothing but praise for Metternich. The ministers and the delegates from the German principalities spoke of the tact and prudence with which he had handled the German Committee; if he had only worked in the month of November as he had worked during the last days, the Congress would have been finished by March, everyone said.

Having set their signatures on the original document the ministers left at once for army headquarters, Talleyrand reluctantly in the general direction of Ghent.

Metternich dined with Gentz on Monday and at one o'clock the following morning his big traveling berline rumbled out over the cobblestones of Ballhaus Square on the first lap of another long journey.

News of Wellington's victory at Waterloo greeted him when he reached Heidelberg a few days later.

7

In early June Laure and the children had parted from *cher Papa* with hugs and kisses and tears, and moved out to Baden for the summer. "Here we are again starting a new correspondence, dear," Laure wrote him, "and though we know it is our only resource during absence, it is nonetheless sad."

It was almost precisely two years since Clemens had left on that other journey, to Gitschin, that was to have lasted six weeks and had taken instead thirteen long months. How long would this new war last? Who could say— three months? Six months? A year or two?

For Laure, a frail woman who had survived almost miraculously her six previous pregnancies, the parting was especially painful. The last birth, that of little Leontine, had nearly cost her life. The child she carried now was a big active child—they had already nicknamed him "little Hermann." Would Clemens be back by the time she gave birth in September, she wondered, and would the pitcher go safely to the well this time again?

The weather was wretched; it poured rain "almost like November, and so cold one can't take off one's heavy lined coat and shawl."

But the children enjoyed themselves, ran about freely, and everyone was well, Marie wrote her father,

> from Maman to the parrot. Polly is the delight of everyone in Baden, always at one of our ground floor windows talking to everyone who passes by, "Pauli, Pauli." He has lost his English accent and instead of saying, "Pretty Polly," he only says "Pauli" with the accent of an old Jew.[65]

When the rain let up the children went for long walks in the country, stopping to drink milk in the cottage of an old peasant woman who invited them to spend the night in her sky-blue cottage.

Once again Laure and Marie kept Metternich posted on all the news. "Princess Bagration," Laure wrote, "has found a banker who has answered for her." The Courland princesses invited Laure to dinner, but she did not go out much these days "because of my big stomach."

The princesses, she heard, had given a luncheon party

> for a certain little Clementine who is at Madame Lange's and who stays in Baden as every year. They say—and this surprises me—that she does not know a word of French. She speaks only good Austrian and kisses everyone's hand.

The "certain little Clementine" was of course Clementine Bagration, Metternich's natural daughter. Laure added for her husband's information:

She is well mannered and well cared for and very pretty but she has
no resemblance to Anybody. Of our family only Clementine has established her old friendship with her. She came to tell me with great
joy that she had met the charming "granddaughter of Madame Lange,"
who had recognized her.[66]

The Metternich children were making new friends that summer too. Most
delightful were two little black girls, daughters of a Brazilian woman who
was *femme de chambre* to the Portuguese ambassador's wife. Marie bathed
with them and was enchanted. She wrote her father:

> They live in the water. The little girls, one three, one eleven, sit
> down on the bottom depth of the water and play together as if they
> were in a room. You can see their eyes and their white teeth at the
> bottom. When they stay down too long Madame Saldanha begs them
> in the name of God to come up again and they appear with peals of
> laughter at our fears.[67]

There was plenty of excitement in Baden in the days of June 1815.

On Thursday, June 15, a new bridge over the river was to be officially
opened. It was a fine day, unusual for that summer; the river sparkled in the
sunshine. The new bridge, a radical feat of engineering, constructed of iron
cast in Bohemia rather than of wood, was decorated with flowers and flags.
A covey of clergy headed by the Archbishop of Vienna had gathered to pronounce the blessing, and the Emperor's brother, Archduke Anton, was to cut
the ribbons.

The band played, the archduke made his speech. Court and clergy walked
in procession across the new bridge. After them rushed pell-mell the whole
mob of delighted spectators, shouting and cheering with the fun and excitement of the occasion.

Just as the crowd reached the middle of the bridge, there was an ominous
sound. The bridge trembled and shivered; a few in the front of the crowd
managed to make it to the far shore. With a thundering screech and crack
the bridge splintered and collapsed. Four hundred people tumbled into the
river, all among the debris of broken planks and girders, among them
Marie and Victor Metternich.

> It was right in the middle [Marie wrote her father] when I felt
> myself suddenly sinking, sinking—and crash! went everything. All the
> people around found themselves in the water.

Two were killed, more than a hundred injured. The Metternich children had
kept their heads above water, Victor clinging to a plank until they were
rescued.

> Adieu, *mon cher Papa* [Marie concluded]. God grant your absence may
> not be long and may the whole French Empire collapse in a moment
> like the Baden bridge.[68]

"Heaven watched over you," Metternich wrote thankfully when he heard of their narrow escape. All the young officers at headquarters, he added, had been "devastated" to learn that Marie had been in danger.

Meantime, along with the excitement of the bridge disaster, everyone in Baden waited anxiously for news of the war.

Wilhelmine, staying with the hospitable Lory Fuchs in her castle Gutenbrunn in Baden, could hardly bear the suspense. There were no letters arriving each day by diplomatic pouch for Wilhelmine from Clemens, bringing the latest news from the war zone. "Dear Gentz," she wrote to Vienna, "for God's sake if you hear something have mercy on me and write. We sit here like princesses enchanted by a spell—as if everyone else were at the far ends of the earth."[69]

Rather complacently Gentz passed this plea along to Metternich at headquarters. "The ladies are dying of boredom in Baden. [The duchess] must realize often enough what it means to have lost such a correspondent as heaven sent her in the year 1813."[70]

In desperation one day toward the end of June Wilhelmine drove into Vienna for news and found a letter just arrived by special courier from Charles Stewart in Belgium. She hurried back with it at once to Baden.

Laure Metternich and the children had just finished dinner and were talking with several of Laure's friends who had dropped by to help her pass the time. All at once Pauline Hohenzollern burst in, "white as death, beside herself and unable to speak a word . . . In the first moments I thought she came to announce the worst news in the world. . . ."

"Good news!" Pauline gasped, collapsing into a chair. "Lord Stewart—dispatch—I can't talk—Napoleon has abdicated. The war is over!"

Everyone began to shout and weep with joy.

"But no! I can't believe it!" cried Marie. "There is no word from Papa."

At that moment a footman brought a letter from Metternich announcing the great victory. "Imagine if it was not a welcome one!" Laure wrote.

"They captured Napoleon's hat and cloak and we must only hope we finally catch him too," Metternich had written.

The Viennese that week, hearing about the hat, shrugged. "*Ja, mein Gott,* he doesn't need a hat when he's gone and lost his head."

The end of dear Papa's letter sent Marie into ecstasy. "Marie will go with me to Italy," he had written.

"*Ah Dieu!*" she wrote her father. "Since yesterday I can see only Italy and peace and the happiness of the whole world!"[71]

XXV

"ALL THE WORLD'S IN PARIS"

1

If it was peace, it was a precarious one.

The second Allied occupation of Paris had the air of a reprise, of *déjà vu* and *déjà fait*. But there were important differences from the occupation of fourteen months before. If the National Guard had carried lilies in the ends of their guns on the day of the King's entry, there were very real cannon in place before the Arc de Triomphe, at the Carousel and at the bridgeheads of the Seine. Nearly every night there were clashes between the royalist guard and Bonapartist crowds.

Twice-restored Louis wobbled precariously on his throne. Instead of Louis le Désiré they were calling him "Louis l'Inévitable" and "Louis l'Impossible." The state of French finances was so bad that the King was said to be living off the revenue Paris police collected from the licensing of prostitutes. To tales of the sorry state of finances punsters retorted, *"Pourtant nous avons un gros revenu."*

The tricolor had been banished, but anti-Bourbonists sported tiny red carnations in buttonholes and tucked into bodices, precipitating recurrent fights with the police. Despite a strictly enforced censorship anti-Bourbon broadsides and cartoons circulated—one showing a fat Louis waddling into France through a pool of blood between a Prussian and an English soldier. In one of the Paris suburbs a hog was paraded through the streets wearing the white lily of the Bourbons stuck in his ears and under his tail, while everyone in the taverns drank to *"le gros Papa."*[1]

Wellington had announced he was entering France as *un pays ami*, and had kept his troops under the strictest discipline. Blücher had announced he was entering *un pays criminel*. The Prussian army crossing northern France had indulged all too freely in looting, arson, rape and murder. The day after the King's entry into Paris Blücher declared he intended to blow up the Jena bridge over the Seine to rid the city of the detestable name that reminded Prussians of their humiliating defeat at the hands of Napoleon. Talleyrand and the King both offered to go and sit on the bridge to protect it. Blücher growled that it might make exploding the bridge a bit more clumsy but none the less desirable.

It was into this uneasy Paris that Metternich rode with the Austrian Emperor and the Tsar on the night of July 10.

The war had been mercifully brief; the only casualties the Austrian Army had suffered crossing France had been from sunstroke, while the bulk of the Russian Army would not arrive in France until September. Neither the Tsar nor Metternich had hastened to put their troops into action. Waterloo had been an Anglo-Prussian victory, and it was Wellington following Castlereagh's orders who had brought Louis back to France, "packed in the baggage of the English army."

Three days after Waterloo the Chamber of Deputies in Paris had demanded Napoleon's abdication, which he gave, reluctantly, in favor of his son. Liberal leaders in the Chamber had sent a delegation to Allied headquarters in Germany declaring they would accept any government for France except that of Louis XVIII—either Napoleon II, the King of Saxony or the Duc d'Orléans.

But, as the armies of Wellington and Blücher pushed rapidly into France, Fouché played kingmaker and warned Wellington that the restoration of Louis XVIII might bring civil war to France. Wellington sent a sharp rejoinder: he had orders from his government to treat on no other terms than the restoration of Louis XVIII.

From Germany the Tsar and Emperor Franz had sent their consent.

Castlereagh and Wellington would play top dog in the second peacemaking, but in the troubled Paris of that hot July they needed support. Wellington had implored the Austrian and Russian sovereigns to hurry; they had left their armies at St. Dizier and ridden to Paris in a post coach.

> The city has an extraordinary look [Metternich wrote Marie]. Everyone cries "Vive le Roi!" without any person knowing what good the king can do by reigning over people who do not wish for order. I would not be in his place for anything in the world, and he will need much skill to be able to keep it.[2]

Nesselrode, moving back into the apartments of Napoleon's son in the Élysée Palace, noticed that they had removed the child's little bed, as if Napoleon's palace were the only place in Paris "where they did not count on the return of the King of Rome."[3]

Meantime, the first order of business was the disposition of Napoleon. After his abdication he had lingered for a few days at Malmaison in late June, among the roses and souvenirs of Josephine. But royalists in Paris were demanding his trial and execution, and the Prussians were demanding that he be shot by a firing squad.

Napoleon hastened on to the port of Rochefort, where he holed up for a few days, trying to make up his mind whether to flee to America or to throw himself on the mercy of his old enemy and ask refuge in England. A British frigate sealed the harbor of Rochefort, but the French skipper of a little sloop was certain he could smuggle the Emperor out of the harbor hidden in a barrel. Napoleon decided on England and wrote the Prince Regent asking his permission to come "like Themistocles to sit at the hearth of the English nation." At dawn on July 15, accompanied by a suite of fifteen officers, sixty servants and an enormous convoy of baggage, wearing his green dress uniform and his two-cornered hat, Napoleon boarded the British frigate *Bellerophon*, asking to be taken to "a country house some ten or twelve leagues from London."

From Paris Metternich wrote Marie Louise, as he had promised, that her husband was well, that he would be taken to Fort George in northern Scotland, where he would be "well-treated and will have as much liberty as is compatible with the certainty that he cannot escape."[4]

But the English Cabinet was nervous about keeping their dangerous prisoner so near the shores of France; there were already signs that he might arouse considerable compassion in England. Lady Holland, musing over a plate of babas, had been heard to murmur, "Poor dear man," while Byron had growled at the news of Waterloo, "I'm damned sorry for it. I didn't know but I might live to see Lord Castlereagh's head on a pole. But I suppose I shan't now."

So it was to be the island of St. Helena in the South Atlantic, where, Liverpool predicted in one of the most unfulfilled prophecies of the nineteenth century, "he will be soon forgotten."[5]

From Baden, where she was taking the waters, Marie Louise thanked Metternich for his news. Word of Napoleon's abdication three weeks before had frightened her all over again that either she might be forced to return to France, or she would be separated from her son, a thought that "made her blood run cold."[6] The King's entrance into Paris had allayed her fears, she wrote Metternich, but she repeated once again, "I was decided under no condition and for no political prospects to return to France." Wessenberg, summoned to Paris, got the same message to carry to her father.[7]

It was clear that summer that Marie Louise had learned two things since leaving France: to be more assertive of her rights as a person, and to practice with some skill the art of diplomacy. Since twice-restored Louis owed his throne to the support of his fellow sovereigns, she reminded her father, would this not be the right moment to press for his agreement to her son's succession in Parma?

Her father answered obliquely. Her interests and those of her son would not be forgotten. On the question of a possible regency he could reassure her more positively.

There is not much to be done about France, for the king totters on his throne, surrounded by rogues. If I declared you and your son were going to occupy it, he would be instantly overthrown.[8]

But a regency could be frightfully dangerous, he wrote, remembering the fate of his aunt, Marie Antoinette. "You and your son could become the most appalling victims." His refusal to allow his daughter and grandson to return to France, however, were earning him "threats and deep hatred," he added.

He did not tell her that the hope of her son's inheriting Parma was growing dimmer. Castlereagh, as well as the Bourbons, opposed it, and Castlereagh that summer was the moving power.

Metternich presently had to inform Marie Louise that her husband was not to be imprisoned in a Scottish fortress after all, but on the rocky isle of St. Helena. That news shocked and depressed her. Indignantly she wrote Wessenberg that if she were a sovereign she would think it an honor to treat a fallen enemy more generously than they were treating Napoleon. "But I think the hearts of sovereigns are made differently from those of ordinary mortals."[9] She begged her father to see that Napoleon was treated with clemency and kindness. And in a skillfully composed letter to Metternich she demonstrated how much she had learned of politics and persuasion. She reminded him of the havoc the Napoleonic marriage he had arranged had wrought in her life. "I shall always be unhappy; what I have suffered has left marks too deep ever to be erased." She had been persuaded into that political marriage "for the good of Austria and Europe." Now in return she asked two favors of her father's Foreign Minister. First, she asked that the sovereigns guarantee her "an independent and peaceful existence," and allow her son to succeed to Parma.

Secondly, she asked Metternich's intervention to ameliorate in any way he could the harsh fate that had been meted out to her husband. "The magnanimity of the sovereigns will not permit that he be meanly treated. They will not want to increase his personal suffering nor exercise any other law against him than that of the conqueror." She would be grateful for whatever Metternich could do; she counted on his help.[10]

But Metternich had no influence on Napoleon's fate. The *Northumberland* would deposit its famous charge on St. Helena in mid-October, and it would be the English who bore the onus of acting as jailers.

Walking through the palace of Napoleon at St. Cloud, when he went to dine one day with Blücher, Metternich nodded when the old Prussian, waving toward the beautiful picture gallery, remarked, "That man must have been a real fool to have had all this and gone chasing off to Moscow."[11]

Not only the French Army and much of the French public but many Austrians of prominence remained outspokenly anti-Bourbon, pro-regency. Gentz regretted that Metternich and Emperor Franz had not insisted on a regency. To be sure there would be some danger, he wrote, but "when one thinks to what heights Austria could be raised in frankly supporting the interest of Napoleon's son. . . ." Instead, Austria would join heart and soul now with England to work for the re-establishment of the Bourbons, however distasteful that chore would be.[12]

Gentz was right in his analysis. While Marie Louise's personal wishes probably did not count much with Metternich—though they had some influence on her father—what decided Metternich finally were the interests of Europe.

Austria's ambition must be subordinated to the unity of the Alliance and the future peace of Europe.

2

Jockies, Jews and Parlez-vous,
    Courtezans and Quakers,
Players, Peers and Auctioneers,
    Parsons, Undertakers,
Modish airs from Wapping-stairs,
    Wit from Norton Falgate,
Bagatelle from Clerkenwell,
    And elegance from Aldgate.

London now is out of town,
    Who in England tarries?
Who can bear to linger there,
    When all the world's in Paris?

So sang Grimaldi, the English music hall star, that summer. And indeed it seemed to be so.

In the Bois among the tents of the British camp could be seen shakos and plumes and red coats. The kilts of His Majesty's Scottish Guard created a sensation. Parisian ladies pointed and giggled, "Mon Dieu! if a big wind came along!"

Along the boulevard of the Temple, where there was a perpetual fair, soldiers of all nations crowded about to watch clowns and jugglers perform on portable stages, to ride on the carrousels, drink gooseberry ale bought at street stalls and munch on Nanterre cakes.

English and Prussian and Austrian officers jostled their way through the crowds in the Palais-Royale, and late at night, after the theater, played *biribi* and *trente-et-un* in the mirrored and gilded gambling rooms of Frascati's and the Cercle des Étrangers. Blücher, having emptied his own and his valet's pockets one night at the Cercle des Étrangers, retired "swearing like a peasant, insulting the croupiers, cursing France and all Frenchmen."[13]

Once again tourists of all nationalities flocked to Paris, haunted the museums, sat on the tree-shaded terraces of Tortoni's and the Café Anglais. The opera was crowded to overflowing. Everyone went to see the new ballet about

Waterloo: National Guard dances in to tell young beauty her lover has been killed; tragic solo follows until English officer who has saved lover dances in with him; everyone joins in joyful finale; stage fills with lilies and Scotsmen in ballet kilts.

At a supper party at the Castlereaghs' after the opera, Lady Granville sat next to Metternich and expressed her shock at the frivolity of the French. "We agreed it was worth coming any distance to see this proof of national character." Though Castlereagh supper parties were exceedingly dull, there were bright spots. "Metternich," Lady Granville informed her sister, "is more entertaining than anybody."[14]

More amusing than the Castlereaghs' were the evenings at Talleyrand's. Once again he received in the mansion on the rue St. Florentin, in the beautiful salon with the painted ceiling, Dorothée at his side, and a cosmopolitan crowd gathered to exchange the latest political wit, to drink tea and play cards for high stakes.

Dorothée had returned from Prussia as soon as she got news of the King's entry. Instead of moving back into the house she had shared with her husband, she went to live at Talleyrand's. The minister's wife, Catherine, had fled to England when Napoleon returned from Elba, and Talleyrand meant to keep her there.

When Frances, Lady Shelley, a pretty young Englishwoman who was infatuated with the Duke of Wellington, accompanied the victor of Waterloo to Talleyrand's, Dorothée flew up to the duke, threw her arms around his neck, kissed him on both cheeks, calling him "her saviour." Frances Shelley was startled and not a little envious at Dorothée's spontaneous display of "the adoration which I also feel for Wellington."

A few nights later, when Frances Shelley, sitting next to Talleyrand at dinner, expressed admiration for Dorothée, he responded, "Ah oui, she is charming and very intelligent. The only thing she has of youth is her naturalness." Pleased with his mot, he repeated it a few minutes later to Dorothée herself, "who kissed him repeatedly on both cheeks," which delighted Talleyrand so much he proceeded to feed her coffee out of his cup "and used his own spoon for the purpose."

The ways of the French continued to astonish and puzzle the English visitors. How could women be fascinated by Talleyrand? Lady Shelley wondered. "He is a frightful object to look at and rolls his tongue about in a disgusting manner. He has a club foot, but in spite of all that the French ladies find him irresistible."

It was, however, neither a smooth nor a cheerful summer in the Talleyrand ménage. Dorothée confided to Frances Shelley that Talleyrand was very downhearted, that he had "lost his spirits and much of his bonhomie."[15] The Allies were taking a hard line toward France, and the second peace promised to be far harsher than the first.

But it was not only political affairs that troubled and discouraged Talleyrand. He had returned to Paris, Comtesse de Boigne recalled, madly in love "like a youth of eighteen." But fond as Dorothée might be of her uncle, it was with Count Clam she was in love. And Clam was now in Paris with Schwarzenberg. Not only did Talleyrand suffer all the torments and miseries of jealousy, but Dorothée's affair with Clam precipitated one of the dramas of that Paris summer.

Dorothée had returned to Paris determined to cut herself loose forever from her unhappy marriage. But divorce was impossible for a Catholic in France and even legal separation extremely difficult for a woman. Edmond, it turned out, was not as complaisant as he had appeared.

Within days of Dorothée's return he challenged Clam to a duel. The duel was fought with sabers on the early morning of Monday, July 31, and it ended when Edmond received a severe slash across the forehead. That night the Duke of Wellington was giving a great ball at his house, attended, Harriet Granville reported, "by four hundred men and forty women." Most Frenchwomen refused to dance in the house of the Waterloo victor, but Dorothée was there, and "she waltzed as if her husband's head had not been laid open in a duel that morning." With an Englishwoman's judgment of the odd ways of the French, Lady Granville shrugged: "I suppose they cannot help dancing."

Dorothée, of course, was not French at all and she appeared at the ball, as Frances Shelley discerned, to muffle if not silence the scandal of the duel.[16]

Pasquier, Minister of Justice and an old friend of Talleyrand, declared:

> It was very difficult to believe, if you had not seen it, that at the very moment when [Talleyrand] should have been exclusively occupied with affairs of state, affairs whose importance and responsibility would have frightened the most consummate statesman, was precisely the moment when, more than sixty years old, he chose to yield to a sentiment whose all-devouring ardor entirely deprived him of all presence of mind.[17]

Charles de Rémusat wrote that "this desperate, slightly senile passion completely dominated him, obsessed him, drove him mad, and was not without influence on public affairs."[18]

3

If London had moved to Paris that summer, so too had Vienna and Baden.

"Now nothing can prevent your coming to Paris," Charles Stewart had written Wilhelmine along with news of Waterloo. In the first week of August she was seen at a great dinner party Stewart gave in the Hôtel Montesquieu, where he had taken up quarters. "The new *régnante* at the court of Prince Charles," Harriet Granville called Wilhelmine. "Lord Stewart came in all over stars and tenderness. I hear there never was anything like his vanity and extravagance."[19]

Wilhelmine had brought fifteen-year-old Emilie with her to Paris: it was time the child saw something of the world. Emilie was growing up to be a delightful companion to Wilhelmine, attractive and bright, with a sharp observing eye, a sparkle of humor and mischief, and a decided flair for writing. The police agent in Baden assigned to watch the movements of Marie Louise, the Duchess of Sagan and other interesting personages, had reported to his chief of the presence in Wilhelmine's household of "a very pretty blond girl called Emilie. Orders have been given that she should pass as having been taken in and adopted by Sagan but she is in reality her natural daughter."[20]

Now in Paris in the warm August days they wandered about the shops, buying pretty things to wear and to furnish the manor house at Ratiborzitz. With Wilhelmine's old friends Wallmoden and Giamboni they dined in chic restaurants, or sat on the shaded terrace of the elegant cafés nibbling sorbets.

Wilhelmine sat for her portrait again to Gérard, this time in the deep green velvet ball gown in which she had appeared at Congress balls, and wearing the Order of Louise the Prussian King had bestowed on her for her patriotic generosity during the late campaigns.

For Wilhelmine, as for Dorothée, the summer was not without complications.

Not only Charles Stewart but Alfred Windischgraetz had been waiting for her in Paris.

As Metternich had had reason to observe, as soon as a rival appeared on the scene, Alfred's flagging devotion at once flamed into new life. Now again he besieged Wilhelmine with anguished pleas, haunted her mother's house where she was staying, enacted scenes of anger and jealousy, deluged her afresh with letters of reproach and recrimination. This time, however, Wilhelmine was proof against the emotional assault. The time had come, she told him, "for a gentle transition from love to warmest friendship."

She reminded him of the previous autumn, the autumn of 1814, when she had sacrificed for his sake

> a love which had become only too deeply interwoven with my whole being, which might have lasted all my life. Nevertheless your return to me and your present attachment blotted out that bitter memory, and I follow now with pain the lesson of a dearly bought experience if I say to you today, dear Alfred, let us be friends and nothing but friends.[21]

Alfred's reproaches pursued Wilhelmine relentlessly, and in the middle of August she wrote him a final, definite letter. Yes, she had once loved him "with all the force of my soul," though his behavior toward her had been such that she should have broken with him long ago. Again she reminded him that she had sacrificed Metternich's love for his sake, "the inclination of my heart and the truest tenderest attachment that I have perhaps ever encountered." She ought never have made that sacrifice, that she knew now only too well; everyone in the world had a right to reproach her for her conduct—

everyone, that is, except Alfred. "Your behavior after that dealt a mortal blow to the love I devoted to you for so long. . . . So have these last 11 months passed."[22]

Now her reason had been restored to her. She must think of her future. Certainly in the back of her mind was the thought that she might marry Stewart. Her advice to Alfred was affectionate and sisterly. Often enough in the early months of their passion he had wounded her by speaking of marrying—but never of marrying her. Now the time had come for him to choose a wife, for the sake of his family whose chief he was, and for himself. "Look for a companion for your life," she wrote, adding tenderly, "It is so easy to love you that you will have an easy choice." And she ended her letter: "Be happy and never forget the friend whose love—so often undervalued—went with you through the years of your youth, and whose faithful attachment to you will last to the end of life."[23]

Wounded and bitter, Alfred lingered on in Paris, hunting with Wellington and gambling recklessly at the Cercle des Étrangers.

Certainly Metternich's path often crossed Wilhelmine's that summer, at dinner parties and in the restaurants and boutiques to which he had introduced her the previous year. He knew very nearly every inch of Paris—at least the cosmopolitan heart of the city. This summer it was his cousin Flora Wrbna and her friend Theresa Jablonowska whom he shepherded about Paris, to the museums and shops and to dine in the fashionable restaurants. They helped him fill the long lists of purchases Laure had requested—"little embroidered babies' bonnets," batiste from Madame Rolland in the rue St. Honoré, blue levantine, white and pistachio bengaline from Chez Pradel, several dozen pairs of gloves and two theater costumes.

No doubt they also shopped for the Empress, who had asked her husband to send her from Paris the latest fashion magazines and stockings from a pattern she enclosed, admonishing him not to pay "over 100 gulden the pair." An imperial price for ladies' stockings!

Gentz too appeared presently in Paris, summoned from the "state of perfect tranquillity," in which he had been enjoying his country villa on the outskirts of Vienna that summer.

His pockets lined with Congress gold, he could afford to travel in luxury, two big carriages carrying his necessary household with him, the beloved Karl Leiden and his cook Bastien going on ahead to see to the preparation of gourmet meals in the inns and the laying of fine linen on the beds, while Gentz himself followed in a second carriage, his valet, a chasseur and his big dog on the box outside, himself cozily ensconced within, in solitary splendor, reading all the way to Paris.

Fearful of crossing western France, where there was still rumor of possible violence, Gentz made a wide detour all the way to Brussels, entering France in the wake of the English army, and passing himself off as an English officer.

The journey from Vienna to Paris, ordinarily a matter of seven days—Metternich had made it more than once in five—took Gentz two full weeks.

Metternich introduced him at once to the culinary pleasures of the great restaurants, to promenades along the boulevards and the quais, and to his favorite tailor and bootmaker. The August days were filled with receptions and dinners and even more engaging forms of entertainment. With Count Schulenburg Gentz visited a well-known bordello, going on immediately afterward to a supper and ball at the Castlereaghs'. At the Théâtre du Vaudeville Gentz and Dalberg ogled a pair of saucy soubrettes dressed up as lady guardsmen in satin-tight uniforms, sent a note backstage proposing a rendezvous and were turned down—but politely and in writing.

4

One distinguished visitor to Paris that summer took in none of the pleasures of the social season.

The Tsar, reported the gossipy Lady Granville, had returned to Paris a changed man. The frivolity of the French shocked him. "He has only been into society three times, has taken a new and grave line, goes walking in his garden and only with the ugly and the old."[24]

At Heilbronn in army headquarters in early June, the Tsar had undergone a profound religious experience, and he was now deeply involved with the preacher-mystic, Julie von Krüdener.

He had reached Heilbronn on the night of June 4, in one of the periodic pits of depression to which he was subject. He sat alone that night in a room in the house that had been taken for him, his Bible open on the table before him. "I thought," he recalled later, "what a consolation the conversation of a pious friend would have been at such a moment." He remembered what he had heard of Madame Krüdener, how she believed that he was destined for some divine mission in the world. "Where can she be at this moment?" he wondered.

The thought had barely flashed through his mind when an aide-de-camp knocked to say that a lady insisted on seeing him at that very late hour, and that nothing would induce her to go away. It was Julie von Krüdener.

Far into the night they talked. She reminded him of his sins of spiritual pride, urged him to put his life in the hands of Christ. Over and over she told him he had been singled out to lead all of Europe into a new religious age. The Tsar sat, head in hands, shedding silent tears.[25]

Barbara Julie von Krüdener, from an aristocratic Baltic family, had been barely eighteen when she married a Russian diplomat twice her age. Intelligent, ambitious, gifted, she found domestic and diplomatic duties intolerably stifling. She left her husband to embark on a series of love affairs and to write a romantic confessional novel, *Valérie*.

Sitting in a window of her house in Riga one day, she saw an admirer tip his hat to her and drop dead in the street. From that day on, so the story went, she had turned to religion.

More likely, having tried her hand at writing and finding that she had nothing more to say in that vein, she turned to another of the very few avenues in which women could achieve celebrity: that of religious mystic. Julie had imagination, charisma and a burning desire to carve a heroic role for herself in the world. She decided on the regeneration of the Christian Church, to be accomplished with the aid of the Tsar of Russia.

Her visit that night in Heilbronn was no accident. In February she had written to Mademoiselle Sturdza, a lady-in-waiting of the Tsarina, that she had important things to tell the Tsar, although "the Prince of Darkness will do all in his power to prevent it." In April she reminded her friend that she had predicted Napoleon's return from Elba six months earlier, as well as the flight of the Bourbons.

In Heilbronn the Tsar confessed to her his deep anxiety about beginning another war without knowing for sure whether it was the will of God. Julie, who was no pacifist and to whom Napoleon was the devil incarnate, could reassure the Tsar on that count. When the delegation of liberal members from the French Chamber of Deputies appeared at headquarters after Waterloo to ask the Allied sovereigns to support either the Duc d'Orléans or a regency, Julie advised the Tsar to turn down their overtures.[26] A letter assenting to the Bourbon restoration went to Fouché, signed by Nesselrode and Metternich.

When the Tsar traveled on to Paris, he arranged for Julie von Krüdener and her party to follow, engaging a mansion for them near the Élysée Palace. Often in the evening he would slip out of a garden door of the Élysée and, accompanied only by a valet, be at Madame Krüdener's in a few minutes to spend the evening in Bible reading and prayer.

Julie von Krüdener was in her element that summer and her religious salon was the most fashionable in Paris.

Evening after evening in her austere, dimly lighted rooms, without carpets or pictures or mirrors, and with only straw-seated peasant chairs for her guests, Julie von Krüdener practiced what Chateaubriand called her "celestial sorceries."

Poets, writers and generals, duchesses and princesses, flocked to the Hôtel Montchenu to hear the famous Madame Krüdener preach and pray in her soft, sweet, persuasive voice.

Not all her guests that summer were as easily swayed as the Tsar. Perhaps the reasonableness of the French mind resists evangelism. Madame Récamier refused to go, and even Chateaubriand confessed that when he wanted to pray, "the devil pushed me to laugh. . . . I liked Madame de Krüdener better when, surrounded by flowers and still living on this miserable earth, she composed Valérie."[27]

One morning, as Madame Krüdener expatiated to a gathering of enthralled listeners on the divine virtues of the Tsar, citing the courage with which he had recently severed his sixteen-year-old liaison with Madame Narischkin, one of the Frenchmen present, Elzéar de Sabran, could not refrain from commenting dryly, "But it's much easier to give up a liaison of sixteen years than one of sixteen days!"

Princess Bagration, who had managed to pacify her creditors, visited the Krüdener salon. But Wilhelmine, whose family were old friends of Julie's, did not appear. Nor did Metternich. He accepted enlightened Catholicism as part of the institutional framework of life, but he had an innate distaste for extremes, whether in religion or in politics.

5

In August Laure Metternich and the children moved from Baden back to the Chancellery, where Laure would await the birth of her child. "My big stomach does not allow me to stay long in one place, and this child is a real devil if I don't shake him up a bit," she wrote.[28] She had hoped Clemens would be back from Paris with the final peace signed and sealed before the child was born, but that event seemed less and less likely.

Nearly every day twelve-year-old Victor went across the square to play with the little King of Rome.

> He has been there several times already [Laure informed her husband] and the little one seems to be very fond of him. He always says when he leaves, "I hope, Monsieur de Metternich, that you will want to play with me again." Victor says he couldn't be nicer and perfectly brought up. Besides Victor enjoys himself like a king there. [The child] has four horses almost life-size and toys made of gold which the little one says he got from his aunt, Princess Pauline.[29]

Two of the little boy's aunts were in Austria just then—Elisa at Brünn, Caroline Murat at Hainburg; the police were watching them closely and they were not given passports to Vienna.

His grandfather, Emperor Franz, had already warned his mother that she would probably have to leave her child behind when she went to Parma, for his own safety's sake. "He has many enemies—you know what I mean," he had written Marie Louise. In Paris in August the White Terror —reprisals of Bourbonists against Bonapartists—was already in progress. La Bédoyère, the young general who had gone over to Napoleon at Grenoble, had been shot, and Ney was about to be court-martialed and sentenced to death.

So Emperor Franz would not have a grandson on the throne of France. What to do with the boy now? Empress Maria Ludovica proposed making him a priest; that would take care of Napoleonic blood threatening future thrones. But Emperor Franz merely wrote his daughter that summer, "We must make an honorable and good person out of him."[30]

On the last night in August, having written Clemens to send her a half dozen bottles of orange water from Paris, Laure went to bed as usual.

The next day Marie, bursting with the joy of her wonderful news, could write her father in Paris:

> Maman was very happily delivered last night of a big baby, only it is not at all a Hermann, *mon cher Papa*, it is a little girl. Schmidt went to bed last night thinking Maman would not go into labor until today. At one o'clock Maman began to feel pains and at 3 o'clock everything was over. She feels marvelous. I just came from seeing her and the little one, who looks more like five weeks old than five hours. She is fatter than Leontine with big dark blue eyes.[31]

By September 5 Laure could take pen herself and write her husband:

> God be praised, here I am in a state able to tell you myself that I am perfectly well. Everything has been for the best, *très cher ami*. Hermine is a real little angel and is getting along beautifully. . . . She is sweet with her little eagle's nose, which truth to tell, is not really so small. . . . I am sure she will resemble you.

But her husband would be deeply disappointed, Laure feared, that she had borne another girl. They had lost two little boys, and on Victor's frail head rested the future of the Metternich clan. "She has only one fault that we both know," Laure wrote sorrowfully, "but then God willed it so."[32]

Marie would not agree. When her mother asked her to add a postscript to one of her letters telling Clemens that the superb camisole and bonnet he had sent from Paris "are much too fine for a person who had the misfortune to bear only a little girl," Marie could not help scribbling her indignation:

> Maman makes acts of contrition as if Hermine were a sin that you would never pardon her. Hermine a sin! Hermine is an angel, that's all there is to it! Maman says to tell you she won't put on the camisole until the day the Empress comes to see her.[33]

A letter arrived promptly by the next courier from Paris that put an end to Laure's fears. Clemens was overjoyed that her confinement had gone safely, and delighted at the birth of another daughter.

"I am much relieved," Laure replied, "to see how well you take the birth of my good charming little treasure whom I already love madly."[34]

Laure recovered quickly from this, her last confinement. But it had as always drained her strength; she went about white as a ghost and painfully thin. She thought wistfully that she must look well by the time her husband returned. When Marie wrote reporting on her mother's health and her own joyful anticipation of the coming journey to Italy, she added, "Maman tells me, dear Papa, that she would like to have a pot of rouge from Mademoiselle Martin, in a blond color. Adieu, I embrace you thousands and thousands of times."[35]

A few days later the Empress came to call on mother and child, Maria

Ludovica looking even paler and more haggard than Laure. "I found her melancholy," Laure wrote. "One could see clearly how a little baby would make her happy."

The night after the Empress's visit to the new baby, Marie wrote dubiously, "You will see, dear Papa, that she will either die on the eve of our departure or else somewhere along the way."[36]

No one knew what caused the dreaded "lung sickness." Most people blamed it on "bad air" and dampness and kept their windows tight shut.

So the young, mortally ill Empress bent over the cradle of the infant Hermine, the Metternich children dutifully kissed her hand, and Marie traveled all the way to Italy with her, where the Empress was to join her husband for a ceremonial journey and Marie to meet her father.

6

The Russian army had finally assembled in France, and in mid-September the Tsar celebrated his name day with a military-religious spectacle on the plains of Vertus, some eighty miles east of Paris.

In a burning sun, Wilhelmine and Dorothée—"more commanded than invited to attend," Humboldt said—watched the review on horseback, along with the sovereigns and generals, while their mother and other ladies who did not ride were ensconced in armchairs under a canopy. On the vast plain, not far from where the spring campaign of 1814 had been fought, some 150,000 Russian troops maneuvered with the precision of machinery, ending with a simulated battle scene.

At the end of the performance, in huge tents set up in the gardens of a nearby château, the Tsar gave a lucullan banquet for his three hundred distinguished guests. The magnificent meal prepared by Chef Carême—lent to the Tsar for the summer—had demanded almost as much energy and organization as the maneuvers themselves. Furnaces and ovens had been hastily built in the barns and courtyards of the château, a whole ice factory bought and moved to the spot; forty cooks, a herd of cattle and innumerable wagonloads of food, wine, linen, silver, porcelain and cooking vessels—all had to be brought from Paris a week before. Among delicacies served that day were fresh oysters, truffled boar's heads in aspic, salmis of partridge in Bordeaux wine, hot and cold soups, twenty-eight different entrées and a dozen desserts. One of the harassed chef's most difficult problems had been to prevent the incursion of Cossacks, who—used to foraging for themselves—did not mind in the least robbing the Tsar's own commissary.[37]

The day following the military review, September 11, was the Tsar's name day and the climax of the fete.

All 150,000 troops gathered in the fields around seven great altars, while the Tsar solemnly led Madame Krüdener, bare-headed, dressed in a long, dark gown as "the ambassadress of Heaven," from one to another of the altars. Mass was sung simultaneously at all seven altars, while the Tsar, his prophetess nearby, consecrated his armies to God. It was, said Alexander, "the most beautiful day of my life."

Vertus was only the beginning, Julie told him, "the living preface of this holy history which is to regenerate everything." The Tsar must proclaim in public his vow to replace worldly politics by the politics of the sacred. The climax was to be Julie von Krüdener's plan for founding a new church.

The Tsar had long been contemplating some written act that would bind the sovereigns together in a kind of mystical brotherhood dedicated to peace. During Christmas week of 1814 he had sketched out such a pledge, and he had intended to present it to his brother sovereigns to sign on New Year's Day. But the Saxony issue was at a boiling point; it was scarcely the moment for such a pledge when the King of Prussia was on the verge of going to war.

During the week after the Vertus review, the Tsar wrote out his act of alliance, based "on the sublime truths which the Holy Religion of Our Saviour teaches." In Madame Krüdener's candlelighted salon he read the draft aloud and asked her guests to join him in prayer that his Allies would sign.[38]

Neither Metternich, Gentz nor Humboldt had attended the Vertus gathering. Gentz was busy drawing up with Capo d'Istria the final peace treaty, and on September 12 Metternich and Gentz enjoyed a very lively dinner party at Véry's, which included Lady Caroline Lamb and her husband, the French actress Mademoiselle Mars, Ferdinand Palffy, Prince Reuss and the Duke of Wellington.

A few days later Emperor Franz with a long face handed Metternich the Tsar's document, the original draft of the Holy Alliance—"a loud-sounding nothing," in Metternich's opinion, "a piece of sublime mystical nonsense," according to Castlereagh. Metternich tried his hand at editing it, but he had the greatest difficulty persuading the Tsar to alter a word.[39]

That week Alexander invited Metternich to dine with him and Madame Krüdener. When Metternich arrived at the Élysée, he was ushered into a small dining room where four places were set at the table. The three seated themselves and the Tsar observed Metternich looking in bewilderment at the fourth place. "That is laid for our fourth guest," the Tsar informed him. "You will not guess who it is so I shall tell you. It is Our Lord Jesus Christ."[40]

On September 26, in a spirit of resignation, Emperor Franz and the King of Prussia put their signatures on the Holy Alliance. Two days later the Tsar left Paris for St. Petersburg.

7

Once again Metternich's calculations of the time needed for peacemaking proved to be widely off margin. He had reckoned on six weeks to complete the Second Peace of Paris; it took four months.

France would not get off so lightly as before. All four Allies agreed that

France must this time bear the cost of the recent war and must contribute her share to the greater security of Europe.

But what stirred the French more bitterly than anything else was the decision to restore to the countries of origin the art objects Napoleon had collected from all over Europe. "Plundering the plunder," the Englishman Croker called it.

The Prussians, without waiting for a treaty, packed up everything they claimed and hustled it off in wagonloads to Berlin. French workmen refused to remove paintings and sculpture from the Louvre. When a group of English soldiers and civilians were deputed to take down the bronze horses of St. Mark's Square in Venice, which Napoleon had mounted on a triumphal arch in the Place du Carrousel, a troop of National Guard and a furious mob intervened and a regiment of Austrian infantry had to be called out in force.

Wellington, who had been greeted everywhere with cheers of "*Vive Vellington!*" in the early occupation days, was hissed when he appeared at the opera and hardly dared show himself on the streets for fear of being assassinated.

The trouble in the Louvre took place on September 19; that night Talleyrand gave a large dinner party with the most elegant ladies of his acquaintance gracing the dinner table. All through the dinner Talleyrand and Wellington argued and shouted furiously at each other across the table. "Stormiest of scenes," Gentz reported—an unusual evening for the usually cool Wellington.[41]

The Tsar, meantime, fresh from the inspiration of the Vertus dedication, had resolved to begin his religious regeneration of French politics. The King had already rid himself of Fouché. Now the Tsar proposed that the King dismiss Talleyrand.

A day or two after his stormy dinner party Talleyrand paid a call on the King to ask his unequivocal support in protesting the proposed peace treaty. Otherwise, he added in the customary formal phrasing of such visits, he would be forced to resign. The King was prepared. "Very well," Louis replied airily, "I accept your resignation."

Stunned, Talleyrand bowed his way out. He was replaced as Foreign Minister by a trusted friend of the Tsar, the Duc de Richelieu, who had spent the years of emigration as governor of Odessa. "A splendid choice"—Talleyrand grimaced bitterly—"certainly the Frenchman who best understands the Crimea."

It was not Talleyrand's worst blow in those weeks of autumn.

Toward the end of September Wilhelmine left for Italy, taking Emilie with her. Stewart was to meet her there, and her sister, Pauline Hohenzollern, was already waiting in Milan.

A week or two later Dorothée followed. Clam was already in Milan with Schwarzenberg. She would spend some weeks there, then journey back to

Vienna with Pauline. She might decide to settle in Vienna, she thought; the city still held for her all the glamor and brilliance of Congress days.

Talleyrand was devastated. He fell at once, according to Pasquier, "into a mental and physical dejection impossible to describe." Hardly had Dorothée left Paris, Count Molé wrote, than Talleyrand "began to wither, to change and to waste away. . . . It was a curious thing to see him, a sixty-year-old man, devoured by a slow fever caused by the absence of a mistress, and to begin to die, quite literally, of disappointed love."[42]

At the Duc de Richelieu's on November 20 the Second Treaty of Paris was finally signed. France was reduced further to her boundaries of 1790, but kept Alsace and Lorraine, which the Prussians had proposed severing. She was saddled with an indemnity of seven hundred million francs and the support of an army of occupation for five years.

Gentz, who had put together the treaty draft, blamed Prussia and England for the harshness of the terms. "Humboldt on one side and Castlereagh on the other," he wrote Nesselrode, who had by then left Paris, "have exhausted every kind of harsh condition, precaution and chicanery to extort from this miserable government the last reparation for every grief Napoleon brought to Europe."[43]

On the same day, prompted by Castlereagh, the four Allies signed a Quadruple Alliance to guarantee the European order as the Vienna Congress and the Second Paris Treaty had shaped it. The Alliance banned forever the succession to power in France either of Bonaparte or "of any of his race"—certainly at Castlereagh's insistence. The little King of Rome would be perpetually exiled from the land of his birth; any dreams of a regency were effectively prohibited.

Certainly the most important section of the treaty was the celebrated Article VI, decreeing that in place of secret bilateral diplomacy, which had led to so many wars in the past, all the powers would meet together in congresses at regular intervals to decide matters of international importance. For the first time in history the idea of group decision making on an international level was written into a binding international agreement.

Years later Metternich claimed for himself that invention of international cabinet meetings, and undoubtedly credit for that vital step in the history of peacemaking procedures does belong to him.

Discussed also in those November days was an "Office of Europe," to be established at Vienna, where problems of a European nature might be handled during the periods between the congress meetings. Gentz, it was suggested, might act as a kind of executive secretary to the Concert of Powers with the title "Secretary-General of Europe." Talleyrand, though out of power and without voice in the government of France, seconded the idea "with much spirit and verve."[44]

There was, finally, a flourish of farewell parties. At the very last conference on November 22 the little group of diplomats who had shared so much since the summer of 1813, when they had met at Ratiborzitz, who had argued together and fought and intrigued and finally put together three important treaties, bade one another "tender adieus."

A little after Saturday midnight Metternich's traveling carriage, with Metternich and Floret and Giroux, rolled out of the courtyard of the Décrès mansion bound for Switzerland and Italy. Emperor Franz had already gone on ahead to Venice, and Marie was to meet him shortly.

Gentz lingered a few days longer in Paris, collecting another batch of jeweled snuffboxes, and making last-minute purchases that would fill two transport wagons.

"Finita la commedia!" he wrote in his diary on his last night in Paris.

CENTRAL EUROPE IN 1815 AFTER THE VIENNA CONGRESS

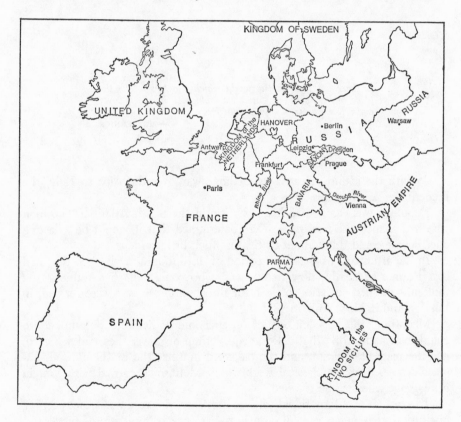

XXVI

BIEDERMEIER FINALE

Is there anything in the world which can today take the place of ink, pens, a conference table with its green cover and a few greater or smaller bunglers?

—METTERNICH

1

So with the sound of carriages rattling away over the Alps to Italy, the Biedermeier Age began.

Napoleon was chained to his rocky isle in the South Atlantic. The men who had shaped the new peace were determined that it would be a lasting one. People could think about cultivating their little gardens.

In the aftermath of that long period of disruption and violence that had cost Europe so dearly—how many lives, who could tell? five million? ten million?—the first societies to work for the abolition of war were formed, in London and in New York, in 1816.

Meantime, the peacemakers of Vienna and Paris were determined to guard their handiwork, that delicate equilibrium of power they had achieved, like the magical equation and the balanced universe the mathematician Laplace described in the classical work which Metternich carried with him in his baggage wherever he traveled.

The system of international cabinet meetings, the very first peace-keeping institution to emerge out of a major war, began to operate—preventive mediation, they might have named it even then. The ministers and sovereigns met at Aachen in 1818, to remove their armies from France and to admit France to membership in the Cabinet. They met again—or some of them— at Karlsbad in 1819, at Troppau in 1820, at Laibach in 1821, at Verona in 1822—to take steps to preserve the fragile structure of their creation.

"There is no longer any such thing as distance in Europe," Metternich exulted with his usual optimism, "thanks to the resolution taken by the sovereigns of meeting in person, at places where they think they can act together for the common good."[1]

Gentz called theirs "diplomacy of the highway."

Unhappily, like a covey of clever surgeons working on the body of Europe, the statesmen had set all the fractures, but their splints kept the patient immobilized. There was no leeway for change in the treaties they had written. And as always, in war's aftermath, there was dissatisfaction, unrest, hope for change—and symptoms of violence.

In October of 1817 students from twelve German universities convened near Eisenach to celebrate the anniversary of the battle of Leipzig—enthusiastic young people for the most part, who wanted to see a truly united Germany take shape. Near the Wartburg, the castle where Martin Luther had hidden during a year of danger, they held sober ceremonies during the day, in the evening less sober ones. Into a huge bonfire they pitched books of a reactionary tinge, together with symbols of military authority—a corporal's stick, a pigtail and a pair of stays. It did not seem like a particularly revolutionary demonstration, but the conservative authorities shivered nervously. All their worst fears about student plots and rebellion seemed realized a year later when a young theological student, Karl Sand, assassinated the reactionary playwright August Kotzebue, who had probably been in the pay of Russia.

"I do not like people to kill in the name of their love of humanity," Metternich remarked when he learned of the murder. He was in Italy just then, in the spring of 1819, sojourning with Marie. The food at the Vatican, he wrote Laure, was wretched, cooked in oil rather than butter, but the fireworks "were the most beautiful I have ever seen."[2]

A series of episodes of violence and threatened violence followed the Kotzebue murder. In Paris the Duc de Berry, nephew of the King of France and a leader of the ultraconservative group, was assassinated as he left the opera. And in London in February of 1820 a plot to kill the entire English Cabinet was uncovered. Not long after, in St. Petersburg, the Semenovsky Guards regiment mutinied, refusing to obey a harsh commanding officer.

Were all the incidents related, the work of "radicals"—"carbonari," Metternich termed them—bent on overturning the existing order? Many thought so—Metternich and Gentz among them.

At Karlsbad in the summer of 1819 Metternich met the King of Prussia and dealt with the student groups and the German universities. Student societies were ordered disbanded, liberal professors were to be discharged, an overseer appointed for the universities, censorship imposed. In England the Six Acts of 1819 clamped down on traditional individual liberties. In France and Russia repressive acts followed the incidents of violence.

The statesmen and sovereigns, nervously glancing over their shoulders, hurried from one summit conference to another, considering what measures to take to preserve, as the famous Article VI of the Paris Treaty stipulated, "the repose and prosperity of Nations, and . . . the Peace of Europe."

Metternich would have been astonished to hear himself called "reactionary." He considered his own views moderate. "True friend of order and public peace," cool, composed, absolutely certain of the rightness of the measures he was taking, he drove about Europe, knowing that he himself went in daily danger of assassination. "My daily battle," he wrote, "is against the ultras of every sort, until finally the poniard of some fool reaches me too. If the fellow does not come at me from behind, he will get a box on the ears that he will remember for a long time—even if he strikes me."[3]

He traveled during those years, hundreds and thousands of miles, with Giroux and Floret, and sometimes Marie or Victor for company, crossing the Alpine passes with ice an inch thick on the carriage windows or inching through mud to the wheel rims. His curiosity and his zest for living were boundless.

In Italy he admired the flowers and the music and the fireflies, visited churches and galleries, artists' studios and marble quarries, collected paintings and sculpture for the long gallery of his villa, rare plants for the glasshouses.

He bought Canova's "Cupid and Psyche," and a copy of his "Venus," which he mounted on a pedestal in the middle of the library in the Chancellery apartments. On the evenings of great balls, when small round supper tables were set up in the library as well as the salons, Venus was apt to intrude herself into the conversation, Metternich noted with humor, for though her front view was of the utmost propriety, "the same cannot be said for the view from behind."

He never passed through Vicenza without going to look at the cool classical buildings of Palladio, so consonant with his own personality and taste.

At home, between long journeys to Italy, to Aachen, and shorter trips to Karlsbad and Königswart, he enjoyed his growing children, his chosen friends, the delightful society of Vienna. He no longer disliked the Austrian capital. "I am back again in my own good city," he wrote.

In the evenings in the Metternich salon his friends gathered. Laure presided at the tea table. Sometimes Marie played spirited waltzes on the piano and guests danced; such fast waltzes were danced in Vienna at that time that no more than three or four couples could whirl at once even in very large salons.

The Metternichs bought a charming house in Baden, and as a reward for his services during the Congress Emperor Franz presented Metternich in 1816 with the splendid estate and castle of Johannisberg on the Rhine, giving him again a pied-à-terre in the countryside of his birth.

In the heady air of peace there was a flurry of betrothals and marriages.

Empress Maria Ludovica had succumbed to tuberculosis on that first Italian journey in the spring of 1816—just as Marie Metternich had predicted. Metternich was helpful in replacing her promptly, with Bavarian Princess Charlotte, the wife discarded by Crown Prince Wilhelm of Württemberg so that he could marry Grand Duchess Catherine. Grateful to Metternich, the new Empress Karoline would be a firm supporter of his policies.

Marie Louise had her heart's desire—the duchy of Parma to rule, and Neipperg at her side. In the summer of 1817 Metternich accompanied the Emperor Franz's second daughter, Leopoldine, to her departure from Leghorn for Brazil, where she was to marry the Portuguese crown prince and eventually become Brazil's first empress.

From Italy he hurried back for a wedding that involved him much more deeply—that of his daughter Marie to Count Joseph Esterházy. It was a suitable match in every way: the young people appeared to be in love, the Esterházys belonged to the top layer of imperial society and were so rich that the couple were given two castles as a wedding present. But to lose this beloved daughter must have wrenched Metternich sorely. On the day of the wedding, September 19, he suffered an attack of hemorrhoids so excruciating that he could not attend the ceremony or the accompanying festivities.

2

Wilhelmine too spent much of the year traveling.

Part of the year she spent in Sagan, which, after the seven-year occupation by French troops, was, Emilie wrote, "like a cornfield after a hailstorm." The fine library of the castle had been looted; scarcely a single work remained whole. To help her restore the library she engaged the old and penniless poet Schink, a friend of her mother's, giving him a pension for life and an excuse to address romantic odes to her on every festive occasion.[4]

Some weeks she would spend in Ratiborzitz, and some weeks at the elegant spa of Karlsbad, where everyone who was anyone in Central Europe gathered to sip the healthful waters and enjoy languid, delightful days. Old friends, old acquaintances, old enemies—even old husbands. Goethe would be there, and Metternich, Schwarzenberg, even old Blücher, in one of his bouts of recurrent madness, going about patting his stomach and announcing that he was again pregnant with an elephant or a bull.

Louis Rohan would be there, dawdling in one or another drawing room —most often Wilhelmine's—and Alfred Windischgraetz, with or without his wife.

In November of 1816 Wilhelmine had addressed to Alfred the very last of the series of letters he kept carefully in the morocco-bound, gem-studded letter-box she had given him. It was a letter of congratulation and good wishes on his forthcoming marriage to Princess Eleonore Schwarzenberg, niece of the field marshal. "I must talk to you, dear Alfred, for the last time in this familiar tone, as I send you my warmest good wishes in the choice you have made." No one, she wrote, took a deeper interest in his happiness; she would always remain his affectionate friend.[5] It was a cool, proper marriage Alfred made, and there were children to carry on the Windischgraetz name. Alfred grew more reserved and proud as he grew older; "der Herrscher," the sovereign, his comrades called him.

The Stewart affair had come rather quickly to an end; Stewart's ungovernable temper, his jealousy and his possessiveness led to stormy scenes that were in the end too tedious. He returned to England, courted a very young orphaned heiress of very great fortune, Lady Frances Vane-Tempest, became embroiled in a lawsuit with her guardians over his conduct of the courtship; he won the lawsuit and eventually the bride.

Young men continued to congregate in Wilhelmine's drawing room— she did not lack for admirers: the Reuss princes, Felix Woyna, Baron Rosty, Count Karl Schulenburg, a major in Austrian service.

Toward the end of the summer, with her sisters Pauline and Jeanne, and her foster daughters Emilie and Marie and Clara Bressler, she would travel to her mother's estate of Löbichau in Saxony. The Duchess of Courland, growing old with remarkable grace, gathered around her each summer a lively house party of fifty or a hundred guests—all ages, of all ranks in society and a wide variety of interests. There were picnics and country excursions and informal balls in the evening, and once a poets' festival in the best romantic tradition, with the duchess crowned Queen of the Fairies.

The young people, with high-spirited Emilie and her cousin Fritz Piattoli as ringleaders, sat at a separate "cats' table" in the dining hall, laughed and flirted and dreamed up jokes and larks and hoaxes. Once they put on a comic ballet called "The Murder of Kotzebue," at which their elders, including Wilhelmine and her mother and sisters, "nearly died laughing."

In late autumn Wilhelmine and her foster daughters would travel on to Italy for a few weeks, returning to Vienna in time for the Fasching season.

Only Dorothée was absent from those summer gatherings at Löbichau.

The brief passion for Clam had burned itself out rather quickly. In February of 1816 she had made up her mind to return to Paris and Talleyrand. In the mansion on the Rue St. Florentin Dorothée reigned from that time on as Talleyrand's dearest friend and his political hostess until his death more than two decades later.

The scandalmongers of Paris enjoyed themselves thoroughly. Mistress of his salon, some sniffed—*bien! maîtresse tout court.* Plain mistress.

An English lady, Miss Mary Berry, visiting Paris that spring, regaled her sister back home with the latest Paris gossip:

> At twelve we left and went to Talleyrand's, that is to say, chez Countess Edmond de Périgord, his niece, whom he has separated from his nephew

to whom she was married (and from whom she made an *échappade* to Italy) and has taken her to live with himself *dans tout l'étendu du terme à ce qu'on dit*. Figurez-vous that she is not five-and-twenty and has a head more like a pretty serpent than anything I ever saw.[6]

Dorothée evidently meant to stay, Miss Berry added, for she had redone her apartments in Talleyrand's house. "They are getting back to India papers, old Indian china and Jars and white silk damask. . . . Everybody," she continued, "is wearing feathers here and their price is enormous."

Whether Dorothée lived with Talleyrand *dans tout l'étendu du terme*, as the titillated Miss Berry suggested, neither she nor he ever revealed. Certainly Dorothée laid down the terms of their relationship, and certainly Talleyrand extracted from her no such promise of eternal fidelity as Metternich had endeavored to impose on Wilhelmine. Dorothée obtained a legal separation from her husband—both were Roman Catholic, divorce was impossible—but in 1820 Edmond suddenly moved back under the Talleyrand roof and remained there until Dorothée bore a child, a daughter Pauline, to whom Talleyrand was deeply devoted all his life. After that Edmond departed, his debts paid, and never again lived under the same roof as Dorothée.[7]

When King Ferdinand of Naples rewarded Talleyrand for his support of the Bourbon cause at the Congress of Vienna, making him a present of the duchy of Dino, Talleyrand deeded it over to his nephew so that Dorothée could be elevated to the title of Duchess of Dino.

Count Molé wrote later on of Dorothée: "The dream of her imagination and the ambition of her whole life has been to govern a man of distinction, a man vested with great power. Nature has given her the talents to fill such a role, even to fill it brilliantly."[8] Yet this can scarcely have been the reason for Dorothée's return to Talleyrand in 1816, for he was out of power and it was impossible to predict whether at his age of sixty-two he would ever have an opportunity to return to a position of influence. "As remarkable for the subtlety of her mind as for the depravity of her heart," Gentz commented on Dorothée on the eve of her return to Paris.[9] But Gentz, hardly an unbiased judge of the "depravity of hearts," could not have understood that an intelligence like Dorothée's would find even such a nice young man as Clam unutterably boring beside the most complex and fascinating political brain in Europe.

My long acquaintance with Monsieur de Talleyrand's expressive powers [Dorothée wrote once] have made me difficult to please where the rest of the world is concerned. The minds I encounter now seem to be slow, diffused, too easily distracted by trivial details; they are forever putting their brakes on like people going cautiously downhill.[10]

Of the four gifted Courland sisters Dorothée was perhaps the one who lived the happiest and most fulfilled life. Able to make decisions and to live with them, able to maintain control over her life, she shaped her life to the greatest independence possible, stretched the limitations society imposed upon women to the utmost.

In the political life of the eighteen-twenties in France Dorothée was not without influence. When Talleyrand went to England as ambassador after the accession of the Duc d'Orléans as King Louis Philippe, Dorothée was at his side.

3

On the surface, at least, Clemens Metternich and Wilhelmine appeared to be friends. Whatever complex and unresolved feelings Metternich continued to harbor under that unruffled composure and appearance of casual indifference, they were certainly feelings he refused to admit to himself.

He sent her clippings from the English papers about Stewart's lawsuit; she wrote thanking him, adding that everything had turned out for the best in that affair, and would he—Metternich—please give her passports to Madame Trogoff to bring to Karlsbad, "for God knows if you will arrive in time to still find me there—if you were only a little more exact—one never knows where one is with you—except in friendship however and in the big things—." To another note she added affectionately, "Adieu, you know that for my peace of mind I must know that you love me a little and for my happiness I need to love you a great deal!" Leaving for Italy, she dashed off a note inviting herself to his house "for a cup of green tea and a chicken wing for my supper."[11]

Yet for Metternich the wounds of that relationship had never quite healed; a kind of festering scar remained on his psyche.

Between Clemens and Wilhelmine there was a last explosive scene that revealed finally how deep had been the roots of his passion for her, how profound the torment of the parting, how unhealed the damage to his ego.

At Karlsbad in the summer of 1818 Wilhelmine hovered anxiously over the sickbed of her seventeen-year-old foster daughter, Clara Bressler, gravely ill with "nerve-fever," while a suitor of long standing, Prince Heinrich Reuss, hovered in the wings, beseeching Wilhelmine to marry him. "She doesn't know what to do," Metternich wrote Laure of Wilhelmine that summer, "pulled this way and that by the despair of her sister and by the continuing proposals of Reuss, by her own desire to marry and just as much her fear of it. She wants to and she doesn't want to; in the end she will [marry] and then no longer want the one she chooses. There you have the last act of the story of her life, all the chapters of which resemble each other more or less."[12]

When Clara was well enough to travel, Wilhelmine took her to Italy. Reuss followed in pursuit. In Florence in November Clara grew ill again and died—a shattering grief to Wilhelmine, who had adopted the girl when she was small, and who, as the years passed, had grown more deeply into the role of mother to her three foster daughters.

Metternich, meantime, had left Karlsbad to journey to the Rhineland, to see his new prize, Castle Johannisberg, for the first time, and continue on to Aachen for the first of the postwar congresses. Everyone had been in the best of tempers, there had been no tension, agreement had been reached even with the Tsar; it had been, in fact, "the prettiest little congress you ever saw."

One evening at a reception at the Nesselrodes', Metternich found himself talking about Napoleon with Dorothea Lieven, wife of the Russian ambassador to England. A few days later the Nesselrodes planned an overnight excursion to Spa. Whether by accident or design the carriage parties were switched on the way home, and instead of returning with her husband, Dorothea found herself riding tête-à-tête with Metternich on the three-hour journey to Aachen. A few days later she came to his rooms.

Princess Dorothea Lieven, with her long, slender neck and shrewd dark eyes, was not so much pretty as distinguished-looking, not so much charming as sharp and sophisticated. She had a gift for amusing conversation, a flair for intrigue; like Clemens Metternich she was cosmopolitan and political to the fingertips.

They were briefly together that autumn in Aachen and Brussels; then she and her husband returned to London, Metternich to Vienna. They saw one another only twice again, at Hanover in 1821, at Verona in 1822; they exchanged long, affectionate, conversational letters, filled with bits of gossip and the political matter of their daily lives. Since they had few common acquaintances and little common frame of reference apart from international politics, both wrote a great deal about themselves—especially Metternich. It was, in fact, a liaison of the diplomatic pouch.

Writing her immediately after his return from Aachen, he adjured her "to be nice to her husband." She took his advice and promptly became pregnant, whereupon he wrote advising her on proper prenatal care. He asked her to look out during her visits to English country houses for rare plants and to send him bulbs or seeds for his Rennweg garden. Dorothea, understanding better the landscape of cities, hardly knew one plant from another. She sent him a pencil and a ring too big for his finger, which he had to wear on his watch chain. They never knew one another very well. Even across the great distances that separated them, Dorothea was easily aroused to jealousy by the mere mention of a woman's name in a letter of Metternich's; he must often have compared her unwillingly to Wilhelmine who was never jealous, who understood all about gardens and knew how to choose gifts.

Hardly had Metternich returned to Vienna in December of 1818 when rumors began to reach him of an affair the Duchess of Sagan was said to be carrying on in Italy with Paul Esterházy. Esterházy, having left his post as Austrian ambassador to England the previous summer, had appeared in Karlsbad, temporarily estranged from his wife. Metternich had not invited

Paul to accompany him to Aachen, as would have been natural, perhaps as a discreet kind of knuckle rapping for leaving his London post without permission. Paul retaliated by going off to Italy; it was said that he had followed Wilhelmine to Florence, then Rome, then Naples, and would soon follow her back to Vienna.

When Wilhelmine returned the first week of January 1819, Metternich went to see her at once—not a visit of friendly welcome but one of outrage. For some reason it infuriated him to think that Paul Esterházy could win her affections—Paul who, as he wrote more than once, stood in the place of a son to him. Confronting Wilhelmine that day Metternich turned on his astonished friend the full force of his long-suppressed rage and bitterness. He railed at her lack of self-control, of will-power, though why her affair with Esterházy differed from his with Lieven does not emerge from his account of the scene.

> I made her weep bitter tears over her conduct. She wept convincingly as happens to her as often as I tell her the truth—and tomorrow she will begin new follies.[13]

Writing Princess Lieven of the confrontation, he called the affair with Wilhelmine "one of my madnesses—I have had few in my life, but I admit to that one because it was so pronounced." The duchess was, he told his new friend

> a person of strong conscience, infinitely sane judgment, of almost imperturbable physical serenity. Eh bien! she commits nothing but follies. She sins seven times a day; she behaves like a mad person and she loves the way one dines.[14]

From that time in his life, the period of his love for her, remained only "a feeling of pain and disgust that I can feel but not describe."

Fragments only of the truth of the relationship appeared in the bitter letters he sent off to Dorothea in London. That it had been Wilhelmine's enduring love for Alfred, her unwillingness to belong exclusively to Metternich as he had demanded, that had brought about the rupture, Metternich did not reveal. Forced to choose, she had chosen Alfred. That blow to his ego Metternich had never accepted.

> Several of my friends who knew the secret [he wrote Dorothea Lieven] could not understand how I could be in love with her. I never was. It was my impossible enterprise I loved and clung to; I abandoned her as a mathematician abandons the solution of squaring the circle. I was out of my mind as a mathematician is when he tries to solve a problem that has no solution.
>
> These same friends could not understand why I did not quarrel to the point of drawing a knife with this woman. I did not quarrel with her because I did not value her enough for that. I do not hate her, for I never loved her.[15]

When Paul Esterházy returned to Vienna from Regensburg, whither Wilhelmine had apparently sent him to try for a reconciliation with his wife, Metternich gave him a stern dressing down—"he's a good boy but he always proceeds without knowing why or how," he wrote of Paul. Clemens gave the young man such good advice as persons in love rarely take. "I had a long serious talk with him and for the moment he is again reasonable."[16]

Metternich could not get Wilhelmine out of his mind. He was obsessed by the ghost of a passion he could not completely exorcise. He wrote Lieven again, a long letter with a much more detailed account of the affair. Wilhelmine, he wrote,

> is clearly mad. . . . I made her acquaintance at least fifteen or sixteen years ago. She was married and she did not want to be any longer. She divorced in order to remarry. Her chosen husband ceased being her lover or even her friend on the day of the marriage. She wanted me as a lover. I did not want to be. She took up with a boring Englishman, Monsieur King. A short time after her liaison began she did not want him any longer and she returned to me. I wanted an affair with her as little the second time as the first.
>
> At the end of three years she took a new lover, only to detest him the day after the affair began. That is when I took her as one takes what one does not love and even what one cares nothing about. . . . She kept her lover for the sake of form. I was free and bored. I saw her when and how I wished. She loved me because I did not love her. At the end of several years I found her free and unhappy. I saw a great deal of her and she asked me if I did not want to enter into more formal relations. I proposed a capitulation: I asked her for six months of fidelity. I felt myself called to maintain her in it: I thought I would do her good in securing peace of mind for her. I never loved her, but I loved the pains I gave to the enterprise. I ended up a bankrupt!
>
> I saw that of all the elements the least possible to meet in her was fidelity. . . . I broke to return no more. The day after the rupture Madame de Sagan wanted to kill herself; I remained faithful to my intent—and she did not commit suicide.
>
> There is the tale of my romance with her; judge for yourself if I ever loved her—judge what I ought to experience today on her behalf! My friends could not understand how I did not hate her. That is because hate is not in me and to hate one must love oneself more than one loves others.[17]

Over those letters from her new lover, of whom she knew so little, Princess Lieven cast an appraising and jealous eye. She could not doubt that much lingered still of his old intense passion for the Duchess of Sagan. Why else would the duchess's new amour trouble him so profoundly? Why else had he exploded in that angry confrontation? Why else did he explain over and over again in letters of ten and twelve pages precisely how indifferent he was to her?

In vain Metternich tried to reassure his new mistress by long distance.

"What could have frightened you in what I told you of Madame de S. ? . . . Madame de S. is no longer a living creature for me, and I do not consider her any longer a creature of reason. She is no more than an object of disgust."[18]

From Wilhelmine's side we know nothing of that angry encounter in January of 1819. Certainly, whatever Metternich had said must have wounded her cruelly. If she had attempted to explain the circumstances in Florence— her grief over her daughter's death, Paul's estrangement from his wife, her isolation and loneliness—two old friends, at loose ends emotionally, consoling one another perhaps—Clemens' anger had not allowed him to listen.

When she left Vienna that spring for Ratiborzitz, then Karlsbad and Löbichau, Wilhelmine had made two decisions. One was that Vienna could no longer be her home.

In Karlsbad that summer rumors spread that the Duchess of Sagan had broken with Paul Esterházy and that she would remarry. The little spa buzzed with the scandal of her choice: Count Karl Schulenburg, seven years younger than she, a major in the Austrian Army and an adjutant to Prince Schwarzenberg, one of the young men who had been dancing attendance on her but had hardly aspired to win her hand. Since only a single career—marriage—was open to women, for a lady of high rank like the duchess to marry down was a clear admission of failure, a loss of status. Such a marriage, Metternich thought, would be "the stupidest, most foolish of all her follies." And he added:

> Of all the men I know [Schulenburg] is least suited to remain even for a year the husband of the Duchess. He is weak, a good fellow, patient and yielding, while to be husband to this woman he needs to have above all other qualities an iron hand, energy, yes, even a kind of impudence.[19]

Early in October Wilhelmine wrote Metternich that she would indeed remarry; it was a serious letter, containing promises for her future life, a kind of "moral testament." In his reply Metternich wrote that he forgave her all the grief she had caused him, and while he knew of no pain he had given her, he asked her pardon just the same. He advised her to be faithful to this man she had chosen. "I feel sorry for Schulenburg," he wrote to Lieven, "if he is marrying her for love. If it is only for self-interest then I despise him."[20]

In Löbichau on an autumn afternoon, wearing a gray silk traveling dress and a white silk hat, Wilhelmine married Karl Schulenburg. Her sisters and her foster daughters wept through the ceremony; they did not believe it would be a happy match. "I cried my heart out," Emilie recalled of the wedding; it was not only in rank that Schulenburg did not equal her mother, but far more importantly, Emilie thought, he lacked her mother's intelligence and largeness of character. Pauline Hohenzollern tried to console her nieces. Their Mama needed a man to look out for her, Schulenburg was not a bad fellow; he had a good head for administration and money matters and would be very useful in looking after Wilhelmine's estates; though seven years younger than she, he was much more experienced—"at least in financial affairs," Pauline added, laughing.[21]

For seven years Wilhelmine did not set foot in Vienna, and if her path crossed Metternich's in those years, it is not recorded. When she and Schulenburg and one or both of her daughters traveled from Sagan to Löbichau to Italy, they by-passed the Austrian capital.

3

During the years of Wilhelmine's absence, the first half of the decade of the eighteen-twenties, a series of terrible tragedies laid waste Metternich's personal life.

Marie had married happily. His other children were growing up and were, as always, a delight to the proud father. Only the youngest, Hermine, gave the parents cause for concern; she had suffered from "bone scrofula" as an infant, which left her lame in one foot.

Metternich's second daughter, Clementine, was a child of such entrancing beauty that people turned to stare at her in the street, which always made her think she had her hat awry or had put on shoes that did not match. "She will soon be fifteen, that age the poets sing, and offers charms only to my eyes," the father wrote.[22] In the summer of 1819 in Baden the English portrait painter Sir Thomas Lawrence had begged the parents to allow him to paint their daughter, and he had depicted her as an enchanting Hebe in an Olympus of clouds and flowers.

But in the winter of 1819 to 1820 Clementine fell gravely ill of lung sickness—clearly consumption, the disease that ravaged the nineteenth century as smallpox had the eighteenth. The doctors treated her with leeches on her chest and throat; for her fever they bled her again and again until she was exhausted and half delirious.

In early May of 1820 the portrait Lawrence had begun in summer arrived from his studio in Italy. The distracted parents could not bear to look at it, but Clementine begged that it be placed near her bed where she could see it. "This, however, we could not do; life and death cannot be placed so close together."[23]

Clementine died on May 11. Metternich spent himself in his work "as one might empty a cup of poison."

There was worse in store.

Hardly had Clementine been carried north to the family tomb in Königswart in Bohemia when Marie began to show symptoms of the same terrible illness. Apparently she had been pregnant and had miscarried. She became pale and thin and listless; her husband brought her to Baden where her mother could care for her.

In July of that year, 1820, only two months after Clementine's death, as Metternich returned from a visit to the Emperor, a messenger met him two post stops out of Vienna with news of Marie's death.

No other loss in his life struck so deeply as the loss of this eldest daughter who had been the joy of his life.

His grief was savage. Despite Laure's pleas he sold the house in Baden almost at once, "the place where I lost half my life." He would never cross the threshold again. Such places, he thought, should be

> leveled to the ground; they should not only be uninhabited but the last trace of them destroyed . . . covered with thorns and high grass like a wilderness, the only picture that has any resemblance to my heart.[24]

He threw himself into his work now, "like a desperate man on the enemies' batteries." He vowed, "Henceforth duty will take the place of life."[25]

Half a year later he wrote Laure, "How I loved that child! She for her part loved me more than a father. For long years she has been my best friend."[26]

He noticed that his hair had turned quite white.

Fearful for the lives of the other children, all of whom suffered bronchial illnesses in the damp Vienna climate, Clemens and Laure made the hard decision to separate the family. Victor would have been sent to a university, but Metternich feared revolutionaries. "I cannot send my son to a German university. He would be murdered there. Nor can I send him to Italy; he would be poisoned." Laure took the children to Paris, and Clemens' cousin, Flora Wrbna, moved into the Chancellery to play hostess at his dinner parties and receptions. "I have no family life," he mourned, "to which the greatest pleasures of life belong. . . . I sit at my writing desk like a bankrupt in a tavern."[27]

Once or twice Laure met him at Castle Johannisberg on the Rhine, but she never ventured to return to Vienna again. By the end of 1824 Metternich learned from her doctors in Paris that his wife was dying of consumption. Laure summoned her failing strength to write him a letter of farewell. It would cost her much to leave this life, she wrote, but she wanted above all else to assure her husband that except for the grief they had suffered together for the loss of their children, she had always been happy. "For that I thank you, my good chivalrous husband. . . . Even now in my forties I would still choose to begin my life all over again in exactly the same way." When he reached Paris in mid-March, he found Laure on her deathbed.[28]

When Wilhelmine returned at last to Vienna in May of 1826, Metternich was one of the first to call on her, the very first to invite her for dinner. On Whitsunday, the eve of his fifty-third birthday, he gave a large dinner party in her honor. His daughter Leontine, who was now fifteen, wrote in her diary that night:

Throng of people for dinner for the Duchess of Sagan. She is as always very beautiful and I do not find her much changed.[29]

He was a widower now; he might have married Wilhelmine as he had once dreamed, as she had once wished. But Wilhelmine had been converted to Catholicism in Rome the previous year. In the eyes of the Church she was still the wife of Louis Rohan. She and Schulenburg still appeared together but it was only a formal relationship. Quite frankly she discussed her situation with Philipp von Neumann; her first two husbands were still living—Schulenburg "has ceased to be her husband."[30]

Metternich, meantime, found himself entranced with an exquisite young girl, Antoinette von Leykam, whose father was a minor bureaucrat in government service and whose mother had been a singer in the Naples opera. Vienna society was shocked in January of 1827 when the Chancellor of Austria, aristocrat of aristocrats and upholder of legitimacy (up to a point only, as many had forgotten) married the pretty twenty-one-year-old girl, who had neither wealth nor social position. Dorothea Lieven in London called Clemens a "political charlatan" and quoted the witty barb of Aimée de Coigny, "*Le chevalier de la Sainte-Alliance a fait une mésalliance.*" But Antoinette was charming and well brought up; she adored the husband, nearly thrice her age, in the wholly uncritical way Marie had once adored him. Surely in marrying Antoinette von Leykam Metternich had sought to replace his beloved daughter. The marriage was happy—but brief. Antoinette bore him a son, Richard, and died within days of puerperal fever, leaving Clemens again a grieving widower. Compounding his sorrow that year of 1829, his son, Victor, who had been serving as a promising young diplomat at the Austrian embassy in Paris, died of the same lung disease that had carried off his mother and his sisters.

In 1830, the year of revolutions and of failed revolutions in Europe, Clemens Metternich again began to appear nearly every day at Wilhelmine's, to talk over political happenings with her. He well knew that few men or women had her sharp perceptions and keen understanding of the currents and crosscurrents of events.

He needed again her "almost imperturbable physical serenity." As always he could count on her discretion. When one day she brought him a piece of political news from Paris that she had got that day in a letter from Dorothée, he begged her "to keep silent on it which she happily knows how to do."[31]

That Wilhelmine's political views were conservative is beyond doubt. But she and her sisters were by no means so inflexible as Metternich in defending the existing order. Her mother, like Talleyrand, had protested the imposition of censorship in France. And during one of those golden summers at Löbichau, when a good male voice was needed for the musical evenings, someone proposed inviting August Binzer, a bearded, long-haired fellow in old-fashioned German clothes, his shirt collar open and worn outside his coat—all the marks of the dangerous student radical. Binzer had indeed belonged to one of the forbidden student secret societies, had climbed to the Wartburg on that October day in 1817, his guitar on his back, and had in fact written the song that was the rallying cry of young German nationalists, "Wir hätten gebauet ein stattliches Haus" (we would have built for ourselves a splendid house).

Should such a fellow be invited to the castle, to spend the summer among all the young Courland relatives? The Duchess of Courland turned to Wilhelmine for a decision. "What difference does all that make?" Wilhelmine had asked. "Is he a decent person? And is that song he wrote pretty? I've never heard it."[32]

So Binzer came to Löbichau, a serious, idealistic young man with a splendid baritone voice. Wilhelmine had long talks with him. By the end of the summer he and Emilie were in love, and though he was penniless and without prospects, Wilhelmine got her half brother, Emilie's father, to consent to the marriage, gave Emilie a fine dowry, and settled an income on the couple for life.

She judged people, Emilie wrote, for what they were.

Of her clear-sighted political thinking, her young friend Baron Prokesch von Osten wrote at that time:

> I am very fond of this woman and I can completely understand how a man could have the most burning passion for her. She has understanding of both head and heart, and in both wings with which she hovers high over the arena of our unhappy times.[33]

When Clemens Metternich became engaged for a third time, to Mélanie Zichy, the daughter of his old friends, he continued his visits to Wilhelmine, and he had to reassure his young fiancee that his attachment for the duchess was purely political. "If she had charms that went beyond her forty-five years, she would still have none for me."[34] Curiously enough, one day Mélanie received a beautiful necklace, with a note attached in Clemens' hand: "It comes from the Duchess of Sagan and me. Love *me* alone and be friendly with the Duchess."[35]

A year or two after his marriage with Mélanie, Wilhelmine sent him from Paris a lithograph of herself, after a portrait Gérard had painted. "Adieu," she wrote him, "I have loved you much too much not to do so always. Tell me that you have kept for me also a little of that interest that my heart always needs."[36]

Metternich's handsome young wife, Mélanie, quick of temper and often hasty in her judgment, passionately curious about everything that went on in the Chancellery, was often indiscreet and politically maladroit. As Metternich's eyesight and hearing dimmed and his success was less assured, he could have used the perspicacity and political judgment of a Wilhelmine, as perhaps he knew only too well.

4

One by one the leading actors in the Napoleonic drama vanished from the stage.

Napoleon himself died on St. Helena in May of 1821, having managed to transmute his life into a legend.

In August of 1822, as Castlereagh was preparing to travel to the congress at Verona, he got up one morning at his country house in Cray and slit his throat from ear to ear with a penknife.

Old Prince Hardenberg had brought along to the Congress of Verona his current *amie*, a Countess Kinsky. She had not looked after her seventy-two-year-old lover very well, had opened the carriage windows so she could better view the landscape, dragged him up and down hundreds of steps in cathedral towers and to several theaters in a single evening. The old statesman caught cold on one of their outings and died of pneumonia in Florence a few weeks after the congress ended.

Tsar Alexander died suddenly and mysteriously in the village of Taganrog on the Black Sea, in 1825, whither the Tsarina Elizabeth had gone to cure her consumption. In his will the Tsar had passed over his nearest brother Constantine, who was ruling over Russian Poland, and bequeathed the rule of Russia to his younger brother Nicholas. In the years that followed a legend spread in Russia that Alexander had not died at Taganrog but had resigned his high office to don the garb and name of a peasant, Fedor Kuzmich, and travel about in Siberia praying and healing the sick. When his tomb was opened in St. Petersburg many years later, it was found to be empty.

In 1832 Goethe died. And the young Duke of Reichstadt, Napoleon's son, once King of Rome and, the hope of the Bonapartists, died at Schönbrunn Palace of consumption, much as Metternich's own son, Victor, had died three years before, the Viennese doctors helpless to arrest the disease.

Gentz lived that decade in sybaritic luxury in his apartment in Rauhensteingasse, where one sank ankle-deep in Persian carpets, according to Emilie von Binzer, and where even the chamber pot, said the envious Grillparzer maliciously, moved at the master's bidding. Gentz dined out, wrote, gossiped, botanized in the gardens of his charming little house in the suburbs. At the age of sixty-five, fresh from a rejuvenating cure at the spa of Badgastein, Gentz fell in love with the beautiful nineteen-year-old ballerina, Fanny Elssler. He made all the classical gestures of the elderly admirer, sent her camellias from his glasshouses, set her up in a little flat in Krugergasse, bought her pearls and Paris dresses, taught her manners, a little French, and, almost, how to spell. He boasted of his conquest in Metternich's salon, confided to his diary the "heavenly hours" he spent with Fanny.

Gentz too died in 1832, physically and fiscally bankrupt, querulous, critical, talkative, amusing and shrewd up to the end. "If I were to write the history of the past fifteen years, it would be one long indictment of Metternich," Gentz told his friend Prokesch shortly before his death.[87] It was an odd friendship between the minister and journalist that had begun in their Dresden days, in 1802; there would be no one to replace Gentz.

Emperor Franz died in 1835, and his retarded, epileptic son Ferdinand was enthroned, with Metternich to guide him.

Talleyrand died in 1838, at the age of eighty-four. Dorothée, who had persuaded him to resign his embassy in England, had also arranged for the cynical old ex-bishop a final reconciliation with the Catholic Church.

Almost alone of the men who had made the peace in 1815, Metternich survived. Longevity was one of his problems. He had long before left off compromising; with the forces of violence and of anarchy that appeared to threaten the peace, there could be, he thought, no compromise.

He began to write his memoirs, remaking history in the process. He wanted to be remembered as a prophet who had foreseen everything exactly as it happened; where he had prophesied wrongly—as in the failed peace attempt of 1813—he rewrote it neatly out of the text. He had opposed the war of 1813 bitterly; now that it was past, he justified it. He had consistently opposed the removal of Napoleon; he had only wished to circumscribe his greed for power. To interfere in the internal affairs of established governments was against the Law of Nations.

Metternich, the old cosmopolitan, child of the Enlightenment, could phrase his political philosophy with great elegance. "We must always view the society of nations as the essential condition of the present world."[38] That "society of nations" was not unlike the well-bred society of men and women in which he himself moved, who if they disagreed politically still agreed on certain permanent rules and rituals that made mutual intercourse possible and agreeable, that preserved a comfortable civilization. Nations had two kinds of interests—those they shared with other nations and those that concerned their internal affairs, themselves alone. When they put their common shared interests first, the world prospered and had peace. When they ignored reciprocity and *bons procédés*—the code of diplomacy—putting their separate and selfish concerns first, then peace was endangered. "For a long time," he wrote the Duke of Wellington once, "I have felt that my native land was Europe."

The American scholar George Ticknor, carrying an introduction from their mutual friend Humboldt, visited Metternich in June of 1836 and dined at the Chancellery.

"I am myself moderate in everything," Metternich told him, Ticknor wrote, "and I endeavor to become more moderate. I have a calm disposition, a very calm one. But I am very often misunderstood. I am thought to be a great absolutist in my policy. But I am not. It is true I do not like democracies; democracy is everywhere and always a dissolving, decomposing principle; it tends to separate men, it loosens society. This does not suit my character. I am by character and habit constructive."

> He asked me [Ticknor went on] who will be our next President. I told him that it will be Van Buren; and that, as I do not desire it, he might consider my opinion at least unprejudiced. He answered, "Neither should I be of Mr. Van Buren's party, if I were in America. I should rather be of that old party of which Washington was originally the head. It was a sort of conservative party, and I should be conservative almost everywhere, certainly in England and America."

It was not for the present he was building, Metternich told Ticknor, but for the morrow. "I care nothing about the past, except as a warning for the future. The present day has no value for me, except as the eve of tomorrow. *C'est toujours avec le lendemain que mon esprit lutte.*"[39]

5

Shortly before Talleyrand's death Wilhelmine had paid her last visit to her sister Dorothée in France.

It must have been soon after her return to Vienna, in the spring of 1838, that she received an anonymous letter threatening blackmail.[40] Certainly a threat to publish details of her personal life could have mattered very little to a woman who had chosen to live her life as she pleased and had never taken any trouble to hide her love affairs from the world. But there were others involved whose families might be embarrassed by the publicity—Windischgraetz, pillar of society and of the Austrian Army, and Metternich, married to the daughter of his old friends the Zichys, with a new young family growing up in his house.

It may well have been at this time that Wilhelmine burned, at Metternich's request, the letters of early 1813 and returned the remainder of his letters to him for his keeping.

During those last months and years of her life, Wilhelmine lived in a state of deep depression. Nothing could lift her spirits any more. "She was so sad, so disheartened, so troubled by everything," Emilie wrote. "She seemed to have attacks of sheer despair."[41]

Both her foster daughters, Emilie and Marie, were married; though they were devoted to her, they had families of their own and both lived some distance from Vienna. Of Gustava Armfelt, her natural daughter, she heard almost nothing, except that the girl had married a cousin and had children growing up in Finland. Only once, when Gustava's half brother came to Vienna from St. Petersburg, he had brought a poignant message. "One's mother remains always one's mother, no matter how great the distance between mother and child."[42]

Wilhelmine was ill much of the time. Her face and legs swelled; daggers of pain shot through her arms. Her doctors diagnosed the illness as gout and shingles; Emilie thought it was poison from the dye her foster mother used to tint her graying hair the color of youth. Women like Wilhelmine could not afford to grow old. Her brain, her talents: nobody had ever really wanted them.

One day at the end of November 1839, in her house in Vienna, Wilhelmine suddenly felt suffocated; before a priest or her sisters could be summoned, her heart stopped beating.

> The Duchesse de Sagan died of apoplexy at 10:15 this morning [Neumann wrote in his diary]. . . . It was in the year 1809 that I first met her. She was then one of the most beautiful women of her day: rich, elegant, witty. She long remained lovely, and indeed only ceased to be so three or four years ago. . . . The news of this death, although not unexpected, has much upset Prince Metternich, who had lived a great deal in the society of the late Duchess.[43]

Young Princess Mélanie Metternich wrote that her husband had been so deeply affected by news of the duchess's death that his grief had quite frightened her.[44]

Very sadly Wilhelmine's sister Jeanne wrote to Dorothée in Paris:

> Everyone who knew her mourns for her and does justice to her great qualities. She did much good and she was certainly a beautiful and rare personality. Whether with all the gifts that Heaven bestowed on her she ever was happy I will not claim, and this doubt is painful for me.[45]

Wilhelmine's estate passed to her sister Pauline. A few years later, after Pauline's death in 1845, her son put all Wilhelmine's possessions on the auction block. It was then that Mélanie Metternich, as a surprise for her husband, bought for him Wilhelmine's writing desk, the handsome desk that had belonged to the Duc de Choiseul, and then to Wilhelmine's father. "It gave my husband great pleasure," Melanie noted in her diary.[46]

Metternich lived on through the eighteen-forties until the revolution of '48 finally swept him out of office. He departed for Brussels by railroad train—that suspect new invention—a dignified old man of seventy-five, wrapped in the cloak of his absolute rectitude, the money for his journey hastily supplied by the Rothschilds.

During his exile old friends came to see him—Dorothea Lieven, tall, gaunt, wrapped in shawls, carrying a green parasol and an outsize fan. Another ghost from his past came to see him as well: it was Princess Bagration, who "had forgotten to grow old." His granddaughter Pauline remembered that visit vividly. The princess's blond curls were gone, her skin was yellow as a lemon, but she dressed still as Isabey had painted her during the Vienna Congress, in a transparent blouse fastened with tiny pink bows, on her head a hat that "an eighteen-year-old shepherdess would have donned only with hesitation." She had scarcely changed in some ways, Pauline noted; she cast flirtatious glances at her elderly host and clung coquettishly to his arm as he led her to the table.[47]

It was Alfred Windischgraetz who commanded the troops that put down the revolution with bloody finality—Alfred, who had once been his bitter rival, who had given Clemens Metternich what he remembered even then perhaps as the most painful hours of his life.

Metternich lived to return to the villa on the Rennweg, eldest of the elder statesmen in the restored monarchy of Franz Josef, lived on to regale young visitors with tales of his meetings with Napoleon. In 1859, as the Italian provinces threatened to break loose from the monarchy, Franz Josef sought advice of the eighty-six-year-old ex-minister. Metternich counseled caution and patience: "For God's sake, Majesty, no ultimatum!" Whatever happened, don't break off diplomatic relations! "It was sent yesterday evening," the young monarch replied. The Italian war that was to signal the break-up of the Austrian empire was in progress when Metternich died a few days later, on June 11, 1859.

In literature of the period, Metternich was enshrined as the cunning Count Mosca in Stendhal's *Charterhouse of Parma*, as the suave persecutor of Andreas Hofer in Landor's *Imaginary Conversations*. But it was in the glittering irony of the Austrian political poet Anastasius Grün that Metternich was most sharply impaled.

In the poem *Salonszene* Grün describes "the one who steers the splendid ship of Austria" moving among his guests in an elegant drawing room where mirrors reflect a thousand candles. The orders sparkle on his breast; he has the same friendly smile for the older ladies of society and for the beautiful young girls. It would almost be a pleasure to be sent to Elba or to the dungeon of Munkács by so polished and charming a man, who with the same enchanting smile praises someone's golden curls—and tears kings' crowns from anointed heads.

Since the statesman is in such a fine humor tonight, will he not speak to a humble petitioner who is waiting, hat in hand, at the door, hoping only for a gracious nod? No reason to fear him: the fellow is sensible, well-bred, carries no dagger hidden under his modest coat.

> Östreichs Volk ist's, ehrlich, offen, wohlerzogen, auch und fein,
> Sieh, es fleht ganz artig: Dürft' ich wohl so frei sein, frei zu sein?

It is the people of Austria asking politely, "May I take the liberty of being free?"[48]

For Wilhelmine was reserved a pleasanter immortality.

In the eighteen-twenties a little girl had grown up on Wilhelmine's Ratiborzitz estate, the child of her housekeeper and her coachman, a sharp-eyed, bright little girl who remembered everything she saw and heard. Years later, when Barbora Panklová had grown up to be Czechoslovakia's celebrated writer Božena Němcová, she set down the recollections of her childhood in the charming story, *Babička* (Granny).

In the figure of the Princess who meets the peasant grandmother on grounds of mutual respect and understanding—rare account in literature of a cross-class friendship between women—Němcová drew a sympathetic portrait of the Duchess of Sagan as she knew and remembered her. And with a writer's sensitive intuition she captured poignantly the tragic essence in the life of a gifted woman who had never found a way to use her gifts.

A legend survives even today among the country people in the Ratiborzitz region of eastern Bohemia, that the talented Němcová herself was not the child of servants at all, but of the Duchess Wilhelmine and of the Austrian Foreign Minister Count Metternich who spent those June days of 1813 under her roof.

It is a legend that would surely have pleased Metternich himself.

NOTES

ABBREVIATIONS

M.F.C. Prague   Metternich Family Correspondence, Central State Archive of Prague

M.-S.C. Prague   Metternich-Sagan Correspondence, Central State Archive of Prague

W.A. Pilsen   Windischgraetz Family Archive, State Archive of Pilsen

H.H.S.A. Vienna   Haus- Hof- und Staatsarchiv, Vienna

P.R.O. London   Public Record Office, London

A.M.A.E. Paris   Archive, Ministère des Affaires Étrangères, Paris

Metternich-Sagan   *Clemens Metternich–Wilhelmine von Sagan: Ein Briefwechsel, 1813–1815*, ed. Maria Ullrichová (Graz and Cologne: Verlag Hermann Böhlaus, 1966)

I. GUNS OR GREEN TABLE?

1. Wilhelm Oncken, *Oesterreich und Preussen im Befreiungskriege* (Berlin: G. Grote'sche Verlagsbuchhandlung, 1876), I, 16, 33.

2. Friedrich von Gentz, *Tagebücher, Aus dem Nachlass Varnhagen's von Ense* (Leipzig: F. A. Brockhaus, 1873), I, 263.

3. Clemens Metternich, *Memoirs of Prince Metternich*, ed. Richard Metternich, trans. Mrs. Alexander Napier (New York: Charles Scribner's, 1880), I, 166.

4. Baron Eugène François Auguste de Vitrolles, *Mémoires et Relations Politiques* (Paris: G. Charpentier, 1884), I, 26.

5. Oncken, I, 30.

6. Ibid., I. 33ff., 390ff.

7. Ibid., I, 60.

8. For details on the operation of the Secret Police and Cipher Office, see Donald Emerson, *Metternich and the Political Police* (The Hague: Martinus Nijhoff, 1968); and Josef Karl Mayr, *Metternichs geheimer Briefdienst* (Wien: Verlag Adolf Holzhausens, 1935).

The term "war hawk" had been invented in November 1811 by the American John Randolph to describe the pro-war party in the United States Congress.

9. Karl Robert Nesselrode, *Lettres et Papiers*, *1760–1850* (Paris: A. Lahure, 1904), V, 12.

10. Ibid., V, 19.

11. Oncken, I, 28.

12. Report of Count Otto, Vienna, February 1, 1813, Vol. 393, No. 438, A.M.A.E. Paris; Friedrich Luckwaldt, *Oesterreich und die Anfänge des Befreiungskrieges von 1813*, in *Historische Studien*, Heft X (Vaduz: Kraus Reprint, 1965), p. 132.

13. Charles Stephen Buckland, *Metternich and the British Government from 1809 to 1813* (London: Macmillan, 1932), pp. 423ff.

14. Report of Count Otto, Vienna, December 28, 1813, Vol. 393, No. 414, A.M.A.E. Paris.

II. EDUCATION OF A DIPLOMAT

1. *Metternich Memoirs*, I, 37.

2. *Metternich-Sagan*, p. 146.

3. Egon Cäsar Conte Corti, *Metternich und die Frauen* (Zurich and Vienna: Europa Verlag, 1948), II, 16.

4. Fresh light has recently been thrown on Clemens Metternich's youthful sojourn in England through the publication of the memoirs of Count Hilarion de Liedekerke Beaufort, who accompanied his father-in-law, Vicomte Désandrouin, on a financial mission to England in 1794 and acted as mentor to the two Metternich brothers, still in their teens. Count Hilarion's journal provides a nearly day-by-day account of the English sojourn, including the frequent visits of the composer Joseph Haydn, then living in London. I am indebted to Georges Englebert for knowledge of this source. See Christiane de Liedekerke Beaufort, *Le Comte Hilarion: Souvenirs et Biographie du premier comte de Liedekerke Beaufort* (Paris: Société Copedith, 1968.)

5. Clemens Metternich, *Lettres du Prince de Metternich à la Comtesse de Lieven, 1818–1819*, ed. Jean Hanoteau (Paris: Librairie Plon, 1909), p. 42.

6. *Metternich Memoirs*, I, 270, 271.

7. Ibid., II, 365.

8. Heinrich Ritter von Srbik, *Metternich: Der Staatsman und der Mensch* (Munich: Verlag F. Bruckmann, 1925), p. 67.

9. Corti, I, 323.

10. *Metternich-Lieven Letters*, p. 176.

11. Corti, II, 224, 269. Clementine Bagration was born in September 1810; Metternich apparently did not see the child until she was fifteen. She married a Count Otto Blume and died during her first childbirth in 1829.

12. Corti, I, 213.

13. Ibid., I, 207, 213.

14. Ibid., I, 215ff.; II, 224, 269.

15. *Metternich-Lieven Letters*, p. 105.

16. Ibid., p. 225.

17. Pauline Metternich-Sandor, *Geschehenes Gesehenes Erlebtes* (Vienna: Wiener Literarische Anstalt, 1920), p. 9.

18. *Metternich-Lieven Letters*, p. 42.

19. Ibid., pp. 102–3

III. THE DUCHESS OF SAGAN

1. *Metternich-Sagan*, p. 22. The original letter telling of the attempt to sell the diamonds bears the date line "Prague, June 11, 1812," when Metternich stayed in Prague after the Dresden meeting with Napoleon.

2. Ibid., p. 137.

3. Ibid., p. 49.

4. In a museum in Castle Náchod in Bohemia a copy of the handbill exists, dated November 10, 1799, offering a reward for the apprehension of Arnoldi and two companions, one an actor, the other a hairdresser, together with an unnamed young woman, who if found was to be given "all possible care." For an account of Jeanne's escapade, see Eugène Vitrolles, *Souvenirs Autobiographiques d'un Émigré, 1790–1800* (Paris: Émile-Paul Frères, 1924), p. 197.

5. Clemens Brühl, *Die Sagan: Das Leben der Herzogin Wilhelmine von Sagan, Prinzessin von Kurland* (Berlin: Steuben-Verlag, Paul G. Esser, 1941), pp. 83ff.

A few months after Vava's birth Wilhelmine and Armfelt confirmed her parentage in a letter addressed to her, which was not to be opened until she was fifteen:

Adelaide Gustava Aspasia, if you have the misfortune to lose your father and mother before the secret of your birth can be revealed to you, know, dearly loved child, that you are the testimony of the truest love that joins the hearts of the undersigned. They have taken care for your fortune and if they have not been able to guide your education according to their desire, their wishes and their blessings will serve as a shield for you in the life you will live. We both sign this act with our own hands, placing thereon our seals, and our hearts pressed one against the other are an eternal pledge to you of our love for you.

Adelaide Gustava Aspasia, you were born the 13 of January in the year 1801 at 4 in the afternoon at Hamburg. Those to whom you appear as daughter have adopted you out of gratitude for your real father, and your baptismal record as their daughter is at Åbo, dated 13 July 1800 [*sic*].

[Signed] Gustave Baron d'Armfelt [and] Cathérine Frédérique Wilhelmine Benigne, Princess of Courland, Duchess of Sagan

Sagan, 19 October, 1801.

The above letter was provided me through the kindness of one of Vava Armfelt's descendants, Baron K. A. Wrede of Helsinki.

6. J. Christopher Herold, *The Mind of Napoleon* (New York: Columbia University Press, 1955), pp. 8, 14; Corti, I, 275.

7. Paul Rachel, *Elisa von der Recke* (Leipzig: Dieterich'sche Verlagbuchhandlung, 1902), I, xxix, footnote.

8. *Metternich-Sagan*, p. 59.

9. Gentz, *Tagebücher*, I, 258.

10. *Metternich-Sagan*, p. 59.

11. Ibid., p. 219.

12. Wilhelm und Caroline Humboldt, *Wilhelm und Caroline von Humboldt in ihren Briefen*, ed. Anna von Sydow (Berlin: Ernst Siegfried Mittler, 1910), IV, 37.

13. Unpublished, Wilhelmine to Alfred, Prague, June 2, 1809, I 4/1, W.A. Pilsen.

IV. DANGERS OF THE TRADE

1. Report of Count Otto, No. 455, Vienna, February 28, 1813, A.M.A.E. Paris.

2. Buckland, p. 261.

3. No. 20, January 9, 1813, and No. 26, February 5, 1813, F.O. Austria 7/99, P.R.O. London.

4. No. 33, March 6, 1813, F.O. Austria 7/99, P.R.O. London.

5. Report of Joseph Danelon to John Harcourt King, Vienna, March 8, 1813, F.O. Austria 7/99, P.R.O. London.

6. No. 33, March 6, 1813, F.O. Austria 7/99, P.R.O. London.

7. Report of Count Otto, No. 460, Vienna, March 8, 1813, A.M.A.E. Paris.

8. King to Castlereagh, No. 31, February 27, 1813, F.O. Austria 7/99, P.R.O. London.

9. Friedrich von Gentz, *Gentz und Wessenberg: Briefe des Ersten an den Zweiten*, ed. August Fournier (Vienna and Leipzig: Wilhelm Braumüller, 1907), pp. 60–61.

10. Nesselrode, *Lettres*, V, 51; Buckland, p. 489, n. 2.

11. No. 36, March 17, 1813, F.O. Austria 7/99, P.R.O. London.

12. Report of Count Otto, No. 455, Vienna, February 28, 1813, A.M.A.E. Paris.

13. Gentz to Wessenberg, H.H.S.A. Vienna, quoted in Corti, I, 570.

14. Nesselrode, *Lettres*, V, 52.

V. GLOOMY SPRING

1. Report of Otto, No. 460, Vienna, March 8, 1813, A.M.A.E. Paris.

2. *Metternich Memoirs*, III, 364.

3. Ibid., III, 363.

4. Émile Dard, *Le Comte de Narbonne, 1755–1813* (Paris: Librairie Plon, 1943), p. 258.

5. Baron Fain, *Manuscrit de Mil Huit Cent Treize* (Paris: Delaunay, 1825), I, 329, n. 1.

6. Luckwaldt, p. 397.

7. Report of Schwarzenberg's interview with Napoleon, Oncken, II, 628ff.

8. Ibid., II, 625.

9. Fain, *1813*, I, 317.

10. Unpublished, Baron Wessenberg, "Souvenirs d'un Voyage et Séjour en Angleterre en 1813 et 1814," Fol. 1–83, H.H.S.A. Vienna; Oncken, II, 301, n. 1.

11. Buckland, p. 506; Nesselrode, V, 83.
12. Oncken, II, 642.
13. Report of Narbonne, No. 15, Vienna, April 19, 1813, A.M.A.E. Paris.
14. Oncken, II, p. 649ff.
15. Ibid., p. 657.
16. Buckland, p. 513.
17. *Metternich-Sagan*, p. 155.
18. *Metternich-Lieven Letters*, p. 111.
19. Emilie von Binzer, *Drei Sommer in Löbichau* (Stuttgart: Verlag von W. Spemann, 1877), p. 37.
20. *Metternich-Sagan*, pp. 149–50.
21. Oncken, II, 657; Fain, *1813*, I, 393, n. 1.
22. Fain, *1813*, I, 430 and n. 1.

VI. HOUSE PARTY IN BOHEMIA

1. Nesselrode, *Lettres*, V, 103.
2. Oncken, II, 331, 660; *Metternich Memoirs*, I, 177–78. The *Memoirs* erroneously state that Nesselrode brought with him a copy of the armistice signed at Pläswitz, which was impossible since Nesselrode had left the Allied headquarters on June 1, before the armistice was concluded.
3. Unpublished, Metternich to Laure, Gitschin, June 6, 1813, M.F.C. Prague.
4. Nesselrode, *Lettres*, II, 98.
5. Dard, p. 271.
6. James Marshall-Cornwall, *Napoleon as Military Commander* (London, Batsford, 1967), p. 237; Fain, *1813*, I, 449.
7. Oncken, II, 383.
8. Ibid., II, 332, 661; Luckwaldt, p. 387.
9. Oncken, II, 341.
10. Ibid., II, 671.
11. Unpublished, Metternich to Marie, Gitschin, June 8; Metternich to Victor, Gitschin, June 12; Metternich to Laure, Budweis, June 1, Gitschin, June 6, June 10, 1813. M.F.C. Prague.
12. Unpublished, Laure to Metternich, Vienna, June 3, June 6, June, 16; Victor to Metternich, Vienna, June 16; Marie to Metternich, Vienna, June 9, June 14, June 17, 1813. M.F.C. Prague.
13. Laure to Metternich, June 6, 1813.
14. Metternich to Laure, June 6, 1813.
15. Marie to Metternich, June 9, 1813.
16. Unpublished, Laure to Metternich, Vienna, June 8, 1813, M.F.C. Prague. An earlier letter of Laure (June 6) informed him that the Duchess of Sagan "is going to Bohemia and not to Baden."
17. Unpublished, Metternich to Laure, Gitschin, June 15, 1813, M.F.C. Prague.
18. *Metternich-Sagan*, p. 23. Metternich's first letter to Wilhelmine, written after his departure from Vienna (probably June 8) has not been found.
19. Nesselrode, *Lettres*, V, 104.

20. *Briefe von Friedrich von Gentz an Pilat,* ed. Karl Mendelssohn-Bartholdy (Leipzig: F. C. W. Vogel, 1868), I, 8.

21. *Metternich-Sagan,* p. 25.

22. Unpublished, Wilhelmine to Alfred, Ratiborzitz, June 17, 1810, I 4/5, W.A. Pilsen.

23. Unpublished, Wilhelmine to Alfred, Prague, September 12, 1811, I 4/53, W.A. Pilsen.

24. Unpublished, Wilhelmine to Alfred, n.p., n.d.; Ratiborzitz, November 11 and 20, 1812, I 4/82, 4/83, 4/95, W.A. Pilsen.

25. *Metternich-Sagan,* pp. 26–27; unpublished, Metternich to Laure, Gitschin, June 22, 1813, M.F.C. Prague.

26. *Gentz an Pilat,* p. 12.

27. Unpublished, Wilhelmine to Alfred, Ratiborzitz, June 16, 1813, I 4/98, W.A. Pilsen.

28. *Metternich-Sagan,* p. 26.

29. *Gentz an Pilat,* p. 15.

30. Unpublished, Wilhelmine to Alfred, Ratiborzitz, June 17, 1813, I 4/99, W.A. Pilsen.

31. Ibid.

32. Ibid.

33. *Metternich-Sagan,* p. 27.

34. Wilhelmine to Alfred, June 16 and 17, 1813.

35. Unpublished, Wilhelmine to Alfred, Ratiborzitz, June 18, 1813, I 4/101, W.A. Pilsen.

36. *Metternich Memoirs,* I, 180, 314.

37. According to Baron Karl vom Stein, who was in Russia during the period of the French invasion, the Russian people felt very bitterly toward the Tsar, blamed him for their misfortunes, "and demanded of the Grand Duchess, then at Jaroslav, that she place herself at their head and seize the government." *See* Stein, *Diary,* November 19, 1814, excerpted in Frederick Freksa, *A Peace Congress of Intrigue,* trans. Harry Hansen (New York: Century Co., 1919), p. 379.

38. Alexander I, *Scenes of Russian Court Life,* ed. Grand Duke Nicholas, trans. Henry Havelock (London: Jarrolds, n.d.) p. 194.

39. *Metternich Memoirs,* I, 181.

40. Ibid., I, 182.

41. Wilhelmine to Alfred, June 18, 1813.

42. *Metternich-Sagan,* p. 28.

43. Unpublished, Wilhelmine to Alfred, Ratiborzitz, June 19, 1813, I 4/102, W.A. Pilsen.

44. Humboldt, *Briefe,* IV, 27.

45. Ibid., IV, 27–28.

46. Ibid., IV, 40.

47. Wilhelmine to Alfred, June 19, 1813.

48. Metternich to Laure, June 22, 1813.

49. Humboldt, *Briefe,* IV, 38.

50. Ibid., IV, 39.

51. Wilhelmine to Alfred, June 19, 1813.

52. Metternich to Laure, June 22, 1813.

53. Wilhelmine to Alfred, June 17, 1813.

54. Unpublished, Wilhelmine to Alfred, Ratiborzitz, June 18 and 21, 1813, I 4/100 and 4/104, W.A. Pilsen.

55. *Metternich Memoirs*, I, 412, n. 66.

56. Binzer, p. 38.

57. *Metternich-Sagan*, p. 28.

58. Unpublished, Laure to Metternich, Vienna, June 21, 1813; Marie to Metternich, June 24, 1813, M.F.C. Prague.

59. Ibid., and Marie to Metternich, Vienna, June 27, 1813, M.F.C. Prague.

60. Unpublished, Laure to Metternich, Vienna, June 18, 1813, M.F.C. Prague.

61. Unpublished, Marie to Metternich, Baden, July 17, 1813, M.F.C. Prague.

62. Unpublished, Laure to Metternich, Vienna, June 23 and 25, 1813, M.F.C. Prague.

63. Ibid., June 23, 1813.

64. Unpublished, Marie to Metternich, Vienna, June 14, 1813, M.F.C. Prague.

VII. ENCOUNTER IN DRESDEN

1. Unpublished, Metternich to Laure, June 22, 1813, M.F.C. Prague.

2. Of the famous encounter in Dresden the only first-hand reports are those of Metternich—the extensive account he wrote out many years later, included in his *Memoirs*, I, 184ff., and the terse, undoubtedly more accurate account written the following day to Emperor Franz: *Memoirs*, II, 538ff. A third—and hitherto unknown and unpublished account—is the letter written to his wife from Dresden on June 28, 1813, two days after the interview, which is copiously excerpted here (M.F.C. Prague).

On the French side all accounts are second-hand, but are valuable as reflecting in at least a fragmentary way Napoleon's views. Caulaincourt's was garnered from a conversation the same evening with Napoleon, and supposedly written down at once. Baron Fain had to be content with what had been heard through the paneling, and what Napoleon told him in the days following (Fain, *1813*, II, 36ff.; Armand de Caulaincourt, "Conversation de M. le Comte de Metternich avec l'empereur Napoléon, telle que S.M. me l'a raconté," ed. Jean Hanoteau, in *Revue d'Histoire Diplomatique* 47–48 [October–December 1933]: 421ff.).

3. *Metternich Memoirs*, I, 184.

4. Fain, *1813*, II, 39.

5. *Metternich Memoirs*, I, 190. A footnote explains, "I do not dare make use of the much worse expressions employed by Napoleon."

6. *Metternich Memoirs*, I, 187.

7. *Metternich Memoirs*, I, 185.

8. Caulaincourt, "Conversation," p. 435.

9. Fain, *1813*, II, 41.

10. Fain, *1813*, II, 43.

11. Caulaincourt, "Conversation," p. 432.

12. Unpublished, Metternich to Laure, Dresden, June 28, 1813, M.F.C. Prague.

13. *Metternich Memoirs*, I, 191ff.

14. Caulaincourt, "Conversation," pp. 439–40.

15. Metternich to Laure, June 28, 1813.

16. Ibid.

17. *Metternich Memoirs*, I, 39.

18. Metternich to Laure, June 28, 1813.

19. *Metternich Memoirs*, I, 195ff.

20. Unpublished, Metternich to Marie, Gitschin, July 2, 1813, M.F.C. Prague.

21. Unpublished, Metternich to Laure, Brandeis, July 8, 1813, M.F.C. Prague.

22. *Gentz und Wessenberg*, p. 80.

23. Fain, *1813*, II, 64.

24. *Gentz an Pilat*, p. 37.

25. Metternich to Laure, July 8, 1813.

26. *Metternich-Sagan*, p. 28.

27. *Gentz an Pilat*, p. 26.

28. Humboldt, *Briefe*, IV, 43.

29. Ibid.

30. *Gentz an Pilat*, pp. 26–27.

31. Ibid.

32. Ibid.

33. *Metternich-Sagan*, p. 28.

34. *Gentz an Pilat*, p. 28.

35. *Metternich-Sagan*, p. 48.

36. Nesselrode, *Lettres*, II, 99.

37. Ludwig Lebzeltern, *Mémoires et papiers de Lebzeltern, un collaborateur de Metternich*, ed. Emmanuel de Lévis-Mirepoix (Paris: Librairie Plon, 1949), p. 264.

38. Unpublished, Metternich to Laure, Gitschin, July 5, 1813, M.F.C. Prague.

39. *Metternich-Sagan*, p. 21. Metternich mistakenly dated this letter "6 June" rather than "6 July." He was on his way to Brandeis when he wrote it— and he left Gitschin for Brandeis on July 6.

VIII. COLD PEACE IN SUMMER

1. Humboldt, *Briefe*, IV, 50.

2. *Gentz und Wessenberg*, p. 81.,

3. Unpublished, Metternich to Laure, Brandeis, July 8, 1813, M.F.C. Prague.

4. M. Adolphe Thiers, *History of the Consulate and the Empire of France under Napoleon* (London: Willis and Sotheran, 1857), XV, 77.

5. Unpublished, Metternich to Laure, Prague, July 14, 1813, M.F.C. Prague.

6. C. K. Webster, *British Diplomacy 1813–1815* (London: G. Bell & Sons, 1921), pp. 6–13.

7. "Metternich's Instructions for the Conference at Prague," *Metternich Memoirs*, II, 541.

8. Ibid., p. 546.

9. Achille Charles, Duc de Broglie, *Personal Recollections, 1785–1820* (London: Ward and Downey, 1887), I, 223–24.

10. Gentz, *Tagebücher*, I, 271.

11. Unpublished, Metternich to Marie, Prague, July 16, 1813, M.F.C. Prague.

12. Unpublished, Metternich to Laure, Prague, July 19, 1813, M.F.C. Prague.

13. *Metternich-Sagan*, p. 30.

14. *Metternich-Sagan*, p. 23. Mistakenly dated by Metternich "12 June" instead of "12 July," this is the confidential letter that accompanied the ostensible one preceding. It was written from Prague, and Metternich was not in Prague until July.

15. Unpublished, Wilhelmine to Metternich, Ratiborzitz, July 12, 1813, M.-S.C. Prague.

16. *Metternich-Sagan*, p. 155.

17. *Gentz an Pilat*, p. 40.

18. Humboldt, *Briefe*, IV, 63.

19. *Metternich-Sagan*, p. 32.

20. Ibid., pp. 34–35.

21. Metternich to Marie, July 16, 1813.

22. Unpublished, Metternich to Laure, Prague, July 17, 1813, M.F.C. Prague.

23. Humboldt, *Briefe*, IV, 60.

24. Nesselrode, *Lettres*, II, 100.

25. Unpublished, Metternich to Laure, Prague, July 26, 1813, M.F.C. Prague.

26. Ibid.

27. Alexander I, *Scenes of Russian Court Life*, p. 193.

28. Unpublished, Metternich to Laure, Prague, July 20, 1813, M.F.C. Prague.

29. Fain, *1813*, II, 75–76.

30. Thiers, XVI, 80–81.

31. Unpublished, Metternich to Laure, Brandeis, August 3, 1813, M.F.C. Prague.

32. Dard, *Le Comte de Narbonne*, p. 277.

33. Corti, I, 386.

34. Nesselrode, *Lettres*, V, 122.

35. Unpublished, Metternich to Laure, Prague, July 31, 1813, M.F.C. Prague.

36. Unpublished, Metternich to Wilhelmine, "the 3 [August 1813], 7 o'clock in the morning," M.-S.C. Prague.

37. *Metternich-Sagan*, p. 156.

38. Unpublished, Marie to Metternich, Baden, July 8, 1813, M.F.C. Prague.

39. Unpublished, Laure to Metternich, Baden, July 9, August 1, 1813; Marie to Metternich, June 24, July 17 and 26, et passim, M.F.C. Prague.

40. Unpublished, Marie to Metternich, Baden, July 22, 1813, M.F.C. Prague.

41. Maria Beatrix to Metternich, Grünberg, June 25, 1813; Marie to Metternich, Baden, August 9, 1813, M.F.C. Prague.

42. Unpublished, Laure to Metternich, Baden, August 3, 1813, M.F.C. Prague.

43. Unpublished, Marie to Metternich, Baden, August 9, 1813, M.F.C. Prague.

44. Unpublished, Laure to Metternich, Baden, August 5, 1813, M.F.C. Prague.

45. Unpublished, Laure to Metternich, Baden, August 12, 1813, M.F.C. Prague.

46. Fain, *1813*, II, 73.

47. Ibid., p. 80.

48. Ibid., p. 90.

49. Gentz, *Tagebücher*, I, 265.

50. Fain, *1813*, II, 93; Thiers, XVI, 107.

51. Unpublished, Metternich to Alfred Windischgraetz, Prague, August 9, 1813, I 3/190, W.A. Pilsen.

52. Unpublished, Metternich to Wilhelmine, n.p., n.d., prob. August 10, 1813, M.-S.C. Prague.

53. Unpublished, Metternich to Laure, Prague, August 10, 1813, M.F.C. Prague.

54. *Metternich Memoirs*, I, 199.

55. Fain, *1813*, II, 201.

56. Broglie, p. 228.

57. *Metternich Memoirs*, I, 200.

58. Corti, I, 390.

59. Dard, *Le Comte de Narbonne*, p. 282.

60. Fain, *1813*, II, 76.

61. Sir Robert Wilson, *Private Diary of Travels, Personal Services and Public Events . . . 1812, 1813, 1814* (London, John Murray, 1861), II, 145; Webster, *British Diplomacy*, pp. 18–19, 97.

Cathcart's unpublished letter to Castlereagh tells of the decision to keep Britain's assent to the mediation effort a secret from Austria (F.O. Russia 65/86, No. 82):

Reichenbach the 12th August 1813

My Lord,

I had the honor of receiving on the 8th instant your Lordship's dispatches No. 45 and 46, conveying to me the Prince Regent's commands to acquaint the Emperor of Russia that His Royal Highness is now ready to accept the mediation of the Emperor of Austria in conjunction with His Allies and upon an express understanding as to the conditions laid down in Your Lordship's dispatch No. 42 and in conformity to the faith of treaties from which Great Britain can under no circumstances recede.

It being His Royal Highness' desire to act in the most entire concert with His Allies, I am further directed to be governed by the sentiments of Their Imperial and Prussian Majesties, and by the state of affairs at the moment as to the steps to be taken in pursuance of this dispatch.

The Emperor [Alexander] having been on a visit to the King in the County of Glatz, and occupied on the succeeding days in the inspection of troops and in making the arrangements with persons sent by the Austrian Government for the march and supply of a large body of troops in Bohemia, it was not possible for me to communicate to His Imperial Majesty the important matter contained in these dispatches till the evening of the 8th instant.

His Imperial Majesty desires me to express for the information of the Prince Regent how very much affected He was by this fresh instance of confidence reposed in Him by His Royal Highness and His Government in leaving it to Him to decide whether it were expedient at this juncture to state the acceptance by Great Britain of the mediation of Austria.

That however He had no hesitation in deprecating the making any overture to that effect at the present moment. That there was no reason to believe that there existed any disposition on the part of France seriously to treat for Peace, and that the acceptance of mediation by another power would undoubtedly if now made form a ground for prolonging the armistice.

That the armistice and the period of negotiation were to end in less than two days and that it was extremely probable that Austria by the time the proposition could reach Her would have quitted Her attitude of neutrality and mediation for that of war.

That with the acquisition of the power of Austria there was every reason to hope that the war might be brought to a happy conclusion.

But that to invite Austria to mediate for England would be to press for a renewal of the armistice at the very moment when it seemed that every preparation was completed by that power for joining the Allies, and engaging with all Her force in a war by the vigorous prosecution of which it was now alone to be expected that a solid, honorable and lasting peace could be obtained.

Upon these grounds it was decided to make for the present no communication either to Count Stadion or to Count Metternich, and to keep the determination of the British Cabinet as much a secret as the disclosures already made by Your Lordship's direction to the Ministers of other powers would permit.

The declaration of war which has been made by Austria immediately after the expiration of the 10th instant has justified the policy of His Imperial Majesty in suggesting this decision.

I have the honor to be, with the utmost respect, My lord, etc.

IX. DEFEATS AND VICTORIES

1. Unpublished, Metternich to Laure, Prague, August 16, 1813, M.F.C. Prague.

2. Unpublished, Metternich to Laure, Prague, August 13, 1813, M.F.C. Prague. Metternich dated this letter erroneously May 13, 1813.

3. Unpublished, Metternich to Laure, Prague, August 20, 1813, M.F.C. Prague.

4. *Metternich-Sagan*, p. 36.

5. Unpublished, Metternich to Laure, Postelberg, August 23, 1813, M.F.C. Prague.

6. Ibid.

7. Unpublished, Wilhelmine to Metternich, Ratiborzitz, August 15, 1813, M.-S.C. Prague.

8. *Metternich-Sagan*, p. 38.

9. Unpublished, Wilhelmine to Metternich, Náchod, August 17, 1813, M.-S.C. Prague.

10. *Metternich-Sagan*, p. 40.

11. Ibid., p. 45.

12. Johann Friedrich Novak, ed., *Briefe des Feldmarschalls Fürsten Schwarzenberg an seine Frau, 1799–1816* (Vienna: Verlag von Gerlach & Wiedling, 1913), p. 330.

13. Unpublished, Metternich to Laure, "At Headquarters in Reichsted near Dippoldiswalde in Saxony, 4 o'clock in the afternoon," August 26, 1813, M.F.C. Prague.

14. Ibid.

15. *Metternich-Sagan*, p. 48.

16. Robert Wilson, *General Wilson's Journal, 1812–1814*, ed. Antony Brett-James (London: William Kimber, 1964), p. 169.

17. Ibid, p. 167.

18. Charles William Vane, Third Marquess of Londonderry, *Narrative of the War in Germany and France in 1813 and 1814* (London: Henry Colburn & Richard Bentley, 1830), p. 120.

19. Wilson, *Journal*, p. 174.

20. Novak, *Schwarzenberg Briefe*, p. 332.

21. *Metternich-Sagan*, p. 42. The original letter is dated "31 August."

22. Alfons von Klinkowström, *Oesterreichs Theilnahme an den Befreiungskriegen* (Vienna: Carl Gerold's Sohn, 1887), p. 51.

23. *Gentz an Pilat*, p. 53.

24. *Metternich-Sagan*, p. 51.

25. Ibid., p. 45.

26. Ibid., p. 50.

27. Ibid., pp. 47ff., 50.

28. Ibid., p. 56

29. *Gentz an Pilat*, p. 52.

30. *Metternich-Sagan*, p. 156.

31. *Gentz an Pilat*, p. 52; Gentz, *Tagebücher*, p. 265.

32. Unpublished, Metternich to Wilhelmine, Teplitz, September 9, 1813, M.-S.C. Prague.

33. *Metternich-Sagan*, p. 58.

34. Metternich to Wilhelmine, September 9, 1813.

35. *Metternich-Sagan*, p. 58.

36. *Klinkowström*, p. 57.

37. *Metternich-Sagan*, p. 60.

38. Ibid., p. 61.

X. WAR CAMP IN TEPLITZ

1. Unpublished, Metternich to Laure, Teplitz, September 11, 1813, M.F.C. Prague.

2. Unpublished, Metternich to Laure, Teplitz, September 18, 1813, M.F.C. Prague.

3. Fain, *1813*, II, 333.

4. For information on Austrian army medical facilities in the years 1813–14, I am indebted to the staff of the Army Museum, Vienna, and to Paul Myrdacz, *Handbuch für k.u.k. Militärärzte*, II (Vienna, 1898), chap. III: "Organisatorische Bestimmungen über den Feld-Sanitätsdienst vom Jahre 1808–1814."

5. Unpublished, Metternich to Marie, Teplitz, September 4, 1813, M.F.C. Prague.

6. Metternich to Laure, September 18, 1813.

7. Unpublished, Marie to Metternich, Vienna, September 19, 1813, M.F.C. Prague.

8. Unpublished, Metternich to Laure, Teplitz, September 14, 1813, M.F.C. Prague.

9. Humboldt, *Briefe*, IV, 116.

10. Ibid., p. 114.

11. Unpublished, Metternich to Laure, Teplitz, September 21, 1813, M.F.C. Prague; *Gentz an Pilat*, p. 70.

12. Klinkowström, p. 52.

13. Frances Balfour, *The Life of George, Fourth Earl of Aberdeen* (London: Hodder and Stoughton, 1922), p. 94.

14. Ibid., p. 99.

15. Humboldt, *Briefe*, IV, 110.

16. Klinkowström, p. 62.

17. Humboldt, *Briefe*, IV, 115.

18. Balfour, p. 84.

19. Friedrich von Gentz, *Briefe von und an Friedrich von Gentz*, ed. Friedrich Carl Wittichen and Ernst Salzer (Munich and Berlin: R. Oldenbourg, 1913), I, 163.

20. *Metternich-Sagan*, p. 60.

21. Ibid., p. 61.

22. Metternich to Marie, quoted in Corti, I, 400.

23. *Metternich-Sagan*, p. 68.

24. Ibid., p. 63.

25. Ibid., p. 64.

26. Ibid.

27. Ibid., p. 55.

28. Unpublished, Metternich to Wilhelmine, n.d. [September 21, 1813], M.-S.C. Prague.

29. *Metternich-Sagan*, p. 66.

30. Unpublished, Wilhelmine to Metternich, Prague, September 23, 1813, M.-S.C. Prague.

31. Unpublished, Metternich to Wilhelmine, Teplitz, September 29, 1813, M.-S.C. Prague.

32. Novak, *Schwarzenberg Briefe*, p. 341.

33. Unpublished, Metternich to Laure, Teplitz, September 28, 1813, M.F.C. Prague.

34. Balfour, p. 104.

35. Wilson, *Private Diary*, II, 145–46.

36. Ibid., II, 136.

37. Klinkowström, p. 79ff.

38. Balfour, p. 89.

39. Castlereagh to Aberdeen, "Private and Confidential," October 15, 1813, in Webster, *British Diplomacy*, pp. 103, 105.

40. *Metternich-Sagan*, p. 68.

41. Ibid., p. 74.

42. Metternich to Marie, October 9, 1813, quoted in Corti, I, 400.

43. *Metternich-Sagan*, p. 76.

44. Ibid., p. 69.

45. Ibid., p. 72.

46. Ibid., p. 77.

47. Balfour, p. 118.

48. *Metternich-Sagan*, p. 255.

XI. LEIPZIG

1. Fain, *1813*, II, 373, n. 2.

2. Ibid., p. 374, n. 1.

3. Ibid., p. 381, n. 2.

4. Novak, *Schwarzenberg Briefe*, p. 347.

5. Fain, *1813*, II, 389.

6. Novak, *Schwarzenberg Briefe*, p. 348.

7. Unpublished, Metternich to Laure, Rötha near Leipzig, October 18, 1813, "11 o'clock in the evening," M.F.C. Prague.

8. *Metternich-Sagan*, p. 81.

9. Humboldt, *Briefe*, IV, 149.

10. Balfour, p. 125.

11. Humboldt, *Briefe*, IV, 151.

12. *Gentz an Pilat*, p. 84.

13. Brühl, p. 188.

14. *Gentz an Pilat*, p. 85.

15. Klinkowström, p. 90.

16. Unpublished, Marie to Metternich, Vienna, October 25, 1813, M.F.C. Prague.

17. Unpublished, Laure to Metternich, Vienna, October 25, 1813, M.F.C. Prague.

18. Klinkowström, p. 769, n.; *Metternich-Sagan*, p. 88.

19. Hudelist to Metternich, November 3, 1813, quoted in Corti, I, 403.

20. Metternich-Sandor, *Geschehenes Gesehenes Erlebtes*, p. 24.

XII. WINTRY PAUSE

1. Novak, *Schwarzenberg Briefe*, p. 354.

2. Balfour, p. 131.

3. Ibid., p. 130.

4. Unpublished, Metternich to Laure, Frankfurt, November 6, 1813, M.F.C. Prague.

5. Wilson, *Private Diary*, II, 216.

6. *Metternich Memoirs*, I, 210.

7. *Metternich-Sagan*, p. 100.

8. Ibid., p. 91.

9. Wilson, *Private Diary*, II, 216.

10. Aberdeen to Castlereagh, Frankfurt, November 9, 1813, F.O. Austria 7/102, P.R.O. London. Also *Metternich Memoirs*, I, 215, and Klinkowström, pp. 770ff. Baron Fain, "Rapport de M. le Baron de Saint-Agnan," in *Manuscrit de Mil Huit Cent Quatorze* (London: Martin Bossange, 1823), pp. 48–55.

11. Copy of letter of Metternich to Caulaincourt, November 10, 1813, No. 33, F.O. Austria 7/102, P.R.O. London.

12. Wilson, *Private Diary*, II, 239.

13. Unpublished, Metternich to Marie, Frankfurt, November 18, 1813, M.F.C. Prague.

14. Lady Burghersh, *Letters*, ed. Rose Weigall (London: John Murray, 1893), p. 80.

15. Metternich to Marie, November 18, 1813.

16. Unpublished, Metternich to Laure, Frankfurt, November 24, 1813, M.F.C. Prague.

17. *Metternich-Sagan*, pp. 93, 95.

18. Ibid., p. 122.

19. Unpublished, Wilhelmine to Metternich, Prague, October 15, 1813, M.-S.C. Prague; *Metternich-Sagan*, pp. 84, 92, 128.

20. *Metternich-Sagan*, p. 103.

21. Ibid., p. 83.

22. Wilhelmine to Metternich, October 15, 1813.

23. *Metternich-Sagan*, p. 82.

24. Ibid., p. 101.

25. Ibid., p. 119.

26. Ibid. pp. 109–10.

27. Gentz, *Tagebücher*, I, 266.

28. *Gentz Briefe*, ed. Wittichen and Salzer, I, 179.

29. Ibid., I, 173.

30. *Metternich-Sagan*, p. 96.

31. *Gentz Briefe*, ed. Wittichen and Salzer, I, 204; *Metternich-Sagan*, p. 124.

32. *Gentz Briefe*, ed. Wittichen and Salzer, I, 201–2.

33. Ibid., I, 206.

34. Unpublished, Metternich to Laure, Frankfurt, December 6, 1813, M.F.C. Prague.

35. Ibid.

36. *Metternich Memoirs*, I, 215.

37. "Résumé of Wessenberg Conversation with Napoleon, Dijon, April 3, 1814," Frankreich Varia 65, H.H.S.A. Vienna.

38. Webster, British Diplomacy, p. 87.

39. Novak, *Schwarzenberg Briefe*, p. 357.

40. Lebzeltern, pp. 286–89.

41. Klinkowström, pp. 777–79.

42. Ibid., p. 775.

43. Novak, *Schwarzenberg Briefe*, p. 356.

44. Unpublished, Metternich to Laure, Frankfurt, December 11, 1813, M.F.C. Prague.

45. Unpublished, Metternich to Laure, Freiburg, December 22, 1813, "2 o'clock in the morning," M.F.C. Prague; *Metternich Memoirs*, I, 222.

46. Balfour, p. 461.

XIII. CHRISTMAS IN FREIBURG

1. Burghersh, p. 160.

2. Franz von Andlaw, *Mein Tagebuch: Auszüge aus Aufschreibungen der Jahre 1811 bis 1861* (Frankfurt am Main: J. D. Sauerlander's Verlag, 1862, I, 25ff.

3. Unpublished, Metternich to Laure, Freiburg, December 16, 1813, M.F.C. Prague.

4. *Metternich-Sagan*, p. 144.

5. *Metternich Memoirs*, I, 220ff.; Alexander I, *Scenes of Russian Court Life*, p. 198.

6. Robert Stewart, Second Marquess of Londonderry, *Correspondence, Despatches, and Other Papers of Viscount Castlereagh, Second Marquess of Londonderry*, ed. Charles William Vane, [Third] Marquess of Londonderry (London, John Murray, 1853), IX, 126.

7. Unpublished, Metternich to Laure, Freiburg, December 22, 1813, M.F.C. Prague.

8. Londonderry, *Castlereagh Papers*, IX, 104.

9. Ibid., IX, 126.

10. Ibid., IX, 142; Klinkowström, p. 219.

11. Unpublished, Metternich to Marie, Freiburg, December 26, 1813, M.F.C. Prague.

12. Unpublished, Marie to Metternich, Vienna, September 17, 1813, M.F.C. Prague.

13. Unpublished, Metternich to Laure, Frankfurt, December 1, 1813, M.F.C. Prague.

14. Unpublished, Metternich to Laure, Freiburg, December 29, 1813, M.F.C. Prague.

15. Metternich to Laure, December 1, 1813.

16. Ibid.
17. Metternich to Laure, December 16, 1813.
18. Unpublished, Metternich to Laure, Basel, January 15, 1814, M.F.C. Prague.
19. Unpublished, Metternich to Laure, Frankfurt, December 11, 1813, M.F.C. Prague.
20. *Metternich-Sagan*, p. 126.
21. Ibid., pp. 141–43.
22. Ibid., p. 98.
23. Ibid., p. 130.
24. Unpublished, Metternich to Wilhelmine, Freiburg, January 2, 1814, M.F.C. Prague.
25. Ibid.
26. *Metternich-Sagan*, p. 172.
27. Ibid., p. 164.
28. Ibid., p. 132.
29. Ibid., p. 105.

XIV. CAMPAIGN IN FRANCE

1. Unpublished, Metternich to Laure, Freiburg, January 9, 1814, M.F.C. Prague.
2. Auguste Fournier, *Der Congress von Châtillon* (Vienna and Prague: Verlag F. Tempsky, 1900), p. 48.
3. Klinkowström, p. 788.
4. Metternich to Laure, January 9, 1814.
5. Balfour, pp. 176–77.
6. Ibid.; also Webster, *British Diplomacy*, p. 131.
7. Klinkowström, p. 798.
8. Humboldt, *Briefe*, IV, 226.
9. *Metternich-Sagan*, p. 181; Humboldt, *Briefe*, IV, 227; C. J. Bartlett, *Castlereagh* (New York: Charles Scribner's Sons, 1966), p. 98.
10. Klinkowström, p. 800.
11. *Metternich-Sagan*, p. 195.
12. Burghersh, pp. 167–69.
13. Unpublished, Metternich to Laure, Langres, January 28, 1814, M.F.C. Prague.
14. *Metternich-Sagan*, p. 193; and unpublished, Metternich to Laure, Langres, January 25, 1814, M.F.C., Prague.
15. Klinkowström, pp. 804–5; Fournier, *Châtillon*, p. 80; Fain, *1814*, pp. 296ff.
16. Novak, *Schwarzenberg Briefe* p. 369.
17. Fournier, *Châtillon*, pp. 64ff.
18. Webster, *British Diplomacy*, pp. 123–25, 141–47.
19. Hardenberg noted in his diary on January 9, 1814: "Metternich dined with me. Agreed to the plan for Saxony" (quoted in Fournier, *Châtillon*, Appendix, p. 361). However, not only did Hardenberg's extreme deafness make it likely that he did not hear correctly, but, significantly, the Tsar and his staff that

week refused to believe that Metternich had agreed to such a sacrifice (Webster, *British Diplomacy*, p. 132). There is no corroboration in Humboldt's letters or elsewhere for Hardenberg's statement, and subsequent discussions on the subject do not bear out the note in Hardenberg's diary.

20. Londonderry, *Castlereagh Papers*, IX, 234; Webster, *British Diplomacy*, p. 138.

21. Klinkowström, p. 262, n. 2.

22. Burghersh, p. 161.

23. Klinkowström, p. 803.

24. Ibid., p. 805.

25. Ibid., p. 804.

26. Unpublished, Metternich to Laure, Langres, February 1, 1814, M.F.C. Prague.

27. Klinkowström, p. 802.

28. Unpublished, Metternich to Laure, Vandoeuvre, February 5, 1814, M.F.C. Prague.

29. Burghersh, pp. 150, 153; C. K. Webster, *Foreign Policy of Castlereagh*, (London: G. Bell & Sons, 1931) p. 505.

30. Fain, *1814*, p. 36ff.; Fournier, *Châtillon*, p. 88.

31. Armand de Caulaincourt, *Mémoires*, ed. Jean Hanoteau (Paris: Librairie Plon, 1933), III, 35.

32. Fournier, *Châtillon*, pp. 88–93; and Floret's Journal, quoted in Appendix, pp. 371–72.

33. Ibid.

34. Ibid., pp. 93ff.; Fain, *1814*, pp. 29–30, 312. The text of the carte-blanche letter and of other correspondence exchanged at this time between Caulaincourt, Napoleon and Metternich is given only in the original edition (1823) of Fain, *1814*.

35. Fain, *1814*, p. 318.

36. In his *Memoirs* (I, 227) Metternich erroneously places the conversation with the Tsar in Langres, but other documents fix it clearly on the night of February 9 at Troyes. Again in his *Memoirs*, Metternich claims to have leapt to the defense of the Bourbons, but both Castlereagh's correspondence and Metternich's own—as well as statements of others close to Metternich, such as his secretary, Baron Binder—disprove this. He did not go over to the Bourbon cause until March 19 or later, and then reluctantly, as did Schwarzenberg. Cf. Novak, *Schwarzenberg Briefe*, p. 372; Webster, *British Diplomacy*, p. 136; Niels Rosenkrantz, *Journal du Congrès de Vienne, 1814–1815* (Copenhagen: Georg Nørregård, 1953), p. 190.

37. *Metternich-Sagan*, p. 204.

38. Fournier, *Châtillon*, pp. 110–11.

39. *Metternich-Sagan*, p. 206.

40. Novak, *Schwarzenberg Briefe*, p. 375.

41. *Metternich-Sagan*, p. 208.

42. Webster, *British Diplomacy*, pp. 147ff., 157–58.

43. Fournier, *Châtillon*, p. 135 and n. 1.

44. *Metternich-Sagan*, p. 207.

45. Fain, *1814* (1823 ed.) p. 323.

46. Klinkowström, pp. 809–10.
47. Fournier, *Châtillon*, p. 256.
48. Klinkowström, p. 811.
49. Fain, *1814*, p. 325.
50. Napoleon I, *Napoleon Self-Revealed*, trans. and ed. J. M. Thompson (Boston and New York: Houghton Mifflin, 1934) pp. 345–46.
51. The account of Metternich's journey to Bray is contained in letters written immediately afterward to Laure and to Wilhelmine. See unpublished, Metternich to Laure, Troyes, February 21, 1814, M.F.C. Prague; and *Metternich-Sagan*, pp. 214ff.

XV. LADIES OF VIENNA

1. Unpublished, Metternich to Marie, Basel, January 17, 1814, M.F.C. Prague.
2. Unpublished, Metternich to Laure, Chaumont, March 13, 1814, M.F.C. Prague.
3. Laure to Metternich, February 16, 1814, quoted in Corti, I, 418; and unpublished, Laure to Metternich, Vienna, March 18, 1814, M.F.C. Prague.
4. Laure to Metternich, January 17, 1814, and Marie to Metternich, January 18, 1814, quoted in Corti I, 416, 428; and unpublished, Metternich to Marie, Bar-sur-Aube, February 7, 1814, M.F.C. Prague.
5. Klinkowström, p. 232.
6. Laure to Metternich, February 10, 1814, quoted in Corti, I, 447.
7. Unpublished, Laure to Metternich, Vienna, May 5, 1814, M.F.C. Prague.
8. Unpublished, Metternich to Laure, Langres, February 1, 1814; Chaumont, March 2, 1814, M.F.C. Prague.
9. *Metternich-Sagan*, p. 196.
10. Ibid., p. 184.
11. Ibid., p. 179.
12. Ibid., pp. 194–95.
13. Ibid., p. 177.
14. Binzer, p. 35.
15. *Metternich-Sagan*, p. 191.
16. Ibid., p. 214.
17. Ibid., p. 153.
18. Ibid., p. 194.
19. Nesselrode, V, 137.
20. *Metternich-Sagan*, p. 77.
21. Ibid., p. 141.
22. Ibid., p. 212.
23. Ibid., p. 205.
24. Ibid., p. 162.
25. Ibid., pp. 149–50.
26. Ibid., p. 198.
27. Ibid., pp. 177, 187, 192.
28. Ibid., pp. 186, 223.
29. Ibid., p. 166.

30. Ibid., p. 185.

31. Unpublished, Metternich to Wilhelmine, Langres, January 30, 1814, M.F.C. Prague.

32. Ibid.

33. Unpublished, Wilhelmine to Metternich, Vienna, February 7, 1814, M.F.C. Prague.

34. *Metternich-Sagan*, p. 212.

35. Ibid., p. 206.

36. Ibid., p. 219.

XVI. NAPOLEON'S SECOND LAST STAND

1. *Metternich-Sagan*, p. 223.

2. Fain, *1814*, p. 79ff.

3. Novak, *Schwarzenberg Briefe*, p. 376.

4. Unpublished, Metternich to Laure, Chaumont, February 27, 1814, M.F.C. Prague.

5. Burghersh, pp. 175–76.

6. Metternich to Laure, February 27, 1814.

7. *Metternich-Sagan*, p. 218.

8. Unpublished, Metternich to Laure, Chaumont, February 25, 1814, M.F.C. Prague.

9. *Metternich-Sagan*, pp. 227–29; Fain, *1813*, II, 39.

10. Klinkowström, pp. 815, 816, 818.

11. Roger Parkinson, *Clausewitz* (New York: Stein and Day, 1971), pp. 311ff.

12. Klinkowström, p. 815.

13. *Metternich-Sagan*, p. 231.

14. Ibid., p. 218.

15. Unpublished, Metternich to Laure, Chaumont, March 13, 1814, M.F.C. Prague.

16. *Metternich-Sagan*, p. 230.

17. Ibid., p. 211.

18. Ibid., pp. 204, 206, 209, 224, 226.

19. C. F. Palmstierna, ed., *My Dearest Louise. Marie Louise and Napoleon 1813–1814*, trans. E. M. Wilkinson (London: Methuen, 1958), p. 82.

20. Georges Lacour-Gayet, *Talleyrand* (Paris: Payot, 1930), II, 325.

21. In his *Memoirs* Talleyrand relates that a careless nurse dropped him in early childhood, crippling him for life, but it is probably untrue. His contemporaries referred to his clubfoot; moreover, the shame and guilt with which such a birth defect was viewed in the eighteenth century would explain why his parents shunned him from his christening literally to adulthood, as his bitterness in his *Memoirs* testifies.

22. *Talleyrand Intime, d'après sa correspondance inédite avec la Duchesse de Courlande* (Paris: Librairie des Auteurs Modernes, n.d.), January 3, January 27, 1814. Pages in the early part of the volume are not numbered.

23. Ibid., January 12, 1814.

24. Ibid., February 15, 1814, p. 94. The Hôtel Talleyrand, at the corner of the rue St. Florentin and the Place de la Concorde is occupied today by the U. S. Information Service.

25. Ibid., January 19, 1814.

26. Prince de Talleyrand, *Memoirs*, ed. Duc de Broglie, trans. Mrs. Angus Hall (New York: G. P. Putnam's Sons, 1891), II, 110ff.; and account of Dalberg, Appendix, p. 186ff.

27. Baron [Eugène François Auguste] de Vitrolles, *Mémoires et Relations Politiques* (Paris: G. Charpentier, 1884), I, 66ff.

28. Ibid., I, 74ff.

29. Ibid., I, 107.

30. Londonderry, *Castlereagh Papers*, IX, 553.

31. Burghersh, p. 195.

32. General [Armand Augustin Louis] de Caulaincourt, *No Peace with Napoleon!* trans. George Libaire (New York: William Morrow, 1936), pp. 19, 22.

33. Commandant M. H. Weil, *Les Dessous du Congrès de Vienne* (Paris: Librairie Payot, 1917) I, 149.

34. Vitrolles, *Mémoires*, I, 128ff.

35. Ibid., I, 134ff.

36. Rosenkrantz, *Journal du Congrès de Vienne*, p. 190.

37. *Metternich-Sagan*, p. 235.

38. Ibid.

39. Palmstierna, p. 135.

40. Burghersh, p. 202; unpublished, Metternich to Laure, Dijon, April 2, 1814, M.F.C. Prague; *Metternich-Sagan*, p. 236.

41. Unpublished, Metternich to Laure, Dijon, March 25, 1814, M.F.C. Prague.

42. *Talleyrand Intime*, March 24, 25, 1814, pp. 182, 183.

43. Ibid., p. 162.

44. Ibid., March 20, 1814, p. 170. This letter of Talleyrand to the duchess, revealing with amazing frankness Talleyrand's political thinking in late March, just before the fall of Napoleon, was not entrusted to the ordinary post but was carried by one of Talleyrand's own servants to Rosny. Instructions were added: "Macoucy will carry this letter to you, which you will burn as soon as you have read it. It is essential. In general, my dear, don't keep any of my letters." Fortunately the duchess did not burn it.

45. Ibid., March 21, 1814, p. 175. Talleyrand writes: "This morning before dinner I was at Madame de Brignole's, who said to me, 'Is it true that you asked the Empress directly if Madame de Périgord would be serving [her] in the month of April?'" Talleyrand denied it. Madame de Brignole replied, "They told me so at the palace." See also March 19, p. 166; March 20, p. 170; March 21, p. 175; and March 22, p. 179.

46. Ibid., January 25, 1814.

47. André Castelot, *King of Rome* (New York: Harper & Brothers, 1960), p. 98ff. Perhaps because of Talleyrand's negative vote, Marie Louise's departure from Paris was uncertain until the very last moment. On March 29 he wrote the

Duchess of Courland that the departure was still up in the air and that he was betting they would not leave. "I have hardly slept at all. I love you," he wrote her (*Talleyrand Intime*, p. 195).

48. Castelot, *King of Rome*, pp. 100–1.

49. Metternich *Memoirs*, I, 237.

50. Unpublished, Metternich to Laure, Dijon, April 7, 1814, M.F.C. Prague. In the instructions given Count Bombelles on his mission to the Comte d'Artois, the King's brother, in Nancy, it was specified that the Austrian Government supported the return of the Bourbons on the following conditions: 1) that the King reign constitutionally; 2) the King give complete royal sanction to the public acquisition of national properties; 3) sanction the public debt 4) maintain in office present public functionaries, both civil and military. (Webster, *British Diplomacy*, p. 173, n. 2.) These surprisingly liberal requirements were not of course honored by Louis XVIII.

51. Wessenberg's own account of his capture and his interview with Napoleon in "Résumé of Wessenberg Conversation with Napoleon, Dijon, April 3, 1814," in Frankreich Varia, 65, H.H.S.A. Vienna. Cf. also Alfred von Arneth, *Johann Freiherr von Wessenberg* (Vienna and Leipzig: Wilhelm Braumüller, 1898), I, 164, and Charles K. Webster, *The Foreign Policy of Castlereagh*, (London: G. Bell and Sons, 1931), p. 508.

52. Unpublished, Metternich to Laure, Dijon, March 31, 1814, M.F.C. Prague.

53. Metternich to Laure, April 2, 1814.

54. Unpublished, Metternich to Marie, Dijon, March 29, 1814, M.F.C. Prague.

55. *Metternich-Sagan*, p. 233.

56. Ibid., p. 237.

57. Ibid., p. 238.

58. Ibid., p. 239.

59. Ibid., p. 242.

60. Text of manifesto in *Talleyrand Intime*, pp. 203–4.

61. Baron de Löwenstern, *Mémoires du général-major Russe Baron de Löwenstern*, (1776–1858) ed. M. H. Weil (Paris: Albert Fontemoing, 1903), II, 372; Caulaincourt, *No Peace with Napoleon!* p. 42.

62. Novak, *Schwarzenberg Briefe*, p. 388; Talleyrand, *Memoirs*, II, 122ff.; Nesselrode, *Lettres*, II, 115; Vitrolles, *Mémoires*, I, 311; Londonderry, *Castlereagh Papers*, IX, 416.

63. Louis Madelin, *Talleyrand* (Paris: Flammarion, 1944), p. 266.

XVII. REUNION IN PARIS

1. Unpublished, Metternich to Laure, Dijon, April 4, 1814, M.F.C. Prague.

2. Burghersh, p. 221ff.

3. *Metternich Memoirs*, I, 239ff.

4. Castelot, *King of Rome*, p. 107.

5. Ibid., p. 110.

6. Novak, *Schwarzenberg Briefe*, p. 388.

7. Vitrolles, *Mémoires*, I, 341.

8. *Metternich Memoirs*, I, 239ff.

9. Jean de Bourgoing, *Marie Louise von Osterreich* (Vienna: Europa Verlag, 1949), p. 277.

10. Ibid., p. 281.

11. Ibid.

12. Metternich to Marie Louise, Paris, April 11, 1814, Frankreich Hofkorrespondenz, Fasc. 9, H.H.S.A. Vienna.

13. Burghersh, p. 225.

14. Ibid., p. 226, n. 2.

15. *Metternich-Sagan*, p. 249.

16. Unpublished, Metternich to Laure, Paris, April 21, 1814, M.F.C. Prague.

17. Unpublished, Metternich to Laure, Paris, April 23, 1814, M.F.C. Prague.

18. Marie to Metternich, quoted in Corti, I, 431.

19. Unpublished, Metternich to Laure, Paris, April 13, 1814, M.F.C. Prague.

20. *Metternich-Sagan*, p. 243.

21. Balfour, p. 189.

22. Metternich to Laure, April 23, 1814.

23. *Metternich-Sagan*, p. 248–49.

24. John Cam Hobhouse, Lord Broughton, *Recollections of a Long Life* (New York: Scribner's, 1909), I, 121.

25. Unpublished, Metternich to Marie, Paris, May 5, 1814, M.F.C. Prague.

26. Unpublished, Metternich to Laure, Paris, May 22, 1814, M.F.C. Prague.

27. Metternich *Memoirs*, I, 242.

28. Ibid.

29. Ibid., II, 551.

30. Caulaincourt, *No Peace with Napoleon!* p. 192.

31. "The English have raised a pig, the French bought it for 18 louis, but it is not worth one napoleon."

32. Webster, *Foreign Policy of Castlereagh*, p. 280ff.; Guglielmo Ferrero, *The Reconstruction of Europe: Talleyrand and the Congress of Vienna, 1814–1815*, trans. Theodore R. Jaeckel (New York: W. W. Norton, 1963), p. 123; *Metternich-Sagan*, p. 252.

33. *Metternich-Sagan*, p. 248.

34. Ibid., p. 243.

35. Ibid., p. 255.

36. Ibid., p. 253.

37. Unpublished, Metternich to Laure, Paris, May 26, 1814, M.F.C. Prague.

38. Unpublished, Metternich to Laure, Paris, May 12, 1814, M.F.C. Prague.

39. Comtesse de Boigne, *Mémoires*, ed. Jean-Claude Berchet (Paris: Mercure de France, 1971), I, 264.

40. Novak, *Schwarzenberg Briefe*, p. 396.

41. Metternich to Laure, April 21, 1814.

42. Unpublished, Laure to Metternich, Vienna, May 5, 1814, M.F.C. Prague.

43. Unpublished, Laure to Metternich, Vienna, May 12, 1814, M.F.C. Prague.

44. Ibid.

45. *Metternich-Sagan*, p. 244.

46. Ibid., p. 223.

47. Unpublished, Metternich to Wilhelmine, Dijon, April 3, 1814, M.-S.C. Prague.

48. *Metternich-Sagan*, p. 252.

49. Ibid.

50. Ibid.

51. Ibid., p. 254.

52. Ibid., p. 246.

53. Gentz, *Briefe*, ed. Wittichen and Salzer, I, 291.

54. This excerpt and those following are from two unpublished letters, Metternich to Wilhelmine, Paris, April 30 and May 4, 1814, M.-S.C. Prague.

55. *Metternich-Sagan*, p. 241.

56. Unpublished, Wilhelmine to Metternich, Vienna, May 2, 1814, M.-S.C. Prague.

57. Laure to Metternich, May 5, 1814.

58. Metternich to Laure, May 2, 1814.

59. *Talleyrand Intime*, May 23, 1814, p. 271.

60. Unpublished, Metternich to Laure, Paris, May 13, 1814, M.F.C. Prague.

61. *Talleyrand Intime*, May 19, 1814, p. 263.

62. Metternich to Laure, May 2, 1814.

63. Burghersh, p. 231.

64. Ione Leigh, *Castlereagh* (London: Collins, 1951), p. 282.

65. Metternich to Laure, May 22, 1814.

66. Unpublished, Wilhelmine to Metternich, n.d., M.-S.C. Prague.

67. Unpublished, Metternich to Wilhelmine, [Paris], May 23, 1814, M.-S.C. Prague. The text of this unpublished letter was kindly furnished me by Dr. Maria Ullrichová, editor of the published letters.

68. Metternich to Laure, May 26, 1814.

69. Unpublished, Metternich to Laure, Paris, June 1 and 3, 1814, M.F.C. Prague.

70. Metternich to Laure, May 22, 1814.

71. Unpublished, Wilhelmine to Metternich, n.d., M.-S.C. Prague.

72. *Metternich-Sagan*, p. 256.

XVIII. POLITICAL COMEDY IN LONDON

1. Unpublished, Metternich to Laure, London, June 12, 1814, M.F.C. Prague.

2. Balfour, p. 187.

3. Lady Caroline Capel, *The Capel Letters* (London, Jonathan Cape, 1955), p. 36.

4. Auguste Fournier, "Londoner Präludien zum Wiener Kongress," in *Deutsche Revue*, 3, No. II (1918), 125ff., 205ff.

5. Alexander I, *Scenes of Russian Court Life*, p. 217.

6. Ibid., "Extract from Memoirs of Princess Lieven," p. 270.

7. Ibid.

8. Ibid., p. 221

9. Ibid., p. 277.

10. Ibid., p. 286.

11. Fournier, "Präludien," p. 206; *Metternich-Sagan*, p. 257; London *Times*, June 10, 1814.

12. Metternich to Laure, June 12, 1814.

13. Ibid.

14. Alexander I, *Scenes of Russian Court Life*, p. 287.

15. Unpublished, Metternich to Laure, Oxford, June 15, 1814, M.F.C. Prague.

16. Ibid.

17. Alexander I, *Scenes of Russian Court Life*, pp. 285–86.

18. Ibid., p. 274.

19. Fournier, "Präludien," p. 208.

20. Alexander I, *Scenes of Russian Court Life*, p. 274.

21. Fournier, "Präludien," pp. 206–7.

22. Ibid., p. 127, n. 1.

23. Unpublished, Metternich to Laure, Paris, June 1, 1814, M.F.C. Prague.

24. Thomas Creevey, *The Creevey Papers*, ed. Sir Hubert Maxwell (New York: Dutton, 1904), p. 197.

25. Talleyrand, *Memoirs*, II, 155–57.

26. Unpublished, Wilhelmine to Alfred, London, June 9, 1814, I 4/105, W.A. Pilsen.

27. Unpublished, Baron Wessenberg, "Souvenirs d'un voyage et séjour en Angleterre en 1813 et 1814," Cahier 16, Fol. 1–83, H.H.S.A. Vienna.

28. *Metternich-Sagan*, p. 257; unpublished, Wilhelmine to Metternich, n.d., M.-S.C. Prague.

29. Wilhelmine to Alfred, June 9, 1814.

30. *Metternich-Sagan*, p. 257.

31. Unpublished, Metternich to Laure, London, June 19, 1814, M.F.C. Prague.

32. Unpublished, Wilhelmine to Metternich, notes from London sojourn, most without date, M.-S.C. Prague.

33. Wilhelmine to Alfred, June 9, 1814.

34. Unpublished, Wilhelmine to Alfred, London, June 24, 1814, I 4/106, W.A. Pilsen.

35. Unpublished, Madame de Merveldt to Madame la Duchesse de Sagan, Hanover Square, June 20, 1814; Wilhelmine to Metternich, n.d., M.-S.C. Prague.

36. Metternich to Laure, June 19, 1814.

37. Unpublished, Metternich to Laure, Paris, July 7, 1814, M.F.C. Prague.

38. Metternich to Laure, June 12, 1814; Laure to Metternich, Vienna, June 25, 1814, M.F.C. Prague.

39. Unpublished, Wilhelmine to Metternich, Paris, July 11, 1814, M.-S.C. Prague.

40. Unpublished, Metternich to Wilhelmine, Munich, July 16, 1814, "in the morning," M.-S.C. Prague.

XIX. INTERLUDE IN BADEN

1. Unpublished, Metternich to Laure, London, June 19, 1814, M.F.C. Prague.

2. Leaflet, "Der Wanderer," July 23, 1814, M.F.C. Prague.

3. Unpublished, Metternich to Wilhelmine, n.d. [summer 1814], M.-S.C. Prague.

4. Unpublished, Metternich to Laure, Paris, May 22, 1814, M.F.C. Prague.

5. Unpublished, Wilhelmine to Metternich, Vienna, July [23, 1814], M.-S.C. Prague.

6. Gentz, *Tagebücher*, I, 277–78, 285–86.

7. *Metternich-Sagan*, pp. 258–59.

8. Gentz, *Tagebücher*, I, 278.

9. Unpublished, Wilhelmine to Metternich, [Vienna], July 25, [1814], M.-S.C. Prague.

10. In the published *Briefwechsel* (p. 35), this letter is mistakenly dated "26 July 1813." The original letter is actually dated only "26 July," but the year is clearly 1814, as the visit of Metternich to Elisa Bacciochi in Neustadt corroborates. Cf. Gentz, *Tagebücher*, I, 286.

11. Frankreich Varia, 65, H.H.S.A. Vienna.

12. Metternich to Laure, May 22, 1814.

13. Gentz, *Tagebücher* I, 287.

14. Ibid., I, 287–88.

15. Ibid., I, p. 289.

16. Unpublished, Wilhelmine to Metternich, n.d., M.-S.C. Prague.

17. Unpublished, Metternich to Wilhelmine, n.d., M.-S.C. Prague.

18. Unpublished, Wilhelmine to Metternich, "Mardi 7 h." [Tuesday, August 2, 1814], M.-S.C. Prague.

19. *Metternich-Sagan*, p. 259.

20. Gentz, *Tagebücher*, I, 293.

21. Ibid., p. 294.

22. *Metternich-Sagan*, p. 260.

23. Ibid., p. 261.

24. Unpublished, Wilhelmine to Metternich, Vienna, "ce 15," M.-S.C. Prague.

25. Lamb to Castlereagh, F.O. 7/Austria, Vienna, August 17, 1814, cipher, marked "Recd. Sept. 6," P.R.O. London.

26. Humboldt *Briefe*, IV, 375.

27. Instructions to Koller, August 16, 1814, and Koller's Report to Metternich, September 7, 1814, cited in Corti, I, 460ff.

28. Nesselrode, *Lettres*, V, 197.

29. Unpublished notes, Wilhelmine to Metternich, August 20, and 22, September 6, [1814], M.-S.C. Prague.

30. Unpublished, Wilhelmine to Alfred, Baden, September 8, [1814], I 4/130, W.A. Pilsen. Unlike most of her letters to Alfred, this letter of farewell was written in German rather than French.

31. Unpublished, Wilhelmine to Metternich, September 9, [1814], M.-S.C. Prague.

32. *Metternich-Sagan*, pp. 262–63.

XX. EUROPE COMES TO A CONGRESS

1. Unpublished, Metternich to Laure, Vienna, September 15, 1814, M.F.C. Prague.

2. *Metternich-Sagan*, pp. 263–64.

3. Unpublished, Metternich to Wilhelmine, Vienna, September 18, 1814, "11 o'clock in the evening," M.-S.C. Prague. The letter quoted above and dated "Vienna, the 19, nine in the morning," is actually the second half of this unpublished letter, begun the night before.

4. Ibid.

5. *Metternich-Sagan*, p. 264.

6. Metternich Report to Emperor Franz on Congress Preparations, London, June 25, 1814, in *Der Wiener Kongress Ausstellung*, Katalog, (Vienna, G. Gistel, 1965), p. 125.

7. *Metternich Memoirs*, I, 252. See also C. K. Webster, *The Congress of Vienna* (New York: Barnes & Noble, 1966), p. 80 and Appendix, pp. 168ff. The *Projet No. 1* (Appendix III, p. 172), which Webster ascribes to Castlereagh, was almost certainly Metternich's put into English translation. The details on the Austrian capital and plans for imperial hospitality could hardly have been known by Castlereagh within three or four days of his arrival. Certain sentences, moreover, suggest literal translation from the French.

8. Friedrich von Gentz, *Dépêches Inédites aux Hospodars de Valachie, 1813–1828*, ed. Count Anton Prokesch von Osten (Paris: E. Plon, 1876), I, 98; *Wiener Kongress Ausstellung 1965*, "Protocol einer Sitzung, 22 Oktober," p. 126; Comte d'Angeberg (Leonard Chodzko), *Le Congrès de Vienne et les Traités de 1815* (Paris: Amyot, 1864), I, 249.

9. *Metternich-Sagan*, p. 265.

10. Gentz, *Tagebücher*, I, 309.

11. Talleyrand, *Memoirs*, II, 153.

12. Ibid., II, 199, and "Instructions for the King's Ambassadors at the Congress," II, 157ff.

13. *Metternich-Sagan*, p. 265; unpublished, Wilhelmine to Metternich, September 25, [1814], M.-S.C. Prague.

14. Rosenkrantz, *Journal du Congrès de Vienne*, pp. 27ff.

15. *Metternich-Sagan*, p. 265.

16. Webster, *Congress of Vienna*, p. 172. Austrian police reports of the Congress period have been compiled by August Fournier, *Die Geheimpolizei auf dem Wiener Congress* (Vienna: F. Tempsky, 1913), and Commandant Weil, *Les Dessous du Congrès de Vienne*.

17. Fournier, *Die Geheimpolizei*, p. 164.

18. Ferrero, *Reconstruction of Europe*, p. 147; Webster, *British Diplomacy*, p. 195.

19. *Metternich-Sagan*, p. 266; unpublished, Wilhelmine to Metternich, "the 28," [September 1814], M.-S.C. Prague.

20. Prince de Talleyrand, *Correspondance Inédite du Prince de Talleyrand et du Roi Louis XVIII, pendant le Congrès de Vienne,* ed. M. G. Pallain (Paris: E. Plon et Cie., 1881), pp. 18ff.

21. Ibid., pp. 10ff.

22. Gentz, *Tagebücher,* I, 312.

23. Humboldt, *Briefe,* IV, 391–92.

24. Weil, I, 193, 205.

25. Unpublished, Metternich to Wilhelmine, "the 11" [October 1814], M.-S.C. Prague.

26. Comte Auguste de La Garde-Chambonas, *Souvenirs du Congrès de Vienne, 1814–1815,* (Paris: Librairie Émile-Paul, 1904), p. 16.

27. Ibid., p. 37.

28. Unpublished, Wilhelmine to Metternich, n.d., M.-S.C. Prague; *Metternich-Sagan,* p. 266.

29. Alville, *Anna Eynard-Lullin et l'Époque des Congrès et des Révolutions,* (Lausanne: Paul Feissly, 1955), p. 406.

30. Talleyrand, *Correspondance Inédite,* p. 25.

31. Ibid., pp. 26–27.

32. Gentz, *Tagebücher,* I, 314. Gentz's and Talleyrand's account of the same events disagree somewhat as to dates. According to Gentz, the dinner at Talleyrand's followed Wednesday's stormy conference (October 5); according to Talleyrand, he and Gentz dined after the conference at Windischgraetz's. Gentz sometimes erred in dates in his diary during the Congress, since, he admitted, he was often so busy he had to summarize a week or two at once. Talleyrand, according to his chef, nearly always gave his great dinners on Tuesdays and Thursdays.

33. Talleyrand, *Correspondance Inédite,* pp. 28ff.

34. Ibid., p. 32.

35. Ibid., pp. 34ff.

XXI. "SIX WEEKS OF HELL"

1. Franz Krones, ed., *Aus dem Tagebuche Erzherzog Johanns von Oesterreich, 1810–1815* (Innsbruck: Verlag der Wagner'schen Universitäts-Buchhandlung, 1891), p. 174.

2. Hilde Spiel, *The Congress of Vienna: An Eyewitness Account,* trans. Richard H. Weber (Philadelphia: Chilton, 1968), p. 85.

3. La Garde-Chambonas, *Souvenirs,* pp. 12–13.

4. Alville, p. 156.

5. Text of Castlereagh's "Confidential Letter" to Hardenberg, October 11, 1814, in Jan de Bourgoing, *Vom Wiener Kongress* (Vienna and Munich: Verlag Georg D. W. Callwey, 1943), p. 368.

6. Talleyrand, *Correspondance Inédite,* p. 30.

7. Unpublished, Metternich to Wilhelmine, October 26, 1814, M.-S.C. Prague.

8. Unpublished, Metternich to Wilhelmine, "the 11," [October, 1814], M.-S.C. Prague.

9. Ibid.

10. Gentz, *Tagebücher*, I, 317.

11. Jean-Gabriel Eynard, *Journal*, ed. Édouard Chapuisat (Paris: Plon-Nourrit, 1914), pp. 17ff.

12. Unpublished, Wilhelmine to Metternich, "the 11," [October 1814], M.-S.C. Prague.

13. Quoted in Webster, *Foreign Policy of Castlereagh*, p. 344.

14. Bourgoing, *Vom Wiener Kongress*, p. 368.

15. Talleyrand, *Correspondance Inédite*, pp. 83–84, n. 2.

16. Gentz, *Tagebücher*, I, 318.

17. Unpublished, Wilhelmine to Metternich, "12 October in the evening," [1814], M.-S.C. Prague.

18. Unpublished, Metternich to Wilhelmine, October 12, 1814, M.-S.C. Prague.

19. Webster, *British Diplomacy*, pp. 206ff.

20. Gentz, *Tagebücher*, I, 318.

21. Ibid., I, 319.

22. Unpublished, Wilhelmine to Metternich, October 14, 1814, M.-S.C. Prague.

23. Gentz, *Tagebücher*, I, 319.

24. Unpublished, Metternich to Wilhelmine, n.d., M.-S.C. Prague.

25. Wilhelmine to Metternich, October 14, 1814.

26. Unpublished, Metternich to Wilhelmine, n.d., M.-S.C. Prague.

27. Gentz, *Tagebücher*, I, 319.

28. Talleyrand, *Correspondance Inédite*, pp. 55ff.

29. Ibid., p. 58, n. 1.

30. Ibid., p. 60.

31. Webster, *Foreign Policy of Castlereagh*, p. 345.

32. Unpublished, Metternich to Wilhelmine, October 16 and 19, 1814, M.-S.C. Prague.

33. Unpublished, Metternich to Laure, Paris, June 3, 1814, M.F.C. Prague.

34. Novak, *Schwarzenberg Briefe*, p. 408.

35. "Programme de la 'Fête de la Paix' pour être exécutée dans les jardins de Son Excellence le Prince Metternich auprès de Vienne," *Metternich Memoirs*, I, n. 81, pp. 424ff.

36. Eynard, pp. 18ff.

37. Countess Bernstorff is quoted in Freksa, *A Peace Congress of Intrigue*, p. 21.

38. Gentz, *Tagebücher*, I, 321.

39. Krones, pp. 178–79.

40. Weil, I, 339; Fournier, *Die Geheimpolizei*, p. 39.

41. Unpublished, Metternich to Wilhelmine, October 19, 1814, M.-S.C. Prague.

42. Ibid. No "attached plan" remains with the correspondence.

43. Gentz, *Tagebücher*, I, 321.

44. Weil, I, 234.

45. Rosenkrantz, p. 54.

46. *Metternich-Sagan*, p. 258. This undated letter, published with the cor-

respondence of July 1814, belongs in all likelihood with the series of letters exchanged between the two in late October 1814.

47. Unpublished, Wilhelmine to Metternich, October 21, 1814, M.-S.C. Prague.

48. Gentz, *Tagebücher*, I, 322.

49. *Metternich-Sagan*, p. 267.

50. In fact, Gentz may never have been shown the memorandum on Saxony. He certainly had not seen it by the following February 1815, when he wrote his memoir on the Vienna Congress and described completely erroneously the terms of Metternich's Saxony proposals (see *Metternich Memoirs*, II, 570). Obviously, Metternich could not trust Gentz's discretion.

51. Webster, *British Diplomacy*, p. 211; Webster, *Foreign Policy of Castlereagh*, p. 345.

52. "Lettre Confidentielle du Ministre d'État et des Affaires Étrangères Prince de Metternich à M. le Prince de Hardenberg," October 22, 1814, in Bourgoing, *Vom Wiener Kongress*, p. 362.

53. Webster, *British Diplomacy*, pp. 212ff.

54. "Memorandum on the best Method of Handling the Polish Question," Webster, *British Diplomacy*, pp. 213ff.

55. Talleyrand, *Correspondance Inédite*, pp. 74ff.

56. Ibid., p. 80.

57. Ibid., pp. 86ff.; Eynard, pp. 73ff.; Stein's Diary, quoted in Freksa, pp. 369ff.

58. "Gentz on the Vienna Congress," in *Metternich Memoirs*, II, 563–64.

59. Corti, I, 477.

60. Rosenkrantz, p. 71.

61. Unpublished, Wilhelmine to Metternich, "Night of 22 to 23 October," [1814], M.-S.C. Prague.

62. Ibid.

63. Quoted in Brühl, *Die Sagan*, p. 241.

64. Ibid., p. 240.

65. Unpublished, Metternich to Wilhelmine, October 26, 1814, M.-S.C. Prague.

66. Gentz, *Tagebücher*, I, 323.

67. Fournier, *Die Geheimpolizei*, p. 235.

68. Weil, I, 443; unpublished, Metternich to Wilhelmine, "the 24," [October 1814], M.-S.C. Prague; unpublished, Wilhelmine to Metternich, "the 25 8bre," M.-S.C. Prague.

69. Metternich to Wilhelmine, "the 24" [October 1814].

70. *Metternich-Sagan*, p. 258. This letter, undated, appears to belong definitely to the series in October, rather than earlier in July, where it is placed in the published letters.

71. Unpublished, Wilhelmine to Metternich, "the 25 8bre," M.-S.C. Prague.

72. Weil, I, 446.

73. Metternich to Wilhelmine, October 26, 1814.

74. Ibid.

75. Unpublished, Wilhelmine to Metternich, October 27, 1814, M.-S.C. Prague.

76. Unpublished, Metternich to Wilhelmine, October 27, 1814, M.-S.C. Prague.

77. Fournier, *Die Geheimpolizei*, p. 236. Also Weil, I. 297, 315, 427 et passim.

78. Novak, *Schwarzenberg Briefe*, p. 410.

79. Fournier, *Die Geheimpolizei*, p. 209; Weil, I, 423.

80. Weil, I, 234, 469.

81. Fournier, *Die Geheimpolizei*, pp. 181, 210; Weil, I, 225, 296, 428; Rosenkrantz, pp. 98, 99.

82. Weil, I, 315–16; also Fournier, *Die Geheimpolizei*, p. 233.

83. *Metternich-Sagan*, p. 267.

84. Ibid., p. 270.

85. Weil, I, 480.

86. Rosenkrantz, December 28, 1814, p. 119.

XXII. CHANGING ALLIANCES

1. Weil, I, 398.

2. *Metternich Memoirs*, I, 252.

3. Gentz, *Tagebücher*, I, 324.

4. Arthur, Duke of Wellington, *Supplementary Despatches, Correspondence and Memoranda* (London: John Murray, 1862), IX, 473.

5. Fournier, *Die Geheimpolizei*, p. 38; Webster, *British Diplomacy*, p. 230; Stein's Diary, quoted in Freksa, p. 372; Talleyrand, *Correspondance Inédite*, p. 87.

6. Freksa, p. 374.

7. Wellington, IX, 473.

8. Metternich to Emperor Franz, November 2, 1814, quoted in Bourgoing, *Vom Wiener Kongress*, p. 146.

9. *Metternich-Sagan*, p. 269.

10. Unpublished, Wilhelmine to Metternich, November 1, 1814, M.-S.C. Prague.

11. *Metternich-Sagan*, p. 270.

12. Webster, *British Diplomacy*, p. 227.

13. Freksa, p. 376.

14. Ibid., p. 377.

15. Talleyrand, *Correspondance Inédite*, pp. 97–98.

16. Ibid., pp. 109–110; Wellington, IX, 477.

17. Rosenkrantz, p. 73.

18. Memorandum of Hardenberg, November 7, 1814, quoted in Bourgoing, *Vom Wiener Kongress*, pp. 154–55.

19. Hans Delbrück, "Friedrich Wilhelm III und Hardenberg auf dem Wiener Kongress," *Historische Zeitschrift* (Munich and Leipzig), Neue Folge, 27 (1889): 259–60; also Bourgoing, *Vom Wiener Kongress*, p. 155.

20. Rosenkrantz, p. 68.

21. Wellington, IX, 476; Fournier, *Die Geheimpolizei*, p. 252; Weil, I, 422.

22. Rosenkrantz, p. 86; Weil, I, 459, 470.

23. Weil, I, 569; Rosenkrantz, p. 72.

24. Paul Müller, *Feldmarschall Fürst Windischgrätz* (Vienna and Leipzig: Wilhelm Braumüller, 1934), p. 13.

25. Friedrich Anton von Schönholz, *Traditionen zur Charakteristik Österreichs: seines Staats- und Volkslebens unter Franz I* (Munich: Georg Müller, 1914), II, 88–89.

26. Gentz, *Tagebücher*, I, 328.

27. Unpublished, Metternich to Wilhelmine, n.d., [prob. November 7, 1814], M.-S.C. Prague.

28. Eynard, pp. 97ff.; Alville, pp. 184ff.

29. Gentz, *Tagebücher*, I, 328.

30. Unpublished, Metternich to Wilhelmine, October 29, 1814, "2 o'clock in the morning." M.-S.C. Prague.

31. Unpublished, Metternich to Wilhelmine, November 4, 1814, "2 o'clock in the morning," M.-S.C. Prague.

32. *Metternich-Sagan*, p. 270.

33. Ibid., p. 271.

34. Unpublished, Wilhelmine to Metternich, November 7, 1814, M.-S.C. Prague.

35. Unpublished, Metternich to Wilhelmine, n.d., [November 7, 1814], M.-S.C., Prague.

36. Unpublished, Wilhelmine to Metternich, November 8, [1814], M.-S.C. Prague.

37. Unpublished, Metternich to Wilhelmine, November 7, [1814], M.-S.C. Prague.

38. Gentz, *Tagebücher*, I, 327, 329.

39. Klinkowström, p. 450.

40. Talleyrand, *Correspondance Inédite*, pp. 145ff.

41. Weil, I, 469, 442.

42. Carl Bertuch, *Carl Bertuchs Tagebuch vom Wiener Kongress*, ed. Hermann Egloffstein (Berlin: Verlag von Gebrüder Pastel, 1916), p. 55

43. *Metternich-Sagan*, p. 270.

44. Weil, I, 444.

45. Rosenkrantz, p. 82. According to Dalberg, Castlereagh explained his conduct in the Saxony affair by what he had found in Austria—"a country without finances and without army and a minister without vigor, that he has judged there was nothing to be had from Austria, and it was for this reason he had decided to support Prussia."

46. Webster, *British Diplomacy*, p. 244; Talleyrand, *Correspondance Inédite*, p. 157.

47. Webster, *British Diplomacy*, pp. 229ff.; pp. 219ff.

48. Ibid., pp. 221–22.

49. Rosenkrantz, p. 64.

50. Talleyrand, *Correspondance Inédite*, pp. 138ff.; p. 164, n. 1.

51. Ibid., p. 170, n. 1.

52. Webster, *Foreign Policy of Castlereagh*, pp. 356–57; Freksa, p. 378; Rosenkrantz pp. 64, 90.

53. Freksa, p. 375.

54. Rosenkrantz, p. 107.

55. Talleyrand, *Correspondance Inédite*, pp. 59–60, 83.

56. Ibid., pp. 148–49.

57. Spiel, p. 87.

58. Eynard, p. 51; Alville, p. 159.

59. Unpublished, Wilhelmine to Metternich, November 22, [1814], M.-S.C. Prague.

60. Unpublished, Metternich to Wilhelmine, November 23, 1814, "1 o'clock in the morning," M.-S.C. Prague.

61. Spiel, pp. 101ff.; Alville, p. 183.

62. Unpublished, Wilhelmine to Metternich, November 19, 1814, M.-S.C. Prague.

63. *Metternich-Sagan*, p. 272.

64. Ibid., p. 273.

65. Clarence Ford, *The Life and Letters of Madame de Krüdener* (London: Adam and Charles Black, 1893), p. 155.

66. Bourgoing, *Vom Wiener Kongress*, p. 196.

67. *Metternich-Sagan*, p. 274.

68. Rosenkrantz, pp. 102–3.

69. Webster, *British Diplomacy*, pp. 248–9.

70. Rosenkrantz, pp. 94, 96, 103.

71. Webster, *British Diplomacy*, p. 251ff.

72. Liverpool to Castlereagh, November 18, 1814, in Webster, *British Diplomacy*, p. 235.

73. Rosenkrantz, p. 105.

74. Ibid., p. 106.

75. Webster, *British Diplomacy*, p. 257. Castlereagh's account of the affair to the London Cabinet was not quite complete. His own memorandum of October 11 on Saxony and another "very compromising" *note verbale* drafted by Cooke also angered the Tsar. Metternich complained to Talleyrand of the "severe embarrassment" in which the revelation of the English notes placed him.

76. Accounts of the succession of scenes in the diplomatic explosion of mid-December are given by Delbrück, "Friedrich Wilhelm III und Hardenberg auf dem Wiener Kongress"; in Bourgoing, *Vom Wiener Kongress*, pp. 214ff.; and in Metternich's own account in his *Memoirs*, I, 326ff.

77. Gentz, *Tagebücher*, I, 339; Eynard, p. 200; Bertuch, p. 67.

78. Freksa, p. 393.

79. Webster, *British Diplomacy*, p. 258.

80. Eynard, p. 207.

81. Freksa, pp. 394ff.; Talleyrand, *Correspondance Inédite*, pp. 181–82.

82. *Metternich Memoirs*, I, 328.

83. Schönholz, II, 126ff.

84. *Metternich-Sagan*, p. 272.

85. Unpublished, Wilhelmine to Metternich, n.d., M.-S.C. Prague.

86. *Metternich-Sagan*, p. 276. This note, undated in the original, has been

tentatively dated in the published form "January, 1815," but it clearly belongs to the series of early December 1814, that pertain to the performance of the first series of *tableaux vivants*.

87. Rosenkrantz, p. 113.

88. Alville, p. 190.

89. Gentz, *Tagebücher*, I, 339.

90. Webster, *British Diplomacy*, p. 260; Wellington, IX, 492.

91. Talleyrand, *Correspondance Inédite* pp. 182, 198–99.

92. Webster, *British Diplomacy*, p. 247.

93. Eynard, pp. 228ff. Eynard is, of course, mistaken about the date of Castlereagh's memorandum on Saxony.

94. Ibid., p. 230.

95. Humboldt, *Briefe*, IV, 444.

96. Unpublished, Metternich to Wilhelmine, December 24, [1814], "2 o'clock in the morning," M.-S.C. Prague.

97. Unpublished, Metternich to Wilhelmine, December 28, [1814], "2 o'clock in the morning," M.-S.C. Prague.

98. Unpublished, Metternich to Wilhelmine, December 29, 1814, M.-S.C. Prague.

99. Unpublished, Wilhelmine to Metternich, December 29, [1814], M.-S.C. Prague.

100. Unpublished, Metternich to Wilhelmine, December 30, [1814], M.-S.C. Prague.

101. Unpublished, Wilhelmine to Metternich, December 30, [1814], M.-S.C. Prague.

102. Gentz, *Tagebücher*, I, 344.

103. Unpublished, Wilhelmine to Metternich, December 31, 1814, M.-S.C. Prague.

104. Unpublished, Metternich to Wilhelmine, December 31, 1814, M.-S.C. Prague.

105. *Metternich-Sagan*, December 31 [1814], "11 o'clock at night," pp. 274–75.

106. La Garde-Chambonas, *Souvenirs*, p. 252.

107. Unpublished, Metternich to Laure, Laibach, May 31, 1816, M.F.C. Prague.

XXIII. A NEW YEAR BEGINS

1. Wellington, IX, 523.

2. Ibid., IX, 526.

3. Eynard, p. 236.

4. Talleyrand, *Correspondance Inédite*, p. 209.

5. Webster, *British Diplomacy*, p. 284.

6. Fournier, *Die Geheimpolizei*, p. 379.

7. Klinkowström, p. 822.

8. Webster, *Foreign Policy of Castlereagh*, p. 380; Webster, *British Diplomacy*, p. 295.

9. Fournier, *Die Geheimpolizei*, pp. 349ff.

10. Rosenkrantz, p. 126.

11. Webster, *British Diplomacy*, p. 295 and n. 1; Rosenkrantz, p. 132.

12. Webster, *British Diplomacy*, p. 290.

13. Klinkowström, p. 823.

14. Talleyrand, *Correspondance Inédite*, p. 256.

15. Rosenkrantz, pp. 123–24; Fournier, *Die Geheimpolizei*, p. 337.

16. Talleyrand, *Correspondance Inédite*, p. 207.

17. Ibid., p. 234, n. 1.

18. Eynard, p. 287.

19. Eynard, p. 292; Alville, p. 224; La Garde-Chambonas, *Souvenirs*, p. 303.

20. Dr. Richard Bright, *Travels from Vienna Through Lower Hungary with Some Remarks on the State of Vienna During the Congress in the Year 1814* (Edinburgh: Archibald Constable and Co., 1818), p. 35.

21. Fournier, *Die Geheimpolizei*, p. 348.

22. *Metternich-Sagan*, p. 275.

23. Unpublished, Metternich to Wilhelmine, January 31, 1815, M.-S.C. Prague.

24. *Metternich-Sagan*, p. 277.

25. Unpublished, Wilhelmine to Metternich, February 8, [1815], M.-S.C. Prague.

26. Fournier, *Die Geheimpolizei*, p. 346; Weil, II, 63–64.

27. Unpublished, Metternich to Wilhelmine, October 26, 1814, M.-S.C. Prague.

28. Rosenkrantz, p. 181.

29. Humboldt, *Briefe*, IV, 482–84.

30. Webster, *Foreign Policy of Castlereagh*, p. 371.

31. Talleyrand, *Correspondance Inédite*, p. 312.

32. Ibid., p. 301; Duff Cooper, *Talleyrand* (London: Jonathan Cape, 1939) p. 259.

33. Metternich *Memoirs*, I, 329–30.

34. La Garde-Chambonas, *Souvenirs*, p. 484; Metternich *Memoirs*, I, 255.

35. Rosenkrantz, p. 176.

36. Ibid.

37. Freksa, p. 196.

38. Rosenkrantz, p. 184.

XXIV. VIENNA'S HUNDRED DAYS

1. André Castelot, *Napoleon*, trans. Guy Daniels (New York: Harper & Row, 1967), p. 522.

2. Ibid., p. 532.

3. Humboldt, *Briefe*, IV, 498.

4. Rosenkrantz, p. 188.

5. Gentz, *Tagebücher*, 365.

6. Unpublished, Wilhelmine to Metternich, March 18, [1815], M.-S.C. Prague.

7. *Metternich-Sagan*, n.d., prob. March 16, 1815, p. 278.

8. Ibid.

9. Madame de Basily-Callimaki, *J. B. Isabey* (Paris: Frazier Soye, 1909), p. 196.

10. Unpublished, Wilhelmine to Metternich, March 6, [1815], M.-S.C. Prague.

11. Unpublished, Wilhelmine to Metternich, n.d., prob. March 20, 1815, M.-S.C. Prague.

12. *Metternich-Sagan*, p. 279.

13. Bourgoing, *Marie Louise*, p. 461.

14. Rosenkrantz, p. 198.

15. Bourgoing, *Marie Louise*, p. 387.

16. Talleyrand, *Correspondance Inédite*, pp. 299, 305–8, 314–15, 323–24.

17. Wessenberg, *Notebooks*, quoted in Bourgoing, *Marie Louise*, p. 607.

18. Weil, II, 338.

19. Rosenkrantz, pp. 192, 193.

20. Castelot, *King of Rome*, p. 166.

21. Ibid.

22. Joseph Fouché, *Memoirs* (Philadelphia: J. B. Lippincott, 1892), p. 422.

23. Bourgoing, *Marie Louise*, p. 467.

24. Humboldt, *Briefe*, IV, 500.

25. *Metternich-Sagan*, n.d., prob. March 23, 1815, p. 279.

26. Günther Elbin, *Macht in Zarten Händen* (Munich: Ehrenwirth Verlag, 1968), p. 250.

27. Weil, II, 478.

28. Elbin, p. 252.

29. Rosenkrantz, p. 202.

30. Gentz, *Tagebücher*, p. 368.

31. Brühl, p. 251.

32. Humboldt, *Briefe*, IV, 503.

33. Weil, II, 356, 377.

34. Rosenkrantz, p. 194.

35. Talleyrand, *Correspondance Inédite*, p. 365; Weil, II, 408; Fournier, *Die Geheimpolizei*, p. 438.

36. Humboldt, *Briefe*, IV, 512.

37. Freksa, p. 42; Gentz, *Tagebücher*, p. 368.

38. Talleyrand, *Correspondance Inédite*, p. 380.

39. Ibid., pp. 485, 376–77.

40. Ibid., pp. 380ff.; Duff Cooper, *Talleyrand*, p. 261.

41. Françoise de Bernardy, *Talleyrand's Last Duchess*, trans. Derek Coltman (New York, Stein and Day, 1966), p. 123; Talleyrand, *Correspondance Inédite*, p. 381; Henri Malo, *Le Beau Montrond* (Paris: Emile-Paul Frères, 1926), p. 164. That the Austrian Government may have collaborated in the mission of Montrond to Talleyrand is suggested by the fact that Montrond traveled with the passport of an attaché of the Austrian embassy in Paris, and arrived in Vienna simultaneously with the Austrian ambassador, Vincent. The latter may have got Montrond through the alerted border guards who had refused to allow Flahaut to pass.

42. Humboldt, *Briefe*, IV, 546.

43. Fournier, *Die Geheimpolizei*, p. 487.

44. Fouché, p. 431; Bourgoing, *Marie Louise*, p. 490.

45. Rosenkrantz, pp. 220–21.

46. Fournier, *Die Geheimpolizei*, p. 446; Bourgoing, *Marie Louise*, p. 499.

47. Klinkowström, p. 604ff. Talleyrand, *Correspondance Inédite*, pp. 402, 407–9; *Gentz und Wessenberg*, p. 86; Rosenkrantz, pp. 223–25.

48. "Report of Ottenfels Mission to Switzerland, 1815," R. A. Metternich 29/4, Sign. 42, Prague. See also Ray Ellsworth Cubberly, *The Role of Fouché During the Hundred Days* (Madison: State Historical Society of Wisconsin, 1969).

49. Bourgoing, *Marie Louise*, p. 495.

50. *Gentz und Wessenberg*, p. 86. Sexist bias even in the presentation of historical documents is evident in the gratuitous footnote appended to this letter by the editor: that these highly intelligent ladies "enjoyed the most evil reputations."

51. Weil, II, 450. The police agent reporting the incident adds that the adieu was so tender it could have for consequence "the arrival in the world of a third illegitimate child for the virtuous princess."

52. Fournier, *Die Geheimpolizei*, p. 484.

53. Ibid., p. 470. The gulden was worth approximately 50 cents; one must multiply by at least 10 to estimate the difference in today's currency.

54. Weil, II, 466.

55. Weil, II, 670.

56. Webster, *Congress of Vienna*, p. 146, n.2; Corti, I, 514.

57. Weil, II, 680.

58. Unpublished, Wilhelmine to Alfred, Vienna, April 22, May 14, 19, 24, and June 1, 1814, I 4/109, 4/110, 4/111, 4/112, 4/114, W. A. Pilsen.

59. Unpublished, Wilhelmine to Alfred, Paris, August 15, [1815], I 4/128, W.A. Pilsen.

60. Brühl, p. 244.

61. Weil, II, 555, 571, 598, 611, 613, 614, 615, 621, 630.

62. Wilhelmine to Alfred, Vienna, April 22, 1814, I 4/109, W.A. Pilsen.

63. Talleyrand, *Correspondance Inédite*, pp. 395, 418, and 419, n. 1.

64. Gentz, *Tagebücher*, I, 384.

65. Unpublished, Marie to Metternich, Baden, June 17, 1815, M.F.C. Prague.

66. Unpublished, Laure to Metternich, Baden, June 14, 1815, M.F.C. Prague.

67. Unpublished, Marie to Metternich, Vienna, August 2, 1815, M.F.C. Prague.

68. Unpublished, Marie to Metternich, Baden, June 14 and 17, 1815, M.F.C. Prague.

69. Brühl, p. 257.

70. Gentz, *Briefe*, ed. Wittichen and Salzer, I, 308.

71. Unpublished, Marie to Metternich, Baden, July 2, 1815; Laure to Metternich, July 3, 1815, M.F.C. Prague; Weil, II, 673; Corti, I, 516.

XXV. "ALL THE WORLD'S IN PARIS"

1. Wellington, XI, 44–45.
2. *Metternich Memoirs*, II, 610.
3. Weil, II, 691.
4. Castelot, *Napoleon*, pp. 566ff.; Metternich *Memoirs*, II, 613.
5. Harriet Countess Granville, *Letters, 1810–1845* (London: Longmans, Green & Co., 1894), I, 57; Wellington, XI, 47; John Marriott, *Castlereagh: The Political Life of Robert, Second Marquis of Londonderry* (London: Methuen & Co., 1936), p. 274.
6. Corti, I, 518.
7. Ibid., pp. 519, 523.
8. Bourgoing, *Marie Louise*, p. 500.
9. Ibid., p. 505.
10. Corti, I, 524.
11. *Metternich Memoirs*, II, 612.
12. Gentz, *Dépêches Inédites*, I, 170.
13. Roger Boutet de Monvel, *Les Anglais à Paris, 1800–1850* (Paris: Librairie Plon, 1911), p. 107.
14. Granville, I, 64–65.
15. Frances Shelley, *The Diary of Frances Lady Shelley (1787–1817)*, ed. Richard Edgcumbe (London: John Murray, 1913), pp. 112, 138.
16. Granville, I, 65ff.; Shelley, p. 130; Weil, II, 702.
17. Bernardy, *Talleyrand's Last Duchess*, p. 126.
18. Ibid.
19. Granville, I, 63.
20. Weil, II, 674.
21. Unpublished, Wilhelmine to Alfred, [Paris], 4 [August 1815], I 4/127, W.A. Pilsen.
22. Unpublished, Wilhelmine to Alfred, [Paris], August 15 [1815], I 4/128, W.A. Pilsen.
23. Wilhelmine to Alfred, 4 [August 1815].
24. Granville, I, 65.
25. Ford, *The Life and Letters of Madame de Krüdener*, p. 165.
26. Francis Ley, *Madame de Krüdener et son Temps* (Paris: Librairie Plon, 1961), pp. 451–57.
27. Ibid., p. 503.
28. Unpublished, Laure to Metternich, Vienna, August 10, 1815, M.F.C. Prague.
29. Ibid.
30. Bourgoing, *Marie Louise*, p. 500.
31. Unpublished, Marie to Metternich, Vienna, September 1, 1815, M.F.C. Prague.
32. Unpublished, Laure to Metternich, Vienna, September 5, 1815, M.F.C. Prague.
33. Unpublished, Marie to Metternich, Vienna, September 5, 1815, M.F.C. Prague.

34. Unpublished, Laure to Metternich, Vienna, September 18, 1815, M.F.C. Prague.

35. Unpublished, Marie to Metternich, Vienna, September 3, 1815, M.F.C. Prague.

36. Marie to Metternich, quoted in Corti, II, 17.

37. M. Antonin Carême, *Le Maître d'Hôtel* (Paris: Firmin Didot, 1823), II, 130ff.

38. Ley, pp. 496ff.

39. *Metternich Memoirs*, I, 260–61.

40. Michel Missoffe, *Metternich, 1773–1859* (Paris: Librairie Arthème Fayard, 1959), p. 227.

41. Gentz, *Tagebücher*, I, 410.

42. Philip Ziegler, *The Duchess of Dino* (New York: John Day Company, 1963), p. 131.

43. Nesselrode, *Lettres*, V, 230.

44. Gentz, *Tagebücher*, I, 429.

XXVI. BIEDERMEIER FINALE

1. *Metternich Memoirs*, III, 69.

2. *Metternich-Lieven Letters*, p. 295; *Metternich Memoirs*, III, 223.

3. *Metternich Memoirs*, III, 264.

4. Binzer, pp. 60–61.

5. Unpublished, Wilhelmine to Alfred, Vienna, November 15, 1816, I 4/131, W.A. Pilsen.

6. Mary and Agnes Berry, *The Berry Papers: Correspondence of Mary and Agnes Berry, 1763–1852*, ed. Lewis Melville (London, John Lane, The Bodley Head, 1914), p. 342.

7. Bernardy, *Talleyrand's Last Duchess*, p. 145ff. Dorothée apparently had another child in 1825, which was not Talleyrand's (See Bernardy, pp. 156–57 and footnote.) To Floret on November 3, 1825, Victor Metternich wrote from Paris:

> Prince Talleyrand and Mme de Dino are spending the winter as you know far from Paris, but you probably do not know that it is to break up a liaison between the latter and Jules de Mornay that the journey to Italy was undertaken. They say in this regard that the blackest of scenes took place between Marshal Soult, father-in-law of the lover, and M. de Talleyrand, during which the Marshal went so far as to call the beautiful Duchess a jade; they say moreover [that she] is pregnant. [Unpublished, Korrespondenz Floret, Fasc. 449, 450, H.H.S.A. Vienna.]

8. Ziegler, p. 73.

9. Gentz, *Tagebücher*, II, 12.

10. Bernardy, *Talleyrand's Last Duchess*, p. 130.

11. Unpublished, Wilhelmine to Metternich, n.d., and one note dated August 7, 1818, M.-S.C. Prague.

12. Corti, II, 71.

13. *Metternich-Lieven Letters*, pp. 110–11.

14. Ibid.
15. Ibid., p. 112.
16. Ibid., pp. 140–41.
17. Ibid., pp. 196–98.
18. Ibid., p. 208.
19. Corti, II, 106.
20. Ibid., pp. 106–7.
21. Binzer, pp. 76–77.
22. *Metternich-Lieven Letters*, p. 142.
23. *Metternich Memoirs*, III, 370.
24. Ibid., III, 502.
25. Ibid., III, 387.
26. *Metternich-Lieven Letters*, p. 319; *Metternich Memoirs*, III, 387.
27. *Metternich Memoirs*, III, 390.
28. Corti, II, 390.
29. Unpublished, Diary of Leontine Metternich, May 14, 1826; in possession of Princess Tatiana Metternich.
30. Philipp von Neumann, *Diaries, 1819–1850*, ed. E. Beresford Chancellor (London: Philip Allan, 1928), II, 15.
31. Clemens Metternich, *Aus Metternichs nachgelassenen Papieren*, ed. Richard Metternich-Winneburg (Vienna: Wilhelm Braumüller, 1880–84), V, 632.
32. Binzer, pp. 114–15.
33. Ibid., p. 77.
34. Corti, II, 311.
35. Ibid., II, 314.
36. Ibid., II, 352.
37. Golo Mann, *Secretary of Europe: The Life of Friedrich Gentz, Enemy of Napoleon*, trans. William H. Woglom (New Haven: Yale University Press, 1946), p. 304.
38. *Metternich Memoirs*, I, 36.
39. George Ticknor, *Life, Letters, and Journals* (London: Sampson, Low, Marston, Searle, & Rivington, 1876), II, pp. 13–17.
40. Neumann, II, 76.
41. Brühl, p. 453.
42. Ibid., p. 443.
43. Neumann, II, 133.
44. Corti, II, 410.
45. Brühl, p. 457.
46. Metternich, *Aus Metternichs nachgelassenen Papieren*, VII, 80.
47. Metternich-Sandor, *Geschehenes Gesehenes Erlebtes*, p. 18.
48. Grün, Anastasius (pseud.) [Anton Count Auersperg], *Sämtliche Werke*, ed. Anton Schlosser (Leipzig: Max Hesses Verlag, 1906), I, 128.

BIBLIOGRAPHY

Unpublished Materials

Central State Archive, Prague (Státní Ustředni Archiv v. Praze)
Metternich Family Correspondence
Metternich-Sagan Correspondence
"Report of Ottenfels Mission to Switzerland, 1815," R.A. Metternich 29/4, sign. 42
State Archive, Pilsen (Státní Archiv v. Plzni)
Windischgraetz Family Archive
Haus- Hof- und Staatsarchiv, Vienna
Baron Wessenberg, "Souvenirs d'un voyage et séjour en Angleterre en 1813 et 1814," Cahier 16, Fol. 1–83
Frankreich Varia, 1814/17, 1–140
Frankreich Hofkorrespondenz, Fasc. 9
Polizei Korrespondenz, 1813–1815
Korrespondenz Floret, Fasc. 449, 450
Diary of Leontine Metternich, Private Collection of Princess Tatiana Metternich.
Archive, Ministère des Affaires Étrangères, Paris
Autriche, Vols. 393, 394, 395: Reports of Count Otto and Count Narbonne
Public Record Office, London
F.O. 7 Austria
F.O. 65 Russia

Contemporary Sources:
LETTERS, DIARIES, MEMOIRS AND COLLECTIONS OF DOCUMENTS

Abrantès, Madame de (Laure Junot). *Mémoires.* Paris: Hachette, 1958.
Alexander I. *Scenes of Russian Court Life. Being the Correspondence of Alexander I with his Sister Catherine.* Edited by Grand Duke Nicholas; translated by Henry Havelock. London: Jarrolds Publishers, n.d. [1915].
Alville. *Anna Eynard-Lullin et l'Époque des Congrès et des Révolutions.* Lausanne: Paul Feissly, 1955.
Andlaw, Franz Freiherr von. *Mein Tagebuch. Auszüge aus Aufschreibungen der Jahre 1811 bis 1861.* Frankfurt am Main: J. D. Sauerländer's Verlag, 1862.
Angeberg, Comte de (Chodzko, Leonard). *Le Congrès de Vienne et les Traités de 1815.* 4 vols. Paris: Amyot, 1864.

Beaufort, Christian de Liedekerke. *Le Comte Hilarion: Souvenirs et Biographie du premier comte de Liedekerke Beaufort.* Paris: Société Copedith, 1968.

Bernstorff, Elise, Gräfin von. *Ein Bild aus der Zeit von 1789 bis 1835, Aus ihren Aufzeichnungen.* 2 vols. Berlin: Ernst Siegfried Mittler und Sohn, 1897.

Berry, Mary and Agnes. *The Berry Papers: Correspondence of Mary and Agnes Berry, 1763–1852.* Edited by Lewis Melville. London: John Lane, The Bodley Head, 1914.

Bertuch, Carl. *Carl Bertuchs Tagebuch vom Wiener Kongress.* Edited by Hermann Freiherr v. Egloffstein. Berlin: Verlag von Gebrüder Pastel, 1916.

Binzer, Emilie von. *Drei Sommer in Löbichau.* Stuttgart: Verlag von W. Spemann, 1877.

Boigne, Comtesse de. *Mémoires.* Edited by Jean-Claude Berchet. 2 vols. Paris: Mercure de France, 1971.

Brett-James, Antony. *Europe Against Napoleon: The Leipzig Campaign, 1813, from Eyewitness Accounts.* London: Macmillan & Co., 1970.

———. *The Hundred Days. Napoleon's Last Campaign from Eyewitness Accounts.* New York: St. Martin's Press, 1964.

Bright, Dr. Richard. *Travels from Vienna Through Lower Hungary with some Remarks on the State of Vienna During the Congress in the Year 1814.* Edinburgh: Archibald Constable, 1818.

Broglie, Achille Charles, Duc de. *Personal Recollections, 1785–1820.* 2 vols. London: Ward and Downey, 1887.

Broughton, John Cam Hobhouse, Lord. *Recollections of a Long Life.* Vol. I, 1786–1816. New York: Charles Scribner's Sons, 1909.

Burghersh, Lady (Priscilla Ann Fane, afterward Countess of Westmorland). *Letters from Germany and France During the Campaign of 1813–14.* Edited by Lady Rose Weigall. London: John Murray, 1893.

Capel, Lady Caroline. *The Capel Letters. Correspondence of Lady Caroline Capel and Her Daughters, 1814–1817.* London: Jonathan Cape, 1955.

Caulaincourt, General Armand de, Duc de Vicence. *Mémoires.* Edited by Jean Hanoteau. 3 vols. Paris: Librairie Plon, 1933.

———. *No Peace with Napoleon!* Translated by George Libaire. New York: William Morrow & Co., 1936.

Clary-et-Aldringen, Prince Charles de. *Trois Mois à Paris lors du Mariage de l'Empereur Napoléon I et de l'Archiduchesse Marie Louise.* Paris: Librairie Plon, 1914.

Creevey, Thomas. *The Creevey Papers.* Edited by Sir Hubert Maxwell. New York: E. P. Dutton Co., 1904.

Croker, John Wilson. *The Croker Papers: The Correspondence and Diaries of the late Right Honorable John Wilson Croker, Secretary to the Admiralty.* Edited by Louis J. Jennings. 3 vols. London: John Murray, 1885.

Czartoryski, Prince Adam. *Memoirs.* 2 vols. London: Remington & Co., 1888.

Eynard, Jean-Gabriel. *Journal.* Edited by Édouard Chapuisat. Paris: Plon-Nourrit, 1914.

Fain, Baron [Agathon Jean]. *Manuscrit de Mil Huit Cent Douze.* 2 vols. Paris: Delaunay, 1827.

———. *Manuscrit de Mil Huit Cent Treize.* 2 vols. Paris: Delaunay, 1825.

————. *Manuscrit de Mil Huit Cent Quatorze*. London: Martin Bossange, 1823.

Feyerlichkeiten bey der Rückkehr Sr. Maj. des Kaisers von Oesterreich nach Wien im Jahr 1814, dann bey dem Empfänge und während der Anwesenheit der fremden Souveräne in Wien in den Jahren 1814 und 1815. Vienna: Johann Baptist Wallishausser, 1816.

Fouché, Joseph. *Memoirs*. Philadelphia: J. B. Lippincott Co., 1892.

Fournier, August. *Die Geheimpolizei auf dem Wiener Kongress*. Vienna: F. Tempsky, 1913.

Frass, Dr. Otto. *Quellenbuch zur österreichischen Geschichte*. Vol. III. Vienna: Birken-Verlag, 1962.

Freksa, Frederick. *A Peace Congress of Intrigue: A Vivid, Intimate Account of the Congress of Vienna Composed of the Personal Memoirs of Its Important Participants*. Translated by Harry Hansen. New York: Century Co., 1919.

Gentz, Friedrich von. *Briefe von Friedrich von Gentz an Pilat*. Edited by Dr. Karl Mendelssohn-Bartholdy. 2 vols. Leipzig: F.C.W. Vogel, 1868.

————. *Briefe von und an Friedrich von Gentz*. Edited by Friedrich Carl Wittichen and Ernst Salzer. 3 vols. Munich and Berlin: R. Oldenbourg, 1913.

————. *Dépêches Inédites du Chevalier de Gentz aux Hospodars de Valachie, pour servir à l'histoire de la politique européene, 1813–1828*. Edited by Count Anton Prokesch von Osten. 3 vols. Paris: E. Plon, 1876.

————. *Gentz und Wessenberg: Briefe des Ersten an den Zweiten*. Edited by August Fournier. Vienna and Leipzig: Wilhelm Braumüller, 1907.

————. *Österreichische Manifeste von 1809 und 1813*. Edited by Dr. Eugen Guglia. Vienna: Verlag von Karl Graefer, n.d.

————. *Staatsschriften und Briefe, 1799–1813*. Munich: Drei Masken Verlag, 1921.

————. *Tagebücher, aus dem Nachlass Varnhagen's von Ense*. 4 vols. in 2. Leipzig: F. A. Brockhaus, 1873.

Granville, Harriet, Countess. *Letters, 1810–1845*. 2 vols. London: Longmans, Green & Co., 1894.

Greville, Charles Cavendish Fulke. *The Greville Diary*. Edited by Philip Whitwell Wilson. Vol. I. Garden City, N.Y.: Doubleday, Page & Co., 1927.

Hardenberg, Karl August von. *Denkwürdigkeiten des Staatskanzlers Fürsten v. Hardenberg*. Edited by Leopold von Ranke. Leipzig: Duncker & Humbolt, 1877.

Humboldt, Wilhelm von. *Humanist Without Portfolio. An Anthology of the Writings of Wilhelm von Humboldt*. Translated by Marianne Cowan. Detroit: Wayne University Press, 1963.

Humboldt, Wilhelm and Caroline. *Wilhelm und Caroline von Humboldt in ihren Briefen*. Edited by Anna von Sydow. 6 vols. Berlin: Ernst Siegfried Mittler & Sohn, 1910.

Kielmannsegge, Countess. *Memoiren der Gräfin Kielmannsegge über Napoleon I*. Dresden: Paul Aretz Verlag, 1927.

Klinkowström, Alfons von. *Oesterreichs Theilnahme an den Befreiungskriegen. Ein Beitrag zur Geschichte der Jahres 1813 bis 1815 nach Aufzeichnungen von*

Friedrich von Gentz nebst einen Anhang, "Briefwechsel zwischen den Fürsten Schwarzenberg und Metternich." Vienna: Carl Gerold's Sohn, 1887.

Krones, Franz, Ritter von, ed. *Aus dem Tagebuche Erzherzog Johanns von Oesterreich, 1810–1815.* Innsbruck: Verlag der Wagner'schen Universitäts-Buchhandling, 1891.

La Garde-Chambonas, Auguste, Comte de. *Souvenirs du Congrès de Vienne, 1814–1815.* Paris: Librairie Émile-Paul, 1904.

———. *Gemälde des Wiener Kongresses, 1814–1815.* Edited by Gustav Gugitz. 2 vols. Munich: Georg Müller, 1914.

La Tour du Pin, Marquise de (Henriette Lucie Gouvernet). *Recollections of the Revolution and the Empire ("Journal d'une Femme de Cinquante Ans.")* Edited and translated by Walter Geer. New York: Brentano's, 1920.

Lebzeltern, Ludwig. *Mémoires et papiers de Lebzeltern, un collaborateur de Metternich.* Edited by Emmanuel de Lévis-Mirepoix. Paris: Librairie Plon, 1949.

Lieven, Princess Dorothea. *Unpublished Diary and Political Sketches of Princess Lieven.* Edited by Harold Temperley. London: Jonathan Cape, 1925.

Ligne, Prince de. *Fragments de l'histoire de ma vie.* Edited by Felicien Leuridant. 2 vols. Paris: Librairie Plon, 1927.

Londonderry, Charles William Vane, Third Marquess of. *Narrative of the War in Germany and France in 1813 and 1814.* London: Henry Colburn & Richard Bentley, 1830.

Londonderry, Robert Stewart, Second Marquess of. *Correspondence, Despatches, and Other Papers of Viscount Castlereagh, Second Marquess of Londonderry.* Edited by Charles William Vane, Third Marquess of Londonderry. 12 vols. London: John Murray, 1853.

Löwenstern, Baron de. *Mémoires du général-major Russe Baron de Löwenstern (1776–1858).* Edited by M. H. Weil. 2 vols. Paris: Albert Fontemoing, 1903.

Martens, G. F. *Recueil de Traités d'Alliance.* 16 vols. Göttingen: Dieterich, 1817–1835.

Metternich, Clemens Lothar Wenzel, Prince von. *Aus Metternichs nachgelassene Papieren.* Edited by Prince Richard Metternich-Winneburg. 8 vols. Vienna: Wilhelm Braumüller, 1880–84.

———. *Clemens Metternich-Wilhelmine von Sagan: Ein Briefwechsel, 1813–1815.* Edited by Maria Ullrichová. Graz and Cologne: Verlag Hermann Böhlaus, 1966.

———. *Lettres du Prince de Metternich à la Comtesse de Lieven, 1818–1819.* Edited by Jean Hanoteau. Paris: Librairie Plon, 1909.

———. *Memoirs of Prince Metternich.* Edited by Prince Richard Metternich; translated by Mrs. Alexander Napier. 5 vols. New York: Charles Scribner's Sons, 1881.

Metternich und seine Zeit: Sonderausstellung 1959 des Haus- Hof- und Staatsarchiv in Wien (Catalog of documents relating to Metternich's life). Vienna: Haus- Hof- und Staatsarchiv, 1959.

Metternich-Sandor, Pauline. *Geschehenes Gesehenes Erlebtes.* Vienna: Wiener Literarische Anstalt, 1920.

Montet, Baronne du. *Souvenirs, 1785–1866.* Paris: Librairie Plon, 1904.

Napoleon I, Emperor of the French. *Correspondance de Napoléon Ier.* 32 vols. Paris: H. Plon et J. Dumaine, 1858–1870.

———. *The Corsican: A Diary of Napoleon's Life in His Own Words.* Boston and New York: Houghton Mifflin Co., 1930.

———. *Napoleon Self-Revealed, in Three Hundred Selected Letters.* Translated and edited by J. M. Thompson. Boston and New York: Houghton Mifflin Co., 1934.

Nesselrode, Karl Robert, Comte de. *Lettres et Papiers, 1760–1850.* 11 vols. Paris: A. Lahure, 1904.

Neumann, Philipp von. *Diaries, 1819–1850.* Edited by E. Beresford Chancellor. 2 vols. London: Philip Allan, 1928.

Nostitz, Karl von (1781–1838). *Leben und Briefwechsel. Auch ein Lebensbild aus den Befreiungskriegen.* Dresden and Leipzig: Arnoldische Buchhandlung, 1848.

Novak, Johann Friedrich, ed. *Briefe des Feldmarschalls Fürsten Schwarzenberg an seine Frau, 1799–1816.* Vienna: Verlag von Gerlach & Wiedling, 1913.

Oncken, Wilhelm. *Oesterreich und Preussen im Befreiungskriege.* 2 vols. Berlin: G. Grote'sche Verlagsbuchhandlung, 1876.

Palmstierna, C. F., ed. *My Dearest Louise: Marie-Louise and Napoleon 1813–1814. Unpublished Letters from the Empress with Previously Published Replies from Napoleon.* Translated by E. M. Wilkinson. London: Methuen & Co., 1958.

Parthey, Lili. *Tagebücher aus der Berliner Biedermeierzeit.* Edited by Bernhard Lepsius. Leipzig: Koehlr & Amelang, 1928.

Pertz, Georg Heinrich. *Aus Stein's Leben.* 2 vols. Berlin: George Reiner, 1856.

Pichler, Karoline. *Denkwürdigkeiten aus meinem Leben.* 2 vols. Munich: Georg Müller, 1914.

Rachel, Paul. *Elisa von der Recke: Tagebücher und Briefe aus ihren Wanderjahren.* 2 vols. Leipzig: Dieterich'sche Verlagbuchhandlung, 1902.

Radziwill, Princess Antoine (Louise de Prusse). *Quarante-Cinq Années de Ma Vie (1770 à 1815).* Paris: Librairie Plon, 1912.

Rémusat, Madame de. *Mémoires.* Paris: Calmann Levy, 1880.

Rosenkrantz, Niels, Ministre des Affaires Étrangères du Danemark. *Journal du Congrès de Vienne, 1814–1815.* Publications des Documents de l'Histoire du Danemark. Copenhagen: Georg Nørregård, 1953.

Rzewuska, Rosalie. *Mémoires (1788–1865).* Edited by Giovanella Caetani Grenier. 2 vols. Rome: Typ. Cuggiani, 1939.

Shelley, Frances. *The Diary of Frances, Lady Shelley (1787–1817).* Edited by Richard Edgcumbe. London: John Murray, 1913.

Spiel, Hilde. *The Congress of Vienna: An Eyewitness Account.* Translated by Richard H. Weber. Philadelphia: Chilton Book Company, 1968.

Talleyrand, Charles Maurice, Prince de. *Correspondance Inédite du Prince de Talleyrand et du Roi Louis XVIII, pendant le Congrès de Vienne.* Edited by M. G. Pallain. Paris: E. Plon et Cie, 1881.

———. *Memoirs.* Edited by the Duc de Broglie; translated by Mrs. Angus Hall. 5 vols. New York: G. P. Putnam's Sons, 1891.

Talleyrand Intime, d'après sa Correspondance Inédite avec la Duchesse de Courlande. La Restauration en 1814. Paris: Librairie des Auteurs Modernes, n.d.

Talleyrand-Périgord, Dorothée. *Souvenirs de la Duchesse de Dino.* Edited by la Comtesse Jean de Castellane. Paris: Calmann-Levy, [1908].

Ticknor, George. *Life, Letters and Journals of George Ticknor.* Vol. II. London: Sampson, Low, Marston, Searle & Rivington, 1876.

Thürheim, Lulu von. *Mein Leben: Erinnerungen aus Österreichs Grosser Welt, 1788–1819.* 2 vols. Munich: Georg Müller. 1913.

Varnhagen von Ense. *Denkwürdigkeiten des eignen Lebens.* 2 vols. Berlin: Wegweiser Verlag, 1922.

Varnhagen, Rahel. *Im Umgang mit ihren Freunden: Briefe 1793–1833.* Munich: Kosel-Verlag, 1967.

Vitrolles, Eugène François Auguste, Baron de. *Mémoires et Relations Politiques.* 3 vols. Paris: G. Charpentier, 1884.

————. *Souvenirs Autobiographiques d'un Émigré, 1790–1800.* Paris: Émile-Paul Frères, 1924.

Webster, Charles Kingsley. *British Diplomacy, 1813–1815: Select Documents Dealing with the Reconstruction of Europe.* London: G. Bell & Sons, 1921.

Weil, Maurice Henri, Commandant. *Les Dessous du Congrès de Vienne.* 2 vols. Paris: Librairie Payot, 1917.

Weissenbach, Dr. Alois. *Meine Reise zum Congress.* Vienna: Wallishauser, 1816.

Wellington, Arthur, Duke of. *Supplementary Despatches, Correspondence and Memoranda.* Edited by his son, the Duke of Wellington. Vols. IX, XI. London: John Murray, 1862.

Der Wiener Kongress: Ausstellung, 1 Juni bis 15 Oktober 1965 (Katalog). Vienna: G. Giestel & Cie, 1965.

Wilson, General Sir Robert. *General Wilson's Journal, 1812–1814.* Edited by Antony Brett-James. London: William Kimber, 1964.

————. *Private Diary of Travels, Personal Services and Public Events . . . 1812, 1813, 1814.* 2 vols. London, John Murray, 1861.

Articles in Journals and Periodicals

Caulaincourt, Armand de, "Conversation de M. le Comte de Metternich avec l'Empereur Napoléon, telle que S.M. me l'a raconté," edited by Jean Hanoteau, in *Revue d'Histoire Diplomatique,* 47–48 (October-December 1933).

Dard, Émile, "Lettres inédites de Dalberg à Talleyrand," *Revue d'Histoire Diplomatique,* 51 (1937).

Delbrück, Hans, "Friedrich Wilhelm III und Hardenberg auf dem Wiener Kongress, "*Historische Zeitschrift* (Munich and Leipzig), 27 (1889).

Fournier, August, "Londoner Präludien zum Wiener Kongress (Geheime Berichte Metternichs an Kaiser Franz)," *Deutsche Revue,* 3, II (1918).

Grunwald, Constantin de, "Metternich et Napoléon," *Revue des Deux Mondes,* 10, XLI (October 1937).

Hillebrand, K., "La Société de Berlin de 1789 à 1815," *Revue des Deux Mondes* 5, LXXXVI (March 15, 1870).

London *Times,* 1814.

Rokyta, Hugo, "Die Gestalt der Schlossherrin in Bozena Nemocová's *Babieka,* ihr Prototyp und deren Erzieherin, die Schwester J. B. Forsters," *Zeitschrift für Slawistik*, 2, X (1968), pp. 244–56.

Sweet, Paul, "Erich Bollmann at Vienna in 1815," *American Historical Review* 46 (1941): 580–87.

Weil, H., "Autour du Congrès de Vienne—la Princesse Bagration, la duchesse de Sagan et la Police Secrète de l'Autriche," *Revue de Paris* 20, III (1913).

Wulffius, Gerhard, "Aus dem Leben Herzog Peters [of Courland]," *Sonderdruck des baltischen Deutschtums* XXI (1974).

History, Biography, Miscellaneous Sources

A SELECTION

Almedingen, E. M. *The Emperor Alexander I.* New York: Vanguard Press, 1964.

Arneth, Alfred Ritter von. *Johann Freiherr von Wessenberg: Ein Österreichischer Staatsmann des neunzehnten Jahrhunderts.* Vol. 1: 1773–1815. Vienna and Leipzig: Wilhelm Braumüller, 1898.

Arrigon, Louis J. *Une Amie de Talleyrand: La Duchesse de Courlande. (1761–1821).* Paris: Flammarion, 1946.

Auernheimer, Raoul. *Metternich: Staatsmann und Kavalier.* Vienna: Ullstein Verlag, 1947.

Balfour, Lady Frances. *The Life of George, Fourth Earl of Aberdeen.* 2 vols. London: Hodder and Stoughton, n.d.

Bartlett, C. J. *Castlereagh.* New York: Charles Scribner's Sons, 1966.

Basily-Callimaki, Madame de. *J. B. Isabey: Sa Vie—Son Temps 1767–1855.* Paris: Frazier Soye, 1909.

Bernardy, Françoise de. *Son of Talleyrand.* Translated by Lucy Norton. New York: G. P. Putnam's Sons, 1956.

———. *Talleyrand's Last Duchess.* Translated by Derek Coltman. New York: Stein and Day, 1966.

Bertaut, Jules. *La Vie Aventureuse de Louis XVIII.* Paris: Lardonchet, 1949.

Bertier de Sauvigny, G. de. *Metternich and His Times.* Translated by Peter Ryde. London: Darton, Longman & Todd, 1962.

Bibl, Victor. *Metternich: Der Dämon Österreichs.* Leipzig and Vienna: Johannes Günther Verlag, 1936.

Bonjour, E., H. S. Offler and G. R. Potter. *A Short History of Switzerland.* Oxford, Clarendon Press, 1952.

Botzenhart, Manfred. *Metternichs Pariser Botschafterzeit.* Münster: Verlag Aschendorff, 1967.

Bourgoing, Jean de. *Marie Louise von Österreich.* Vienna: Europa Verlag, 1949.

———. *Vom Wiener Kongress: Zeit- und Sittenbilder.* Vienna and Munich: Verlag Georg D. W. Callwey, 1943.

Boutet de Monvel, Roger. *Les Anglais à Paris, 1800–1850.* Paris: Librairie Plon, 1911.

Breycha-Vauthier, Arthur. *Aus Diplomatie und Leben: Maximen des Fürsten Metternich.* Graz, Vienna and Cologne: Verlag Styria, 1964.

Brinton, Crane. *The Lives of Talleyrand.* New York: W. W. Norton, 1936.

Brühl, Clemens. *Die Sagan: Das Leben der Herzogin Wilhelmine von Sagan, Prinzessin von Kurland.* Berlin: Steuben-Verlag, Paul G. Esser, 1941.

Brunier, Ludwig. *Elisa von der Recke.* Bremen: Verlag J. Kuhlmann's Buchhandlung, 1873.

Buckland, Charles Stephen. *Metternich and the British Government from 1809 to 1813.* London: Macmillan and Co. 1932.

Carême, M. Antonin. *Le Maître d' Hotel.* 2 vols. Paris: Firmin Didot, 1823.

Castelot, André. *King of Rome.* New York: Harper & Brothers; 1960.

———. *Napoleon.* Translated by Guy Daniels. New York: Harper & Row, 1971.

Cecil, Algernon. *Metternich: A Study of His Period and Personality.* London: Eyre & Spottiswoode, rev. ed. 1943.

Christophe, Robert. *Napoleon on Elba.* Translated from the French by Len Ortzen. London: Macdonald, 1964.

Cooper, Duff. *Talleyrand.* London: Jonathan Cape, 1939.

Corti, Egon Cäsar Conte. *Metternich und die Frauen.* 2 vols. Zurich and Vienna: Europa-Verlag, 1948.

Coudray, Helene du. *Metternich.* New Haven: Yale University Press, 1936.

Cubberly, Ray Ellsworth. *The Role of Fouché During the Hundred Days.* Madison: State Historical Society of Wisconsin, 1969.

Darby, W. Evans. *International Tribunals.* London: J. M. Dent, 1904.

Dard, Émile. *Le Comte de Narbonne, 1755–1813.* Paris: Librairie Plon, 1943.

Elbin, Günther. *Macht in Zarten Händen—Dorothea Herzogin von Kurland.* Munich: Ehrenwirth Verlag, 1968.

Emerson, Donald E. *Metternich and the Political Police: Security and Subversion in the Hapsburg Monarchy 1815–1830).* The Hague: Martinus Nidjhoff, 1968.

Engelman, Fred L. *The Peace of Christmas Eve.* New York: Harcourt, Brace & World, 1960.

Feckes, Elisabeth. *Dorothea, Herzogin von Dino und Sagan.* Krefeld: J. B. Kleinsche Druckerei, 1917.

Ferrero, Guglielmo. *The Reconstruction of Europe: Talleyrand and the Congress of Vienna, 1814–1815.* Translated by Theodore R. Jaeckel. New York: W. W. Norton & Co., 1963.

Ford, Clarence. *The Life and Letters of Madame de Krüdener.* London: Adam and Charles Black, 1893.

Fournier, August. *Der Congress von Châtillon: Die Politik im Kriege von 1814.* Vienna and Prague: Verlag F. Tempsky, 1900.

———. *Napoleon I.* 2 vols. Translated by Margaret Baker Corwin and Arthur Dart Bissell; edited by Edward Gaylord Bourne. New York: Henry Holt, 1911.

Griewank, Karl. *Der Wiener Kongress und die Europäische Restauration 1814/15.* Leipzig: Koehler & Amelong, 1954.

Grün, Anastasius (pseud.) [Anton Count Auersperg], *Sämtliche Werke,* ed. Anton Schlosser (Leipzig: Max Hesses Verlag, 1906), I, 128.

Grunwald, Constantin de. *La Vie de Metternich.* Paris: Calmann-Levy, 1938.

Guglia, Eugen. *Kaiserin Maria Ludovica.* Vienna: Verlag von Carl Graeser, 1894.

Gulick, Edward Vose. *Europe's Classical Balance of Power.* Ithaca, N.Y.: Cornell University Press, 1955.

Helfert, J. Alexander, Freiherr von. *Maria-Louise, Erzherzogin von Oesterrich, Kaiserin der Franzosen.* Vienna: Wilhelm Braumüller, 1873.

Herold, J. Christopher. *The Age of Napoleon.* New York: American Heritage, 1963.

————. *The Mind of Napoleon. A Selection from his Written and Spoken Words.* New York: Columbia University Press, 1955.

Hyde, H. Montgomery. *The Strange Death of Lord Castlereagh.* London: Heinemann, 1959.

International Commission for the Teaching of History. *The Congress of Vienna and Europe.* Oxford, London, etc.: Pergamon Press, 1964.

Kircheisen, Friedrich Max. *Napoleon.* Translated by Henry St. Lawrence. New York: Harcourt, Brace & Co., 1932.

Kissinger, Henry A. *A World Restored.* New York: Grosset & Dunlap, 1964.

Kraehe, Enno E. *Metternich's German Policy.* Vol. I: *The Contest with Napoleon, 1799–1814.* Princeton, N. J.: Princeton University Press, 1963.

Lacour-Gayet, Georges. *Talleyrand (1754–1838).* 3 vols. Paris: Payot, 1930.

Leigh, Ione. *Castlereagh.* London: Collins, 1951.

Leisching, Hugo. *Der Wiener Kongress.* Vienna: Artaria, 1893.

Ley, Francis. *Madame de Krüdener et son Temps, 1764–1824.* Paris: Librairie Plon, 1961.

Lockhart, John Gilbert. *The Peacemakers.* London: Duckworth, 1932.

Luckwaldt, Friedrich. *Oesterreich und die Anfänge des Befreiungskrieges von 1813.* In *Historische Studien.* Vaduz: Kraus Reprint, 1965.

Madelin, Louis. *Talleyrand.* Paris: Flammarion, 1944.

Malo, Henri. *Le Beau Montrond.* Paris: Émile-Paul Frères, 1926.

Mann, Golo. *Secretary of Europe: The Life of Friedrich Gentz, Enemy of Napoleon.* Translated by William W. Woglom. New Haven: Yale University Press, 1946.

Marriott, John A. *Castlereagh: The Political Life of Robert, Second Marquis of Londonderry.* London: Methuen & Co., 1936.

Marshall-Cornwall, General Sir James. *Napoleon as Military Commander.* London: B. T. Batsford, 1967.

Mathy, Helmut. *Franz Georg von Metternich, Der Vater des Staatskanzlers.* Meisenheim am Glan: Verlag Anton Haim, 1969.

Mayr, Josef Karl. *Metternichs geheimer Briefdienst, Postlagen und Postkurse.* Vienna: Verlag Adolf Holzhausens, 1935.

Missoffe, Michel. *Le Coeur Secret de Talleyrand.* Paris: Librairie Académique Perrin, 1956.

————. *Metternich, 1773–1859.* Paris: Librairie Arthème Fayard, 1959.

Müller, Paul. *Feldmarschall Fürst Windischgrätz.* Vienna and Leipzig: Wilhelm Braumüller, 1934.

Nicolson, Harold. *The Congress of Vienna: A Study of Allied Unity, 1812–1822.* New York: Viking Compass Edition, 1968.

Oechsli, Wilhelm. *History of Switzerland, 1499–1914.* Translated from the German by Eden and Cedar Paul. Cambridge: Cambridge University Press, 1922.

Ohquist, Johannes. *Ein König und Sein Günstling.* Bonn: Ludwig Röhrscheid Verlag, 1940.

Orieux, Jean. *Talleyrand ou le Sphinx Incompris*. Paris: Flammarion, 1970.

Pakenham, Simona. *In the Absence of the Emperor: London–Paris 1814–1815*. London: Cresset Press, 1968.

Parkinson, Roger. *Clausewitz: A Biography*. New York: Stein and Day, 1971.

Rössler, Hellmuth. *Graf Johann Philipp Stadion*. 2 vols. Vienna, Munich: Verlag Herold, 1966.

Schönholz, Friedrich Anton von. *Traditionen zur Charakteristik Österreichs: seines Staats-und Volkslebens unter Franz I.* 2 vols. Munich: Georg Müller, 1914.

Schwarzenberg, Karl Fürst. *Feldmarschall Fürst Schwarzenberg, Der Sieger von Leipzig*. Vienna and Munich: Verlag Herold, 1964.

Sorel, Albert. *L'Europe et la Révolution Française*. 8 vols. Paris: E. Plon Nourrit, 1903–6.

Spiel, Hilde. *Fanny von Arnstein oder Die Emanzipation, Ein Frauenleben an der Zeitenwende 1758–1818*. Berlin: S. Fischer Verlag, 1962.

Srbik, Heinrich Ritter von. *Metternich: Der Staatsmann und der Mensch*. 2 vols. Munich: Verlag F. Bruckmann, 1925.

Sweet, Paul R. *Friedrich von Gentz: Defender of the Old Order*. Madison: University of Wisconsin Press, 1941.

Talleyrand. *Catalogue de l'Exposition Talleyrand*. Paris: Bibliothèque Nationale, 1965.

Theiss, Viktor. *Erzherzog Johann, der steirische Prinz*. Graz: Hermann Böhlaus, 1950.

Thiers, M. Adolphe. *History of the Consulate and the Empire of France Under Napoleon*. Translated by D. Forbes Campbell. 20 vols. London: Willis and Sotheran, 1857.

[Thürheim, Andres Graf von]. *Der k.k. Österreichische Feldmarschal Fürst Windisch-Grätz: Eine Lebensskizze aus den Papieren eines Zeitgenossen der Stürm Jahre 1848 und 1849*. Berlin: Verlag von Richard Wilhelmi, 1886.

Vallotton, Henry. *Metternich*. Paris: Fayard, 1965.

Vries-Gunzburg, Irène de. *Catherine Pavlovna, Grande Duchesse Russe, 1788–1819*. Amsterdam: J. M. Meulenhoff, 1941.

Webster, Charles Kingsley. *The Congress of Vienna, 1814–1815*. New York: Barnes & Noble, 1966.

———. *The Foreign Policy of Castlereagh, 1812–1815*. London: G. Bell & Sons, 1931.

Wolf, Adam. *Fürstin Eleonore Liechtenstein, 1745–1812*. Vienna: Carl Gerold's Sohn, 1875.

Wostry, Wilhelm. *Prag in der deutschen Freiheits Bewegung*. Prague: Verein für Geschichte der Deutschen in Böhmen, 1914.

Ziegler, Philip. *The Duchess of Dino*. New York: John Day Company, 1963.

INDEX